978-1487803926
W0028367

AN IDEOLOGICAL HISTORY
OF THE
COMMUNIST PARTY OF CHINA

(Volume 3)

www.royalcollins.com

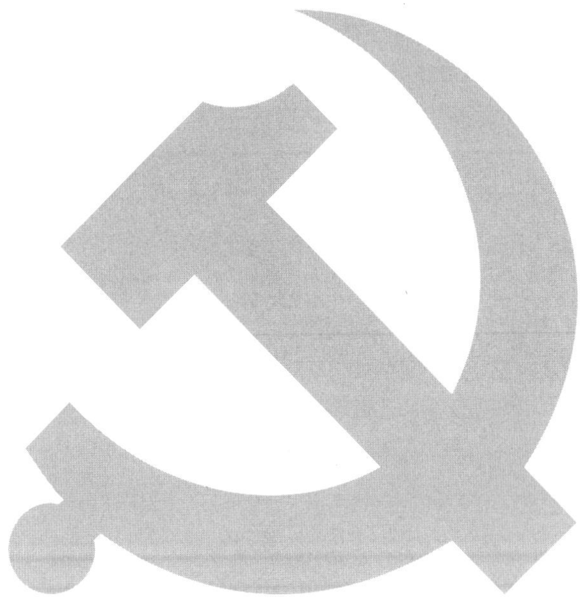

An Ideological History of the Communist Party of China

(Volume 3)

Wu Guoyou and Ding Xuemei

Zheng Qian (Chief Editor)
Translated by Sun Li and Shelly Bryant

——— *Books Beyond Boundaries* ———
ROYAL COLLINS

An Ideological History of the Communist Party of China, Volume 3

Wu Guoyou and Ding Xuemei
Translated by Sun Li and Shelly Bryant

First English Edition 2020
By Royal Collins Publishing Group Inc.
BKM ROYALCOLLINS PUBLISHERS PRIVATE LIMITED
www.royalcollins.com

Original Edition © Guangdong Education Publishing House, China
All rights reserved.

No part of this publication may be reproduced, stored in a retrieval system, or transmitted, in any form or by any means, electronic, mechanical, photocopying or otherwise, without the written permission from the publisher.

Copyright © Royal Collins Publishing Group Inc.
Groupe Publication Royal Collins Inc.
BKM ROYALCOLLINS PUBLISHERS PRIVATE LIMITED

Headquarters: 550-555 boul. René-Lévesque O Montréal (Québec) H2Z1B1 Canada
India office: 805 Hemkunt House, 8th Floor, Rajendra Place, New Delhi 110 008

ISBN: 978-1-4878-0392-6

We are grateful for the financial assistance of B&R Book Program in the publication of this book.

Contents

Introduction		3
Chapter 1:	***The Preparation for a New Era of Reform and Opening Up and the Restoration and Reestablishment of the Correct Line***	9
	I. Generation of Political Reconciliation on the Path to Progress	9
	II. Theoretical Recognition and Addressing Ideological Resistance	20
	III. Partial Deliberation on the Shift of Focus in the Work of the Party and the State	45
	IV. The Central Working Conference and the Third Plenary Session of the Eleventh CPC Central Committee in 1978	52
Chapter 2:	***The Overall Rectification of the Disorder and Adjustment of Social Relations in the New Context***	65
	I. Launch of The Full Redressing of Injustices and False Charges	65
	II. Proper Handling of Lingering Historical Issues	82
	III. Proper Adjustment of Social Relations in the New Context	110
	IV. Restoration of the Party's Ethnic and Religious Policies	118

Chapter 3: Strengthening the Party's Leadership in Ideology and Culture and in Scientific Evaluation of Mao Zedong's Historical Position — 135

I. Negating Class Struggle as the Key and Reaffirming the Four Cardinal Principles — 135

II. Reexamining the Criterion of Truth — 152

III. Adoption of the Resolution on Some Historical Issues in the Party After the Founding of the People's Republic of China — 159

Chapter 4: The Proposition of Building Socialism with Chinese Characteristics and the Formulation of a Comprehensive Reform Program — 173

I. The Proposition of Socialism with Chinese Characteristics — 173

II. Formulation of the Program for Economic Restructuring and the Reform and Opening Up in Full Swing — 192

III. Clarification of the Theme of the Times and Development of External Relations — 202

IV. Proposal of the Notion of "One Country, Two Systems" and the Launch of Peaceful Reunification — 225

Chapter 5: The Theory of the Primary Stage of Socialism and the Proposal of the Three-step Strategy — 239

I. The Theory of the Primary Stage of Socialism and the Establishment of the Party's Basic Line — 239

II. The Three-step Development Strategy — 258

III. Further Clarification of the Objectives of Reform of the Political System — 268

IV. The New Path to Strengthening the Party's Construction through Institution Building — 279

Chapter 6: ***The Formation of the Third Generation of Central Collective Leadership and the Initial Establishment of the Guiding Role of Deng Xiaoping Theory***   ***301***

   I. Comprehensive Governance and Rectification and a Series of Principles for Balanced Development   301

   II. The 1989 Political Storm and the Formation of the Third Generation of the Central Leadership Collective   322

   III. The Publication of Deng Xiaoping's Southern Talks and the Initial Establishment of the Guiding Role of Deng Xiaoping Theory   326

Chapter 7: ***The Socialist Market Economic System and the Basic Program of the Initial Stage of Socialism***   ***343***

   I. The Ultimate Goal of the Reform of the Market Economic System and the Formulation of the Program of Action   343

   II. The Overall Development of Reform of the Socialist Market Economy System   352

   III. The Important Juncture of Historical Development and the Great Banner of Deng Xiaoping Theory   357

   IV. Formation of the Basic Program for the Primary Stage of Socialism   363

Chapter 8: ***The Development of Socialist Democracy with Chinese Characteristics and the Socialist Spiritual Civilization***   ***369***

   I. Active Promotion of the Construction of Socialist Democratic Politics   369

   II. Implementation of the Basic Strategy of the Rule of Law in the Country   379

   III. Practical Enrichment and Development of Socialist Spiritual Civilization   381

   IV. Development of Advanced Socialist Culture with Chinese Characteristics   386

Chapter 9: The Cross-Century Development Strategy of Reform and Opening Up and the Development of Socialism with Chinese Characteristics — 397

I. Formulation of the Strategy for Reform, Opening Up, and Modernization in the New Century — 397

II. The Deepening of the Reform of State-owned Enterprises — 403

III. Adherence to "One Country, Two Systems" for the Great Cause of National Reunification — 413

IV. Forging a Comprehensive Pattern for Foreign Relations in the New Century — 421

V. Forging Ahead with Military Revolution with Chinese Characteristics — 429

Chapter 10: The Advancement of the New Great Project of Party Building and the Formation of the Important Concept of the "Three Represents" — 443

I. Further Clarification of the General Objectives and Tasks of Party Building and the Continuation of the New Great Project — 444

II. The Training and Selecting of Leading Cadres with Competence and Integrity to Build a Qualified Team — 457

III. Strengthening the Party's Work Style and the In-depth and Persistent Struggle Against Corruption — 461

IV. The Formation of the Important Concept of the "Three Represents" and the Establishment of Its Leading Position — 468

Chapter 11: The Proposal of Building a Moderately Well-off Society in a Comprehensive Way and a Scientific Outlook on Development — 479

I. The New Goal of Building a Moderately Well-off Society in a Comprehensive Way and the Reform Program for Improving the Market Economy — 480

II. The New Situation of Deepening Reform and Development
and the Proposal of a Scientific Outlook on Development ... 497

III. Major Strategic Decisions for Scientific Development ... 506

IV. Strengthening the Party's Governing Capabilities and
Advanced Nature ... 512

V. Adherence to Peaceful Development for Building a
Harmonious World ... 516

Chapter 12: *The Implementation of a Scientific Outlook on Development and the Building of a Harmonious Socialist Society* ... ***523***

I. A New Summary of the Theoretical System of Socialism
with Chinese Characteristics ... 524

II. New Requirements for Building a Moderately Well-off
Society in a Comprehensive Way and the Overall Layout
of the "Four-in-One" Construction ... 527

III. Deepening Reform in Administrative Systems and
the New Deployment of Rural Reform ... 536

IV. A Summary of Thirty Years of Reform and Opening Up
and the Implementation of the Scientific Outlook on
Development ... 545

Postscript ... ***553***

Notes ... ***555***

Index ... ***565***

AN IDEOLOGICAL HISTORY
OF THE
COMMUNIST PARTY OF CHINA

(Volume 3)

INTRODUCTION

The Development of Innovation in the Party's Guiding Ideology and the New Era of Reform and Opening Up

At the end of 1978, the Third Plenary Session of the Eleventh National Congress of the Communist Party of China achieved a great turning point for both the Party and the state, which demonstrated that the CPC had pulled itself up again after severe setbacks and led all the people of the nation to carry out Reform and Opening Up and reexamine the path of socialist modernization. Since that time, China has entered a new period of reform and opening up. In this historical context of an intensified reform and opening up, the localization of Marxism in China made a second historic leap. Over the previous thirty years, the development and innovation of the Party's guiding ideology had gone through four stages.

The first phase, which involved "restoring order out of chaos and initiating the reform," it extended from the Third Plenary Session of the Eleventh National Congress of the CPC to the Twelfth National Congress of the CPC in 1982 (1978–1982). At this stage, the work of rectifying disorder was carried out comprehensively, marking the initial start of Reform and Opening Up. Rural areas began to allocate production to households, and coastal areas started to set up special economic zones. In line with Reform and Opening Up, in the field of political thought, China began to reform the leadership system of the Party and the state, adopting the Resolution of the Central Committee of the Communist

Party of China on Some Historical Issues of the Party Since the Founding of the People's Republic of China. In view of the situation at this historical turning point and the new requirements of Reform and Opening Up, the second generation of central leaders, with Deng Xiaoping as its core, resolutely ceased to use the slogan "class struggle as the priority," and decided on the political line of focusing on economic construction. After making the strategic decision to pursue Reform and Opening Up, the Party also put forward the basic idea of adhering to the four basic principles and the fundamental concept of "one central task, two basic points." In the previous four years, as Deng Xiaoping said, the Party had shifted its focus "from taking class struggle as the priority to enhancing productivity, from seclusion to openness, and from clinging to outdated practice to reform on all fronts," marking the beginning of "a new cause of building socialism with Chinese characteristics."[1]

The second phase, focused on "comprehensive reform, governance, and rectification," stretched from the Twelfth National Congress of the CPC to Deng Xiaoping's Southern Talks in 1992 and the Fourteenth National Congress of the CPC (1982–1992). In 1982 at the Twelfth National Congress of the CPC, when the Party set the program of ushering in a new era of modernization and the goal of building a moderately well-off society by the end of the 20th century, at the Third Plenary Session of the Twelfth National Congress of the CPC in 1984, the Party made the decision to reform the economic structure. Under the guidance of the spirit of the Twelfth National Congress and the Third Plenary Session, the Reform and Opening Up policy was fully implemented. At the Thirteenth National Congress of the CPC in 1987, the Party systematically illustrated the theory of the initial stage of socialism and the Party's basic line during this initial stage, outlined the theory of building socialism with China characteristics, and clarified the "three-step" development strategy. At this stage, reform spread steadily from the countryside to the city, moving from the economic field to other fields to further the reform, strengthen governance, and accelerate the development of the Pudong district in Shanghai and Hainan Province. In carrying forward the Reform and Opening Up policy, the Party withstood the severe test brought on by domestic political turmoil and an upheaval in the international situation, making a smooth transition from the old leadership to the new. In the first five years of reform during the previous decade, the focus of reform moved from the countryside to the city, spreading steadily to various areas, with the newly opened regions extending from the coast to the interior. In the next five years, the focus was put on governance and rectification, in hopes of coordinating internal and external relations and dealing with various contradictions, which laid a solid foundation for healthy socioeconomic progress. At this stage, the overall trend was that the market orientation of economic restructuring became more evident.

The third phase included "deepening reform and accelerating the establishment of a socialist market economic system," spanning from Deng Xiaoping's Southern Talks and the Fourteenth National Congress of the CPC to the turn of the century (1992–2000). At the end of 1980s and the beginning of 1990s, China faced an important historical juncture. With Deng Xiaoping's Southern Talks and the Fourteenth National Congress of the CPC, the Party firmly grasped its historical direction, despite various interferences, and made China's Reform and Opening Up move in the correct direction towards the establishment of a socialist market economic system. This was a key step toward China's ultimate destiny. Therefore, Deng Xiaoping's Southern Talks and the Fourteenth National Congress of the CPC, the two major inter-connected events of the time, marked a new stage of China's socialist Reform and Opening Up and its drive toward modernization. The Fourteenth National Congress of the CPC initially established throughout the Party the guidance of Deng Xiaoping's theory of building socialism with Chinese characteristics. Since the Third Plenary Session of the Fourteenth National Congress of the CPC in 1993, when the reform of the socialist market economic system was formulated, the Party furthered reform in various fields and quickened the pace of opening up. Lifting the banner of Deng Xiaoping Theory, the Party put forward at the Fifteenth National Congress the basic program of the initial stage of socialism and formulated the goals and tasks of cross-century development for the cause of Reform and Opening up. At the end of the 20th century, China initially established a socialist market economic system and fulfilled ahead of schedule the first two tasks of the "three-step" strategy, with the overall living standard of urban and rural residents reaching a moderately well-off state. The reform at this stage was generally clear and targeted at economic restructuring. The establishment of a socialist market economic system became a conscious, active historical process in China. The main target of the reform was the highly centralized planned economic system with little vitality. It focused on the reform of the micro-subject with little drive for self-development or market-oriented vitality, so as to realize the transition from a planned economic system to a socialist market economic system.

The fourth phase of scientific and harmonious development focused on building a well-off society in a comprehensive way in the new century (2001–2008). This was the key period for profound changes in China's economic system, social structure, interest patterns, and ideology. After the Fifteenth National Congress of the CPC, the third generation of central leaders, with Jiang Zemin as the center, came to forge the important thought of the "Three Represents," and established it as the guiding ideology of the CPC at the Sixteenth National Congress. Subsequently, the CPC Central Committee, with Hu Jintao as its General Secretary, put forward a series of important strategic thoughts, such as a focus on the people and a comprehensive, coordinated, and sustainable scientific development concept. The cause of socialism with Chinese characteristics took an overall "four-in-one" layout incorporating economic, political, cultural, and social construction. Focusing on perfecting the socialist market economy system, deepening the reform of the administrative management system with the establishment of a public service-oriented government as its major concern, implementing the overall strategy of regional coordinated development, and deepening the construction of a new socialist countryside, China accelerated social construction, shifting the focus to improving people's livelihood and striving to achieve harmonious, scientific development. The general characteristics of the reform at this stage can be summarized as "comprehensive improvement," "good and efficient," "overall planning for harmony," and "four-in-one." The overall trend was to move steadily towards harmonious, scientific development.

Since the Third Plenary Session of the Eleventh National Congress of the CPC, China had ushered in remarkable achievements, presenting profound changes in its people, in Chinese socialism, and in the Communist Party of China. Over the past thirty years, the Party developed more steadily than at any other stage in its 90-year history, avoiding major twists and turns or setbacks, and developed more thoroughly and rapidly than at any other time in the sixty prior years since the founding of New China. In terms of the development and innovation of the Party's guiding ideology, its greatest achievement was the second historic leap in the localization of Marxism in China. At the practical level, this leap opened up the path of socialism with Chinese characteristics, while at the theoretical level, it created a theoretical system of socialism with Chinese characteristics, including Deng Xiaoping Theory, the important concept of the "Three Represents," and the concept of scientific development.

Over the past thirty years of Reform and Opening Up, the localization of Marxism in China has undergone remarkable changes. The history of the Communist Party of China was formerly the history of the localization of Marxism in China, but from now on it will be the history of the development of Chinese Marxism. The development and innovation of the guiding ideology of the CPC will continue to develop in the direction of the localization, modernization, nationalization, and popularization of Marxism. The connotation of "China's reality" will become richer, the methods of "combination" and "adjustment" will keep pace with the times, and the path of the localization of Marxism in China will become broader. In this way, the theory of the localization of Marxism in China will continuously reflect the distinct spirit and the practical requirements of the times, allowing it to constantly forge ahead.

CHAPTER 1

The Preparation for a New Era of Reform and Opening Up and the Restoration and Reestablishment of the Correct Line

I

Generation of Political Reconciliation on the Path to Progress

During the transitional period from 1976 to 1978, the atmosphere of political reconciliation was mainly achieved by restoring Deng Xiaoping's leadership, reinstituting the college entrance examination system, and redressing the Tiananmen Incident.

1. Restoring Deng Xiaoping's Leadership and Redressing the Tiananmen Incident

After the crushing of the Gang of Four, although the political forces supporting the Cultural Revolution were overthrown at the top level of the Central Committee, the issue concerning the Party's and the nation's top leadership, which had a bearing on China's future and destiny after the Cultural Revolution, failed to make substantial progress at that time.

Hua Guofeng, appointed in the last stage of Mao Zedong's life as Chairman of the Central Committee of the CPC, Chairman of the Central Military Commission, and Premier of the State Council, leaned heavily on the Politburo of the Central Committee to act upon the will of the people and took decisive measures to smash the Gang of Four and end the Cultural Revolution. In the process of toppling the Gang of Four, Hua Guofeng played an important central role in the leadership. The masses were encouraged and celebrated the victory.

At the beginning of the dismantling of the Gang of Four, Hua Guofeng focused on criticizing the Gang of Four to solve problems, stabilized the situation, and gained support both inside and outside the Party. The investigation into various factions and organizations tied to the Gang of Four then followed on a nationwide scale, restoring normal production and work order and recovering the national economy. These efforts achieved remarkable results. There was, however, a self-contradictory problem that had not been properly resolved. On the one hand, the Gang of Four was unveiled and criticized, while on the other, the investigation was highly restricted in terms of the harm caused by the extreme left line of the Gang of Four, especially the part concerning Mao Zedong's own errors in his later years. In this way, the work of redressing the wrongs and injustices of the Cultural Revolution moved extremely slowly, and the rectification of some major issues was hindered.

As early as October 26, 1976, Hua Guofeng told the head of the central publicity department that the government should not criticize what Chairman Mao had said or given approval to. On November 18, Wang Dongxing said at the publicity work conference of the Central Committee of the CPC that Chairman Mao already had the No. 4 document on the Deng Xiaoping issue, so it would not be wrong to stick to what Chairman Mao had said and instructed. On February 7, 1977, *Two Newspapers and One Magazine* published an editorial entitled "Studying Documents to Grasp the Key Links," which clearly put forward the policy of the "Two Whatevers." It reads "We will firmly uphold whatever decisions Chairman Mao has made, and we will always follow whatever instructions Chairman Mao has given." The "Two Whatevers" aimed to safeguard Mao Zedong's "banner," including the mistakes of the Cultural Revolution, but it was conflicted with the way the situation had actually developed. After the Cultural Revolution, in view of the growing calls inside and outside the Party for the redressing of the Tiananmen Incident and the revival of Deng Xiaoping, in his speech at the Central Working Conference in March, Chen Yun put forward four points affirming the Tiananmen Incident and fully supported Deng Xiaoping's renewed involvement in the leadership of the Central Committee. Wang Zhen offered the same opinion in his speech, winning widespread support. Ye Jianying and Li Xiannian, two vice-chairmen of the Central Committee, also clearly endorsed it. Under these circumstances, Hua Guofeng recommended "having Comrade Deng Xiaoping come to work at the right time." In July 1977, the Third Plenary Session of the Tenth National Congress of the CPC officially reinstated Deng Xiaoping's post and position.

Once Deng Xiaoping's leadership was restored, the Tiananmen Incident (also known as the April 5th Movement), when people mourned for Premier Zhou Enlai and condemned the Gang of Four, and which was suppressed by the Gang of Four in 1976, was also to be redressed. However, the political identity and situation remained uncertain for those who had participated in the April 5th Movement in Tiananmen Square and were thus "in the same difficulty" as Deng Xiaoping. Therefore, the movement for redressing the Tiananmen Incident sprang up spontaneously among the people. Sixteen teachers of the Chinese Language Teaching and Research Group of the Beijing Second Foreign Language College (with the signature of "Tong Huaizhou"[1] collected and spread mimeographed copies of *Tiananmen Poetry*, and people rushed to buy, reprint, and spread it. It had a great social impact. Another example was Zong Fu, a worker in Shanghai who wrote a four-act drama entitled "In the Silent Spot" to celebrate the April 5th Movement in Tiananmen Square and expose the ugly face of the Gang of Four and its followers. The play was staged first in Shanghai, then in Beijing, causing a sensation. In addition, the first issue of the periodical *Chinese Youth* reported the story of Han Zhixiong, a young worker in Beijing during the April 5th Movement (which was severely criticized by Wang Dongxing and later retracted). It can be said that the Tiananmen Incident was later redressed not out of nothing, but because of the unremitting bottom-up efforts and persistent struggle of the push for social justice.

It was not until November 14, 1978, with the approval and consent of the Central Committee of the CPC, that the Standing Committee of the Beijing Municipal Committee of the CPC formally adopted the decision to rectify the Tiananmen Incident, which was announced in the *Beijing Daily* on November 15. The announcement read, "On Qingming, the Tomb-Sweeping Day, in 1976, the masses went to Tiananmen Square to mourn our beloved Premier Zhou out of their infinite love, remembrance, and deep condolences, and out of deep hatred for the heinous crimes committed by the Gang of Four against the country and the people. It reflected the aspirations of millions of people throughout the country and was entirely a revolutionary action. Cases of comrades persecuted as a result should be redressed and their reputations restored." However, it was obviously not enough for such a nationwide event to be reported only by local newspapers.

Zeng Tao, President of the Xinhua News Agency, Hu Jiwei, editor-in-chief of the *People's Daily*, and Yang Xiguang, editor-in-chief of the *Guangming Daily*, took keen note of the report. A special news item was issued with the above passage taken out of the full text, under the headline, "The Beijing Municipal Committee of the Communist Party of China Declares that the Tiananmen Incident Completely a Revolutionary Action," immediately highlighting the significance of the news. The Xinhua News Agency did not send the news to the Politburo of the CPC for examination and approval, nor did it report to any member of the Standing Committee. Afterwards, even Hu Yaobang questioned Hu Jiwei, asking, "Why didn't you inform me of such an important matter?" At that time, Zeng Tao and others considered it better to keep things this way, so that the Xinhua News Agency could take the full responsibility for this matter. Everyone appreciated Zeng Tao's courage and determination.

After discussion among members of the Standing Committee of the CPC, Hua Guofeng, announced on behalf of the Central Committee at the Central Working Conference then being held that the Tiananmen Incident was a revolutionary mass movement and should be completely and publicly redressed. In this way, the Tiananmen Incident was finally redressed.

2. Partial Redressing Unjust, False, or Erroneous Charges

During the Cultural Revolution, there were a large number of unjust, false, and erroneous charges. The injustices of a considerable number of social groups involved in the whole country, both inside and outside the Party, could not be redressed, and their basic political and working rights and subsistence could not be guaranteed. Therefore, after toppling the Gang of Four, the most direct and urgent appeal of the entire society was to eliminate unjust and false cases as soon as possible. This became the ardent expectation and strong desire of the broad social strata, including leading cadres at all levels who had suffered serious persecution.

In July 1977, the Third Plenary Session of the Tenth National Congress of the CPC decided to restore Deng Xiaoping's leadership, signaling a clear political rationale. The political report of the Eleventh National Congress of the CPC in August pointed out, "Some problems remaining from earlier reviews of cadres should be dealt with seriously and properly as soon as possible. Those who are capable of working but not yet assigned to any post should be offered jobs as soon as possible. Those who are old or physically weak and unable to work should be taken proper care of. Those who are awaiting the conclusion of the review should be given immediate attention as well. All the slander the Gang of Four imposed on others should be discarded." These important messages paved the way for further clarification of historical issues concerning truth and falsehood. In the minds of those who were not relieved, the light of hope concerning their fate and future, as well as those of their families and relatives, began to grow brighter.

Hu Yaobang was then the executive vice president of the Party School of the Central Committee of the CPC. He had been considering how to accelerate the fight against unjust and false cases and implementing the cadre policy. On October 7, 1977, with the support of Hu Yaobang, the *People's Daily* published a full-page article entitled "Correcting the Error of the Cadre Route Imposed by the Gang of Four." The article clearly pointed out that some comrades, especially leaders, had not been able to act upon the Party's cadre policy because of the pernicious influence of the Gang of Four. As a result, some cadres with an awareness of the political line and high measure of working competence had not yet been assigned jobs. Many of the cadres under review had not yet been granted a proper conclusion, and some of the negative elements who had mixed into the cadre teams had not yet been dealt with. All these issues indicated that the implementation of the Party's cadre policy remained a challenging task. The article emphasized that the government should dare to break through the resistance and overthrow the false statements and wrong conclusions imposed on many cadres by the Gang of Four.

This article aroused widespread social resonance. In a little over a month, the relevant departments of the Central Committee had received more than 10,000 letters from cadres and the masses, all expressing their agreement with the views of the article and the measures proposed. The *People's Daily* also continued to publish editorials on the conscientious implementation of cadre policies and published excerpts from the letters from readers to report on the implementation of cadre policies in some parts of the country. This further stimulated the people's desire to wash away their grievances, and they tried to address the problem as quickly as possible through petitions and letters of appeal.

However, the implementation of the cadre policy and the redress of unjust and false cases still faced great resistance. Primarily, in the organizational departments of the Central Government and some regions and units, there were people working for or affected by the Gang of Four faction, and they would always look for various excuses to delay implementing the Party's cadre policy. That aside, there were also many people who had lingering fears and worries that dealing with the remaining problems concerning the censorship of cadres, especially correcting those wrong cases, would negate the achievements of the Cultural Revolution. A typical example was Shu Tong, the former first Secretary of the Shandong Provincial Party Committee, who went to the Central Organizational Department to request the implementation of policies and the distribution of work. Unfortunately, he was blocked by the then head of the Central Organizational Department, even without accommodations at the guesthouse of the Department. There were more than 6,000 cadres like Shu Tong who were "shelved" or "put aside" in the central and state organs alone. Those cadres continued petitioning, but in vain.

This incident shocked Hu Yaobang and strengthened his determination to push ahead the implementation of the cadre policy. Drawing upon Dante's line in *Divine Comedy*, "If we don't go to hell, then who would?"[2] Hu Yaobang stated, "What we say is that if we don't go into the frying pan, then who would?" This was the critical moment against a fierce new typhoon. Since the first step had been firmly and steadily taken, it was important to never retreat, but instead to strive to further the breakthrough that had been made. Hu Yaobang also pointed out that currently the cadre issue remained a daunting task requiring the people to go the distance with great determination. He once again arranged for the comrades of the Central Party School to write a second critical essay entitled "The Earnest Implementation of Chairman Mao's Cadre Policy," condemning such acts as stubbornly adhering to the wrong organizational route.

At this time, veteran comrades such as Ye Jianying, Deng Xiaoping, and Chen Yun also believed that the leadership of the organizational departments must be strengthened, and some sections adjusted and replenished. Hu Yaobang was then highly recommended as the Minister of the Central Organizational Department.

Hu Yaobang was appointed to the Central Organizational Department on December 15, 1977. At eight o'clock that morning, the front courtyard of the Central Organizational Department was filled with excited people celebrating, and setting off firecrackers. All the cadres and workers welcomed the new minister with trust and anticipation, which reflected the strong desire of the masses and cadres to thoroughly redress unjust and false cases. Since then, the number of letters and visits had increased. In January 1978, the number of petitioners was up to hundreds per day and that of letters up to six sacks, some letters directly addressed to Hu Yaobang.

With the support of Deng Xiaoping, Chen Yun, and other veteran comrades, Hu Yaobang, a "young red soldier" who had joined the Chinese Red Army of Workers and Peasants at the age of fourteen, selflessly and courageously broke through the restrictions and taboos imposed by the "Two Whatevers" and drastically organized and led the Central Organizational Department to conduct a series of urgent work on implementing the cadre policy and redressing unjust and false cases.

At the first working meeting of the Central Organization Department, Hu Yaobang pointed out that it was the due responsibility of the organizational departments to redress unjust and false cases and implement the cadre policy. He said that the major cases during the Cultural Revolution alone included the Tiananmen Incident, the 61-people issue, the Peng Dehuai case, the Tao Zhu case, the Wang Renzhong case, the Inner Mongolia "insider party" issue, the so-called "traitor group" issue in Northeast China, the "traitor group" issue of Ma Mingfang in Xinjiang Autonomous Region, the "current counter-revolutionary" cases concerning the appeal for justice for Liu Shaoqi, "vicious attacks on the great leader," and "vicious attacks on Vice-Commander Lin," where the people involved were beheaded. No one knew exactly how many were victims of such incidents. The previous political movements before the Cultural Revolution, as well as some unjust and false cases before the founding of New China, including those in the central soviet area of the CPC in the 1930s, constituted "countless cases," while the current situation of the Central Organizational Department was "treading on thin ice."

Hu Yaobang made it clear that it was the primary task of the organizational departments to clean up the unjust and false cases that had occurred since the founding of New China and during the Cultural Revolution and implement corresponding policies. It was also necessary to come to a thorough settlement regarding the remaining historical problems before the founding of New China, which were not solved or not entirely settled due to the historical conditions at that time or the influence of the war. No matter how difficult the task, it was necessary that the people be determined to "brave the world." He also said to those present at his speech that if any old comrades who had been wronged and wrongfully accused came to him, he would meet them and talk to them without hindrance, and that all letters addressed to "Hu Yaobang" must be sent to him promptly, with no one else taking the initiative to act on his behalf, let alone withholding the letters.

According to statistics, the Central Organizational Department received 1,730 files of 391,363 cases, with 669 senior cadres investigated, 320 of whom had been identified as having serious problems or contradictions with the people, accounting for 47.8% of the number of people reviewed. Among them, there were 213 vice ministerial cadres, 71 official or alternate members of the Central Committee, 10 members of the Politburo of the Central Committee, 10 members of the Secretariat of the Central Committee, and seven vice premiers.

From March to April 1978, Hu Yaobang organized and guided the Central Organizational Department to hold seminars with the central and state organs, and some provinces, autonomous regions, and municipalities directly under the Central Government to study the difficult cases. He personally attended the meetings to participate in discussions or speeches, offer proposals on handling hundreds of long-standing and difficult cases, decide on policy boundaries, and put forward four criteria for implementing the cadre policy. These policies were 1) for those involved in cases with no conclusion, a conclusion needed to be drawn as quickly as possible, and if the conclusion was incorrect, correction needed to be made based on facts. 2) For those not yet offered a job opportunity, work needed to be assigned appropriately, with the elderly and the infirm properly considered. 3) For those who had passed away, a realistic conclusion needed to be drawn and proper arrangement made for their families. 4) Those whose families and children were negatively affected should be properly settled as well. The general policy was to seek truth from facts, and the approach was to follow the mass line.

Under the chairmanship of Hu Yaobang, for the purpose of liberating the cadres and redressing the unjust and false cases, the Central Organizational Department issued more than forty guiding documents, published over a dozen articles in newspapers and journals, and more than thirty issues comprising nearly 100,000 words of policy comments in the *Organization Newsletter*. During the days he spent working in the Central Organizational Department, Hu Yaobang was busy dealing with numerous letters almost every day. On average, 33 letters concerning cadres ranking above deputy offices and prefectural Party Secretaries were dealt with each day, with the record being of 200 letters handled in one day. According to one cadre of the Central Committee, during that year, 902 letters were handed down to the Cadre Censorship Bureau by Hu Yaobang himself. Through Hu's tireless effort and meticulous work, and that of the comrades of the Central Organizational Department, issues concerning a considerable number of middle- and senior-level cadres were settled, with their work re-assigned and living arrangements properly made.

As Hu Yaobang said, "A grievance redressed is a huge relief." By July 1978, 5,344 cadres of central and state organs were re-assigned jobs and placed according to policies, accounting for 87.2% of the cadres previously to be allocated jobs in the 53 units of central and state organs, which played a leading role in emancipating thought and rectifying chaos. By August, nine of the principal leaders in twenty provinces, autonomous regions, and municipalities directly under the Central Government were dismissed because of their involvement in the usurpation of power by the Gang of Four, accounting for about one third of the total number of principal leaders in these areas. The Central Government also made major adjustments to the leading bodies of fourteen provinces, autonomous regions, and municipalities directly under the Central Government, and 23 ministries and bureaus, which secured the organizational issues and stabilized the situation, restored and developed the national economy, and furthered the struggle against censorship.

3. Restoring the College Entrance Examination System to Offer Equal Opportunities for Young Students

On October 21, 1977, the *People's Daily* published the news of the resumption of the college entrance examination under the striking headline "Proper University

Enrollment: Hope of the Entire Nation." The resumption of the college entrance examination marked the beginning of the reform and development of China's education in this new historical period, and also the prelude to the magnificent Reform and Opening Up in China in the 1980s. At the end of this year, thousands of young intellectuals took part in the college entrance examination. With years of knowledge accumulation at the grassroots level, most only made brief, hasty preparations, and with anxiety and excitement, they rushed to examination halls that had been hastily set up in various places, and people in such capacities as rural practitioners, factory apprentices, people demobilized from troops, or those unemployed participated in and witnessed the first college entrance examination after the Cultural Revolution, which changed the times and the fate of an entire generation. That year, 5.7 million people across the nation enrolled in the national college entrance examination. The age range of the candidates was unprecedentedly large, ranging from 13 to 37 years old. The number of those finally accepted was only 272,000, making it the most competitive year in the college entrance examination since the founding of New China.

The recruitment occurred at the end of the year, and many failed to grasp the opportunity to register for the first restored college entrance examination due to personal, family, or social reasons. Fortunately, the college entrance examination was only partially resumed in 1977. In 1978, the national unified examination for college recruitment was restored, with the Ministry of Education organizing test paper writing, with provinces, autonomous regions, and municipalities directly under the Central Government organizing the examination, paper marking, and recruitment at local colleges and universities. According to Deng Xiaoping's instructions, "While the lists of examinees for physical tests are issued, the examination results of all examinees should also be announced. The Admission Committee of the county (district) is to notify the unit the candidate works for, which in turn will inform the individuals." Making the results public was an important measure to enhance the openness and transparency of the examination and recruitment. It played an important role in changing the social atmosphere and eliminating unhealthy tendencies such as "going through the back door," favoritism, or fraud.

Due to the interruption of regular recruitment in colleges and universities for ten years, more than 30 million young people and students were eligible for registration in China. Colleges and universities were recovering from the devastation of the Cultural Revolution, and with limited teaching staff and school buildings, they were unable to take in many students. In 1978, the Ministry of Education decided to restore and add 60 key universities and 55 ordinary universities, and it requested colleges and universities to do everything possible to expand recruitment. As a result, in 1978, 6.1 million candidates registered for the national college entrance examination, and 402,000 were admitted, an unprecedented scale that is unimaginable today.

When the bar was lifted, all poured in. The wave of talent that had remained pent up for eleven years surged overnight. More than 670,000 people were fortunate enough to be admitted into the halls of higher education. More than 11 million young people registered for the college entrance examination. This involved the consideration of countless families, units, and people from all walks of life, bringing about extensive social impact.

As a result of the abolition of the recruitment model based on "the recommendation of the masses and the approval of the leadership," in which power and family background were of central concern in recruiting college students from workers, peasants, and soldiers in the Cultural Revolution, the restored examination system followed the principle of a standardized examination and merit-based selection, and the new model extended the recruitment to high school graduates from the previous eleven years and young people from all walks of life. Many who had not dared to imagine such opportunities in the past now managed to alter their destiny by "standing on their own two feet." The phenomenon of the "zero-score hero" during the Cultural Revolution was gone forever. The restoration of the college entrance examination sparked enthusiasm for studies in an entire generation of young people and initiated a mechanism of fair competition.

Many candidates failed to be admitted because of family problems, since the overall rectification was not yet implemented in 1977. Even so, the examinees and parents no longer gave up or remained silent, but rushed to appeal or petition, partially settling this sort of problem. In light of this, the *People's Daily* published a commentator's article entitled "Resolute Implementation of the Party's Policy on the Political Examination of College Entrance Examination," criticizing the error of the political examination of the candidates not mainly depending on their political performance, but on the political and historical problems of their families and relatives, and pointing out that this biased, irresponsible approach was extremely damaging and seriously interfered with the implementation of the Party's policies. With the further development of the guiding ideology, the problem of overemphasizing the so-called "class route" in the college entrance examination recruitment was rectified.

After the toppling of the Gang of Four, one large shift in the overall social structure was that the atmosphere of social reconciliation was beginning to take shape. The emergence of this change was largely due to the gradual dissolution of the highly tense political relations in Chinese society that had existed for a long time. Apart from the resumption of the college entrance examination, at the National Science Congress in March 1978, Deng Xiaoping proposed the important view that "science and technology is productivity and a great revolutionary force to push historical progress forward," and reiterated that the vast majority of intellectuals were already part of the working class, thus reversing the "left-leaning" policy toward intellectuals that had prevailed over the years. A "spring" of respecting knowledge and talent had arrived, and intellectuals in various fields, including science, education, literature, and art, were greatly encouraged. It was generally felt that a long-lost atmosphere of "reconciliation" that united the people throughout society was accelerating the restoration and reconstruction of normal, orderly social life. The entire society was filled with renewed vitality.

II

Theoretical Recognition and Addressing Ideological Resistance

The ten-year civil strife of the Cultural Revolution not only caused serious damage to the national economy, but also great confusion in theory and ideology. With the recovery and development of the national economy in 1977, theoretical circles began to rectify various wrong ideas that had spread during the Cultural Revolution by exposing and criticizing the fallacies of the Gang of Four in economic theory, and to steadily restore the correct Marxist economic theory, the Party's concept of seeking truth from facts, and the correct criterion for testing truth to give full play to their roles in socialist construction.

1. Discussion of the Issue of Commodity, Circulation, and Labor-Based Distribution in Economic Theoretical Circles

The type of planned economy advocated by Stalin was a highly centralized planned economic mode. For this reason, the commodity economy had always been in an awkward position in China. For many years, the commodity economy was regarded as a type of capitalism, and even the simplest commodity exchange in rural markets was described as capitalism. Under the guidance of this ideology, the development of the commodity economy in China was greatly restricted, and the commercialization of agricultural products was very low, while industrial products were far from meeting the needs of the people's daily life, nor could they provide enough machinery, fertilizers, and pesticides for agricultural development. With a single commodity circulation channel, people had to acquire their necessary goods through "supply," and some of the hard-to-come-by commodities could only be purchased in the form of "ration coupons." This was characteristic of a shortage economy in an underdeveloped commodity economy. After the toppling of the Gang of Four, in order to eliminate the shortage economy, the issue of developing the commodity economy was first proposed. In fact, there was no point developing economic construction without developing a commodity economy, which required stripping the "capitalist" label attached to commodity production and circulation.

On December 5, 1977, the State Council issued the Notice on Convening the National Conference for Urban and Rural Areas to Learn from Daqing and Dazhai, pointing out that socialist commodity production and circulation were essentially different from that of capitalism. There was not a surplus in China's current commodity production, but a deficit. With the systems of both public ownership and collective ownership coexisting, socialist commodity production should have been greatly boosted. Only in this way could China strengthen socialist economic power, eliminate urban and rural capitalist activities, and strengthen the material basis of the dictatorship of the proletariat. It was necessary to promote socialist production and socialist commodity circulation with great confidence. Although this notice bore the linguistic features of that era, such as touching upon the importance of commodity production and circulation from the perspective of "eliminating urban and rural capitalist activities," it ultimately succeeded in pointing out that there were essential differences between the socialist and capitalist commodity economy, and the suggestion that China develop the commodity economy rationally and vigorously at that time was of great significance.

On July 7, 1978, Hua Guofeng delivered a speech at the National Conference on the need for the financial and trade sectors to learn from Daqing and Dazhai. This speech, drafted by several comrades in theoretical circles and revised multiple times by Hu Qiaomu, analyzed the relationship between the economic development and the guaranty of supply, which was basically the interrelationship between production, exchange, distribution, and consumption, all of which were indispensable. Production was the decisive factor in the total production process, while exchange, distribution and consumption also played a vital role in production. The speech also emphasized that commercial development was a "strong engine" of industrial and agricultural production, which had a great social impact.

In order to promote the rational and vigorous development of commodity production and circulation, the theoretical group of the Finance and Trade Section of the State Council drafted the article "Rejecting the Reactionary Fallacy of the Gang of Four in Slandering Socialist Commodity Production," and expounded the proper understanding of socialist commodity production. The article pointed out that commodity production must be allowed to exist in a socialist society, through which the urban and rural areas could be closely connected. Only by vigorously developing commodity production and circulation could China meet the needs of national construction and the people's livelihoods. Vigorously developing the socialist commodity economy was a prerequisite for the mutual promotion of industry and agriculture. Although there were still problems with these discussions, it was a major step beyond the earlier view that the commodity economy was the hotbed of capitalism and distorted talk suggesting that rural community members raising three ducks were socialist, while those raising five ducks were capitalists.

After the progress in renewed acknowledgement of commodity production and exchange, there were obstacles to clarify the leftist influence on distribution as it involved Mao Zedong. As early as 1958, Mao Zedong regarded the wage and bonus systems as "the bourgeois legal right," believing that these things were a retrogression of military communist life during the war, and he had tried to restore the supply system. In 1974, when meeting Danish Prime Minister Paul

Hartlin, Mao said, "In short, China is a socialist country. Before the liberation, it was just like any capitalist country, but now we have the eight-tier wage system, labor-based distribution, and currency exchange. It is not too different from the old one, but ownership is different now," and "this type of distribution can be restricted only under the dictatorship of the proletariat."

The Gang of Four exaggerated to the extreme the remark that "labor-based distribution is not too different from that of the old society." In 1975, Zhang Chunqiao published his article "On the Overall Dictatorship over the Bourgeoisie" and Yao Wenyuan published his "On the Social Basis of Lin Biao's Anti-Party Group," both claiming that labor-based distribution was the legal right of the bourgeoisie and an important economic basis for the emergence of the new bourgeois members, and that labor-based distribution "can be restricted only under the dictatorship of the proletariat." As the article made use of Mao Zedong's speech, it seemed that "abolishing the bourgeois legal right" became a classic interpretation of the Marxist explanation of socialist distribution, which was widely reported and publicized in various newspapers and magazines at the time. As a result, the principle concerning labor-based distribution and material interests was totally negated, which led to great confusion in theory and great trouble in practice.

In January 1977, some people suggested openly criticizing Zhang Chunqiao and Yao Wenyuan. Wang Dongxing, who was in charge of publicity at that time, disagreed on the grounds that Chairman Mao had read the two articles and he could have, instead of completely rejecting their views, merely criticized the wrong ideas in the articles without mentioning their names. This actually set a restricted area for the reinterpretation of labor-based distribution. However, this did not prevent the continued steady discussion of labor-based distribution. In February 1977, the Institute of Economics of the State Planning Commission, in coordination with the Institute of Economics of the Chinese Academy of Sciences, the State General Administration of Labor, and Peking University, decided to hold a national seminar on economic theory, starting with criticizing the fallacy of the Gang of Four on the issue of labor-based distribution. In April, more than one hundred theoretical workers from over thirty units in Beijing attended the seminar. In June, the second seminar was held, with more than four hundred theoretical workers from nearly one hundred units in Beijing attending the meeting.

In July, shortly after his comeback, Deng Xiaoping responded to the discussions in economic circles. He said that the article on labor-based distribution was good as a whole, but not bold enough. On August 3, while talking to Yu Guangyuan and others about the article on labor-based distribution, Deng said that it was basically well-written and tenable, but somewhat vague and needed revision based on discussion. He pointed out that it should be clearly stated that appropriate material rewards should be encouraged, with more gains for more work and less gains for less work. On August 8, he pointed out at the symposium on scientific education that labor-based distribution was nothing more than more gains for more work, less gains for less work, and no gains for no work. In terms of both theory and practice, there were many specific problems to be solved, which was an issue concerning not only the scientific and educational circles, but the nation as a whole.

"It is nothing more than more gains for more work, less gains for less work, and no gains for no work." With his distinctive remark, Deng Xiaoping promoted ideological emancipation in the economic circle. On August 9, the *People's Daily* published an article entitled "Refuting Yao Wenyuan's False View on the Emergence of the Bourgeoisie through Labor-based Distribution" to openly criticize his fallacy. From the end of October to the beginning of November, the economic circle held a third seminar on labor-based distribution. In addition to more than 500 theoretical workers from units in Beijing, more than 300 theoretical workers from 23 provinces, municipalities, and autonomous regions also participated, with over 100 speakers. More articles were published in the *People's Daily*, *Guangming Daily* and *Economic Research*, and the debate within economic circles gradually extended to the entire society.

From February 6 to March 5, 1978, the Fifth Session of the National People's Congress was held. The government's work report clearly affirmed that "throughout the socialist historical period, it is important that we adhere to the principle of no pain, no gain, and of each working in his or her capacity, with labor-based distribution." It pointed out that in distribution, it was important to avoid the disparity between high and low incomes and equal distribution, and that it was important to act upon the principle of more pay for more work and less pay for less work. It was further noted that all community teams should conscientiously implement the quota management and grading systems to achieve equal pay for equal work for male and female employees, that employees' wages in state-owned enterprises should be set based on a working time and supplemented on a piecemeal basis in an hourly wage plus reward system, and that allowances should be provided for jobs with high labor intensity and poor working conditions. The principle of labor-based distribution was to be included in the Constitutional Amendment adopted by the conference.

Based on Deng's proposal, the research office of the State Council wrote articles on labor-based distribution. On March 28, when meeting with Hu Qiaomu, Deng Liqun, and Yu Guangyuan, who were in charge of the research office, Deng Xiaoping said, "I've read the draft of this article. It is well-written and clearly states that the nature of labor-based distribution is socialist, not capitalist. Yet improvements are needed to tie the article to the practical problems existing in the current labor-based distribution."

How do these ideas relate to practical problems? Deng Xiaoping discussed his own thought processes in regards to this issue.

He noted that it was necessary to follow the principle of distribution based on the quantity and quality of labor. The wage level of an employee mainly depended on how good his work was, how sophisticated his skills were, and how significant his contribution was. Distribution could only be done based on labor, not on political background or qualifications. A low wage policy was to be implemented, and it was to be a fairly long-term policy. At the time, the maximum wage of a Level 8 worker was more than one hundred yuan. In the coming years, with the development of production, the wages at all levels needed to be increased. The salaries of primary school teachers were too low, and they needed to be raised, since a good primary school teacher had a very heavy workload. In the future, primary school teachers who taught well would be rated as exceptional, in terms of salary. All trades and professions needed to set up exceptional ranks to encourage people to stay in lifelong careers.

An assessment system needed to be implemented. The assessment had to be strict, comprehensive, and regular in all walks of life. It needed to have clear-cut rewards and penalties. Those who did well or poorly would receive different remuneration based on assessments. The bonus system was to be restored, with bonuses given to inventors and those who made special contributions. Those who made great achievements in scientific research would be offered a pay raise in addition to other rewards for their inventions. The royalty system would also be restored and revised according to the new environment. There were many things to do in order to implement the principle of labor-based distribution. Some problems needed to be investigated and solved systematically, and some systems needed to be restored or established. The purpose was to encourage everyone toward greater progress.

On May 5, with Deng Xiaoping's and Li Xiannian's revision, the *People's Daily* published an article entitled "Implementing the Socialist Principle of Labor-based Distribution" in the name of a special commentator, which thoroughly demonstrated the socialist nature of labor-based distribution and its various forms of remuneration, while also systematically clearing up theoretical errors and confusion in connection with the issue of labor-based distribution. The publication of the article sparked widespread social repercussions. At the same time, it was criticized by the leaders who insisted on the "Two Whatevers." Wang Dongxing openly criticized the article at a small conference, claiming that "it actually pointed the finger at Chairman Mao's thought." In contrast, Deng Xiaoping thought it was a Marxist article. He also said to the head of the Chinese Academy of Social Sciences that the principle would be lost if concessions were made in theory.

In August, the Economic Research Institute of the Chinese Academy of Social Sciences and other institutions held a special seminar on the implementation of the principle of labor-based distribution in rural areas, with the participation of comrades from seventeen provinces, autonomous regions, and municipalities directly under the Central Government and its relevant departments. Attendees to the conference generally agreed that egalitarianism was the main trend in current agricultural distribution at the time. Some participants called for the implementation of the principle of material interests to ensure good management, so that people would give more weight to their own achievements in terms of material interests. This principle was not allowed in the past, but was to be emphasized from this point and applied in practical work. Given the current situation, it was important not to confine the line of thinking to a few certain concepts. Some economists pointed out that over the previous twenty years, the government had invested greatly in agriculture, but without much progress in return, which pointed to the need to identify the causes linked to production relations. To boost agriculture, it was necessary to strengthen the material basis of agricultural production, but it was even more necessary to earnestly implement the policy of equal-value exchange and labor-based distribution.

From October 25 to November 2, at the fourth symposium on labor-based distribution, the question of whether the combination of labor-based distribution with commodity production and currency exchange would produce a new bourgeoisie was discussed. Most participants believed that socialist labor-based distribution, commodity production, and currency exchange would not produce capitalism, nor would they give rise to a new bourgeoisie. In this regard, according to systematic social surveys, some participants also pointed out that not a single bourgeois member was produced by labor-based distribution.

At this stage, the discussion on labor-based distribution was conducted on a large scale and over a long period, which mainly resulted in clarification of several issues. First, it noted that labor-based distribution was a socialist principle of distribution, and by no means a capitalist element. Further, it found that the right of exchange of equal amounts of labor in labor-based distribution was both equal and unequal. There was no hierarchy in labor-based distribution, which did not produce capitalism and bourgeois members. And finally, it pointed out that bonuses and piecework wages were not the results of revisionism and should be restored. Under the situation of rectifying the previous chaos, the discussion of labor-based distribution played a positive role in clarifying the people's vague understanding.

At the same time, theoretical circles were also conducting criticism of the Gang of Four's labeling development of production as "solely focused on productivity." After discussion, some consensus had been reached on several issues. First, it was determined that true socialism should be a higher mode of production than capitalism, and accordingly it should create higher productivity. Socialism was not compatible with poverty, and poverty was not an essential requirement of the socialist system. Further, the Chinese government was developing socialist construction in a country with relatively backward productive forces. It was thus necessary to take the path from rags to riches, so that the nation could flourish rapidly and become a socialist, modernized, strong nation. To achieve this goal, it was necessary to develop productivity. In addition, the contradiction that China faced then was still the contradiction between productivity and productive relations, which was mainly manifested in the factors hindering productivity in productive relations and the superstructure, which contradicted and clashed with the requirements of productivity development, and the solution lay in the development of social productivity. Finally, productive relations had to conform to the nature of productivity. According to this principle, it was necessary to alter the underdeveloped productive relations to pave the way for productivity development, while also guarding against the exaggerated counteractions of productive relations. If productive relations moved too fast or hastily, exceeding the level of productivity development, it would hinder the development of productivity, or even destroy it.

Deng Xiaoping also expressed his views on this issue. In October 1977, when he met with Canadian guests, he said that the Gang of Four denied the importance of productivity, and the development of productivity was labeled as the "sole focus on productivity." This was one of the major debates between other leaders and the Gang of Four. How could distribution on demand and communism be achieved if productivity was not greatly enriched? Marxism and Leninism did not mention the term "sole focus on productivity," and it was not a scientific expression. In December, when meeting with Australian guests, Deng said, "How can we demonstrate the superiority of socialism as Lenin put it? What is superiority? Is it superiority without work or study? Is it superiority if people's living standard goes downward rather than upward? If this is the superiority of socialism, we might as well do without."

In addition, theorists offered a theoretical analysis of the time when leftist errors were prevalent and doing things based on economic laws was regarded as something contrary to a correct political line. At that time, a representative article was drafted by Hu Qiaomu, Yu Guangyuan, and Ma Hong, entitled "Acting in Accordance with the Economic Laws Accelerating the Four Modernizations." This article was first delivered by Hu Qiaomu at an informal meeting of the State Council and published in the *People's Daily* on October 6, 1977. The article elaborated several issues. It first noted that economic laws were objective, not subject to the people's will. It went on to say that although economic laws were objective, they did not automatically guarantee that people would act in accordance with objective economic laws, which must be studied and applied consciously. Further, to follow economic laws, it was important to excel in scientific management and enhance the functions of economic organizations and means. Specifically speaking, China needed to promote the contract system, develop professional companies, strengthen the role of banks, and develop economic legislation and jurisdiction. These discussions provided some guidance for solving the problems in the actual economic situation. Some effective economic management approaches, such as quality-based remuneration and piecework wages, had already begun to be re-implemented.

2. The Historical Reflection of Literary and Art Circles

After the toppling of the Gang of Four, the so-called "black line dictatorship of literature and art" was completely overthrown. With the liberation of film, drama, and other excellent literary and artistic works, which had long been restricted, mass organizations such as literary federations and writers' associations resumed their work. Various literary and artistic creations gradually became active, and some literary and artistic works reflecting on the trauma of the Cultural Revolution soon emerged. After ten years of a cultural desert, simply restoring the works from before the Cultural Revolution was far from sufficient to meet the needs of society. Without new works reflecting the fate of ordinary people in recent years, it was difficult to change the withered literary and artistic scene. In a transitional period such as this, reportage with strong documentary features was the first type of artistic work to break through the barriers that naturally existed.

The form of reportage, which was closest to people's real life, could present readers with the living conditions of protagonists they were not familiar with and yet were keen on knowing, as well as presenting the truth about the events concerned. After toppling the Gang of Four, a cultural spring was ushered in first in the field of science education, and sensitive writers captured the breath of spring. In particular, the stories of Chinese scientists who had been committed to their aspirations during the decade of chaos and persevered in scientific research at the cost of their lives were in themselves vivid and touching enough to move the reader, even without elaboration.

Xu Chi, the leading writer of the old generation, took up his pen to record the footprints of scientists who had been drowned by the political atmosphere of fanaticism and ignorance, yet remained committed to revitalizing China's scientific and technological undertakings, continuing to work in obscurity. He enthusiastically eulogized the scientists who were willing to stay alone and selfless in difficult times, writing in succession "Geological Light," "Goldbach's Conjecture," and "The Evergreen Tree of Life," among other documentary writings. The emergence of these works injected vigor and vitality into the literary and artistic forms that had been destroyed and distorted in the decade of turmoil.

"Goldbach's Conjecture," published in the first issue of *People's Literature* in 1978, vividly depicted the perseverance of Chen Jingrun, a mathematician, in his diligent pursuit and perseverance as he overcame the world's most advanced mathematical problems, his commitment to the cause of science, and his precious qualities of not yielding to evil forces or being shaken by the lure of profit in the face of political storms. This was a truthful reproduction of the feelings of the new generation of intellectuals committed to scientific exploration. The *People's Daily* reprinted this reportage in two full pages, a rare event in the history of the *People's Daily*.

Subsequently, a series of documentary works that extolled Chinese scientists were released one after another. From those historical narratives, readers came to know the names of the leading figures as well as China's young and middle-aged elites in scientific research and its scientific and technological community. These included geologist Li Siguang, biologist Tong Dizhou, quantum chemist Tang Aoqing, physicist Xie Xide, mathematician Chen Jingrun, botanist Cai Xitao, engineering physicist Wu Zhonghua, hydrologist Zhang Guangdou, mathematician Hua Luogeng, scientific "iron man" Chen Chi, and Wu Jichang, a model cotton planter. People lamented that it was under an extremely weak material foundation and the impact and interference of the leftist political tendencies in recent years that these groups of individual scientists with common ideals made scientific achievements at world class levels, winning the respect of all. These works of reportage exerted a huge impact and made a great impression in terms of rationality, emotion, and values, igniting and eliciting rational thinking throughout Chinese society.

Around the same period, works dubbed as "scar literature," revealing the trauma of the Cultural Revolution, began to emerge. In the eleventh issue of 1977, *People's Literature* published the short story "Head Teacher" by Beijing writer Liu Xinwu, which is known as the seminal work of "scar literature." In the story, the author depicted two typical images of middle school students – the hooligan, Song Baoqi, and the Secretary of the Youth League, Xie Huimin. The Cultural Revolution seemed to have left quite different impressions on the two middle school students, but both their souls were branded with the indelible scars caused by the ultra-leftist thought trends of the period. Xie Huimin is viewed as "the first artistic typical character in the new period of literature." Liu Xinwu, the author, said that the story was written out of a "long-standing discontent" with the Cultural Revolution, "which embodies a strong dissatisfaction with the Gang of Four's cultural despotism."

After its publication, the story provoked strong reactions from readers.[3] Several reflections on the painful work of the Cultural Revolution were published in newspapers and periodicals. A typical example was "The Scars," published in *Wenhui Newspaper* on August 1, 1978. This tragic story revealed the hardships of life and the "internal wounds" of the soul of Chinese society that had been caused by the extreme left line and the "theory of descent," especially among young people. This extremely stimulating theme touched more directly on the hidden pain of real society, which evoked reflections on the past for the sake of the future, making a considerable impact on the entire nation.

The reason the story "The Scars" provoked such great repercussions in society and resonated with a large number of people was that it expressed the inexplicable pain deep inside the people at that time, though there were different critical opinions on the themes and thoughts reflected in the story itself. There were some debates at the symposium held in Shanghai and Beijing, but whether most were for or against it, literary works of this kind soon became a trend and were later collectively referred to as "scar literature." In fact, this phenomenon was a historical reflection of the great pain the people inevitably endured in the process of returning to reason after China's period of great social turbulence. Although this sort of reflection was only preliminary and superficial, it urged more people to think deeply about the leftist errors that had been so prevalent in the recent past.

The historical reflection elicited by scar literature soon became the persistent proposition of rational thinking during the transition from the traditional to the modern. The evolution of humanity had suffered a breach in the development of China over the previous decades. The far-reaching cause of this breach was the May 4th Movement, which basically negated the fundamental thinking of pre-Qin scholars, and its more recent cause was the Cultural Revolution, which subverted the tradition of science and democracy that had set in after the May 4th Movement. The consequence was that the humanistic spirit gradually cultivated in modern China was sacrificed as the cost of drastic changes in that era, and the core values transmitted by the Chinese nation over a long period were interrupted. Though it was possible to restore them after the interruption, the wound or scar remained and could not be restored to its original form. During the ten years of the Cultural Revolution, human, social, and ideological problems began, and they continued to loom in the twenty or thirty years that followed. Among various people and strata of society, new and old causes of illness presented themselves in every aspect. This was a truly grave problem.[4] Only with the return of the rationality of social values, with the economic and social development after Reform and Opening Up, and the prosperity of the country, to a certain extent, would it return to the issue of humanity. The human condition of a civilized society could never be completely avoided.

Literature played a leading role in opening up rational thinking in ideological and cultural circles at that time, while drama played a more unique role in mobilizing people's thoughts and feelings at the ground level. In March 1978, the Peking People's Art Theatre staged the play *Song of the Heart*, by Su Shuyang. This was the first political drama to be staged after the restoration of the theatre. The play depicted medical workers, represented by the old intellectual Fang Lingxuan. In order to carry out the instructions of Premier Zhou Enlai and develop new drugs for treating coronary heart disease, these workers launched a thrilling struggle with the followers of the Gang of Four. It profoundly exposed the enormous internal wound caused by the retrogressive actions of the Gang of Four, extolled Fang Lingxuan's persistent pursuit of science, and harshly criticized the despicable deeds of Fang Jisheng, a trendy figure and a disciple of the Gang of Four. The performance of this play and the four-act drama "In the Silent Place," written by Zong Fuxian, a Shanghai worker, were highly praised and widely watched.

In the commentary of the *People's Daily* at that time, the purpose of these plays was "to get the history that had been turned upside down by the Gang of Four back onto the track in the form of literature and art, to utter what millions of people have on their minds, and to express the strong feelings they hold deep down." The Gang of Four was criticized by Chinese literary circles in various artistic forms and in vivid language, which opened the door for historical reflection on the Cultural Revolution and pushed forward the tide of ideological emancipation at that time.

3. A Discussion on the Criterion of Truth

Discussions in the field of economic theory and the historical reflection of the literary and arts communities led the way in breaking through the taboos of the times and played the role of "chiseling through the wall and transmitting light." However, under the rigid shell of the "Two Whatevers," it was still difficult to clarify thoroughly the rights and wrongs of the Cultural Revolution and its predecessors. However, as Hu Yaobang had said, since the nation had firmly taken the first step, it would never retreat. Rather, it would strive to expand the breakthroughs that had been made thus far. Therefore, in view of the "Two Whatevers," it was necessary to wield the weapon of criticism.

The older generation of revolutionaries within the Communist Party of China had both lofty political prestige and rich experience in long-term struggle. They now revealed their ideological weapon, which was seeking truth from facts.

On September 5, 1977, Nie Rongzhen published the article "Restoring and Developing the Party's Fine Traditional Style" in the ninth issue of *Red Flag* magazine. Nie stated that the idea of seeking truth from facts was the most valuable theoretical legacy left by Mao Zedong. He wrote, "To adhere to the realistic working style, we must adhere to the correct attitude toward Marxism-Leninism and Mao Zedong Thought. When we study and apply Marxism-Leninism and Mao Zedong Thought, we must grasp the essence of the spirit, study its stands, viewpoints, and methods, take its basic principles as guidelines for action, and firmly oppose taking some expressions of Marxism-Leninism and Mao Zedong Thought out of context as dogmas divorced from time, place, and conditions." He went on, "All correct ideas vary with specific time, place, and conditions. If not, they will become metaphysics [...] We should always hold onto the guideline of seeking truth from facts at all times, seeing both sides of a story, and taking action suited to the particular time, place, and conditions. Otherwise, we deviate from the most fundamental core of Mao Zedong Thought."

On September 19, Xu Qianqian emphasized the importance of adhering to the principle of seeking truth from facts by discussing the struggle between the Party and Zhang Guotao and the Gang of Four regarding the issue of the military. He pointed out, "It is dangerous to follow whoever has the greatest power, without discriminating the right from the wrong route, as some people do. Of course, it is not easy to identify the correct route or the wrong one." Therefore, it was necessary to "fully and accurately understand and master Marxism-Leninism and Mao Zedong Thought."

On September 28, in his article "Adhering to the Revolutionary Style of Seeking Truth from Facts," Chen Yun sharply criticized the rampant idealism and metaphysics of the Gang of Four. The article pointed out that it was common for the Gang of Four and their followers to take the words of classical Marxist writers out of context to oppress and ruin the public, the Party, and the nation, and that they seriously damaged the fine tradition and style of the Party, which Chairman Mao has been cultivating for a long time, not only greatly undermining the Party's practical and realistic style, but also openly created a "theoretical" basis for their subjective idealism. What they were touting was "anti-empiricism as the outline." In fact, they denied practical experience as the basis of knowledge and the correctness of work based on the actual situation. They further rejected Mao's theory of practice, which was seeking truth from facts.

Chen Yun pointedly noted, "Seeking truth from facts is not an ordinary style of work, but a fundamental ideological line of Marxist materialism. If we insist on Marxist-Leninist doctrine and Mao Zedong Thought, we must insist on seeking truth from facts. If we depart from the revolutionary style of seeking truth from facts, then we will depart from Marxism-Leninism and Mao Zedong Thought and become idealists divorced from reality. This will lead our revolutionary work to failure. Therefore, whether to adhere to the revolutionary style of seeking truth from facts is in fact one of the fundamental signs of distinguishing true Marxism-Leninism and Mao Zedong Thought from the false ones."

The older generation of revolutionaries stressed the importance of adhering to the fundamental ideological line of seeking truth from facts. They opposed the misuse of some words or phrases of Mao Zedong Thought that led to misinterpretation. On this issue, the "Two Whatevers" was intended precisely to safeguard all of Mao Zedong's teaching, including his erroneous theory and practice in his later years. To address this difficult issue, in July 1977, after he returned to work, Deng Xiaoping immediately proposed at the Third Plenary Session of the Tenth Central Committee that it was necessary to understand Mao Zedong Thought accurately and thoroughly, adhere to the scientific system of Mao Zedong Thought, and actively advocate adherence to the basic view of seeking truth from facts, so as to guide the people to view Mao and his thought in an objective way.

However, since Mao had just passed away and the cult of personality continued to have an enduring impact on the Party, it was extremely difficult to achieve "thoroughness and accuracy." This required an objective criterion that placed all people and things under it. Otherwise, it would be impossible to break away from the shackles of the "Two Whatevers," and the guiding principle of emancipating the mind and seeking truth from facts would be difficult to re-establish. This was bound to slow down the process of restoring order and aggravate the stagnation of work in various fields. With this in mind, the criterion of testing truth was put forward.

At the end of 1977, more than 800 senior and mid-level cadres studying in the Central Party School focused on discussing the history of the Party since the Cultural Revolution. A prominent problem in the discussion was what criteria should be used to recognize and judge the historical rights and the wrongs. For this reason, Hu Yaobang, the vice-president who presided over the regular work of the Central Party School at that time, guided theoretical workers in the Party School to write, after several revisions, a document guiding the study of Party history, clearly putting forward two guiding principles. The first was that the basic principles of Marxism-Leninism and Mao Zedong Thought should be applied accurately and thoroughly. The second was that practice was the criterion for testing truth and distinguishing between right and wrong. Under the guidance of these two principles, theoretical workers in the Party School began to write articles on the criterion of truth in view of the influence of the "Two Whatevers."

In March 1978, the editorial department of the *People's Daily* published an ideological commentary entitled "There is Only One Criterion" in response to the confused understanding of the issue of truth criterion. It clearly pointed out that "there is only one criterion of truth, that is, social practice." After it was published, the article provoked the objection of those who argued that Marxism-Leninism and Mao Zedong Thought were the criteria for testing truth. As a result, the editorial department decided to continue publishing articles to further clarify this issue.

In early April, the *Guangming Daily* was preparing to publish in the "Philosophy Issue" a feature written by Hu Fuming, a teacher of philosophy at Nanjing University, entitled "Practice is the Criterion for Testing Truth." The new editor-in-chief Yang Xiguang, who had just returned from the Central Party School, was keenly aware of the importance of the issues discussed in this article to political and ideological circles in China at that time, so he decided to remove it from the "Philosophy Issue," add something more specific to the situation at that time, then publish it on the front page. At this time, the original author, Hu Fuming, traveled to Beijing to attend a theoretical seminar, and the news agency asked him to discuss the revisions with the theoretical research team of the Central Party School. After revisions, the manuscript was processed twice by the editors of the newspapers and sent to the theoretical research room of the Central Party School for further revision and polishing before the final draft was completed.

After Hu Yaobang's examination and approval, the article "Practice is the Sole Criterion for Testing Truth" was first published on May 10, 1978 in the *Theoretical Dynamics* of the Central Party School, and the next day, the *Guangming Daily* published it in the form of a special commentator's article. On the 12th, the full text was reproduced in the *People's Daily*, the *PLA Daily*, and many provincial and municipal Party newspapers, and the Xinhua News Agency issued a news release as well.

This article condensed the collective wisdom of theoretical circles at that time, providing a large number of facts illustrating that practice was not only a criterion for testing truth, but the only criterion. Any theory should be constantly tested by practice. The reason Marxism was recognized as truth was that it had been proven by the long-term practice of millions of people. The dialectical materialist epistemological viewpoint on the dialectical unity of absoluteness and relativity of the standard of practice was that any thought and theory must undergo the test of practice, constantly and continuously, and without exception. That was the notion of truth development, which was the example revolutionary mentors set for later generations to see the principle of testing truth through practice at work.

Given the situation in the ideological and political field at that time, the article emphasized that the Gang of Four and its system of cliques had been destroyed, but the spiritual shackles imposed on the people by the Gang of Four were still far from being completely shattered. The tendency criticized by Mao Zedong that "only what is written in the Bible is right" remained. In theory as well as in practice, the Gang of Four had set up many "forbidden zones" to imprison people's minds. It was absolutely essential to break through these taboos and differentiate the right from the wrong. Mao reasoned that there was no forbidden zone in science, so wherever there is a "forbidden zone" beyond practice and which regarded itself as the absolute, there would be no science and no real Marxism or Mao Zedong Thought, but only obscurantism, idealism, and cultural autocracy.

The end of the article pointed out that socialism was for China an inevitable kingdom with unknown regions. In order to accomplish the great task of building socialism, China was faced with many new problems which required exploration and study. It was wrong to be contented with the established rules of Marxism-Leninism and Mao Zedong Thought and even use the ready-made formulas to restrict, contain, and cut short the infinitely rich and rapidly developing revolutionary practice. Rather, it was important to have the responsibility and vision of the Communists, daring to study the actualities of real life, the exact facts of the world, and the new problems emerging in new practices. Only in this way would it be possible to have a proper mentality toward Marxism and gradually move from the kingdom of necessity to that of freedom, and in this way successfully carry forward the new long march.

In fact, the article "Practice is the Sole Criterion for Testing Truth" demonstrated time and again a common-sense philosophical proposition of Marxism, containing no particular theoretical innovation in itself. However, under the specific historical conditions immediately after the end of the Cultural Revolution when the "Two Whatevers" still fettered people's thinking, the power of its distinct tendencies and clear targets was absolute. As soon as the article was published, it immediately provoked different reactions from various fronts and caused a great sensation both inside and outside the Party, marking the beginning of the national debate on the criterion of truth.

On May 12, when the *People's Daily* reprinted the article, the person in charge of the newspaper received a phone call accusing the article of "making a mistake in its direction."

On May 17, Wang Dongxing, then Vice-Chairman of the Central Committee of the Communist Party of China, criticized two articles, entitled "Practice is the Sole Criterion for Testing Truth" and "Implementing the Socialist Principle of Labor-based Distribution," published by *People's Daily* on May 5. He said that neither article was carefully examined before publication, and there were many discussions both inside and outside the Party targeting Mao's thought. This, he said, was inappropriate for a Party newspaper. He questioned, "which Central Committee's view this is" and stated that "we need to look into it, learn from it, and unify our understanding to ensure this sort of thing will never happen again." He demanded that the Central Propaganda Department "look into it more closely."

On May 18, at the National Conference on Education held by the Ministry of Propaganda and the Symposium of the Secretary of Culture and Education and the Minister of Propaganda of various provinces and municipalities, Zhang

Pinghua, Minister of Propaganda, asked participants to comment on the article "Practice is the Sole Criterion for Testing Truth," and to express different opinions. He said, "We should not assume that what is reported in the *People's Daily* or issued by the Xinhua News Agency is a final conclusion [...] Chairman Mao in his lifetime told the comrades in charge of the administration of provinces and municipalities that no matter where something comes from, including that from the Central Government, it should be examined to test whether it is fragrant or smelly, instead of following it blindly."

On June 15, Wang Dongxing convened a meeting with the heads of the Ministry of Propaganda, the directly affiliated organs of the Central Committee, and relevant news organizations. At the meeting, he criticized the article "Practice is the Sole Criterion for Testing Truth" and several other articles once again, and called out Hu Yaobang, reminding him to be more cautious when writing articles for the newspaper. In particular, he referred to two commentator's articles, pointing out that they were quite inappropriate, and warned everyone to be scrupulous and not focus on instant gratification. He believed that the inadequacies of propaganda would be exploited by enemies both in China and abroad, and by both Soviet and American powers and reactionaries. They would cause trouble in the relationship between members of the Standing Committee of the Politburo, between Chairman Mao and Chairman Hua, and between workers and farmers. It would be a grave, alarming matter to be taken advantage of by a variety of enemies.

In July, members of the Central Committee in charge of propaganda visited Shandong Province. In Jinan, they made a speech to the comrades in charge of the Shandong Provincial Committee, where they talked about the criteria of truth. The conclusions drawn included 1) don't abandon the flag, 2) don't drop your weapons, and 3) don't make a U-turn.

In this political context, many newspapers and magazines were actively involved, while *Red Flag* magazine remained silent for a long period. This silence was another clear manifestation of attitude. When the person in charge of the magazine mentioned that the attitude of *Red Flag* was being censured by the broad masses of cadres and people inside and outside the Party, Wang Dongxing said, "You should not be afraid of being isolated. There's nothing to be afraid of. The *Red Flag* will not take part in the discussion."

At a time when the discussion of truth criteria was suppressed and many felt burdened, Deng Xiaoping and other revolutionaries of the older generation stepped up to offer strong support. On May 30, in talks with several leaders, Deng made a targeted comment, saying, "One is not allowed to speak differently from Chairman Mao, nor is one allowed to say something that Chairman Mao or Chairman Hua has not said. You must only copy exactly Chairman Mao's or Chairman Hua's speech. This is not an isolated phenomenon. It is a reflection of a current trend of thought."[5] He stressed that the most fundamental and important thing in Mao Zedong Thought was seeking truth from facts, but at this time, even practice as the criterion for testing truth was in question.

On June 2, at the meeting of the political work of the entire military, Deng once again discussed this issue and commented that "some of our comrades speak of Mao Zedong Thought every day, but often forget, abandon, or even oppose such fundamental Marxist concepts and practice as Comrade Mao Zedong's seeking truth from facts, proceeding from reality, and combining theory with practice. Moreover, some people believe that whoever persists in seeking truth from facts, proceeds from reality, and combines theory with practice is guilty of a heinous crime. In essence, they advocate doing nothing more than merely copying the original words of Comrades Marx, Lenin, and Mao. Otherwise, they would say it is against Marxism, Leninism, and Mao Zedong Thought and violates the spirit of the Central Government. The question they have raised is not a minor one, but a matter of how to view Marxism-Leninism and Mao Zedong Thought."

On July 21, Deng Xiaoping specifically spoke to Zhang Pinghua, Minister of the Central Propaganda Department, asking him not to issue prohibitions or set up taboo areas, and not to pull back the emerging, lively political progress.[6]

On August 19, in a talk with the head of the Ministry of Culture, Deng Xiaoping said, "I have stated that the article 'Practice is the Sole Criterion for Testing Truth' is of Marxist nature and can stand any test. I agree with what is stated in this article."

On September 16, when listening to the report of the Standing Committee of the Jilin Provincial Committee, Deng said more directly, "At present, many people both inside and outside the Party are in favor of upholding the banner of Mao Zedong Thought. What is upholding? How to uphold? As we all know, there is an argument called the "Two Whatevers." Is it not very famous? Whatever documents Comrade Mao Zedong has read or commented on cannot be touched, and whatever Comrade Mao Zedong has done and said cannot be touched. Is this upholding the banner of Mao Zedong Thought? Definitely not. In doing so, we would only do harm to Mao Zedong Thought. The basic point of Mao Zedong Thought is to seek truth from facts, that is, to combine the general principles of Marxism-Leninism with the specific practice of the Chinese revolution."

In his speech at the State Council on September 9, Li Xiannian also expressed support for the discussion of the criterion of truth. He said that the destructive ruling of Lin Biao and the Gang of Four disrupted many theoretical issues, including the relationship between theory and practice, and caused confusion in thinking, which needed to be clarified. He emphasized that practice was the only criterion for testing truth. He pointed out that everything that has been proven by long-term social practice to be in conformity with objective laws, and the interests of the majority of people should be carried out resolutely and clung to until the end. Whether policies, plans, and measures were correct or not must be tested by the criterion of whether they worked for the interests of the people.

In order to commemorate the 85th anniversary of Mao Zedong's birth, the *Red Flag* invited Tan Zhenlin to write an article in memory of Mao Zedong's leadership in the struggle in Jinggangshan. When the article was completed, the editors found that beyond merely tracing the history, it also stated the fact that practice was the criterion for testing truth. This was apparently contrary to the *Red Flag*'s "non-involvement" attitude, but the author was reluctant to modify it and requested it be submitted to the Standing Central Committee for a decision. Having read the article, Hua Guofeng, Deng Xiaoping, Li Xiannian, and other leaders agreed to publish the article in the *Red Flag*.

Deng Xiaoping and Li Xiannian also criticized the *Red Flag* in their comments. Deng wrote, "I think this article is good, at least not wrong. If the *Red Flag* does not want to publish it, it can be transferred to the *People's Daily*. Why is the *Red Flag* not involved? It should be, and it should publish articles with different views. It seems that not being involved is in itself a kind of involvement." Li commented, "I've read this article and feel what Comrade Tan Zhenlin has mentioned are historical facts which should be published. Otherwise, the *Red Flag* is in too passive a position, as it has been up until now."

When the central high-level discussion on the criterion of truth launched a further struggle against the "Two Whatevers" faction, theoretical circles, academia, and the press acted accordingly. Encouraged by the concern and support of the older generation of revolutionaries, they withstood various pressures from the "Two Whatevers" faction, continuing to write articles and hold seminars to further the discussion.

Most people supported the fact that practice was a criterion of testing truth, but some questioned whether it was the only criterion. They believed that practice was a criterion of truth, but Marxism should be another criterion. This was quite a widespread ideological understanding at the time. As a result, the *People's Daily* invited Xing Bensi, from the Philosophy Research Institute of the Chinese Academy of Social Sciences, to publish an article entitled "Issues Concerning the Criteria of Truth" in response to the above doubts. This article held that the viewpoint that practice and Marxism were both truth violated the monism of dialectical materialism, resulting in confused theory. Cognitively speaking, this was a confusion between truth and the criterion of truth. Marxism was truth, but just as any truth cannot be proved by itself, it could not prove itself and needed to be proved by practice. At the same time, Marxism could not be used as a criterion to test other truths. Another confusion occurred between taking Marxism as both the guiding principle of revolutionary practice and as the criterion of truth, which were two different issues. From a philosophical point of view, it was absolutely wrong to deny the decisive role of practice when recognizing the reaction of theoretical cognition to practice. This sort of reaction could never take the place of practice as the criterion of testing truth.

In the face of various censures that practice was the sole criterion of testing truth, theorists gave a convincing reply and refutation. Among them, a comparatively systematic, sharp, and critical one was found in the article "A Fundamental Principle of Marxism" published by the *People's Liberation Army Daily* on June 24 in the name of a special commentator, which clearly pointed out that "the most powerful refutation to agnosticism, skepticism, and other philosophical eccentricities is practice. In a well-known quote Engels criticized Hume's and Kant's agnosticism and skepticism, which is of great relevance today." Marxist epistemology acknowledged that practice was the true yardstick. Agnosticism and skepticism could gain their foothold only when there was no objective criterion (i.e., practice) of testing truth, and it was by no means true that agnosticism and skepticism would become popular because of the establishment of an objective criterion of truth. Holding the opposite view was another shocking "reversal."

In view of this inversion, the article pointed out sharply, "Marxist theory is science, not superstition. A theory must be tested in practice before guiding the practice, and a theory is not unchangeable, but is constantly supplemented, revised, enriched, and developed in practice." Therefore, it was important not to stop at the old conclusions and slogans. Admittedly, it was not easy to change the old slogans. As the article noted, "The reason is that, apart from the fact that people's thinking often lags behind reality, some people's interests are more or less linked with those old slogans. These who verbally express their concern that revisions of some old slogans and propositions might lead to the negation of the entire revolution and the theoretical system (which is clearly a fanciful rhetoric) are actually afraid that some of their own interests would be affected as a result." For example, if the Party put practice as the sole criterion for testing truth, where should it put Mao Zedong Thought and Chairman Mao Zedong's words? The article pointed out that for those who uttered such irrational comments, one question still remained. Chairman Mao said that the revolutionary practice of millions of people was the only yardstick to test the truth, and there was no other way. Where was this instruction of Mao to be placed? And what did truly acting upon Mao's instructions entail?

This article, over ten thousand words long, was logical and highly pertinent. It was called a sister article to "Practice is the Sole Criterion for Testing Truth." It was published with the concern and support of Luo Ruiqing, Secretary-General of the Central Military Commission. When the article was finished, the *PLA Daily* newsagent sent it to Luo for review, and he read it closely three times, made five phone calls, consulted relevant works, and put forward detailed advice for revision to ensure the article was impeccable. This former general suffered persecution during the Cultural Revolution, and he broke his leg and had an amputation, but before he went to the Federal Republic of Germany for treatment, he called Hu Jiwei, the head of the *People's Daily*, and said, "If this article is to be beaten, I would like to get fifty beatings first." This risk-taking spirit demonstrated the clear-cut attitude of Luo Ruiqing in supporting the discussion of truth criteria, though he was never able to stand again, despite receiving treatment in the Federal German Hospital.

Practice as the criterion of testing truth was an unquestionable and irrefutable issue in the field of natural science, but natural scientists were actively involved in the debate. In mid-May, under the oversight of Fang Yi, the National Science and

Technology Commission, Chinese Academy of Science, and the leading Party group of the Chinese Association of Science and Technology held a joint meeting to discuss the relevant articles and made a decision to support the discussion. On July 5, the Seminar on the Relationship Between Theory and Practice, organized by the theoretical group of Chinese Academy of Science and Chinese Society of Natural Dialectics, was held in Beijing. Many scholars in the fields of natural science and the social sciences participated in the discussion and made speeches. The scientists employed a large number of examples from the history of science to illustrate that when conflicts occur between an original theory of natural science and new experimental facts, the breakthroughs of old theories and the creation of new theories must both resort to practice. Their arguments in natural science played a special supporting role in this great discussion in the field of ideological and political education.

From July 17 to 24, the Institute of Philosophy of the Chinese Academy of Social Sciences and the Editorial Department of Philosophical Research invited more than 160 theoretical workers from central and state ministries, Party schools, colleges and universities, scientific research institutes, and news organizations in provinces, municipalities, and autonomous regions to hold seminars on the relationship between theory and practice. At the seminar, many social scientists made speeches, which fully affirmed the practical significance of the discussion. After the seminar, representatives of many provinces and municipalities went back to convey the message, and the discussion on the criterion of truth was spread to every part of the nation.

In the second half of 1978, theoretical circles, academic circles, literary and artistic circles, and the press all actively devoted themselves to the discussion of the criterion of truth. According to incomplete statistics, by the end of the year, more than 650 monographs on the discussion of the truth criterion were published in the central and provincial newspapers and periodicals. As the discussion continued, these articles were published one after another, forming a widely recognized upsurge in discussion among the people, with theoretical circles as the main force, affecting the whole country and all levels of society.

In this upsurge in discussion, there was a noticeable phenomenon, which was that, along with the launching of the discussion on the criterion of truth, most provincial Party and government leading organs and the leading organs of the large military region launched the discussion on the criterion of truth in succession.

Many principal leaders of provinces, autonomous regions, municipalities, and military regions had publicly written articles or made speeches, expressing their support for the view that practice was the sole criterion for testing truth and extolling the theoretical and practical significance of this discussion. This was rare in the history of the Party and the People's Republic of China. Their speeches were generally related to the actual situation of the whole country and their particular region at that time. They not only pointed out the theoretical significance of the discussion, but also emphasized its political significance. At the very least, this demonstrated that the discussion of the criterion of truth had indeed become a major political issue of great concern to the Party, the army, and the people of the entire nation, that the correct view that practice was the sole criterion for testing truth was strongly supported by more senior cadres, and that the yardsticks of power, obscurantism, idealism, and cultural dictatorship had increasingly lost their markets.

The discussion of the criterion of truth not only restored the role of practice as the criterion of testing truth, but also provided a sharp ideological weapon to break through the confinement of the "Two Whatevers" and a theoretical basis for accurately summarizing the lessons of the Cultural Revolution and remedying it and other past historical errors. As is pointed out in the article "Practice is the Sole Criterion for Testing Truth," there are only obscurantism, idealism, and cultural authoritarianism when there is a self-assigned absolute "forbidden zone." The discussion of the criterion of truth greatly facilitated people's ideological emancipation, quickened the pace of rectifying chaos, and made necessary ideological preparations for the Communist Party of China to break the ideological shackles of the "Two Whatevers," re-establish the practical and realistic guiding principles, and successfully navigate this great historical turning point.

More importantly, this movement, which was later called a great ideological emancipation in the history of modern Chinese thought, laid the foundation for the exploration of the socialist path with Chinese characteristics and a range of theoretical innovations and practical development after Reform and Opening Up.

III

Partial Deliberation on the Shift of Focus in the Work of the Party and the State

The ideological emancipation brought about by the discussion of the criterion of truth promoted a new exploration of China's socialist path by the Communist Party of China. With the end of the Cultural Revolution and the rapid increase in China's exchanges with other countries, this new exploration gained a broader vision. China began to learn from different countries' experience of economic construction, and from there, it gradually and clearly determined its own basic policy of opening up.

1. A Large Number of Chinese Leaders' Visits and the Increasing Awareness of Reform and Opening Up

Since 1978, China changed the practice of Party and government leaders' rare visits to other nations, as had been the norm during the Cultural Revolution period. That year alone, 13 Chinese Vice-Premiers and leaders above the level of vice-chairman led delegations for visits 21 times, spanning 51 countries. Among them, Deng Xiaoping himself visited eight countries four times. These visits not only improved China's foreign relations, but also enabled senior Party and state officials to have a more direct, comprehensive understanding of the development and changes in the international situation in recent years. The strong feeling commonly espoused among the visiting leaders was that China's economic, scientific, and technological development lagged far behind the world's most advanced levels.

At the National Science Congress in March 1978, some comrades mentioned that the development of the world economy was more closely related to science and technology, and that the development of the national economy and industries mainly depended on the development of science and technology. One of the most important reasons for China's economic backwardness was its underdeveloped technology. Compared with the world's most advanced levels, China's science and technology in most areas were about 15 to 20 years behind, and in some areas there were even larger gaps. Therefore, if China intended to push the economy forward, it must first earnestly learn the world's most advanced technology. If it closed its eyes and ears, not knowing the trends, changes, and levels of international scientific and technological development, it would not be able to catch up with or surpass the world's most advanced nations. These opinions captured the attention of the leaders of the CPC Central Committee and the State Council.

On May 17, 1978, the State Council set up a leading group for the introduction of new technologies to study and formulate plans for the introduction of advanced technologies from abroad. Then, the leaders of the State Council and the comrades in charge of various departments and localities visited and inspected developed Western countries and regions to understand the level and the experience of economic development there. On the eve of the delegation led by Vice Premier Gu Mu of the State Council visiting Western Europe, Deng Xiaoping specifically asked the group to make a detailed study into the stage to which its modern industry had developed, and how its economic work was managed. It was important for China to learn from the advanced experience of capitalist countries.

When Chinese leaders went abroad, capitalism had passed the "golden age" of great development after the Second World War. During the first half of the 1970s, capitalist countries suffered their most serious economic crisis after the war. In 1974 and 1975, the GDP of the United States, Japan, the Federal Republic of Germany, the United Kingdom, France, and Italy all showed negative growth. In the second half of the 1970s, the Western economy was in stagflation, and its recovery was weak. Under such circumstances, developed countries were willing not only to expand trade with China, but they did provide preferential loans to and even make investments in China.

Through visits and inspections, these leading comrades saw not only the gap in China's economic development, but many good opportunities provided by the international situation for China's development at that time. Upon returning, they proposed to the Central Government that China should make full use of the current favorable conditions, absorb foreign funds as much as possible, introduce a large number of foreign advanced technology and equipment, learn from their advanced managerial expertise, and speed up its modernization drive. When reporting to the CPC Central Committee and the State Council on his visits, Gu Mu said in particular that Western Europe had the experience of utilizing foreign capital and introducing advanced technology when its economy took off. Why couldn't China do that? The opinions and suggestions put forward by these comrades were filed into documents and circulated among the leaders of various departments of the central and state organs, bringing about major results.

2. Proposal for Holding and Reform of the State Council's Retreat Meeting

The understanding of the world's most advanced levels provoked reflection on the experience and lessons of China's economic construction. How to draw upon this experience and speed up construction became an increasingly pressing problem facing the entire Party.

During this period, Deng Xiaoping stated on various occasions that there was a better international condition for China to make use of the advanced achievements in the world as the starting point for its development. In the past, when the Gang of Four interfered with construction, it had not been clear what the rest of the world looked like. With the rapid development of the world economy, China still had some old concepts in mind, preventing it from focusing on the present to identify and address problems. In this way, the Four Modernizations would only be an empty dream, even if they were discussed every day. Compared with the world's most advanced level, China was underdeveloped not only in technology, but in management as well. The country's system, including the institutional system, was basically modeled after that of the Soviet Union, which was underdeveloped with overstaffed and overlapping institutions and increasing bureaucracy. There were many institutional problems to be reevaluated. These views gradually become the consensus of the Party leadership.

From July 6 to September 9, 1978, the State Council held bimonthly meetings to study how to speed up China's drive toward modernization. On the basis of summarizing the experience and lessons learned since the founding of New China, the leaders of all departments put forward at their meetings suggestions for reforming the economic management system and introducing advanced foreign technology and equipment.

Several leading comrades who returned from their visits introduced the current international situation and the experience of foreign economic development. The State Planning Commission put forward suggestions on actively expanding exports and increasing foreign trade ports, and the Ministry of the Machinery Industry put forward the idea of combining the introduction of new technologies with the reform of the domestic management system. In addition, the State

Administration of Labor proposed the reform of the wage system to effectively mobilize and motivate staff and workers. In his speech, Hu Qiaomu enumerated the drawbacks of simply relying on administrative methods to manage the economy, stating that this method "should be narrowed to a minimal scope, the maximum amount of economic work should be transferred from the government administration to the enterprise operation, and enterprises should try to narrow the management of pure administrative methods and expand the management relying on economic means."

In the concluding speech of the meeting, Li Xiannian clearly put forward the idea of carrying out a policy of Reform and Opening Up to the outside world. He pointed out that in the past two decades, China had reformed the economic system more than once. He added, "But in the aspect of enterprise management system, we tend to focus more on the transfer of administrative power, often fluctuating in the old-fashioned way between empowering and disempowering, which makes it difficult to meet the requirements of economic development [...] The reform we are going to carry out now must take into account the motivation of the central departments, local governments, and enterprises, considering the economic benefits and development prospects of large enterprises and professional companies, with an aim of managing the modern economy with modern management methods." He pointed out that the current international situation was favorable to China, so it should have the courage and ability to make use of the advanced technology, equipment, funds, and organizational experience of foreign countries to speed up its construction. It was imperative that this rare opportunity not be missed, as it would be much quicker for development than trying to start from scratch behind closed doors.

On September 30, the Central Committee transmitted the speech and was ready to discuss it further at the forthcoming Central Working Conference.

Shortly after the meeting, the National Planning Conference convened by the State Council pointed out that the economic front should undergo three transformations. First, from top to bottom, China must turn its attention to the struggle for production and the technological revolution. Second, it should shift its attention from bureaucratic management systems and methods that ignored economic effects and work efficiency to scientific management working in accordance with economic laws and integrating democracy and centralization. Third, it should shift from the closed or semi-closed state of economic and technological exchanges between different capitalist countries to actively introducing advanced technologies, making use of foreign funds, and boldly entering the international market.

On October 11, Deng Xiaoping said in his speech at the Ninth National Congress of China's Trade Union that the realization of the Four Modernizations "is a great revolution that fundamentally changes the underdeveloped economic and technological situation of our country and further consolidates the dictatorship of the proletariat. If the revolution is to dramatically change the backward productivity we see at the moment, it should inevitably change in many ways the relations of production, the superstructure, the management mode of industrial and agricultural enterprises, and the state's management mode of industrial and agricultural enterprises, so as to be adapted to the needs of the modern economy." Therefore, "all economic fronts not only need major technological reforms, but also major institutional and organizational reforms, which are in line with the long-term interests of our people. Otherwise, we cannot get rid of the backward state of production technology and management."

Motivated by the above ideas, in 1978, China signed 22 contracts with developed Western countries to import set projects. Although there was a tendency to be overeager for success in import work, the imported projects, ultimately provided more advanced technical equipment and a higher starting point for China's modernization construction. For example, the introduction of complete sets of equipment in Shanghai Baoshan Iron and Steel Works enabled China to learn world-class production technology and management methods, and it shortened the gap between China's iron and steel industry and the world's most advanced level by at least 20 years. Both ideological preparations and practical attempts showed that the general policy of Reform and Opening Up was ready to emerge.

3. Brewing and Putting Forward the Idea of Shifting the Focus of the Party's and State's Work

The idea of shifting the focus of work in the Party and the state was brewing much earlier in the senior leadership of the party. As early as the tenth day after the toppling of the Gang of Four, on October 16, 1976, Li Xiannian called Chen Yun to ask for his views on the future work. After deliberation with Wang Zhen and Yao Yilin, Chen Yun put forward several suggestions, one of which was "vigorously grasping production so as to enable the national economy to recover and develop rapidly." This was the earliest material that planned for the shift focus in the work.

In September 1978, after concluding his visit to North Korea, Deng Xiaoping made an unusual inspection of the three northeastern provinces, Tangshan, Tianjin, and other areas, which was an important effort to push forward the turning point of history.

On the way to make inspection, Deng repeatedly appealed to the comrades in charge of local affairs to emancipate the mind and seek truth from facts. According to the current international and domestic conditions, it was important to think, ask questions, and solve problems rather than set up forbidden zones. The harm of forbidden zones was to make people rigid in their thinking and not approach problems based on their own conditions. In short, it was necessary to seek truth from facts and turn to the intellect to initiate a revolution. Having introduced advanced technology and equipment, it was important to follow advanced international management methods and economic laws. It was likewise necessary to revolutionize rather than modify or patch and mend. The key was to advocate and educate all cadres to think critically and to boldly conduct reform on things that were unreasonable. It was time to change the superstructure.

He also stressed time and again that the most urgent task facing China was to develop productivity. China was too poor and backward to be responsible for its people. It was a socialist country. The fundamental manifestation of the superiority of the socialist system was that it could facilitate social productivity to develop rapidly at a speed that the old society did not have, so that the people's growing material and cultural needs could be met. From the point of view of historical materialism, the results of correct political leadership ultimately lay in the development of social productivity and the improvement of people's material and cultural life. It was important to think about how much had been done for the people. Therefore, it was necessary to accelerate the development of productivity and improve the people's material and cultural life.

It was for this reason that Deng Xiaoping proposed that the mass movement to expose and criticize the Gang of Four should be ended in a timely manner, and that the focus of the work of the Party and the state should be shifted to socialist modernization. This was a great strategic mindset. When listening to the report of the Standing Committee of the Shenyang Military Region of the Communist

Party of China on the campaign aimed at exposing and criticizing the Gang of Four, he said, "You can carry on the movement, but what is the bottom line? This will never be an absolutely completed thing. You can't go too long with the movement or you will get tired of it. There is always an end to the campaign exposing and criticizing the Gang of Four. We can't go on for another three or five years. After a while, we need to finish it and turn to normal work." After leaving the northeastern provinces, he reiterated this opinion to the relevant comrades of the Central Committee and received the support of other leading comrades there. This made it possible for the shift of work to become a major overarching decision.

On October 11, Deng Xiaoping made his view clearer in a speech at the trade union's ninth conference. He pointed out that the struggle to expose and criticize the Gang of Four had won a decisive victory in a wide range of areas throughout the country. He said, "We have been able to start new tasks on the basis of this victory." At this point, the Party Central Committee and the State Council called for speeding up the pace of realizing the Four Modernizations. "This is a great revolution that fundamentally changes the backward situation of our economy and technology and further consolidates the dictatorship of the proletariat." He hoped that the delegates at the meeting would "discuss the current situation in depth so as to unite all members and fight for this great task on the basis of a complete victory in the struggle against the Gang of Four."

At this time, quite a number of people realized that in order to achieve the goal of socialist modernization and to put into effect the plan for Reform and Opening Up as soon as possible, it was important to shift the focus of the work of the Party and the state to modernization. There were basically no divergent views within the Party. However, in the guiding ideology of modernization, the Party members were divided in their understanding. Some comrades still adhered to the guiding ideology of the "Two Whatevers" and believed that to realize the Four Modernizations, "we must adhere to the principle of class struggle and seize all the three revolutionary movements of class struggle, production struggle, and scientific experiment." Most comrades, on the other hand, advocated that in the process of modernization, China needed to adhere to the guiding ideology of seeking truth from facts and, first of all, rectify the chaos. This divergence in guiding ideology inevitably led to a fierce ideological confrontation on the issue of shifting the focus of work.

IV

The Central Working Conference and the Third Plenary Session of the Eleventh CPC Central Committee in 1978

The period from the Central Working Conference in 1978 to the Third Plenary Session of the Eleventh Central Committee of the CPC had a significant impact on the Party and the state in the process of moving towards a great historical turning point after the toppling of the Gang of Four. With the Third Plenary Session of the Eleventh Central Committee of the CPC, the Party and the state launched a great new journey of Reform and Opening Up.

1. The Central Working Conference Held in 1978

On November 10, 1978, the Central Committee Working Conference was held in Beijing. The conference was attended by 219 leading comrades from provinces, municipalities and autonomous regions, major military regions, and central departments, along with some veteran comrades who held important positions in the central, local, and military forces. The participants were divided into six groups by region. This was an extremely important central meeting in preparation for the Third Plenary Session of the Eleventh CPC Central Committee.

At the opening meeting, Hua Guofeng announced that the topics to be addressed at the meeting were 1) the Decision on Accelerating Agricultural Development and the Rural People's Commune Work Regulations (Draft), 2) the implementation of the National Economic Plans for 1979 and 1980, and 3) Li Xiannian's speech at the State Council meeting. Before discussing these issues, the Politburo decided to discuss the issue of shifting the focus of the Party's work to the socialist drive toward modernization that would begin the following year.

In his speech, Hua Guofeng did not mention the discussion of truth standards or the change of guiding ideology, nor did he mention the issue of redressing injustices and falsehoods, which were of general concern both inside and outside the Party at that time. He said that the basis for shifting the focus of work was that the mass movement of exposing and criticizing the Gang of Four had been successfully completed for the most part, and new tasks should be put forward to adapt to current developments. He noted, "The main problems of one stage have been solved, and we need to go on to a new stage." This meant that the shift of the focus of work was only a change in the work stage, not a change in the fundamental guiding ideology or the Party's political line. Influenced by this, in the documents on agriculture submitted to the conference for discussion, the idea of "grasping the revolution and promoting production" was still followed, and the general evaluation of the "great harvest for more than ten consecutive years," which was popular in the Cultural Revolution and concealed the truth, continued. Obviously, it was unsatisfactory to those comrades who hoped to sort out the guiding ideology and the rights and wrongs of major historical issues.

Since the group discussion on November 11, some people had raised the issue of remedying and reversing major cases of misjudgment, such as the Tiananmen Incident. On the 12th, Chen Yun spoke in the Northeast Group and first put forward his view on resolving the lingering historical problems. He said that realizing the Four Modernizations was the urgent aspiration of the Party and the people of the whole country at that time. Stability and unity were also matters of concern to the Party and the people of the country. In order to ensure stability and unity, "the Central Government should consider and make decisions on lingering issues with great impact or involving a wide range of aspects." Then, he raised six major lingering historical issues, such as redressing the issue of 61 comrades, including Bo Yibo, the Tiananmen Incident, and the conclusion about Tao Zhu and Peng Dehuai. Once these major issues of concern were raised, they had strong repercussions, and the atmosphere at the conference became quite lively. The focus of each group's speeches soon turned to the issue of redressing injustices and wrongs, especially the Tiananmen Incident. Almost all the groups suggested that redressing injustices and wrongs should be done as quickly as possible.

Under these circumstances, the Central Committee approved the announcement by the expanded meeting of the Standing Committee of the Beijing Municipal Committee of the Communist Party of China on the Tiananmen Incident. All the persecuted comrades would be put right and their reputations would be restored. On the 15th, the Xinhua News Agency reported on the incident under the heading "Tiananmen Incident, An Entirely Revolutionary Action." On the 16th, the *People's Daily*, *Guangming Daily*, and other major newspapers and magazines published the news, which inspired the masses and cadres. Subsequently, the provincial Party committees of Henan, Zhejiang, and Jiangsu solemnly declared that the cases concerning comrades who were persecuted during the Qingming Festival in 1976 for mourning Premier Zhou and opposing the Gang of Four were completely redressed, and their reputations were restored.

As for other major misjudged cases raised at the meeting, some comrades pointed out that the Central Committee had settled these issues in the past and that it would be inappropriate for the Central Committee not to come out and state its attitude clearly. Otherwise, cadres and the masses would feel dissatisfied. It was therefore best for the central authorities to make these issues clear before shifting the focus of work.

Under these circumstances, the Standing Committee of the Politburo of the Central Committee discussed these views. On November 25, on behalf of the Politburo of the Central Committee, Hua Guofeng announced at the meeting that the Central Committee had decided to openly and thoroughly redress the Tiananmen Incident, the so-called February Countercurrent, and the Bo Yibo Group of more than sixty traitors. It further determined the past erroneous treatment of Comrades Peng Dehuai, Tao Zhu, and Yang Shangkun, and some major local events were dealt with by the Party committees of provinces, autonomous regions, and municipalities directly under the Central Government in a pragmatic manner based on the circumstances. The Central Special Task Force was to finish its work and hand over all its cases to the Central Organizational Department, and Kang Sheng and Xie Fuzhi had aroused great indignation among the people and had to be exposed and criticized. Later, on December 14, when the Central Working Conference issued Hua Guofeng's speech, it added, on the basis of public opinion, the recognition that it was wrong to "fight against the right-leaning style of overturning cases," and revoked all the documents of the Central Committee concerning the "fight against the right-leaning style of overturning cases." These decisions basically solved several major issues that had been strongly appealed to by cadres and the masses for the previous two years, and the comrades present at the meeting were immediately put at ease. Everyone spoke freely and thought was more liberated. Some comrades even suggested that the Cultural Revolution should be reexamined and reevaluated. They believed that "Liu Shaoqi's bourgeois headquarters" did not exist at all, and that the evaluation of the Cultural Revolution and its "70% of achievements and 30% of errors" was not convincing. However, it was not yet mature enough to fully discuss and definitely settle the issue.

Having settled some major lingering historical issues, the meeting also held a heated discussion on the divergence of views concerning the criteria of truth. Some comrades still believed that discussing the standard of truth was in fact "advocating suspicion of everything and guiding people to discuss Chairman Mao's mistakes, which is not in line with the principles of the Eleventh National Congress." This view was criticized by most comrades, who also criticized the heads of the *Red Flag* and the Central Propaganda Department who had taken a negative attitude in the previous discussion, hoping that the latter would adjust their attitude as soon as possible. Most people felt that the divergence on this issue was essentially the difference in two guiding principles. If the problem was not solved and right and wrong were not clearly distinguished, the shift of work focus would not go smoothly. After sharp ideological confrontation, some comrades who did not know enough about the significance of this discussion turned around and offered self-criticism. The Central Committee was also asked to make a clear statement on this discussion, so as to thoroughly settle the ideological line.

In discussing other issues, most people shook off the bondage of the Two Whatevers, carried forward the tradition of seeking truth from facts, seriously reflected on the guiding ideology and some policies of the previous years, and boldly put forward criticisms and suggestions.

Guiding the key shift in work was a very crucial issue. Some comrades believed that "we should continue to take class struggle as the key link" in our construction. Many comrades pointed out that the problem of class struggle in the period of construction should be reconsidered to clarify vague ideas. This was an issue that had to be resolved by the Party in the work of guiding modernization. Some comrades pointed out that the shift of the focus of work was not a change in the general nature of the Party's specific work, but a fundamental change of historical significance. In the future, except in the event of outbreak of war, it was necessary to take the struggle for production and technological revolution as the priority, and this must remain the sole priority. Some comrades also questioned the years-long proposition that "class struggles and the struggle for production and scientific experiment should be carried out with equal focus." They believed that this proposal had misplaced priorities and that focus should be given to the production struggle as the center. After heated discussion, most believed that the problem of class struggle in the socialist period should be reconsidered, thus opening up the way to deny the policy of "taking class struggle as the key point."

In discussing the two agricultural documents, many comrades expressed their strong dissatisfaction with the documents' avoidance of grim reality and its empty talk of "the superiority of the people's commune" and "the great harvest for more than ten consecutive years." They pointed out that there were nearly 200 million people in the country whose rations were less than 150 kilograms, and the per capita food supply was less than that in 1957. This was mainly the result of the past policy that restricted farmers too much, resulting in agriculture failing to develop rapidly due to the "left-leaning" mistakes. Some comrades stated that China should not be afraid of rich farmers. If it was believed that rich farmers would lead to capitalism, then China would remain poor from generation to generation. How would revolution be carried out then? Many suggestions were put forward for the restoration and development of agriculture as soon as possible. In his speech, Chen Yun proposed that in three to five years, "20 million tons of grain can be imported every year. We can't be rigid in every aspect. We must first stabilize the farmers. To stabilize this part is to stabilize the majority... and society will be stable then... This is the most vital economic measure." These opinions and suggestions attracted the attention of the Central Government, and the two documents on agriculture were rewritten based on public opinion.

In discussing Li Xiannian's concluding speech at the State Council meeting, many people supported the reform of the management system and the implementation of the policy of opening to the outside world. At the conference, a number of materials were published on how other countries, Hong Kong, and Taiwan had developed their economy rapidly. Many attendees proposed changing the past practice of having "neither domestic nor external debt," making full use of the favorable international situation, absorbing as much foreign capital as possible, introducing a large number of advanced technologies and equipment, and speeding up construction. It was suggested that the Standing Committee of the National People's Congress should enact laws on receiving foreign loans, borrowings, and investments as soon as possible so as to encourage foreign business owners to set up joint ventures in China. These opinions further solidified the previous formulation of the policy of Reform and Opening Up, and the time for formal decision-making on Reform and Opening Up was ripe.

The conference also discussed Party building, building the country's democracy and legal system, and other similar issues. In light of the painful lessons of the Cultural Revolution, the participants talked about the need to restore the Party's fine tradition of democratic centralism and strengthen the socialist democracy and building the legal system, and proposed a series of measures to strengthen the Party and the country's democratic construction.

Deng Xiaoping closely observed the process of the conference. Based on the discussion and the questions raised, he felt that the manuscript he had prepared for his speech was no longer applicable. Rather, he thought it more appropriate to clarify more pertinently the most critical and urgent issues. He thus personally wrote an outline that listed seven issues, including (1) emancipating the mind and inspiring motivation, (2) promoting democracy and strengthening the legal system, (3) looking backwards to move toward the future, (4) overcoming bureaucracy and overstaffing, (5) allowing some areas to improve first, (6) strengthening the liability system and making decisions, and (7) "new problems." Based on this outline, several comrades redrafted the speech for him.

On December 13th, the conference held the closing ceremony. Hua Guofeng, Ye Jianying, and Deng Xiaoping each made speeches. In his speech, Hua Guofeng offered a self-criticism on the issue of the "Two Whatevers," admitting that "the two statements are not thought through… To varying degrees, they have fettered our thinking and are not conducive to the practical implementation of the Party's policies, or to the activation of ideas within the Party." He announced that the Third Plenary Session of the Eleventh Central Committee would be convened after the meeting to further define the principles and tasks of the Party after the shift of the focus of its work.

Ye Jianying made three suggestions. (1) There should be good leadership, especially in the Central Committee. (2) To promote democracy and strengthen the legal system, the Standing Committee of the National People's Congress should shoulder the responsibility of formulating laws and improving the socialist legal system as soon as possible. (3) It was essential to study diligently and emancipate the mind. He pointed out that "our socialist modernization drive is not only a great improvement in social productivity, but also a profound social revolution of the economic base and the superstructure." Many people were not yet ready for such a revolution and their minds were not sufficiently liberated. Therefore, "we must break all the superstitions caused by feudalism and liberate our minds from their shackles."

Deng Xiaoping made an important speech entitled "Emancipating the Mind, Seeking Truth from Facts, and Looking Forward Together." In this speech, he pointed out that "first of all, we need to emancipate the mind. Only when our minds are emancipated can we properly take Marxism-Leninism and Mao Zedong Thought as our guide, solve the lingering problems from the past, and settle a range of new problems [...] Without breaking ideological rigidity and liberating the minds of cadres and the masses, there will be no hope for the Four Modernizations."

Deng Xiaoping offered a summary of the heated discussion on the criterion of truth that had pervaded the Party over the previous six months. He pointed out that the discussion on whether practice was the sole criterion for testing truth was in fact a debate on whether to emancipate the mind. It was necessary and of great significance to carry out this debate. "If a party, a country, or a nation proceeds from mere book knowledge, with rigid ideology and prevailing superstition, it will stop moving forward and lose its vitality, and the Party and the country will perish." At that time, in order to restore the tradition of seeking truth from facts, it was necessary to emancipate the people's minds and overcome ideological rigidity in all fields. In this sense, "the debate on the criterion of truth is indeed a question of ideological line, a political issue, and a matter concerning the future and destiny of the Party and the country."

Deng Xiaoping emphasized that one of the most important conditions for emancipating and mobilizing the mind was to truly implement the democratic centralism of the proletariat. At this stage, it was necessary to emphasize democracy. The Party had to create the conditions for democracy and strengthen socialist democracy and the rule of law. This conference solved some problems that still remained from the past, distinguished some people's merits and demerits, and corrected cases of major injustices and wrongs, which met the requirements to emancipate the mind. The purpose was to look ahead and make a smooth shift of the focus onto the Party's work.

Regarding the reform to be implemented, Deng said that in order to look ahead, the government must study new situations and solve new problems in a timely manner. At the time, China's economic and management work was overstaffed, overlapping, procedurally complicated, and inefficient. Empty political talk often drowned everything else. This was not the responsibility of some particular comrades, but a result of the fact that reform had been promptly initiated. At the same time, if reform was not then carried out, the cause of modernization and socialism would be buried.

He also pointed out that in the future, special attention should be paid to strengthening accountability in the management system. For any task or construction project, the system of defining tasks, personnel, quantity, quality, and time should be implemented. In terms of economic policy, it was necessary to allow some areas and some people be the first to make more money and live a better life because of their hard work and great achievements. In this way, good models would exert a great impact on their neighbors, drive other regions, and make the national economy develop substantially. "This is a strategic policy, a policy that can influence and drive the entire national economy."

Deng Xiaoping's speech not only raised and answered a series of fundamental questions at this turning point in history, but also summarized the work conference of the Central Committee and provided a guiding ideology for the upcoming Third Plenary Session of the Eleventh Central Committee. Therefore, this speech had in fact become the keynote speech of the Third Plenary Session of the Eleventh Central Committee of the CPC.

After the closing meeting, the conference continued its two day discussion, which ended on December 15. With the promotion of the older generation of revolutionaries and the joint effort of the overwhelming majority of the comrades participating in the meeting, the 36-day Central Working Conference finally shook off the shackles of the "Two Whatevers" policy and turned the meeting that was originally intended to discuss economic work into a meeting to rectify the overall chaos and create new prospects.

2. The Third Plenary Session of the Eleventh Central Committee

On the basis of the significant achievements of the Central Working Conference, the Third Plenary Session of the Eleventh Central Committee of the Communist Party of China was held in Beijing from December 18–22, 1978. The meeting was attended by members of the Central Committee, alternate members of the Central Committee, and responsible comrades from relevant departments of the Central Committee, a total of 290 people. At the opening meeting, Hua Guofeng announced that the main task of this plenary session was to discuss and adopt the proposal of the Politburo of the Central Committee to shift the focus of the Party's work to socialist modernization beginning the following January. The meeting deliberated and adopted two documents on agriculture, namely the Decision of the Central Committee of the Communist Party of China on Issues to Accelerate Agricultural Development (Draft) and the Rural People's Commune Work Regulations (Draft for Trial Implementation). It reviewed and approved the national economic planning arrangements for 1979 and 1980, and it discussed personnel issues and the election of the Central Disciplinary Inspection Commission.

Previously, after 36 days of thorough discussions at the Central Working Conference, the participants reached consensus on several major issues. Accordingly, the plenary session decided to put an end to the nationwide mass movement to expose and criticize Lin Biao and the Gang of Four in a timely and decisive manner, and to shift the focus of the Party's work to socialist modernization after 1979. In the future, class struggle in the socialist society should be solved in accordance with the principle of strictly distinguishing and correctly handling two kinds of contradictions of different natures, in line with the procedures prescribed by the Constitution and the law, instead of confusing the boundaries of two kinds of contradictions of different natures or undermining the political situation of stability and unity required for socialist modernization. Since the policy of "taking class struggle as the main line" was put forward, this was the first time that the Party had formally made such clear restrictions and regulations on class struggle, which politically guaranteed the realization of the shift of work focus.

Under Deng Xiaoping's guiding principles of emancipating the mind, seeking truth from facts, and looking forward with unity, attendees at the meeting discussed the Party's ideological line in depth. They agreed that only under the guidance of Marxism-Leninism and Mao Zedong Thought could the people emancipate the mind, seek truth from facts, proceed from reality, and integrate theory with practice. Then, the Party could smoothly shift the focus of work. The plenary highly appraised the discussion concerning practice as the sole criterion for testing truth, believing that it was of far-reaching historical significance for promoting the emancipation of the mind and rectifying the ideological line of all Party members and the people.

On the basis of a careful summary of the experience and lessons learned since the founding of New China, it was generally felt that after the shift of work priorities, it was important not to continue to use the previous management system and methods, but to boldly reform the traditional ones and explore new ways of development in accordance with the needs of the drive toward modernization.

The communiqué of the plenary session pointed out that, according to the new historical conditions and practical experience, China should adopt a series of new and important economic measures, carry out serious reforms in the economic management system and methods, actively develop equal and mutually beneficial economic cooperation with other countries on the basis of self-reliance, and strive to adopt the world's most advanced technology and equipment. This in fact made the previous preparation of Reform and Opening Up the general policy of socialist modernization construction, and the shift of the focus of work likewise became the beginning of a new revolution by the Party through Reform and Opening Up, exploring a new path of socialist construction.

In discussing agricultural issues, the plenary session proposed a series of policies and measures to promote agricultural development, such as raising the purchase price of agricultural products, and agreed to issue the Decision of the Central Committee of the Communist Party of China on Issues of Accelerating Agricultural Development (Draft) and the Rural People's Communes Work Regulations (Draft for Trial Implementation) to provinces, autonomous regions, and municipalities directly under the Central Government for discussion and trial implementation. After rewriting the document, it pointed out the backward situation of agriculture in China and put forward a series of policies and measures to speed up the development of agriculture. It emphasized that "the autonomy of production teams should be respected," the democratic rights of farmers should be effectively guaranteed politically, and the material interests of farmers should be fully covered economically, thus starting the rural reform in practice.

In reviewing the arrangements of the national economic plan for 1979 and 1980, the plenary session affirmed the views of the Central Working Conference on the adjustment of the national economy and put forward the policy that capital construction must be carried out actively and based on the specific situation, thus beginning to correct the guiding ideology of economic construction.

The plenary session affirmed the decision of the Central Working Conference to rectify and reassess the merits and demerits of some important leaders for a series of major misjudged cases. It reiterated the principle of seeking truth from facts and correcting mistakes to solve the remaining problems of history, thus initiating the fight against all unjust and false cases, and comprehensively clearing up and thoroughly resolving the Cultural Revolution and its previous major historical issues, both right and wrong.

The plenary session also made a series of decisions, such as strengthening socialist democracy and construction of the legal system, improving the democratic centralism of the Party, improving Party regulations and discipline, and implementing serious Party discipline. It also put forward the task of strengthening the socialist legal system, and institutionalizing and legalizing democracy. It emphasized that the state must have national laws, and the Party must have discipline. All Party members and Party cadres were to abide by this Party discipline.

While resolutely correcting the leftist errors of the Cultural Revolution and some of its previous mistakes, the plenary session affirmed Mao Zedong's achievements and thought. The communiqué of the plenary session pointed out that Mao Zedong's great merits in his neutrality in the long-term revolutionary struggle were indelible. At the same time, it pointed out that requiring a revolutionary leader to have no shortcomings or mistakes was neither Marxist nor consistent with Mao's historical evaluation of himself. The lofty task of the Central Committee on the theoretical front was to lead and educate the whole Party and the people of the whole country to understand Mao's great achievements historically and scientifically, to master the scientific system of Mao Zedong Thought completely and accurately, to integrate the general principles of Marxism-Leninism and Mao Zedong Thought with the concrete reality of socialist modernization construction, and to develop the thought under new historical conditions. This made it possible not only to point out and correct Mao Zedong's errors in his later years, but also to objectively respect the history of the Party and the people, so as not to lose its direction and basic foothold.

After careful deliberation, the plenary elected Chen Yun as a member of the Politburo of the Central Committee, a member of the Standing Committee of the Politburo, and vice-chairman of the Central Committee. Deng Yingchao, Hu Yaobang, and Wang Zhen were elected as members of the Politburo. Huang Kecheng, Song Renqiong, Hu Qiaomu, Xi Zhongxun, Wang Renzhong, Huang Huoqing, Chen Zaidao, Han Guang, and Zhou Hui were elected as members of the Central Committee and their names were submitted to the Twelfth National Congress for confirmation. The Central Commission for Discipline Inspection was elected with Chen Yun as its first secretary, Deng Yingchao as the second secretary, Hu Yaobang as the third secretary, Huang Kecheng as the standing secretary, and Wang Heshou as the deputy secretary. On December 25, the Politburo of the

Central Committee held a meeting and decided that Hu Yaobang would be the Secretary-General of the Central Committee of the Communist Party of China and the Minister of the Central Propaganda Department, that Hu Qiaomu and Yao Yilin would be the Deputy Secretary-General of the Central Committee of the Communist Party of China, and Wang Dongxing would be relieved of his concurrent post as the Director of the Central Office. These organizational measures provided a reliable guarantee for the smooth realization of the shift in priorities and the implementation of the principles and policies set by the plenary. Although Hua Guofeng was still the chairman of the CPC Central Committee at that time, Deng Xiaoping actually became the central leader of the CPC Central Committee in terms of embodying the correct guiding ideology of the Party and deciding on the major principles and policies of reform, opening up, and modernization.

A series of important decisions made at the Third Plenary Session of the Eleventh Central Committee in the ideological, political, economic, and organizational fields indicated that the Party had re-established the ideological, political, and organizational lines of Marxism. The plenary session not only started to rectify the overall chaos caused by the Cultural Revolution and its previous leftist errors, but also laid a solid foundation for the Party's new exploration of the road to socialist construction under the correct guiding ideology.

While the focus of the Party's and the state's work had begun to shift strategically, the Party's guiding ideology and China's socialist cause had also begun to shift from "class struggle as the core" to "productivity development as the center," from closed or semi-closed to open to the outside world, and from a highly centralized planned economic system to a vibrant socialist market economic system, with the guideline shifting from Mao Zedong Thought to Deng Xiaoping Theory. These changes not only set off a revolution to shake off poverty and backwardness in China, but also break through the old mode of socialist construction which had lagged behind the times and become increasingly rigid, and to create a new path and theory of socialist construction with Chinese characteristics. Deng Xiaoping's report "Emancipating the Mind, Seeking Truth from Facts, and Looking Forward with Unity" was a declaration that opened up a new era and path and created a new theory of socialist construction.

After twenty-nine years of a circuitous historical path, China's socialist cause had finally embarked on the path to victory. The Third Plenary Session of the

Eleventh Central Committee was the symbol of realizing this great historical transformation and the starting point of opening up new paths and theories. In the communiqué of the plenary session, one remark was particularly striking: "To realize the Four Modernizations requires a substantial increase in productivity, which necessarily requires a variety of changes in production relations and superstructure that are not suited to the development of productivity, in all unfit approaches of management, activities, and of thinking." With such historical demands, China began to usher in a new era of reform and opening to the outside world.

CHAPTER 2

The Overall Rectification of the Disorder and Adjustment of Social Relations in the New Context

I

Launch of The Full Redressing of Injustices and False Charges

After the Third Plenary Session of the Eleventh Central Committee of the Communist Party of China, with the progress and deepening of the whole Party's work to rectify the disorder, society initiated efforts in every area aimed at broadly redressing injustices and false charges and adjusting social relations. This brought about widescale liberation of the people's minds and mobilized enthusiasm in all sectors of society.

1. Further Defining a Series of Major Policy Principles to Redress Unjust, False, and Wrongful Charges

The work of redressing unjust and false charges was generally to be carried out in two stages. The first stage began with the toppling of the Gang of Four and lasted until just before the Third Plenary Session of the Eleventh Central Committee of the Communist Party of China. During this stage, the redress of the cases of some important figures and events in the history of the Party created favorable political conditions for that historical turning point. However, at this stage, the work of redressing injustices, falsehoods, and wrongs was not smooth. Due to the deep-rooted influence of the errors of expanding class struggle within the Party and the fact that during the previous two years, the principal leaders of the Party Central Committee maintained a series of leftist errors in Mao Zedong's later years, pushed forward the erroneous policy of the "Two Whatevers," and delayed the correction of those events, there were many obstacles in the process of rectification, and the work proceeded only partially and slowly.

The convening of the Third Plenary Session of the Eleventh Central Committee of the Communist Party of China created the conditions for large-scale redressing of injustices, falsehoods, and wrongs. After the meeting, a large-scale movement against unjust, false, and wrong charges and the implementation of cadre policy were launched rapidly and comprehensively throughout the country. According to the documents published by the Central Organizational Department, at this time, the work of eliminating injustice and false and wrongful charges made breakthroughs mainly in several areas.

In the process of redressing unjust and false cases and implementing cadre policy, the Central Committee issued the Notice on Removing All Rightists' Hats, the Notice on Rehabilitation and Correction of Right Opportunists, the Notice Concerning the Processing Measures of Central Documents in Clearing up Historical Problems, the Notice on Redressing the Cases Concerning Yang, Yu, and Fu, the Notice on Redressing the "North China Territorial Doctrine," the Notice of Conveying the Message of Redressing the Case of Comrade Liu Shaoqi, and other key documents. It transmitted and approved the Central Organizational Department's "Investigation Report on 61 People's Cases," the Sichuan Provincial Committee's "Notice on Several Issues for Attention in Implementing Policy," the Shanghai Municipal Committee's "Request on Solving the So-Called January Revolution," the Central Organizational Department's "Report on Redressing the Case Concerning the Fiction of Liu Zhidan," the Party Group of the Supreme People's Court's "Request on Re-examination and Correction of Unjust, False, and Wrong Charges," the Central Organizational Department's "Request on Issues Concerning Completing Re-examination and Correction of Unjust and Wrong Cases to the End," and other documents. In these documents and comments, in accordance with the fundamental principle of seeking truth from facts established at the Third Plenary Session of the Eleventh Central Committee, the Central Committee determined the policy of "Two No Matters," that is, any false words and any incorrect conclusions and handling, no matter when and under what circumstances, no matter what level of organizations or individuals decided and approved them, should all be remedied. A complete remedy should be launched if it was completely wrong, and a partial remedy offered for partial wrongs. The focus should be on settling problems while maintaining stability, attention should be placed on general issues rather than dwelling on details, and no problems should be allowed to linger. As for the large number of financial compensation issues concerning property confiscation and wage deduction, the Central Government decided to "take a political approach with appropriate financial subsidies," as well as follow the major policies of "those in charge being responsible and hands-on, and the entire Party's being involved."

According to the relevant documents and spirit of the Central Committee, in accordance with the instructions of the leading comrades of the Central Committee, and in view of the practical problems encountered in the implementation of the cadre policy, the Central Organizational Department alone or in collaboration with the Central United Front Department, the Ministry of Public Security, the Ministry of Education, the State Science and Technology Commission, and the Overseas Chinese Office of the State Council studied and formulated a series of specific policy provisions to redress unjust and false charges and implement the cadre policy.

Before the Third Plenary Session of the Eleventh Central Committee, on the basis of in-depth investigation and repeated argumentation, the Central Organizational Department successively formulated the Notice on the Correct Treatment of the Family and Children of the Personnel Under Examination, the Notice on the Serious Historical and Political Problems of Parents and Issues Not Affecting Children, the Notice on Opinions on Implementing the Policy of Rural Grassroots Cadres, the Notice of Opinions on Implementing the Party's Intellectual Policy, and other documents concerning policies formed the basic framework of the guiding ideology, principles, and policies for eliminating injustices and false cases and implementing the cadre policy.

After the Third Plenary Session of the Eleventh Central Committee, according to the arrangement of the Central Committee, Hu Yaobang was appointed Secretary-General of the Central Committee and Minister of the Central

Propaganda Department, and Song Renqiong was appointed Minister of the Central Organizational Department. With the comprehensive development of eliminating unjust and false cases and implementing the cadre policy, the Central Organizational Department, in view of the new problems encountered in the work, accelerated the research and formulation of eliminating unjust and false cases and implementing the policy provisions in cadre policy work on the basis of in-depth investigation and research, in accordance with the spirit and requirements of the Third Plenary Session of the Eleventh Central Committee. According to preliminary statistics, from 1979 to 1982, nearly 30 specific policies and regulations were formulated by the Central Organizational Department, or by the Central Group, in collaboration with the relevant departments of the central and state organs on a certain aspect, which further improved the policy system of eliminating injustices and falsehoods and implementing cadre policy work. The formulation and implementation of these principles and policies greatly promoted the unity and improvement of the understanding of organizations and leaders at all levels in dealing with unjust and false cases and in implementing cadre policy work, standardized the methods and procedures in specific work, enabled organizations at all levels to deal with unjust and false cases, and implemented cadre policy work with principles and rules to follow, which ensured the elimination of unjust and false cases and put the implementation of the cadre policy on a healthy track.

2. Further Emancipating the Mind and Promoting the Work of Redressing Injustices, Falsehoods, and Wrongs

After the Third Plenary Session of the Eleventh Central Committee, in the work of eliminating unjust and false cases and implementing cadre policies, the leftist impact on the minds of leaders and staff of some units and regions were not yet thoroughly eliminated. Especially under the influence of the "Two Whatevers," the mind was not emancipated. Some cases were delayed as they were studied and settled. For the tasks assigned by various superiors that needed to be settled and were not difficult to handle, some people simply refused to follow up and even thought the implementation of the policy was going too far. The problem was that the leaders of individual regions and units, because of their factionalism, passively confronted the implementation of the cadre policy and refused to address some of the remaining problems. Some even covered the lingering problems up. In response to these problems, the relevant departments of the Central Committee first needed to strengthen the implementation of the spirit of the Third Plenary Session of the Eleventh Central Committee, publicize the Party's ideological line of emancipating the mind and seeking truth from facts, and further eliminate the leftist influence, especially the interference of the "Two Whatevers." It was then necessary, through the elimination of major injustices and falsehoods, to facilitate people's ideological emancipation, the fight against injustices and falsehoods, and the implementation of the cadre policy. For example, the redressing of Liu Shaoqi's case, the greatest injustice in the Cultural Revolution, greatly facilitated the further emancipation of the minds of the cadres and the masses and effectively drove the redressing of injustices and falsehoods and the implementation of the cadre policy. In addition, the formulation and issuance of documents clearly stipulated that those who resisted the spirit of the Third Plenary Session of the Eleventh Central Committee and stubbornly refused to follow it, or, because of factional interference, deliberately delayed or passively confronted the implementation of the cadre policy, must be handled seriously and with the necessary organizational measures.

In the process of eliminating unjust and false cases and implementing the cadre policy, due to lack of understanding of the importance, continuity, and arduousness of the work, some leaders and staff did not put forth their best effort, feeling contented with partial work, and even closed their working offices without proper revision or evaluation. Given this situation, the Party organizations at all levels strengthened education on the importance and arduousness of the implementation of the cadre policy, so as to make them realize the far-reaching historical and practical significance of the implementation of the cadre policy and the historical responsibilities they shouldered. Emphasis was laid on the elimination of injustices and false or wrongful cases, the need for the cadre policy to go to the distance, and the idea that Party organizations should be responsible for the political life of every comrade. It was important not to be satisfied to note that 80% or 90% of the problems had been solved. As long as there was one wrong case that was not corrected, then for this comrade, his problem was 100% unsolved. It was thus necessary to do a solid job with each case and each individual, so that the Party's work would stand the test of history. Meanwhile, the requirements of inspection and the acceptance work were put forward, and evaluation standards were formulated.

In view of the problems of neglecting thorough and meticulous ideological work and of the few people to whom the policy was applicable or their relatives making unreasonable demands or even making trouble, the Central Organizational Department required all levels of organizational departments to strengthen political and ideological work in eliminating unjust and false cases and implementing the cadre policy. It was necessary to be patient and meticulous in carrying out the ideological work of policy targets. Leading comrades at all levels were to personally persuade persecuted comrades and their family members, encouraging them to take heart, work hard, and be united as they looked forward to contributing to the realization of the Four Modernizations. It was emphasized that the implementation of policies should focus on solving problems politically instead of dwelling upon details. It was important to strengthen political care for those who were eligible for the cadre policy, to strictly follow the Party's policies, and to criticize and educate those who made trouble.

3. New Progress in the Rehabilitation of Misjudged Cases in the Cultural Revolution

Under the guidance of the spirit of the Third Plenary Session of the Eleventh Central Committee and through the effort of the whole Party, by the end of 1982, the task of redressing unjust and false cases in the Cultural Revolution had been basically completed, and the decisive victory of redressing unjust and false cases and implementing cadre policy had been achieved. A total of 2.3 million cadres and nearly 20,000 grouped cases of injustice, falsehood, and wrongdoing were reviewed and put on file in the nationwide fight against the Cultural Revolution, including a number of major cases that had a great influence on the whole Party, the whole country, and even the world.

a. *Receiving of censorship materials from the Central Special Task Force to review and redress a large number of cases concerning senior cadres.*

The Third Plenary Session of the Eleventh Central Committee of the CPC decided to withdraw the leading group of the Central Project and submit all the files to the Central Organizational Department. In order to implement the decision of the plenary session, on December 19, 1978, Wang Dongxing, Ji Dengkui, and Wu

De, former heads of the Central Project Leading Group, summoned comrades from the Central Project Group and the Central Organizational Department to convey the decision on the transfer of the plenary session. Hu Yaobang, Minister of Central Organization, Chen Yeping, Vice Minister of Public Security, Zhao Cangbi, Minister of Public Security, and three other special officials in charge of the Special Case Office and the Central Organizational Bureau attended the meeting. At the meeting, it was announced that the first office, the third office of the Central Project Review Group, and the office of the May 16 Joint Project Review Group would be withdrawn as of that day. All project materials were to be submitted to the Central Organizational Department for processing. During the transfer process, not one page of material was to be destroyed. On the morning of December 20, Chen Yeping, Vice Minister of the Central Organizational Department, conveyed the spirit of the handover meeting at the meeting of ministries, departments, and directors, and made specific arrangements for receiving and reviewing work. He selected special personnel to form a receiver organization and put them to work without delay. By the end of February 1979, the transfer of project materials had been completed. The Central Organizational Department received 1,730 volumes and 391,363 pieces of materials handed over by the former Central Project Team, involving 669 people under review.

Subsequently, the Central Organizational Department immediately carried out a review of counter-offensive work. According to statistics, 213 cadres at or above the level of deputy ministers of central and state organs and deputy governors of provinces, autonomous regions, and municipalities directly under the Central Government (including cadres at this level in the army) were included in the special examination of the Central Committee. Among them, there were 10 members of the Eighth Politburo, 10 members of the Secretariat of the Central Committee, 71 members of the Central Committee and alternate members of the Central Committee (excluding those examined by provinces and municipalities), 7 Vice Premiers of the State Council, and marshals and generals of the Southern Expedition and the Northern War. There were former Party Committee secretaries of the Central Bureau, provinces, autonomous regions, and municipalities directly under the Central Government, as well as heads and Deputy Governors of the Central Organs and Ministries of the Experts, professors, writers, engineers, and technicians, and even a small number of residents and students. The people under review were classified as "320 persons with serious problems or involving contradictions between the masses and the enemy, accounting for 47.8% of the persons under review."

With so many major important cases, it was obviously impossible to quickly reach a realistic conclusion by relying solely on the work of the Central Organizational Department. In view of this, the Central Organizational Department took the following measures: 1) All leading comrades who had been delegated by the Central Task Force to other places and were still supervising their work went back to Beijing and their relevant units. After the Third Plenary Session of the Eleventh Central Committee, the Central Organizational Department took greater initiative on this issue. After the meeting, Peng Zhen and Zhang Jieqing returned to Beijing. Wang Guangmei, who had formerly been detained, returned, and other comrades were also brought back by their previous units. 2) Some comrades were assigned work first and their cases reviewed and redressed for conclusion, so that these leading comrades could go to work as early as possible. 3) According to the principle of handling cases by the whole Party and the mass line, it was necessary to refer the cases to those comrades' previous units for review, then send them to the Central Organizational Department for review and to the Central Committee for examination and approval, thus greatly speeding up the progress of the review. Over time, these measures achieved good results. From 1979 to 1980, the cases of 445 people, including Peng Zhen, Lu Dingyi, Tao Zhu, Liu Lantao, Xi Zhongxun, An Ziwen, Qian Ying, Hu Qiaomu, Shuai Mengqi, Zhao Yimin, Lin Feng, Tan Zhenlin, Li Lisan, and Wang Renzhong, were reviewed for conclusion directly by the Central Organizational Department and submitted to the Central Committee for approval.

b. A number of key cases with great influence were completely redressed.

1) *The complete reversal of the 7/20 Incident in Wuhan.* The 7/20 Incident in Wuhan took place on July 20, 1967, when masses of workers, peasants, and soldiers marched in the streets to oppose the plots initiated by the Gang of Four to engage in disrupting the army, damaging civil-military relations, supporting armed struggle, smashing and looting, and destroying production, in hopes of reasoning with them. Afterwards, Lin Biao and the Gang of Four described the 7/20 Incident as a "thoroughly counter-revolutionary incident," falsely accusing Wang Renzhong and Chen Zaidao, the main leaders of the Hubei Provincial

Committee and the Wuhan Military Region Party Committee, of acting "behind the scene" in the 7/20 Incident, and turning a group of leading cadres of the Party, government and army into "a clique of capitalists" within the Party and the military. Those participating in or supporting the march by the broad masses of cadres and masses were also severely persecuted. In the struggle to denounce and criticize the Gang of Four, the Hubei Provincial Committee, the Provincial Reform Committee, and the Party Committee of the Wuhan Military Region, in accordance with the requirements of the masses of cadres and people, studied the case and believed that Lin Biao and the Gang of Four had completely distorted the facts and confused the right and wrong by describing the 7/20 Incident as a "counter-revolutionary incident," and that all slander imposed on the PLA and the masses of cadres and people should be reversed. He also reported to the Central Committee the Request on Addressing the 7/20 Incident in Wuhan. In November 1978, the Central Committee of the Communist Party of China transmitted the request of the Hubei Provincial Party Committee, the Provincial Reform Committee, and the Party Committee of the Wuhan Military Region, which completely reversed the 7/20 Incident in Wuhan.

2) *Rectifying the so-called "February countercurrent" problem.* Around February 1967, in response to Lin Biao, the Gang of Four, Kang Sheng, and Chen Boda inciting the notion of "overthrowing everything, waging an all-round civil war" in an attempt to disrupt the army and the whole country and usurp power, and in addressing questions such as whether the Cultural Revolution required the Party's leadership, whether veteran cadres should all be defeated, and whether the army should be stabilized, representing the will of the broad masses of Party members and the people, at meetings of the Central Military Commission and the Politburo of the Central Committee, Tan Zhenlin, Chen Yi, Ye Jianying, Li Fuchun, Li Xiannian, Xu Qianqian, Nie Rongzhen, and other leading comrades of the Central Politburo and the Military Commission, strongly criticized the erroneous practices in the Cultural Revolution and made a rightful and sharp attack against Lin Biao, the Gang of Four, Kang Sheng, and Chen Boda. The struggle against them, however, was stifled and attacked as the "February countercurrent." After crushing the Lin Biao Group, Mao Zedong put forward the idea of redressing the "February countercurrent" and pointed out that the matter was clear and that it was time to stop talking about that case. After the toppling of the Gang of Four, at the Central Working Conference in 1978, the

Central Committee pointed out that the "February countercurrent" was entirely a set of deliberate and false accusations made by Lin Biao, whose purpose was to overthrow the old commanders and deputy prime ministers opposing him, and ultimately to overthrow Zhou Enlai and Zhu De. The Central Committee decided that all comrades who had been wronged in this case would have their reputations restored and all comrades who had been implicated and punished would be put back in their positions. The false statements about the so-called "February countercurrent" in various documents and materials from earlier times should be abolished.

3) *The case of the "61 traitors" brought to an end.* The so-called "61 traitors" case was a major political case which stirred up domestic and foreign sensations during the Cultural Revolution. The so-called "traitors" referred to 61 CPC members, such as Bo Yibo, who were released from Caolanzi prison in Beiping in 1936 with the special approval of the CPC Central Committee. During the Cultural Revolution, only 40 of these people were still alive, 22 of whom held leading posts as secretary of provincial Party committees, vice-governor, vice-minister of the central organs or above, and Vice-Premier of the State Council. At that time, not only were those forty old comrades persecuted, but almost all their families, relatives, friends, and subordinates were drawn into trouble as well. Thousands of people were censured and persecuted. Regarding this case, in June 1978, Deng Xiaoping issued instructions in a letter of appeal concerning the "61 people's cases" that "this problem must be dealt with, and it is also a matter of seeking truth from facts." In accordance with the spirit of these instructions, the Ministry of the Central Committee reviewed the case. On December 6 of the same year, the Central Committee agreed to and forwarded the Ministry of the Central Committee's "Investigation Report on the 61 People's Case," pointing out that it was a major error, and comrades who had been wrongly treated were to be compensated with proper job positions, so as to publicly rectify this major grievance.

4) *Redressing the persecution of cadres and masses in the "January Revolution."* The so-called "January Revolution" was the period from January 4, 1967, when Zhang Chunqiao and Yao Wenyuan returned to Shanghai, to February 5, when they established the Shanghai People's Commune, during which they started in Shanghai and sought to carry out a conspiracy to seize overall power.

In 1966, Zhang Chunqiao and Yao Wenyuan colluded with Lin Biao, Chen

Boda, and Jiang Qing to incite "the rebellion against the Shanghai Municipal Committee." On January 4, 1967, Zhang Chunqiao and Yao Wenyuan returned to Shanghai to further incite public opinion that "there is no need to hold any expectation for the Municipal Committee anymore… The basic problem at present is to take the leadership back from the capitalists" and so on, stating the need to overthrow everything and seize overall power. On January 6, they held the meeting of "overthrowing the Municipal Party Committee" in the name of all rebel organizations in the city, publicly berated leading comrades of the Shanghai Municipal Party Committee, dragged hundreds of cadres above the bureau level to the meeting spot to accompany those being publicly berated, and announced that Cao Diqiu would no longer be recognized as secretary and mayor of the Shanghai Municipal Party Committee. In fact, they seized power in Shanghai and established the so-called Shanghai People's Commune on February 5. From that time, the whole country was plunged into a tidal wave of power seizure, which in many places even turned into physical conflict, resulting in the paralysis or semi-paralysis of the leading organs of the Party and government in many places, and further damaged social order and industrial and agricultural production. The so-called January Revolution was actually a conspiracy plotted by Lin Biao, Chen Boda, and the Gang of Four. It was an important step for them to disrupt the entire country and achieve the general usurpation of the Party's power.

In December 1978, the Shanghai Municipal Committee decided that the case of Cao Diqiu, who was publicly criticized in the January Revolution, and of all the persecuted cadres and the masses should be redressed. In January 1979, the Central Committee of the Communist Party of China transmitted the Request on Solving the January Revolution issued by the Shanghai Municipal Committee, which was a complete redressing of the cases concerning the cadres and masses criticized and persecuted in the so-called January Revolution.

5) *Redressing the "Yang, Yu, Fu Incident."* In March 1968, in order to disrupt and divide the army and to usurp the Party's power, Lin Biao and the Gang of Four produced the so-called "Yang, Yu, Fu Incident." Yang Chengwu (alternate member of the Eighth Central Committee of the Communist Party of China, Standing Committee of the Central Military Commission, acting Chief of the General Staff), Yu Lijin (political member of the Air Force, Second Secretary of the Party Committee of the Air Force), and Fu Chongbi (commander of the Beijing garrison area) were falsely accused of "overturning the case of the

February Countercurrent." They fabricated Yang Chengwu's "collusion with Yu Lijin to seize leadership of the Air Force," "collusion with Fu Chongbi to seize power of Beijing," "compilation of Jiang Qing's special black materials," "ordering Fu Chongbi to rush three times to Diaoyutai to capture people in the Central Cultural Revolution," and "beating Jiang Qing." They claimed that Yang's "black background" was related to "Ye (Jianying), Nie (Rongzhen), Chen (Yi), and Tan (Zhenlin)." They falsely accused Yu Lijin as a traitor and slandered "Yang, Yu, and Fu as the black behind the scenes force of 5/16," and so on. The issue of "Yang, Yu, and Fu" was also written in the communiqué of the Twelfth Plenary Session of the Eighth Central Committee and the Ninth Political Report of the Ninth Congress of the CPC, and called "the evil wind of overturning the case of the February Countercurrent." They cruelly persecuted Yang Chengwu, Yu Lijin, and Fu Chongbi and attacked a large number of comrades throughout the country, some of whom were disabled or killed, to great consequence. In March 1979, the Central Committee issued the Notice of Open Rehabilitation of Yang, Yu and Fu, pointing out that the so-called "Yang, Yu, Fu Incident" was a complete injustice of Lin Biao and the Gang of Four anti-Party groups. The Central Committee decided to publicly rectify the incident. All slanderous and untrue statements were to be abandoned, and the previous documents issued by the Central Government were to be revoked. Compensation was to be paid for comrades persecuted to death or maimed as a result of this case and their reputations restored.

6) *Redressing the case of the so-called North China Territorial Doctrine.* In March 1968, Lin Biao and the Gang of Four fabricated the charges of the North China Territorial Doctrine and the Jin-Cha-Ji Territorial Doctrine in the process of creating the "Yang, Yu, Fu Incident." From that time, the Beijing Military Region repeatedly opposed the so-called North China Territorial Doctrine, aiming directly at Nie Rongzhen, Xu Qianqian, Luo Ruiqing, and Yang Chengwu, who had served as the main leaders in North China. Some leading comrades in the Beijing Military Region were charged with non-existent crimes, brutally attacked, and persecuted, affecting a large number of comrades, disturbing people's thinking, undermining the unity and construction of the army, and bringing about serious consequences. In December 1979, the Central Committee issued the Notice on the Rehabilitation of the So-Called North China Territorial Doctrine, pointing out that Lin Biao and the Gang of Four had slandered and defamed the glorious

history of the Jin-Cha-Ji Military Region, the North China Military Region, and the Beijing Military Region solely because of the former's counter-revolutionary political needs. They regarded the Beijing Military Region as a serious obstacle to their counter-revolutionary coup, so they had repeatedly set off a vicious wave against North China Territorial Doctrine and used every means they could to bring down the old generation of proletarian revolutionaries formerly working in North China and some leading comrades in the Beijing Military Region at that time, attempting to realize their plot to usurp the Party's power. The Central Committee officially declared that the so-called Jin-Cha-Ji Territorial Doctrine and North China Territorial Doctrine were sheer slander and false accusations and should be completely overthrown. All relevant materials were to be revoked, and the cases concerning all comrades who suffered from persecution or were affected as a result would be redressed and their reputation restored.

7) Redressing the case of Liu Shaoqi and a large number of comrades affected by it. The case of Liu Shaoqi, Vice-Chairman of the Central Committee and Chairman of the People's Republic of China, was the greatest national injustice committed during the Cultural Revolution and in the history of the Republic.

After the toppling of the Gang of Four, cadres and the masses both inside and outside the Party requested and suggested to the Central Committee that Liu Shaoqi's case should be reviewed. In February 1979, the Central Committee decided that the case of Liu Shaoqi would be reviewed by the Central Commission for Discipline Inspection and the Central Organizational Department. In February 1980, after serious discussion at the Fifth Plenary Session of the Eleventh Central Committee of the Communist Party of China, the Resolution on Redressing the Case of Comrade Liu Shaoqi was unanimously adopted and it was noted that the three major crimes of working as a traitor, a secret enemy agent, and a "blackleg" imposed on Comrade Liu Shaoqi in the original review report, as well as various other crimes, were all deliberate framings by Lin Biao, Jiang Qing, Kang Sheng, and Chen Boda. It was wrong for the Twelfth Plenary Session of the Eighth Conference of CPC to adopt the resolution of "expelling Liu Shaoqi from the Party forever and revoking all his positions inside and outside the Party…" Liu Shaoqi was acknowledged as a great Marxist and a proletarian revolutionist who struggled for communism all his life. "As one of the outstanding leaders of the Party and the country, he made indelible contributions to the construction of our Party, the Democratic revolution, the socialist revolution, and the socialist construction of our country… The slander, false accusations, forged materials, and all false statements against comrade Liu Shaoqi issued in the past should be completely overturned."

The Twelfth Plenary Session of the Eighth Conference of the CPC decided to revoke the charges imposed on and the resolution against Liu Shaoqi and to restore his reputation as a great Marxist and proletarian revolutionist, one of the main leaders of the Party and the state. All unjust, false, and wrongful charges related to Liu Shaoqi's case should be rectified by the relevant departments. On March 19, 1980, the Central Committee of the Communist Party of China issued the Notice of Transmitting the Resolution on Redressing the Case of Comrade Liu Shaoqi.

In this spirit, the plenary session called on Party organizations at all levels to actively and responsibly continue to settle similar unresolved or partially resolved issues. Following the spirit of the Fifth Plenary Session of the Conference of the CPC, on April 18, 1980, the Ministry of Organizational Affairs transmitted the notice issued by the Guizhou Provincial Party Committee, Notice of Rectifying or Remedying the Unjust, False, and Wrong Cases As a Result of Comrade Liu Shaoqi's Case and Thorough Implementation of the Party's Policy, requesting all local departments to complete all the rectification of cases concerning Liu Shaoqi and other unjust, wrong, and false cases during the Cultural Revolution. On May 17, the Liu Shaoqi Memorial Conference was solemnly held in Beijing. More than 10,000 Party and state leaders and representatives from all facets of the capital participated in the memorial conference. The rectification of Liu Shaoqi's case brought a complete rectification throughout the country of tens of thousands of people suffering as a result of the injustice committed against Liu. Through the redressing of this case, which had the greatest impact throughout nation, the cadres further emancipated their minds and facilitated the redressing of other cases of injustice, falsehood, and wrongdoings.

8) *Redressing the case of comrades framed by the so-called First Big Character Posters in the country.* At the beginning of the Cultural Revolution, Nie Yuanzi, General Secretary of the Party Branch of the Department of Philosophy of Peking University, and others launched the so-called First Big Character Poster that framed the Party Committee of Peking University and Lu Ping (Secretary of the Party Committee of Peking University), Song Shuo (Vice-Minister of Science Department of Peking University), and Peng Peiyun (Vice-Secretary of

the Party Committee of Peking University), which was praised by Mao Zedong. Lin Biao, Jiang Qing, Kang Sheng, and Chen Boda took the opportunity to persecute Lu Ping, Song Shuo, Peng Peiyun, and other people on various charges. It not only broadcasted the content of the big character posters on the radio, but also organized commentators' articles in the *People's Daily* to give great praise, which had had an extremely negative impact on the entire country. This was a major injustice that occurred in the early days of the Cultural Revolution. In February 1979, the Beijing Municipal Committee of the Communist Party of China decided to completely redress the case concerning the Party Committee of Peking University and Lu Ping, Song Shuo, and Peng Peiyun. In August 1980, the Central Organizational Department transmitted the Notice of Redressing the Case of Comrades Falsely Accused in the So-called First Big Character Posters issued by the Beijing Municipal Committee, which completely reversed this injustice.

9) *Redressing cases concerning the so-called "mafia" and "fake party."* During the Cultural Revolution, under the influence of Lin Biao and the ultra-leftist line of the Gang of Four, the underground party organization of the former 38th troop led by Yang Hucheng was framed as a "mafia" and "fake party." Many of the veteran comrades in the organization were falsely accused of being "true Kuomintang, false Communist Party" members, "traitors," and "secret agents," and were for this reason brutally persecuted. After the toppling of the Gang of Four and the investigation by the Shaanxi Provincial Committee, it was noted that the so-called "mafia" and "fake party" accusations were totally unfounded. With the consent of the Central Committee, in February 1981, the Central Organizational Department transmitted the Shaanxi Provincial Party Committee's Request for Redressing the Cases Concerning the Underground Party Organization of the Former 38th Troop Led by Yang Hucheng Being Framed as a "Mafia" and "Fake Party." For the underground party organization of the former 38th troop led by Yang Hucheng and the underground party members who suffered persecution in this case, all slander and untruths were drawn to a complete end, and the follow-up work was handled well.

10) *Redressing the case of the so-called Red Flag Party.* During the Yan'an Cadre Trial Campaign in 1943, Kang Sheng launched forced confession letters and created the trumped up Red Flag Party case. Underground Party members in Gansu, Henan, Shaanxi, Sichuan, Hunan, Hubei, Yunnan, Guizhou, Zhejiang, and

Guangxi were framed as the Red Flag Party. Many underground Party members were labelled as "special agents," "traitors," and "secret agents." In the late stage of the Yan'an Cadre Trial, the Central Committee found that Kang Sheng's so-called Red Flag Party was a false case, and they corrected it in time. However, due to the historical conditions at the time, no comprehensive conclusion was reached. During the Cultural Revolution, this historical issue resurfaced, and many comrades were once again framed and cruelly persecuted, and some were even mutilated to death or maimed. In order to thoroughly settle the remaining problems of the so-called Red Flag Party and eliminate the negative consequences of Kang Sheng's false case, in September 1981, the General Office of the Central Committee issued the Circular of Notice on Redressing the Case of the Underground Party Organizations in the Gansu, Henan, and Shaanxi Provinces Framed as the Red Flag Party, announcing the Central Committee's decision to redress the underground Party organizations in relevant provinces (autonomous regions) framed as the Red Flag Party, overturn all the slander imposed on them, and completely put an end to the persecution of comrades in this case.

11) *Redressing the case of Pan Hannian and restoring his reputation.* Pan Hannian was an old Party member who held various important leading posts both inside and outside the Party. He made great contributions to the Party's cultural work and united front work, especially in carrying out covert struggles against the enemy. After 1955, due to the serious neglect of the particularity of the covert struggle against the enemy, the distinction between right and wrong, and between the enemy and ourselves was blurred, and Pan Hannian was mistakenly classified as an "internal enemy." He was arrested and detained for examination, and later convicted, sentenced, and expelled from the Party. He was wronged and tortured for more than 20 years, until his death in 1977. Because Pan Hannian's problems also involved many comrades who had worked with him, they similarly suffered grievances over a long period. In March 1981, the Central Committee of the CPC ordered the Central Commission for Discipline Inspection to review Pan's case. For this purpose, the Central Commission for Discipline Inspection consulted and studied various materials in detail. It also made an investigation into dozens of comrades who had worked with Pan Hannian in the past. The results of the review showed that the conclusion that Pan Hannian was a "secret agent" was not valid and should be negated. This was a major case of injustice after the founding of New China. On August 23, 1982, the Central Committee issued a document

solemnly announcing to the whole Party that it would restore the reputation of Pan Hannian, and that the cases of comrades implicated in Pan's case who had been wrongly dealt with should also be subjected to a realistic review and rectification and properly dealt with.

c. Reviewing and Redressing the Cases of Numerous Party and State Leaders, Provincial and Ministerial Cadres, and Celebrated Personages from All Walks of Life.

During the Cultural Revolution, a large number of important leaders of the Party and the state were attacked and persecuted. After the Third Plenary Session of the Eleventh Conference of CPC, the Central Committee of the CPC reviewed the issues of Liu Shaoqi, Peng Dehuai, He Long, Tao Zhu, Peng Zhen, Bo Yibo, Yang Shangkun, Zhang Wentian, Lu Dingyi, Tan Zhenlin, Xi Zhongxun, Huang Kecheng, Wang Renzhong, Song Renqiong, Luo Ruiqing, and other leading comrades of the Party, the state, the government, and the army. The issue of the martyr Qu Qiubai, the early leader of the Party, was also brought to light.

Before the Cultural Revolution, there were 1,253 cadres at or above the level of vice-governors and vice-ministers throughout the country. One thousand eleven people were affected by the Cultural Revolution, accounting for 81% of the total number of cadres at this level. Among them, 453 people, accounting for 36% of the total, were falsely accused as "traitors," "secret agents," "counter-revolutionary revisionists," "agents of bourgeois headquarters," and "carrying out the revisionist line" (not counting those directly examined by the former central task force). The so-called censorship of these cadres was mostly a fabrication of false accusations, or an unlimited exaggeration of one point to create negative labels, so that those comrades suffered serious mental and physical damage, with forty comrades dying during the "censorship" period and many others suffering lifelong disabilities.

After the toppling of the Gang of Four, the Central Committee entrusted the Central Organizational Department with the task of reviewing or trying the sentences of 453 deputy governors and cadres above deputy ministers from 1978 to the end of 1980. During the Cultural Revolution, 85 people were classified as contradictions between the enemy and the masses, all of whom were redressed and their reputation restored. As for those cases with historical conclusions that escalated during the Cultural Revolution, most maintained the conclusions reached before the Cultural Revolution. After the implementation of the policy, those who were in good health and able to work took up leading posts. Those who were not in good health were properly placed. Those who died unjustly were redressed, and those affected by these cases and their family members were properly treated, with the elimination of any remaining impact from the injustices.

d. Redressing the departments of the Central Government that were wrongly criticized or falsely framed in the Cultural Revolution.

The main goals at this time were 1) to cancel the wrong conclusion that the "three pacifications and one reduction, three surrenders and one annihilation" made on the Foreign Liaison Department of the Central Committee of the Communist Party, 2) to completely redress the so-called Palace of Hell in the Central Propaganda Department, 3) to remove the label of the "capitulationist line" on the National United front and ethnic and religious departments, 4) to redress the wrong case of labeling the former Ministry of Culture as the "ministry of imperial officials, of talented men and beautiful women, of foreign dead people," 5) to redress the case that the General Political Department of the People's Liberation Army was framed as the Palace of Hell, 6) to revoke the Memo of the Army Literary and Art Works Symposium in February 1966, 7) to overturn the conclusion that the so-called "revisionist line" was enforced on the educational front, and 8) to revoke the Memo of the National Conference on Educational Work in 1971. After the Third Plenary Session of the Eleventh Conference of the CPC, Party organizations at all levels further reviewed and rectified the issues of a large number of well-known figures in literary and artistic circles, sports circles, scientific and technological circles, and health circles.

II

Proper Handling of Lingering Historical Issues

Dealing properly with lingering historical problems was an important part of the work of rectifying the chaos and disorder of the times. It was also an arduous task to deal with unjust and false cases and implement the cadre policy.

Due to the influence of erroneous leftist ideas in previous political movements, mistakes in work, and the special historical conditions of the war years, some complex problems had not been addressed in a timely way, and for this and various other reasons, a large number of historical problems remained to be settled. According to preliminary statistics, millions of cases remained unsettled from before the Cultural Revolution, involving millions of people and affecting tens of millions more.

With the recovery and development of the Party's principle of seeking truth from facts, the fight against cases of injustices and falsehoods, and the deepening and development of the implementation of the cadre policy, the appeals for resolving the problems left over from the history before the Cultural Revolution gradually increased and the voices became increasingly strong. It was not only an inevitable requirement for the Party to emancipate the mind, seek truth from facts, fight against unjust and false cases, and implement the in-depth cadre policy, but there was also a direct link with the fight against unjust and false cases during the Cultural Revolution. Many unjust, wrong, and false cases in the Cultural Revolution were caused by Lin Biao and the Gang of Four, who purposefully restored the historical issues that had been previously dealt with and accused them of various charges. Therefore, with the further development of eliminating injustices and falsehoods and implementing the cadre policy, many historical problems would inevitably be involved. If these problems were not properly handled, it would be difficult to mobilize these cadres and the masses, to consolidate stability and unity, and to thoroughly restore and develop the Party's principle of seeking truth from facts.

Shortly after the implementation of the cadre policy and the launch of the fight against injustices and falsehoods, the review and correction of the remaining problems in the anti-Rightist and Four Purifications movements was put on the agenda. The Central Committee issued relevant documents, clarified relevant policies and regulations, and began to review and rectify the historical problems existing before the Cultural Revolution.

After the Third Plenary Session of the Eleventh Conference of the CPC, especially when the task of eliminating unjust and false cases in the Cultural Revolution was basically completed, the focus of eliminating unjust and false cases and implementing the cadre policy shifted to properly handling the lingering historical problems. A large number of important lingering historical issues such as "anti-Rightists," "anti-right-tendency," "Four Purifications," the "underground party," "intelligence workers," "people killed accidentally during the Soviet area purge," "the purge of Trotskyism in the Huxi area of Shandong Province," and the "breakthrough of the Central Plains" were each dealt with in turn. This work was not completed until the Thirteenth National Congress was held in 1987.

How to deal actively and properly address the lingering historical issues was related to whether the rectification of unjust and false cases and the implementation of the cadre policy could be carried out steadily and healthily, and whether the overall situation of stability and unity could be maintained. To this end, the Central Organizational Department and the relevant departments of the central state organs mainly focused on two aspects to provide guidance on the macro level.

1. Efforts to Eliminate Various Forms of Resistance and Interference

In the early stage of dealing with lingering historical problems, resistance and interference mainly came from the left. Some people continued to view the lingering historical issues from the leftist point of view, failing to correct the mistakes made in defining the nature of those issues.

After the Third Plenary Session of the Eleventh Conference of the CPC, another mistake occurred in the work of reviewing and dealing with the lingering historical issues. Some people held a negative attitude toward everything, demanding that all the issues in the political movements since the founding of New China and those lingering historical problems from before the founding of New China should be addressed afresh, and their voice was gaining traction. Letters and visits were becoming more frequent, and even things that should not be changed were altered. In response, in June 1979, the Central Organizational Department held a Symposium on Implementing the Cadre Policy. At the meeting, the leaders of the Central Organizational Department clearly pointed out that the cases of injustice, falsehood, and misjudgment during the Cultural Revolution were different from those before the Cultural Revolution. The old cases before the Cultural Revolution were to be settled based on the principles of dialectical and historical materialism, of seeking truth from facts, and of timely correction of mistakes. In general, it was important to deal with issues according to the circumstances, conditions, and policies of their time. The principles and policies for dealing with the problems remaining from the time before the Cultural Revolution were proposed. After the meeting, with the approval of the Central Committee, the Central Organizational Department issued the Notice of Opinions on Handling Cases from Before the Cultural Revolution. The document pointed out that, in addition to the Central Government's stipulation involving the corrections of those wrongfully labeled as the "rightists," the wrong cases in the anti-Rightist struggle since 1959, and the review of the wrong cases in the Four Purifications Movement, other cases could be approached on a case-by-case basis and reviewed and dealt with in the course of routine work. They differed in principle from a large number of unjust, false, and wrong cases caused by the serious interference and destruction of Lin Biao and the Gang of Four during the Cultural Revolution. Without any historical analysis of these old cases and a general review based on the current policy viewpoints, there would inevitably be some confusion regarding right and wrong and unnecessary ideological confusion, impairing stability and unity and distancing cadres and the masses both inside and outside the Party. Old historical cases should be handled cautiously based on their specific situations. For those who had made mistakes, their cases would not be further reconsidered if they had been appropriately dealt with according to the Party's policy at that time, even if the treatment was slightly harsher but the main factual basis remained unchanged. If, according to the Party's policy at that time, the main basis for the previous treatment of individuals was incorrect or they were wrongly expelled from the Party membership and public office and defined as the contradiction between the enemy and the mass, their cases should be reviewed and corrected. For those who were wrongly expelled from the Party and had been doing well later and had the qualifications for Party membership, they could resume their Party membership or re-join the Party.

In order to make a more accurate and thorough job of reviewing the lingering historical issues, the Central Organizational Department held a symposium in Yichang, Hubei Province, in January 1983. The event was attended by relevant comrades from seventeen provinces, municipal Party committees, and some central state organs. At the meeting, participants shared their experiences in the work, analyzed difficulties encountered, offered suggestions and measures to address the problems, and further determined the principles and tasks of the work. After the meeting, the Central Organizational Department issued a notice and published the Summary of the Symposium on the Review of Unjust and False

Cases before the Cultural Revolution," pointing out that such cases before the Cultural Revolution were mainly the result of the limited knowledge at that time and the mistakes made in the work, which were fundamentally different in nature from those deliberately produced under the specific historical conditions of the Cultural Revolution and by the counter-revolutionary groups led by Lin Biao and Jiang Qing. Reviewing and correcting the unjust, wrong, and false cases before the Cultural Revolution and addressing the lingering historical issues should follow the spirit of the Party since the Third Plenary Session of the Eleventh CPC Conference and the policy stipulations of the Central Organizational Department, such as the Notice of Opinions on Handling Cases from Before the Cultural Revolution, take into account the historical background, and look at the specific cases comprehensively and historically on the basis of factual materials. It was important to persist in seeking truth from facts, correct mistakes, and actively, steadily, and systematically correct all unresolved cases of injustice and falsehood.

In this work, the Party had to pay attention to preventing two kinds of deviations. The first was to continue to address old historical cases from the leftist point of view and refuse to correct the mistakenly defined issues, or even refuse to correct the mistakes made in handling or approving the cases. The other was to change things that should not be changed based on the view of negating everything. For cases from before the Cultural Revolution, all those concerning people who had lodged complaints or had failed to lodge complaints but were spotted by the organizations needed to be reviewed, focusing on larger or major cases, public cases, cases designated as contradictions between the enemy and the mass, and cases involving mistaken expulsion from the Party or public office. The handling of cases was to be based on facts and guided by the Party's policies. If the original conclusion was based mainly on falsehood, it was to be completely reversed, while if the basis was correct but the determination of the nature of the cases was wrong, it should be corrected. If on the other hand, the facts were clear, the evidence conclusive, and the conclusion correctly handled, or if there was no major discrepancy in the main basis and the determination of its nature was basically appropriate, but with slightly harsher treatment than was warranted, the cases did not need to be rectified, though proper care should be taken concerning those comrades' lives and daily needs. After redressing the unjust, wrong and false cases, it was important to focus on solving problems politically, to make effective persuasion and reasoning, and to properly handle the follow-up work in accordance with the relevant provisions.

Through these two meetings and the documents issued afterwards, the progress of the work in properly dealing with lingering historical problems were appropriately enhanced and deepened.

2. Formulating Correct Guidelines and Policies for Handling Lingering Historical Issues

Applying polices to properly handle lingering historical problems was a great responsibility, directly related to the identification and evaluation of some martyrs who had shed blood for the revolution and to the political life of some comrades. It was necessary to strictly follow the principles and policies of the Central Committee. Therefore, it was particularly important to formulate correct policies and principles for doing so.

Under the leadership of the Central Committee and the guidance of the older generation of revolutionaries, the relevant departments of the Central Committee and the central state organs successively formulated the Notice on Removing All Rightist Labels, the Plan for Implementing the Decision of the Central Committee to Remove All Rightist Labels, Notice on Rehabilitation and Correction of Right Opportunists, Notice of Opinions on Handling Cases before the Cultural Revolution, Supplementary Notice of Opinions on Handling Cases from Before the Cultural Revolution, Notice of Issuing the Summary of the Symposium on Review of Unjust, Wrong, and False Charges from Before the Cultural Revolution, Notice of Transmitting Opinions of the Party Group of the Ministry of Railways on Reviewing Unjust, Wrong, and False Charges Since the Founding of the People's Republic of China, Notice of Transmitting the Report of the Organizational Department of the Jiangsu Provincial Committee on Investigating and Reviewing Unjust and False Charges from Before the Cultural Revolution, and other policy provisions for dealing with lingering historical issues, clearly putting forward the principles, guidelines, and policy boundaries in dealing with issues from before the Cultural Revolution, strictly stipulating the scope, focus, and boundaries for approval in the review process. Practice subsequently proved that these policies and regulations played an important role in timely unification of understanding in all sectors, specifying the direction of work, and properly handling the problems still lingering from before the Cultural Revolution.

In the process, the major lingering historical problems entrusted by the Party Central Committee, the relevant departments of the central state organs, and the Central Government to the relevant provinces and municipalities mainly fell into several categories.

1) *Reviewing and correcting unjust, wrong, and false charges in the anti-Rightist campaign.* During the rectification campaign conducted throughout the Party in 1957, a very small number of bourgeois right-wing elements took the opportunity to advocate the so-called "big bang" and launched an unrestrained attack on the Party and the new socialist system, in an attempt to replace the leadership of the Communist Party. Under these circumstances, it was necessary and correct for the Central Committee to decide to counter the attack of the Rightists. However, the anti-Rightist campaign was greatly expanded, and a number of intellectuals, patriots, and cadres were misclassified as rightists, resulting in unfortunate consequences. As Deng Xiaoping pointed out, "The problem is that, with the evolution of the movement, the scope of attack has been widened and the weight of the attack has been too heavy. A large number of people have not been properly handled and were too heavily punished. They have suffered grievances for many years and cannot bring their wisdom into full play for the people. This is not only their personal loss, but also the loss of the whole country."[1]

In 1959, the Party Central Committee issued instructions on removing the rightist label step by step in several batches. By 1964, in a series of five batches, the majority of people classified as rightists had their labels removed.

After the toppling of the Gang of Four, in the work of redressing unjust and false charges and implementing the cadre policy, the issue of the rightists' "label-removing" and correcting was raised again. Since the ideological imprisonment of the left was not yet broken at that time, the Cultural Revolution had not yet been completely denied. As a result, there were great obstacles to proper handling of this issue, with many criticisms and under extremely difficult circumstances.

In the spring of 1978, the relevant departments of the Central Government organs held a meeting in Yantai, Shandong Province, to study how to properly handle lingering historical issues concerning the anti-Rightist struggle. At the meeting, there was consensus on the issue of "label removal," but there was still disagreement on the correction of the improper division of the Rightist. After the meeting, the Central United Front Department and the Ministry of Public Security drafted the Request for Removing All Rightists' Labels and sent it to the Central Committee. After research and approval, in April 1978, the Central Committee of the Communist Party of China issued the Notice on the Removal of All Rightists' Labels, and decided to remove all the other labels.

Later, following Hu Yaobang's proposal, the Central Organizational Department wrote a report to the Central Committee suggesting that the Rightists who had made mistakes in the struggle against the Rightists should be corrected according to the principles of seeking truth from facts and correcting mistakes. To this end, in August 1978, the relevant departments of the central state organs convened another meeting to study the issue of the correction. At the meeting, some people still insisted on removing the labels with no correction. Some thought that the rights and wrongs of the past had passed, and that there was no need to clear the accounts in such detail. At this point, they thought it sufficient to uniformly remove the labels of the Rightists, who were now treated as equals. Some thought that in any case, every place and department must keep some "models" and the labels should not all be removed. Some even questioned that if hundreds of thousands of Rightists were corrected, wouldn't the whole Party be in disorder? Comrades who insisted on both label removal and correction believed that it was necessary to adhere to the principle of seeking truth from facts and correcting mistakes when they occurred. They also pointed out that only by correcting all cases of injustice and falsehood could right and wrong be distinguished, strengthening unity for the development of the cause. After heated debate, the latter's opinion was approved by the majority of comrades present at the meeting.

In September 1978, on the basis of the principles of seeking truth from facts, resolving disputes, and correcting mistakes, the Central Committee approved and transmitted the Plan for Implementing the Central Committee's Decision to Remove All Rightists' Labels drafted by the Central Organizational Department, the Central Propaganda Department, the Central United Front Department, the Ministry of Civil Affairs, and the Ministry of Public Security, and issued a notice, deciding to review and correct the cases of those wrongly classified as

Rightists. This document pointed out the direction for correctly dealing with the remaining problems in the anti-Rightist struggle and formulated basic policies and approaches.

In order to do a thorough job of removing and correcting the Rightists' labels, five departments – the Central Organizational Department, the Central Propaganda Department, the Central United Front Department, the Ministry of Public Security, and the Ministry of Civil Affairs – jointly established the Label Removal Office. A Right-Wing Correction Office was set up within the Central Organizational Department to take charge of the work. In order to promote the work, on January 4, 1979, the Central Organizational Department also published the article "Prompt Correction of the Misjudged Rightists' Cases" in Issue 33 of *Organizational Communications*. This article offered a concrete analysis of the rectification of the Rightists, clarified some vague understandings, and put forward some concrete measures. In order to withstand pressure and overcome resistance, the older generation of revolutionaries represented by Deng Xiaoping gave great support to the work. Deng Xiaoping emphasized that "it is a necessary and important political measure to remove all the Rightists' labels, correct the treatment of the majority of them, and assign them appropriate work."[2]

Under the correct leadership of the Central Committee, with the resolute support of the older generation of revolutionaries and the joint efforts of the relevant departments of the central state organs, and through painstaking and meticulous work, obstructions to removing Rightists' labels and correcting the wrong classification of the Rightists was finally broken.

In February 1979, the Central Organizational Department and the Central United Front Department jointly held a national meeting exchanging insights gained from experience in the right-wing review and correction work. The Central Party School, the Ministry of Public Security, and the Yongcheng County Committee of Henan Province discussed their experience in emancipating the mind and doing thorough work in reexamination and correction. Leading comrades of the Central Organizational Department and the Central United Front Department also spoke at the meeting, emphasizing the great importance of carrying forward the spirit of the Third Plenary Session of the Central Committee and dealing with remaining historical issues in a pragmatic manner. For the first time, they raised the issue of "the mistake of escalation made in the 1957 anti-Rightist struggle," emphasizing that "correcting the wrongly classified

Rightists means correcting our mistakes in the struggle against the Rightists... No matter what level of organization or individual has approved the final decision, all mistakes must be corrected." This was a meeting for the exchange of insights gained from experience and for the emancipation of the mind. Subsequently, similar meetings were held in provinces, autonomous regions, and municipalities directly under the Central Government, and even in prefectures and counties. From that time, in view of the new situations and acute contradictions arising in the work, the Party Central Committee also issued a notice on the policy issues concerning the follow-up resettlement of the corrected Rightists who were wrongly classified, which thoroughly settled the problems lingering after the struggle against the Rightists, in terms of policy provisions. By the first half of 1981, the work had been successfully completed, and more than 540,000 cases against Rightists had been corrected nationwide, accounting for more than 98% of the total of 550,000 Rightists. For the 270,000 people who lost public offices, their posts were restored, their jobs reassigned, or their lives resettled, and adjustments were made to the previously improper work arrangements. In addition, correction policies were implemented for more than 315,000 people classified as "middle-Rightists" and "anti-socialist elements" and their relatives who had been affected. The successful completion of the work not only "liberated" hundreds of thousands of comrades who were wrongly classified as rightists, but also relieved the suffering of a large number of relatives and friends affected by the faction and stimulated their enthusiasm for building socialism.

2) *Reviewing and correcting the unjust, wrong, and false cases in the struggle against Rightist deviations.* From July 2 to August 16, 1959, the Central Committee of the Communist Party of China successively held an expanded meeting of the Politburo and the Eighth Plenary Session of the Eighth CPC Conference in Lushan, Jiangxi Province, also called the Lushan Conference. In the latter part of the Lushan Conference, Peng Dehuai was wrongly criticized, and then the struggle against rightist deviation was wrongly conducted throughout the Party. The resolution of the Eighth Plenary Session of the Eighth CPC Conference on the so-called "Peng Dehuai, Huang Kecheng, Zhang Wentian, and Zhou Xiaozhou-led Anti-Party Group" was totally wrong. The resolution proposed that Peng Dehuai and other comrades should be transferred from their posts in the Ministry of National Defense and retain their posts as members of the Politburo, monitoring the after effects. The plenary session also adopted the resolution

Fighting for the Defense of the Party's General Line and Against Rightist Opportunism. According to the resolution, "Rightist opportunism has become the main danger within the Party at present. Uniting the whole Party and the people, defending the general line, and repelling the attack of rightist opportunism have become the main tasks of the Party today. Thus, the struggle against rightist deviations spread to the whole Party. In the struggle against rightist deviations, a large number of Party members and cadres have been wrongly criticized and dealt with, and some comrades have been wrongly classified as rightist opportunists. In the Cultural Revolution, under the interference of the ultra-leftist trend of thought, these comrades were therefore attacked, criticized, and punished in various ways."

The struggle against rightist deviations was a major mistake in the Party's political life after the founding of New China. It seriously damaged the democratic life of the Party from the Central Committee to the grassroots level, wrongly attacked a large number of comrades who dared to seek truth from facts, reported the actual situation to the Party, and put forward criticisms, in this way encouraging the harmful tendencies of exaggeration, falsehood, and cults of personality within the Party.

After the 7,000 People's Congresses in 1961 and 1962, the Central Committee decided to screen those who had been designated as rightist opportunists (or as right opportunist mistakes) since 1959, and a great deal of work was done and many cases were redressed and corrected. However, since the leftist mistakes were not fundamentally corrected at that time, the work was not done thoroughly. Later, after the Tenth Plenary Session of the Eighth CPC Conference, the work was suspended as a result of the opposition against the rightists' case-reversals. In the Four Purifications Movement and the Cultural Revolution, with the interference of ultra-leftist thought, many places redefined and criticized the rightist opportunists or rightist mistakes that had been redressed and corrected in 1961 and 1962, and for those who had not yet been redressed or corrected, many were therefore attacked, persecuted, or subjected to disciplinary sanctions. Many suffered from various punishments such as dismissal from Party or League membership, demotion, salary reduction, assignments to remote areas to work, and removal from public office. After the toppling of the Gang of Four, in the early stages of putting an end to unjust and false cases and implementing the cadre policy, some veteran comrades put forward suggestions and requirements for the rectification of comrades who were wrongly criticized in the struggle against rightist deviations. At the Third Plenary Session of the Eleventh CPC Conference, the case of Peng Dehuai was redressed. In July 1979, the Central Committee officially issued the Notice on the Redressing and Correction of Rightist Opportunists. The notice emphasized that in the struggle against rightist deviation after 1959, all rightist opportunists or rightists wrongly classified as a result of reporting the actual situation or putting forward different opinions within the Party was to be redressed and corrected, and all policies concerning political and daily life were to be properly implemented.

Following the issuance of these documents, the Central Disciplinary Inspection Commission, with the assistance of the Central Organizational Department, handled the remaining issues in the anti-Rightist movement promptly and properly, in accordance with central deployment.

3) *Reviewing and Correcting the Wrongs and Injustices in the Four Clean-ups Movement.* The Four Clean-ups Movement was a large-scale mass movement initiated and led by the Party. In February 1963, the Central Working Conference decided that a socialist education campaign focused mainly on the Four Clean-ups (clearing accounts, warehouses, finances, and work assignments) should be carried out in rural areas, and the Five Oppositions (anti-corruption and theft, anti-speculation, anti-extravagance and waste, anti-decentralization, and anti-bureaucracy) campaign should be carried out in urban areas. From the end of 1964 to the beginning of 1965, the Central Working Conference, under the chairmanship of Mao Zedong, the Central Working Conference discussed and formulated Current Issues Present in the Rural Socialist Education Movement, also called the 23 Articles. In this document, the Four Clean-ups were defined as "purifying politics, economy, organization, and ideology," emphasizing that the nature of this movement was to solve the "contradiction between socialism and capitalism," putting forward the more leftist viewpoint that the focus of this movement was to rectify "those in power who take the capitalist path within the Party." Although the Four Clean-ups Movement played a particular role in solving the problems of the cadres' style of work and economic management, many grassroots cadres were unduly attacked because issues of different natures were all treated as class struggle or signs of class struggle within the Party. During the Cultural Revolution, Lin Biao and the Gang of Four further complicated issues by creating chaos.

In May 1978, Li Jingquan, the former First Secretary of the Southwest Bureau, presented to the Central Committee a report on the Remaining Problems of the Four Clean-ups Movement in Guiyang City. Deng Xiaoping instructed, "I agree to this report, and this matter may be reported to the Central Committee by the Central Organizational Department and the Provincial Committee after their discussion of a policy and method for handling it." In July of the same year, the Guizhou Provincial Committee submitted to the Central Committee the Request on the Situation of the Remaining Issues in the Four Clean-ups Movement in Guiyang City and the Opinions on Handling Them. In August of the same year, the Central Committee of the Communist Party of China approved the request of the Guizhou Provincial Committee. The Central Committee's reply pointed out that during the Four Clean-ups Movement in Guiyang City, some comrades' problems were improperly identified and handled only partially, confusing two types of contradictions of different natures and hurting some comrades the process. At present, it was necessary to correct it based on facts, restoring and developing the Party's fine tradition, implementing the Party's policies, mobilizing the enthusiasm of cadres and Party members, and strengthening unity. For all comrades who participated in the work of the Four Clean-ups and those who were criticized or punished in the movement, proper rectification should be done to ensure that no individuals would be held accountable, that personal grievances would not be dwelled upon, and that matters would proceed from the overall situation, with all parties united and jointly fighting against the enemy to make new contributions to the development of Guizhou. In the same month, the twelfth issue of *Organization Newsletter* published an article entitled "Errors in the Four Clean-ups Should Also be Corrected." This article was written in accordance with the spirit of the Central Committee's approval of Guiyang's Four Clean-ups Request Report. The article requested that the cases in the Four Clean-ups that were indeed mistaken should also be corrected in a pragmatic manner. This article gave an answer to the ideological concerns about whether correcting the wrong cases in the Four Clean-ups was to reverse the Four Clean-ups, whether the achievements of the Four Clean-ups would be negated, and whether it would cause trouble. It also noted the importance of adopting a positive, prudent policy to correct the wrong cases in the Four Clean-ups, and solving the problems and stabilizing the situation. It was important to focus on solving problems politically, promoting stability and unity, and forming a good situation. Later, the Central Organizational Department put forward some specific provisions and work requirements for reviewing and correcting unjust and false cases in the Four Clean-ups Movement. In accordance with the spirit of the Central Committee, all localities and departments throughout the country began to review and correct the erroneous cases in the Four Clean-ups Movement.

In view of the great difference and particularity between Guizhou's Four Clean-ups Movement in 1964 and that of the rest of the country, in December 1983, the Guizhou Provincial Committee once again submitted to the Central Organizational Department the Request on the Complete Settlement of the Four Clean-ups Issue in Guizhou and again requested the Central Committee's approval. Entrusted by the Central Committee, the Central Organizational Department drafted the Opinions on Addressing the Four Clean-ups Issue in Guizhou Province (Draft) to the Guizhou Provincial Committee, which was approved by the Central Committee in June 1984 in the name of the Central Committee of the Communist Party of China. In the reply, it was pointed out that the Four Clean-ups movement in Guizhou in 1964 was carried out under the erroneous guiding ideology of leftist deviation. At that time, it was recognized that the Provincial Party Committee had made a qualitative mistake on the rightist opportunistic path. It was totally wrong to estimate and analyze that the "Guiyang Municipal Committee formed a counter-two-sided revolutionary regime." And it was "absolutely correct to completely rectify the resulting injustices and wrongs." According to the spirit of the relevant provisions of the Central Committee, "erroneous conclusions and documents concerning the Four Clean-ups issue in Guizhou were automatically invalidated... The Central Committee believed that the leading cadres of the Guizhou Provincial Party Committee, the Guiyang Municipal Party Committee, and other places carrying out the Four Clean-ups Movement were good comrades. At that time, the two thousand cadres appointed by the Central Committee to participate in the Four Clean-ups Movement in Guizhou were also good comrades. At present, strengthening unity among cadres is of great significance for creating a new situation in Guizhou." From then on, all provinces, autonomous regions, and municipalities directly under the Central Government made a comprehensive and thorough review and correction of the wrongs and falsehoods in the work of the Four Clean-ups Movement in accordance with the spirit of the Central Committee. A total of

630,000 cases of wrongs and falsehoods in the Four Clean-ups Movement were corrected through national review.

4) *Properly Handling the Problems Lingering after the Party's Underground History.* In the early days of the founding of New China, in the general clean-up of under-ground Party organizations, some underground Party comrades were mishandled and unfairly treated, resulting in many lingering problems due to insufficient understanding of the complexity of the underground struggle, of the historical environment and characteristics of the underground struggle, and certain errors in the course of their work. During the Cultural Revolution, some comrades of the underground Party were slandered and persecuted. In July 1981, Hu Yaobang instructed in a visitor's letter that the lingering historical problems of the underground Party should be well focused and addressed fairly and impartially, starting with those in Fujian Province. The Central Organizational Department sent letters to Fujian and other provincial committees conveying Hu Yaobang's instructions. The Fujian Provincial Party Committee attached great importance to this issue, and the Secretary of the Provincial Party Committee took responsibility for it. It took more than three years to thoroughly review and properly address lingering historical problems in Fujian's underground Party.

In accordance with the spirit of these instructions, the Yunnan Provincial Committee immediately began to address the lingering problems in the work of clearing up underground Party members in Yunnan. In March 1982, the Central Organizational Department issued the Report of the Yunnan Provincial Party Committee on Solving the Historical Problems of Yunnan's Underground Party and the Yunnan, Guangxi, and Guizhou Border Troops and the Report on Restoring the Political Reputation of Comrade Zheng Boke, which were approved by the Central Committee. All the slanderous and false statements imposed by the Provincial Military Control Council and the Provincial Reform Commission on Yunnan's underground Party and the border troop in the Cultural Revolution were overthrown, and a large number of resulting cases of injustice, falsehood, and wrongdoing were eliminated. At the same time, it also reversed the inappropriate conclusions made regarding Yunnan's underground Party and the border troop in several political movements before the Cultural Revolution and the wrong criticisms made by the Provincial Party Committee on Zheng Boke, the main leader of Yunnan's underground Party in the 1950s. It fully affirmed that Yunnan's underground Party and the border troop had worked hard in the multi-ethnic border areas located some distance from the Central Government, and had made great achievements and contributions to the liberation of Yunnan. In August 1982, the Ministry of Central Organizations approved and issued the Report of the Organizational Department of the Shaanxi Provincial Committee on the Situation of Underground Party Organizations in Northwest United University and Opinions on the Handling of Party Membership of Relevant Personnel.

On the basis of this earnest summary of the experience of dealing with lingering historical problems in the underground Party in these areas, the Central Organizational Department held a symposium on dealing with the historical problems of the underground Party in sixteen provinces, autonomous regions, and municipalities directly under the Central Government in December 1984, and conducted a serious study of and deployment for dealing with the historical issues of the underground Party. After the meeting, with the approval of the Secretariat of the Central Committee, the Central Organizational Department issued a circular on the issuance of the Summary of the Symposium on Handling the Historical Issues of the Underground Party (hereinafter referred to as the Summary). The Summary affirmed that the underground Party organizations and the guerrilla armed forces led by the underground Party throughout the country had fought bravely during the White Terror over a long period and made their due contributions to the cause of the liberation of the Chinese people. It pointed out that the historical issues of the underground Party mainly referred to the wrongly handled grievances, false cases, and Party membership issues concerning the guerrilla armed forces, secret peripheral organizations, and their members, including those established before liberation and led by the local underground Party organizations or the underground Party organizations. In dealing with these problems, it was important to follow the Resolution on Historical Issues of the Party After the Founding of the People's Republic of China and the relevant policies and guidelines of the Central Committee, adhere to the principle of seeking truth from facts and correcting mistakes, and settle any issues fairly and impartially. It was necessary not only to distinguish right from wrong and solve problems, but also to maintain stability and unity. There was to be no investigation into individual responsibility. Emphasis was to be placed on political solutions, and appropriate remedies were to be made for comrades who had been wrongly handled for long periods in terms of political and living situations. The Summary also put forward suggestions for how to deal with lingering problems in the underground Party. From that time, this work was carried out on a national scale. In November 1985, the Central Organizational Department issued a Circular on Dealing with the Historical Issues of the Underground Party, requiring all organizational departments to continue to do a thorough job of dealing with the historical issues of the underground Party, in accordance with the spirit of the Central Committee and basically completing the implementation of the policy before the Thirteenth National Congress. In addition, specific replies were made concerning subsidizing Party comrades from the underground who were wrongly treated over a long period of time.

With the correct leadership of the Central Committee and the joint efforts of relevant provinces and municipalities, the work was basically completed before the Thirteenth National Congress. The remaining historical issues of the underground Party were properly handled, the revolutionary image of the underground Party was restored, rights and wrongs were distinguished, and the unity of the Party was strengthened.

5) *Carefully Implementing the Policy on Intelligence Workers.* This was an important task after the implementation of the cadre policy. The Party's intelligence reconnaissance work played an important role in revolution and construction both in the war years and in the construction years. However, after the founding of New China, in all previous political movements, especially in the Cultural Revolution, with the ideological influence of leftist errors, the special situation of intelligence reconnaissance was neglected, resulting in the mishandling of many intelligence investigators and leading cadres, which led to many unjust or false charges. After the Third Plenary Session of the Eleventh CPC Conference, Party organizations around the country corrected some unjust and false charges among intelligence investigators in their efforts to fight against injustice and falsehoods and implement cadre policies. In particular, the Central Committee exerted a great influence on Pan Hannian, who suffered great injustice for many years. However, the lingering historical problems of these intelligence investigators were rather complicated. In some areas and departments, for lack of sufficient understanding about the policies, practices, and characteristics of the Party's intelligence reconnaissance work, and with no policy basis for dealing

with the issues concerning intelligence investigators under specific conditions, the problems of some intelligence investigators were mishandled and the follow-up work was either not carried out or not done thoroughly.

As a result, in April 1986, the Party Group of the State Security Department and the Central Organizational Department submitted to the Central Secretariat the Request on the Serious Implementation of the Policy for Intelligence Detective Personnel. The Secretariat of the Central Committee instructed that the implementation of the policy on intelligence investigators was a serious political task, and all localities and relevant departments should earnestly implement it. In carrying out the policy, it was important to fully consider the particularity of information work, conduct comprehensive and factual analysis and investigation according to the Party's policies and strategies for the struggle against the enemy in different periods, and closely integrate the historical environment and actual situation at that time. In dealing with specific problems, it was important to deal with them in the spirit of a general rather than a detailed approach, and leniency rather than strictness. In May of the same year, with the consent of the Central Committee, the General Office of the Central Committee of the Communist Party of China transmitted the request report. In July, the Ministry of State Security and the Ministry of Central Organizations jointly held a symposium in Beijing on the implementation of intelligence investigators' policies in provinces, autonomous regions, and municipalities directly under the Central Government. Emphasis was laid on the study of the implementation of the Central Committee's directives on the implementation of the policy for investigators and the Circular of the General Office of the Central Committee of the Communist Party of China, further deepening the understanding of the importance of doing this work well, defining the guidelines and guiding principles for the work, as well as the measures to be taken, and making corresponding work arrangements. After the meeting, the implementation of the intelligence investigator policy was carried out in 24 provinces, municipalities, and relevant ministries and commissions of central state organs.

All provinces and municipalities attached great importance to this work, and some provinces set up specialized agencies to undertake it. However, due to the particularity, complexity, and arduousness of implementing the policy of intelligence investigators, the work was not completed until the early 1990s. The entire country made remarkable achievements in settling unjust and false cases and implementing the policy of intelligence investigators for tens of thousands of people.

In the history of intelligence reconnaissance work, the national policy of eliminating unjust and false charges and implementing intelligence reconnaissance personnel was unprecedented, and it produced remarkable results. It fully embodied the Party's spirit of solicitude and thorough responsibility for intelligence investigators, which laid down the heavy burden carried by comrades and children of their families who had been wrongly handled for many years. It played a positive role in winning friends, uniting comrades, mobilizing the enthusiasm of the majority of comrades on the intelligence and reconnaissance front, enhancing cohesion, and promoting the development of the cause of national security.

6) *Rectification for the Novel* Liu Zhidan. In 1962, with Kang Sheng's prompting, the unpublished novel *Liu Zhidan* was criticized at the Beidaihe Central Working Conference and the Tenth Plenary Session of the Eighth CPC Conference. After the meeting, a long-term special review was conducted of the novel itself, the author of the novel, Li Jiantong, the reviewers Xi Zhongxun and Liu Jingfan, who had read the manuscript, and the comrades of the Workers' Publishing House who had overseen the creation of the novel. At the beginning of the Cultural Revolution, the review of the project had not been completed and no formal conclusions had been reached. During the Cultural Revolution, Kang Sheng, together with Lin Biao and the Gang of Four, carried out greater political persecution in connection to *Liu Zhidan*. Yao Wenyuan published an article publicly declaring that *Liu Zhidan* was an anti-Party novel and that the comrades who wrote and supported the book were anti-Party elements. After that, Party members who had been examined by the special project suffered more severe persecution and more people were implicated. Leading comrades who had read manuscripts and supported this creation, a group of veteran cadres and Party members in the former Shaanxi-Gansu revolutionary base areas, and even some comrades who had participated in the review of this project were persecuted to varying degrees, and some were even persecuted to death. Li Jiantong was designated as "the backbone of Xi Zhongxun's anti-revolutionary group's anti-Party activities through novels." Until May 1977, with the conclusion of the review of Liu Jingfan's works by the Central Special Task Force, Liu Jingfan was still

said to have "collaborated with Xi Zhongxun to support the anti-Party novel *Liu Zhidan* to redress Gao Gang's case."

Reviewed by the Central Organizational Department in 1979, the facts showed that *Liu Zhidan* was not an anti-Party novel. On the contrary, it was a fairly good novel eulogizing the older generations of proletarian revolutionaries and tracing the history of revolutionary struggle. It was entirely legitimate for Comrade Xi Zhongxun and other comrades to be concerned about the creation of the novel and express their opinions on how to polish it, which were not activities of anti-Party conspiracy groups at all. Looking at the case from beginning to end, the so-called case of anti-Party activities connected to the writing of the novel *Liu Zhidan* was a major mistake made by Kang Sheng. It was a modern literary prison intensified by Lin Biao and the Gang of Four in the Cultural Revolution. For this reason, in August 1979, the Central Committee approved the Central Organizational Department's Report on the Fiction of *Liu Zhidan*. By publishing articles in newspapers and periodicals to distinguish right and wrong, to rectify the falsely framed comrades, and to do a good job in the follow-up, this major mistake was fairly settled and won the hearts of the people.

7) *Redressing the Case of the So-Called Peng, Gao, and Xi Anti-Party Group.* The so-called Peng Dehuai, Gao Gang, and Xi Zhongxun Anti-Party Group was fabricated after the Tenth Plenary Session of the Eighth Conference of the Communist Party, when Kang Sheng presided over the special examination of Xi Zhongxun. He took advantage of his authority, gave "instructions," and carried out random criticism and a series of other activities to expose and criticize the Peng, Gao, and Xi Anti-Party Group. In 1965, the Outline of Xi Zhongxun's Anti-Party Issues, approved by Kang Sheng, was handed out and communicated among cadres at all levels, plotting to "thoroughly eliminate the evil influence of Peng, Gao, and Xi." As a result, not only were Peng Dehuai and Xi Zhongxun framed and persecuted, but a group of comrades who had worked with them were affected as well. During the Cultural Revolution, Kang Sheng, Lin Biao, the Gang of Four, and their representatives in Shaanxi further made a fuss about the so-called Peng, Gao, and Xi Anti-Party Group, saying that "the enemy in Shaanxi is serious… Peng Dehuai, Gao Gang, and Xi Zhongxun take Xi'an in Shaanxi as their base." In the name of "purifying the team," they made "checking black lines" and "digging black roots" to classify the former Northwest Bureau, the Shaanxi

Provincial Committee, the Provincial People's Committee, the Xi'an Municipal Committee, and the Municipal People's Committee as "five black nests," regarding them as the "old forces" of Peng, Gao and Xi who should be totally destroyed. Since the founding of New China, most of the members of the four standing committees of the Provincial Committee had been classified as "traitors," "special agents," and "hardcore disciples of Peng, Gao, and Xi." They imprisoned more than 50 leading cadres of the Northwest Bureau, the Shaanxi Provincial Party Committee, and the Xi'an Municipal Party Committee, convicted them of various charges, and imposed fascist persecution on them.

In 1979, after a review by the Shaanxi Provincial Committee, the so-called Peng, Gao, and Xi Anti-Party Group was extremely absurd, purely slanderous, and patently false. As a result, many cases of injustice, falsehood, and errors ensued, and a large number of cadres and masses were attacked, which caused serious damage to Shaanxi's work. Although the Central Government had redressed the cases of Peng Dehuai and Xi Zhongxun, considering that the so-called Peng, Gao, and Xi Anti-Party Group had a profound impact in Shaanxi Province involving a number of people and sectors, the Shaanxi Provincial Committee of the Communist Party of China believed that it was still necessary to officially declare that these false charges should be completely redressed. In January 1980, with the consent of the Central Committee, the Organizational Department forwarded the Request for the Complete Redressing of the So-called Peng, Gao, and Xi Anti-Party Group issued by the Shaanxi Provincial Party Committee of the Communist Party of China, which thoroughly redressed the false case.

8) *Properly Addressing the Issue of Wrongfully Murdered People in the Soviet Area During the Anti-Revolt Campaign.* The problem of people mistakenly killed in the course of eliminating the counter-revolt in the soviet area was a major historical issue that had a wide influence and involved a large number of people. From 1930 to 1935, under the influence of the erroneous leftist line, the Central Soviet Area, Western Hunan and Hubei, Hubei-Henan-Anhui, Western Fujian, Sichuan-Shaanxi, Shaanxi-Gansu, and other major soviet areas successively carried out campaigns to eliminate the AB League, the Restructuring Party, the Social Democratic Party, the Third Party, and the Abolition Party. A large number of Party members were mistakenly imprisoned or killed. In the Resolution on Several Historical Issues passed at the Seventh Plenary Session of the Sixth Conference

of CPC in 1945, it was clearly pointed out that "due to the entanglements of the wrong anti-revolutionary policy and sectarianism in the cadre policy, a large number of outstanding comrades were falsely handled and framed, resulting in extremely painful losses within the Party… After investigation, cases of all comrades who have been falsely dealt with should be redressed, their reputation restored, and their names remembered." However, due to the limitations of the historical conditions at that time, there was no time to settle this issue before the founding of New China. The Central Committee only put forward its opinions on how to properly deal with this issue in 1954. The Central People's Government issued a circular on the handling of wrongfully murdered people and their families during the Second Revolutionary Civil War. In accordance with the spirit of the circular, the cases of nearly 20,000 people were redressed in Jiangxi, Fujian, Hubei, and other provinces. Other provinces also advanced the redressing of the main leading cadres of the Party, government, and army who were wrongfully murdered. It was clear a thorough job had been done, but the issues of most of the people were not yet settled. After the Third Plenary Session of the Eleventh Conference of the Communist Party of China, many relatives and some veteran comrades of the wrongfully murdered people repeatedly urged a thorough solution to lingering historical issues. The leading comrades of the Central Committee instructed the Central Organizational Department and the Ministry of Civil Affairs to study and propose solutions. In March and June 1983, the Central Committee of the Communist Party of China and the State Council approved two ministries' opinions on this issue. The State Council approved the Circular of the Ministry of Civil Affairs Regarding Opinions on Dealing with Mistakenly Killed Persons During the Second Revolutionary Civil War. The Organizational Departments of Hubei, Anhui, Henan, Fujian, Jiangxi, Sichuan, and Shaanxi Provinces worked closely with civil affairs departments to conduct in-depth and detailed review work.

Under the leadership of the Central Committee and the efforts of relevant provinces and municipalities, after three years of hard work, the unjust, wrong, and false cases in the Soviet areas' anti-revolt campaign were thoroughly redressed, and the issues of the persons who were wrongly killed or mishandled or the follow-up work with their widows were properly handled, thoroughly addressing this major lingering historical issue that had dragged on for decades.

9) *Redressing the Case of Ji Zhentong and Huang Zhongyue, Famous Generals of the Ningdu Uprising.* In June 1979, twelve veteran comrades, including Ji Pengfei, Li Da, Huang Zhen, Wang Youping, Yuan Xuezu, and Su Jin, wrote to the Central Committee to report that Ji Zhentong and Huang Zhongyue of the former Fifth Red Army were wrongly killed in 1934. They suggested that the cases should be redressed and their reputation restored. Following the instructions of the leading comrades of the Central Committee, the Central Organizational Department sent people to investigate more than seventy veteran comrades and consulted relevant archival materials. Ji Zhentong was the commander of the 74th Brigade of the 25th Divi-sion of the 26th Route Army of the Kuomintang, and Huang Zhongyue was the head of the first regiment of the Brigade. On December 14, 1931, they took part in the Ningdu Uprising led by Zhao Bosheng, a member of the Communist Party of China, and Dong Zhentang, an important general, which shocked the whole country. After the uprising, thousands of officers and soldiers were incorporated into the Fifth Troop of the Red Army, and Ji Zhentong was accepted as a special member of the Communist Party of China. He served as the commander-in-chief of the Legion and Huang Zhongyue as the commander of the 15th Army. In the spring of 1932, the National Security Bureau discovered that a small number of officers headed by Ji Zhentong and Huang Zhongyue had attempted to withdraw their teams. The two were classified as counter-revolutionaries and imprisoned. They were later executed on the eve of the Long March because of the influence of Wang Ming's left-leaning line. For this case, Comrade Ye Jianying instructed, "I heard Chairman Mao say (probably in Yan'an) that the killing of Ji Zhentong and Huang Zhongyue was wrong. Now I think this grievance should be cleared." From the review of the Central Committee, Ji Zhentong and Huang Zhongyue had made great contributions to the Ningdu Uprising, which had had a great influence and should be affirmed. Ji Zhentong and Huang Zhongyue had their own patriotic anti-Japanese ideas. The Party had absorbed Ji as a special Party member and decided to send him to the Soviet Union for study, and he was politically reliable. He Yingqin once sent people to contact Ji Zhentong and Huang Zhongyue for counter-measures, but in vain. Although Ji and Huang did not report their contacts to the organization, the enemy's counter-plot did not succeed. Ji said that it was not possible to pull the team out of the Soviet area, which was credible. It was wrong to classify Ji

Zhentong and Huang Zhongyue as counter-revolutionaries and to execute them in violation of the resolutions of the Chinese Soviet Executive Committee. It was thus necessary to redress the case and restore their reputation and Ji's Party membership. In August 1981, the Secretariat of the Central Committee approved the Central Organizational Department's Request for Redressing the Case of Comrade Ji Zhentong and Comrade Huang Zhongyue of the Former Fifth Red Army Regime. The merits of Ji Zhentong and Huang Zhongyue in the uprising were appropriately evaluated. In this way, this wrongful case, which had stood for nearly half a century, was fairly and reasonably settled.

10) *Redressing the Clearing-up of the Trotsky Doctrine Incident in the Huxi Area*[3]. The Clearing-up of the Trotsky Doctrine Incident in the Huxi Area lasted from August to November 1939, developing from the Lakeside Prefectural Committee, then expanding to the whole border area of Jiangsu, Shandong, and Henan. In this incident, a large number of cadres were arrested and killed, resulting in serious losses. In November 1939, Luo Ronghuan and Guo Hongtao, the leaders of the Shandong Branch of the Communist Party of China, rushed to the Huxi area to take urgent measures to stop the development of the incident. From 1940 to 1945, the Central Committee and the Shandong Branch made several reviews and affirmed that Wang Xuren, the former head of the Organizational Department of the Lakeside Prefectural Committee, was the one who initiated the Clearing-up of the Trotsky Doctrine Incident out of thin air. However, due to the limitations of the historical conditions at that time, there was no definite conclusion concerning the nature of the incident, which led to the incomplete handling of many lingering issues. Some of the families of the murdered comrades were labeled "relatives of the anti-revolutionaries" during the Cultural Revolution. The Shandong Provincial Committee re-examined this historical case of injustice in accordance with the directive of the Central Committee on redressing unjust, wrong, and false cases. In May 1983, the Shandong Provincial Committee of the Communist Party of China (CPC) submitted to the Central Committee the Report on the Treatment of the Remaining Issues of the Clearing-up of the Trotsky Doctrine Incident in the Huxi Area, pointing out that this case was not a matter of escalation. In 1939, there was no factual basis for the campaign aimed at eliminating Trotskyists and Trotskyist organizations. None of the seven so-called "genuine Trotskyist disciples" originally identified was proven genuine

after detailed investigation. This was a major case of injustice, falsehood, and wrongdoing, which needed to be completely reversed. Comrades who had been wrongfully killed or mishandled would be redressed. The children or families affected were to be redressed as well, in hopes of eliminating the influence of the case. With the approval of the Central Committee, in December 1983, the Central Organizational Department transmitted the Report of the Shandong Provincial Committee of the Communist Party of China on the Treatment of the Remaining Issues of the Clearing-up of the Trotsky Doctrine Incident in the Huxi Area, which completely reversed this wrongful case that had carried on for years.

11) *Redressing the So-Called Trotskyists Case in the Fourth Division of the New Fourth Army and the Huaibei and Huainan Bases in 1941.* In October 1984, the Organizational Department of the Central Committee of the Communist Party of China and the General Political Department of the Liberation Army made the Decision on the Elimination of the So-called Trotskyists Case of the Fourth Division of the New Fourth Army and the Huaibei and Huainan Bases in 1941. The decision pointed out that during the period from May 1938 to March 1940, when the CPC branch of the Guangxi Student Army was established and retreated to the Huainan and Huaibei bases, under the direct leadership of the Anhui Provincial Labor Committee, the Party Committee of Hubei, Henan, and Anhui Provinces, and the Lihuang Municipal Committee, it mobilized and organized the masses, adhered to the anti-Japanese forces behind the enemy lines, propagated the policy of the Party's anti-Japanese national united front and the anti-Japanese political propositions, and protected the underground Party. After the members of the Communist Party of China and the progressive masses of the Guangxi Student Army arrived at the New Fourth Army and the Huainan and Huaibei bases, they made positive contributions to the armed struggle against Japan and the construction of the base areas. In the past, there had been no basis to classify the Communist Party branch of the Guangxi Student Army as a Trotskyist organization and to examine dozens of comrades on the basis of the "Trotskyist problem." The so-called Trotskyists case was an instance of complete injustice. In order to eliminate the influence of this historical injustice, it was now decided that the cases of the Communist Party Branch of the Guangxi Student Army and of all the relevant comrades who had been wrongfully examined, handled, and executed, would be redressed and their reputation were to be restored. The Party

organizations of the relevant regions and units were to conscientiously clean up archives and materials in accordance with the relevant provisions of the Central Committee and do a thorough follow-up work.

12) *Properly Handling the Historical Issues of the Breakthrough on the Central Plains.* In August 1980, Zheng Shaowen and Zhang Zhiyi wrote to the Central Committee requesting that the remaining problems of the breakthrough on the Central Plains be properly solved based on facts. In response to the letter, Hu Yaobang gave important instructions to the relevant departments to properly solve the problem.

In 1946, under the heavy siege of 300,000 troops of the Kuomintang, the Central Plains Army and the Party and government organs in the Central Plains Liberated Area carried out a strategic transfer breakthrough. Because of the pressing situation, in order to preserve its strength, the Party's Central Plains Bureau formulated some special policies, mobilized a large number of comrades who could not break through with the army to demobilize and conceal, and in the process of breaking through, many comrades were dispersed. Some of them, due to demobilization, concealment, and alienation, were unfairly treated regarding issues such as Party membership, work periods for the revolution, and conclusions of historical issues. On May 29, 1957, two comrades, Zheng Weisan, former Secretary of the Central Plains Bureau, and Chen Shaomin, Minister of the Organizational Department, wrote to the Central Organizational Department to elaborate on the situation. Before the breakthrough of the Central Plains in 1946, the situation was so urgent that a large number of local cadres could not follow the army. In order to preserve their strength, the following decisions were made at that time: 1) to use social relations as much as possible to disguise themselves in other liberated areas, 2) to use social relations as much as possible to conceal themselves, and 3) if they were spotted by the enemy and could not hide any more, to surrender themselves to the enemy as soldiers of the New Fourth Army or members of peasant associations. As long as they did not expose their Party membership and did not surrender as Party members, they could go back to the army and not be considered surrenderers, though things would be different if they surrendered as Party members. This was a decision made in exceptionally difficult circumstances. If this decision was wrong, the Party took responsibility for it. The Central Organizational Department forwarded the letter to the Party committees of Hubei and Henan Provinces for their attention when dealing with the surrender of Party members in the Central Plains Liberated Areas. However, it did not attract the attention it deserved at that time. In the early days of the founding of the People's Republic of China, when dealing with the historical issues of the breakthrough on the Central Plains, some comrades did not take into account the historical background at that time and conduct enough specific analysis, and so were too harsh in deciding on the nature of the incident. In particular, in the Cultural Revolution, some comrades were assaulted afresh and the nature of the incident was more severely determined.

According to the instructions of the leading comrades of the Central Committee, the Organizational Department of the Hubei Provincial Party Committee and the Party group of the Provincial Civil Affairs Department made a serious investigation of the historical issues of the breakthrough on the Central Plains. They put forward Opinions on Handling the Historical Issues of the Demobilized, Concealed, and Left-Behind Personnel During the Breakthrough on the Central Plains, pointing out that the lingering issues of demobilized, concealed, and left-behind personnel during the breakthrough on the Central Plains should be handled in accordance with the basic spirit of the Central Organizational Department's Opinions on Redressing Unjust, Wrong, and False Cases and Further Implementing the Cadre Policy, along with the letter of Comrades Zheng Weisan and Chen Shaomin approved by the Central Organizational Department on June 6, 1957. In line with the principle of seeking truth from facts and correcting errors, the Central Organizational Department carried out a thorough clean-up of the problems, adopted a positive and prudent attitude, and properly settled the lingering issues. The conclusion of the review dealt with the incorrect problems concerning Party membership, work arrangement, retirement, and other follow-up work, as well as the calculation of working periods, and the issues of being treated as demobilized soldiers and being recognized as martyrs. In July 1981, the Central Organizational Department transmitted the Opinions of the Organizational Department of the Hubei Provincial Committee and the Party Group of the Provincial Civil Affairs Department on Dealing with the Historical Issues of the Demobilized Hidden and Left-Behind Personnel During the Breakthrough on the Central Plains. Relevant provinces, municipalities, and departments promptly organized review and correction. Through reexamination and correction, more than 50,000 cases of demobilized, concealed, and left behind personnel were settled, and the cases mishandled in the early days of the founding of New China were corrected, bringing this historical issue to a proper resolution.

13) *Properly Handling the Lingering Issue of the Undetermined Martyrs Killed in the Sino-American Cooperative Organization (SACO) Prison on the Eve of Chongqing's Liberation.* After the Third Plenary Session of the Eleventh CPC Conference, the Organiza-tional Department of the Central Committee of the Communist Party of China entrusted the Organizational Department of Sichuan Province to re-investigate and verify the undetermined martyrs killed in the prison of SACO in the days leading up to Chongqing's liberation. Through an in-depth investigation conducted by the Organizational Department of the Sichuan Provincial Committee, 83 people's issues were identified. Party organizations brought these to practical and realistic conclusions. Among them, 64 people, including Xi Maozhao and Zhang Luping, had adhered to the nobility of Communist Party members in prison, fought bravely and unyieldingly, and given their lives with peace of mind. They had shown their impressive and exemplary deeds and were recognized as revolutionary martyrs. This issue, which had been delayed for more than thirty years, was finally brought to an appropriate resolution. On November 20, 1986, the Xinhua News Agency also made a special report on this matter.

Through dealing with the major historical issues mentioned above, the progress of properly handling the historical issues was widely promoted throughout the country. All provinces, municipalities, autonomous regions, ministries, and commissions likewise reviewed, cleared up, and properly handled the historical issues of their respective regions and departments. According to preliminary statistics, in properly dealing with lingering historical problems, nearly 2 million lingering historical cases from before the Cultural Revolution were reviewed and dealt with nationwide. By 1987, before the Thirteenth National Congress, the work of properly dealing with historical issues nationwide had basically ended. By properly dealing with the lingering historical problems, the Party greatly mobilized the enthusiasm of its cadres and the masses, consolidated social stability and unity, promoted the fight against injustices and falsehoods, and implemented the cadre policy to ensure the successful completion of this work before the Thirteenth National Congress.

III

Proper Adjustment of Social Relations in the New Context

While dealing with large-scale cases and redressing instances of injustice, falsehoods, and wrongdoing, the Party Central Committee also studied and dealt with some historical problems, adjusted social relations, and implemented various policies.

1. Comprehensively Implementing the Policy of Intellectuals and Solving the Practical Problems of Intellectuals

Implementing the policy of intellectuals was an important part of the work of eliminating unjust and false cases and implementing the cadre policy, running through the whole process. It began in 1978, and was successfully completed before the Thirteenth National Congress in 1987. There was a fine tradition of patriotism among Chinese intellectuals, and under the Party's long-term education, the overwhelming majority of intellectuals supported the leadership of the Communist Party of China and loved the socialist motherland. However, due to the leftist prejudice and discrimination against intellectuals that had long been simmering, many intellectuals were impacted to varying degrees in previous political movements. During the Cultural Revolution, countless intellectuals were once again severely attacked and persecuted. After the toppling of the Gang of Four, Deng Xiaoping delivered an important speech at the National Science Congress in March 1978, expounding the basic principles of Marxism concerning the position and role of science and technology in social development, pointing out that the intellectual workers serving socialism were part of the working class and stressing the necessity of creating a more ambitious scientific and technological team in China. Deng Xiaoping's exposition stating that intellectuals were part of the working class greatly inspired the enthusiasm of the majority of intellectuals to love the Party and work toward building a socialist motherland. At the same time, it cleared the obstacles and pointed out the direction for large-scale implementation of the intellectuals policy.

From October to November 1978, the Central Committee organized a seminar on the implementation of intellectuals policies. The meeting held that the situation of intellectuals had undergone profound changes and that the policy of "unity, education, and transformation" for intellectuals put forward in the early days of the founding of the People's Republic of China was no longer applicable to the current situation. At present, it was important to do a good job in implementing the policy of intellectuals. On November 3, the Central Committee issued a circular entitled Opinions on Implementing the Party's Intellectuals Policy, which put forward six requirements for the implementation of the Intellectuals Policy. First, a correct estimate of the intellectuals' ranks should be made. Second, it was important to continue to do a thorough job in reviewing and redressing unjust, false, and misjudged cases. Third, it was necessary to fully trust and employ intellectuals so they were granted status, authority, and responsibility. Fourth, it was important to assign them to appropriate positions so that they could make the best use of their talents. Fifth, efforts needed to be made to improve working and living conditions. And finally, it was important to strengthen leadership and improve work style. Following the issuance of the document, the work of broadly implementing the policy on intellectuals was steadily carried out nationwide, and the social fashion of respecting knowledge and talent began to emerge.

Hu Yaobang paid close attention to the work and devoted great effort to it. He gave many important instructions regarding the challenges encountered in the implementation of the policy on intellectuals. According to Hu Yaobang's instructions and the request of the Central Committee that the redressing of cases of injustices and falsehoods should be basically completed and the cadre policy should be implemented before the Thirteenth National Congress, the Central Organizational Department, together with the relevant departments, paid close attention to the inspection and supervision of the implementation of the intellectuals policy and took the work as one of the key tasks of the Central Organizational Department during this period.

In May 1985, the Central Organizational Department and the Central United Front Department jointly held a National Symposium on the implementation of the intellectuals policy, focusing on how to accomplish the tasks specified by the Central Committee to basically complete the implementation of the intellectuals policy before the Thirteenth National Congress, and proposed the establishment of a separate hierarchical responsibility system. Leading organs at all levels and in all sectors, especially comrades in organizational departments, were to go to the grassroots level personally, supervise and inspect the work, help solve difficult problems, and do a solid job in implementing the policy on intellectuals.

In September 1986, with the approval of the leading comrades of the Central Committee, the Organizational Department issued the Notice on Inspecting and Implementing the Intellectuals Policy, pointing out that some regions and departments had basically completed the task of implementing the policy on intellectuals and solving the lingering historical problems, and most of the regions and departments planned to complete it in the second half of the year. In order to ensure the quality of their work, those that had completed the task were required to carry out a thorough inspection, and specific requirements for the scope and content of the inspection, organization, leadership, steps, and methods were also put forward. In November, the Organizational Department of the Central Committee of the Communist Party of China held three national meetings exchanging insights gained from experience in the implementation of intellectuals policies in Dalian, Wuhan, and Beijing. According to statistics in 25 provinces, districts, and municipalities, a variety of problems encountered by more than 7.1 million people were solved in the implementation of intellectuals policies.

The above measures and work greatly facilitated the in-depth development of the implementation of the policy of intellectuals. With the care of the central leadership and the joint efforts of various regions and departments, this important project, which lasted several years and involved an arduous task, was basically completed before the Thirteenth National Congress of the Communist Party of China.

2. Removing Labels for Landlords and Rich Peasants and Settling the Issue of the Status of Landlords' Children

On January 11, 1979, in accordance with the relevant provisions of the Rural People's Commune Work Regulations (Draft Trial Implementation) adopted by the Third Plenary Session of the Eleventh Central Committee, the Central Committee made the Decision on the Label Removal Issue of Landlords and Wealthy Peasants and the Status of the Children of Landlords (hereinafter referred to as the Decision). The Decision declared that all landlords, rich peasants, counter-revolutionaries, and "bad elements" who had abided by government decrees and worked honestly for many years and had done nothing wrong would be treated as rural people's commune members upon removing their labels, subject to the mass appraisal and the county revolutionary committee's approval. The members of the landlords' and the rich peasants' families were all members of the commune and enjoyed the same treatment as other members of the commune. In the future, their enrollment for school, recruitment for army, membership of the League and Party, and assignment of work would mainly depend on their political performance, without discrimination. The children of landlord and rich peasant families would all be members of the community and should no longer be viewed as members of landlords' or rich peasants' families. The Decision also called for organizing cadres and the masses both inside and outside the Party to study the Party's policies conscientiously and do a thorough job of ideological education.

This decision put an end to the political discrimination imposed on at least 20 million people, who now started to enjoy their rights of citizens and a new political life. According to the Xinhua News Agency, by November 1984, the last batch of landlords, rich peasants, counter-revolutionaries, and bad elements in the country had been successfully relieved of these labels. Those who were wrongly assigned these labels were also redressed, and those who had gone abroad and left the country were likewise relieved of their labels, and their families were notified accordingly.

3. Restoring the Status of Former Industrial and Commercial Workers

On November 12, 1979, the Central Committee of the CPC approved the Request on the Differentiation of Workers from Former Businessmen issued by the Central United Front Department and six other departments, which clearly pointed out that when private industry and commerce were jointly operated by public and private sectors in 1956, a large number of peddlers, handicraftsmen, and other workers were brought into public-private joint ventures and collectively referred to as private personnel. It was inappropriate to treat them as bourgeois businessmen. They should be distinguished from the former bourgeois businessmen and their original status as workers was to be clarified. In accordance with the spirit of this document, after over a year's work, more than 700,000 small businesses, hawkers, small handicraftsmen, and other workers throughout the country were distinguished from the former businessmen, and their status as workers was restored. In this way, the remaining historical issues in the socialist transformation were properly settled and the mistakes made at that time were corrected. At the same time, according to the Regulations of the Central Committee on Some Specific Policies Concerning the Former Businessmen and Industrialists, the former businessmen and industrialists were also removed of their labels as capitalists or agents of the capitalists.

4. Removing the Historical Restrictions on the Appointment of Some Cadres

In the latter part of the work of eliminating unjust and false cases and implementing the cadre policy, the Central Organizational Department also made a systematic clearance of some special documents on cadre review that had been issued after the founding of New China, amending or abolishing those documents which were influenced by leftist ideology or no longer applicable due to the changed circumstances, and reviewing and correcting the cases of cadres that had been mishandled, including some cadres who had been restricted in their employment for many years.

Restricting the appointment of some cadres was a special method adopted by the CPC in order to adapt to the war years and other special circumstances. In the war years and the early days of the founding of New China, owing to the restrictions of objective conditions, it was difficult to clarify some cadres' political history or social relations and to draw positive or negative conclusions on them. Therefore, when issuing their appointments, the Party organizations assigned them to secondary positions and observed them closely for further investigation. Such temporary measures were necessary at that time, but even some time after the founding of New China, this method had not been changed, but instead continued to be used. In the Cultural Revolution, some areas and units abused this method and arbitrarily drew conclusions that some comrades were restricted in their appointment, seriously damaging the enthusiasm of some cadres and the masses. On February 1, 1979, the 38th Issue of *Organization Newsletter* published the article "Restricting the Appointments of Cadres Should Not be Indiscriminately Applied." It pointed out that after nearly thirty years of national liberation and repeated political movements and organizational reviews, some comrades had turned out fine, displaying no problems, or despite facing some problems, they still consistently performed well during the long-term investigation. Organizationally, it was important to remove past doubts about them, abolish the conclusion of "restricting their appointment," give them political trust, and boldly employ them based on their morality and talent. It was clearly pointed out that in the future, cadres were generally not to be subject to "restricted appointment." It was only for very few people who, without restriction, were likely to endanger the cause of socialism that necessary restriction was needed in their appointment. However, before their problems were thoroughly clarified, those who were skilled should be given appropriate opportunities to play their roles and continue to be educated and inspected in the appointment process. In October 1983, with the consent of the Central Secretariat, the Central Organizational Department issued the Opinions on Removing the Historically Restricted Appointment of Certain Cadres. The document pointed out that before and after the founding of New China, during the process of examining cadres and eliminating counter-revolutionaries, the Central Committee and the Central Organizational Department had made restrictions on the appointment of cadres with political and historical problems. These regulations were necessary under the historical conditions at that time. However, after a long period of revolutionary struggle and training, the vast majority of these restricted cadres had performed well or fairly well. Some comrades had made important contributions to the Party and the people. In order to facilitate rational deployment of cadres and give full play to their positive role in the construction of the Four Modernizations, the original regulations needed to be changed.

In order to do this work well, in September 1984, the Organizational Department of the Central Committee of the Communist Party of China forwarded the Report on the Pilot Work of Removing the Historically Restricted Use of Some Cadres by the Examination Offices of the Changchun Municipal Party Committee and the Nong'an County Committee. In September 1986, the Organizational Department of the Central Committee of the Communist Party of China reported to the Central Committee the Request for Change of the Opinions on Restricting the Use of 41 Cadres at or Above the Vice-ministerial Level, which was approved by the leading comrades of the Central Committee. The document pointed out that according to the relevant provisions of the Central Organizational Department approved by the Central Committee in July

1981 Opinions on Changing the Restricted Use of Cadres Who Made Mistakes After Arrest and Captivity and by the Central Organizational Department in the October 1983 Opinions on Releasing the Historically Restricted Use of Some Cadres, opinions on 41 comrades with previously restricted appointment were to be revoked, cancelled, or dismissed based on their individual situations. Departments and commissions of provinces, autonomous regions, and municipalities directly under the Central Government and central state organs also carried out the work actively and steadily on the basis of the suggestions of the Central Committee and in accordance with the administrative authority of cadres. Before the Thirteenth National Congress, the work of lifting the restricted use of some cadres was basically completed.

5. Implementing the Party's Ethnic and Religious Policy

From 1980 to 1981, the Secretariat of the Central Committee of the Communist Party of China held successive meetings in Tibet, Yunnan, Xinjiang, Inner Mongolia, and other provinces and autonomous regions to earnestly settle the issues of implementing the Party's ethnic policy. The Central Committee and some local Party committees also removed the labels for comrades designated as "local nationalists."

In March 1982, the Secretariat of the Central Committee of the Communist Party of China issued a document on religious issues in the socialist period, clarifying the Party's basic views and policies on religious issues. Around this time, the activities of patriotic religious organizations were restored, temples and monasteries were restored and reopened, and the Party's religious policy was implemented.

6. Implementing Policies for Foreign Experts and Work Teams Working in China

In September 1981, a foreign expert working in China wrote a letter to a leading comrade of the Central Committee requesting that the conclusions of the examination be revised. After research, the leaders of the Central Organizational Department suggested that the implementation of policy on foreign experts and team workers should be thoroughly reviewed, and that the solution should be submitted to the Central Secretariat for overall consideration and approval. The leading comrades of the Central Committee agreed and instructed that the foreign expert's "requirements are reasonable and should be completely reviewed without leaving any lingering problems. It is absolutely necessary to conduct a comprehensive review of the implementation of policies related to foreign friends."

Following the instructions of the leading comrades of the Central Committee, the Central Organizational Department and the Ministry of Public Security reconsidered the conclusions of and implemented policies for Israel Epstein and his wife, the foreign experts and the experts formerly working in the Foreign Language Bureau, Sidney Shapiro, a British expert formerly working at the Xinhua News Agency, and Isabel Crook, a British expert formerly working at the Foreign Language Institute. The Central Organizational Department and the Ministry of Public Security also informed the State Bureau of Foreign Experts and other units about the implementation of policies for foreign experts. According to the survey, most of the foreign experts affected by the Cultural Revolution in these units were reexamined, their reputation restored, their wages reimbursed, and their jobs reallocated. However, there were still many problems that needed to be settled properly.

To this end, the Party Group of the Central Organizational Department and the Ministry of Public Security submitted to the Central Committee the Report on the Implementation of Policies for Foreign Experts and Allies, affirming the important contributions made by foreign experts to China's revolution and construction, pointing out that they should be respected by the Party and the people of the entire nation, and requesting relevant units to earnestly carry out a comprehensive policy for foreign experts and allies to clear up problems promptly and to eliminate adverse effects. The wrongs against experts who were hurt in the Cultural Revolution were to be completely redressed politically, fully taken care of in their lives, and enthusiastically supported in their work. A series of principles and policies for the implementation of the Party's cadre policy should be fully and conscientiously implemented among foreign experts and allies. Moreover, it was important to take into account their characteristics and offer them preferential treatment. In March 1982, the Central Committee of the Communist Party of China approved the report of the Party Group of the Central Organizational Department and the Ministry of Public Security. After the issuance of the documents, the relevant units followed through the implementation of policies for foreign experts working in China and dealt with them appropriately with no delay. Thus, the negative influence was eliminated, and foreign experts and allies working in China were able to wholeheartedly serve the construction of socialist modernization, while also easing the negative international influence.

This nationwide effort to fight against unjust and false cases, adjust social relations, and implement various policies took some time, involving a wide range of players across a broad range, a move unprecedented in the Party's history that led to the problems being thoroughly settled. The settlement of these historical problems and the implementation of the Party's policies effectively mobilized the enthusiasm of all sectors of society, consolidating and developing the patriotic united front, which played an important role in promoting the ideological emancipation of the whole Party, the overall rectification of the organizational front, consolidating and developing the political situation of stability and unity, guaranteeing socialist modernization, and realizing the great cause of the reunification of the motherland.

IV

Restoration of the Party's Ethnic and Religious Policies

In the Cultural Revolution, the work on the ethnic and religious fronts, like that of other fronts, was seriously damaged and hampered by the leftist guiding ideology. Ethnic and religious institutions were abolished, and ethnic and religious work was imposed with false charges. After the toppling of the Gang of Four, the top priority in the field of ethnic and religious work was to heal the trauma the decade of chaos had wreaked, adjust ethnic and religious relations, reiterate and restore the Party's ethnic and religious policies, formulate guidelines for ethnic and religious work under the new situation, and carry out pioneering work.

1. Restoring the Party's Ethnic Policy

Reaffirming, implementing, and adhering to the Party's ethnic policy required the working institutions and people to carry out the task. At the first meeting of the Fifth National People's Congress in 1978, it was decided that the National Ethnic

Affairs Commission of the People's Republic of China would be restored and Yang Jingren would be appointed its chairman. In 1979, the Second Session of the Fifth National People's Congress decided to restore the National Committee of the National People's Congress, with Abe Awang Jinmei, Vice-Chairman of the Standing Committee of the National People's Congress, concurrently serving as Chairman-member. Other ethnic working institutions and institutions for Ethnic Affairs at various levels were also restored.

Shortly after the Third Plenary Session of the Eleventh Conference of the Communist Party of China in April 1979, the Central Committee chaired an ethnic frontier defense conference. This conference was of historic significance for consolidating the frontier defense of the motherland, promoting national unity, and "putting an end to chaos" in the ethnic work. One of the main purposes of the meeting was to discuss the task of ethnic work in the new period. Since most of the border areas in China were inhabited by ethnic minorities, and in order to build and consolidate the border, safeguard the reunification of the motherland, and develop good stability and unity, it was important to do a thorough job in ethnic work and to promote national unity, common development, and prosperity. In response to Lin Biao's and the Gang of Four's destruction of ethnic policies and ethnic work, the conference reiterated a series of policies that had been proved correct in practice, including ethnic, religious, and united front policies. It focused on the practice of ethnic work after the founding of New China and summed up the experience and lessons. First, it noted the importance of adhering to the principle of integrating theory with practice and working based on the real situation. The situation in the border minority areas was complex. To carry out the Party's line, principles, and policies and realize the general task in the new period, it was necessary to combine the ethnic and regional characteristics of border minority areas. Further, it was important to adhere to the long-standing view of ethnic issues. The socialist stage was a period of common development and prosperity for all ethnic groups. In the whole socialist historical stage, ethnic work was arduous, so it was important to give weight to ethnic issues, conscientiously implement the Party's ethnic policy, and earnestly respect the equal and autonomous rights of ethnic minorities. In addition, it was important to adhere to the proletarian view of the nation and constantly strengthen the great unity of the people of all ethnicities on the basis of consolidating the alliance between workers and peasants. Consolidating the unity of the country and the unity of all ethnicities in the country was the basic guarantee for speeding up the realization of the general task in the new period. Finally, it was necessary to adhere to the principle of combining state support with self-reliance and to accelerate the economic and cultural construction in border minority areas. Practice had already demonstrated that the development of economic and cultural construction in frontier ethnic minority areas depended on the local people of all ethnic groups to carry forward the revolutionary spirit of arduous struggle and self-reliance. At the same time, the state needed to adopt a policy of active support and prioritization, sincerely and actively helping ethnic minorities develop economic and cultural construction. This was an important task of the state in its ethnic work. The Central Committee of the Communist Party of China approved the report of the meeting, demanding that the whole Party should attach great importance to ethnic work, re-publicize ethnic policies, check the implementation of ethnic policies, and effectively solve existing problems.

In September 1979, the Central Committee of the Communist Party of China approved the Guidelines and Tasks of the United Front in the New Historical Period, issued by the National Conference on United Front Work. The main point regarding strengthening the work of ethnic minorities was that, according to the instructions of the Central Committee of the Communist Party of China, rebroadcasting of the ethnic policy should be carried out universally, thoroughly, and vigorously among the whole Party and the people of all ethnic groups, and the implementation of the ethnic policy should be thoroughly monitored. It was important to effectively solve the problems existing in ethnic relations and eliminate all factors that were not conducive to national unity. It was likewise necessary to educate cadres and people of all ethnic groups, especially those of the Han ethnicity, helping them fully understand the importance of strengthening national unity and doing a thorough job of ethnic work, while constantly improving the consciousness of implementing ethnic policies. It was important to treat ethnic minorities as equals, respect their equal, autonomous rights, their language and writing, their customs, and their religious beliefs. At the same time, it was pointed out that the Party's policy of freedom of religious belief should be fully implemented.

To implement the Party's ethnic policy, it was important not only to do a thorough job in ethnic minority areas, but also to attach importance to ethnic work in mixed or scattered areas. In October 1979, the Central Committee of the Communist Party of China and the State Council approved the Report of the Party Group of the Central People's Committee on the Work of Mixed and Diaspora Ethnic Minorities, pointing out that the struggle to expose and criticize Lin Biao and the Gang of Four had gained great victories, but the remaining impact of Lin and the Gang of Four had not been eradicated, ethnic and religious policies in many areas had not been implemented conscientiously, and some cases of wrongs and falsehoods had not been corrected. There were many problems in the work of mixed and scattered minorities, which required effective measures if they were to be settled properly. Effective measures should be taken to ensure their equal rights, actively help minorities develop their economy and culture, earnestly respect the customs and habits of minorities, implement the policy of freedom of religious belief and strengthen the leadership of the Party, and restore and improve institutions for ethnic work at all levels. In accordance with the instructions of the Party Central Committee and the State Council and the views of the Party group of the National People's Committee, Party committees and all levels of government had organized and inspected the work of the mixed and scattered inhabitants, formulated measures, and implemented the Party's ethnic policy. Much work had already been done in this regard.

In order to educate cadres of all ethnicities and the broad masses of the people on ethnic policies, the Central Propaganda Department, the United Front Department of the Central Committee of the Communist Party of China, and the National People's Committee held a symposium on the propaganda of ethnic policies in December 1979. They deployed the issue of re-education on ethnic policies and decided to concentrate on a period of time and conduct a wide-ranging publicity and education campaign on national ethnic policy and national unity. In January 1980, the three ministries and commissions approved the summary of the convening meeting, pointing out that it was of crucial importance to carry out ethnic policy education. The emphasis of re-education was to overcome Han nationalism, which was the key to adjusting ethnic relations and consolidating national unity. At the same time, attention had to be given to preventing and overcoming general and local nationalism. The objects of the education included cadres and the masses, mainly leading cadres. Both the Han and minority ethnic groups needed to be educated, especially the Han. Re-education was to be combined with checking the implementation of ethnic policies and solving practical problems. From the central to the local government, and in combination with the inspection of the implementation of ethnic policy, religious policy, and united front policy, the re-education regarding the ethnic policy was carried out, which solved some outstanding problems in ethnic relations, raised the awareness of the masses of cadres and cadres on ethnic policy, safeguarded the consciousness of national unity, and made preliminary improvements in ethnic relations. For example, the Xinjiang Uyghur Autonomous Region concentrated on ethnic policy and national unity propaganda and education, promulgated and implemented the Code of Strengthening National Unity, formulated the Convention on National Unity, held a general Congress of commendation for national unity and progress in the whole autonomous region, and carried out activities aimed at promoting national unity and progress. The General Office of the Central Committee of the Communist Party of China forwarded the documents of the Party Committee of the Xinjiang Uyghur Autonomous Region, pointing out that it was an important task for Party committees at all levels in all ethnic autonomous areas and ethnic mixed areas to conscientiously implement the Party's ethnic policy and constantly strengthen national unity. It was important to formulate practical measures to do a thorough job of ethnic policy education and promote the great development of national unity.

To restore and adhere to the Party's ethnic policy, it was important to adhere to and implement the policy of regional ethnic autonomy. The first task was to restore the system of regional autonomy for ethnic minorities, and the second was to train cadres of ethnic minority descent. In 1979, the Central Committee of the Communist Party of China and the State Council decided to restore the original administrative divisions of the Inner Mongolia Autonomous Region, that is, administrative regions previously assigned to Liaoning, Jilin, Heilongjiang, Gansu, and Ningxia Provinces or Autonomous Regions during the Cultural Revolution were to be reallocated back to the jurisdiction of the Inner Mongolia Autonomous Region. Ethnic regional autonomy, which was interrupted by the ten years of unrest, was restored. At the same time, a number of new national autonomous areas were built. From 1979 to the end of 1988, 53 new national autonomous areas were built throughout the country. Training the cadres of ethnic minorities was the key to implementing the policy of regional autonomy for ethnic minorities, allowing the autonomous ethnic groups to truly take charge of their own affairs and exercise the management of their own internal matters. The Constitution of the People's Republic of China, promulgated in 1982, restored and developed some important principles of regional ethnic autonomy in the 1954 Constitution, and made a series of important amendments and supplements on the basis of the changes in the state conditions in the new period of socialist construction, further expanded the rights of autonomy in ethnic autonomous organs, and clearly stipulated that ethnic autonomous areas should be relegated to ethnic cadres. On the one hand, the autonomous right to arrange and manage the local economic and cultural construction independently demonstrated that the state and the people's governments at higher levels helped ethnic minorities develop their economic and cultural undertakings, which fully embodied the spirit of respecting and guaranteeing the democratic rights of the ethnic minorities to manage their own internal affairs. In the new period of Reform and Opening Up, the policy of regional ethnic autonomy had not only recovered from the destruction of the decade-long turmoil, but had also made new progress. After the Third Plenary Session of the Eleventh Conference of the Communist Party of China, a large number of ethnic minority cadres returned to their posts as a result of "rectifying the disorder" and "redressing unjust, false, and wrong cases." From the central to local levels, efforts were intensified to train ethnic minority cadres, and many effective measures were taken. The number of ethnic cadres grew rapidly, reaching 1.84 million by 1988.

2. New Policies for Work in Tibet

Tibet had long been a place of a special sensitivity in the relations of ethnic groups in China. Tibet began to solve its various historical problems in 1977, including the review and redressing of cadres who lost their jobs during and before the Cultural Revolution, rearranging leading patriotic members to be elected deputies to the National People's Congress, members of the Political Consultative Conference, or to serve in government organs at all levels throughout the country or in the region, and generously releasing all prisoners who participated in the 1959 Tibetan Rebellion. In November 1978, a week after the Central Working Conference, Deng Xiaoping conveyed to the West his willingness to reconcile with the Dalai Lama. Three months later, Deng Xiaoping met with representatives of the Dalai Lama in Beijing and said to him personally, "The Dalai Lama is welcome to come back, and more people are welcome to return and have a look."

In February 1980, Hu Yaobang, General Secretary of the Central Committee, first turned his focus to the issue of Tibet. From March 14 to 15, 1980, he chaired a symposium on Tibetan work and heard a report from the head of the Party Committee of the Tibet Autonomous Region of the Communist Party of China. Hu Yaobang stressed at this meeting that, in order to speed up Tibet's construction, it was important to further emancipate the people's minds, implement policies, resolutely eliminate the pernicious influence of the left-leaning line, correct the leftist economic policy, boldly train and promote Tibetan cadres, and gradually reach the stage that the party and government organs above the county level could take Tibetan cadres as the main body. Religiously, it was necessary to treat Lamaism with caution, deal with the historical problems of the escalation and the misclassification of rich peasants, monitor the work of the Dalai Lama clique and the relatives of the outgoing Tibetans who remained at home, mobilize all positive factors, and consolidate stability and unity. On April 7, the Central Committee approved the summary of the meeting and issued a circular. In late May, Hu Yaobang, Wan Li, and a group of more than ten heads of relevant central departments visited Tibet. On May 29, Hu Yaobang made a report at the cadres' congress at and above the county level of the Tibet Autonomous Region, pointing out that Tibet should do six important things, including resolutely implementing the policy of recuperation and rest, implementing a more flexible economic policy than the Mainland, and restoring and developing Tibetan culture and science. The most important were, first, the proposal that Tibet be given "full and independent autonomy." If the Central Government's policy did not conform to the actual situation in Tibet, it could be executed with flexibility or not implemented at all, while if the central policy was not conducive to national unity and the development of productive forces, it did not have to be implemented. Next, it was important to strengthen unity between the Han and Tibetan cadres by gradually withdrawing the Han cadres and replacing them with Tibetan cadres. Within two or three years, more than two-thirds of the state's full-time cadres would be Tibetan cadres. For cadres working in Tibet, Hu Yaobang both encouraged and criticized them, believing that "Han cadres working in Tibet have fulfilled their historical tasks" and proposing that 80% of the Han people should withdraw from Tibet. According to Hu Yaobang's opinions, the Tibet Autonomous Region submitted to the Central Committee the Requests for Large-scale Redeployment of Cadres and Workers Into and Out of Tibet, suggesting that, in addition to retaining some leading cadres and the technical backbone, most of the Tibetan personnel should be transferred back east in stages and offered retirement. On August 6, the Central Committee and the State Council approved the report. From 1980 to the end of 1981, more than 20,000 cadres were transferred to Tibet in two batches, mostly the "veteran Tibetans" who went to Tibet in the 1950s and 1960s. In 1986, it was decided that 17,000 cadres and workers (including retirees) would be redeployed from Tibet.

The Central Government's policy on Tibet had exerted a great influence on the minority areas of Inner Mongolia, Xinjiang, Yunnan, Qinghai, Ningxia, and Gansu. On May 31, 1980, during a short stay in Golmud, Hu Yaobang said to the head of Qinghai Province, "The six items we mentioned at the cadre meeting of the Tibet Autonomous Region basically conform to the situation of Qinghai Province and can be carried out according to our research." Hu Yaobang and Wan Li both stressed that the policy should be relaxed and the right of regional ethnic autonomy should be fully exercised. Its purpose was to promote the policy of settling issues from Tibet to other ethnic areas. Subsequently, the Party committees of Gansu, Inner Mongolia, Ningxia, Guangxi, and other provinces and autonomous regions held meetings to study the instructions of the Central Committee of the Communist Party of China on Tibet work and Hu Yaobang's Tibetan speech, and decided to solve local problems in accordance with the instructions of the Central Committee on Tibet work. After this, the Secretariat of the Central Committee of the Communist Party of China discussed the work of Yunnan, Xinjiang, and Inner Mongolia in turn, forming a summary of ethnic work in Yunnan, Xinjiang, and Inner Mongolia.

In the early 1980s, the Party began to adjust its ethnic policy, focusing on improving ethnic relations. However, the official notice 'Tibet in Contemporary China' pointed out that a large number of Han people and cadres had withdrawn from Tibet, which had been done "roughly," and a number of human resources who were urgently needed in Tibet had also been transferred, which had a great impact on various sectors of Tibet's work, especially on science and technology, education, healthcare, and financial sectors. Deng Liqun politically criticized the withdrawal of large numbers of cadres from Tibet. Some domestic scholars also raised objections to the decision to withdraw cadres from Tibet on the basis of national security considerations.

3. Restoration and Adjustment of Religious Policies

After 1957, the Party's leftist errors in religious work gradually grew, further developing in the mid-1960s. In particular, during the Cultural Revolution, Lin Biao and the Gang of Four made use of these leftist errors from ulterior motives, wantonly trampled on the scientific theories of Marxism-Leninism and Mao Zedong Thought on religious issues, totally denied the Party's correct policy on religious issues from the founding of New China, and fundamentally abolished the Party's work on religion. They forcibly prohibited the normal religious activities of believers, regarded patriots in religious circles and even ordinary believers as "dictatorship objects," and created many cases of injustice, falsehood, and errors in religious circles. They also regarded the customs and habits of some ethnic minorities as religious superstitions and forcibly prohibited them. In some places, they even suppressed believers and undermined national unity. Their use of violence to address religious issues resulted in the development of covert and scattered religious activities, and a small number of "bad elements" made use of this condition to engage in illegal or criminal activities under the cover of religious activities.

After the Third Plenary Session of the Eleventh CPC Conference, the Party's correct principles and policies on religious issues were gradually restored. At this time, the core of religious policy adjustment was to grant the freedom of religious belief to a certain extent. On December 1, 1978, the Central United Front Ministry convened a National Symposium on religious work. It proposed that the main tasks of religious work in the coming period were to earnestly implement the policy of freedom of religious belief, properly arrange places for religious activities, and unite the broad masses of believers to participate in socialist construction. It proposed to restore and improve religious institutions and resume the activities of patriotic religious groups. The CPC Central Committee transmitted the summary of the meeting.

In 1979, many national religious groups and local religious organizations resumed their activities. The clergy of each religious sect returned to the temples and churches and presided over the teaching once again. Some national and religious festivals that had been banned for many years were also restored.

On January 25, 1980, the Central Committee approved the request of the United Front Ministry for the convening of a national conference of religious groups. That year, the Chinese Islamic Association, the Chinese Taoist Association, the Chinese Catholic Patriotic Congress, the Chinese Christian Three-Self Patriotic Movement Committee, and the Chinese Buddhist Association held meetings to elect leaders of various religious groups, formulate rules of activities, and resume work. One hundred sixty-four provincial religious groups and more than 2,000 county-level religious groups were successively restored and established throughout the country. On July 16, the State Council approved the report of the Bureau of Religious Affairs, the State Construction Commission, and other units, returning all the property rights of religious organizations to those organizations or returning at a discount payment those that could not be refunded. They also returned the occupied temples and churches and the deposits of religious organizations. In some large and medium-sized cities, historically famous places for religious activities and places where Christians lived together, especially in minority areas, a number of temples, monasteries, and churches were restored in a planned, systematic way. On April 1, 1983, the State Council approved the opening of 163 national key Buddhist and Taoist temples in Han majority areas. The government provided financial subsidies for the maintenance of some temples, monasteries, and churches. According to preliminary statistics, from 1980 to 1991, the Central Government allocated more than 140 million yuan in subsidies for the maintenance of temples, monasteries, and churches. By 1992, more than 60,000 places of religious worship had been reopened throughout the country. Since 1980, the China Buddhist College, the China Islamic Economics College, the China Christian Nanjing Jinling Union Theological College, the China Catholic Theological and Philosophical College, the China Taoist College, and the China Tibetan Language Department Senior Buddhist College were restored and built, along with 41 local religious colleges. In March 1982, the Central Committee of the Communist Party of China put forward the Basic Views and Policies on Religious Issues in the Socialist Period of China, emphasizing the long-term nature of religious issues under socialist conditions, and criticizing the ideas and practices of attempting to eliminate religion with one strike by administrative order or other coercive means. It reaffirmed the policy of respecting and protecting freedom of religious belief, but did not allow religion to interfere in the political affairs of the country.

From August 29 to September 7, 1979, Zhao Puchu, the deputy president of the Chinese Buddhist Association, and Ding Guangxun, vice-chairman of the

Chinese Christian Patriotic Movement Committee, participated in the Third World Conference on Religion and Peace (WCRP), held in Princeton, New Jersey, USA. In October, the Chinese Muslim pilgrimage group was allowed to make pilgrimages to Mecca for the first time since the Cultural Revolution, indicating that the CPC was willing to resume international contact among domestic religious circles, at least on a provisional basis. However, the Party was highly vigilant about the infiltration of foreign groups into domestic religions. On March 4, 1980, the Central Committee of the Communist Party of China and the State Council approved the Request on Resisting Foreign Groups' Religious Infiltration into Domestic Religions proposed by the Religious Affairs Bureau and other departments, pointing out that the harm of foreign religious infiltration should be fully considered, and both internal and external work should be done to prevent and limit its impact as much as possible.

Looking back on the basic situation of religious work in this period, it is evident that the basic task of the Party and the government in religious work was to firmly implement the policy of freedom of religious belief, consolidate and expand the patriotic political alliance of all ethnic and religious circles, strengthen their patriotic and socialist education, mobilize their positive factors and build a strong, modernized socialist country to achieve the great cause of reunification of the motherland, to oppose hegemonism, and to safeguard world peace. Under the guidance of these fundamental tasks, all Party members, Party committees at all levels, and especially departments in charge of religious work at all levels had earnestly summed up and absorbed the Party's historical experience in both positive and negative aspects of religious work since the founding of New China, further understood and grasped the objective law of the occurrence, development, and extinction of religion, overcome all difficulties and obstacles, and firmly put the Party's religious policy on the scientific track of Marxism-Leninism and Mao Zedong Thought.

4. Implementing the United Front Policy and Developing the Patriotic United Front

After the toppling of the Gang of Four, the organizations and activities of various democratic parties were gradually restored. After the Third Plenary Session of the Eleventh Conference of the Communist Party of China, the work of the

United Front of the Communist Party of China was restored in an all-round way, with the full-scale development of rectifying chaos and the start of Reform and Opening Up. These democratic parties began to play the role of participating in and discussing politics and democratic supervision in the nation's political life, and the theory of the Party's united front was enriched and developed.

In June 1979, in his opening speech at the Second Session of the Fifth CPPCC National Committee, Deng Xiaoping analyzed the situation of every class in Chinese society, pointed out clearly the new tasks and changes facing the United Front in the new era, and put forward the two concepts of "socialist laborers and patriots who support socialism." He pointed out, "Our United Front has become a broad alliance of socialist workers and patriots who support socialism, led by the working class and based on the workers-peasants alliance. The task of the United Front and the CPPCC in the new era is to mobilize all positive factors, make efforts to turn negative factors into positive ones, unite all forces that can be united, work with one heart and one mind, work together, maintain and develop a stable and united political situation, and strive to build our country into a powerful modern socialist country."[4] Shortly afterwards, the Central Committee of the Party further proposed that "for revolutionary and patriotic United Front, the largest issue now is Taiwan's return to the motherland and reunification of the motherland."[5] In accordance with this directive, the Fourteenth National United Front Work Conference, held in August 1979, used the term "revolutionary patriotic united front." The meeting held that in the new era, within the United Front, there were still contradictions between socialist workers, peasants, intellectuals, and other patriots who supported socialism, but there was no fundamental conflict of interests. It was important for the basic policies and methods of the revolutionary patriotic United Front to proceed from the fact that the main contradictions in the country had changed, strictly distinguish between two types of contradictions of different natures, correctly regard the proper handling of contradictions among the people as the central topic, strictly abide by socialist democracy and socialist legal system, correctly handle contradictions within the United Front, and actively help non-Party figures in all fields. New progress and contributions were made in realizing the Four Modernizations. For all those who loved the motherland, "as long as they are in favor of reunifying the motherland, they should be united even if they are not in favor of the socialist system."[6]

In October of the same year, the Central Committee approved the Guidelines and Tasks of the United Front in the New Historical Period at the National United Front Work Conference. This document made a practical and realistic analysis of the fundamental changes in the social class situation over the previous 30 years following the founding of New China and clearly explained the nature, principles, and tasks of the United Front in the new era. The document pointed out that the industrial and agricultural alliance, the foundation of the United Front, had entered a new stage in which the task of realizing socialist modernization was the central task. The vast majority of intellectuals, including the overwhelming majority of the intellectuals from the old society, were already part of the working class and an important backbone force in realizing modernization. All ethnic groups in China had formed a new type of ethnic relations of socialist unity, friendship, mutual assistance, and cooperation. In the process of modernization, the socialist consistency between all ethnicities was to be further developed, and patriots of different ethnicities and religions would likewise make great progress. China's capitalist class no longer existed as a class. On the path of socialist transformation, they had withstood various tests in the struggle between the Party and Lin Biao and the Gang of Four. The overwhelming majority supported the leadership of the Party and the socialist system. Now, as self-supporting workers or state cadres, they were contributing to the Four Modernizations. The democratic parties in China had become part of the socialist laborers and of the political alliance supporting the socialist patriots, which were all political forces serving socialism under the leadership of the Communist Party of China. Some of the people who were originally part of the conflict between the Party and the enemy, such as those war criminals who had been granted amnesty and former Kuomintang officers ranked above county and regiment level who had been generously released, were transferred to the people after long-term transformation. Class struggle was no longer the main contradiction in Chinese society. With the strategic shift of the focus of the Party's work and the fundamental change of the domestic class situation, the United Front in the new period should be called the revolutionary patriotic United Front, which was a broad alliance of all socialist workers and patriots. In the new historical era, the guiding principles and tasks of the United Front were to unite all forces that could be united, mobilize all positive factors in China and abroad, strive to turn negative factors into positive ones, maintain and develop a stable and united political situation, and work together to build China into a modern socialist power and to realize Taiwan's return to the motherland

and the great cause of the reunification of the motherland. This document not only helped eliminate the influence of leftist errors on the work of the United Front, but also promoted the implementation of the Party's policies.

Soon afterwards, the Party Central Committee proposed the concept of a "patriotic united front." Although the concept of the revolutionary patriotic United Front had greatly developed compared with the previous understanding of it, it still could not cover a wider range of united front targets, nor could it fully adapt to the tasks and requirements under the new historical conditions. In June 1981, the Sixth Plenary Session of the Eleventh Conference of the Communist Party of China adopted the Resolution on Several Historical Issues of the Party Since the Founding of the People's Republic, which clearly pointed out, "We must unswervingly unite all forces that can be united to consolidate and expand the patriotic united front."

The Fifteenth National United Front Work Conference, held from December 1981 to January 1982, further clarified the "patriotic united front," emphasizing that the United Front in the new era was still a "magic weapon" of the Party. The meeting held that for a long time, due to the influence of leftist ideology, there had been a wrong tendency to ignore or even abandon the United Front. Understanding the importance and long-term nature of the United Front was a prerequisite for doing a thorough job in united front work. Hu Yaobang's speech pointed out, "In the new historical period, through the long historical period ahead, the United Front will remain necessary and important, will continue with great vitality, and will remain a great, potent weapon of our Party."[7] The conference further clarified the scope and targets of the patriotic united front in the new era and proposed that there were two United Fronts in the new period. One was the international anti-aggression and expansion United Front, and the other was the National Patriotic United Front. The National Patriotic United Front was the widest united front for all socialist workers and patriots who supported socialism and the reunification of the motherland.

For a long time to come, the target of united front work was not less, but more, and the scope of united front work was not narrower, but wider. United front work targeted at the national scale could be divided into ten areas: democratic parties; non-Party celebrities, especially patriots; non-Party intellectuals; former Kuomintang military and political personnel who initiated uprisings and surrendered; former and current businessmen; leading figures of ethnic minorities;

patriotic religious leaders; relatives and friends of people going to Taiwan who remained in the Mainland; compatriots from Taiwan, Hong Kong, and Macao; and returned overseas Chinese and overseas Chinese.[8]

The concept of the "patriotic united front" was the development of the Party's united front theory, which accurately expressed the characteristics of the times of the United Front in the new era. In developing from a "revolutionary patriotic united front" to a "patriotic united front," without changing its original nature, a more conducive approach to strengthening unity was to include more targets of the United Front. This change not only developed the theory of the Party's United Front, but also made the policy of the united front more suitable to the social reality of China in the new era. The patriotism of the patriotic United Front was essentially socialist patriotism, but the scope was broader than socialism, including patriots who advocated the reunification of the motherland but did not necessarily support socialism or who were suspicious of socialism. The patriotic United Front was a combination of principle and flexibility.[9] Mao Zedong put forward the eight-character policy of "long-term coexistence and mutual supervision" as early as April 1956, addressing the relationship between the Communist Party, the democratic parties, and other non-Party patriotic nationalists in the united front. The eight-character policy objectively reflected the history and reality of the Chinese revolution. It not only reflected the long-term coexistence of the Communist Party of China and democratic parties, but also reflected the equal status of the democratic parties. However, from the late 1950s to the end of the Cultural Revolution, the correct policy of dealing with the relationship between the CPC and the democratic parties was not well implemented. In particular, at one point during the Cultural Revolution, the work and activities of the democratic parties were forced to stop. After the Third Plenary Session of the Eleventh Conference of the Communist Party of China, the Party reiterated the principle of "long-term coexistence and mutual supervision" with all democratic parties. Deng Xiaoping also made it clear that "this is a long-term unchanged policy."[10]

In the new period of Reform and Opening Up, with the profound changes in class relations underway in Chinese society, the class boundaries of democratic parties in China gradually faded away, and in essence it became a party of socialist workers. In order to adapt to this change, the Communist Party of China further developed the "Eight-Character Principle" guiding the relationship between democratic parties into the "Sixteen-Character Principle." At the Fifteenth National United Front Work Conference held in January 1982, Hu Yaobang pointed out that Party members should "make friends with all non-Party personages, and move from general to genuine friendship so as to build the relationship of mutual respect in honor and disgrace," and "we should make clear to all Party members that in the new historical era, we must make friends with non-Party members and truly build the relationship of 'mutual respect in honor and disgrace.'"[11] This is the first time that the Communist Party of China put forward the eight characters in the united front work that were translated "mutual respect in honor and disgrace."

In September of the same year, Hu Yaobang, in his report to the Twelfth National Congress of the Communist Party of China, for the first time linked the slogan "long-term coexistence and mutual supervision" with the slogan "liver and gall, honor and disgrace and coexistence." He proposed that the Party should continue to adhere to the principle of "long-term coexistence, mutual supervision, and mutual respect in honor and disgrace" and strengthen its cooperation with democratic parties, non-Party democrats, ethnic minorities, and religious patriotic cooperation.[12] In November of the same year, in his speech at the opening ceremony of the fifth session of the CPPCC National Committee, Deng Xiaoping also emphasized the sixteen-character policy of "long-term coexistence, mutual supervision, and mutual respect in honor and disgrace," which was formally defined as the basic guiding principle of the relationship between the CPC and the democratic parties in the new era. The Sixteen-Character Principle was in line with the objective reality of the new period of Reform and Opening Up and socialist modernization. It was conducive to giving full play to the role of democratic parties and democrats, encouraging them to participate in the common management of state affairs, long-term cooperation, and closer unity between the CPC and democratic parties.

After the Twelfth National Congress of the Communist Party of China, with the full implementation of Reform and Opening Up and the implementation of the policy of "one country, two systems," the United Front further undertook the dual tasks of serving socialist modernization and the great cause of the reunification of the motherland, with a wider range of objects and richer content. In this context, the Sixteenth National United Front Work Conference, held from the end of November to December 1986, put forward the idea of "two alliances," namely, an alliance based on socialism composed of all the workers and patriots of the Mainland, and an alliance based on patriotism and support for the reunification of the motherland, including Taiwanese compatriots, compatriots in Hong Kong and Macao, and overseas Chinese. The alliance of these two areas not only constituted the whole of the United Front in the new period, but also constituted an important new feature of socialism with Chinese characteristics.

CHAPTER 3

Strengthening the Party's Leadership in Ideology and Culture and in Scientific Evaluation of Mao Zedong's Historical Position

I

Negating Class Struggle as the Key and Reaffirming the Four Cardinal Principles

After extensive discussion on the criterion of truth, especially after the Central Working Conference and the Third Plenary Session of the Central Committee, the errors of the "Two Whatevers" were seriously criticized and the Party's ideological line of seeking truth from facts was re-established. However, the differences and disputes within the Party centered on the ideological line had not yet been completely eliminated. Moreover, there were two kinds of erroneous tendencies in the Party and society. One was that those affected by leftist errors were still in a rigid or semi-rigid state. They were skeptical about the lines, principles, and policies of the Third Plenary Session of the Eleventh Central Committee and even had feelings of resistance. The other was that there was a wrong tendency among some people to negate socialism and the leadership of the Party. In order to ensure the realization of the shift of focus in the Party's work and to smoothly drive the cause of modernization under the changing situation, the Central Committee required adherence to the Four Basic Principles.

1. Proposal of the Basic Political Thought of Modernization Under the New Situation

The climax of ideological emancipation came to China in 1979. On the first day of the New Year, Deng Xiaoping spoke highly of the new political situation and social atmosphere at a symposium held by the CPPCC National Committee, putting forward for the first time the political basis of modernization. Deng said that the political situation proposed by Chairman Mao in 1957, which was centralized and democratic, disciplined and free, lively and vigorous, and with a unified will and individual peace of mind, had come into being the previous year. Generally speaking, this type of atmosphere was regarded as a lively political situation. It was important to carry forward and persevere in this trend across the country and in all aspects of the Party, government, army, and people. This was the political basis for realizing the Four Modernizations, and without such a political situation, the Four Modernizations could not be realized. For quite some time, China had not been managing the relationship between democracy and centralism well, and democracy had diminished. For this reason, it was necessary to promote democracy more ardently.[1]

Deng Xiaoping's speech represented the spirit of the Central Committee and was the collective consensus of the leaders of the Central Committee of the CPC. On January 2, when Hu Yaobang reported to Hua Guofeng on the political and ideological situation of the country, Hua Guofeng also stressed that it was imperative to unswervingly improve the democratic life of the Party and country. This was a political policy decided by the Third Plenary Session of the Central Committee, and adherence to it was imperative. Party members and cadres were to be well guided. Party committees and newspapers at all levels should guide the healthy, orderly development of democratic life and avoid detours.

After a great change, especially for China, which had just gone through the Cultural Revolution and was stepping out of the shadow of the "Two Whatevers," reexamining and establishing the political foundation of China's modernization construction was the core of the entire historical turning point. Therefore, as soon as the issue of the political basis for the movement was raised, it immediately brought about a wide range of social repercussions. Major media outlets such as the *People's Daily* and the *People's Liberation Army Daily* constantly published editorials and signed articles and investigative reports to further elucidate the political basis of the construction of modernization. In less than a month, the *People's Daily* published articles such as "People's Representatives are to be Elected by the People," "Democracy and the Rule of Law are Political Guarantees for Realizing the Four Modernizations," "Promoting Democracy and Realizing the Four Modernizations," "There Must be a Sound Democratic Life Within the Party," and "Proletarian Democracy and Proletarian Dictatorship," emphasizing that "realizing socialist modernization is inseparable from developing socialist democracy. The Four Modernizations must be accompanied by political democratization" and calling for "expanding this democratic style to the whole Party, the whole army, and the people of all ethnic groups, as requested by the Third Plenary Session of the Central Committee."[2]

It was in such a social atmosphere that preparations for the theoretical work meeting were begun. The meeting on theoretical work was initially proposed by Ye Jianying. Regarding the specific period when this proposal was put forward, the *Ye Jianying Chronology*, the authoritative work on Ye Jianying's life and activities, did not record it, but Hu Yaobang's speech at the meeting of theoretical work and the *Deng Xiaoping Chronology* provided important evidence.

Hu Yaobang pointed out in his Introduction to the Meeting of Theoretical Work that the previous May, an important development of the ideological and theoretical front began discussing the idea that practice was the sole criterion for testing truth, which caused a storm on the China's ideological and theoretical front. The previous September, the journal *Red Flag* carried a long article entitled "Reviewing the Theory of Practice on the Basis of Marxist Epistemology of Practice Standard," which was sent to the Standing Committee of the Central Committee. Comrade Ye Jianying suggested that the Central Committee hold a meeting on theoretical work, presenting different opinions and, on the basis of full democratic discussion, coming to a unified understanding and a solution to the problem.[3]

On October 14, 1978, Deng Xiaoping mentioned in his talk with Wei Guoqing that Ye Jianying had proposed holding a meeting on theoretical work, not wishing to speak behind the scenes.[4]

Subsequently, in his speech at the closing meeting of the Central Working Conference, Hua Guofeng formally noted that at this meeting, many comrades had presented different situations and raised many questions on the notion that "practice is the sole criterion for testing truth," put forward critical opinions to some comrades, and created favorable conditions for holding a theoretical meeting. Due to the large number of issues and limited time in this central working conference, it was impossible to spend much time solving these problems. In accordance with Ye Shuai's proposal, comrades of the Politburo of the Central Committee convened a theoretical meeting after the Third Plenary Session of the Eleventh Central Committee of the Communist Party of China to further address this problem. The preparations for the theoretical meeting were overseen by Hu Yaobang.

On January 7, 1979, Hu Yaobang wrote to the Standing Committee of the Politburo of the Central Committee to submit the introduction drafted as the opening statement of the theoretical meeting and the notice of the meeting for review. In the letter Hu said, he had come up with an idea for the opening of the meeting for theoretical work. First, he suggested inviting about 200 theoretical workers in Beijing to meet in late January or early February over a period of roughly twenty days. The group would then take a few days off to report to the Central Government. Afterward, another 200 or so theorists from all over the country, totaling about 400 people, would be invited for another meeting spanning about ten days. The first part of the meeting was mainly a combination of discussion, group discussion, and speeches at the conference, so that participants could open their minds and speak freely. At the second session, Hu intended to invite Hua Guofeng, Ye Jianying, and Deng Xiaoping to speak and guide the group to focus on some important issues that needed to be settled urgently in connection with the ideological and theoretical front. Democracy should come first, then centralization, as the unification of ideas would help the Party to do a better job in theoretical matters once the focus of the Party's work had shifted.

The draft and letter of Hu Yaobang's Introduction to the Meeting of Theoretical Work received the consent of the Standing Committee of the Politburo. Hua Guofeng was the first to express his approval.

On January 9, Hu Yaobang presided over the ministerial meeting of the Ministry of Publicity and Propaganda, formally setting the specific agenda of the theoretical meeting. First, the starting time of the meeting was to be January 18.

Second, conference venues would include the Friendship and Jingxi Hotels. Third, the Congress was to be divided into two parts. The first part would be a twenty-day session (ten days before and after the Spring Festival), with 200 delegates, mainly from Beijing, plus one from each province, municipality directly under the Central Government, and autonomous region, and taking the form of a group meeting. The second part was to be a ten-day session, with 400 delegates (200 each from Beijing and local governments) in the name of the Central Committee of the CPC and inviting the Chairman and Vice-Chairman of the Central Committee to address the meeting, with the General Assembly forming the main body. There would be a week's recess between the two sessions. In addition, leading group members of the theoretical meeting would be Hu Yaobang, Hu Qiaomu, Huang Zhen, Zhu Muzhi, Hu Jiwei, Yu Guangyuan, Zhou Yang, Tong Dalin, Wu Lengxi, Wu Jiang, and Hu Sheng. Finally, members of the drafting group of the conference documents would include Hu Yaobang, Hu Qiaomu, Yu Guangyuan, Wu Jiang, Ruan Ming, Lin Jianqing, and Li Honglin.

Although the conference not only went longer than the original plan, it also adjusted its procedure and content. The meeting of theoretical work officially began on January 18, with Hu Yaobang's careful preparation.

2. Convening of the Meeting on Theoretical Work

Hu Yaobang presided over the opening ceremony of the conference. At the beginning of the meeting, he announced the list of those leading groups and the names of the convenor of each of the five groups.

The convenor of each group was also the head and deputy head of each subsequent group. In addition, twenty special invitees, all veteran Party members, were notified that they could decide whether to participate in the meeting based on their physical heath and work, and documents and briefings would be given to them in either case.

At the opening meeting, Hu Yaobang delivered a speech, the main content of which was the Introduction to the Meeting on Theoretical Work. In his speech, Hu spoke highly of all the things ideological and theoretical circles had achieved in the rectification work since 1977. He believed that the ideological and theoretical work of the previous two years had been the best and most rewarding rectification work in terms of its scale, its role in the combat, and the improvement of the theoretical level of the entire Party since the founding of the People's Republic of China. He praised the theorists as vanguard fighters on the ideological and theoretical front. The emergence of a group of outstanding generals had reinforced the strength of the Marxist theoretical team, which was a great harvest. He said that it was a rare thing in history for theoretical work to become a truly mass activity as it had at this time. A look around would find just how rare the deep interest the Chinese public took in theoretical issues was in the world. There were not many people who took such interest in theory. This was a valuable aspect of China's national spirit.

In his speech, Hu suggested a general guiding principle for how to adapt the theoretical propaganda to the shift seen in the focus of the work of the Party and the state. He said that the fundamental task of theoretical propaganda work after this shift of the focus could be summed up as: 1) a need to closely integrate the universal truth of Marxism-Leninism and Mao Zedong Thought with the great practice of realizing the Four Modernizations, 2) a need to study and solve new problems, 3) a need to make China's ideological and theoretical work progress beyond the actual work, and 4) a need for continual enrichment and practical developments of Marxism-Leninism and Mao Zedong Thought, which would guide China toward a victorious completion of the New Long March.

The meeting was to be held in groups beginning the following day. On January 22, Hu Yaobang conveyed to the General Assembly some of Deng Xiaoping's opinions on the meeting to discuss theoretical work. Deng emphasized that it was important to have open minds in the course of discussion. How much more was there to discuss besides the criterion of truth? Those items could be discussed more quickly. Many theoretical issues had not been clarified, such as democracy, the legal system, and economic management. The Cultural Revolution could also be discussed. "The question of continuing revolution under the dictatorship of the proletariat can also be discussed. In the future, we should not mention 'holding high Chairman Mao's banner' but 'holding high the banner of Mao Zedong Thought.'" According to the spirit of Deng Xiaoping's instructions and the preliminary discussions of the various conference groups after the beginning of the meeting, Hu Yaobang again made a speech, summed up a number of major issues, and submitted them to the conference for further study. These problems included how to discuss the standard of truth in depth, the class struggle in the socialist period, and how the Party's basic theory came into being, the experience and lessons of theoretical work since the founding of New China, the evaluation of the Cultural Revolution, and its nature, requirements, and lessons, socialist democratic issues, the prominence of propaganda related to individual issues, and other issues.

Subsequently, discussion at the meeting became more enthusiastic. Statements from each group were sent to the Secretariat of the General Assembly, which issued detailed briefings to each participant. As a result, the exchange of information was timely. A total of 262 briefings were issued at this stage. Despite Hu's explicit request that conference materials and discussions should not be spread beyond participants, the briefing was widely disseminated, which resulted in a large number of disseminators and a rapid expansion of the impact of the conference in society.

Almost at the same time that the Central Committee held a meeting on theoretical work, the same conference was held in Shandong, Shanghai, Fujian, Guangdong, Liaoning, Hunan, Jiangsu, and other provinces and cities before Spring Festival. The attendance was generally 50 to 60 people, though the meeting in Shanghai included 300 people.

The first stage of the theoretical meeting ended in mid-February 1979, and the second stage began in late March. In the second stage, in addition to the personnel of the former central unit, Party members from all provinces and municipalities (mainly the secretary and minister responsible for ideological and propaganda work of the Party Committee) were invited, as planned, to participate, with a total of 400 to 500 people. The theoretical meeting lasted until April 3.

From the progress of the first phase of the conference, the meeting of theoretical work adhered to the democratic atmosphere restored at the Third Plenary Session of the Eleventh Central Committee of the CPC and adhered to the principle and direction of liberating thought. It not only continued to criticize the wrong guiding ideology of the "Two Whatevers," but also hit the so-called "forbidden zone," and dealt with many important theoretical issues, such as class struggle in the socialist period. Some propositions, theories about continuing revolution under the dictatorship of the proletariat, whether intra-Party struggle was a reflection of social class struggle, what stage China's socialism was in, standing against personal superstition, socialist democracy, economic theory, practical issues, and so forth were all discussed in depth and debated in many ways, providing a valuable reference for decision-makers in the Central Committee.

Many issues proposed for discussion at the meeting were gradually resolved through research and practice in later years, which played a role in promoting the formation and development of the theory and cause of socialism with Chinese characteristics.

However, at this meeting, due to the lack of comprehensive analysis of the situation after the Third Plenary Session of the Eleventh Central Committee of the Communist Party, the lack of systematic analysis and research on the rapidly changing ideological situation and insufficient theoretical preparation, some delegates' speeches also had obviously erroneous tendencies and vague understandings. This situation was intertwined with the complex social environment, which brought new challenges to the new socialist construction.

3. Presentation of Social Instabilities in the New Situation

Before holding the meeting on theoretical work, there were some social contradictions caused by many lingering problems from the Cultural Revolution. Some people took the opportunity to make trouble and put forward various unreasonable requirements that could not be achieved under the current conditions. They also incited the masses to shock Party and government organs, occupy offices, practice a sit-in or hunger strike and block traffic. Particularly serious was that, through the incitement of these people, riots became the trend in many places, seriously undermining the work order, production order, and social order. In this process, there appeared a trend of thought that doubted or even denied the leadership of the Communist Party, the socialist system, the dictatorship of the proletariat, and Mao Zedong Thought. From late October 1978, the Xidan Wall of Democracy became the main spot for such propaganda and activities.

On January 6, 1979, Ren Wanding and seven others posted a mimeographed leaflet entitled "Declaration of Human Rights in China," announcing the establishment of the so-called China Human Rights Alliance, putting forward twelve programs and handing them to foreign journalists, claiming that "this alliance requires the support of human rights organizations and the public of all countries around the world" and demanding that the President of the United States "take care of" China's human rights. A worker in Beijing organized a Citizen's Appeal Group with some petitioners. With the support of some organizations, she demonstrated in Tiananmen Square with a banner that read,

"Anti-hunger, Anti-persecution, Human Rights, and Democracy." She petitioned at Xinhua Gate and was watched by thousands of people, causing serious traffic jams. On January 18, Beijing detained the worker, and seven organizations such as the China Human Rights League and mimeographed publications, namely the "Joint Statement," planned to hold a 10,000-person complaint conference at the Xidan Wall of Democracy, after which they petitioned at Zhongnanhai. Other non-governmental organizations and publications beside the Xidan Wall of Democracy were active as well. It was at this time that Wei Jingsheng and his "Exploration" began to draw attention.

Wei Jingsheng was a worker in the Beijing Park Service Management Office and the editor-in-chief of the mimeographed newsletter "Exploration." From December 1978 to March 1979, he wrote articles and distributed publications, calling Marxism-Leninism and Mao Zedong Thought "a better bandage than that of a quack." He slandered the state system of proletarianism in China as "a feudal monarchy in the cloak of socialism," and incited the masses to "stop believing in the stability and unity of dictators" and "gather anger toward the criminal system of creating the miserable situation of the people," and instigated the public "to seize power from these lords." Some of the articles he wrote were posted on the walls of Xidan and others in "Exploration." The publication was widely posted, distributed, and sold in Beijing and Tianjin.

In addition, there were eight workers in Guiyang who initiated the establishment of the Enlightenment Society. The headquarters in Guiyang and Beijing set up branch offices, which grew to include more than thirty people. They advocated "democracy," "freedom," and "human rights" like those touted in the capitalist world. In March 1979, the main head of the Enlightenment Society set up the Thaw Society in Beijing, declaring that "class struggle, violent revolution, and all forms of dictatorship should be abolished." Similar organizations and journals also appeared in Guangzhou, Wuhan, and Shanghai.

There were different understandings within the Party and theoretical circles concerning how best to address these new aspects of the ideological and theoretical circles. Some people had sympathy for or even supported these new social trends in ideological and social issues.

At the meeting on theoretical work, some people suggested that "the Central Government should express its support for the Wall of Democracy." Some people said, "Even under socialist conditions, democracy is won by the people themselves. It can only be achieved by breaking the resistance of bureaucrats and opportunists and by breaking the oppression of bureaucrats with excessive centralization of power. Democracy must not depend on the gift of anyone […] The main problem now is that democracy has not been developed enough or too much, and should not be rectified." Others said, "What we should be vigilant about now is not the tendency to emancipate our minds and democracy too much, let alone launch a new anti-right campaign. It is the 'left' that is not properly criticized. If we put forward an anti-right campaign, it will hinder the criticism of the 'left' campaign, affect the emancipation of our minds, and maybe even make us regress. The so-called 'right' must not be regarded as a remarkable tendency to be countered. As for some exceptional cases, we should rely on actual work for guidance. For these kinds of questions, we should remain sober in thought, but in theoretical propaganda, there is no need to publicly object to them as a tendency." Individuals suggested that a column for "The Wall of Democracy" should be set up in the newspaper, and large-character newspapers should be selected. Others said that Mao Zedong Thought should also be divided into two parts, which should include the understanding that Mao Zedong Thought also contains some mistakes. Others thought that "without Chairman Mao there would be no New China" and "Chairman Mao's achievements cannot be overestimated." These talks and discussions clearly demonstrated that the meeting on theoretical work had deviated from the new situations and problems.

4. A Preliminary Response to Tendencies Toward New Errors

Various new situations both inside and outside the Party, especially the various discussions at the Party's meeting on theoretical work, provoked great vigilance in Deng Xiaoping. He was keenly aware of the seriousness of the problem. As a result, after March 1979, he gave many speeches and talks and clearly put forward the necessity of adhering to the Four Basic Principles.

On March 16, 1979, Deng Xiaoping pointed out at the report meeting of the Central Committee on the situation of Vietnam's self-defense and counter-attack war that "Chairman Mao's Great Banner must be Safeguarded." He said that to deny Chairman Mao was to deny the People's Republic of China and the whole history of the Party. Without Chairman Mao, there would be no

New China. This was a matter of history. It meant that without Mao Zedong Thought to guide it to victory in the revolution, China would still be struggling in the dark. When the Party wrote articles, it was important to pay attention to safeguarding Chairman Mao's Great Banner and never harm it in any way. Class enemies at home and abroad hoped that China would fall into confusion on such important issues. It was important, then, to tell Party members and the people not to be fooled. The key at this point was stability and unity. The purpose of dealing with the lingering problems was to concentrate on looking forward. In response to the excessive behavior of some young intellectuals demanding resettlement, he seriously pointed out that if young intellectuals were engaged, what would happen if they were disruptive and rushed to the authorities? Were the lessons of the past not enough? Was there any hope of realizing the Four Modernizations? What else did stability and unity mean? All leading organs had devoted their energies to dealing with these matters. They had no energy to carry out the Four Modernizations. What hope did they have for the improving the people's lives and the development of the national economy? Partial and whole, immediate and long-term issues should be addressed. Everyone in the country should be educated regarding these issues. He said that some people were so envious of foreign human rights movements, so why not organize a refutation? The Wall of Democracy was addressed to US President Carter and supported his human rights. What human rights did imperialism have? How many people did imperialism kill and how many people did imperialism help Chiang Kai-shek kill in China? Imperialism said human rights were only for those who were eligible. Why not educate people with these living facts? He pointed out that the arrest of bad elements who incited disturbances was absolutely correct, according to law.[5] Deng Xiaoping's speech first sounded an alarm to the senior cadres of the Party, then conveyed it to the cadres of counties and regiments within the Party, demonstrating the attitude of the Central Committee.

On March 27, Deng Xiaoping talked with Hu Yaobang and Hu Qiaomu about some of the main points and ideas he intended to highlight at the Party's meeting on theoretical work. He said that it was time to talk about the four principles of adhering to the socialist road, adhering to the dictatorship of the proletariat, adhering to the leadership of the Party, and adhering to the basic principles of Marxism-Leninism and Mao Zedong Thought.

Deng Xiaoping asked whether it was socialist public ownership or capitalist private ownership that should be pursued. As long as the work was done well and construction was carried out according to economic laws, it was important to affirm that socialist public ownership was better than capitalist private ownership and that socialism was better than capitalism. In talking about the leadership of the Party, it was necessary to discuss history. Without the CPC, there would be no new China, and without the CPC, there would be no socialism. Which of the difficulties encountered was not overcome under the leadership of the Party? Evaluation of Chairman Mao must be made in light of these facts. At that time, the speeches were not very prominent or were of insufficient weight. With the October Revolution and the acceptance of Marxism-Leninism, the Communist Party of China and New China came into being. These were inseparable from Chairman Mao, who had put forward the theory of dividing the three worlds, which helped the Party get rid of international isolation even without a proletarian dictatorship. In order to address the realistic conditions in China and abroad, it was necessary to also prevent the restoration of capitalism.

Deng Xiaoping went on to say that democracy and the rule of law needed to be addressed, and that the relationships between democracy and centralization, between immediate interests and long-term interests, and between personal interests and national interests needed to be discussed. In regards to democracy, he noted that it was important to clarify what constituted socialist democracy by analyzing the activities of several illegal organizations. The question was, could China not stick to the four principles? Would it be acceptable to fail to take the bad elements in society seriously? This could be more powerful and targeted. If there are too many empty words, their relevance would not be evident, nor would they be convincing or capable of mobilizing the people. Instead, the masses should be mobilized to fight these bad elements. At the same time, he pointed out that democracy was under highly centralized guidance, and this centralization was highly democratic. It was important to carry democracy forward, give full play to the wisdom of the people, and mobilize their enthusiasm. Only on the basis of democracy was it possible to combat bureaucracy and the will of various senior officials. However, without a high degree of centralization on the basis of democracy, these goals could not be achieved. When considering the Party's leadership, it was important to emphasize the need for unified leadership and authority. Without unified leadership of the Party, there would be no efficiency. With unified leadership of the Party, as long as such leadership was correct, adjustments could be made and construction done quickly, but nothing would be achieved without unification. Lenin put great emphasis on centralization, unity, and discipline, and China's revolutionary war was likewise won through a high degree of concentration and discipline.

Deng Xiaoping sternly pointed out that the Wall of Democracy actually had a program. Those who made use of democracy or used the Wall of Democracy to spoil things, sell information, and make foreign accusations should be banned. It was important to separate the few bad elements from the masses, and the masses should be mobilized to fight these bad elements. Unless the riots were stopped and these bad elements opposed, there would be no hope for the Four Modernizations. Most of the people in Shanghai and Beijing opposed the destructive activities and strange remarks of various illegal organizations, whose actions were similar to those of Lin Biao and the Gang of Four. These people feared a world will without chaos, so it was important to ask everyone, especially young people, not to be deceived by them. Their essence, ideological system, and organizational purpose were directed at socialism, the dictatorship of the proletariat, the Communist Party, Marxism-Leninism, and Mao Zedong Thought.

In this talk, Deng Xiaoping also criticized the existing problems in theoretical circles. He said that the ideological and theoretical front could not be said to have fully carried out the shift of work focus, as there was a tendency among some to be obsessed with settling old accounts. The spirit of the Third Plenary Session of the CPC Central Committee had been little publicized, and some specious and even extreme propositions had emerged. This was not good, not conducive to unity or forward-looking, not conducive to mobilizing the enthusiasm of the people, and not conducive to commitment to the Four Modernizations. Why not put greater emphasis on publicizing the Party's positive traditions? Traditional education included discipline, diligence, and general consideration. It emphasized that theory should serve politics. At that time, the biggest domestic political issue was to unite and wholeheartedly look forward to the Four Modernizations. In carrying out the Four Modernizations, many difficulties would be faced, so it was important to prepare the masses. Many new questions needed to be studied and addressed by theoretical circles. In those days, there was a lack of such theorists.[6]

5. Formal Proposal of the Four Basic Principles

On March 30, the third day after the resumption of the theoretical meeting, Deng Xiaoping delivered the famous speech "Adhering to the Four Basic Principles" at the Central Committee of the Communist Party of China, on behalf of the Great Hall of the People.

This speech was very pertinent, but it did not discuss the current issues alone, instead deeply expounding on the unique political foundation and connotation of the construction of Chinese-style modernization.

Deng Xiaoping suggested that adhering to the Four Basic Principles was the basic condition for realizing the Four Modernizations and clearly emphasized that the Four Basic Principles was one of the basic connotations of the Four Modernizations of the "Chinese Style" just put forward.

Deng Xiaoping pointed out that in the past, the democratic revolution had to be adapted to the situation in China and followed the path of encircling the cities in the countryside, as launched by Mao Zedong. Now, in order to carry out construction, it was likewise necessary to adapt to China's current situation and take a Chinese style path to modernization.

In order to realize the Four Modernizations in China, it was necessary to note at least two important characteristics. The first was the weak foundation. The long-term destruction of imperialism, feudalism, and bureaucratic capitalism had made China a poor, backward country. After the founding of New China, great achievements had been made in its economic construction. A relatively complete industrial system had been established, and a number of technical experts had been trained. The average annual growth rate of industry and agriculture in China from Liberation to the previous year was relatively high, compared to the rest of the world. However, due to its weak foundation, China was still one of the poorest countries in the world. China's scientific and technological strength was insufficient. Generally speaking, the level of science and technology in China lagged behind the world's most advanced countries by twenty or thirty years. Over the previous three decades, China's economy had gone through two cycles of rise and decline. Specifically, Lin Biao and the Gang of Four had caused great damage to the national economy in the decade spanning 1966 to 1976, with extremely serious consequences. Now, it was necessary to adjust, that is, to further eliminate these serious consequences.

The other characteristic was that the population was large and the amount of cultivated land was small. At the time, there were more than 900 million people in the country, 80% of whom were farmers. Many people had both advantages and disadvantages. With the insufficient development of production, food, education, and employment had become serious problems. It was important to greatly strengthen work in family planning, but even if the population did not increase over the next several years, the problem of China's large population would continue for a period of time. China's land was vast and abundant, which was an advantage. However, there were many resources that had not been carefully explored, exploited, or utilized, so they were not the real means of production. Though the land area was vast, the amount of cultivated land was small. It was not easy to change this situation of little cultivated land and a large population, especially of farmers. This had become a feature that had to be considered in China's drive toward modernization. Chinese-style modernization had to start from China's own characteristics. For instance, modern production needed only a small number of people, and China's population was so large, so how could these factors be balanced? Without broad consideration, China would face a social problem of insufficient employment in the long run. There were many problems in this area, which needed to be jointly studied by all Party members in the practical and theoretical work of the Party. It was important to find appropriate ways to properly address these issues.

Deng Xiaoping then turned to point out that the Central Committee believed that if China hoped to realize the Four Modernizations, it had to adhere to the Four Basic Principles in ideology and politics. This was a fundamental prerequisite for realizing the Four Modernizations. These four points were 1) it was necessary to adhere to the socialist road, 2) it was necessary to adhere to the dictatorship of the proletariat, 3) it was necessary to adhere to the leadership of the Communist Party, and 4) it was necessary to adhere to Marxism-Leninism and Mao Zedong Thought.

Deng Xiaoping said that it was well-known that these Four Basic Principles were not new things, and that they had been consistently upheld by the Party for a long time. Since the toppling of the Gang of Four and the Third Plenary Session, the Central Committee had been adhering to a series of principles and policies. Practically and theoretically, the Party had criticized the pseudo-socialism of the Gang of Four, which advocated universal poverty in an extreme leftist form. The

Party had adhered to the principles of socialist public ownership and distribution according to work and to the principle of giving priority to self-reliance, striving for foreign aid as a supplement, and learning and introducing foreign advanced technology to develop socialist economic construction. It was important to act in accordance with objective economic laws. That is to say, the Party must adhere to scientific socialism.

The CPC had smashed the feudal fascism of the Gang of Four, reversed a large number of injustices, solved a series of lingering historical problems, consolidated the dictatorship of the proletariat, and restored and developed socialist democracy, especially after the Third Plenary Session of the Central Committee, a lively political situation which Mao Zedong had hoped to achieve for many years before his death.

It had further restored the three major styles of work of the damaged Party, perfected the democratic centralism of the Party, strengthened the unity of the whole Party, and also the unity of the Party and the masses, thus greatly enhancing the prestige of the Party and strengthening its leadership over national and social life.

It had broken the spiritual shackles created by Lin Biao and the Gang of Four, insisted that leaders were human beings rather than gods, adhered to the scientific system of mastering Marxism-Leninism and Mao Zedong Thought completely and accurately, and adhered to proceeding from reality and seeking truth from facts. This restored the true face of Mao Zedong Thought and safeguarded Mao's lofty position in the history of the Chinese revolution and throughout the world as a great revolutionist.

Deng Xiaoping clearly pointed out that, nevertheless, the Central Committee believed that it was still necessary to emphasize and publicize these Four Basic Principles. On the one hand, for the time being, some comrades in the Party were still deeply poisoned by Lin Biao and the ultra-leftist trend of thought espoused by the Gang of Four, and a few had even spread rumors and slander, attacking a series of principles and policies adopted by the Central Committee after the toppling of the Gang of Four, especially after the Third Plenary Session of the Central Committee, which violated Marxism-Leninism and Mao Zedong Thought. On the other hand, a few people in society were spreading suspicions or misgivings. Opposing these Four Basic Principles, some comrades in the Party not only did not recognize the danger of this trend of thought, but even supported it directly or indirectly, to some extent. Although these types of people were few, both inside and outside the Party, their roles could not be ignored just because they were small in number. Facts had proven that they could and had done great harm to the Party's cause. Therefore, on the one hand, it was important to continue to resolutely eliminate the Gang of Four virus, help those comrades who had been poisoned by it to come to their senses, and severely attack the reactionary remarks spread by a very small number of people that defamed the Central Committee of the Party. On the other hand, great efforts were required to resolutely fight against the trend of doubting the Four Basic Principles mentioned above. Both trends of thought ran counter to Marxism-Leninism and Mao Zedong Thought and hindered the progress of the Party's drive toward socialist modernization.

After this, Deng Xiaoping emphatically criticized the trend of doubting ideology or opposing the Four Basic Principles from the right, which was clear, profound, and very convincing. In his summary, he pointed out that the Central Committee believed that it was important to repeatedly emphasize adhering to these Four Basic Principles, because some people (though it was only a very small number) were trying to shake these principles. This was absolutely unacceptable. Every member of the Communist Party, particularly its ideological and theoretical workers, must never waver in this fundamental position. If any of these Four Basic Principles were shaken, it would in turn shake the whole cause of socialism and modernization.

At the historic turning point when the Party and the state were setting out to rectify the chaos and shift the focus of their work to the drive toward socialist modernization, on behalf of the Central Committee, Deng Xiaoping put forward for the first time the Four Basic Principles in clear, complete terms and made a profound, systematic exposition of them, which had a far-reaching, significant impact. From that time, as an important theme of the Party's political life, the Four Basic Principles became the basis for the Party to formulate various policies, and they were enriched and improved through the development of practice. In 1982, the Four Basic Principles were formally enshrined in the Party Constitution and the Constitution, becoming the common will of the whole Party and the people of the entire country. The Thirteenth National Congress of the Communist Party of China took adhering to the Four Basic Principles as a fundamental point of the Party's basic line in the primary stage of socialism. The Fourteenth National Congress listed it as the basic content of Deng Xiaoping's theory of building socialism with Chinese characteristics. At the Fifteenth National Congress, the theory of peace was established as the guiding ideology of the Party, and the Four Basic Principles were strongly reiterated as an integral part of Deng Xiaoping's theory. The Four Basic Principles were a lofty generalization of the long-term historical experience of the Party and state, and they served as a common political basis for the unity and struggle of the entire Party and the people.

II

Reexamining the Criterion of Truth

After the meeting on theoretical work, the rightest trend of opposing the Four Basic Principles was quickly defeated. However, the long-standing ideological rigidity or semi-rigidity was difficult to overcome in the short term, and the leftist ideological tendency was still quite serious and had become the main resistance to rectification of the chaos.

1. The Criterion of Truth in Discussing the Problem of Supplementary Lessons

Since the Third Plenary Session of the Eleventh Central Committee, the Party had promoted democracy and emancipation of the mind. However, the work itself had just begun. Some people believed the Party had gone too far, while some mistakenly attributed the chaos that once appeared in society to the Third Plenary Session of the Central Committee, believing that this chaos was caused by the promotion of democracy and emancipation of the mind. Others opposed the Four Basic Principles with the line of the Third Plenary Session of the Eleventh Central Committee and believed that the Four Basic Principles were "correcting the deviation" from the Third Plenary Session of the Central Committee. All manner of incorrect opinions in cadres' ideology demonstrated that continuing to emancipate the mind and overcome ideological rigidity was still a major long-term task to be addressed on the ideological and theoretical front. At the same time, this situation also showed that the discussion of the criterion of truth carried out before the Third Plenary Session of the Central Committee had not been conducted seriously in some regions and units and had not been deeply rooted in the hearts of the people, so that some people were still in a rigid state of mind and were still blindly following "mere doctrine." Therefore, continuing in-depth discussions on the criterion of truth and further correcting the Party's ideological line was still an important, and even urgent task. In this context, while implementing the line of the Third Plenary Session of the Eleventh Central Committee and the spirit of the meeting in the work of communicating theory, all localities raised the issue of truth standards and discussed the issue of "make-up lessons."

On May 21, 1979, the *People's Liberation Army Newspaper* published a commentary entitled "Unswervingly Continuing to Implement the Spirit of the Third Plenary Session of the Central Committee." The article pointed out some ideological and cognitive problems in the process of carrying out the spirit of the Third Plenary Session of the Central Committee. The article noted that practice is the only criterion for testing truth and plays a key role in emancipating the mind. However, discussion of this issue had not been carried out very well in many units of the army. Why discuss the criterion of truth? Why couldn't the test of truth be anything other than practice? Why were emancipation of the mind and activation of thought so crucial? If the mind was rigid and practice proceeded from the original approach, the vitality of the Party, the state, and the nation would cease to boom. Many comrades in the army had not made this clear. The article stated, "Comrades in the army should make up for this lesson and study the documents of the Third Plenary Session of the Central Committee again." The article uses the term "make-up lesson" and clearly required such revision. This was the earliest and clearest proposal for "make-up lessons" in the discussion of the criterion of truth.

On May 22, 1979, the *People's Daily* reprinted this article prominently. The title used by the *People's Daily* was "Reviewing the Documents of the Third Plenary Session of the Central Committee and Supplementing the Lesson on the Standard of Truth." This was the first time that the *People's Daily* explicitly proposed such "make-up lessons."

2. Responses of Various Regional Departments to the Discussion of Supplementary Lessons on the Standard of Truth

After May 1979, heads of various departments made speeches, analyzed the situation, and pointed out that the main problem at the time was still the emancipation of the mind. Local Party committees and propaganda departments also held meetings, emphasizing that practice was the only criterion for testing truth while continuing to carry out in-depth discussions on the criterion of truth. The central and local Party organ newspapers also published a large number of articles on this issue.

In mid-May, Feng Wenbin, Vice Principal of the Central Party School, pointed out that the main obstacle to the implementation of the principles and policies of the Third Plenary Session of the Central Committee was still the ideological rigidity of some cadres. He said, "At present, in many places, education regarding the distinction between the two ideological lines is not very common or in-depth. Some comrades have said, 'The general situation of ideological emancipation is that the Central Committee has begun, some places have begun, and many places have not started yet.' Therefore, it is absolutely necessary to continue to propagate the ideological line of dialectical materialism, liberate ourselves from the spiritual shackles of Lin Biao and the Gang of Four, dare to consider new problems, and raise and solve new problems in the new Long March."[7]

In mid-May, the principal person in charge of the Sichuan Provincial Committee of the Communist Party of China delivered a speech at the Second Plenary Session of the Provincial Party Committee, pointing out that, from the perspective of the ideological situation of Party members, especially senior and middle-level cadres, it was relatively easy to unify thought on the Four Basic Principles. However, it was still a major challenge to continue emancipating the mind, and especially to integrate Marxism-Leninism and Mao Zedong Thought with the reality of the Four Modernizations. Much less was done to study new situations and solve new problems. He said that there was still rigidity and semi-rigidity in the Party's ideology. A considerable number of comrades still had lingering problems to be solved, and it would take a long time and great effort to solve them. He thus proposed that the Party should further study, publicize, and implement the spirit of the Third Plenary Session of the Central Committee and unify adherence to the Four Basic Principles with the emancipation of the mind.

The head of the Anhui Provincial Party Committee pointed out at the working meeting of the Provincial Party Committee held in May that it was imperative to distinguish the mainstream from the tributaries, in view of the situation. In the previous period, some people from the right took advantage of the opportunity to promoting democracy and emancipating the mind to spread suspicion and denial of the Four Basic Principles, and a very small number of people in society also appeared to support anarchy and extreme democratization. This was a tributary. After conveying and implementing the speech of the leading comrades of the Central Committee on the Four Adherences, the situation in this regard had changed rapidly. It was important not be confused by these tributaries. At that point, there was another wrong trend of thought that denied the Third Plenary Session of the Central Committee. Some people seized such tributary phenomena and exaggerated them, then attacked the Party's line as "right" and "biased" in regards to the principles and policies of the Third Plenary Session. It was likewise important to give full attention to this trend of thought, which appeared in the face of leftism. This showed that many people's thought was still in a rigid state. For this reason, it was important to correctly understand the situation, firmly adhere to the political direction, continue to carry out the spirit of the Third Plenary Session of the Central Committee, continue to emancipate the mind, and lead the discussion on the question of truth standards to a deeper level. This discussion surpassed any other theoretical discussion that had arisen on the ideological front since the founding of New China, and it was another Marxist educational and ideological emancipation movement with far-reaching significance after the Yan'an Rectification Movement.

The head of the Jiangxi Provincial Party Committee delivered a speech at the working meeting of the Provincial Party Committee held in May, calling on Party organizations at all levels throughout the province to adhere to the principles of emancipating the mind, activating the machine, seeking truth from facts, uniting and looking forward, and uniting ideas both inside and outside the Party into the spirit of the Third Plenary Session. The working meeting of the Jiangxi Provincial Committee held that as long as the Party adhered to the resolution of the Third Plenary Session of the Central Committee, the ideological line emphasized emancipation of the mind and practice as the only criterion for testing truth, engaged in in-depth practice, conducted investigations and studies, and followed the mass line, some problems and difficulties that might emerge at that time could be completely resolved.

In early June, the head of the Guangdong Provincial Party Committee pointed out at the provincial cadres' meeting at the prefectural, municipal, and county levels that attention should be paid to opposing interference from both "left" and "right" erroneous ideological trends. Comparing the two ideological trends of the left and right, the leftist trend of thought was more likely to confuse people and do more harm, which called for universal vigilance. The emergence of these left and right ideological trends was not due to the implementation of the spirit of the Third Plenary Session of the Central Committee. On the contrary, the Party had not yet fully implemented the spirit of the Third Plenary Session of the Central Committee. Rather, it had only preliminarily implemented it, which was the "beginning," not an "excess." Therefore, it was important to continue to earnestly study the documents of the Third Plenary Session of the Central Committee. In many places, it would be necessary to supplement the discussion of the standard of truth and continue to educate the people on the ideological line of dialectical materialism.

At the expanded meeting of the Standing Committee of the Hubei Provincial Committee, the head of the committee pointed out that in the previous point, within the Party and among cadres, there were divergent views on the principles and policies of the Third Plenary Session of the Central Committee, and there appeared to be a trend of doubting or opposing the spirit of the Third Plenary Session. A few comrades believed that after the Third Plenary Session of the Central Committee, "the policy was right." This misunderstanding was due to the lack of a comprehensive and correct understanding of the principles and policies of the Third Plenary Session of the Central Committee, which confused the inevitable problems in the process of implementing the spirit of the Third Plenary Session with the principles and policies set by it. Therefore, it was important to continue to emancipate the mind and eliminate the influence of the ultra-leftist trend remaining among the cadres.

The head of the General Political Department of the PLA also encouraged the entire army to continue to learn the lesson that practice was the sole criterion for testing truth and to further eliminate the pernicious influence of Lin Biao and the Gang of Four on the far-left line. Immediately, the Standing Committee of the Party Committee of the Navy expanded its meeting and decided to start studying and discussing the point that practice was the only criterion for testing truth in the navy. It was important to earnestly address the ideological line and make up for the lack of education regarding the discussion of the criterion of truth.

3. Nationwide Discussion of the Criterion of Truth

Some leaders in the Central Committee, especially Deng Xiaoping, attached great importance to supplementary lessons on the discussion of truth standards. On July 29, 1979, when he met all the participants in the enlarged meeting of the Standing Committee of the Party Committee of the Navy, he made a speech, pointing out, "From the beginning, many people opposed the argument that practice is the sole criterion for testing truth, but the vast majority of cadres and masses throughout the country have gradually accepted it." The debate was not over yet. At that time, the Navy was considering reviewing those lessons, which was very important. The discussion of the standard of truth was a basic construction. Without addressing the problem of the ideological line and emancipation of the mind, the correct political line could not be drawn up and implemented. It was important, then, not to underestimate the argument that practice was the only criterion for testing truth. The significance of this debate was so great that its essence was not to adhere to Marxism-Leninism and Mao Zedong Thought.

In mid-August of that year, Deng Xiaoping visited Tianjin. At that time, the Tianjin Municipal Committee of the CPC was holding an expanded meeting of its Standing Committee. Deng Xiaoping listened to the work report of the Standing Committee of the Municipal Party Committee and made an important speech on implementing the principles and policies of the Third Plenary Session of the CPC Central Committee and deepening the understanding of the Party's political, ideological, and organizational lines in the new era, especially the discussion that carrying out in-depth practice was the test of truth standards. In line with the spirit of Deng Xiaoping's speech, the head of the Tianjin Municipal Committee proposed that in an effort to adhere to the political line of the Third Plenary Session of the Eleventh Central Committee, Party members should adhere to emancipation of the mind and carry out a major discussion on the issue of truth standards. It was imperative that great efforts to make up for this lesson be conscientiously put forth by everyone, from the municipal Party committee down to the grassroots units. Leading comrades at or above the district, county, and bureau levels should study it with particular diligence.

On September 29, 1979, Ye Jianying delivered a speech to the Congress celebrating the 30th anniversary of the founding of New China. In his speech, he suggested, "We should conduct an extensive and in-depth study and discussion on the standard of truth on all fronts and in all industries, from leading organs to grassroots units, and carry out education on the ideological line of dialectical materialism nationwide. In particular, the main cadres in charge should take the lead in emancipating the mind with a clear banner. The responsibility of leaders lies in further guiding the thoughts of the masses and cadres to the political line of realizing the Four Modernizations."[8] This speech was discussed and adopted by the Fourth Plenary Session of the Eleventh Central Committee, and it was regarded as a supplementary lesson for the discussion of truth standards made by the Central Committee.

Around this time, under the unified leadership and deployment of the Party committees in various places or units, the provinces, autonomous regions, municipalities directly under the Central Government, and PLA forces had conducted "remedial lessons" on the issue of truth standards. Beginning in the summer and autumn of 1979, the "remedial course" on the standard of truth was carried out nationwide, and it reached its climax in the autumn and winter of that year. This "make-up lesson" greatly exceeded the discussion in 1978 in both breadth and depth, especially at the grassroots level. It had strong resonance among the cadres and the masses at the grassroots level and formed a trustworthy discussion. In fact, this major discussion lasted until June 1981, when the Sixth Plenary Session of the Eleventh Central Committee of the Communist Party of China passed the Resolution on Some Historical Issues in the Party since the Founding of the People's Republic of China, and basically completed the rectification of the disorder in guiding ideology, marking the end of the "remedial lesson."

The "remedial lesson" on the discussion of the criterion of truth was not only a continuation of the discussion on the criterion of truth under the new situation in 1978, but also a great movement toward popularization of the Marxist ideological line. At the same time, it was also further propaganda and an implementation of the spirit of the Third Plenary Session of the Eleventh Central Committee.

III

Adoption of the Resolution on Some Historical Issues in the Party After the Founding of the People's Republic of China

After the Third Plenary Session of the Eleventh Central Committee, the Party conducted a large-scale rectification of the damage caused by Lin Biao and the Gang of Four in various fields. At the same time, it also cleaned up and corrected some leftist errors that had occurred before the Cultural Revolution. On this basis, the Party comprehensively reviewed and summarized the history of socialist revolution and socialist construction since the founding of New China and drafted and adopted the Resolution on Some Historical Issues of the Party since the Founding of the People's Republic of China.

1. Objective Requirements for Summing Up Historical Experience and Lessons

As early as the Third Plenary Session of the Eleventh Central Committee of the Communist Party of China, Deng Xiaoping raised the question of summing up the history of the Cultural Revolution. He pointed out that the shortcomings and mistakes in the course of the Cultural Revolution should in due course be summed up as lessons, which was necessary for unifying the understanding of the Party. The Cultural Revolution was a stage in the historical development of socialism in China. It was necessary to summarize it, but it was not necessary to do so in a rush. To make a scientific evaluation of such a historical stage, it was important to conduct serious research. Deng Xiaoping's opinion was accepted by the entire Party and written in a communiqué of the plenary meeting.

After this plenary session, the Central Committee began to carry out specific work in this area. In September 1979, on the eve of the 30th anniversary of the founding of New China, the Central Committee organized some cadres engaged in theoretical work to conduct a comprehensive study and summary of the 30-year history of the founding of New China, drafted a speech, then held extensive consultations both inside and outside the Party. From September 25–28, the Fourth Plenary Session of the Eleventh Central Committee was convened by the

Central Committee to discuss and adopt the speech delivered by Ye Jianying on China's 30th National Day.

On September 29, Ye Jianying made a long speech on behalf of the Central Committee, the Standing Committee of the NPC, and the State Council at the Congress celebrating the 30th anniversary of the founding of New China. He made a comprehensive review of the thirty-year history since the founding of New China, pointing out that great achievements had been made over the previous thirty years, and it was totally wrong to fail to see these great achievements. Of course, the road had not been smooth, but had in fact been made up of a mix of smooth development and serious setbacks. Compared with the arduous efforts made by people throughout the country and the advantages that the socialist system played, the achievements made thus far were still insufficient. The Party still needed to earnestly sum up its experiences and lessons and strive to achieve even greater things.

In his speech, Ye Jianying recalled that just three years after the founding of New China, the Party had healed the wounds caused by the long war, successfully completed the remaining tasks of the Democratic revolution, and restored the national economy to a level higher than had ever been reached in the history of old China while carrying out the anti-American struggle and aid to the DPRK.

Then, in 1956, the socialist transformation of agriculture, the handicraft industry, and capitalist industry and commerce was successfully realized, the first Five-Year Plan for the development of the national economy was completed, and brilliant achievements in socialist revolution and construction were realized. However, in the face of these great victories, the Party grew overly cautious. In 1957, it committed the error of enlargement in its attempt to counter the attack of bourgeois right-wing elements. In 1958, the guidance of economic work violated the objective law, left the principle of in-depth investigation and research and all experimentation, and committed the errors of blind command, exaggeration, and the "Communist wind." In 1959, the struggle against so-called right opportunism was inappropriately launched within the Party.

Speaking of the Cultural Revolution, Ye Jianying pointed out that the starting point of launching the Cultural Revolution was anti-revisionism and self-defense. For a ruling proletarian party, of course, it was crucial to always be vigilant and prevent it from taking the revisionist road of oppressing the people at home and pursuing hegemony abroad. The problem was that when the Cultural Revolution was launched, the situation inside the Party and at home was estimated in a way that went against reality, and there was no accurate explanation of what revisionism actually was. Further, the Party left the principle of democratic centralism and adopted wrong principles and methods of struggle. For their counter-revolutionary purposes, Lin Biao and the Gang of Four took advantage of this mistake and pushed it to the extreme. They carried out a decade-long counter-revolutionary destruction of the country, causing a great catastrophe to the people and the most serious setback to the socialist cause since the founding of New China.

After reviewing China's history since the founding of the People's Republic, Ye Jianying summed up several experiences and lessons. These included that 1) the fundamental purpose of socialist revolution was to liberate productive forces. Therefore, after the proletariat had gained national political power and established the socialist system, it needed to firmly focus on economic construction, vigorously develop social productive forces, and gradually improve people's lives. 2) After the establishment of the socialist system, the domestic class and class struggle situation must be analyzed scientifically and objectively, and correct policies and methods needed to be adopted. 3) It was important to correctly understand the relationship among the masses, classes, political parties, and leaders, which was particularly important in a socialist society. 4) It was important to further improve the Party's discipline and socialist legal system, effectively safeguard the democratic rights of all Party members and citizens, and institutionalize and legalize intra-Party and socialist democracy.

Ye Jianying's speech showed that the Communist Party of China was a great proletarian party that was open and aboveboard and dared to admit its mistakes. At the same time, it also showed that after a long period of setbacks and mistakes, the CPC had correctly summed up the lessons in its work, thus growing more mature.

2. Correct Evaluation of Mao Zedong and Scientific Understanding of Mao Zedong Thought

At that time, when summing up the history after the founding of New China, the Central Committee encountered the complex problem of how to evaluate the merits and demerits of Mao Zedong's life scientifically and correctly. This was because, on the one hand, Mao was the main leader of the Communist Party of China and the main founder of the People's Republic of China. He was also a beloved leader of the Chinese people and had created immortal merits for the Chinese revolution and the liberation of the Chinese nation. On the other hand, he committed serious leftist errors in his later years, which led to the disaster of the Cultural Revolution. At the same time, how to evaluate Mao was an unavoidable issue in the course of summarizing the history of the Party after the founding of New China. Whether such a leader could be evaluated or not was the key factor for the success of the Party's efforts to rectify the recent chaos.

After the Third Plenary Session of the Eleventh Central Committee of the CPC, with the development of rectifying the chaos and the gradual correction of leftist errors, and especially with the deepening of the discussion on the criterion of truth, the long-standing cult of personality was broken. People no longer regarded Mao as a god, and they no longer regarded him as a perfect revolutionary leader. At that time, there were two biases regarding the treatment of his merits and demerits. One bias was that some people still could not rid themselves of the influence of personal worship and did not recognize the fact that Mao had made mistakes. Another bias was that some people, out of their resentment for the consequences of the leftist errors to the Party, the country, their families, or individuals, espoused a more extreme mentality, blaming Mao for all the mistakes that had been made. Obviously, these two biases were not conducive to making a correct evaluation of Mao, correcting leftist errors, and scientifically summing up China's historical experience. In response to this situation, the CPC Central Committee, especially Deng Xiaoping and other older revolutionaries, called on the people to emancipate their minds and break through taboos. At the same time, they also paid great attention to guiding people to treat Mao's merits and demerits realistically and understanding Mao Zedong Thought comprehensively and accurately.

On March 30, 1979, in his speech Adhering to the Four Basic Principles, Deng Xiaoping pointed out that a series of victories in China's revolution and construction could not be separated from Mao Zedong Thought, and Mao's life had made immortal contributions to the Chinese people. But Mao, like anyone else, had his shortcomings and errors. In analyzing his shortcomings and errors, of course, it was important to recognize individual responsibility. But more importantly, it was necessary to analyze the complex historical background. Only in this way could history be treated fairly and scientifically, that is, employing a Marxist treatment of history and historical figures.

In August 1980, when Deng answered questions from Italian journalist Oriana Fallaci, he expounded on the CPC's evaluation of Mao and its attitude toward Mao Zedong Thought. He pointed out that Mao's achievements were primary. He was the main founder of the Communist Party of China and the People's Republic of China. What he did for the Chinese people could not be erased. He saved the Party and the people from crisis many times. Without Chairman Mao, the Chinese people would, at the least, have had to grope in the dark for a longer period. Mao Zedong Thought was the guiding ideology of the Party. Mao Zedong Thought was mainly Mao's thinking, but it was not his own creation. It included the contributions of the older generation of revolutionaries who had participated in the establishment and development of Mao Zedong Thought.

Concerning the errors Mao committed in his later years, Deng pointed out that there were some unhealthy factors and ideas in Mao's later years, mainly some leftist ideas. The errors began in the late 1950s. He did not carry out the proper style of work, such as democratic centralism and the mass line, and did not formulate or form a good system. As a result, he led the way to the Cultural Revolution. Mao made political mistakes, and they were not small mistakes. On the other hand, the mistakes were exploited by two counter-revolutionary groups, Lin Biao and the Gang of Four. Their aim was to conspire to seize power. So it was important to distinguish Mao's mistakes from the crimes of Lin Biao and the Gang of Four. Mao's mistakes were secondary. It was important to be realistic about his later mistakes, just as it was important to continue in Mao Zedong Thought.

From Deng's answers to reporters' questions, it can be seen that the correct evaluation of Mao's merits and demerits by the CPC was in sharp contrast to the practice of the Soviet leader Khrushchev totally denying Stalin's merits in the International Communist movement, demonstrating the greatness and maturity of the Communist Party of China.

After that, from March 1980 to June 1981, in the process of drafting the Resolution on Several Historical Issues in the Party after the Founding of the People's Republic of China, organized by the Central Committee, Deng repeatedly emphasized the importance of establishing Mao's historical position and adhering to and developing Mao Zedong Thought. He pointed out that evaluation of Mao and elaboration of Mao Zedong Thought were not only related to Mao's personal problems, but also to the whole history of the Party and the nation. Mao's errors must be criticized unequivocally, but also realistically, analyzing various situations and adhering to Mao Zedong Thought, and the Party went on to educate a whole generation with Mao Zedong Thought. The goal now was to put the chaos right, that is, put the chaos created by Lin Biao and the Gang of Four in order, criticizing Mao's mistakes in his later years and returning to the correct track of Mao Zedong Thought.

Other veteran Party members likewise abandoned their personal grievances and made contributions to the correct evaluation of Mao's merits and demerits from the perspective of the interests of the Party and the people, playing an exemplary role.

Huang Kecheng, an old Communist Party member persecuted by leftist errors for many years, beginning in 1959, was a leader who was criticized and dealt with by Mao Zedong at the Lushan Conference. At that time, he still highly affirmed Mao's historical achievements. In November 1980, at a meeting of the Central Discipline Commission, he talked about how to evaluate Mao Zedong and his attitude towards Mao Zedong Thought. Starting from history, he reviewed Mao's great contributions to the Chinese revolution. At the same time, he pointed out that it was important to have a correct attitude towards Mao's mistakes. If Mao was to blame for all the mistakes made by the Party since the founding of New China, that was not in line with historical facts. In the past, the old Communists did their part to liberate China and build a new China. All, therefore, had a share of the credit. It would likewise be unfair to credit all the mistakes on one person, as if the rest had no share. It was more in line with historical facts and materialism to share the responsibilities. Huang Kecheng said emphatically that some comrades had said many extreme words about Chairman Mao, and some even said nothing about him. Huang believed this was wrong. It was not only a fundamental violation of the facts, but also a great disadvantage to the Party and the people. It was understandable that some comrades, especially those who had been attacked and persecuted, felt some indignation. In Mao's later years, Huang too had suffered greatly, but he did not think it appropriate to be emotional in dealing with a matter of such great importance. It was important to proceed from the fundamental interests of the Party and the country as a whole.

Huang Kecheng's speech was later published as an article in the *People's Daily* on April 10, 1981. His articles had tremendous social repercussions. Many people were deeply moved after reading this article. Such an old comrade who had suffered so much still treated history impartially and without resentment. How should others, then, vent their personal grievances? It was the spirit of seeking truth from facts and the broad mind of the older generation of revolutionaries that set an example for the whole Party and the people to correctly evaluate Mao Zedong and correctly understand Mao Zedong Thought, uniting the views of the Party and the people on Mao Zedong.

3. Drafting and Adoption of the Resolution on Some Historical Issues of the Party after the Founding of the People's Republic of China

With the intensification of the work of rectifying the chaos and the gradual agreement of the entire Party and the people on the evaluation of Mao Zedong's merits and weak points, the conditions for a comprehensive summary of the Party's history since the founding of New China had gradually matured. As a result, the Central Committee began to draft the Resolution on Some Historical Issues of the Party after the Founding of the People's Republic of China.

Shortly after Ye Jianying delivered his speech on China's 30th National Day, the Central Committee began drafting the Resolution on Several Historical Issues of the Party after the Founding of the People's Republic of China in November 1979. Under the leadership of the Politburo and the Secretariat, Deng Xiaoping, Hu Yaobang, and other leaders of the Central Committee presided over this work. Hu Qiaomu was mainly responsible for the specific work of the document drafting group. Deng Xiaoping attached great importance to the drafting of the resolution and put forward many guiding opinions on the drafting and revision of the draft resolution.

In March 1980, the drafting group put forward a preliminary proposal for the resolution. On the 19th of that month, Deng proposed three opinions on the drafting of the resolution. 1) Establishing Mao Zedong's historical position and adhering to and developing Mao Zedong Thought are the core issues. 2) In the thirty years after the founding of the People's Republic of China, it was important to make a realistic analysis of the major events, which were correct and which were wrong, including the merits and demerits of some responsible comrades, and make a fair evaluation. 3) It was important to make a basic summary of the past through this resolution. This summary was meant to be rough rather than detailed. The purpose of summarizing the past was to guide everyone to unite and look forward. On April 1, he also put forward his views on the overall design of the draft resolution and his views on the seventeen-year history of the Cultural Revolution after the founding of New China.

On June 27, after reading the draft resolution, Deng Xiaoping pointed out that the focus should be on what Mao Zedong Thought was, what Mao was right about, and criticizing what was wrong, but it was also appropriate to say that acknowledging Mao's mistakes alone could not thoroughly address the problem. Rather, the most important thing was a systemic approach. Deng Xiaoping's talk showed his superb ability and level of insight into problems and observation as a great Marxist.

In October 1980, the draft resolution was discussed for twenty days among 4,000 senior cadres. During the discussion, everyone spoke freely, offering many good opinions, but some people still put forward extreme opinions during the discussion too. Some people even thought that Mao Zedong should be held responsible for all the mistakes made before and during the Cultural Revolution.

In line with this situation, speaking with the head of the Central Committee on October 25, 1980, Deng Xiaoping pointed out that, without mentioning Mao Zedong Thought, it was inappropriate to evaluate Mao's merits and weak points, that the old workers would not agree, that the poor middle peasants who had been liberated during the land reform would not agree, and that a large number of cadres associated with them would not agree either. The banner of Mao Zedong Thought could not be thrown away. Losing this banner actually negated the glorious history of the Party. This part of Mao Zedong Thought in the draft resolution could not be avoided. This was not just a theoretical issue, but was even more a political one, and it was a very big political issue both in China and abroad. If the Party did not write or failed to write this part of its history properly, it may as well not do anything about the whole resolution. If it did not adhere to Mao Zedong Thought, it would make great historical mistakes. Mao's mistakes must be criticized unambiguously, but it was important to be realistic and analyze various situations so that not all the problems were arbitrarily attributed to personal qualities. Mao was not an isolated individual, but had been the leader of the Party until his death. His mistakes should not be overstated, and it was contrary to historical facts to overwrite and blacken Mao, which was in fact to blacken the Party and the country.

In March 1981, Deng Xiaoping pointed out that the outline of the draft resolution could be determined, and the achievements of the first seven years of the founding of New China were universally recognized. It could be affirmed that the ten years before the Cultural Revolution were generally good and had basically developed along a healthy path. There had been twists and turns and mistakes, but the achievements outweighed the divergences. This part of the Cultural Revolution should be summarized. Compared with the mistakes made in the previous seventeen years, the Cultural Revolution was a serious overall mistake. Its consequences were extremely serious and still had an impact at that time. On April 7, Deng spoke to the head of the drafting group about his views on some issues in the Cultural Revolution. First, it was important to recognize the legitimacy of the Twelfth Plenary Session of the Eighth Central Committee and the Ninth Congress. Even during the Cultural Revolution, there had still been a Party. Further, great achievements were made in foreign affairs during the Cultural Revolution. At the same time, Chen Yun also made important comments on the revision of the draft resolution, putting forward two opinions on the draft resolution on March 24. One was to add a special remark on the history of the Party before the founding of the People's Republic and write about the Party's sixty years. In this way, Mao's achievements and contributions would be more comprehensive, establishing his historical position and adhering to and developing Mao Zedong Thought would have a comprehensive basis. The other was to suggest that the Central Committee advocate learning, with emphasis on learning Mao Zedong Thought and his philosophical works. Deng attached great importance to these two opinions. Two days later, he conveyed them to the drafting group of the resolution. Before and after this, Chen Yun also put forward several opinions on the draft resolution, including 1) the errors in the Party's work in the thirty-two years since the founding of New China must be written accurately and the conclusions should be realistic, and they should also be finalized, 2) it was important to add a paragraph reviewing the twenty-eight years of history before the founding of New China, 3) it was important to fully affirm Mao's historical achievements, and 4) it was important to write about international help to China.

In May 1981, the Politburo invited more than forty people to discuss the draft resolution for twelve days. On the basis of this discussion, the drafting group made repeated revisions.

On May 19, Deng Xiaoping pointed out at the enlarged meeting of the Politburo that the document on historical resolutions should be produced as soon as possible, and it should not be left too long. In order to get it out at the earliest possible date, the present method was to hold an expanded meeting of the Politburo. More than seventy people spent time and energy deliberating on and correcting the manuscript. After that, at the Sixth Plenary Session of the Central Committee they made plans to publish it on the 60th anniversary of the founding of the CPC.

Subsequently, according to Deng Xiaoping's opinion, the Politburo invited more than seventy people to discuss the draft resolution for twelve days. After the amendment, 130 representatives of democratic parties were consulted regarding their views and opinions, and further amendments and improvements were made to the content of the resolution. In June 1981, the Sixth Plenary Session of the Eleventh Central Committee held a serious, detailed discussion on the draft resolution. Deng made important comments on the draft resolution at the meeting.

In this way, after more than a year, the draft resolution had undergone a process of drafting, discussing, and revising. During this process, there were four or five extensive discussions. Through brainstorming, collective revision, and gathering the wisdom of the entire Party, the majority of comrades' opinions were gradually unified and the purpose of drafting the resolution had been achieved.

On this basis, the Central Committee held the Sixth Plenary Session of the Eleventh Central Committee from June 27–29, 1981. The plenary session considered the Resolution on Several Historical Issues of the Party after the Founding of the People's Republic (referred to as the Resolution). After thorough discussion, the plenary unanimously adopted the Resolution. Using Marxist dialectical materialism and historical materialism, the Resolution made a correct summary of the major historical events of the Party in the thirty-two years since the founding of New China, especially the Cultural Revolution.

The most important contributions of this historical document included:

1) It evaluated Mao Zedong's historical status scientifically and realistically, and fully expounded the great significance of Mao Zedong Thought as the

guiding ideology of the Party. The Resolution pointed out that Mao was a great Marxist and a great proletarian revolutionist, strategist, and theorist. Throughout his life, his contribution to the Chinese revolution was far greater than his faults. He established indelible merits for the founding and development of the Party and the People's Liberation Army, for the victory of the cause of liberation of the Chinese people of all ethnicities, for the founding of the People's Republic of China, and for the development of its socialist cause.

The Resolution fully expounded Mao Zedong Thought, pointing out that it was the application and development of Marxism-Leninism in China and the correct theoretical principle and summary of the experiences of the Chinese revolution proved through practice. It was the crystallization of the collective wisdom of the Communist Party of China. Many outstanding leaders of the Party had made important contributions to its formation and development. Mao's scientific works were his concentrated summary. The scientific system of Mao Zedong Thought mainly included the following items: the construction of the revolutionary army and military strategy; policies and strategies; ideological, political, and cultural work; and the construction of the Party. Among these components, there were three basic aspects: seeking truth from facts, mass line, and independence, which were the living soul of Mao Zedong Thought.

The Resolution distinguished Mao's mistakes in his later years from Mao Zedong Thought and pointed out that it was totally wrong to attempt to deny the scientific value of Mao Zedong Thought because of Mao's mistakes in his later years. At the same time, it was totally wrong to adopt a dogmatic attitude towards Mao's speech, or to refuse to admit that Mao made mistakes in his later years and to try to persist in these mistakes in his new practice. Mao Zedong Thought, which had undergone a long historical test and become a scientific theory, must be distinguished from Mao's mistakes in his later years. Mao Zedong Thought was the precious spiritual wealth of the Party, which would guide its actions for a long time.

The exposition of Mao Zedong Thought in the Resolution not only scientifically summarized and defined the first theoretical achievement formed by the Party on the road toward the localization of Marxism, but also opened up a road for inheriting and developing this theory, thus continuing to promote the cause of the localization of Marxism.

2) It offered a scientific summary of the Party's history, especially the thirty-two years after the founding of New China. Regarding the seven years (1949–1956) when the socialist transformation was basically completed, the Resolution held that the guiding principles and basic policies set by the Party during this period were correct and that the victory achieved was glorious. The establishment of the socialist system was the deepest and greatest social change in the history of China and the basis for all its future progress and development. As for the ten years (1957–1966) when it began to build socialism comprehensively, the Resolution held that it had made great achievements, but also suffered serious setbacks. All the achievements of the previous ten years were made under the collective leadership of the Central Committee headed by Mao Zedong. Later, owing to complex subjective and objective reasons such as insufficient experience, there was a subjective deviation in the analysis of the situation and the understanding of the national conditions, leading to mistakes such as the expansion of class struggle and the rash advance of economic construction, including long-term general mistakes such as the Cultural Revolution, which caused serious setbacks and losses to the cause of socialism.

The Resolution completely negated the Cultural Revolution (May 1966–October 1976). It pointed out that the Cultural Revolution caused the Party, the country, and the people to suffer the most serious setbacks and losses since the founding of New China. Mao's main arguments for launching the Cultural Revolution were neither in line with Marxist-Leninist doctrine nor with China's reality. The arguments summarized as "the theory of continuing revolution under the dictatorship of the proletariat" were totally wrong in estimating the class and political situations of the Party and the state at that time. History had determined that the Cultural Revolution was a case of civil disorder initiated by the wrong leaders and exploited by the Lin Biao and Jiang Qing cliques, which brought serious disaster to the Party, the country, and the people.

The resolution made several comments on the two years of wandering and advancing after the toppling of the Gang of Four. The crushing of the victory of the Jiang Qing Anti-Revolutionary Group in October 1976 brought China into a new historical period of development. However, in the first two years, the strong demands of comrades inside and outside the Party for correcting the mistakes of the Cultural Revolution met with serious obstacles. This was due to the fact that the political and ideological confusion caused by the Cultural Revolution in the previous ten years could not be easily eliminated in a short period. At the same time, Hua Guofeng, then chairman of the Party Central Committee, continued to commit leftist errors in his guiding ideology. The Third Plenary Session of the Eleventh Central Committee, held in December 1978, was a great turning point of far-reaching significance in the history of the Party after the founding of New China. The plenary session ended the situation in which the Party's work had been wandering and advancing since October 1976. It began to correct the leftist deviation that had occurred during the Cultural Revolution comprehensively and earnestly and achieved a series of victories in rectifying the chaos, thus bringing about a positive economic and political situation in China.

3) The Resolution also marked the first time that the Party pointed out that its socialist system was still in its infancy and that the socialist system needed to go through a long process to move from imperfection to perfection. This recognition was a step further than had been taken before. On the basis of a correct summary of historical experience, this paper offered a preliminary summary of the socialist construction road that the Party had gradually established after the Third Plenary Session of the Eleventh Central Committee, which was suitable for China's national conditions, noting several key points, including 1) after the basic completion of the socialist transformation, the main contradiction to be solved in China was the contradiction between the increasing material and cultural needs of the people and the backward social productive forces, and the focus of the work of the Party and the state must be shifted to the socialist modernization construction centered on economic construction. 2) Socialist economic construction must proceed from the national conditions of China to systematically achieve the goal of modernization. 3) The transformation and perfection of production relations must be adapted to the conditions of productive forces, and there was no fixed pattern for the development of socialist production relations. It was important to create specific forms of production relations that were suitable to the situation and advance in each stage in accordance with the requirements of the development of productive forces in China. 4) The transformation and perfection of production relations must be adapted to the conditions of productive forces. 5) It was one of the fundamental tasks of the socialist revolution to gradually build a highly democratic socialist political system. 6) Socialism must have a high level of spiritual civilization. Efforts should be made to improve the position and role of education, science, and culture in the construction of modernization. 7) Improving

and developing socialist national relations was of great significance to China's multi-ethnic country. 8) It was important to strengthen the modernization of national defense construction, which should be compatible with the country's economic construction. 9) It was important to persist in opposing imperialism, hegemonism, colonialism, and racism, and safeguarding world peace. 10) The Communist Party of China must be built into a party with sound democratic centralism.

Although the individual expressions of these main points changed in subsequent documents, their basic spirit and main content embodied the preliminary results of the Party's reexamination of the road to socialist construction under the new historical conditions. The adoption of the Resolution on Some Historical Issues of the Party after the Founding of the People's Republic of China was of great significance to the Party's construction and the political construction of the country. It further unified the thought and understanding of the Party and the people, strengthened the unity of the Party and the people of all ethnicities, and marked the Party's successful accomplishment of the task of rectifying chaos in its guiding ideology. Immediately after the resolution was promulgated, it received a strong response throughout the Party and the people, and it was widely and enthusiastically supported. At the same time, the adoption and publication of this resolution also had a great impact overseas and internationally.

CHAPTER 4

The Proposition of Building Socialism with Chinese Characteristics and the Formulation of a Comprehensive Reform Program

I

The Proposition of Socialism with Chinese Characteristics

From September 1–11, 1982, the Communist Party of China held the Twelfth National Congress in Beijing. This was the most important national congress in the history of the Party after the Eighth Congress.

At the Third Plenary Session of the Eleventh Central Committee held in December 1978, a series of important decisions concerning the future and destiny of the Party and the country were put forward, the wrong policy of the Two Whatevers was criticized, a push was made to fully and accurately grasp the scientific system of Mao Zedong Thought, clear definitions were formulated for the guiding principles of emancipating the mind, seeking truth from facts, and looking forward in unity, and use of the slogan of "taking class struggle as the guideline" was decisively terminated. The strategic decision was made to shift the focus of the Party's work to the drive toward socialist modernization.

1. Preparatory Work for the Twelfth National Congress of the Communist Party of China

The transformation achieved at the Third Plenary Session of the Eleventh Central Committee indicated that the Party had fundamentally broken through its long-term leftist mistakes, corrected the Party's guiding ideology, re-established Marxist ideological and political and organizational lines, ended the lingering issues in the Party's work since October 1976, and explored the construction path and the Party's basic line according to China's national conditions. It laid a foundation and ushered in a new period of socialist modernization in China.

After the Third Plenary Session of the Eleventh Central Committee, the Party carried out large-scale work to rectify the chaos, systematically settling many problems that had been lingering since the founding of New China and also new issues in the current situation. Centering on the theme of shifting the work focus of the entire Party and the country to economic construction, the Party concentrated on the development of social productive forces and carried out socialist modernization in China, focusing on construction and reform. The issue of how to further map out China's reform, opening up, and modernization, and to explore the path to building socialism with Chinese characteristics had become a new topic facing the whole Party. It was against this backdrop that the Twelfth National Congress was held.

In order to hold the Party Congress successfully and smoothly, the Central Committee spent more than two years making preparations. As early as February 1980, the Fifth Plenary Session of the Eleventh Central Committee officially decided to hold the Twelfth National Congress ahead of schedule. The Plenary Session also stipulated the main agenda of the Twelfth National Congress, the allocation of delegates and the way to produce them.

The plenary held that since the Eleventh Congress of the CPC, and especially since the Third Plenary Session of the Eleventh Central Committee, the situation in China and abroad had undergone significant changes and development. With the shift of the work focus of the whole Party, the cause of socialist modernization had begun to embark on a track of healthy development. The political, ideological, and organizational lines of the Party as determined by the Third and Fourth Plenary Sessions of the Fourth Central Committee had been widely accepted by the people. The ultra-Leftist line pursued by Lin Biao and the Gang of Four and their organizational and ideological remnants had been further exposed and criticized. In addition, a large number of unjust and false cases that had been lingering had since been rectified, and the Party's policies had been widely implemented throughout the country. On this basis, the entire Party, the entire army, and the people of the entire country were closely united around the Central Committee, struggling for the great cause of socialist modernization and the implementation of the principles of readjustment, reform, rectification, and improvement of the national economy. Rapid reports on various fronts, such as agriculture, industry, finance and trade, education, science, culture, politics, national defense, and diplomacy, were frequently circulated. A situation of stability, unity, and vitality was developing. These facts proved that the lines, principles, and policies carried out by the Central Committee were correct. China had basically moved from the serious chaos caused by Lin Biao and the Gang of Four during the previous ten years to a positive situation with strong leadership, order, direction, and objectives for progress, along with the necessary conditions and confidence for victory. This was a great achievement the Party had made in overcoming tremendous difficulties.

The plenary session pointed out that across the country, the great practice of the people of all ethnicities marching toward the Four Modernizations had now put forward to the Party a series of major problems that needed to be solved promptly and without losing time, including the determination of a long-term plan for the development of the national economy, the determination of an economic system suitable for the development of the national economy, and the determination of an educational plan and system conducive to the development of the national economy. With the change in the domestic situation, a series of important issues in the political life of the country and in the life of the Party, as well as some important ideological and theoretical issues, also needed to be addressed accordingly in order to facilitate the development and consolidation of a stable, united, and lively political situation and the smooth progress of modernization. In order to settle these urgent problems, the Central Committee was required to convene the Twelfth National Congress earlier than planned. The Central Plenary Session unanimously adopted a decision to convene the Twelfth National Congress in advance, with the specific time to be decided by the Politburo of the Central Committee.

The plenary session initially settled on the main agenda for the Twelfth National Congress. It was stipulated that the number of delegates to the Congress would be 1600, and each electoral unit was to elect alternate delegates in proportion to one tenth of the number of its delegates. Each province, autonomous region, municipality directly under the Central Government, central state organ, PLA headquarters, military and military branches, and major military regions were to hold Party congresses at the appropriate level. After full deliberation, the method of differential election would be adopted and votes cast by secret ballot.

After the Fifth Plenary Session of the Eleventh Central Committee of the Communist Party of China was held, the Central Committee immediately began the preparatory work for the Twelfth National Congress.

Regarding the election of representatives to the Twelfth National Congress, in order to do this work well, the Politburo adopted Opinions on the Election of Representatives to the Twelfth National Congress in April 1980. In accordance with the spirit of the resolution of the Fifth Plenary Session of the Central Committee of the Communist Party of China, the document put forward specific opinions on issues concerning the election of deputies, along with requests that the principles of democratic centralism be adhered to throughout the Party congresses or conferences. Representatives attending the Twelfth National Congress were to be fully deliberated and elected by means of a differential election by secret ballot. Party committees of provinces, municipalities, and autonomous regions should strengthen leadership and hold Party congresses or conferences of counties and municipalities. At the same time, it was important to make preparations for the congresses or conferences of representatives of provinces, autonomous regions, and municipalities directly under the Central Government. After thorough deliberation, a preliminary list of candidates attending the Twelfth National Congress should be proposed. The preliminary list of candidates representing the congresses should only be obtained by Party leaders. The opinions of the majority representatives should be fully reflected throughout the electoral process. Elections for units in various regions should be completed by the end of November.

In this document, the Politburo of the Central Committee also stipulated in principle the proportion of representatives of all parties. About 15% of the total number of representatives were female Party members, about 6% were well-known labor models and war heroes, about 15% were professionals in science, technology, culture, education, health, and sports, and no less than 5% were representatives of ethnic minorities. At the same time, delegates were to be younger, with those under 55 making up no less than two-fifths of the class.

The Politburo also made the Decision on the Inappropriate Representatives of the Twelfth National Congress and Candidates for Central Committee Members of the CPC, pointing out that in order to make sure a considerable proportion of the deputies to the Congress and the Central Committee Members were elected by the Congress, the Party's leading bodies should be able to meet the demands of the arduous task of socialist modernization. To prove the long-term continuity of the Party's line, principles, and policies, to ensure the Party's centralized leadership and long-term stability, and on the basis of the proposals of many veteran comrades and the masses inside and outside the Party, the spirit of the Fifth Plenary Session of the Central Committee and the principles of the New Party Constitution (Draft), the Central Committee decided that veteran comrades who were old enough to lose their ability to work and take care for themselves should not be candidates for a place in the Twelfth National Congress. This was an important step in abolishing the cadre tenure system and gradually updating the leadership.

He added that there were roughly three criteria for the best Congress. 1) The line it had laid down was correct. 2) The leading group it had elected was prestigious and was recognized and supported by the overwhelming majority of Party members. 3) Its methods embodied the principle of democratic centralism and fully followed the mass line. When discussing how the elected representatives were truly representative, Hu Yaobang asked comrades in the organizational departments to study and examine the issues carefully under the leadership of Party committees at all levels, so as to ensure that the conditions for the current representatives were adequate and that those who were not qualified should not be included. The Party should fully deliberate and truly obtain the consent of the majority of Party members rather than rely on a limited few. The list was not confidential, and the leaders should elicit opinions among Party members through deliberation and discussion. It was important to not fear change. This too was a form of dialectic. A Party Congress should be held to carry forward democracy within the Party, improve its life, and strengthen the lively education of its leadership. In accordance with the resolution of the Fifth Plenary Session of the Eleventh

Central Committee of the CPC and the spirit of the relevant instructions of the Central Committee, Party organizations of provinces, autonomous regions, municipalities directly under the Central Government, central organs, and the People's Liberation Army convened Party congresses or representative meetings, elected representatives to the Twelfth National Congress, and completed the election work on schedule.

Further preparatory work for the Twelfth National Congress came in the form of the revision of the Party Constitution, which was also under way. From the winter of 1979, under the leadership of the Standing Committee of the Politburo of the Central Committee, various relevant units of the Central Committee held discussions on mobilizing a group of cadres and conducted investigations in many parts of the country to seek opinions and draw up a draft. In January 1980, Deng Xiaoping put forward many important guiding opinions on the revision of the Party Constitution. Under the leadership of the Central Committee, a Party Constitution Amendment Group, chaired by Deng Xiaoping and Hu Yaobang and specifically under the charge of Hu Qiaomu, was set up to discuss and revise the original draft numerous times and form the first version of the revised draft. In February 1980, it was submitted to the Fifth Plenary Session of the Eleventh Central Committee for discussion. Based on the opinions of the Plenary Session, it made its first revision. In April, it was sent by the Secretariat of the Central Committee to the entire Party for discussion and to some non-Party figures for comments. The second major revision was made in May 1980. In June of the same year, Party organizations and all representatives of the Twelfth National Congress of the Central Committee, government, and army were sent to all provinces, autonomous regions, municipalities directly under the Central Government, and major military regions for comments. A third revision was made in July.

On the basis of the above preparations, the Politburo of the Central Committee held an expanded meeting in Beijing in late July 1982. Over 130 people in charge of the Central Committee and the provinces, autonomous regions, and municipalities directly under the Central Government attended the meeting. The meeting discussed some important issues related to the Twelfth National Congress.

On August 6, 1982, the Central Committee held the Seventh Plenary Session of the Eleventh Central Committee of the CPC. The meeting was attended by 185 members of the Central Committee, 112 alternate members, and 21 participants. Hu Yaobang, Ye Jianying, Deng Xiaoping, Zhao Ziyang, Li Xiannian, Chen Yun, and Hua Guofeng, all standing members of the Politburo of the Central Committee, presided over the meeting.

The plenary session decided to hold the Twelfth National Congress on September 1, declaring publicly to the whole Party and the people that the Eighth National Congress's good tradition of making its congresses completely open to the people should be restored and the secret practice of the Ninth National Congress of the Communist Party of China be abandoned. The plenary session considered and adopted the report of the Central Committee on the Twelfth National Congress and the draft Constitution of the Communist Party of China (Amendment), and decided to submit the two documents to the Twelfth National Congress for consideration.

On August 30, the preparatory meeting for the Twelfth National Congress was held in Beijing. Four items on the agenda of the General Assembly were determined, the twelve presidiums consisting of 252 people were elected, and Zhao Ziyang was elected Secretary-General of the General Assembly. At the meeting, Hu Yaobang put forward the tasks of the Twelfth National Congress, which was to make a successful summary of the great historical turning point achieved in the previous six years, especially since the Third Plenary Session of the Eleventh Central Committee. At the same time, he would determine the Party's grand goals and combat tasks in the new period, so that the Party could take the lead of the people of all ethnic groups in the country in the construction of socialist modernization with a new outlook and increased capacity. The meeting adopted the Decision on Confirming the Supplementary Central Committee Members at the Third Plenary Session and the Fourth Plenary Session of the Eleventh Central Committee. The presidium of the Congress elected a standing committee of 31 members, including Hu Yaobang, Ye Jianying, Deng Xiaoping, Zhao Ziyang, Li Xiannian, Chen Yun, Hua Guofeng, Xu Qian, Nie Rongzhen, Peng Zhen, and Deng Yingchao, which passed the report of the Committee for the Qualification of the Twelfth National Congress and the agenda of the congress. Up to this point, the preparatory work for the Twelfth National Congress had been successfully completed.

2. Convening the Twelfth National Congress of the Party

The Twelfth National Congress of the Communist Party of China was officially held from September 1–11, 1982, in Beijing. There were 1,545 formal delegates and 145 alternate delegates, representing more than 39 million Party members. The main agenda of the Congress included three items: 1) to deliberate and adopt the report of the Central Committee to determine the program for the comprehensive opening up of a new situation in socialist modernization; 2) to deliberate and adopt the new Constitution of the Communist Party of China; and 3) to elect a new Central Committee, a Central Advisory Committee, and a Central Commission for Discipline Inspection in accordance with the provisions of the new Constitution.

The meeting was chaired by the Presidium of the General Assembly and the Standing Committee of the Presidency. The opening ceremony was attended by representatives of democratic parties and non-partisan democrats. The Executive Chairman of the General Assembly, Deng Xiaoping, delivered an opening speech.

In his opening speech, Deng reviewed China's history since the Seventh National Congress of the CPC and clarified the important historical position of the Twelfth National Congress. He said, "The Seventh National Congress of the Party, held in 1945 under the chairmanship of Comrade Mao Zedong, was the most important congress of our Party in the period of democratic revolution after the founding of the Party. That Congress summed up the historical experience of the circuitous development of the democratic revolution in China for more than twenty years, formulated correct programs and strategies, overcame erroneous ideas within the Party, unified the understanding of the entire Party on the basis of Marxist-Leninist Theory and Mao Zedong Thought, and achieved unprecedented unity throughout the Party. The Congress laid the foundation for the victory of the new democratic revolution throughout the country… Since the Third Plenary Session of the Eleventh Central Committee, our Party has restored correct policies in all aspects of economic, political, and cultural work, studied new situations and experiences, and formulated a series of new and correct policies. Compared with the time of the Eighth National Congress, our Party now has a much deeper understanding of the laws of socialist construction in our country and has much more experience. It has greatly strengthened its consciousness and firmness in carrying out our correct principles. We have ample grounds to believe that the correct program formulated by this Congress will surely open up a comprehensive new phase of socialist modernization, make our Party, our socialist cause, our country, and our people of all ethnicities flourish and develop."

In this opening speech, Deng Xiaoping also summarized the Party's historical experience and put forward the guiding ideology of taking the road of socialism with Chinese characteristics. He pointed out, "In our drive toward modernization, we must proceed from the actual situation in China. Whether in revolution or in construction, we should pay attention to learning and drawing lessons from foreign experience. However, we can never succeed by merely copying other countries' experience and models. We have learned many lessons in this respect. Combining the universal truth of Marxism with the concrete situation in our country and taking our own path and building socialism with Chinese characteristics are the basic conclusions we draw from our long-term historical experience. This basic conclusion is the correct understanding and application of the objective laws of socialist construction held by the Communist Party of China, as well as the concentrated expression of the will, aspirations, and demands of the people of all ethnicities within our country. Under the guidance of this ideology, China's Reform and Opening Up and construction of modernization have made tremendous achievements and successes."

In his opening speech, Deng also reviewed the situation and put forward three major tasks facing the Chinese people in the 1980s, namely, to accelerate the socialist drive toward modernization, strive for the reunification of the motherland, including Taiwan, and oppose hegemony and maintain world peace. Among these three tasks, the core was economic construction, which was the basis for solving international and domestic problems. He stressed that for some time to come, at least until the end of the 20th century, it would be necessary to grasp four tasks: carrying out institutional reform and economic restructuring; building a team of younger, knowledgeable, professional revolutionary cadres; building a socialist spiritual civilization; combating criminal activities that undermined socialism in the economic and other fields; and studying earnestly. On the basis of the new Party Constitution, rectifying the Party's style of work and organization was the most important guarantee for China to adhere to the socialist path and concentrate its efforts on the drive toward modernization.

At the Twelfth National Congress of the Communist Party of China, on behalf of the Eleventh Central Committee, Hu Yaobang made a political report to the General Assembly entitled "Creating a New Situation in the Construction of Socialist Modernization in a Thorough Manner." The report was divided into six parts: 1) historic transformation and new great tasks, 2) promoting the overall rise of the socialist economy 3) striving to build a high level of socialist spiritual civilization, 4) striving to build a high level of socialist democracy, 5) adhering to an independent foreign policy, and 6) making party building a hardcore principle for leading the cause of socialist modernization.

The report reviewed the Party's history since the Third Plenary Session of the Eleventh Central Committee and the tremendous achievements made on all fronts and proposed the general tasks of the Party in the new historical period. This was meant to unite the people of all ethnicities throughout the country, work hard for self-reliance, gradually realize the modernization of industry, agriculture, national defense, and science and technology, and build China into a highly civilized and highly democratic socialist country. During the five years from this Congress to the next, it was important to vigorously promote the construction of socialist material and spiritual civilization in accordance with the requirements of these general tasks and proceed from the current situation. It was important to continue to improve socialist democracy and the legal system, conscientiously rectify the Party's style of work and organization, and strive for a fundamental improvement in the state's financial and economic situation. At the same time, working with all patriotic people, including Taiwanese, Hong Kong, and Macao compatriots and overseas Chinese, to promote the great cause of reunification of the motherland was a crucial step. Together with the people of the world, the Chinese people should continue to fight against imperialism and hegemony, safeguarding world peace.

Starting from China's concrete reality and focusing on the overall task, the report formulated the strategic objectives, strategic priorities, and a series of principles and policies for China's economic construction. The report pointed out that among all the tasks aimed at comprehensively opening up a new situation, the first was to push forward the economic construction of socialist modernization and promote the overall rise of the socialist economy. In the twenty years from 1981 to the end of the 20th century, the overall goal of China's economic construction was to quadruple the total annual output value of industry and agriculture in the country, i.e. from 710 billion yuan in 1980 to about 28 trillion yuan in 2000, on the premise of constantly improving economic benefits. In order to achieve the above strategic objectives, it was important to solve the problems of agriculture, energy, transportation, education, and science. Taking these as strategic priorities and solving these problems on the basis of comprehensive balance, China could promote the rapid growth of consumer goods production, promote the development of industry and other production and construction undertakings, and guarantee the improvement of the people's lives.

In order to achieve this goal over the next twenty years, two steps in strategic deployment were necessary. The first ten years would mainly be spent laying a solid foundation, accumulating strength, and creating the necessary conditions. The second ten year period would bring about a new period of economic revitalization, which was an important decision made by the Party Central Committee after a comprehensive analysis of China's economic situation and development trends. During the period of the Sixth Five-Year Plan, from 1981 to 1985, it was important to continue to unswervingly implement the principles of readjustment, reform, rectification, and improvement, maintain a strict economy and oppose waste, and shift all economic work to a track centered on economic benefits. It was important to concentrate efforts on adjusting the economic structure in all aspects, consolidate and improve the preliminary reforms already under way in the economic management system, and work out the overall plan and implementation steps for reform. During the Seventh Five-Year Plan period, from 1986 to 1990, extensive technological transformation of enterprise and gradual reform of economic management systems should be carried out. At the same time, the rationalization of enterprise organizational structure and various aspects of economic structure would be completed. In the 1980s, a series of necessary capital construction and "tackling key issues" of a series of major scientific and technological projects must also be carried out in the fields of energy and transportation. As long as the above work was done well, China could solve its lingering historical problems and lay a solid foundation for economic growth in just ten years. By the 1990s, China's economic development would surely be much quicker than that in the 1980s, and China's economy would enter a period of full economic boom.

The report highly affirmed the significance and role of building a socialist spiritual civilization and pointed out that efforts must be made to build this civilization. The report pointed out that while building high-level material civilization, China should strive to build a high level of socialist spiritual civilization as well, which was a strategic policy issue in the process of building socialism. The historical experience of socialism and the current situation in China indicated that whether or not it adhered to such a policy would be closely related to the rise and fall of socialism. The relationship between spiritual and material civilization in socialist construction was very close. The construction of the material civilization was the indispensable foundation for the construction of the socialist spiritual civilization. The socialist spiritual civilization not only played a major role in promoting the construction of the material civilization, but also ensured the correct direction for its development. The two civilizations were each the mutual conditions and purposes for the other. The report pointed out that building a socialist spiritual civilization was not an easy task, especially at that time. It was important to put maximum effort into adapting to the new conditions in the construction period, conscientiously doing a thorough job of building a socialist spiritual civilization, and stoking the enthusiasm of the masses for building socialism with revolutionary ideas and a revolutionary spirit.

The report also pointed out that building a high degree of socialist democracy was one of the Party's fundamental goals and tasks. The report stressed the need to continue to reform and improve the country's political and leadership systems in accordance with the principle of democratic centralism, and to extend socialist democracy to all aspects of political, economic, cultural, and social life. It was equally important to develop democratic management of enterprises and institutions, develop mass autonomy in grassroots societies, and closely integrate the construction of socialist democracy with the construction of the socialist legal system, so as to institutionalize and legalize socialist democracy.

Regarding China's foreign policy, the report pointed out that a combination of patriotism and internationalism had always been China's fundamental starting point for dealing with foreign relations, and it adhered to an independent foreign policy. China's foreign policy was based on the scientific theories of Marxism-Leninism and Mao Zedong Thought, and it proceeded from the fundamental interests of the Chinese people and the people of the world. It had a long-term overall strategic basis. It would never accommodate temporary events, or be instigated and provoked by anyone, and under no circumstances would the Party ever seek hegemony. At the same time, the report pointed out that the Party adhered to the principle of independence, full equality, mutual respect, and non-interference in internal affairs on the basis of Marxism and developing relations with the Communist Party of all countries and other working class political parties. All parties should respect and help each other, and China should make greater contributions to the world.

The report emphasized that party building should be a strong core in leading the cause of socialist modernization. In order to strengthen the Party's construction in the new period, the Twelfth National Congress made many fundamental amendments to the Party Constitution of the Eleventh National Congress. The general principle of revising the Party Constitution was to adapt to the characteristics and needs of the new era, put forward stricter requirements for Party members, improve the combat effectiveness of Party organizations, and uphold and strengthen the leadership of the Party. The new Constitution cleared the leftist mistakes in the Constitution of the Eleventh National Congress and inherited and developed the advantages of the Constitutions of the Seventh and Eighth National Congresses. The report pointed out that in order to make party building the core force leading the cause of socialist modernization, it was necessary to perfect the democratic centralism of the Party, improve the leading institutions and cadre system, cultivate the revolutionary, younger, intellectualized, and professional cadres, strengthen the work of the Party among workers, peasants, and intellectuals, and closely link the Party with the masses within three years. It was important to carry out Party consolidation in a planned, systematic manner, so as to fundamentally improve the Party's style.

Hu Yaobang's report centered on the construction of socialism with Chinese characteristics, and from the perspective of political, economic, cultural, and diplomatic work and party building, he outlined a blueprint to achieve this magnificent goal. By integrating theory with practice, it addressed a series of major issues in the socialist revolution and construction of China and had a strong impact in all sectors. From September 2–4, delegates attending the Twelfth National Congress spent three days heatedly discussing the report. Everyone spoke freely and was in high spirits. The atmosphere of the meeting was quite lively.

On the afternoon of September 5, the Bureau of the General Assembly held a meeting. Hu Qiaomu, Deputy Secretary-General of the General Assembly, explained the suggestions and opinions made by the delegates during the group discussion on the report of the Eleventh Central Committee and the draft Constitution of the Communist Party of China, and made revisions on the report and the draft Constitution accordingly. The Conference adopted the draft resolutions on the report of the Eleventh Central Committee and the Constitution of the Communist Party of China and decided to submit the two draft resolutions to the General Assembly for adoption. The meeting also determined to submit the list of candidates for the Central Committee, the Central Advisory Committee, and the Central Disciplinary Inspection Commission proposed by the Bureau to all delegates for discussion, and adopted the election methods for the three Committees for consideration by the General Assembly.

On the afternoon of September 6, a plenary meeting was held. The General Assembly adopted a resolution on the report of the Twelfth Central Committee and approved the report made by Hu Yaobang on behalf of the Eleventh Central Committee. The resolution of the General Assembly held that the line, principles, and policies since the Third Plenary Session of the Eleventh Central Committee were correct and the work had been fruitful. He noted, "The correct program and a series of principles and policies put forward in the report to create an overall new situation of socialist modernization should be the basic basis for the Party's work in the future." The General Assembly also adopted the Constitution of the Communist Party of China and the resolution on the Constitution proposed by the Eleventh Central Committee. The resolution required the whole Party to earnestly study the Party Constitution and to strive to make all Party members truly understand the general outline of the Party Constitution and its provisions, so as to enhance the understanding of all Party members, especially all cadres and Party members, allowing full preparations for the comprehensive rectification of the Party's style and organization to be made and for the party building to become a strong leading core for the cause of socialist modernization.

Ye Jianying and Chen Yun delivered speeches at the Sixth Congress, expressing their support for Deng Xiaoping's opening speech, Hu Yaobang's political report, and the Constitution of the Communist Party of China, and emphatically expounding the issue of the alternation of old and new cadres' cooperation. Ye Jianying said, "Our Party is a vibrant one. After this congress, there will be a group of young, energetic comrades who will take up leading posts and other leading positions within the Central Committee. This is an important symbol of the prosperity and development of the Party's cause. Our older generation of comrades is sincerely delighted to see this situation." At the same time, he quoted the poem of Tang Dynasty poet Li Shangyin, saying that "the young phoenix sings better than the old one" as a way of praising the young comrades, adding that he sincerely "hoped that the young comrades who came up to work would cooperate closely with the old comrades, shoulder heavy burdens, and go forward bravely," and later rise to the top and surpass the old comrades. He expressed hopes that the old comrades who retired would not retreat from their thoughts, but should fill their calendar in their later years with practical actions, always keeping in mind the interests of the Party and the people and continuing to do what they could.

Chen Yun analyzed the situation of the Party's cadres and expounded the significance and principles of cooperation and exchange between new and old cadres. He said, "Solving the problem of succession of cadres is an important task facing the whole Party. To solve this problem, first of all, veteran cadres should steadily withdraw from the leading group, and veteran comrades who remain in the front line for the time being should guard well in major issues, diligently pass on fine traditions, and guide the young cadres." He focused on promoting thousands of young and middle-aged cadres into leading bodies at all levels. He stressed that "thousands of promotions must be made, not just dozens or hundreds." Only in this way could the Party have enough cadres to take over the work of veteran cadres. However, "for those who rebelled with Lin Biao and Jiang Qing, those who held serious Gang of Four ideas, and those who preferred the work of beating, smashing, and robbery during the Cultural Revolution, none of them should be promoted, and those who have been promoted must be resolutely removed from the leading group." He said that on the one hand, the Party should boldly promote the younger cadres, while on the other, it should undertake a serious political examination. It should pay more attention to morality than competence, which was to say, it should truly promote those who were strong in Party spirit, had a decent style of work, and dared to adhere to principles. He believed that as long as the transfer of cadres was properly handled, the cause of the Party would definitely enjoy enduring prosperity.

On the morning of September 9, the Presidency of the General Assembly met to establish the official lists of candidates for the three committees on the basis of the results of the pre-election and adopted a draft resolution on the report of the Central Disciplinary Inspection Commission in its work. In the afternoon, delegations held group meetings to consider the list of candidates proposed by the Bureau.

From the morning of October 10 through the following day, plenary meetings were held to elect members of the Central Committee and the Central Advisory Committee. After full preparation had been made, the General Assembly democratically elected 210 members of the Central Committee and 138 alternate members to form a new Central Committee. Of the 348 central and alternate committee members, 211 were newly elected, accounting for 65% of the total, 171 were under 60 years of age, accounting for 49.1% of the total, and 122 had a college education, accounting for 35.1% of the total. In terms of knowledge and specialization, they had greatly improved when compared with the previous Central Committee. The Central Committee also preserved eight senior revolutionaries, Ye Jianying, Deng Xiaoping, Li Xiannian, Chen Yun, Xu Qianqian, Nie Rongzhen, Peng Zhen, and Deng Yingchao, who all enjoyed great prestige in China and abroad. At the same time, the new Central Advisory Committee, which had never before been established in the history of the Party, elected 172 members, all of whom were veteran comrades with over forty years of Party membership, a record of great contributions to the Party, and rich experience in leadership. One hundred thirty-three members of the Central Commission for Discipline Inspection were also elected.

The emergence of these three committees embodied Deng Xiaoping's principle of establishing three committees and further implementing the alternation of old and new cadres in the Reform of the Leadership System of the Party and the State. It provided a reliable organizational guarantee for strengthening and improving the leadership of the Party, for the long-term stability of the Party and the state, and for the realization of an overall new situation of socialist construction.

On September 11, at the close of the Twelfth National Congress, Li Xiannian delivered his closing speech. He spoke highly of Hu Yaobang's report and the new Party Constitution, as well as the achievements of the Congress. He called for extensive, in-depth publicity, learning from the spirit of the Twelfth National Congress, taking practical measures to implement them in a down-to-earth manner, and achieving its great goals systematically.

From September 12–13, the Twelfth Central Committee held its first plenary session. Hu Yaobang and Zhao Ziyang presided over the meeting. At the plenary session, Wan Li, Xi Zhongxun, Wang Zhen, Wei Guoqing, Ulanhu, Fang Yi, Deng Xiaoping, Deng Yingchao, Ye Jianying, Li Xiannian, Li Desheng, Yang Shangkun, Yang Dezhi, Yu Qiuli, Song Renqiong, Zhang Tingfa, Chen Yun, Zhao Ziyang, Hu Qiaomu, Hu Yaobang, Nie Rongjun, Ni Zhifu, Xu Qianfu, Peng Zhen, and Liao Chengzhi were elected as the Politburo. Members elected Yao Yilin, Qin Jiwei and Chen Muhua as alternate members of the Politburo of the Central Committee.

Hu Yaobang, Ye Jianying, Deng Xiaoping, Zhao Ziyang, Li Xiannian, and Chen Yun were elected members of the Standing Committee of the Central Politburo.

Hu Yaobang was elected General Secretary of the Central Committee, Wan Li, Xi Zhongxun, Deng Liqun, Yang Yong, Yu Qiuli, Gu Mu, Chen Pixian, Hu Qili, and Yao Yilin were elected Secretary of the Secretariat of the Central Committee, and Qiao Shi and Hao Jianxiu were alternate secretaries.

At the plenary session, Deng Xiaoping was selected as Chairman of the Central Military Commission, Ye Jianying, Xu Qianqian, and Nie Rongzhen as the Vice-Chairmen, and Yang Shangkun as the Standing Vice-Chairman.

The plenary approved Deng Xiaoping as the director of the Central Advisory Committee, Bo Yibo, Xu Shiyou, Tan Zhenlin, and Li Weihan as deputy directors, Wang Ping as standing member, Chen Yun as the first Secretary of the Central Discipline Inspection Committee, Huang Kecheng as the second secretary, Wang Heshou as standing secretary, Wang Congwu, Han Guang, Li Chang, Ma Guorui, and Han Tianshi as secretary, and Ma Guorui, Han Tianshi and eleven others as the Standing Committee members.

The Twelfth National Congress of the CPC was an important meeting. In the history of the Party and of socialist construction in China, it held great status as a result of the great achievements it made.

3. The Major Contributions and Historical Position of the Twelfth National Congress

The conference clearly put forward the proposition of "building socialism with Chinese characteristics." Deng Xiaoping's theory of taking the path of socialism with Chinese characteristics had great guiding significance for China's reform, opening up, and socialist modernization.

Primarily, the Twelfth National Congress successfully realized the alternation of the old and new leadership within the Party. This was one of the main topics of the Twelfth National Congress, and it aimed at addressing the problems of cadres becoming more revolutionary, younger, more knowledgeable, and more professional. From the perspective of the history of the international communist movement, the issue of the succession of the Party's top leaders had always been a major issue related to the future and destiny of the Party and the country, but it was also a problem that had not been well addressed and had included many painful lessons. The Twelfth National Congress actively and effectively explored this issue.

In addition, the General Assembly formulated and adopted a new Party Constitution. The Party Constitution was the fundamental law of the Party. All previous Party Congresses attached great importance to the revision and formulation of the Party Constitution. The Twelfth National Congress of the Party formulated a new Party Constitution with distinctive features, in order to make party building the strong core to lead the cause of socialist modernization, greatly improve the political quality of the whole Party, and enhance the fighting capacity of the Party. Its characteristics were that 1) it had a relatively substantial "general outline," which summarized the nature of the Party and its general tasks in a more complete and concise manner and made Marxist provisions for how the Party could correctly play its leading role in national life, and 2) its ideological, political, and organizational requirements for Party members and Party cadres were higher than those stipulated in previous Party Constitutions. Building on historical experience and lessons, the new Constitution stressed that organizations at all levels, from the central to the grassroots level, must strictly abide by the principles of democratic centralism and collective leadership, and clearly stipulated that "no form of personal worship shall be allowed." It made many new provisions for improving the system of the Party's central and local organizations, strengthening the Party's disciplinary and inspection organs, and strengthening the construction of the Party's grassroots organizations. The new Party Constitution adopted at the Twelfth National Congress was formulated by gathering the wisdom of the whole Party and summing up the Party's historical experience.

Further, the Twelfth National Congress enriched and developed Marxism in relation to some specific theoretical issues. On the issue of the basic characteristics of socialism, the report of the Twelfth National Congress put forward new content for socialist characteristics, namely, socialist spiritual civilization and a high degree of socialist democracy. In this way, the basic characteristics of socialism included not only productive relations and productivity, but also the superstructure and ideology, making it more comprehensive and complete. On the issue of the socialist ownership structure, the report of the Twelfth National Congress pointed out that the socialist state-owned economy occupied the leading position in the overall national economy, but it needed to coexist in many forms over a long period. On the issue of socialist planning and the socialist market, past discussions often emphasized planning while excluding the market. The Twelfth National Congress put forward the principle of giving priority to the planned economy and supplementing market regulation. Under this principle, it was important to correctly divide the scope and boundaries of mandatory planning, guiding planning, and market regulation. On the issue of class struggle in the socialist period, the report of the Twelfth National Congress pointed out that after the elimination of the exploiting class as a class, most of the contradictions in society were not in nature a class struggle. Class struggle was no longer the main contradiction in Chinese society, but class struggle could continue to exist within a certain range of Chinese society for a long time and could even intensify under certain circumstances. In addition, the report of the Twelfth National Congress also made new statements on the construction of spiritual civilization and the Party. These new understandings enriched and developed the treasures of Marxist theory.

Finally, the Twelfth National Congress of the CPC scientifically summarized the historical experience of the Party. Based on the actual situation within China, it formulated the grand goal of creating a new situation of socialist construction and a series of more complete and correct policies, principles, and measures. It put forward the general task and line of the Party for the new historical period, combining economic construction, political construction, and ideological and cultural construction so that they could occur simultaneously. With the goal of building socialism, this was put forward for the first time in the history of socialist construction in China, and it was also a first in the international communist movement. The Twelfth National Congress thoroughly opened up a new phase of socialist modernization in China. After the Twelfth National Congress, China's Reform and Opening Up and drive toward socialist modernization entered a period of vigorous development.

II

Formulation of the Program for Economic Restructuring and the Reform and Opening Up in Full Swing

With the advancement of rural and urban economic reform, the substance of the reform greatly exceeded the scope of developing commodity production and commodity exchange as originally envisaged. The orientation of developing the commodity economy and market regulation had become more obvious. It further touched on the core of the directive planning system of the planned economy. Some deeper contradictions and problems were exposed, leading to fierce disputes. The focus of the debate was whether China's current economy was a commodity economy, and whether it was necessary to establish an economic system compatible with the commodity economy.

1. Conflict Over the Theory of the Socialist Commodity Economy

At that time, quite a number of people believed that the socialist economy was a planned economy, not a commodity economy. Since it was a planned economy, the economic system should also be compatible with a planned economy. Of course, this opinion could easily occupy the moral high ground, because in many people's eyes, there had been a lot of discussion in the classical works of Marxism. Quoting "the old ancestors," would arm the speaker with sharp theoretical weapons, and the idea that socialism was a commodity economy could be easily refuted.

However, before and after the Third Plenary Session of the Eleventh Central Committee, many economists adhered to the concept of the commodity economy. As early as 1959, Wang Xuewen and Qi Qi jointly published an article in *Economic Research*, putting forward the idea of the "planned development of the commodity economy." After the Third Plenary Session of the Eleventh Central Committee, Zhuo Jiong, an economist of the old generation in Guangdong, wrote an article in the spring of 1979, unambiguously putting forward that it was necessary to eliminate the product economy and develop the commodity economy. In that same year, at a seminar on the law of socialist economic value held in Wuxi, Professor Hu Zhaopei of Xiamen University also explicitly put forward the view that the "socialist economy is a planned commodity economy on the basis of public ownership." In 1979, Deng Liqun, Vice President of the Chinese Academy of Social Sciences, published an article in the 11th issue of the *Financial and Trade Economy*, advocating that the socialist economy at this stage was a commodity economy.

In October 1979, the Preliminary Opinions on the Overall Conception of Economic System Reform issued by the Reform Group of the Financial and Economic Committee of the State Council stated clearly that the socialist economy at that stage in China was a commodity economy with public ownership of the means of production and coexistence of various economic components. It was necessary, then, to establish an appropriate economic system. Although two attributives were added to this passage, the objective of the reform was clearly to establish an economic system that was compatible with the commodity economy. According to Professor Yang Qixian, who participated in drafting the Opinions, this part was added by Xue Muqiao.

During this period, Chen Yun was also considering how to reform the planned economic system. In March 1979, he concluded in the outline of his research on Planning and Market Issues that "in the past 60 years, the main demerits of the planned work system in both the Soviet Union and China include focus only on the 'planned and proportionate' economy, but not the 'market regulation' under the socialist system. Market regulation refers to the regulation according to the law of value. In some aspects of economic life, it can be regulated by means of 'non-interference by the government' or 'blind' production." This was the earliest written expression proposed by the Party on the role of market regulation under the planned economic system. Throughout the 1980s, the relationship and proportion between plan and market remained part of the mainstream discourse within the Party and theoretical circles. In 1981, Chen Yun summarized this statement as the "planned economy is the main factor, and market regulation is the supplement."

Economic, ideological, and theoretical circles had been debating whether China should opt for a planned or commodity economy, but since 1982, the situation had changed dramatically. In early May of that year, the State Economic Reform Office (which was changed into the Commission for Economic Reform in 1983) and the Economic Center of the State Council jointly held a large-scale seminar to discuss theoretical issues related to economic reform. The seminar was divided into eight groups with more than 200 participants. The main theme of the seminar was to affirm the planned economy, which was regarded as the socialist economic system. Some scholars pointed out that the commodity economy was a theoretical summary of real life, while commodity production and commodity exchange were the basic content of the commodity economy, and there was no essential difference. However, the dominant view was that there was commodity production and commodity exchange in a socialist society, which could not be viewed as a commodity economy.

Because no new progress had been made in theory, the Twelfth National Congress of the Communist Party of China, held in September 1982, emphasized the principle that a "planned economy is the main factor, and market regulation is the supplement," pointing out that "China implements the planned economy on the basis of public ownership. Planned production and circulation are the main body of China's national economy... We must carry out plans for the production and distribution of the means of production and consumption related to the national economy and people's livelihood in the state-owned economy, and especially for the backbone enterprises related to the overall economic situation... For the collective ownership economy, some directive indicators should also be issued according to needs."

The Twelfth National Congress affirmed that China still implemented a planned economy and should implement mandatory plans and indicators, which was an inevitable stage in understanding and "crossing the river by testing the stones" in the early stage of China's reform. In this case, the theory of the commodity economy naturally fell into an awkward position. In 1982 and 1983, the criticism of the notions of a "socialist commodity economy" and a "planned commodity economy" in newspapers became increasingly heated. Some scholars believed that "a basic feature of the socialist economy should be a planned economy, not a commodity economy [...] The foothold of a planned commodity economy is still a commodity economy. If the planned economy is abstracted and no longer exists, where does the 'plan' come from?" Others believed that if China generalized its economy as a commodity economy, the essential difference between a socialist and capitalist economy would be blurred. "The essential feature of a socialist economy can only be that of a planned economy... To reduce the socialist economy to a commodity economy is, of course, only a historical retrogression. In fact, if there is no planned economy, there will be no socialism. Of course, some scholars believe that it is correct to regard the existence of mandatory plans as an important symbol of differentiating the socialist planned economy from a capitalist market economy."

For a time, newspapers and public opinion were full of severe criticism of the "commodity economy theory." Xue Muqiao, who advocated the theory of the commodity economy, was even criticized as having bad roots as an intellectual. After this fierce criticism, Xue Muqiao finally made a concession, pointing out that "the most important feature of the socialist economy is not the commodity economy, but a planned economy based on the public ownership of the means of production and the existence of commodity production and exchange."

On September 6, 1982, Liu Guoguang, an economist of the Chinese Academy of Social Sciences, published an article entitled "Adhering to the Basic Direction of Economic System Reform" in the *People's Daily*, emphasizing the importance of guiding plans and reducing the scope of mandatory plans. On September 21, the *People's Daily*, in the name of its commentator, published a long article on the front page, criticizing Liu Guoguang without naming him.

The article repeatedly emphasized the importance of mandatory plans, that "market utilization is not equal to market regulation," and that "mandatory plans are not only necessary under the specific circumstances in which the national economy is being adjusted, but also for the production and distribution of products related to the national economy and the people's livelihood, as well as for the backbone enterprises related to the operation of the economy under general conditions." It was necessary, and was in fact the key to the principle that the planned economy be the dominant one and market regulation the supplementary one. Liu Guoguang's article was sent to the *People's Daily* before the Twelfth National Congress of the Communist Party of China and was published just before the event, contradicting the spirit of the political report of the Twelfth National Congress. From the autumn of 1982 to 1983, the forces defending the mandatory plan were quite strong. Deng Liqun, who wrote an article in 1979 advocating the commodity economy, also stood among the ranks of those criticized.

In fact, an important reason for such high-profile criticism of the commodity economy in 1982 and 1983 was a macro-interpretation of China's economy after the Twelfth National Congress, that is, the relationship between market regulation and the planned economy, just like the relationship between birds and cages. That is, if birds are an invigoration of the economy, cages are national plans. It was important to enliven the economy and market regulation, which could only play a role within the scope permitted by the plan and could not be divorced from the guidance of the plan. This was tantamount to saying that the ongoing reform of state-owned enterprises was a "change in the cage." Another piece of the political background was the fight against "mental pollution" in 1983. At that time, some people criticized the idea of the commodity economy as a target of "spiritual pollution." Fortunately, this deviation was quickly corrected by the Central Government. The process of China's reform always opened up a new realm of "another village with bright flowers and dark willows." At the climax of the criticism of the commodity economy, new changes were brewing.

2. Divergences and Breakthroughs in the Reform of the Planning Management System

In 1983, the Central Committee of the Communist Party of China and the State Council prepared to promote an "initial macro-reform" strategy. Where was the entry point for initial macro-reform? It was the "directive planning system" of the product planned economy system, that is, the planned management system. The planned management system controlled the overall situation of the planned economy system. Before anything else, then, the reform of the planned management system was the entry point for promoting the initial macro-reform strategy from an overall perspective.

From August to December 1983, under the leadership of the Secretariat of the Central Committee of the Communist Party of China, a leading group on the reform of the planned management system was set up, with a working group on the reform of the planned management system. The main members of the working group were from the State Planning Commission and the State Council's System Reform Office, which was located in the South District Security Building in Zhongnanhai. The task of the Working Group on the Reform of the Planning and Management System was to propose plans for reform. This work lasted from August to December 1983. Because there were different opinions in the discussion, and there was a great gap between them, most of the time was spent debating these issues, which were represented by two main opinions.

The first opinion was that state-owned enterprises should expand their autonomy in production and operation, expand the scope of market regulation, and implement the principle that enterprises bear their own profits and losses. This would narrow the scope of the mandatory plan, and correspondingly narrow the scope of national pricing products.

The second opinion mainly emphasized two points. 1) Mandatory plans should be implemented for all important products related to the national economy, whether they were in shortage or surplus. The scope of mandatory plans could and should not be narrowed. 2) State-owned enterprises could not implement a system of self-responsibility for profits and losses, nor could they implement the relative system of self-responsibility for profits and losses, since state-owned enterprises were reluctant to accept low-cost directive production plans and product allocation plans because of their own profit and loss system.

The debate was intense and deep. Wang Zhuo, an economist who participated in the discussion, recalled several things that happened during the discussion. The first one was that Rezső Nyers, known as the father of Hungarian reform, visited China. When he visited the State Planning Commission, some members of the Commission asked him whether Hungary had really cancelled the mandatory plan. Some of the people present clearly expressed doubts about this. When Nyers visited the Ministry of Material and other ministries, some work units raised similar questions, expressing doubts about the cancellation of Hungary's mandatory plan. Nyers was deeply puzzled about this. When he arrived at the State Council's reform office, he asked why some ministries and commissions in China believed that Hungary had abolished the reform of its mandatory plan. He found it disappointing that they thought so. This showed that the central ministries and commissions at that time generally disagreed with the reform of diminishing the mandatory plan, and even less with the reform of canceling the mandatory plan.

The second was that at a briefing attended by leading comrades from various ministries and commissions, some people named Wang Zhuo as the one promoting the argument of commodity production in the discussion. At that time, whoever advocated the development of commodity production was regarded as a heretic. Wang Zhuo was ready to speak in response. Liao Jili, a reformer of the State Council, immediately protected Wang, saying that this was not the case, so he blocked the other member's aggressive opinions, and there was no need for Wang to speak further.

A third issue was that at the same meeting, a well-known economist spoke disapprovingly of reforms that narrowed the scope of mandatory plans. After the meeting, some comrades began to criticize him as a reformer on paper. When the political trend changed, they immediately changed their original arguments.

Further, several different opinions originally discussed in the Working Group on the Reform of the Planning and Management System later became known to Party members outside the meeting. Accordingly, some people in the Policy Research Office of the Central Committee of the Communist Party of China wrote letters to the leading comrades of the Central Committee of the Party, saying that some people were again stirring up controversy over the mandatory plan. This was originally a dispute between right and wrong in reform issues, but it was painted with a political color, resulting in the failure of this useful debate to achieve the desired results.

After several months of work, the Working Group on the Reform of the Planning and Management System finally produced a compromise between the two opinions. After the meeting, it was revised many times and no reasonable documents were formed. However, the macro-reform strategy had not failed, and the "big debate" had not ended. In 1984, this systematic project of China's reform continued, making breakthroughs and major achievements. This was the Decision of the Central Committee of the Communist Party of China on Economic System Reform adopted by the Third Plenary Session of the Twelfth Central Committee of the Communist Party of China on October 20, 1984. This decision recognized for the first time that China had a planned commodity economy.

3. Drafting and Adoption of the Decision of the Central Committee of the Communist Party of China on Economic System Reform

The members of the drafting group of the Decision of the Central Committee of the Communist Party of China on Economic System Reform were from the drafting group of the work report of the Sixth National People's Congress

Government, including Yuan Mu, Gao Shanquan, Gui Shifu, Wang Ninzhi, Xie Minggan, and Yang Qixian. At first, Yuan Mu was in charge of preparing the outline. This outline had been discussed many times, but it always failed to escape the confines of the idea that the planned economy was primary and market regulation was the supplement. At this time, some believed that in order to get out of this cycle, a breakthrough must be made in the issue of the commodity economy. That is to say, the target mode of reform needed to be changed from the idea that the planned economy was primary, supplemented by market regulation, to the notion of a planned commodity economy. However, the views of the drafting group on this issue were very different.

In July and August 1984, the Central Committee of the CPC met in Beidaihe. Under the chairmanship of Hu Yaobang, the drafting group twice discussed the outline. Not satisfied with the outline, Hu repeatedly stressed that this was a historic document that must be well written. He also said that Zhao Ziyang should listen to his views on economic issues and put forward the idea of developing various economic components. Hu strengthened the drafting group, adding Lin Jianqing, Lin Zili, Gong Yuzhi, and Zheng Bijian to it. Yuan Mu was replaced by Lin Jianqing as the person in charge.

After returning to Beijing's Yuquan Mountain from Beidaihe, Hu Yaobang and Zhao Ziyang both went up to the mountain to chair the discussion. When talking about the relationship between planning and market, Zhao Ziyang said, "I tend to write about the planned commodity economy." During this period, many people made suggestions to Zhao Ziyang. For example, in August, more than a dozen economists, such as Dong Fureng, Tong Dalin, and Yu Guangyuan, held a meeting in Beijing's Baiwan Village to insist on the formulation of the planned commodity economy. They wrote a conference briefing for Zhao Ziyang stating their reasons. It was evident that Zhao Ziyang initially established the concept of the planned commodity economy and listened to various opinions.

Zhao Ziyang twice convened a drafting group to discuss it in Zhongnanhai. During the last discussion, Deng Liqun was invited to join the members of the drafting group. Zhao Ziyang asked everyone, "Is there any problem in theory?" Yang Qixian replied, "In theory, it can stand." Zhao Ziyang asked, "Is there any contradiction with the Constitution?" Zheng Bijian replied, "There is no contradiction. The Constitution does not stipulate that the planned economy is primary and market regulation is the supplement." Zhao Ziyang announced that the meeting was over. As everyone stood up to leave, Zhao asked Deng Liqun, "Mr. Deng, what do you think?" Deng Liqun replied, "That's what I said in 1979." This is one of history's many intriguing details.

On September 9, Zhao Ziyang wrote to Hu Yaobang, Deng Xiaoping, Li Xiannian, and Chen Yun, suggesting that China's economic system should be summarized as follows:

1) China's planned economy is not a market economy.
2) The spontaneous and blind regulation of production and exchange through the market is limited to small commodities, three types of agricultural by-products, and service repair industries, which play a supporting role in the entire national economy.
3) The planned economy is not equal to a mandatory plan. Directive plan and mandatory plan are both concrete forms of a planned economy. For now and quite a long time in the future, China's policy should be to gradually narrow down the mandatory plan and expand the guiding plan.
4) Directive plans are mainly regulated by economic means. Directive plans must also consider the role of economic laws, especially the law of value. The socialist economy is a planned commodity economy based on public ownership. Planning should be realized through the law of value, and the law of value should be used to serve the plan. The expression "plan first, law of value second" is not exact and should not be used in the future.

Zhao Ziyang's letter was quickly endorsed by four Standing Committees of the Politburo. On September 11, the Central Committee convened about 1,500 people to discuss the draft for comments, including members of the Beijing Central Committee, alternate members, members of the Chinese Customs Commission, members of the Central Discipline Commission, leading comrades of various departments of the Central Committee, responsible comrades of provinces, municipalities, and major military regions, and heads of 26 major enterprises. Through discussion, participants strengthened their understanding of the necessity and urgency of economic restructuring, especially urban restructuring. They agreed to include the planned commodity economy in the Decision of the Central Committee of the Communist Party of China on Economic restructuring (hereinafter referred to as the "Decision") at the Third Plenary Session of the

Twelfth Central Committee. At the same time, the title of the fourth part of the manuscript, "Reforming the Planned System and Consciously Applying the Law of Value," was changed to "Consciously Applying the Planned System of the Law of Value to Develop the Socialist Commodity Economy."

"But the decision to write it in does not mean that everyone has thought through it," Yang Qixian said. Because of the controversy, the evening before the formal writing of the Decision, he added, "But under socialist conditions, labor, banks, land, and mines are not commodities." In fact, this meant that the commodity economy was limited to the production of products, not including the factors of production, and was thus not a complete commodity economy system.

The decision on reform of the economic system adopted at the Third Plenary Session of the Twelfth Central Committee clarified the necessity and urgency of speeding up the reform of the whole economic system focusing on cities and stipulated the direction, nature, tasks, and basic principles and policies of the reform.

The most outstanding contribution of this Decision was to break through the traditional concept of opposing the planned economy and the commodity economy, confirming that China's socialist economy was a planned commodity economy on the basis of public ownership, that it was the self-improvement and development of the socialist system, and that the basic task of reform was to further implement the policy of invigorating the economy at home and implementing it abroad. The policy of opening up would gradually establish a socialist economic system with Chinese characteristics, full of vigor and vitality, and promote the development of social productive forces.

Focusing on the basic task of reform, the Decision clearly pointed out the main problems to be addressed, namely, the establishment of a vibrant socialist economic system, the enhancement of the vitality of enterprises as the central link of economic system reform, the establishment of a planning system that consciously applied the law of value to develop the socialist commodity economy, the establishment of a reasonable price system and giving full attention to the role of economic leverage, the implementation of the separation of responsibilities between the government and enterprises and giving proper play to the functions of government agencies in managing the economy, the establishment of various forms of economic responsibility systems and earnest implementation of the principle of distribution according to work, active development of various economic forms to further expand economic and technological exchanges abroad and at home, employment of a new generation of people to create a large contingent of socialist economic management cadres, and the strengthening of the leadership of the Party and ensuring that reform proceeded smoothly.

This Decision clarified a series of basic issues such as the direction, tasks, and requirements of China's reform. It was a programmatic document guiding China to carry out comprehensive reform of its economic system. Although it had not yet raised the issue of establishing a socialist market economic system in terms of its reform objectives, the proposal of planned commodity economic objectives on the basis of public ownership had contained a clear market orientation, which was a major breakthrough in socialist economic theory. Deng Xiaoping gave it a high appraisal, believing that it was a political economy that combined the basic principles of Marxism with the practice of socialism in China.[1]

In practice, it had been proven that the publication and implementation of the Third Plenary Session of the Twelfth Central Committee's Decision on Economic System Reform was another step in emancipating of the minds of cadres and the masses. After this plenary session, the economic reform focusing on cities began to focus on expanding the autonomy of enterprises, carrying out a pilot joint-stock system, reforming ownership structure, changing the employment system, and implementing the director's responsibility system.

III

Clarification of the Theme of the Times and Development of External Relations

After the Third Plenary Session of the Eleventh Central Committee, when the Party and the state shifted the focus of their work to the construction of socialist modernization centered on economic construction, while diplomatic work and other similar work served as the center of economic construction and the focus of socialist modernization construction. In order to meet this need, the Party and the state adjusted their diplomatic strategies.

1. Adjustment of International Strategies and Diplomatic Guidelines

In centering economic construction, it was necessary to have good external conditions. That is to say, a peaceful international environment was essential to economic construction. However, determining how to create a peaceful international environment was a question restricted by many factors. Deciding how to correctly analyze and estimate the international situation and adopt correct foreign strategies and policies was one of the most important aspects of the work at that time.

1) *Preliminary adjustment of Chinese leaders' understanding of war and peace.* When New China was founded, in order to resist and break the hostility, isolation, and blockade of the United States, the Chinese government adopted a "preferential" foreign policy and allied with the Soviet Union. This was necessary in the international environment at that time. In the late 1950s, the Soviet Union pursued a chauvinism typical of great powers, forcing China to accept claims that undermined China's sovereignty and exerting political, economic, and military pressure, which led to the rapid deterioration of Sino-Soviet relations. By the 1970s, the United States, one of the two superpowers at the time, had contracted strategically due to its weakening in the Vietnam War, while the Soviet Union, which was in the stage of strengthening its military power, had taken the opportunity to expand dramatically, seriously threatening world peace and China's security. In this international situation, the Chinese government has adjusted its foreign policy, adopted a "one-side line" and implemented the diplomatic strategy of uniting with the United States and resisting the Soviet Union. Implementing this strategy not only effectively safeguarded China's own security, but also greatly curbed the momentum of the global expansion of the Soviet Union.

After the end of the Cultural Revolution, deciding how to analyze and judge the international situation and formulate foreign strategies and policies on this basis had become a major issue in China's foreign relations. In December 1977, the Central Military Commission convened a meeting. Hua Guofeng, Chairman of the Central Committee of the Communist Party of China, made a speech on the international situation, especially on the issue of war and peace. He believed that because imperialist and social imperialist systems in themselves brewed war, the Soviet Union and the United States would eventually fight for hegemony.

Therefore, another world war was inevitable, and sooner or later it would break out. It was important to seize the opportunity and make appropriate preparations. However, compared with the world war caused by the US-Soviet hegemony, the biggest threat to China's security was in fact the war of aggression launched by the Soviet Union. Because the Soviet Union's revisionists aimed ultimately to destroy China, they were its main and most dangerous enemy. In this regard, China needed to make adequate and sufficient evaluations and find a foothold for the preparation for a Soviet attack on it, even for a swift, sudden attack. China needed to prepare for the worst situation and not take any chances. The veteran comrades present at the meeting should prepare for another big war in their lifetime.[2] To a certain extent, this understanding represented the views of the Chinese leaders at that time. Such an understanding demonstrated that the sense that the crisis of war, especially the war of aggression against the Soviet Union against China, was inevitable and imminent.

Despite the fact that the world war and the Soviet invasion of China seemed inevitable and imminent, Chinese leaders needed to strive to postpone the war and gain time in order to build up their national defense forces. There were certain favorable conditions for delaying the outbreak of war, including Mao Zedong's theory of delineating the three worlds and his revolutionary diplomatic line and the thorough treatment of the international anti-hegemonic united front they provided. In addition, the Soviet Union's revisionists' global strategy was not yet mature. After the failure of the United States in Southeast Asia, their global strategy was defensive and world war was not imminent. This meant that China could gain some time to delay the outbreak of war. However, it was difficult to determine how long it would take to delay the outbreak of war, considering the severe estimation of the danger of war. There was a great possibility of five or more years without fighting, or only two, three, or four years. In any case, it was important to make thorough preparations before the outbreak of war.[3] However, before the outbreak of war, China had to make use of peacetime to rapidly build up a strong economic force and national defense. To do so at low or medium speed would not suffice. It had to be high speed.[4]

At the beginning of 1980, these basic estimates of the international situation remained unchanged. China still believed that the contradictions in the world would continue to develop, the international situation would become more turbulent, and factors leading to war would continue to grow. However, in view of the international political reality that war had not yet erupted and the domestic political reality that China had not yet prepared for war, Chinese leaders still hoped to postpone the arrival of the war as far as possible. Deng Xiaoping suggested that "we may strive for more time not to fight" and "we can strive to delay the outbreak of war."[5] He added, "It is good for us to strive for a longer period of time, for the modernization of our army, for the improvement of our combat effectiveness and for our preparations for war."[6] At this time, while insisting that "large-scale world war is inevitable," it seemed to have begun to alleviate the high sense of urgency regarding an "imminent" world war.

Since then, however, Chinese leaders' views on war and peace had gradually begun to adjust with the development of the international situation. On January 16, 1980, Deng Xiaoping said at the meeting of cadres of the Central Committee of the Communist Party, "We are confident that if the struggle against hegemony is well carried out, we can delay the outbreak of war and strive for a longer period of peace."[7] He also proposed the view that the US-Soviet strategic deployment should be disrupted through the struggle against hegemony in order to delay the outbreak of war. Deng's sense of the imminent crisis of war was further alleviated and his confidence in long-term peace further strengthened. As the judgment of the danger of war eased, Deng extended the period of postponing war and striving for peace proposed a few years earlier from five years or less to ten years or even twenty years. When he met with World Bank President McNamara in April 1980, he said that it seemed there were still some storms in the world that needed to be weathered, and China needed to look ahead and take effective measures. The dangers of the 1980s could be overcome and it was possible to strive for a peaceful environment for twenty years. China needed a long-term peaceful environment for development.[8] Although the international situation was not stable at that time, especially after the Soviet invasion of Afghanistan at the end of 1979, the international situation was more turbulent. However, Deng continuously prolonged the period of peace he could strive for, demonstrating that his views of the world situation and war and peace had undergone a more obvious, essential change. He had begun to shift his focus from highlighting the dangers of war to striving for longer periods of peace, and emphasized that China should seize this time of peace to develop its economy rather than prepare for war.

2) *A new summary of the theme of the world era.* With major changes in its relations with several major powers, China soon noticed the positive role of

such changes. At the end of 1970s, the international situation was still quite turbulent, and at the end of 1979, the Soviets invaded Afghanistan. In view of this international situation, the standpoint of China's foreign relations was "to strive for more time without war," "to delay the outbreak of war,"[9] and "to seize time" for construction.

After the establishment of diplomatic relations between China and the United States, China strengthened the "one-line" strategy of uniting with the United States and resisting the Soviet Union. This was not only for the sake of national security, but also for the need to accelerate opening up. However, there were always some obstacles to the normal development of Sino-US relations, the most important of which was the Taiwan issue. Shortly after the establishment of diplomatic relations between China and the United States, the US Congress passed the Taiwan Relations Act, damaging Sino-US relations. On August 17, 1982, Sino-US relations basically stabilized when the two governments issued a joint communiqué on a systematic solution to the issue of arms sales from the United States to Taiwan, but the US government later failed to live up to its promises. This being the case, China began to distance itself from the United States.

In 1982, given the need to strive for peace, postpone war, and seek more balanced foreign relations, the Chinese government began to take the opposition to hegemony, the maintenance of world peace and the strengthening of solidarity, and cooperation with the third world as its basic foreign policy in the new era. As for the implementation of such a policy, Deng Xiaoping emphasized, "Our proposal to safeguard world peace is not empty talk, but is based on our own needs, which clearly meets the needs of the people of the world, especially those of the third world. Therefore, opposing hegemony and safeguarding world peace are our real policies and the guiding principles of our foreign policy."[10]

In September of the same year, Hu Yaobang also stated publicly in his report to the Twelfth National Congress, "China adheres to an independent foreign policy and develops relations with other countries under the guidance of the Five Principles of Peaceful Coexistence." By the mid-1980s, the international situation had apparently eased. Not only had US-Soviet relations improved, but Sino-Soviet relations had loosened. According to this new change in the international situation, in May 1984, Deng Xiaoping explicitly suggested that the "peace issue" and "north-south issue" had become the two prominent issues in the world. On

March 4, 1985, when he met with Japanese guests, he further made the judgment that peace and development were the two major issues in the contemporary world. He said, "The real major problem in the world today is a global strategic one. One is peace, the other is the economy or development. Peace is a matter of East and West, and development is a matter of North and South. Generally speaking, it can be summarized in the four words north, south, east, and west." The theme of the era of peace and development laid an important cognitive foundation for the transformation of diplomatic strategy in the new era.

3) *Re-establishing an independent foreign policy.* On September 1, 1982, Deng Xiaoping solemnly declared in his opening speech to the Twelfth National Congress that independence and self-reliance were China's footholds in the past, present, and future. The Chinese people cherished their friendship and cooperation with other countries and people, and cherished even more their right to independence through long-term struggle. No foreign country should expect China to be its vassal or to swallow the bitter fruits that harmed its interests.

Obviously, Deng Xiaoping's remark was aimed at the changes in Sino-US relations in the previous period, demonstrating the solemn position of the Chinese government and announcing the change of its diplomatic strategy.

Deng Xiaoping also pointed out in his speech that the three major tasks of the Chinese people in the 1980s were to intensify the socialist modernization drive, strive for the reunification of the motherland, including Taiwan, and oppose hegemony and safeguard world peace. Among these three tasks, the core was economic construction, which was the basis for settling international and domestic problems.

Deng's speech clearly pointed out that the goal of China's diplomatic strategy was to create a positive international environment for China's domestic drive toward socialist modernization, which embodied the principle of diplomatic work serving as the center of economic construction.

In his political report to the Twelfth National Congress, Hu Yaobang, General Secretary of the Central Committee of the Communist Party of China, comprehensively expounded China's adherence to independent foreign policy. He declared, "China will never be dependent on any big country or group of countries, nor will it yield to the pressure of any big country [...] The Five Principles of Peaceful Coexistence apply to our relations with all countries, including socialist countries."

Independence and peaceful coexistence were the foreign policies that New China had been implementing since its establishment. However, from the 1950s to the end of the 1970s, due to the limitations of the international environment and historical conditions at that time, during the implementation of the strategy of "one-side" and "one-line," there was a tendency of "drawing lines with the United States" and "drawing lines with the Soviet Union," which to some extent affected the implementation of the foreign policy of independence and peaceful coexistence, while in the diplomatic work, it affected China's foreign policy with countries that had friendly relations with the United States or with the Soviet Union.

After the 1980s, Deng Xiaoping added new connotations to the foreign policy of independence and peaceful coexistence, based on China's long-standing diplomatic experience and new changes in the international situation. Among these, the new connotation of independence and autonomy was "non-alignment" and did not depend on any big country or group of countries. The new connotation of the principle of peaceful coexistence was the relationship between countries and did not alienate other nations according to the similarities and differences in social system and ideology. Regardless of the similarities and differences in social system and ideology, state-to-state relations were to be based on the five principles of peaceful coexistence. Deng Xiaoping believed that dividing the front and deciding on affinity and alienation based on the social system or ideology was not reliable. Only by transcending the similarities and differences of social system and ideology and universally implementing the five principles of peaceful coexistence could normal state-to-state relations be developed, international cooperation be enhanced, and world peace be maintained. China adhered to the independent foreign policy of non-alignment and universally implemented the principle of peaceful coexistence, which was widely praised and supported by the international community.

China regarded the maintenance of world peace and the promotion of human progress and development as its fundamental objectives in its diplomatic work. To maintain world peace, it was necessary to first stop the arms race and implement genuine disarmament. To this end, the Chinese government changed some of its past views and practices on disarmament issues, participated actively in various international disarmament activities, and put forward many new proposals and propositions on this issue. For example, the goal of disarmament should be the complete prohibition and thorough destruction of nuclear weapons. The United States and the Soviet Union, which had the largest nuclear arsenals in the world, needed to take the lead in stopping the testing, production, and deployment of all types of nuclear weapons and drastically reduce all types of nuclear weapons in their respective regions at home and abroad.

In order to prevent an outbreak of nuclear war, the Chinese government also proposed that all states that owned nuclear weapons should take up the obligation to commit to never being the first to use nuclear weapons under any circumstances, especially not to use or threaten to use them against non-nuclear countries or non-nuclear areas. On this basis, an international convention to which all states with nuclear capabilities were parties should be held to ensure the prohibition of the use of nuclear weapons. While nuclear disarmament was being carried out, conventional arms should likewise be substantially reduced, and no country should develop, test, or deploy space weapons in any way. An international convention for the complete prohibition and thorough destruction of chemical weapons should be concluded at an early date, and in order to ensure the implementation of disarmament, disarmament agreements must provide for necessary and effective verification measures.

Considering that the issue of disarmament concerned the security interests of all the world's nations, the Chinese government also proposed that disarmament should not be monopolized by a few major powers and that disarmament agreements between them should not harm the interests of other countries. All countries in the world, regardless of size or military strength, should enjoy the equal right to participate in the discussion and resolution of disarmament-related issues and achieve effective disarmament in accordance with the principles of fairness, rationality, comprehensiveness, and balance.

In addition to these fair and reasonable proposals, the Chinese government also took a series of practical actions on disarmament issues. For example, in 1985, the number of military posts would be reduced by 1 million, military production would be converted to civilian production, and a large number of military facilities would be converted to civilian or military-civilian sharing. At the same time, a large number of defense expenditures had been cut. By the early 1990s, the proportion China's military expenditure made of its GDP was the lowest in the world. The Chinese government's reasonable proposals and practical actions on arms reduction won universal welcome and praise from the international community.

Deng Xiaoping's international strategic thought and diplomatic theory proposed in the new era and the adjustment of the Chinese government's foreign policy and principles made China's independent and peaceful foreign policy more rational and created a new situation for China's diplomatic work, thus contributing to China's socialist modernization, maintaining world peace, developing friendly cooperation with other countries, and promoting common prosperity. It played an important role and made great contributions to world peace.

2. Developing Friendly, Peaceful, Relations Between Major Powers

While Chinese leaders' views about the issue of war and peace were changing, the relationship between China and several major powers was changing as well.

1) *The sound development of Sino-Japanese relations.* In October 1978, after the conclusion of the Treaty of Peace and Friendship between China and Japan, bilateral relations in the fields of politics, economy, science, technology, and culture gained a good development momentum. In December 1979, Japanese Prime Minister Masayoshi Ōhira officially visited China. During this visit, both sides agreed that although the systems of China and Japan were different, in order to deepen mutual understanding and trust, it was necessary to further strengthen intergovernmental dialogue and promote exchanges at all levels between the two countries. During this visit, the leaders of the two countries focused on the issue of economic cooperation between China and Japan. They agreed that it was desirable for China and Japan to further cooperate in the fields of resources and energy. The two sides reached agreements on Sino-Japanese cooperation in exploration and exploitation of oil in the Bohai Sea and in the development of coal and other resources. From 1979 to 1983, Japan would provide 330 billion yen ($1.5 billion) in loans from the Overseas Economic Cooperation Fund for construction projects such as Qinhuangdao Port, Shijiusuo Port, Beijing-Qinhuangdao Railway, and Yanshi Railway. From April 1980, Japan would offer Chinese products preferential tariff treatment. During Ohira's visit, the two sides also signed an agreement on cultural exchange. Sino-Japanese economic cooperation was greatly advanced with Ohira's visit.

In 1982, on the 10th anniversary of the normalization of diplomatic relations between China and Japan, Premier Zhao Ziyang of the Chinese government and Prime Minister Zenko Suzuki of Japan exchanged visits. During his visit to Japan at the end of May and the beginning of June 1982, Zhao Ziyang put forward three principles for developing Sino-Japanese relations. First, based on the Sino-Japanese Joint Statement and the Sino-Japanese Treaty of Peace and Friendship, it was important to actively develop economic relations between the two countries on the basis of existing friendly, peaceful relations. Second, Sino-Japanese economic relations should follow the principle of equality and mutual benefit, taking into account their respective needs and capabilities. Third, developing such economic relations was in line with the fundamental interests of the Chinese and Japanese people and the desire of friendship across many generations. It should be long-term, stable, and free from the influence of international turbulence. The three principles of Sino-Japanese relations proposed by China received positive responses from Prime Minister Suzuki and the Japanese government. In September of that year, Prime Minister Suzuki returned to China. Deng Xiaoping told Prime Minister Suzuki that, in a nutshell, resumption of Sino-Japanese relations meant that the two peoples would continue to be friendly from generation to generation, which was in line with China's national policy.

In November 1983, General Secretary Hu Yaobang visited Japan. Prime Minister Nakasone Yasuhiro proposed to add a principle to Sino-Japanese relations, adding to the original three principles of "peace and friendship, equality and mutual benefit, long-term stability," the idea of "mutual trust." Hu Yaobang agreed. According to the agreement between the two sides during this visit, the China-Japan Friendship Committee for the 21st Century was established in 1984, with the participation of representatives from all walks of life in China and Japan. That same year, 3,000 young Japanese visited China. The following year, 500 young people from China visited Japan.

In March 1984, Prime Minister Nakasone Yasuhiro visited China. In April 1985, Chairman Peng Zhen visited Japan. The exchange of visits between the leaders of the two countries made positive contributions to the establishment of the four principles of Sino-Japanese relations and the establishment of long-term, stable Sino-Japanese friendly, cooperative relations. During this period, exchanges and cooperation between China and Japan in the fields of economy, culture, science, and technology were more active. By 1989, the total trade volume between China and Japan had reached 18.9 billion US dollars, 2.7 times the total trade volume in 1979, making Japan China's second largest trading partner, ahead of the United States. The two countries made progress in financial cooperation and technology transfer. During his visit to China in December 1979, Prime Minister Yokohama Ohira officially announced that the Japanese government had cooperated in financing six large-scale projects proposed by China and decided to provide China with the first batch of low-interest government loans of 50 billion yuan in 1979, with an annual interest rate of 3%, a repayment period of 30 years, and a 10-year moratorium. This was called government development assistance, or official development aid (ODA). In 1984, 470 billion yen ($2.1 billion) was provided for the second batch of low-interest loans. In December 1984, Japan agreed to provide China with a second batch of energy development loans of about $2.4 billion. In 1988, Japan put forward the third batch of low-interest loans of 810 billion yen, mainly for 42 key projects during the Eighth Five-Year Plan period. New progress was also made in the joint development of offshore oil fields between China and Japan. The two sides signed five contracts with a total investment of US$800 million. In order to promote and guarantee the smooth development of economic cooperation between the two countries, the two governments signed an agreement to avoid double taxation between China and Japan in 1983.[11] The increasingly close economic cooperation between China and Japan effectively promoted their respective economic development and brought great benefits to both sides.

Admittedly, while China and Japan had made good progress in their relations, there were also problems. For example, in 1979 and 1980, Japan violated China's sovereignty on the Diaoyu Island issue, and in the spring of 1982, there was a "textbook incident." At that time, when examining the textbooks of history for primary and secondary schools, the Ministry of Culture in Japan changed the history of the Japanese military invasion of China, calling "aggression" by the term "entry," and "all-round invasion" by the phrase "all-round attack" against China. It even framed the "Nanjing Massacre" in the terms "the Japanese army's killing of Chinese soldiers and civilians as a result of the great loss and indignation incurring in the fierce resistance of the Chinese army," making excuses for Japanese militarism. In 1985, the Japanese Prime Minister and other government members formally visited the Yasukuni Shrine for war criminals. Although these events affected the smooth development of Sino-Japanese relations to a certain degree, on the whole, the development of bilateral relations in this period was relatively good.

2) *Sino-US relations advance with enhanced understanding.* China and the United States formally established diplomatic relations in 1979. In order to further strengthen the understanding between China and the United States and promote the development of Sino-US relations, Deng Xiaoping paid an official visit to the United States at the invitation of President Carter in early 1979. This was the first visit by a Chinese leader to the United States since the founding of the People's Republic of China, and it was warmly welcomed by the American government and people. During his visit to the United States, Deng Xiaoping and President Carter exchanged views on the international situation, especially Vietnam's invasion of Cambodia with the support of the Soviet Union. The two sides also focused on the Taiwan issue and Sino-US relations. During the visit, China and the United States signed scientific and technological cooperation agreements and cultural agreements, agreements on cooperation in education, commerce, and space, and agreements on consular relations and mutual establishment of consulates-general, and decided to negotiate on the signing of trade, aviation, and maritime agreements. During his visit, Deng Xiaoping had extensive contact with people from all walks of life in the United States.

The establishment of diplomatic relations between China and the United States and Deng Xiaoping's visit to the United States promoted the development of Sino-American relations in various fields. In August 1980, China and the United States signed the Sino-American Civil Aviation Agreement, the Sino-American Maritime Transport Agreement, and the Sino-American Textile Agreement in Washington. Sino-US trade volume increased markedly, and cultural exchanges also developed rapidly. However, some erroneous practices of the United States on the Taiwan issue remained major obstacles to the smooth development of Sino-US relations.

After the formal establishment of diplomatic relations between China and the United States, President Carter proposed to the US Congress on January 26, 1979, the Legislative Adjustment Bill on the relationship between the United States and Taiwan. He said that he would continue to maintain business, cultural, and other relations with Taiwan on an unofficial basis. This meant that he would establish the American Association in Taiwan to deal with related affairs. In discussing the bill, the two houses of the US Congress proposed a series of amendments which seriously violated the principle of the communiqué on the establishment of diplomatic relations between China and the United States and obviously interfered with China's internal affairs. This could not help but arouse strong opposition from the Chinese side.

At the end of March 1979, the two houses of the American Congress passed the Taiwan Relations Act, whose basic spirit and many specific provisions violated the communiqué on the establishment of diplomatic relations between China and the United States and recognized basic principles of international law. This was particularly manifested in the idea of "guaranteeing Taiwan's security" and the nature of US-Taiwan relations. The Taiwan Relations Act declared, "The President shall promptly inform Congress of any threat to the security of the people of Taiwan or to the socio-economic system of Taiwan and any danger to the interests of the United States arising therefrom, and that the President and Congress shall, in accordance with the constitutional procedure, decide on any appropriate action by the United States to deal with such danger." In fact, in disguised form, these provisions restored the US-Taiwan Joint Defense Treaty, which in the communiqué of the establishment of diplomatic relations between China and the United States was to be terminated, and explicitly interfered in China's internal affairs.

The Taiwan Relations Act also stipulated in the form of law that the United States should continue to provide so-called "defensive materials" and "defensive services" to Taiwan. The law stipulated that the recognition of the People's Republic of China should not in any way affect the tangible or intangible property owned by the Taiwan authorities in the United States before the establishment of diplomatic relations between China and the United States. However, according to international law, after the United States recognized the Government of the People's Republic of China as the sole legitimate government of China, the United States was obliged to deliver to the People's Republic of China the official property of China in the United States formerly occupied by the Taiwan authorities in a timely manner for acceptance by the People's Republic of China. Many provisions in the Taiwan Relations Act actually regarded Taiwan as an independent political entity, trying to make the relationship between the United States and Taiwan official.

On April 10, Carter signed the Taiwan Relations Act, making reservations only on individual issues, indicating that he would exercise the "discretion" granted to the US President by the Act in a manner consistent with the Sino-

US diplomatic agreement. In turn, China was indignant about the enactment of the Taiwan Relations Law. On April 19, when Deng Xiaoping met with the delegation of the Foreign Committee of the US Senate to China, he pointed out that the political basis for normalization of Sino-US relations was that there was only one China, and that understanding had been disrupted. China was not pleased with the Taiwan Relations Act passed by the US Congress. One of the most essential problems of this bill was that it did not actually recognize that there was only one China.[12] On April 28, the Chinese Foreign Ministry, in a note to the US Embassy in China, pointed out that the Act on Relations with Taiwan was in essence a deliberate attempt to continue to regard Taiwan as a "state" and the Taiwanese authorities as a "government," and that many of its provisions violated the principles of the Sino-US diplomatic communiqué. "The United States will abide by the understandings reached with the People's Republic of China on the establishment of diplomatic relations," the US Embassy in China said in a July 6 reply. "The final US-Taiwan Relations Act passed by Congress does not conform to the wishes of the government in every detail, but it provides the President with sufficient discretionary powers so that he can adhere fully to the law in line with the normalization approach." The law would have been enforced, but instead, Congress eventually passed the bill.[13]

Following the Taiwan Relations Act incident, the United States increased arms sales to Taiwan. After long-term negotiations between China and the United States, the August 17 communiqué was reached in 1982, which further determined the principles and directions for resolving the issue of arms sales to Taiwan. This was an important step toward removing obstacles to Sino-US relations.

In January 1984, Premier Zhao Ziyang of the State Council visited the United States at the invitation of President Reagan to exchange views with the president and other leaders of the US government on the international situation and major international issues of interest to both sides. In April of the same year, Chinese leaders paid a return visit to the United States at President Reagan's invitation. President Li Xiannian visited the United States in July 1985, and Vice President Bush visited China in October that same year. The visits between the leaders of the two countries continued the exchange of views on bilateral relations and major international issues. One of the core issues was the Taiwan issue. Obviously, only by removing the obstacle to the Taiwan issue could a truly reliable foundation for stable, lasting development of Sino-US relations be established.

Although there were always obstacles between China and the United States on the Taiwan issue, the overall momentum of the development of economic, trade, and scientific and technological exchanges and cooperation between the two countries was positive. The economic and technological cooperation between China and the United States gradually developed. By the end of 1986, US direct investment contract agreements in China totaled more than 2.627 billion US dollars. Among those investments, joint ventures represented 400 million US dollars, and nearly 600 million US dollars were invested in the cooperative development of offshore oil. A total of sixty-two Sino-US joint ventures were approved, accounting for 6% of the total number of Sino-US joint ventures in China. The total amount of investment and projects was second only to Hong Kong, ranking first in all countries. After the signing of the agreement on scientific and technological cooperation between the Chinese and American governments in 1979 and 1986, the Communist Party of China and the United States signed twenty-seven official protocols on scientific and technological cooperation, with more than 500 Sino-US cooperation projects and more than 5,000 personnel exchanges.[14]

In 1972, trade between the two countries was almost zero. By 1985, the United States had become China's third largest trading partner. From 1981 to 1986, the cumulative bilateral trade volume exceeded 35.3 billion US dollars. This included $5.9 billion in 1981, $5.28 billion in 1982, $4 billion in 1983, $6.1 billion in 1984, $7.4 billion in 1985, and $7.3 billion in 1986.[15]

During his visit to China in May 1983, US Commerce Secretary Baldrige informed the Chinese government that President Reagan had relaxed the new regulations on technology exports to China, changed China from the "P" group of countries classified by the US export control to the "V" group, and included China in the category of friendly African Union countries. On June 21 of that year, the United States officially promulgated this provision. In October 1985, the United States opened up to China the export of 27 types of equipment in different commodity sectors. The United States also loosened its exports of technology to China.

However, China and the US also had problems in economic, trade, and technical cooperation. Domestic trade protectionism in the United States posed a threat to the development of Sino-US trade and economy. For example, the US repeatedly restricted China's textile imports. From 1972 to 1986, China's trade deficit with the United States totaled 18.4 billion dollars.[16] Because the United States insisted on more stringent conditions than other developed countries, the Sino-US investment agreement was not negotiated for several years, and the United States still had many restrictions on the export of advanced technology to China, which needed to be examined by the United States National Security Review and the Paris Coordination Commission.

3) *Sino-Soviet relations developed through a process of "ice-breaking."* After the 1960s, Soviet leaders seriously violated the spirit of the Sino-Soviet Treaty of Friendship, Alliance, and Mutual Assistance, leading to a serious deterioration of relations between the two countries. By the late 1970s, the Soviet Union continued to maintain and strengthen its military pressure on China's northern border, which posed a serious threat to China's security. This violated the Sino-Soviet Treaty of Friendship, Alliance, and Mutual Assistance. In view of this, in accordance with the relevant provisions of the Sino-Soviet Treaty of Friendship, Alliance, and Mutual Assistance, the seventh meeting of the Standing Committee of the National People's Congress decided on April 3, 1979, that the treaty should not be extended after its expiration. On the same day, Chinese Foreign Minister Huang Hua met with the Soviet Ambassador to China, Shcherbakov, and handed him a note from the Chinese government to the Soviet government, informing the Soviet side of this decision of the Standing Committee of the Chinese People's Congress.

In 1982, talks between China and the United States regarding arms sales to Taiwan made progress, and Sino-US relations saw a new high point, which in turn had a good impact on Sino-Soviet relations. On March 24, Soviet leader Brezhnev delivered a speech in Tashkent, expressing his willingness to improve relations with China. Taking note of the message from the Soviet side, Deng Xiaoping immediately instructed the Ministry of Foreign Affairs to respond to it. On March 26, the Ministry of Foreign Affairs held a press conference and issued a brief statement on Sino-Soviet relations. The following day, the *People's Daily* issued a statement to this effect prominently on its front page, which aroused a broad international response. In the summer, Deng Xiaoping invited several leaders of the Central Committee and the Ministry of Foreign Affairs to meet and proposed that major action should be taken to convey information to the Soviet Union and strive for a great improvement in Sino-Soviet relations. At the same time, there were principles for doing so, and the Soviet Union must do something to facilitate it, so it was suggested that the Soviet Union take the initiative to settle the "three major obstacles."[17] Subsequently, the competent officials of the foreign ministries of China and the Soviet Union made diplomatic visits to one another. On August 10, the Director-General of the Soviet Union and European Department of the Chinese Foreign Ministry visited Moscow in the name of inspecting the work of the embassy, and while there, they suggested holding political consultations at the vice-foreign ministerial level. On the 20th, the Soviet side submitted a memorandum of understanding as an official reply, agreeing to discuss bilateral relations with China at any time, any place, and any level in order to "remove obstacles to the normalization of relations." In view of the positive reaction of the Soviet side, Deng Xiaoping immediately decided to reopen the Sino-Soviet negotiations after hearing the report of the Ministry of Foreign Affairs.[18] After this, the two sides agreed to establish official channels of dialogue and hold alternate political consultations between special envoys at the Deputy Foreign Minister level in Beijing and Moscow to discuss how to normalize relations between the two countries. In September, Hu Yaobang said in his report to the Twelfth National Congress that as long as the Soviet Union took practical steps to remove the security threat to China, Sino-Soviet relations would probably normalize. Whatever the situation of Sino-Soviet relations, China would maintain and develop the friendship between the two peoples. He responded positively to the speeches of Soviet leaders on their China policy. In October, the two countries resumed political dialogue and held the first consultation at the Deputy Foreign Minister level. China proposed the removal of three major obstacles, namely, withdrawing troops from Mongolia and the Sino-Soviet border, withdrawing troops from Afghanistan, and prompting Vietnam to stop its aggression against Cambodia and withdraw troops from Cambodia. This was the key to the normalization of Sino-Soviet relations. Regrettably, the Soviet Union opted for non-recognition and refused to discuss the "three major obstacles" under the pretext of not harming the "interests of the third countries."

After that, when several Soviet leaders died, China sent delegations headed by members of the Politburo, foreign ministers, secretaries of the Central Secretariat, and Vice-Premiers to the Soviet Union to attend their funerals. Through high-level contacts, China affirmed the cause of socialist construction in the Soviet Union, expressed good wishes for improving Sino-Soviet relations, and promoted the Soviet Union's tangible actions in the normalization of Sino-Soviet relations.

In December 1984, Vice Premier Arkhipov of the Soviet Union visited China, raising Sino-Soviet bilateral contacts from the level of Vice Foreign Minister to the level of Vice Prime Minister. The Economic, Trade, and Science and Technology Commission was established. The Economic and Technical Cooperation Agreement for the Construction and Reconstruction of Industrial Projects in China and the Exchange and Payment Agreement were signed from 1986 to 1990. Bilateral trade increased, border trade resumed, the scope of cooperation expanded, and bilateral relations improved significantly.

In March 1985, Gorbachev became General Secretary of the CPSU Central Committee. In October 1985, Deng Xiaoping asked the Romanian leaders who had visited China to take a message to Gorbachev, saying that if the Soviet Union urged Vietnam to withdraw its troops from Cambodia, he would like to meet Gorbachev. In November, the Soviet side said that the time was ripe for the Soviet Union and China to hold a meeting at the highest level and resume relations between the two parties. It suggested that they should meet in the easternmost parts of the Soviet Union or in China to discuss the normalization of Soviet-Chinese relations. In July 1986, Gorbachev delivered a speech in Vladivostok, saying that the Soviet Union would withdraw six regiments from Afghanistan by the end of 1986, that it was discussing with Mongolia the withdrawal of "a considerable part of the Soviet army" from Mongolia, that it was possible to divide the boundary line between China and the Soviet Union along the Sino-Soviet border river based on the main channel, and that "the Soviet Union was willing to discuss with China most seriously at any time and at any level" the issue of supplementary measures for the establishment of a good-neighborly situation.[19] China cautiously welcomed this, making a positive gesture and agreeing to resume border negotiations. In September, Deng Xiaoping pointed out that if the Soviet Union took a solid step towards eliminating the three major obstacles between China and the Soviet Union, especially on the issue of stopping Vietnam's aggression against Cambodia and withdrawing its troops from Cambodia, he would like to meet Gorbachev anywhere in the Soviet Union.[20]

In February 1987, Sino-Soviet border negotiations were formally resumed with the improved atmosphere in bilateral relations. After two rounds of negotiations and years of stalemate, progress was finally made. From August 27 to September 1, 1988, Vice Foreign Minister Tian Zengpei and Vice Foreign Minister Igor Rogachev of the Soviet Union held a working meeting in Beijing regarding the situation in Cambodia. The two sides reached an internal understanding. On September 16, Gorbachev delivered another speech in Krasnoyarsk, a major town in Siberia, suggesting that "the Soviet Union intends to proceed immediately to prepare for its most senior meeting."[21] On the basis of the Sino-Soviet Vice Foreign Ministers' Working Meeting and Gorbachev's September 16 speech, on September 28, Chinese Foreign Minister Qian Qichen and Soviet Foreign Minister Shevardnadze, who attended the 43rd United Nations General Assembly, met in New York. The two sides believed that discussions on Cambodia should continue. From December 1–3, Chinese Foreign Minister Qian Qichen was invited to pay an official visit to the Soviet Union. This was the first official visit of a Chinese foreign minister to the Soviet Union since 1957. The main task was to prepare for the Sino-Soviet Summit. From February 1–4, 1989, Soviet Foreign Minister Shevardnadze paid a return visit to China in preparation for a high-level meeting between China and the Soviet Union. On February 6, the two sides also issued a statement on Cambodia and the date of Gorbachev's visit to China. The statement said that "the two sides advocate a just and reasonable political solution to the Cambodian issue as soon as possible, and express their willingness to make efforts to promote the realization of this goal." Further, the two sides believed that Vietnam's withdrawal from Cambodia was an important part of the political solution to the Cambodian issue. The two sides noted Vietnam's announced decision to withdraw all its troops from Cambodia no later than the end of September 1989, and hoped that its implementation would facilitate the negotiation process of resolving other aspects of the Cambodian issue. The two sides also agreed to continue discussions on resolving the Cambodian issue."[22] In this way, the most important obstacle in the "three major obstacles," namely, the Cambodian issue, was basically resolved.

The other two obstacles were relatively easy to solve. In January 1987, the Soviet Union announced that in the next four to six months, the Soviet Union would withdraw a motorized infantry division and other parts of its troops from Mongolia. In December 1988, Gorbachev announced in a speech to the General Assembly that the Soviet Union would withdraw 75% of its troops from Mongolia within two years, and on May 15, 1989, the withdrawal process began. Regarding the withdrawal of troops from Afghanistan, Gorbachev announced in his Vladivostok speech in July 1986 that the Soviet Union would withdraw its troops from Afghanistan and hold negotiations with the regimes of Pakistan, Kabul, and the United States under the auspices of the United Nations. On April 14, 1988, the Quartet signed an agreement on a political solution to the Afghan problem in Geneva, which stipulated that the Soviet Union would begin withdrawing from May 15, 1988. The withdrawal of Afghan troops was completed within nine months, and Soviet troops were completely withdrawn from Afghanistan by February 15, 1989. To this point, the "three major obstacles" affecting bilateral relations had basically been resolved and the road to high-level meetings between China and the Soviet Union was finally clear.

On May 15–18, 1989, at the invitation of President Yang Shangkun, Gorbachev, Chairman of the Presidium of the Supreme Soviet Union and General Secretary of the Central Committee of the Soviet Communist Party, paid an official visit to China. During this visit, Gorbachev held meetings with President Yang Shangkun, General Secretary of the Central Committee of the Communist Party of China Zhao Ziyang, and Premier Li Peng of the State Council, but the most crucial meeting was a high-level meeting with Deng Xiaoping on the morning of May 16.

Before the meeting, Deng Xiaoping first defined the theme of the meeting as "ending the past and opening up the future."[23] At the same time, he emphasized that "the normalization of Sino-Soviet relations is on the basis of the five principles of peaceful coexistence."[24] On this basis, Deng Xiaoping laid down the guidelines for the meeting, insisting on not evading differences or dwelling upon old accounts so as to seek common ground, focusing on the future, and discussing a new type of good-neighborly and friendly relations based on the five principles of peaceful coexistence.[25] Through this high-level meeting, the two neighboring countries of China and the Soviet Union finally ended decades of abnormal state relations and re-established normal state relations. On the evening of the 16th, Zhao Ziyang, General Secretary of the Central Committee of the Communist Party of China, met with Gorbachev, indicating that Sino-Soviet relations between the two parties had also been normalized.

On May 18, China and the Soviet Union issued a joint communiqué in Beijing, outlining the agreement reached at the high-level meeting between China and the Soviet Union. The communiqué formally affirmed the norms of the relations between the two countries, which were unanimously determined by the top leaders of both countries. It was different from both the alliance in the 1950s and the confrontation in the 1960s and 1970s. It was a normal state of non-alignment, non-confrontation, non-targeting third countries, and good-neighborly and friendly relations.

3. Developing and Expanding Peripheral Diplomacy and Multilateral Diplomacy

After the 1980s, with the adjustment of China's diplomatic strategy, while focusing on promoting the development of diplomacy between large countries, China also vigorously developed peripheral and multilateral diplomacy, achieving positive results. From 1983 to 1987, China established diplomatic relations with ten countries, bringing the total number of diplomatic countries to 135. The main leaders of the Chinese government and the Party made friendly visits to 46 countries, and Vice-Premier leaders, government envoys, and foreign ministers visited 77 countries. China received visits from more than 90 heads of state, government heads, vice-presidents, vice-premiers, and foreign ministers. China and foreign senior parliamentary leaders exchanged 113 visits, and China participated in 64 international conventions, signed 12 bilateral consular treaties, and many other operational agreements, which laid the foundation for China to develop friendly cooperation with other countries throughout the world.

Particularly noteworthy was the significant improvement in relations with surrounding countries. From 1984 to 1987, China's leaders visited Pakistan, Bangladesh, Sri Lanka, Thailand, Myanmar, and Nepal. Trade and friendly exchanges between China and Mongolia increased, and the two countries signed new consular treaties. China and Laos negotiated the normalization of relations, and the two countries resumed the exchange of ambassadors. After many contacts with Indonesia, relations between China and Indonesia improved, and direct trade between the two sides resumed.

On the whole, China's foreign relations developed well, and their effects were quite noticeable.

1) *Relations with neighboring countries.* China attached great importance to properly handling lingering historical problems with its neighbors, and it made some adjustments to its policies toward Southeast Asian countries. It also paid attention to strictly distinguishing between inter-party relations and state relations,

which greatly improved bilateral relations between China and Southeast Asian countries. At the same time, it also put forward a five-point policy for resolving the Sino-Indian border issue, so that China and India resumed high-level mutual visits and border negotiations.

2) *Relations with developing countries.* China attached great importance to pragmatic cooperation, put forward four principles of economic cooperation (namely, equality and mutual benefit, seeking practical results, diversification of forms, and common development), and carried out diversified forms of economic cooperation. This provided a deeper economic basis for China's relations with developing countries.

3) *Relationship between China and Western European countries.* In the late 1970s, China established diplomatic relations with all Western European countries except Andorra, Liechtenstein, Monaco, and the Vatican. China also specifically suggested accelerating economic cooperation between China and Western European countries through joint ventures, cooperative development, compensation trade, processing of incoming materials, and processing of incoming samples, especially through joint development of petroleum, coal, and non-ferrous metal resources. From the early 1970s to the early 1980s, China signed cooperation agreements with many Western European countries in the fields of trade, economy, science and technology, culture, civil aviation, and maritime transport. In 1978 and 1979, trade and textile agreements were signed with the European Community. After 1980, the European Community granted preferential treatment to China. Overall, during this period, China's trade with Western Europe increased significantly, and other forms of economic cooperation also made a gratifying start. China introduced some advanced technologies from Western European countries and began to introduce some of the funds required for modernization from Western European countries. The common aspiration of "developing in peace" laid a solid foundation for China's relations with the vast number of Western European countries and opened up broad prospects. After 1983, China's trade with Western European countries continued to grow. In 1985, the trade volume reached 9.575 billion US dollars, an increase of 40.7% over 1984. In 1986, the trade volume reached 11.339 billion US dollars, an increase of 39.3% over 1985, but China's trade deficit remained large.[26]

4) *Taking advantage of status in international organizations.* In international organizations, China took advantage of its international status as one of the five

permanent members of the United Nations, actively participated in multilateral diplomatic activities centered on the United Nations, and acceded to 64 international conventions, playing an important role in promoting world peace and development. In promoting development, China emphasized that it was a developing country and strove to strengthen its relations with other developing countries. It enacted its positive role in promoting North-South dialogue, South-South cooperation, and developing international economic and technological cooperation. In March 1986, Zhao Ziyang clearly listed multilateral diplomacy as one of the important aspects of China's independent, peaceful foreign policy in his report on the work of the government at the fourth session of the Sixth National People's Congress, saying, "China adheres to the purposes and principles of the Charter of the United Nations, supports the work of the United Nations organizations in accordance with the spirit of the Charter, and actively participates in the activities for world peace and development conducted by the United Nations and its specialized agencies. China extensively participates in various international organizations, carries out active multilateral diplomatic activities and strives to enhance cooperation among countries in various fields."[27] By the end of 1986, China had entered almost all important fields of intergovernmental multilateral diplomacy, participated in nearly 400 international organizations, and ratified and acceded to more than 130 international conventions. China had eleven permanent multilateral diplomatic institutions in various countries and ten representative offices of the United Nations and its specialized agencies in China.[28] At the 39th session of the General Assembly in 1984, Ni Zhengyu, a famous Chinese jurist, was elected to serve as a judge in the International Court of Justice, – the first person from the People's Republic of China to hold such a position in the history of this important institution. In November 1986, Chinese jurists were elected as members of the International Law Commission.

In the area of multilateral economic and technical assistance, China actively participated in and made efforts to promote cooperation in various fields. By the end of 1986, China and the World Bank had signed and put into effect a total of 4.15 billion US dollars in loans, including 1.6 billion US dollars in soft loans, accounting for 39% of the total. Forty-one loan projects were mainly in education, health, agriculture, transportation, hydropower, energy, and other fields. In 1981 and 1986, China borrowed its first two credit loans from the International Monetary Fund, totaling 1.048 billion SDRs. Over the previous seven years, the

United Nations Development Programme, UNFPA, and UNICEF pledged more than $800 million in unpaid technical assistance to China and arranged about 600 projects. During the same period, China made pledges to the United Nations economic institutions. By the end of 1986, it had contributed 25.48 million yuan and 25.51 million yuan in convertible currencies.[29] This played a positive role in promoting China's economic construction and strengthening international economic and technological cooperation. In the first ten years after the start of Reform and Opening Up, with the new round of adjustments to foreign principles and policies, China's diplomacy had begun its comprehensive development. An international environment conducive to China's modernization and Reform and Opening Up had taken its initial form.

IV

Proposal of the Notion of "One Country, Two Systems" and the Launch of Peaceful Reunification

After the Third Plenary Session of the Eleventh Central Committee of the Communist Party of China, the leading group of the CPC Central Committee, with Deng Xiaoping as its core, creatively put forward the scientific concept of "peaceful reunification – one country, two systems" in accordance with the major changes in the international and domestic situation and in the light of the fundamental interests of the country and the nation, and ultimately made it a basic national policy of China.

1. The Origin of the Scientific Concept of "One Country, Two Systems" and Peaceful Reunification of the Motherland

The principle of "one country, two systems" and peaceful reunification of the motherland was the inheritance and development of the Central Committee's policy toward Taiwan since the founding of New China. In 1949, the Chinese People's Liberation Army had proved invincible, and "overthrowing Chiang Kai-shek and liberating China" soon became a reality. Chiang Kai-shek fled to Taiwan in despair. Since that time, the two sides of the Taiwan Strait had unfortunately separated. Faced with the situation of separation between the Mainland and Taiwan, Mao Zedong and others had been unremittingly exploring and seeking means for reunification of the motherland, putting forward a series of principles and policies toward Taiwan.

From 1949 to 1955, the CPC's Taiwan policy could be summarized as "relying solely on force" to solve problems. On December 31, 1949, the Central Committee of the Communist Party of China issued a Letter to Commanders on the Front Line and Compatriots of the Whole Nation, pointing out that the reactionary rule of imperialism and the Kuomintang had been overthrown forever. The task in 1950 was to liberate Hainan Island, Taiwan, and Tibet and wipe out the last remnants of the Chiang Kai-shek Group. By May 1950, with the exception of Tibet, the Chinese Mainland had been completely liberated. The Chinese People's Liberation Army was actively preparing to cross the sea to liberate Taiwan with high morale. However, soon after the outbreak of the Korean War, the seventh fleet of the United States Navy invaded the Taiwan Strait to prevent China from liberating Taiwan by force. Subsequently, China sent volunteers to fight in North Korea, and the liberation of Taiwan was temporarily put on hold. After the Korean War, the Chinese government repeatedly reiterated its policy of resolving the Taiwan issue by force. In 1955, the Chinese army crossed the sea and liberated Jiangshan Island and Dachen Island.

In May 1955, the CPC changed its policy toward Taiwan. On May 13, Zhou Enlai first put forward at the Fifteenth Meeting of the Standing Committee of the National People's Congress that there were two possible ways to liberate Taiwan. The first was through war, and the second through peace. The Chinese people were willing to strive for the peaceful liberation of Taiwan under certain conditions. This was not said lightly, but was a solemn promise approved by Mao Zedong. In April 1956, Mao Zedong put forward the notion that "harmony is precious," "patriotism is for all," and "there is no preference in patriotism." On June 28 of the same year, Zhou Enlai delivered a new message to the world at the third session of the First National People's Congress, saying, "Our government has repeatedly pointed out that there are two possible ways for the Chinese people to liberate Taiwan, namely, the way of war and the way of peace. The Chinese people are willing to strive for the peaceful way to liberate Taiwan under certain conditions. There is no doubt that if Taiwan can be peaceful, it will be most beneficial to our country, to all the Chinese people, and to peace in Asia and the world... Now, on behalf of the government, I formally express our willingness to consult with the Taiwan authorities on the specific steps and conditions for the peaceful liberation of Taiwan, and I hope that the Taiwanese authorities will send representatives to Beijing or other appropriate places to start such discussions with us at such a time as they deem appropriate."

At the same time, the Central Committee of the Communist Party of China sent a letter to Chiang Kai-shek through Zhang Shizhao in Hong Kong, saying that "the tomb-side hubs in Fenghua remain, and the flowers and plants in Xikou remain the same" in the hope of prompting feelings of homesickness in Chiang Kai-shek. On July 16, 1956, Zhou Enlai met with Hong Kong journalist Cao Juren in Beijing. This was a mysterious figure who had a special relationship with senior members of both the Kuomintang and the Communist Party. Zhou Enlai said in his interview, "The Kuomintang and the Communist Party have cooperated twice. The first cooperation was the success of the Northern Expedition of the National Revolution and the second cooperation was the victory of the War of Resistance. These are facts. Why not cooperate for a third time? We are not surrendering to each other, but talking to each other. As long as the regime is unified, all the other matters can be discussed and proper arrangements made."

Mao Zedong later personally received Cao Juren, demonstrating the great importance he attached to this matter. In the interview, Mao said that if Taiwan were reunified with the Mainland, the people there would continue to live their own way of life, like fish in the water specific to them. This was similar to the fish in Mao'ergai, which might fail to survive elsewhere. Mao also said that when Chiang Kai-shek cut ties with the United States and linked to the Mainland, his roots would still remain, and he would survive and develop in his own way. His army could be preserved. Mao would not force him to cut down his troops or to streamline his administration. Rather, he would be allowed to carry on with the Three People's Principles. Later Zhou Enlai summed it up as "one guideline with four principles," that is, the guideline that Taiwan must be reunified with the Mainland, and the principles that 1) after the reunification of Taiwan and the Mainland, with the exception of diplomatic issues, all military and political powers and personnel arrangements would be decided by Chiang Kai-shek, 2) all insufficient funds for military and political construction would be allocated by the Central Government, 3) social reform in Taiwan would be slowed down and settled through consultation, and 4) mutual agreements between the two sides would be made that neither would undermine the other's unity. In fact, this already contained the basic idea of "one country, two systems."

However, the Kuomintang did not respond positively to the CPC's overtures toward peace. On the contrary, it continued to deploy a large number of troops to Jinmen and Mazu, while the United States intensified its activities behind the scenes in an attempt to make the Kuomintang accept its plot of "governance by division of the Strait." Under such circumstances, in order to fight against the reactionary spirit of the United States and Chiang Kai-shek, and to maintain "contact" between the Mainland, Taiwan, Penghu, Jinmen, and Mazu in the form of warfare, the Fujian Front Force of the People's Liberation Army (PLA) was ordered in August 1958 to "fire with artillery" and lash out at Large and Small Jinmen Islands, and the Dadan and Erdan islands. Despite the attack, China's policy of giving priority to emancipation by force and supplementing with peaceful struggle remained unchanged. In the period of the Cultural Revolution, because of the influence of leftist ideology, the government's policy toward Taiwan turned tough, that is, it was a stage of "continuing to maintain military confrontation and concentrating on diplomatic struggle."

2. Preliminary Conception of the Policy of Peaceful Reunification of the Motherland in the New Period

In the late 1970s, with the relative relaxation of the international situation, China faced a new situation in its diplomacy. China resumed normal relations with the United States and Japan in turn. Both the United States and Japan recognized that the People's Republic of China was the only legitimate government of China, and that Taiwan was part of China's territory. By 1978, 116 countries had established diplomatic relations with the People's Republic of China, while only 23 countries and regions had maintained diplomatic relations with Taiwan.

On New Year's Day, 1979, the Standing Committee of the National People's Congress issued "A Letter to Taiwanese Compatriots," which marked the comprehensive determination of the Chinese government's policy of peaceful reunification. The Communist Party of China pointed out in its Letter to Taiwan, "Today, the realization of China's reunification is the aspiration of the people and the general trend of the times. It is universally acknowledged that there is only one China and that the government of the People's Republic of China is the only legitimate government in China. The recent signing of the Treaty of Peace and Friendship between China and Japan and the normalization of relations between China and the United States are more evidence that no one can stop the tide. At present, the motherland is stable and united, and the situation is better than ever before. The people of all ethnic groups on the Mainland are working together to achieve the great goal of the Four Modernizations. We earnestly hope that Taiwan will return to the motherland as soon as possible and jointly develop the great cause of nation building. Our leaders have expressed their determination to consider the actual situation and accomplish the great cause of reunification of the motherland. In resolving the reunification issue, they should respect the current situation of Taiwan and the opinions of people from all walks of life in Taiwan and adopt reasonable policies and measures so as not to cause losses to the people of Taiwan."

It went on, "The Chinese government has ordered the People's Liberation Army to stop shelling on the islands of Jinmen from today on. There is still a military confrontation between the two sides in the Taiwan Strait, which can only create artificial tension. We believe that this military confrontation should first be ended through negotiations between the government of the People's Republic of China and Taiwanese authorities in order to create the necessary preconditions and a safe environment for exchanges between the two sides in any field."

"A Letter to Taiwanese Compatriots" not only symbolized the comprehensive determination of the policy of peaceful reunification by the Chinese government, but also contained the germination of the idea of "one country, two systems." Shortly after the publication of the "Letter," Deng Xiaoping, during his visit to the United States, explained the Chinese government's policy toward Taiwan to the relevant parties in the United States, saying, in accordance with China's wishes, it fully hoped to solve this problem peacefully, because it was more beneficial to the country and the people. China no longer used the term "emancipating Taiwan," and as long as it achieved the reunification of the motherland, it would "respect the current concrete system there." This was actually the first time that a "one country, two systems" approach was put forward publicly as a means for settling the Taiwan issue.

On December 6 that year, Deng Xiaoping concretized the idea of "one country, two systems" when he met with visiting Japanese Prime Minister Yoshihiro Ohira. He said that for Taiwan, China's conditions were very simple. That is, Taiwan's system and lifestyle would remain unchanged, and Taiwan's non-governmental relations with foreign countries would remain unchanged, including foreign investment in Taiwan and non-governmental exchanges. As a local government, Taiwan could have its own self-defense and military force. There was only one condition, that is, Taiwan should be an integral part of China. As a local government in China, it would have full autonomy.

On September 30, 1981, Ye Jianying, Chairman of the Standing Committee of the National People's Congress, issued nine guidelines on the peaceful reunification of Taiwan. These were:

1) In order to put an end as soon as possible to the unfortunate situation in which the Chinese nation had been divided, China proposed to hold bilateral negotiations between the Communist Party of China and the Chinese Kuomintang, to carry out the third cooperation and jointly complete the great cause of reunification of the motherland. The two sides could first send representatives for contact and to fully exchange views.
2) The people on both sides of the Taiwan Strait were eager to exchange information, reunite with their relatives, conduct trade, and enhance understanding. China suggested that the two sides work together to facilitate the exchange of posts, commerce, family visits, tourism, and academic, cultural, and sports exchanges, and reach relevant agreements.
3) After the reunification of the country, Taiwan could enjoy a high degree of autonomy as a special administrative region, even retaining its army. The Central Government would not interfere in Taiwan's local affairs.
4) Taiwan's current social and economic system, its way of life, and its economic and cultural relations with foreign countries would remain unchanged. Private property, housing, land, enterprise ownership, legal inheritance rights, and foreign investment would be inviolable.
5) Taiwanese authorities and representatives from all walks of life could hold leading positions in national political institutions and participate in state administration.
6) When Taiwan's local finance met any difficulty, the Central Government could make allowances at its discretion.

7) People of all ethnic groups and from all walks of life in Taiwan could return to the Mainland as they pleased to settle, in order to ensure proper arrangements, non-discrimination, and freedom of movement.
8) Taiwanese businessmen and entrepreneurs were welcome to invest in the Chinese Mainland and set up various economic undertakings to ensure their legitimate rights, interests, and profits.
9) It was everyone's duty to reunify the motherland. China warmly welcomed people of all ethnic groups, people from all walks of life, and people from all people's groups in Taiwan to provide suggestions through various channels and in various ways.

At this point, the Communist Party of China had in fact outlined the basic content of "one country, two systems."

3. Formal Proposal of "One Country, Two Systems"

In January 1982, Deng Xiaoping formally put forward the concept of "one country, two systems" for the first time in a talk, pointing out that the nine principles proposed by Ye Jianying were actually "one country, two systems." Later, the leaders of the Party and the state made speeches on this idea on different occasions. In September that year, Deng Xiaoping held talks with British Prime Minister Thatcher on the Hong Kong issue. He said that the issue of recovering Hong Kong's sovereignty could likewise be solved by "one country, two systems." This demonstrated that the policy of "one country, two systems" to solve the reunification of the motherland had expanded from Taiwan to Hong Kong and Macao.

That December, the Constitution of the People's Republic of China, amended and adopted at the Fifth Session of the Fifth National People's Congress, took into account the special circumstances of Taiwan, Hong Kong, and Macao, legally affirmed the policy of establishing special administrative regions after the recovery of sovereignty over Hong Kong and Macao and the reunification with Taiwan while maintaining the unchanged capitalist system in these areas. Article 31 of the Constitution stipulated that the state would establish special administrative regions when necessary. The system implemented in the special administrative region would be prescribed by the law of the National People's

Congress in accordance with the specific circumstances. This affirmed the idea that two different social systems could be implemented in a unified country in the form of a fundamental national law.

On June 26, 1983, Deng Xiaoping received a visiting American guest, Yang Liyu, a famous professor at Seton Hall University in New Jersey, and his party. During the interview, according to the opinions discussed by the Politburo of the Central Committee, Deng Xiaoping elaborated on the essence and concrete ideas of the policy of peaceful reunification of the motherland in view of some doubts held by the Taiwan authorities. He said, "The core of the problem is the reunification of the motherland. Peaceful reunification has become the common language of the Kuomintang and the Communist Party. But it's not that I swallow you, or vice versa. It's two systems in one country. We will adhere to the principle of peaceful reunification. After the reunification of the motherland, Taiwan's local government can develop its own set of internal policies and have its own independence. Judicial power and final adjudication power will be maintained within the local government. The army will be independent. The Mainland will not send military and political personnel to Taiwan. Taiwan's party, political, and military systems will be managed by Taiwan itself, and the Central Government will set aside posts for Taiwan." Deng Xiaoping also said that the implementation of "one country, two systems" was meant to accomplish the great cause of reunification, which had not been completed by his predecessors. If the KMT and the CPC worked together to accomplish this, the history of Chiang's family would be better written.

At that time, the domestic Chinese news media did not pay special attention to the reception of Deng Xiaoping's speech. A month later, Yang Liyu published an article in the Hong Kong journal *Wide Angle Lense*, introducing the meeting and the main content of Deng's talk. Deng Xiaoping's speech immediately had wide repercussions in Hong Kong, Macao, Taiwan, in China, and abroad, and it was widely praised as "Deng's Six Articles." The publication of "Deng's Six Articles" marked the complete formation of the concept of "one country, two systems." In May 1984, this scientific concept was formally written into the Report on Government Work adopted by the Second Session of the Sixth National People's Congress, which became a basic national policy with a legal guarantee.

Regarding the nature of "one country, two systems," Deng answered this question to different people on different occasions. The most concise, concrete, understandable, and memorable remarks were made when he met respectively with the Hong Kong Business Group and Hong Kong celebrities such as Zhong Shiyuan on June 22–23, 1984. He said, "Our policy is to implement 'one country, two systems,' specifically, in the People's Republic of China, to implement the socialist system on the Mainland with a billion people, while the capitalist system remains in Hong Kong and Taiwan."

"One country, two systems" was a complete scientific concept. The premise was one China. Without this premise, reunification was impossible. One China referred to the People's Republic of China. It did not allow for "two Chinas," "one country, two governments," "one China, one Taiwan," "two equivalent political entities," "the Republic of China in Taiwan," or "Taiwan is a sovereign and independent country" in any form, overt or disguised.

Under the premise of one China, the main body of the country would be socialist. Deng pointed out that the main body of China must be socialist. In Mainland China, it was important to unswervingly adhere to the socialist system. After the founding of the People's Republic of China in 1949, through the joint efforts of all the people throughout the country, socialism had laid a solid foundation in the Mainland. Practice had proven and would continue to prove that only socialism could save and develop China. Therefore, it was necessary to adhere to socialism on the Mainland. On the premise of adhering to the one-China principle, while practicing socialism in the Mainland, capitalism would be practiced in Taiwan, Hong Kong, and Macao. In these areas, the current social and economic systems remained unchanged, the way of life remained unchanged, and the existing laws remained basically unchanged. The army was also allowed to remain in Taiwan. This system would remain unchanged for a long time.

The policy of "one country, two systems" had great repercussions both in China and abroad. On August 27, 1984, the Hong Kong newspaper *Ming Pao Daily* published an editorial saying that "one country, two systems" was "the basic principle of Marxism today." In 1984, the American paper *Overseas Chinese Daily* published an editorial entitled "Major Events in the History of International Relations." It held that the future implementation of "one country, two systems" between Hong Kong and Mainland China would have a far-reaching impact on China's overall reunification and world affairs. Taiwanese authorities had refused to hold peace talks with the Chinese Communist Party, and they had made many statements against national justice on the Hong Kong issue. The result was that

Taiwan would lose more people's hearts both in China and abroad. It was the Party's hope that Taiwanese authorities would change course and follow the trend of history. If not, it would be too late to change course.

4. Beginning Negotiations on the Return of Hong Kong and Macao in Accordance with the Principle of "One Country, Two Systems"

Although the concept of "one country, two systems" was mainly put forward to solve the Taiwan issue, it was first successfully applied to solve the Hong Kong and Macao issues. The Hong Kong issue was a lingering historical problem from the British colonialists' aggression against China. Hong Kong included three parts: Hong Kong Island, Kowloon, and the New Territories. It had been China's territory since ancient times. After the Opium War in 1840, Britain forced the Qing government to sign three unequal treaties, namely the Nanjing Treaty, the Beijing Treaty, and the Special Article on the Development of Hong Kong Border Sites, which occupied Hong Kong, Kowloon, and the New Territories and plunged Hong Kong into British colonial rule. All previous Chinese governments after the 1911 Revolution did not recognize these unequal treaties, and they had many negotiations with Britain to recover Hong Kong. On the eve of the founding of New China, due to the special internal and external environment, the CPC Central Committee and Mao Zedong decided to "temporarily leave Hong Kong aside." After the founding of the People's Republic of China in 1949, the Chinese Government adopted the policy of "long-term planning and full utilization" toward Hong Kong. It did not recognize the three unequal treaties imposed by imperialism on China. However, considering historical factors, it temporarily maintained the status quo and settled them peacefully through negotiation at the appropriate time.

According to these unequal treaties, the New Territories, which covered 92% of Hong Kong's total area and concentrated on Hong Kong's major energy and industrial sectors, would expire on June 30, 1997. With the approaching of the expiration of the New Territories lease, the question of whether the New Territories land contract could go beyond 1997 became more and more urgent, and investors hesitated to move forward. In order to extend the period of governance of Hong Kong, in March 1979, British Governor Murray MacLehose visited Beijing to try to discover the attitude of the Chinese government toward the Hong Kong issue.

During the meeting, Deng Xiaoping pointed out that China had always believed that Hong Kong's sovereignty belonged to the People's Republic of China, but that Hong Kong had a special status. The Chinese government's position would not affect investors' interests. That is to say, for a long period in the 20th and early 21st centuries, Hong Kong could pursue its capitalism and the Mainland could pursue its socialism.

At the beginning of 1981, Deng pointed out that the Hong Kong issue was on the agenda, and China needed to have a clear policy and attitude. Subsequently, he directed the establishment of a panel on Hong Kong to discuss countermeasures. In December of that year, the Central Secretariat made a decision to regain Hong Kong's sovereignty on July 1, 1997. In April 1982, when Deng Xiaoping met with former British Prime Minister Heath, he expounded the basic position of the Chinese government on the settlement of the Hong Kong issue and made it clear that it was time to consider dealing with it.

In June 1982, when Deng met with eminent Hong Kong figures, he formally announced the basic position and principles of the Chinese government in dealing with Hong Kong's problems. First, China must recover Hong Kong in 1997 and resume the exercise of sovereignty no later. Second, it must maintain Hong Kong's prosperity and stability on the basis of resuming the exercise of sovereignty. At the same time, a research group approved by the Central Committee traveled to Hong Kong and, through investigation and research, drew up twelve policies to address Hong Kong's problems, with "one country, two systems" as the core. The main spirit of the twelve policies was to restore sovereignty, maintain the same system, administer Hong Kong by Hong Kong's people, and exercise a high degree of autonomy. These policies further embodied the principle of "one country, two systems" to solve the Hong Kong issue, thus laying the foundation for Sino-British negotiations to resolve the Hong Kong issue.

On September 24, 1982, when Deng Xiaoping met with visiting British Prime Minister Thatcher, he clearly stated the basic position of the Chinese government on the Hong Kong issue. First, the issue of sovereignty was not negotiable. China left no room to maneuver on this issue. It was on this premise that China and Britain negotiated ways of resolving the Hong Kong issue. Further, after China recovered Hong Kong in 1997, it would adopt a policy suitable for Hong Kong. Hong Kong would continue to practice capitalism. In addition, the governments of China and the United Kingdom should properly discuss how to avoid major fluctuations in Hong Kong in the fifteen years from that time until 1997.

With the above principles put forward by Deng Xiaoping, Sino-British negotiations on Hong Kong had officially begun. The whole negotiation lasted two years and was divided into two stages. The first stage was from September 1982 to June 1983, when the two sides initially consulted on some principles and procedural issues and China finally completed the formulation of its policy toward Hong Kong. The second stage was from July 1983 to September 1984, when the two sides conducted substantive negotiations to form an agreement text on Hong Kong between China and the UK on the basis of Chinese policy.

In September 1984, the two sides reached an agreement. On December 19, the heads of state of China and Britain formally signed the Joint Statement on Hong Kong between the two governments in Beijing, announcing that the government of the People's Republic of China resumed the exercise of sovereignty over Hong Kong on July 1, 1997, and that the British government would return Hong Kong to China on that day. During the transitional period from the date of entry into force of the Joint Declaration to June 30, 1997, the British government was responsible for the administration of Hong Kong and the Chinese government cooperated. The two-year negotiations between China and Britain came to a successful conclusion. On May 27, 1985, the two governments met in Beijing and exchanged the instruments of ratification of the Sino-British Joint Statement and its three annexes, and the Joint Statement came into force. Hong Kong then entered the transition period before China resumed its sovereignty.

After Hong Kong entered the transitional period, the Chinese government began to enact the Basic Law of the Hong Kong Special Administrative Region. On April 10, 1985, when the Third Session of the Sixth National People's Congress approved the Sino-British Joint Statement, it decided to establish the Drafting Committee of the Basic Law of the Hong Kong Special Administrative Region to be responsible for the drafting of the Basic Law. On July 1, the Drafting Committee of the Basic Law of the Hong Kong Special Administrative Region was formally established and began its work. In February 1990, on the basis of extensive consultation and repeated amendments, the Drafting Committee of the Basic Law of the Hong Kong Special Administrative Region considered the draft Basic Law at its ninth plenary meeting and submitted it to the National People's Congress for consideration and adoption. On April 4, the Third Session of the Seventh National People's Congress deliberated and adopted the Basic Law of the

Hong Kong Special Administrative Region of the People's Republic of China and three annexes: the Method for the Formation of the Chief Executive of the Hong Kong Special Administrative Region, the Method for the Formation and Voting Procedures of the Legislative Council of the Hong Kong Special Administrative Region, the National Law Enforced in the Hong Kong Special Administrative Region, and the Regional Flag of the Hong Kong Special Administrative Region Regional Emblem Design. Sino-British cooperation in solving the Hong Kong issue has basically gone smoothly through the 1980s.

With the start of the process of Hong Kong's return, the issue of Macao's return was also put on the agenda. As early as 1974, the Portuguese government announced that it would abandon all its overseas colonies and recognize that Macao was not a colony but a Chinese territory. In February 1979, China and Portugal established diplomatic relations. The two sides reached an understanding on the Macao issue, with the Portuguese government recognizing Macao as China's territory. The two sides agreed to resolve the issue through negotiations between the two governments at an appropriate time.

In the autumn of 1984, the Chinese and British governments reached an agreement on the Hong Kong issue, and the conditions for China and Portugal to resolve the Macao issue through negotiation reached maturity. On October 6, when he met Ma Wanqi, a well-known Macau personality, Deng Xiaoping further elaborated on the principles for solving the Macau problem. The settlement of the Macau problem would also be carried out in accordance with the same principles applied to the Hong Kong problem, namely, the "one-country two-systems" and "Macau people governing Macau," which would remain unchanged for fifty years. In June 1986, the Chinese and Portuguese governments began negotiations regarding Macao. On April 13, 1987, the prime ministers of the two governments formally signed the Joint Statement of the People's Republic of China and the Government of Portugal on Macao in Beijing. The statement declared that Macao was China's territory and that the Government of the People's Republic of China would resume the exercise of sovereignty over Macao on December 20, 1999. On January 15, 1988, representatives of the two governments exchanged instruments of ratification of the joint declaration in Beijing, and Macao formally entered a transitional period before its return.

CHAPTER 5

The Theory of the Primary Stage of Socialism and the Proposal of the Three-step Strategy

I

The Theory of the Primary Stage of Socialism and the Establishment of the Party's Basic Line

During the Twelfth and Thirteenth National Congresses of the Communist Party of China, guided by the spirit of the Twelfth National Congress, the entire Party and people throughout the country made significant efforts to create a new situation for the construction of socialist modernization and made progress through study and exploration. On this basis, the Thirteenth National Congress of the CPC was held in 1987. Symbolized by this Congress, the Party's basic line was formally established in preliminary form.

1. **Preparing for and Convening the Thirteenth National Congress of the CPC**

On October 25, 1987, the Thirteenth National Congress of the Communist Party of China was convened at the Great Hall of the People. The Thirteenth National Congress was agreed to at the Sixth Plenary Session of the Twelfth Central

Committee of the Communist Party of China in September 1986. Since then, the CPC Central Committee had undertaken the preparatory work for the Thirteenth National Congress of the CPC, mainly dividing the work into two areas.

The first area concerned the election of deputies to the General Assembly. According to the relevant resolutions of the Sixth Plenary Session of the Twelfth Central Committee, the number of deputies to the Thirteenth National Congress was to be 1,950. The central requirement was that the composition of representatives should be extensive. Ethnic minority Party members and female Party members were to make up an appropriate proportion. Special attention was to be paid to the election of a specific number of young and middle-aged Party members who had made outstanding achievements in socialist modernization and various reforms.

Through democratic elections, 1,936 representatives with broad representation were elected. Among them, 75.7% were cadres of various levels, 18.9% were economic, scientific, technological, cultural, educational, sports, and health personnel, and 5.4% were well-known labor models and combat heroes. Women accounted for 14.9%. Ethnic minorities accounted for 10.8%, 59.5% of whom had college education or above. Among the delegates, the old Party members who joined the Party in the early days of its founding to the various periods of the War of Liberation accounted for a certain proportion, with the majority of them having joined the Party after the founding of New China. Among the delegates were some of the older generation of proletarian revolutionaries, as well as vigorous, outstanding young and middle-aged Party members, with those under 55 years of age accounting for 58.8%.[1]

The second area of focus in the preparatory work was the preparation of documents for the General Assembly. The Central Committee set up a drafting group for political reports, and the overall drafting work was carried out under the care and guidance of Deng Xiaoping.

On March 21, 1987, Zhao Ziyang, then head of the drafting group, made a written report requesting Deng Xiaoping to elaborate on the conception of drafting the outline of the report for the Thirteenth General Assembly and put forward a concrete preliminary idea of drafting the political report. The report was intended to be composed of seven parts, including 1) what historical changes had taken place in China since the Third Plenary Session of the Central Committee, including the Twelfth National Congress, 2) the line since the Third Plenary

Session of the Central Committee was a Marxist line based on China's national conditions, emphasizing that China was at the initial stage of socialism, which was the foundation for it to adopt the present policy rather than other policies, 3) the resulting economic development strategy, 4) the task of developing the socialist commodity economy and the direction of China's economic system reform, 5) the task of building socialist democratic politics and the principles of the reform of China's governance system,6) the tasks of strengthening and improving the Party's leadership, including the leadership system of the ruling Party, democracy within the Party, and supervision of the Party's leaders, cadres, and ethos, and 7) the necessity of avoiding both leftist and rightist tendencies in the theoretical and ideological guidance was emphasized. The two basic points of the line since the Third Plenary Session of the Central Committee were to adhere to the four basic principles and to invigorate Reform and Opening Up. It was pointed out that creative theoretical exploration must be carried out in the new practice.

The request also suggested that the Thirteenth National Congress political report should be based on the primary stage of socialism. Why should the Party base its argument on the theory of the primary stage of socialism? The request stated that to confirm that China was in the primary stage of socialism was first to clearly state that it was constructing socialism and could not go back to capitalism, that Westernization was harmful to the country and the people, and that China was currently experiencing socialism in the primary stage, which could only be achieved step by step, rather than in hurried pursuit of success or purity. It seemed that, from the viewpoint of the initial stage of socialism, it was possible to clarify the major problem of avoiding leftist and rightist tendencies, and to clarify the nature and basis of China's reform. If so, it would be very helpful to unifying the nation's understanding both inside and outside the Party and to encourage better understanding of the long-term stability of Party policies in other countries outside China. The request concluded by stating that if there was general agreement, the drafting of the report was ready to follow this line of thought. It was expected that a rough draft would be produced in early May and submitted to the Central Committee for consideration in Beidaihe in July. Further instructions were thus requested.

Four days later, Deng Xiaoping gave instructions, saying, "This plan is good."

On November 16, 1987, when Deng Xiaoping met with the Chairman of the Socialist Party of Japan, Torui Hoko, he said that the report of the Thirteenth

National Congress of the CPC was a collective creation which gathered the wisdom of thousands of people, and many of its ideas had not been put forward by Deng himself. Rather, while it contained many of his views and opinions, most were actually collective opinions.

When the first draft of the political report of the Thirteenth National Congress came out, the Central Committee invited all democratic parties, leaders of relevant organizations, and some patriotic non-Party nationalists, non-Party intellectuals, and people from ethnic and religious circles to hold a week-long symposium to seek different views on the draft of the Thirteenth National Congress of the CPC. At the meeting, people from all walks of life expressed their opinions and put forward many valuable amendments and suggestions.

On October 20, 1987, the Seventh Plenary Session of the Twelfth Central Committee of the Communist Party of China discussed and adopted the report of the Central Committee to the Thirteenth National Congress, discussed and adopted the Amendment to Some Provisions of the Constitution of the Communist Party of China, and unanimously agreed to submit the two documents to the Thirteenth National Congress for consideration. Preparations for the Thirteenth National Congress of the Communist Party of China had been completed up to this point.

On the morning of October 25, the Thirteenth National Congress convened at the Great Hall of the People. The delegates, with the support of 46 million Party members, gathered at the Great Hall of the People and attended the opening ceremony of the Congress with red badges of attendance. Among them were the older generation of proletarian revolutionaries, as well as the outstanding young and middle-aged people who had contributed to Reform and Opening Up. The NPC Standing Committee's non-Party vice-chairman, the NPC's non-Party vice-chairman, the heads of democratic parties, the All-China Federation of Industry and Commerce, and patriotic non-Party nationalists, ethnic minorities, and religious personages were invited to attend the opening ceremony as guests, taking their seats at the rostrum. Members of the Twelfth Central Committee, the Central Advisory Committee, the Central Discipline Inspection Committee, some veteran comrades within the Party, and other relevant members of the Party attended the meeting.

Deng Xiaoping presided over and opened the conference. Zhao Ziyang made a political report on behalf of the Twelfth Central Committee. The report consisted of seven parts: 1) historic achievements and the tasks of the conference, 2) the primary stage of socialism and the Party's basic line, 3) the strategy of economic development, 4) the reform of the economic system, 5) the reform of the political system, 6) strengthening Party building in Reform and Opening Up, and 7) striving for new victories for Marxism in China.

The report clearly put forward and elaborated the theory of the socialist stage, that is, first, Chinese society was already a socialist society, and it must adhere to socialism. Second, Chinese socialist society was still in its infancy. China must proceed from this reality and not go beyond this stage. The primary stage of socialism in China did not refer to the initial stage that any country would go through when it entered socialism, but referred specifically to the particular stage that China would inevitably go through in building socialism under the conditions of backward productivity and an underdeveloped commodity economy. This stage would take at least a hundred years.

According to the theory of the primary stage of socialism, the report formulated the Party's basic line in this stage, that is, to lead and unite people of all ethnicities throughout the country, take economic construction as the center, adhere to the four basic principles, and adhere to Reform and Opening Up, self-reliance, and work hard to build a prosperous, democratic, and civilized modern socialist country.

The report summarized twelve basic points in the theory of building socialism with Chinese characteristics, namely 1) emancipating the mind, seeking truth from facts, and taking practice as the sole criterion for testing truth, 2) building socialism by following its own path in accordance with national conditions, 3) building socialism with a long initial stage under backward economic and cultural conditions, 4) the fundamental task of building a socialist society being developing productive forces and concentrating on modernization, 5) the socialist economy being a planned commodity economy, 6) reform as an important driving force for the development of socialist society, and opening up as a necessary condition for the realization of socialist modernization, 7) socialist democratic politics and socialist spiritual civilization being important features of socialism, 8) adhering to the Four Basic Principles and to the general policy of Reform and Opening Up as the two main characteristics of socialism being integrated and indispensable to each other, 9) the reunification of the country to be achieved by "one country, two systems," 10) the Party style of the ruling party being related to the life and death of the Party, 11) the principle of independence, full equality, mutual respect and non-interference in internal affairs, and the development of the Party's relations with foreign countries or other political parties, and 12) peace and development as the themes of the contemporary world. The report formally formulated a "three-step" economic development strategy. The first step was to double the 1980's GNP and solve the problem of food and clothing for the people. The second step was to again double the GNP by the end of the 20th century, so that the people's livelihood could reach a prosperous level. The third step was to reach the level of moderately developed countries in the mid-21st century, with the per capita GNP reaching the level of moderately developed countries, the people living a relatively prosperous life, and the nation basically achieving modernization.

The report also formulated a program of action to speed up the reform of the economic and political systems, formally putting the reform of the political system on the agenda of the entire Party. Concerning the reform of the economic system, the central link of transforming the operating mechanism of enterprises was to carry out the coordinated reform of planning, investment, price, finance, and foreign trade in stages, gradually establishing the basic framework of the new system of the planned commodity economy. Carrying out the reform of the political system was to promote the advantages and eliminate the disadvantages and build socialist democratic politics with Chinese characteristics. The long-term goal of the reform was to establish a complete, highly democratic legal system and an efficient, dynamic socialist political system. The short-term goal of the political system reform was to establish a leadership system conducive to improving efficiency, enhancing vitality, and mobilizing enthusiasm in all areas.

In addition, the report clearly put forward the criterion of productivity, that is, to take its conduciveness to the liberation and development of social productivity as the criterion for testing reform measures and other Party policies.

After eight days of intensive, orderly work, the Thirteenth National Congress successfully completed all tasks. The Thirteenth Central Committee, the Second Central Advisory Committee, and the Central Discipline Inspection Committee were elected by the Congress. The General Assembly adopted relevant resolutions and concluded on November 1 in a democratic, united atmosphere.

Under the great banner of building socialism with Chinese characteristics and under the leadership of the Thirteenth Central Committee, all Party members were called upon to adhere to the Party's basic line, firmly grasp the "one center, two basic points" stipulated in this basic line, strengthen the unity of the Party, strengthen the close ties between the Party and all the people of the country, work with one heart and one spirit, work hard, and forge ahead. It was important to strive to achieve the grand goal of socialist modernization.

The Congress stressed that the whole Party should resolutely implement the basic line laid down by the Congress at the primary stage of socialism, conscientiously implement the resolutions adopted by the Congress, strive to complete the tasks put forward by the Congress, and lead the people of all ethnicities to continue to advance along the socialist road with Chinese characteristics. During the Congress, political parties and organizations from many countries called to offer their congratulations. Representatives of democratic parties and non-party patriotic nationalists from all over the country also congratulated the Congress, and the Politburo expressed its gratitude to them.

On November 2, the First Plenary Session of the Thirteenth Central Committee was held. At the meeting, members of the Politburo, Wan Li, Tian Jiyun, Qiao Shi, Jiang Zemin, Li Peng, Li Tieying, Li Ruihuan, Li Ximing, Yang Rudai, Yang Shangkun, Wu Xueqian, Song Ping, Zhao Ziyang, Hu Qili, Hu Yaobang, Yao Yilin, and Qin Jiwei were elected. Others elected included Ding Guangen as alternate member of the Politburo, standing committee members Zhao Ziyang, Li Peng, Qiao Shi, Hu Qili, and Yao Yilin, General Secretary of the Central Committee Zhao Ziyang, Secretary of the Central Secretariat Hu Qili, Qiaoshi, Rui Xingwen, Yan Mingfu, and alternate Secretary Wen Jiabao. It was also decided that Deng Xiaoping should be Chairman of the Central Military Commission, Zhao Ziyang first Vice-Chairman, and Yang Shangkun Standing Vice-Chairman. The plenary approved Chen Yun as the director of the Central Advisory Committee and Qiao Shi as the Secretary of the Central Disciplinary Inspection Committee.

It is noteworthy that a large number of younger comrades were selected in the new Central Committee, while a group of older proletarian revolutionaries with outstanding contributions and high morality retired. This was a vivid reflection of the prosperity of the Party's cause and its abundance of successors, providing a reliable guarantee for the continuous, stable implementation of its correct line.

Compared with the previous leading bodies of the Central Committee, the average age of the members in the Politburo of the Central Committee, the Standing Committee of the Politburo, and the Secretariat of the Central

Committee had decreased significantly. The average age of the members of the Twelfth Central Committee and the alternate members was 59.1 years, while it was 55.2 years for the Thirteenth Central Committee. This fully demonstrated the prosperity and vitality of the Party's cause, with its abundance of successors. At this congress, Deng Xiaoping, Li Xiannian, Chen Yun, and other older proletarian revolutionists withdrew from the Central Committee and the Politburo, playing a vital role in further rejuvenating the central leading organs and in the alternation of the old and the new leading organs.

This Congress was a democratic, united, open congress that comprehensively promoted reform and construction. It was also a congress that made the Party more vibrant and vigorous.

2. Deepening the Understanding of the "Primary Stage of Socialism" and Its Historical Significance

A correct understanding of the historical stage of Chinese society was the primary issue facing the construction of socialism with Chinese characteristics and the fundamental basis for formulating and implementing correct routes and policies. To build socialism with Chinese characteristics, the first issue was, definitely, to recognize China's national conditions. On this issue, both the Soviet Union and China offered profound lessons.

The Soviet Union was the first socialist country in the world. Its greatest merit lay in the transformation of socialism from theory to reality. However, in a country like the Soviet Union, no ready-made successful experience was offered to teach later socialist nations how to build socialism. At that time, the situation in the Soviet Union was quite gloomy. Domestic hostile forces intended to overthrow the Soviet regime, and international enemies intended to stifle the socialist system, which had not yet been firmly established. Faced with internal and external pressures, the Soviet people, under the leadership of the Communist Party of the Soviet Union, had overcome various difficulties. Socialism had not only stabilized its foothold in the Soviet Union, but also enjoyed a flourishing atmosphere. On the basis of practice, Lenin put forward that from the Communist point of view, denying political parties meant jumping from the eve of the collapse of capitalism (in Germany) to the highest stage of communism, rather than to its lower and intermediate stages. In the third year after the overthrow of the bourgeoisie, Russia was still in the initial stage of transition from capitalism to socialism, that is, to the lower stage of communism. Just twelve years after Lenin's death, Stalin declared in 1936 that Soviet society had basically realized socialism and established a socialist system, that is to say, the system of the first or lower stage of communism, which was also referred to by Marxists. Three years later, Stalin declared, "We are moving towards communism." This approach was obviously aggressive. After Stalin's death, Khrushchev pushed the rush to advance toward communism to the extreme. Following the proposal of the Twenty-First National Congress of the Soviet Communist Party to China regarding the launch of the comprehensive construction of communism, Khrushchev proposed at the Twenty-Second National Congress of the Soviet Communist Party in 1961 that the Soviet Union should basically build a communist society within twenty years. The new program adopted at the Twenty-Second CPSU Congress was that "our generation will live under the Communist system." In boasting of the significance of the program, Khrushchev said, "The three programs of the Soviet Communist Party are like a three-stage rocket. The first level has separated us from the capitalist world, the second level has raised it to socialism, and the third level has the task of leading it onto the communist track."

Twenty years later, the plan was completely defeated, which showed that the Soviet Union's estimation of its stage of social development was not in line with reality. It was not until the 1980s that some countries in the Soviet Union and Eastern Europe began to re-evaluate their social development stages.

The Communist Party of China had also gone through a detour in recognizing the historical stage of China. After twenty-eight years of hard work, the CPC had won a great victory in the new democratic revolution, and in a relatively short period of time, it had achieved the restoration of the national economy and the realization of socialist transformation, establishing a socialist system in China. As for China's national conditions, Mao Zedong offered an analysis at the Second Plenary Session of the Seventh Central Committee, saying that China's industry and agriculture accounted for about 10% of the national economy, and before the War of Resistance Against Japanese Aggression, about 10% of the national economy was modern industry and 90% was agriculture and handicraft industry. This was the manifestation of the oppression of China by the imperialist and feudal systems, the economic manifestation of the semi-colonial and semi-feudal social nature of the old China, and the basic starting point of everything in the period of the Chinese revolution and for a fairly long period after the victory of the revolution. From this point of view, a series of problems in strategy and policy had arisen in the Party.

Based on this analysis, Mao Zedong proposed the major economic policies that should be implemented after the Second Plenary Session of the Seventh Central Committee of the CPC. After the founding of New China, in the process of socialist transformation, the Party adjusted some policies suggested at the Second Plenary Session of the Seventh Central Committee according to the new situation, carrying on the basic spirit. However, after the basic completion of the socialist transformation, it failed to do thorough investigation and analysis of the new national conditions. In terms of what stage of development Chinese society was at during that period, proper conclusions should have been drawn from the fact that 10% of modern industry and 90% of agriculture and handicraft industry made up China's national economy. Unfortunately, the Party was too excited about the victory of the socialist transformation at that time, and thus divorced from reality, and so took a tortuous road.

The Third Plenary Session of the Eleventh Central Committee of the Communist Party of China signaled a major turning point in China's history. With the development of rectifying the chaos, the Party began to deal with the social development stage when it analyzed the tortuous road and the causes of development errors since the founding of New China. In 1979, Ye Jianying pointed out in his speech at the 30th National Day, "Compared with the capitalist system, which has a history of three or four hundred years, socialism is still in its infancy [...] Our country is still a developing socialist country." This already contained the idea that socialism was at the initial stage.

In the Resolution of the Sixth Plenary Session of the Eleventh Central Committee of the Communist Party of China on Some Historical Issues of the Party since the founding of the People's Republic of China, adopted in 1981, it was clearly pointed out for the first time that China's socialist system was still in its infancy, but there was no doubt that China had established a socialist system and entered a socialist society, and any viewpoint that denied this basic fact was wrong.

The political report of the Twelfth National Congress of the Communist Party of China in 1982 stated that Chinese socialist society was still in the primary stage of development and that material civilization had not yet developed.

The Resolution of the Sixth Plenary Session of the Twelfth Central Committee of the Communist Party of China on the Guidelines for the Construction of Socialist Spiritual Civilization, adopted in 1986, stated that China was still in the primary stage of socialism. It was necessary not only that distribution be made according to work and that the socialist commodity economy and competition be developed, but also to develop various economic components over a long historical period, with public ownership as the main body. With the goal of common prosperity, some people were encouraged to become prosperous first.

These three important documents put forward the important theoretical proposition that China was in the "primary stage of socialism," and they made clear and scientific exposition, but they did not play a full role.

The political report of the Thirteenth National Congress of the Communist Party of China systematically expounded for the first time this issue of great theoretical and practical significance in theory, taking it as the basis for the report's entire argument, affirming clearly that China was in the primary stage of socialism and clarifying the two meanings of the primary stage of socialism (i.e., that Chinese society had become a socialist society and must adhere to socialism, and that its socialist society was still in its infancy).

The primary stage of socialism in China referred not only to the first stage or the first stage in the development sequence, but also to a special stage of development in the maturity of socialist society in a country with an underdeveloped economy and culture. It meant two things. First, in terms of social nature, China was already a socialist society, not in a transitional period. Therefore, it must adhere to the socialist direction and road, not go back to capitalism, go for "wholesale westernization," or make up "capitalist lessons." Any tendency toward retrogression, deviating from the socialist track, was the same as a social owner, incompatible with the nature of righteousness. Second, from the point of view of the degree of development, the maturity of China's socialist society was still very low and only at the primary stage, not at a higher stage. It was therefore important to proceed from this most basic, most important national condition and objective reality to carry out construction and reform, instead of demanding too much, seeking too hastily, rushing to succeed, and doing things beyond what was possible at the current stage. The proposition of the scientific judgment of the primary stage of socialism had not only drawn a clear line with the transitional period, but also with the higher stage of socialism, which put the Party's line, principles, and policy on a scientific basis, thus avoiding the repetition of the leftist mistakes of the previous transcendental stage.

China was in the primary stage of socialism, which was determined by its productivity level. The political report of the Thirteenth National Congress noted that on the one hand, as the socialist economic system was based on the public ownership of the means of production, the socialist political system of the people's democratic dictatorship and the guiding position of Marxism in the ideological field had been established, while the exploiting system and the exploiting class had been eliminated, the national economic strength had increased tremendously, and the cause of education, science, and culture had been established. As a result, China had developed considerably. On the other hand, with a large population and a weak foundation, per capita GNP still ranked bottom in the world. The prominent scenarios were that there were more than 1 billion people, with 800 million of them living in the countryside, basically using hand tools to cook food, while some modern industries coexisted with a large number of industries that lagged behind the modern level by decades or even centuries. Some economically developed areas coexisted with the vast underdeveloped and poor areas, as did a small amount of science and technology with advanced levels. The general level of science and technology was not high, illiteracy and semi-illiteracy still accounted for nearly a quarter of the population, and these co-existed with a more advanced technology and literacy. The backwardness of productive forces determined that the socialization of production required for the development of socialist public ownership was still very low, the commodity economy and domestic market were not developed, the natural economy and semi-natural economy accounted for a considerable proportion of the economy, and the socialist economic system was not mature. In terms of superstructure, a series of economic and cultural conditions were needed for the construction of a highly socialist democratic politics. Very inadequate, feudalist, capitalist, decadent ideas and small production habits still had a wide impact on society, often invading the Party cadres and the national civil service. This situation showed that China was still far from going beyond the primary stage of socialism.

The primary stage of socialism in China carried on through a rather long historical stage. As pointed out by the Thirteenth National Congress, the socialist transformation of the private ownership of the means of production in China from the 1950s to the basic realization of socialist modernization would take at least a hundred years, and this all belonged to the primary stage of socialism.

At this stage, the main contradictions China was facing were the contradiction between the growing material and cultural needs of the people and backward social production. Therefore, in order to solve the main contradictions, China needed to put the emancipation and development of social productive forces in the most prominent position, focusing all the while on economic construction.

China was in the primary stage of socialism, which was not a general case, but a specific one. It not being a general case meant that it was not the initial stage that any country would experience once it became a socialist society. Developed capitalist countries or capitalist countries with medium level of development did not need to go through such a "primary stage" after they became socialist societies. Being a specific case meant that the specific historical stage that a country like China, formerly economically and culturally backward, must go through when it became a socialist society, which was the "primary stage." Then what kind of historical stage was the primary stage of socialism in China? The Thirteenth National Congress offered its description.

Generally speaking, the primary stage of socialism in China was a stage of gradually shaking off poverty and backwardness, a stage of gradual transformation from an agricultural country based on manual labor with a majority agricultural population to a modern industrial country with a majority non-agricultural population, a stage of transformation from a semi-natural economy with a large proportion to a highly developed commodity economy, a stage of establishing and developing a vibrant socialist economic, political, and cultural system through reform and exploration, and a stage when the whole nation would rise up, work hard, and realize the great rejuvenation of the Chinese nation.

Starting from the reality of the primary stage of socialism, it was important to concentrate efforts on modernization. China needed to adhere to comprehensive Reform and Opening Up, take public ownership as the main body, and vigorously develop the commodity economy. It was important to take stability and unity as the premise and strive to build democratic politics, and to take Marxism as the guide and strive to build China's spiritual civilization.

It was of great theoretical and practical significance for the Communist Party of China to recognize afresh the concept that China was in the primary stage of socialism. In theory, it enriched and developed Marxist theory on the stages of socialist development, and provided a scientific basis for the Party to formulate correct lines and policies. In practice, it guided China's reform, opening up, and construction along the track of scientific socialism and helped prevent leftist and rightist errors. Those who did not see that China was already socialist would tend to commit rightist errors, while failing to admit that China was in the primary stage of socialism might lead to leftist mistakes. Both left and right were rooted in the fact that they were divorced from reality and the national conditions and failed to recognize that China was in the primary stage of socialism.

3. Further Elaboration on "One Center, Two Basic Points"

Based on the judgment that China was in the primary stage of socialism, the political report of the Thirteenth National Congress put forward the basic line of the Party's primary stage of socialism, which was, "Leading and uniting the people of all ethnicities throughout the country, centering on economic construction, adhering to the four basic principles and to Reform and Opening Up, self-reliance, and hard work, and striving to build China into a strong, affluent, democratic, highly civilized socialist modernized nation."

This basic line was not easily achieved. The basic or general line referred to the fundamental guiding principle of the Party's overall situation at a large historical stage. Other principles and policies must be subordinate to and serve the basic or general line. Because the basic line was of great importance, the top leaders of the Party attached great importance to the formulation of it.

During the period of democratic revolution, the first generation leading collective of the Central Committee, with Mao Zedong at its center, formulated the correct general line, namely, "the revolution of the masses led by the proletariat against imperialism, feudalism, and bureaucratic capitalism."

Under the guidance of this general line, the Communist Party of China led all the people of the country to drive out the Japanese aggressors, defeat Chiang Kai-shek, and establish a new China.

The founding of the People's Republic of China marked the basic end of the new democratic revolution and the beginning of the socialist revolution. In this period, China was in the period of transition from new democracy to socialism. The general line of the Party in the transitional period was, "the period from the founding of the People's Republic of China to the basic completion of socialist transformation is a transitional period." The general line and task of the Party in this transitional period was to gradually realize the socialist industrialization of the country and the socialist transformation of agriculture, rival and capitalist industry, and commerce over a fairly long period of time. Practice had proven that this general line was correct. By carrying out this general line, China's socialist system had been established and its socialist industrialization had taken a substantial step forward.

After China became a socialist society, the Party put forward the general line of "building socialism with vigor and striving for the upper reaches, quickly and economically." As for this general line, the Resolution of the Central Committee of the Communist Party of China on Certain Historical Issues adopted in 1981 made the following comments, "In 1958, the general line of socialist construction and its basic points adopted at the Second Session of the Eighth National Congress of the Communist Party of China were correct in that they reflected the general desire of the broad masses of the people to urgently change the backward economic and cultural situation in China, but its shortcoming was that objective economic law was neglected." This evaluation was realistic. By implementing this general line, China has witnessed a "great leap forward" in the over-development of productive forces and a "people's communization" in the over-eagerness to change production relations during the transition. The result was haste, but not speed. It violated economic law and was thus punished by the law. Since then, some achievements had been made on the one hand, but on the other hand, mistakes had been made as well, even fumbles, widening the gap between China and developed countries and hindering the exertion of the advantages of socialism.

In the Cultural Revolution, the Party's basic line put forward at the Ninth National Congress of the CPC that the whole socialist historical stage was a wrong leftist line with "class struggle as the main line." It was not a "lifeline," but a "death line," leading to the collapse and turmoil of the country.

History was the mirror of prosperity and succession. Some of the Party's basic or general lines throughout its history had both successful experiences and lessons gained from failure. Faced by this history, the Party was thinking, and its leaders were thinking, *Why did one route lead to victory while the other to failure? What was the reason?* The result of thinking was undoubtedly of great significance to the formation of the Party's basic line in the primary stage of socialism. Its direct result was that the Party had gradually formed its basic line in the primary stage of socialism on the basis of summing up previous historical experience.

As early as eighteen years before the concept of "the primary stage of socialism" was put forward, Zhou Enlai laid the initial foundation for the formation of this basic line in his Government Work Report at the First Session of the Third National People's Congress in December 1964. Zhou Enlai pointed out in his report that the main task of developing the national economy in the future was to build China into a powerful socialist nation with modern agriculture, industry, national defense, and science and technology in a short historical period, to catch up with and surpass advanced nations. In order to achieve this great historical task, starting with the Third Five-Year Plan, China's national economic development could be considered in two steps. The first step was to establish an independent and relatively complete industrial and national economic system. The second step was to realize the modernization of agriculture, industry, national defense, and science and technology across the board, so that China's economy would be at the forefront of the world.

This assumption had not been realized during the interference of the leftist error, but its historical status could not be underestimated. The Third Plenary Session of the Eleventh Central Committee of the Communist Party of China, held at the end of 1978, re-established the correct ideological line, negated the leftist line of "taking class struggle as the main line," persisted in shifting the focus of work to economic construction, and formulated the basic policy of Reform and Opening Up, which laid a solid foundation for the formulation of the Party's basic line at the primary stage of socialism.

After the Third Plenary Session of the Eleventh Central Committee, the Party stressed on many occasions that it should seize the center of economic construction, adhere to the four basic principles, and carry out Reform and Opening Up. After the successful completion of the task of settling the chaos, the Twelfth National Congress of the Communist Party of China put forward the general task of the Party in the new historical period, that is, to unite the people of all ethnicities throughout the country, to work hard for self-reliance, to gradually realize the modernization of industry, agriculture, national defense, and science and technology, and to build China into a highly civilized, democratic socialist country.

In September 1986, the Sixth Plenary Session of the Twelfth Central Committee of the Communist Party of China put forward the overall layout of socialist modernization, which included focusing on economic construction, unswervingly carrying out economic and political system reform, firmly strengthening the construction of spiritual civilization, and making all these aspects coordinate and promote each other. This "overall layout" already contained the main substance of the basic lines summarized at the Thirteenth Central Committee of the CPC, but remained incomplete.

On January 28, 1987, the Central Committee pointed out in the Circular on Several Issues Concerning the Current Anti-bourgeois Liberalization that the route since the Third Plenary Session of the Eleventh Central Committee had been to build socialism with Chinese characteristics on the basis of China's reality. The basic points of this line were 1) to adhere to the four basic principles, and 2) to adhere to the policy of reform, opening up, and invigorating the country. The proposition of the "two basic points" made the most direct preparation for the final formation of the basic line.

Under such conditions, the Thirteenth National Congress clearly put forward and summarized the basic line of the Party in the primary stage of socialism on the basis of putting forward the theory of the primary stage of socialism.

The main points of the Party's basic line in the primary stage of socialism were "taking economic construction as the center, adhering to the Four Basic Principles, and adhering to Reform and Opening Up," that is, "one center, two basic points." "One center, two basic points" represented Deng Xiaoping's efforts toward and policy of rejuvenating the country. At the Third Plenary Session of the Eleventh Central Committee, Deng Xiaoping led the implementation of the shift of the strategic center and decided on the basic national policy of Reform and Opening Up. From then on, China was led to a new field and a new era. However, Deng Xiaoping felt there was something missing. At the theoretical meeting in early 1979, he promptly put forward the idea that China should adhere to the Four Basic Principles. From that time on, Deng held onto the central link of economic construction, grasping two basic points, and promoting the sustainable and healthy development of Chinese society. When some people generalized the Party's basic line in the primary stage of socialism as "one center, two basic points," Deng Xiaoping expressed his appreciation and thought it well summarized.

The "one center and two basic points" were interlinked, interdependent, and indispensable. "Centering on economic construction" ran through the whole process of completing the fundamental task of socialism and was the line for developing social productive forces. It not only revealed and stipulated the central position of economic construction in the overall work of the Party and the state, but also stipulated and demanded that all other work must be obeyed and serve the central position of economic construction in order to ensure the development of social productive forces. Why should the Party insist on taking economic construction as the center? This was because the fundamental task of socialism was to develop productive forces, especially because China's socialist system was not born out of a developed capitalist society, nor of a developing capitalist society like Russia, but of a semi-colonial and semi-feudal society with a weak foundation. Although great progress had been made in developing productive forces since the founding of New China, achievements, however, were still quite backward compared with developed countries. It was thus necessary to adhere to economic construction as the center, carry out socialist modernization, and concentrate all effort on the development of productive forces. The two basic points of adhering to Reform and Opening Up and adhering to the Four Basic Principles were tightly centered on economic construction, that is, the central task of developing productive forces. The basic characteristics of the primary stage of socialism were underdeveloped productive forces, immature production relations, and an imperfect superstructure. Therefore, it was important to persist in reform. Reform and Opening Up was the only way to develop social productive forces and realize socialist modernization in China. The Four Basic Principles were the fundamental guarantee for the development of social productive forces and socialist modernization. The "two basic points" were also the unity of adhering to the socialist orientation and the self-improvement and development of the socialist system.

The "one center, two basic points" were mutually restrictive and reinforcing. Based on the objective requirement of productivity development, the center was to develop productivity, and the "two basic points" functioned like wings of an aircraft, balancing the main fuselage in the central position. The two basic points were guided by the "one center" and at the same time, they themselves disciplined each other.

The Party's basic line in the primary stage of socialism not only stipulated "one center, two basic points," but also set out the Party's goal for struggle. This was the struggle to build China into a prosperous, democratic, and highly civilized modern socialist country. Prosperity, democracy, and civilization, in fact, included the requirements of economy, politics, ideology, and culture. This was not only a trinity of modernization goals, but also three important aspects of socialism with Chinese characteristics.

"Prosperity and strength" were the goals and requirements in the field of social economy. A socialist society must be rich rather than poor. For the first time, the Thirteenth National Congress had put "prosperity and strength" into the Party's goal for struggle.

"Democracy" was the goal and requirement of political construction. Socialist democracy was far higher than capitalist democracy in its essence. Socialist democracy required the broad masses of people to participate in the management of the state and society, and to truly "be the masters of the country."

"Civilization" referred to spiritual civilization, which was the goal and requirement in the field of social ideology and culture. Socialist spiritual civilization was an important feature of socialism. To build socialism with Chinese characteristics, it was important to eliminate all kinds of ignorance and backwardness lingering from the old society. For a long time, the Party's understanding of socialism had not been completely clear, and it had not formulated a goal for scientific struggle that was in line with China's national conditions, which was an important manifestation of this lack of awareness.

The trinity of prosperity, democracy, and civilization reflected the Party's new understanding of socialism. This was a major achievement in the renewed recognition of China's national conditions and socialism after the Third Plenary Session of the Eleventh Central Committee.

The Party's basic line at the primary stage of socialism stipulated the strength to achieve the goal of struggle. This was "leading and uniting people of all ethnicities." Since the socialist transformation of ownership had basically been completed, the exploiting class as a class had been eliminated. Except for a few hostile elements, the people of all ethnicities under the leadership of the CPC were the staunch forces for accomplishing the tasks of the primary stage of socialism.

The basic line of the Party in the primary stage of socialism put forward the requirement of accomplishing various tasks in terms of mental state, namely "self-reliance and hard work." What did China depend on for its development? What did China's achievement of the trinity of prosperity, democracy, and civilization depend on? Foreign aid was clearly important, but it was not the Party's basic point. China's foundation was self-reliance. That is to say, it relied mainly on the people's own strength, enthusiasm, and creativity.

The Chinese people had a bright tradition of perseverance in the face of difficulties. It was with this spirit of ardent struggle that they overcame difficulties and strove for numerous victories. This spirit was China's secret weapon for overcoming the enemy in the revolutionary war era. It was also necessary to achieve the goal of prosperity, democracy, and civilization. To accomplish the historic task of realizing the great rejuvenation of the Chinese nation in the primary stage of socialism required the Chinese people of all ethnicities to actively participate in the wave of reform and construction with a proactive attitude. Only in this way could China be among the highly civilized nations in the world.

II

The Three-step Development Strategy

In 1979, Deng Xiaoping began to design the specific blueprint of China's modernization and gradually formed a strategic concept of "two-step development" to achieve an economic "quadrupling" and to reach the stage of "a moderately well-off society" by the end of the 20th century.

The Third Plenary Session of the Eleventh Central Committee of the Communist Party of China shouldered the heavy burden of history, decided to shift the focus of the work of the whole Party and the attention of the people to the socialist modernization drive, reiterated the goal of realizing the Four Modernizations in the 20th century, and put forward the specific path, principles, methods, and measures for realizing the Four Modernizations. It should be said that the Third Plenary Session of the Central Committee established the overall goal of the economic development strategy of "realizing the Four Modernizations" and put forward the basic principles to achieve this goal. But what was the blueprint for the Four Modernizations? In what ways and through what steps could it be achieved? At that time, the understanding of it was more abstract and general.

1. New Thoughts on China's Modernization Development Strategy

After the Third Plenary Session of the Eleventh Central Committee, the second generation of central leadership, with Deng Xiaoping at its center, began to think seriously about and arduously explore how to realize China's modernization. In March 1979, Deng Xiaoping put forward in his speech Adhering to the Four Basic Principles, "In the past when we carried out democratic revolution, we needed to take into consideration China's specific situation and follow the path blazed by Comrade Mao Zedong to start from the rural areas to encircle the cities. At present, we should also adapt ourselves to China's situation and take a Chinese-style path of modernization." He also pointed out that "Chinese-style modernization must proceed from the characteristics of China." Deng summed up two important characteristics that must at least be seen in order to realize China's modernization. One was that China had a weak economic foundation, and the other was that it had a large population and a small amount of arable land. Deng pointed out that these two characteristics determined that the starting point of China's construction of modernization was very low, so the time required to realize modernization would be long. China could only gradually and systematically realize modernization on the basis of this low starting point. Later, the Politburo and the State Council discussed and researched how to realize socialist modernization in China. They believed that "in order to achieve modernization, we must proceed from China's national conditions." The Central Working Conference held in April 1979 analyzed China's national conditions and pointed out that it was a large country with a population of over 900 million, of which more than 80% were farmers. The communists had won the revolution thirty years earlier, but the economy was still quite backward, and the people's living standards were still very low. It was a contradiction that China was poor and needed a large amount of money for modernization, while the people needed to improve their lives. It was also a contradiction that China should modernize and employ fewer people, while it had a large labor force that needed employment. China could only carry out the Four Modernizations under such contradictions, which was the reality and the basic starting point that had to be considered when planning China's construction blueprint.

It was based on the actual situation in China that Deng Xiaoping began to conceive the specific blueprint for China's modernization. This was not only the need for modernization, but also the inevitable result of the logical development of Deng Xiaoping's thought. On December 6, 1979, Deng held a meeting with Japanese Prime Minister Masayoshi Ōhira, who visited China. In reply to his question about how he conceived the blueprint for China's modernization, Deng said, "The Four Modernizations we aim to achieve are the Four Modernizations of Chinese style. Even by the end of this century when our Four Modernizations has achieved some of our goals, the average GNP remains quite low. We have to make great effort even to reach the level of the wealthier countries in the Third World, such as those with an average GNP of $1,000. Even at that level, we will still be backward compared with Western developed countries. I can only say that China will still be a moderately well-off society." For the first time here, Deng concretized the goal of the Four Modernizations into reaching the level of average GNP of $1,000 and reaching the "moderately well-off" state. The concepts of $1,000 and "moderately well-off" were also formed in this conversation. More than a month later, Deng Xiaoping said when he spoke of his answer to Prime Minister Ōhira's question, "This answer was certainly inaccurate, but it was not casual." According to Deng's analysis, the Chinese people at this time had only more than $200. If they reached $1,000, it would increase their income three times. Those in Singapore and Hong Kong made more than $3,000. It would not be easy for China to reach that level. Because of the vast land and large population, conditions were very different. However, it should be said that if China's gross production really reached an average of $1,000 per person, the life of the Chinese would be much better than theirs, and even better than those with $2,000.

If Deng Xiaoping's talk with Prime Minister Ōhira was the first time that he talked with foreign guests about his vision for the next twenty years, then in his speech on Current Situation and Tasks in January 1980, he not only relayed his talk with Prime Minister Ōhira, but also for the first time put forward his vision to the whole Party. He pointed out that the plans for the Four Modernizations of Chinese style should be completed in two steps over the next two decades. Therefore, the 1980s were very important and decisive. If the Party laid a good foundation in this decade, then in the next decade, there would be real hope for it to realize the Four Modernizations of Chinese style.

According to Deng Xiaoping's conception, in June 1981, the Sixth Plenary Session of the Eleventh Central Committee of the Communist Party of China proposed that the goal of modernization should be achieved systematically and in stages. In November 1981, the Fourth Session of the Fifth National People's Congress stipulated the "moderately well-off level" as the goal of China's economic development. The meeting held that the pace of economic development during the Sixth Five-Year Plan period could not be too fast, while the Seventh Five-Year Plan was expected to be higher than the Sixth Five-Year Plan period, making the following ten years more hopeful. The meeting proposed that China should strive to quadruple the gross output value of industry and agriculture within twenty years, so as to make people's lives reach a moderately well-off level. By September 1982, at the Twelfth National Congress of the Party, Deng Xiaoping's "moderately well-off" level was formally put forward and determined as the strategic goal of the Party and the people to the end of the 20th century. The report of the Twelfth National Congress pointed out that in the twenty years from 1981 to the end of the 20th century, the overall goal of China's economic construction was to quadruple the total annual output value of industry and agriculture throughout the country on the premise of constantly improving economic benefits, that is, from 710 billion yuan in 1980 to about 2,800 billion yuan in 2000, and for the people's material and cultural life to reach a well-off level. In order to achieve the goal of this twenty year struggle, the Party should take two steps in strategic deployment. In the first ten years, it should lay a good foundation, accumulate strength, and create the necessary conditions. In the next ten years, it should enter a new period of economic revitalization.

By the end of the 20th century, after the goal of "two steps" to achieve a "well-off level" was put forward, Deng began to further conceive the economic development goal of China in the middle of the 21st century from 1984, thus gradually forming a complete "three steps" strategic economic development goal.

2. The Gestation and Elaboration of the "Three-step" Development Strategy

The "three-step" development strategy had been brewing even before 1984. The original formulation included the goal of realizing the Four Modernizations by the end of the 20th century. Later, the Party gradually realized that this task could not be accomplished so quickly. Therefore, it used the term "reaching a moderately well-off level." Although the term "realizing the Four Modernizations by the end of this century" was still used sometimes, its meaning had gradually changed, and it was no longer used in the sense of completion, but in the sense of a stage. Under these circumstances, the Twelfth National Congress of the Communist Party of China put forward in September 1982 the goal of quadrupling the average GNP. Since a moderately well-off level could be achieved only by the end of the 20th century, it would take an even longer time to reach the level of modernization. In December 1980, Deng Xiaoping put forward in his speech Implementing the Principle of Adjustment, Guaranteeing Stability and Solidarity that after reaching the moderately well-off level, "we should continue to advance and gradually achieve a higher degree of modernization." In November 1981, the government Work Report of the Fourth Session of the Fifth National People's Congress pointed out that by the end of the 20th century, when people's lives had reached a moderately well-off level, China's economy could begin from a new starting point and reach the level of more developed countries relatively quickly. It was evident that at this time, the goal of reaching the level of comparatively developed countries in several steps had begun to brew. However, before 1984, the conditions for clearly putting forward the "three-step" development goals were not yet available, because whether the "moderately well-off" goal could be achieved remained to be tested. Shortly after the end of the Twelfth Party Congress, on October 14, 1982, Deng Xiaoping asked the responsible comrades of the State Planning Commission to report to him, asking, "Is the goal of quadrupling the average GNP by the end of the 20th century feasible? The Twelfth National Congress of the Communist Party of China stated that it was possible, and I believe it is, but whether it is practical or not depends on future work... Now we must concentrate on long-term planning. The key to the long-term planning is to prepare in the first ten years for the next ten years... There is a timing issue concerning the preparation, and we must take it seriously." What Deng had said indicated that if China did not seize the time and take it seriously, the goal of quadrupling the average GNP would be in danger of failure.

After the Twelfth National Congress of the Communist Party of China put forward the goal of quadrupling the GNP in 1982, the question that had been lingering in Deng's mind was, "Will the goal of quadrupling GNP by the end of this century be achieved?" From 1982 to 1984, China's economic development was rapid, greatly exceeding the economic growth rate stipulated in the Sixth Five-Year Plan. The rural reform made significant breakthroughs. In 1984, China's grain production reached the highest level in history, and urban reform began. The national situation was gratifying.

At the beginning of 1983, Deng Xiaoping visited the area south of the Yangtze River. He traveled through Jiangsu and Zhejiang Provinces, then to Shanghai. On the way, he saw that the situation was very good. People were very happy, many new houses had been built, the market was enjoying an abundant supply, and the cadres were confident. Seeing these vivid scenes, Deng noted that "it seems that there is great hope for the Four Modernizations." When he returned Beijing, speaking with several responsible comrades of the Central Committee, Deng proposed that quadrupling the average GNP by the end of the 20th century required a more comprehensive, specific plan, and that all provinces, autonomous regions, and municipalities directly under the Central Government should have their own specific plans, providing a clear idea of the goals. In March 1984, speaking with Japanese Prime Minister Nakasone Yasuhiro, Deng made it clear that "the goal of quadrupling will not fail." In June, when Deng met with the delegation of the Japanese Committee of the Second Sino-Japanese Non-official People's Conference, he said confidently that, according to the development of China's economy in recent years, "the goal of quadrupling GNP by the end of this century will surely be achieved." On October 1, at the celebration ceremony of the 35th anniversary of the founding of the People's Republic of China, Deng solemnly declared that the situation in recent years showed that the ambitious goal of quadrupling the GNP, proposed at the Twelfth National Congress, could be achieved. Considering that the realization of "a moderately well-off society" had become a realistic goal for the end of the 20th century, Deng began to consider China's economic development strategy across the turn of the century and design a grand blueprint for China's development in the 21st century, considering the future and long-term interests of the Chinese nation.

On April 18, 1984, Deng Xiaoping met with British Foreign Secretary Jeffrey Howe. Around this time, Deng clearly pointed out that achieving a moderately well-off society by the end of the 20th century was only the "smallest goal" of the Four Modernizations. So, how long would it take to achieve the "big goal" of the Four Modernizations, that is, to basically achieve modernization? In his conversation with Jeffrey Howe, Deng first envisioned this issue. He said that compared with the big goal, the development during recent years was only the beginning. After reaching the level of a moderately well-off society, it was necessary to approach the level of developed countries in the first thirty to fifty years of the 21st century. After this, Deng mentioned this idea on many occasions.

On May 29, he met with Brazilian President Figueiredo and said that China was still very poor, with a GNP per capita of only US$300, but it had the ambition of reaching $800 per capita by the end of the 20th century. Eight hundred dollars was not much for developed economies, but it was quite ambitious for China. More importantly, on such a basis, with another thirty to fifty years of development, China would be able to approach the level of developed countries. Subsequently, in three conversations on June 30, October 6, and October 22 that year, Deng stated his assumption in roughly the same language, that by the end of the 20th century, the per capita GNP would reach $800 instead of $1,000. This was because he considered that at the end of the 20th century, China's population would be more than one billion, roughly restricted to about 1.2 billion. If the GNP quadrupled and the population grew to 1.2 billion, then the per capita GNP would be a little more than $800. Later, Deng used the flexible term "800 to 1,000 dollars," but he sometimes still said "800 dollars" or "1,000 dollars." In addition, Deng Xiaoping's goal at that time was to be "close to the level of developed countries," and the time needed was "thirty to fifty years," which was not exactly the same as what he later said.

In 1985, Deng Xiaoping's concept of "three steps" had also advanced. In his speech at the National Conference on Scientific and Technological Work on March 7, 1985, he pointed out that China had struggled for decades to eradicate poverty. The first step was to reach a moderately well-off level at the end of the 20th century, that is, neither rich nor poor, and having a better life. The second step was, for another thirty to fifty years, to make people's lives more prosperous by approaching the level of developed countries economically. This was the overall situation. Deng's remarks involved something new compared with those in 1984. First, he used the words "the first step" and "the second step," which prepared for the later generalization of "the three steps." Second, he explained the "moderately well-off level," that is, neither rich nor poor, but with a better life. Third, he put "making people's lives richer" along with "reaching the level of developed countries" as the goal for struggle. Fourth, it pointed out that this was the "overall situation" of the whole Party and country. On March 25, 1985, when Deng Xiaoping met with American journalists, and on April 15, 1985, when he met with Tanzanian Vice President Ali Hassan Mwinyi, he said that the first step was to achieve a moderately well-off level by the end of the 20th century. From the end of 1979, when this goal was put forward, to the end of the 20th century, there were twenty years. On the basis of a GNP of $1 trillion, in another thirty to fifty years, or more precisely, in another fifty years, China might get closer to the level of developed countries and achieve its goal of the second step. It would take seventy years to do this well. In these two talks, Deng clearly extended the time span of China's economic development strategy from twenty years to seventy years, and divided the development goals into two steps, thus making the strategic objectives and strategic deployment increasingly clear. In September 1985, the Communist Party of China convened a national conference of representatives. Deng pointed out at the meeting that people then said that China had undergone significant changes. He said to some foreign guests that these were only minor changes. Quadrupling and reaching a moderately well-off level could be said to be a mid-term change. By the middle of the 21st century, China would be close to the level of developed countries. That would be the big change. Deng here used the terms of "small change," "medium change," and "big change." These "three changes" clearly showed the three stages of economic development, which were very close and similar to his later "three steps."

By 1987, Deng Xiaoping's "three-step" strategic concept had been formed. The positive situation in economic development in 1985 and 1986 showed that most of the main targets of the Seventh Five-Year Plan could be completed ahead of schedule, which meant that the first strategic goal of doubling the GNP by 1990 could be achieved earlier than expected. This made Deng more confident and clearer about future economic development. On March 8, 1987, Deng said to visiting Tanzanian President Mwinyi that over the previous eight years, China had gained experience and noticeable achievements in construction. "In the first ten years, from 1981 to 1990, doubling the gross national product is quite likely and can be completed ahead of schedule. In the second decade, from 1991 to the end of this century, the GNP will double again, which is also feasible in terms of development trends. In the eight years since the Third Plenary Session of the Eleventh Central Committee, people's lives have indeed improved significantly. By the end of this century, although our per capita GNP is not much, it will exceed $1 trillion annually. With this foundation, it is hopeful to reach the level of moderately developed countries."[2] Deng Xiaoping actually put forward the strategic concept of "three steps" here, but he did not explicitly use the words "the first step," "the second step," and "the third step." Deng also changed here the strategic goal of China's development from "approaching the level of developed countries" to "reaching the level of moderately developed countries" in the mid-21st century. On April 16 that year, Deng Xiaoping used the criterion of "moderately developed countries" again in his speech to the members of the Drafting Committee of the Basic Law of the Hong Kong Special Administrative Region. For the first time, Deng quantified the target as "4,000 US dollars per capita" and "6 trillion RMB of gross national product." Thus, the strategic objectives of China by the middle of the 21st century were clearly visible. On April 30, when Deng Xiaoping met with Spanish Deputy Prime Minister Alfonso Guerra, he made a clear and complete statement on the strategic objectives of the "three-step" economic development for the first time. Deng pointed out that China's original goal was to double the GNP per capita in the 1980s. Based on 1980 figures, when the per capita GNP was only US$250, doubling it would mean US$500. The second step was to double it by the end of the 20th century, reaching $1,000 per capita. Achieving this goal meant entering a moderately well-off society and turning a poor China into a moderately well-off one, with the GNP exceeding $1 trillion. Although the per capita GNP was still very low, the strength of the country increased greatly. What was more important was the third step, which would quadruple the GNP per capita in the first thirty to fifty years of the 21st century, reaching roughly $4,000 per capita. By doing so, China would reach a moderately developed level. This was its ambition. At this point, Deng Xiaoping's conception of the "three-step" economic development strategic goal of China's modernization had been formed.

3. Establishment of the "Three-step" Economic Development Strategy

According to Deng Xiaoping's conception and the basic national conditions of the primary stage of socialism in China, the Thirteenth National Congress of the Communist Party of China, held in October 1987, formally developed the "three-step" economic development strategic goal of socialist modernization. The report of the Thirteenth National Congress proposed, "After the Third Plenary Session of the Eleventh Central Committee of the Communist Party of China, the strategic deployment of China's economic construction is generally divided into three steps. The first step is to double the 1980 gross national product (GNP) and solve the necessities of food and clothing for the people. This task has been basically accomplished. Second, by the end of the 20th century, the GNP will be doubled and the people's livelihood will reach a moderately well-off level. Third, by the middle of the 21st century, the per capita GNP will reach the level of moderately developed countries, the people's livelihood will be relatively prosperous, and modernization will be basically realized. And then, on that basis, we will move on." The formulation of the "three-step" economic development strategy solved the major issues related to the overall situation, such as the objectives and steps of China's modernization construction, and would have a long-term and profound impact on China's development in the coming decades.

Compared with China's previous development strategy, the characteristics of the "three-step" economic development strategy of socialist modernization construction lay in several areas. The first was that it was realistic. Compared with the goals of "overtaking Britain and catching up with the United States in fifteen years" and "realizing the Four Modernizations by the end of this century," this was a small goal, but it was a realistic one. The early realization of the first strategic goal of "three steps" offered strong proof of this. The second area was that it aimed to improve people's material and cultural living standards as a starting point and a foothold. Using "food and clothing," "moderately well-off," and "prosperity" as the goals of modernization, so that people could understand and feel more clearly and directly the realization process of this goal, which could in turn mobilize the enthusiasm and strengthen the confidence of the people, was in line with the fundamental purpose of socialism. In addition, it was clear, concrete, and quantitative. Quantitatively translating the target into "1,000 US dollars" and "4,000 US dollars" helped make the target clear, specific, and easy to operate and measure. Further, it was linked to the world economy. This goal, measured by the US dollar, was to consider and compare China's economy in the broad scope of the world, to make the gap between China and developed countries clear at a glance, and to place China's economy in the context of the development of the world economy. Finally, it was both an economic and a political objective. The fundamental task of socialism was to develop productive forces, and modernization was the biggest political issue in China. Whether it could achieve the strategic goal of the "three steps" was related to the future and destiny of socialism. Therefore, it was not only an economic development goal, but also a political one.

Realizing the strategic goal of the "three steps" was of great significance. It was a strategic goal for China to gradually eliminate poverty and become wealthy. Achieving this strategic goal would not only greatly enhance China's comprehensive national strength, improve people's lives, greatly enhance its international influence and contributions to mankind, but also better reflect the superiority of the socialist system. Deng pointed out that "to prove that socialism is really superior to capitalism, we must take the third step, and we can't boast about it yet." China had a large population. By the middle of the 21st century, with a population of 1.5 billion and a per capita GNP of 4,000 US dollars, China's annual GNP would reach 6 trillion US dollars, which was much higher than the US GDP of $4.97 trillion in 1987. "This is not only a way out for the third world, which accounts for three-quarters of the world's total population, but also a way to show all of mankind that socialism is the only way and that socialism is superior to capitalism."

The strategic goal of the "three-step" economic development constituted an important part of the theory of building socialism with Chinese characteristics and was the concrete implementation plan and fundamental embodiment of the central task of socialist modernization. Some of the major guidelines, principles, and policies for building socialism with Chinese characteristics revolved around and served this development strategy. This strategy pointed out the direction for building socialism with Chinese characteristics in the primary stage of socialism. It was predictable that as long as China continued to follow the path of socialism with Chinese characteristics, Deng Xiaoping's strategic goal of the "three steps" in the drive toward modernization would surely be achieved.

III

Further Clarification of the Objectives of Reform of the Political System

With the further development of economic system reform, the task of political system reform was given a more urgent place on the agenda of the Party. As early as the Third Plenary Session of the Eleventh Central Committee, the task of political system reform began to attract people's attention. In 1980, Deng Xiaoping solemnly proposed the important task of political system reform in his speech Reform of the Party and State Leadership System at the enlarged meeting of the Politburo of the Central Committee. The Central Government had planned to gradually implement political system reform from that time on, but for various reasons the political system reform was not fully implemented until 1986.

1. Deep Understanding of the Importance and Urgency of Promoting Reform of the Political System

With the development of the situation, political system reform was inevitably put on the agenda again. On June 10, 1986, when Deng Xiaoping listened to the report of the Party members in charge of the Central Committee on the current economic situation, he pointed out that it was impossible to adapt to the situation without carrying out reform of the political system. Reform should include the reform of the political system, and it should be regarded as a symbol of the progress of reform. Deng also stressed that all comrades, especially those in the Secretariat of the Central Committee, should consider reform of the political system and find someone to sort it out. Before the Thirteenth National Congress, he demanded that the relationship between the Party and the government be straightened out, the content of the political system reform be clarified, the scope of the political system reform be defined, and the blueprint of the political system reform be formulated.

A series of ideas put forward by Deng Xiaoping laid a foundation for the discussion of political system reform and the design of the scheme framework. In 1986, the Central Committee decided to set up a seminar group on the political system of the Central Committee. This group consisted of five heads of the Central Secretariat, the Central Advisory Committee, the State Council, and the Standing Committee of the National People's Congress. It conducted discussions under the direct leadership of the Standing Committee of the Politburo of the Central Committee.

The Central Political System Reform Seminar Group organized practical and theoretical workers from relevant departments and established seven thematic groups to discuss and demonstrate the separation of Party and government, intra-Party democracy, institutional reform, cadre and personnel system reform, socialist democracy, the socialist legal system construction, and basic principles of reform. At the same time, the Central Party School was asked to set up a seminar group to conduct in-depth investigation and research in parallel with these thematic groups, to listen extensively to the views of the CPPCC, mass organizations, and other parties, to study carefully the historical experience of the political system since the founding of New China, especially the practical experience of reform since the Third Plenary Session of the Eleventh Central Committee, and to combine it with these thematic groups. China's practical research drew lessons from foreign political system structure and operation experience, and put forward various reports on thematic discussions.

The Central Political System Reform Seminar Group gradually formed a general plan for the reform of the political system on the basis of the thematic report and the research results of the theoretical circles put forward by the thematic group. This plan was agreed in principle by the Politburo of the Central Committee and submitted to the Seventh Plenary Session of the Twelfth Central Committee in October 1987. After thorough discussion, the plenary session agreed in principle to the General Idea of Political System Reform and decided to include the basic substance of the idea in the report of the Central Committee to the Thirteenth National Congress for discussion at the Congress.

Based on the concrete situation in China at the primary stage of socialism and the needs of socialist modernization construction, the report of the Thirteenth National Congress expounded the objectives, tasks, and principles of reform on the basis of in-depth analysis of the necessity and urgency of political system reform, putting forward a blueprint for China's political system reform.

2. Setting the Target for Political System Reform

The Thirteenth National Congress divided the objectives of political system reform into long-term and short-term goals. The long-term goal of political system reform as stipulated in the Thirteenth National Congress was to establish a highly democratic, complete legal system and an efficient, dynamic socialist political system. The short-term goal was to establish a leadership system conducive to improving efficiency, enhancing vitality, and mobilizing the enthusiasm of all sectors. Regarding the main content of the reform, the Thirteenth National Congress proposed seven aspects of reform in the near future.

> 1) It was important to separate the Party from the government and strengthen the Party's system construction. The key to the reform of the political system was the separation of Party and government. The leadership of the

Party was political leadership, that is, the leadership of political principles, political direction, major decision-making, and the recommendations of important cadres to state organs of power. The main ways for the Party to exercise political leadership in state affairs were to make the Party's propositions become the will of the state through legal procedures, to drive the broad masses of the people through the activities of Party organizations and the exemplary role of Party members, and to realize the Party's line, principles, and policies. In order to realize the separation of the Party and the government, it was necessary to adjust the Party's organizational form and working organization, strengthen the Party's system construction, and enhance the Party's understanding of the separation of the Party and the government. Only in this way could the desired goal be achieved.

2) Decentralization should be furthered. The phenomenon of excessive concentration of power was not only manifested in the excessive concentration of power of administrative, economic, and cultural organizations and various mass organizations in the leading organs of the Party, but also in the excessive concentration of power at the grassroots level in the leading organs at higher levels. This not only trapped the leading organs in administration and kept them from extricating themselves, but also robbed the grassroots units of autonomy and made it difficult to fully mobilize the enthusiasm of the people. The Thirteenth National Congress established the general principle of decentralization, which meant that everything fit for the subordinate administration should be decided and implemented by the subordinate departments.

3) The government should be reformed. Large and overstaffed government institutions, with too many levels, unclear responsibilities, and mutual harrying were the main reason for the formation of bureaucracy. Government institutions needed to be reformed from top to bottom. The principle of reform was to implement simplification, unity, and efficiency. The Thirteenth National Congress recommended that the State Council immediately begin to formulate a plan for the reform of the Central Government institutions and submit it to the First Session of the Seventh National People's Congress for approval and implementation.

4) Reform of the cadre and personnel system was needed. The key point of reform was to establish the national civil service system, that is, to

formulate laws and regulations and to scientifically manage the personnel who exercised the state administrative power and performed state affairs in the government according to law. At the same time, according to the principles of separating the Party from the government, separating the government from the enterprise, and combining closely and reasonably restricting the management of people and affairs, classified management needed to be carried out for all kinds of personnel. The main points were that the leaders and staff of Party organizations were to be managed by Party committees at all levels, the leaders and staff of state organs of power, judicial organs, and prosecution organs were to be managed by establishing a system similar to that of national civil servants, and the leaders and staff of mass organizations and managers of enterprises and institutions were, in principle, to be managed by their organizations or units in accordance with their respective articles of association or regulations.

5) It was important to establish a system of consultation and dialogue. This system was not only conducive to correctly handling and coordinating various social interests and contradictions, but also to promoting the work of leading organs at all levels to be based on listening to the opinions of the masses, receiving supervision, and avoiding mistakes. The basic principles of establishing consultative dialogue were to carry forward the fine tradition of "coming from the masses, going to the masses," to improve the openness of the activities of leading organs, to let the people know the important situation, and to discuss major issues with the people.

6) It was necessary to improve some systems of socialist democratic politics. These systems included first strengthening the people's Congress system, then improving the multi-party cooperation and political consultation system led by the Communist Party, followed by strengthening the construction of mass organizations, then improving the electoral system, followed by strengthening the institutionalization of democratic life at the grassroots level, and finally, further improving the system of regional national autonomy.

7) It was important to strengthen the construction of the socialist legal system. All aspects of the country's political, economic, and social life, as well as all aspects of democracy and dictatorship, should be governed by law, strictly enforcing the law, and prosecuting violations. Beginning with

the blueprint of political system reform put forward by the Thirteenth National Congress of the Communist Party of China, China's political system reform had gradually entered the stage of targeted, systematic, coordinated reform, in contrast to the earlier stage of partial reform.

On November 14, 1987, the new Politburo of the Central Committee held its first plenary meeting and discussed and adopted the Rules for the Work of the Thirteenth Central Politburo (Trial Implementation), the Rules for the Work of the Standing Committee of the Thirteenth Central Politburo (Trial Implementation), and the Rules for the Work of the Thirteenth Central Secretariat (Trial Implementation). These three rules and the later working rules of the State Council further straightened out the relationship between the Politburo of the Central Committee and its Standing Committee, and the Central Secretariat and the Plenary Session of the Central Committee. The Central Secretariat became an administrative body that no longer had decision-making functions. The Standing Committee of the Politburo regularly reported to the Politburo, and the Politburo regularly reported to the Plenary Session of the Central Committee. The number of plenary sessions of the Central Committee was also increased, from once a year to twice a year. At the same time, it also clarified the respective functions, scope of work, and working methods of the Central Committee and the Central People's Government, and provided preliminary norms for the relationship between the Central Committee of the Party and the highest administrative organs of the state to form a reasonable pattern in accordance with the requirements of the separation of Party and government functions. This was an important step in the democratic construction of the Party and the country.

At the same time, the Party began to exercise a margin election within the Party. According to the differential election method prescribed by the Central Committee of the Communist Party of China, the Thirteenth National Congress was elected by 20%, the members of the Central Committee by 5%, and the alternate members by 12%. The results of the thirteenth general election of the Communist Party of China were that ten candidates for the Central Committee were not elected, sixteen candidates were candidates for the Central Committee, and 4 members of the Commission for Discipline were not pre-elected. At the provincial level, the differential election was carried out in the election of the Standing Committee of the Provincial Party Committee, the chairman and vice-chairman of the Standing Committee of the People's Congress of provinces, autonomous regions, and municipalities directly under the Central Government, and the governors and vice-governors of provinces. In the provincial elections after the Thirteenth National Congress, eleven chairmen of the Standing Committee of the National People's Congress of the provinces, autonomous regions, and municipalities directly under the Central Government, eight governors and chairmen of the provinces and autonomous regions carried out a differential election, and 99 candidates recommended by the people's representatives of 28 provinces, autonomous regions, and municipalities directly under the Central Government were listed as formal candidates, of which twelve were elected, including four chairmen of the Standing Committee of the National People's Congress, two vice-chairmen presidents, and a President of the High Court. This was unprecedented in the history of people's political power elections since the founding of New China, and it had broad repercussions in China's political life.

According to the requirement of separating the functions of the Party and the government and improving the principle of the Party's leadership, the direct subordinate organs of the Central Committee were reformed in 1988. The Central Committee had 26 existing directly affiliated working institutions, of which eight had been abolished, three had been rebuilt, fifteen had been retained, and five had been newly established. After the adjustment, there were 23 working institutions and institutions directly under the Central Committee. In the process of reform, attention needed to be paid to clarifying the responsibilities of the Party's working and administrative departments, straightening out the relationship between the Party's working bodies and government agencies, transferring the work to the relevant government departments that should be undertaken by the government departments, and no longer setting up leading groups and offices overlapping with the Central Committee and the departments of the State Council. Provinces, autonomous regions, and municipalities directly under the Central Government accordingly formulated some rules and reformed their specific organizational forms and working methods. Generally, Party committees did not have full-time secretaries in charge of government work. They abolished their counterparts in Party committees' offices, streamlined Party committees' institutions, and reduced their full-time cadres.

In enterprises, according to the Draft Law of the People's Republic of China on Industrial Enterprises Owned by the People adopted by the First Session of the Seventh National People's Congress, the enterprise implemented the responsibility system of the factory director (manager), who was the legal representative of the enterprise, was in the central position of the enterprise, led the production, operation, and management of the enterprise, and bore overall responsibility for the construction of the material and spiritual civilization of the enterprise. The grassroots organizations of the CPC in enterprises guaranteed and supervised the implementation of the Party's and the state's policies in their enterprises. These provided the legal basis for the separation of Party and government functions in enterprises. After the promulgation and implementation of the Enterprise Law, the factory director (manager) responsibility system had been widely implemented in enterprises throughout the country, and the pattern of separation of Party and government functions in enterprises had basically taken shape.

3. The Reform of Government Institutions and the Initiation of the Reform of the Cadre and Personnel Systems

According to the blueprint of political system reform designed by the Thirteenth National Congress, the reform of government institutions and the cadre and personnel systems had been put on the agenda. The First Session of the Seventh National People's Congress, held from March 25 to April 14, 1988, approved the Plan for the Reform of the State Council's Institutions. When Li Peng wrote the Report on the Work of the Government, he expounded the goals, principles, and key points of the reform of government institutions. He said that the long-term goal of the reform of government institutions was to gradually establish an administrative system with complete functions, reasonable structure, coordinated operation, flexibility, and efficiency with Chinese characteristics, in accordance with the principles of separation of Party and government, of government and enterprise, and focused on simplification, unity, and efficiency. To achieve this goal, long-term effort was needed. In the next five years, effort needed to be made to create conditions to gradually straighten out the relationship between the government, enterprises, institutions, and people's organizations, between government departments, and between the central and local governments.

The State Council's Institutional Reform Program determined that twelve ministries and commission-level institutions had been abolished, nine ministries and commissions had been newly established, and 32 had been retained. Together, the original 45 had been adjusted to 41, and Xinhua News Agency had been transformed into a public institution. In addition, the number of directly affiliated organs of the State Council had been adjusted from 22 to 19, the number of offices has been adjusted from four to seven, the number of national bureaus under the centralized management of ministries and commissions from 14 to 15, and the number of non-permanent organs from 77 to 44. The staff that had been streamlined made up about 20% of the total.

Compared with the reform in 1982, the biggest difference in this institutional reform of the State Council was that it was carried out in accordance with the requirements of the reform process of political and economic systems, with the transformation of functions as the key, in line with the system construction within the government and in conjunction with the preparatory work for the implementation of the national civil service system. In practice, it was important to grasp the key of transforming functions, decompose functions according to the principle of separation of government and enterprise, transfer the functions of direct management of enterprises, lay down the functions of direct management of money and goods, and strengthen the functions of decision-making, consultation, regulation, supervision, and information reserved for the Central Government. At the same time, it also strengthened the social management functions originally undertaken by the Party departments but which should have been undertaken by the government departments. On this basis, the staffing establishment was determined according to their new functions. According to their functions, departments undertaking the same or similar business should be cancelled, and their business should be undertaken by a single department. General economic departments did not have counterpart professional organizations, and the management of industry was to be undertaken by the competent departments. Only divisions and departments should be set up within the ministries and commissions to reduce the management level within the departments. The institutional reform of the State Council promoted the transformation of the government from direct to indirect management. It also facilitated the reduction of overlapping functions and institutions, and the enhancement of institutional vitality and the improvement of work efficiency. This laid a good foundation for further reform and local institutional reform.

The reform of Central Government institutions also required the corresponding convergence of local reforms. For this reason, the Office of Institutional Reform of the State Council began preparations in August 1988. Previously, in May 1986, the pilot work of local institutional reform had been carried out in sixteen medium-sized cities. In 1989, with the approval of the State Council, four cities with separate plans, including Ha'erbin, Qingdao, Wuhan, and Shenzhen, and nine counties, including Jicheng in Hebei Province, Yuanping in Shanxi Province, Zhuozi Mountain in Inner Mongolia Autonomous Region, Shangyu in Zhejiang Province, Hua County in Henan Province, Bao'an in Guangdong Province, Qionglai in Sichuan Province, and Dingxi in Gansu Province were designated to carry out institutional reform pilot projects. After gaining experience at different levels and with different types of reform pilot projects, the pilot projects were expanded in 1991. After the pilot project, not only did the pilot unit itself achieve results in the institutional reform, but it also made the ideas of local institutional reform clearer. According to this experience, the State Council envisaged progressively promoting the reform of local institutions. The basic idea was to start with straightening out relations and transforming functions, then carry out the reform of local institutions, including straightening out the relationship between the central and local governments and the relationship between local governments at all levels, rationally divide functions and powers and transforming the functions of local governments at all levels in accordance with the requirements of separation of government and enterprise, and then strive to implement the scientific administrative decision-making, the perfection of the administrative execution system, the rationalization of the administrative supervision system, and the improvement of the operational mechanism of the administrative management.

The establishment of the national civil service system was the key point of the reform of the cadre and personnel system determined by the Thirteenth National Congress. According to the plan of the Thirteenth National Congress, the Ministry of Personnel had been set up as a national civil servant administration institution. After the establishment of the Ministry of Personnel, it began to formulate regulations for the management of national civil servants. At the same time, it carried out pilot projects in six departments, namely, the Audit Office, the General Administration of Customs, the National Statistical Bureau, the State Tax Administration, the State Building Materials Bureau and the State Environmental Protection Bureau. In 1991, two cities, Ha'erbin and Shenzhen, were selected for the pilot project of the local civil service system. The pilot projects of the six departments of the State Council began with the classification of posts in connection with the institutional reform. The determination of government functions was not only the basis for the establishment of institutions, but also the premise for the establishment of the civil service system. It was undoubtedly a great progress to shift from a situation in which the functions were unclear and people were chosen based on their own circumstances to clearly distinguished functions and choosing personnel based on job requirements. From April 1989, the six departments carried out a pilot job classification project on the basis of the "three determinations" scheme. By the end of June 1990, 2,618 jobs were surveyed, analyzed, and evaluated, and job classification criteria and ranking were worked out.

Another important aspect of the civil service system was the civil service examination recruitment and training system. From 1987 to 1988, the provincial examination system was adopted in thirteen supplementary civil servants departments, such as politics, law, industry and commerce, taxation, and so on. More than one million people across the country signed up for the test, employing more than 80,000 people. In January 1989, the Central Organizational Department and the State Personnel Department issued the Circular on the Measures for Examination and Assessment of Supplementary Staff of State Administrative Organs, which required supplementary staff of administrative organs at or above the county level to implement the Measures for Examination and Assessment. Its procedures included publishing announcements, qualification examinations, written examinations, interviews, physical examinations, assessments and employment. The examination system had existed throughout Chinese history, with the imperial examination system formed through thousands of years of history being the main way China had always selected officials. The examination and employment system for civil servants was not the revival of the traditional imperial examination system, but an important reform of the past cadre selection system to meet the needs of modern social life. This method of an examination open to the public and selection of the best recruits had a positive impact on the implementation of the principle of competition in cadre personnel management, strengthening democratic supervision, preventing unhealthy tendencies in employment, and ensuring the quality of recruits.

Great strides were also made in the reform of the personnel system in enterprises and institutions. In May 1988, the Ministry of Organizations and Personnel of the Central Committee formulated Opinions on the Reform of the Cadre and Personnel System by Introducing Competition Mechanism into Enterprises Owned by the People, requiring the introduction of competition mechanism into enterprise personnel management and the selection of enterprise managers through public bidding, the appointment of managers at all levels within enterprises to carry out various forms of appointment system, employing them systematically, and giving selecting and appointing enterprises the right to appoint and dismiss and individuals the right to be appointed and resign. In 1991, the Central Organizational Department and the Ministry of Personnel issued the Provisional Regulations on the Management of Employed Cadres Under the System of Public Ownership, which unified the provisions on employment, mobilization, retirement, and treatment, so as to further improve the system of employing cadres within enterprises.

By the end of 1990, the number of appointed cadres in enterprises nationwide had reached 1.7 million, of which more than 90% were employed from workers. Practice had proven that the employment system for enterprise cadres was relatively successful. Therefore, many public institutions also used similar methods for inviting tenders to select cadres to produce their own leaders. The appointment system for professional and technical posts was widely implemented among scientific and technological cadres.

IV

The New Path to Strengthening the Party's Construction through Institution Building

Whether China's Reform and Opening Up and socialist modernization could achieve the desired goal was determined by many factors, one of the most important of which was the situation of the Communist Party of China as the ruling party. Since the Third Plenary Session of the Eleventh Central Committee, while leading the reform and economic construction, the CPC firmly grasped the key link of strengthening the Party's self-construction. While strengthening the Party's ideological and political construction, it made great effort to strengthen the Party's organizational construction and style of work, gradually embarking on a new way of strengthening the Party's construction through construction of its systems.

1. Completion of the New Round of Party Consolidation

At the time of the Twelfth National Congress, the Central Committee decided to carry out a comprehensive rectification of the Party's style and organization in stages and in batches over a period of three years, beginning in the second half of 1983.

From October 11–12, 1983, the Second Plenary Session of the Twelfth Central Committee of the Communist Party of China was held in Beijing. In accordance with the decision of the Twelfth National Congress of the Communist Party of China, the Plenary Session deployed the work of Party consolidation in a comprehensive way. The plenary session issued the Decision of the Central Committee of the Communist Party of China on Party Integration (hereinafter referred to as the Decision). The Decision analyzed the necessity and urgency of Party consolidation and put forward the general purpose and requirement of Party consolidation, namely, under the guidance of Marxism-Leninism and Mao Zedong Thought, relying on the revolutionary consciousness of all Party comrades, correctly utilizing the sharp weapon of criticism and self-criticism, carrying out Party discipline, exposing and solving the serious problems of ideology, style of work, and organization existing in the Party, aiming to achieve a fundamental improvement in the Party's style of work, improving the ideological and working level of the whole Party, strengthening the ties between the Party and the people, and striving to make Party building a strong core of the cause of socialist modernization.

The Decision clearly stipulated that the task of this Party consolidation was to unify Party members' thinking, rectify their style of work, strengthen discipline, and purify the organization. The specific explanation, as offered in the Decision, was:

1) The idea of unification is to further achieve a high degree of ideological and political consistency throughout the Party and correct all erroneous tendencies that violate the Four Basic Principles and the Party's line since the Third Plenary Session of the Eleventh Central Committee.
2) Rectifying the style of work is meant to carry forward the revolutionary spirit of serving the people wholeheartedly, correcting all kinds of acts of utilizing power for personal gain, and opposing the irresponsible bureaucracy of the Party to the people.
3) Strengthening discipline involves adhering to the organizational principle of democratic centralism, opposing unorganized and undisciplined patriarchal systems, factionalism, anarchism, and liberalism, and changing the weak and scattered situation of Party organizations.
4) Purifying organizations involves cleansing the Party, in accordance with the provisions of the Party Charter, of those who consistently oppose and endanger the Party.

The Decision stipulated that the steps for rectifying the Party were to move from the Central Government to the grassroots Party organizations, and they were to be rectified in stages and batches from top to bottom. In order to rectify the Party organizations in each unit, it was necessary to first lead the leading group and cadres, then the Party members and the masses from top to bottom. The basic methods of rectifying the Party were to carry out criticism and self-criticism, distinguish right from wrong, correct mistakes, and purify the organization on the basis of conscientious study of documents and raising ideological awareness. In the process of Party consolidation, ideological education should be strengthened from beginning to end, with a view to improving the ideological awareness of the majority of Party members. The Decision announced the establishment of the Central Steering Committee for Party Integration.

According to the Party consolidation decision and the deployment of the Party consolidation Steering Committee of the Central Committee of the Communist Party of China, the comprehensive Party consolidation was actually carried out in three phases. The first phase was carried out in central and state organs, ministries and commissions, provinces, autonomous regions, municipalities directly under the Central Government, and major units of the PLA. In order to strengthen the leadership of the first phase of Party consolidation, the Central Steering

Committee for Party Consolidation and the Central Military Commission had dispatched ninety groups of Party consolidation liaison officers with 850 participants, and set up guidance groups for Party consolidation work in ten sections of central and state organs. During this period, the Central Steering Committee for Party Integration had successively issued eleven notices and other documents. These documents gave specific instructions on the study of documents in Party consolidation, listening attentively to the opinions of non-Party friends and non-Party masses, the formation of two sets of work teams for Party consolidation and business consolidation, and on issues such as comparative inspection, rectification and reform, organization and processing, registration of Party members, review and summary, and consolidation and development of Party consolidation. They not only offered timely guidance for the work of the first phase of Party consolidation at all stages, but also gave specific instructions on various aspects of Party consolidation and development. The work of Party consolidation played an important role.

The second phase was carried out in Party organizations of enterprises, undertakings, colleges and universities, and scientific research institutions at the local, county, and equivalent levels. From February 28 to March 6, 1985, the Central Steering Committee for Party Integration convened the second session of the Party Integration Working Conference and deployed the second phase of party integration. In response to several unhealthy tendencies that interfered with the construction and reform of the Party and society at that time, the Central Steering Committee for Party Consolidation stressed in its circular that strengthening the party spirit of Party members, correcting new unhealthy tendencies, ensuring the smooth progress of reform, and promoting the healthy development of the political and economic situation should be the prominent focus of Party consolidation at the local and county levels. In order to grasp the basic situation of the second phase of Party consolidation work, the Central Steering Committee for Party Consolidation dispatched seven groups of inspectors to various places to investigate the situation, uncover problems, sum up experiences, and put forward suggestions.

The third phase was carried out in the grassroots Party organizations in the vast rural areas. On November 24, 1985, the Central Steering Committee for Party Consolidation issued a circular on the deployment of the work of Party consolidation in the countryside and made a comprehensive arrangement on the specific requirements, methods, and steps of the work of Party consolidation in rural areas. Provinces, autonomous regions, and municipalities directly under the Central Government sent 630,000 publicity and liaison workers to the countryside to help consolidate the Party. From May to June 1986, the Central Steering Committee for Party Rectification held a seminar on Party Secretary's Party Rectification in different provinces, autonomous regions, and municipalities directly under the Central Government, which further clarified the basic guiding ideology of Party consolidation in rural areas. It was requested that the solution of serious power-seeking and serious violations of law and discipline among Party members and cadres in districts, townships, and villages should be given prominent priority and be earnestly done, and that the rural leadership should be effectively strengthened.

In the spring of 1987, the three-and-a-half-year national Party consolidation work was basically completed. On May 26, Bo Yibo, the Standing Vice-Director of the Steering Committee of the Central Committee for Party Consolidation, made a report entitled "Basic Summary of Party Consolidation and Further Strengthening Party Construction" and an overall appraisal of party integration. Bo Yibo concretely pointed out that achievements in the unification of ideas included: 1) Through careful and systematic study of the Party consolidation documents, the Party had clarified many ambiguous understandings, deepened its understanding of the socialist line with Chinese characteristics since the Third Plenary Session of the Eleventh Central Committee, and clarified its adherence to reform, opening up, invigorating the economy, and vigorously developing socialism. It determined that the planned commodity economy was the only way to build a prosperous, democratic, and civilized socialist country and further improved the consciousness of implementing these Marxist principles and policies. 2) By carrying out the education of completely denying the Cultural Revolution, the Party members made it clear that both factions in the Cultural Revolution carried out their activities under the guidance of the leftist theory of "taking class struggle as the guiding principle" and "continuing revolution under the dictatorship of the proletariat," which were generally wrong, thus promoting the further elimination of the pernicious influence of factionalism and leftist tendencies and laying a more solid ideological and political foundation for strengthening the Party's unity and inspiring the Party members' spirit of reform and innovation. 3) Through the education on Party spirit, ideals, and purposes, the situation of some Party members' weak communist ideals and sense of serving the people had been changed, so that the majority of Party members had raised their ideological awareness and strengthened their ability to resist the decadent erosion of capitalist and feudalist ideas.

The progress made in rectifying the style of work included: 1) All localities made great effort to investigate and deal with some cases of serious violations of law and discipline, the abuse of power for personal gain, and serious irresponsible bureaucracy by Party members, which had basically stopped the new unhealthy tendencies of Party and government cadres running enterprises and improved the Party's style to varying degrees. 2) It promoted the transformation of the work of leading organs at all levels, reduced bureaucracy, and strengthened the idea of serving the grassroots level. Leading Party members in many regions and departments had taken the lead in going deep into the grassroots level, conducting investigations and studies to solve practical problems in construction, reform, and mass life, thus bringing the relationship between the Party and the masses closer. 3) In rural Party consolidation, most had carried out financial clearance work. Party members and cadres took the lead in returning long-term arrears of public funds and property and in doing practical work for the masses, which was welcomed by the peasant masses.

The main achievements in strengthening discipline and purifying organizations were: 1) Cleaning up the "three kinds of people" and those who made serious mistakes in the Cultural Revolution. Party organizations at all levels spent a great deal of energy on members who participated in the special verification of Party consolidation, overcome various difficulties and obstacles, and had done a good deal of arduous investigation and evidence-gathering work. On the basis of several checks conducted before the Party consolidation, which dealt with 400,000 people, another 5,449 "three kinds of people" and 43,074 people who made serious mistakes were addressed throughout the country (excluding Guangxi Zhuang Autonomous Region). 2) The tradition of carrying out criticism and self-criticism and regularly participating in organizational activities within the Party had been restored and developed, and the Party members' concept of organizational discipline had been strengthened. After rectification, some Party organizations that were in a paralyzed and semi-paralyzed state made a marked improvement. 3) Through the registration and organizational processing of Party members, a number of members with serious problems or who were unqualified were dealt with. There were 33,896 expulsions, 90,069 non-registrations, 145,456 suspended registrations, and 184,071 detainees for Party inspection, removal of Party posts, and suggestions to non-Party organizations for removal of non-Party posts, serious warnings, and warnings. 4) A number of weak, scattered leading groups had been adjusted, and about half of the leading groups above the county level had been enriched to varying degrees. Through adjustment and enrichment, the construction of leading groups had been promoted. A group of outstanding young and middle-aged Party members with strong Party spirit, decent style, and the ability to lead the masses to resolutely implement the Party's current policies had entered leading posts at all levels.

The weightiest aspect of this Party consolidation work was to clear up the "three kinds of people" hidden in Party organizations at all levels (referring to those who followed the Lin Biao and Jiang Qing Counter-revolutionary Group for rebellion in the Cultural Revolution, those with a serious gang mentality, and those who beat, smashed, and robbed others), to eliminate the hidden dangers affecting Party unity and interfering with Party building, and to purify Party organizations.

It was clear that there were still some shortcomings in the Party consolidation work, such as the unbalanced development of the work, some units including some high and intermediate leading organs of the party and government, failing to thoroughly complete the four basic tasks of the Party consolidation, and some even doing perfunctory work, thus affecting and damaging the reputation of the Party consolidation work among the masses. Units that had done fairly well in Party consolidation had also left behind some problems in Party conduct and other aspects, which needed to be addressed in the regular Party building work in the future.

2. The New Stage of the Party's Cadre Construction

Mao Zedong once said when he talked about the importance of the Party's cadre construction, "After the political line is determined, cadres are the decisive factor." Throughout his life, Mao attached the greatest importance to the cultivation of Party cadres. Chen Yun once said that from the Zunyi Conference to the victory of the War of Resistance Against Japanese Aggression, one of Mao's incomparable achievements was to train a generation of cadres, including the early leaders and a group of cadres from "the years 1937 and 1938."

After the Third Plenary Session of the Eleventh Central Committee, the second generation of the leading team of the Central Committee, with Deng Xiaoping at its core, gradually found a way to build socialism with Chinese characteristics, formed a set of correct principles and policies, and created a new situation of socialist modernization. Deng was not intoxicated by this, but further extended his antenna, considering how to ensure that the cause initiated by the older generation of revolutionaries could succeed.

As early as August 18, 1980, when Deng addressed the enlarged meeting of the Politburo of the Central Committee, he first proposed that cadres should pursue the Four Modernizations. On December 25 that year, Deng clearly put forward the Four Modernizations standard for cadres at the Central Working Conference under the theme of Implementing the Readjustment Policy and Ensuring Stability and Unity. He said that on the foundation of adhering to the socialist path, it was important to make cadres younger, more knowledgeable, and more professional, and gradually formulate a sound cadre system to ensure it. The three criteria of younger, more knowledgeable, and more professional were put forward, with the added note that they must first of all be revolutionary, so the premise was to adhere to the socialist road.

On July 2, 1981, Deng Xiaoping delivered a speech at the Symposium of Party Secretaries of provinces, autonomous regions, and municipalities directly under the Central Government. The topic was The First Task of Old Cadres: Selecting Young and Middle-aged Cadres. After analyzing the importance of promoting young and middle-aged cadres, he put forward the goal and plan of training and selecting young and middle-aged cadres. He suggested that comrades discuss whether they could put forward a five-year plan – or four years would be better – until 1985. On the issue of cadres, he suggested two plans, a five-year plan and a ten-year plan. In the first five years, 50,000 people would be selected and put into suitable posts for practice. It was important to put forward a request that during the five years, leading members, members at the level of departments and bureaus, and members at the level of provinces, autonomous regions, and municipalities who were about 40 or 50 years old had gradually achieved their respective proportions. In the next five years, it would be possible to determine which level of leadership members (for example, provincial, municipal, autonomous region, ministerial level) should, except for special circumstances, not exceed the age limit.

At the Twelfth National Congress of the Communist Party of China, Deng Xiaoping delivered an opening speech. He put the realization of the Four Modernizations of the cadre ranks as the top priority in his current work. At this congress, being "revolutionary, young, knowledgeable, and professional" was written into the new Party Constitution adopted by the Twelfth National Congress as the goal of building a contingent of cadres with Chinese characteristics.

The Four Modernizations construction of the cadre contingent was to apply the principle of both morality, talent, integrity, and specialization to the construction of the cadre contingent, which reflected the objective requirements of the cause of socialist modernization in China. Revolution meant that cadres must uphold the political and ideological lines established since the Third Plenary Session of the Eleventh Central Committee, embrace the Party spirit, not factionalism, adhere to the socialist path, and have a strong sense of enterprise and responsibility. On the premise of revolution, the younger generation was to select a large number of outstanding young and middle-aged cadres to leading posts at all levels, so that the cadres of the Party and the leading organs at all levels of the country could form an echelon structure and be full of vigor and vitality. Intellectualization and specialization required leading cadres to have a certain level of education and knowledge, to master and apply knowledge of modern natural science, social science, and management science, and to carry out scientific leadership and management in socialist modernization. This had fundamentally altered the earlier tendency to emphasize family origin, length of party membership, and seniority in the selection criteria of leading cadres.

In order to realize the Four Modernizations of the cadre contingent, it was necessary to abolish the life-long system of leading cadres' posts. This was a key point, and a difficult one. In this regard, the Party and the State took the following four measures in abolishing the life-long cadre system:

1) *Establish the tenure system of cadres' posts.* The Constitution of the People's Republic of China, adopted at the Fifth Session of the National People's Congress, abolished the lifelong system of cadre posts in the form of a fundamental national law. The Constitution stipulated that the term of office of the highest leadership in various countries should be five years, and that no more than two consecutive terms would be allowed.

2) *Establish a cadre retirement system.* In 1982, the Central Committee of the Communist Party of China issued the Decision on the Establishment of a Cadre Retirement System, which stipulated that the main comrades in charge at the ministerial and provincial levels of the central and state organs should not exceed 65 years of age in office, 60 years of age in deputy posts, and 60 years of age in general for cadres at the department and bureau levels. Individuals who had not reached retirement age may retire early if in poor health. After the retirement of cadres, the treatment of political life remained unchanged. According to the spirit of the document, by the end of 1982, more than 7,260 veteran cadres in the organs directly under the Central Committee of the Communist Party of China and the central state organs had gone through retirement procedures. In August 1982, at the Seventh Plenary Session of the Eleventh Central Committee of the Communist Party of China, Liu Bocheng and Cai Chang withdrew from leading posts. In September 1985, at the Fourth Plenary Session of the Twelfth Central Committee of the Communist Party of China, 64 veteran comrades, such as Ye Jianying, Deng Yingchao, Xu Qian, and Nie Rongzhen, requested that they no longer serve as members of the Central Committee and alternate members of the Central Committee. Thirty-seven veteran comrades, such as Li Jingquan, Xiao Jinguang, and He Changgong, requested that they no longer serve as members of the Central Customs Commission, and thirty veteran comrades, such as Huang Kecheng and Wang Congwu no longer served as members of the Central Discipline Commission.

Deng Xiaoping, who advocated the abolition of the lifelong system of leadership, had long hoped that he would gradually step down from the political stage, because he realized that too great a reputation was a burden on him, and too much personal weight for any individual was also a burden on the Party and the state. Many countries based their policy toward China on whether he was ill or dead, but it was abnormal and dangerous to base a country's destiny on the prestige of one or two people. In case of personnel changes, such an approach would lead to instability. No matter what happened, an accident would be irremediable. Deng did not wish to see such a situation. Therefore, as early as November 2, 1979, he stated at a meeting of senior cadres that if the Party allowed him to retire then, he would do so immediately. He noted that he said this in earnest.

On September 2, 1986, when Deng Xiaoping met with the American journalist Mike Wallace, he said that he advocated the abolition of the life-long system and the establishment of a retirement system. When he had spoken to the Italian journalist Oriana Fallaci, he had said that he would work until 1985, and it was now more than a year past that. He was thinking about when to retire, and he personally wanted to retire soon.

In 1987, before the Thirteenth National Congress of the Communist Party of China, Deng Xiaoping formally put forward his desire to retire in order to abolish the lifelong system of cadres' leading posts. At this time, the Central Committee had repeatedly considered Deng Xiaoping's own views and those both inside and outside the Party, and it was decided that he would resign from other posts except Chairman of the Military Commission of the Party and the State. From that time, he stopped asking about the daily work of the Central Committee and achieved a half-retreat.

3) *Reduce the number of deputy and part-time jobs.* In August 1980, Hua Guofeng was no longer concurrent Premier of the State Council. Deng Xiaoping, Li Xiannian, Chen Yun, Wang Zhen, and Wang Renzhong were no longer concurrent Vice Premiers. In 1982, the number of deputy posts was reduced during the institutional reform of the Central Committee and the State Council. The number of Vice-Presidents of the State Council was reduced from thirteen to two. According to the statistics of 38 ministries and committees, in addition to part-time ministers and directors, there were 167 full and vice-ministers, 338 fewer than the original 505 and a 67% reduction. Their average age was 58 years, a 6-year reduction. Cadres with a university education level originally accounted for 52%, an increase from the previous 37%. According to the statistics of 28 ministries and committees, 720 departments and bureaus were originally set up, but now they had been reduced to 488, a reduction of 32%. The number of directors and deputy directors was reduced from 2,450 to 1,398, a reduction of 43%. Their average age had been 59, but now it was reduced to 54. The number of cadres with university education increased from 36% to 49%.[3]

4) *Establishment of a consultancy system.* In 1981, Deng Xiaoping put forward the idea of establishing an advisory system, saying that, besides the Central Committee, an advisory committee should also be set up to "accommodate some old comrades," and the advisor should not be in the present position, so that he could give up his position to the young people. At the same time, the advisor was also a kind of position, and his rank was no less than that of the members of the Party committees at the same level. It was easier for the old comrades to

move into this position. Clearly, a consultant was not a lax position, but played a "guiding or mentoring" role, which was "to help the young to get on the horse, and give them a ride." Deng Xiaoping's intention was deeply seated, because China's leadership not only had an aging problem, but also an issue of inheritance. To solve these two problems, the establishment of the consultancy system was a good compromise. In September 1982, the Central Advisory Committee was formally established, and Deng was elected Director of the Committee.

The establishment of the Central Advisory Committee made historic contributions to ensuring the long-term stability of the Party and the country at a historical turning point. After the establishment of the Chinese Customs Commission, the Central Committee of the CPC did much fruitful work in helping the Party maintain its unity and social stability, and in promoting reform, opening up, and modernization.

Deng expected to abolish the Advisory Committee after another ten years, or fifteen at most. By 1992, the Central Advisory Committee was just ten years old. Over the previous ten years, the cooperation and alternation between the new and old cadres of the Party progressed smoothly. At the same time, the Advisory Committee lasted for two sessions, and its members were old. As a transitional measure, its mission had been completed. In view of this, the Central Advisory Committee proposed to the Fourteenth National Congress that no Central Advisory Committee should be established after this Congress. After careful and thorough discussion, the Central Committee decided not to set up the Central Advisory Committee of the Party and the Advisory Committee of provinces, municipalities, and autonomous regions.

These measures created favorable conditions for the selection of young and middle-aged cadres and the realization of the goal of the Four Modernizations of the Party's cadre contingent. The Central Committee seized this opportunity to speed up the construction of the Four Modernizations of the Party's cadres.

From 1984 to 1985, the Central Government adjusted the leading bodies at all levels. In the previous year or so, there were 47 newly appointed ministers, directors and bureau directors directly under the Central Committee and the State Council, and 80 vice-ministers, vice-directors, and bureau deputy directors directly under the State Council. Nearly 100 young and middle-aged cadres were newly selected. The average age of the leading bodies of 81 departments of the State Council before the adjustment was 56.6 years old, which had decreased by five years. The proportion under 55 years old increased from 10% to 30%, and those with an educational level of junior college increased by 27.5% to 71%. During the same period, the average age of the standing committees of the Party committees of 29 provinces, autonomous regions, and municipalities directly under the Central Government, as well as the heads and deputy governors, chairmen, and mayors decreased from 57 to 53 years old, with 90% under 55 years old and 80% with a higher education level. In the same period, the leading bodies of 3,000 large and medium-sized backbone enterprises in China were adjusted to form an echelon structure, with cadres in their 40s as the main body. According to the statistics of 2,900 enterprises, 20% of the 18,000 leading cadres were under 40 years old, 63% were between 41 and 50 years old, and the average age was 45. Seventy-four percent of factory directors had an educational level higher than junior college, and 89% of them had higher education, 40% higher than before. Eighty-one percent of the Party secretaries had an education level above technical college, 70% higher than before. In order to accelerate the realization of the youth of cadres, the National Congress was held in 1985. This was a conference focusing on resolving the problem of lowering the average age of cadres. At this meeting, 131 veteran leaders withdrew from the Party's main leading bodies and 179 new leaders were elected. Newly elected Central Committee members and newly appointed ministers and provincial Party committee secretaries were generally in their 50s, and some were in their early 40s. This was an unprecedented catalyst in the history of the Communist Party of China. Deng Xiaoping said that matter deserved a special chapter in the history of the Party.

In view of the fact that a considerable number of veteran cadres of leading bodies at all levels had to withdraw from their posts for a period of time, there would be a disconnection if there were not a sufficient intake of new recruits as reserve forces. For this reason, the Central Committee decided to establish a reserve cadre system and a contingent of excellent young and middle-aged cadres under 50 years of age, especially around 40 years of age, as the main body. They would be put into practical work as a test. They would be further tested by organizations and the masses with real work achievements, and those with outstanding performance would be promoted and employed in a timely manner.

By strengthening the Four Modernizations construction of the cadre contingent, China's cadre contingent began to take on a new look. On the premise of revolutionization, a large number of young and middle-aged cadres stepped into leading posts, forming a cadre force with echelons of old, middle-aged, and young people with rich experience and vigorous vitality, and its combat effectiveness and cohesion were strengthened. Of course, there was still a long way to go in the construction of the Four Modernizations of the cadre contingent, and there were still many tasks to be done and many contradictions to be overcome.

3. Correcting Various Unhealthy Tendencies Within the Party

Party conduct was the concentrated reflection of the Party's spiritual outlook, directly related to the image of the Party and prestige of the Party among the people. Therefore, in the process of Reform and Opening Up, the Central Committee attached great importance to a range of unhealthy tendencies and worked hard to resolve them seriously.

First, it was forbidden for the Party and government cadres, their children, and their spouses to run businesses and engage in unhealthy practices. After the Third Plenary Session of the Twelfth Central Committee, as the focus of China's reform shifted from rural areas to cities, entering a stage of comprehensive reform, economic development entered a new round of growth, and the country witnessed a business boom, some party and government organs and cadres were consciously or unconsciously involved in it, creating a peculiar landscape in economic life. Before the comprehensive reorganization of companies in 1988, more than 470,000 companies were registered in China. Among the numerous companies, there were central-level companies run by the Party, government, and army departments and national mass organizations, subsidiaries run by the children of officials in various regions, and "remaining-heat companies" run by retired veteran cadres. Among them, a considerable number of companies did not divide government from enterprise or government from business, and were often sold for huge profits. Some companies operated in disorder and deviated from China's actual situation to offer high wages and welfare. A few people abused their power to embezzle, steal, speculate, and take bribes, which seriously interfered with the establishment of a sound socialist economic order for clean government, aggravated the contradiction of unfair social distribution, and affected social stability.

The Central Committee of the Communist Party of China maintained a sober understanding of the situation of the Party and government organs in running businesses and the serious harm it brought. On December 3, 1984, the Central Committee of the Communist Party of China and the State Council issued the Decision on the Strict Prohibition of Business and Enterprise Running by Party and Government Organs and Party Members and Cadres. It was made clear that Party and government leading organs at all levels, especially economic departments and their leading cadres, should correctly play their functions in leading and organizing economic construction, adhering to the principle of separation of duties and business, and carrying forward the style of honesty, integrity, and impartiality. It was forbidden to use their power to run businesses, set up enterprises, seek private interests, and gain profits from the people. The Central Committee called on leading organs and comrades at all levels of the Party and government to maintain a clear mind, adopt a clear attitude, and resolutely put an end to corruption.

However, after banning cadres in Party and government organs from doing business, new situations arose. Unexpectedly, the children and spouses of some leading cadres took part in doing business. On May 23, 1985, the Central Committee of the Communist Party of China and the State Council issued the Decision on Prohibiting the Business of the Children and Spouses of Leading Cadres, which stipulated that all the children and spouses of leading cadres at or above the county and regiment levels were not allowed to do business except in state-owned, collective, and Sino-foreign joint ventures. On July 9, the General Office of the Central Committee of the Communist Party of China and the General Office of the State Council issued the Supplementary Notice on the Non-concurrent Employment of Cadres of Party and Government Organs as Economic Entities, making relevant provisions.

For a period of time, most of the enterprises run by the Party and government organs were suspended or decoupled from the Party and government organs. Most of the Party and government cadres who participated in business-running enterprises returned to the organs or resigned from the leading positions of the Party and government. However, the unhealthy trend was like waste grass, "despite the burning of the wildfire, coming to life with a spring breeze." Some party and government organs and cadres still adopted various methods to continue to run businesses, some party and government cadres continued to hold concurrent positions in enterprises, some family members used the relationship between leading cadres to influence business enterprises, and some serious illegal acts in business enterprises, especially involving some leading cadres, could not be solved properly.

In order to resolutely stop the tendency of Party and government organs and cadres to run businesses, on February 4, 1986, the Central Committee of the Communist Party of China and the State Council issued the Provisions on Further Restricting Party and Government Organs and Party and Government Cadres from Doing Business and Running Enterprises, which required that Party committees and governments at all levels resolutely implement the Central Committee's provisions and implement the decrees and prohibitions. Those who refused to implement the law would be dealt with seriously, and the leaders would be held accountable. Discipline committees and administrative departments for industry and commerce at all levels were to closely cooperate with organizations, personnel, auditing, banking, and judicial departments to supervise implementation.

Through the implementation of the spirit of this document, the problems of the Party and government organs and cadres in running businesses were preliminarily solved.

Further, it was important to investigate and deal with the problem of bribery of Party and government cadres. In the process of prohibiting Party and government cadres from running businesses and doing wrong things, the problem of graft and bribery of Party and government cadres was also investigated and dealt with.

As the commodity economy was becoming more active, and administrative, market, and enterprise actions had not yet been regulated by the legal system, corruption, such as power and money exchange, was most likely to breed and spread. In view of the new characteristics of building a clean, honest party in the new situation, on June 30, 1987, the Central Discipline Commission issued the Decision on Firmly Investigating and Punishing the Bribery of Communist Party Members, pointing out that in recent years, in China's foreign economic activities, the corrupt acts of taking and demanding bribes, which were common in feudal and capitalist societies, had spread in some places and departments. This situation aroused strong dissatisfaction both inside and outside the Party and in China and abroad. This required the Party's great attention and its resolute action to severely investigate and punish bribery and bribe-soliciting. For this reason, the Central Discipline Inspection Commission made three decisions. 1) All Party members, especially leading cadres, who violated the criminal law by taking or soliciting bribes were to be expelled from the Party, and all Party members who solicited bribes by any means must take the initiative to explain their situations. If not, when they are found out, they would be removed from the Party regardless of the seriousness of the circumstances. 2) Normal "kickbacks" in economic activities were not to be taken by anyone as personal gains for any reason or excuse, but were to be turned over to the state or the unit, and the violators would be dealt with seriously in accordance with Party rules and discipline. 3) Party organizations at all levels, including disciplinary inspection organs, should conscientiously strengthen the education, management, and supervision of Party members and never allow the act of trading the Party principles. Party members who solicited or accepted bribes were to be investigated and dealt with resolutely. If they allowed bribes and refused to deal with them, their Party organizations would be held accountable.

After a period of great effort, due to these powerful measures, the unhealthy trend of taking and soliciting bribes was basically stopped, but it had not been eradicated. Therefore, the Party Central Committee called on the whole Party to fight tirelessly against this corruption.

Finally, the unhealthy tendencies of selecting and appointing cadres in overseas affairs should be severely shaken. After the Third Plenary Session of the Eleventh Central Committee, great achievements had been made in selecting and appointing cadres. However, there were still some problems, which were prominent. For instance, some leading cadres did not abide by the Party's principles and violated organizational and personnel discipline. Some chose people according to their personal likes and dislikes, or on the basis of their own advantages and disadvantages, or from the feudal clan and sectarian concept. Some used various means to promote and appoint their children, relatives, and friends through "back door" methods. Some traded positions for profits and made transactions. Some did not fight for rank treatment for the cadres of their system or unit according to the policy and upgraded their units. Some ignored their duties and principles, or even sought personal gain through power. The examples were endless.

In order to stop the unhealthy trend of selecting and appointing cadres, on January 6, 1986, the Central Committee of the Communist Party of China put forward eight provisions for the selection and appointment of cadres. 1) Leading cadres must follow the Party's principles in employing cadres in an exemplary manner and maintain the discipline of organizational and personnel work. 2) Selection and appointment of cadres must strictly follow democratic recommendations, widely listen to opinions and put forward selection targets, organize personnel departments for examination, and report to the Party Committee after collective discussion and decision according to cadre management authority, conduct further examination by higher organizational departments, then submit to the Party Committee for discussion and approval. 3) To select and appoint leading cadres, it was necessary to fully follow the mass line. 4) Before deciding to promote cadres, strict examination must be carried out according to the moral and talent conditions required for the proposed post. 5) The selection of cadres must be discussed and vetted collectively by the Party committee. 6) Promotion of cadres should be based on the selection and appointment of comrades who had undergone practical training. 7) It was strictly forbidden to set up additional institutions without authorization, to improve the specifications of institutions, and to increase the number of leading cadres. 8) Organizational and personnel departments at all levels must conscientiously perform their duties and act as staff and assistants of Party committees.

From the beginning of 1986, the Central Organizational Department had plenty of investigation and research work and put forward some ideas and principled opinions on the establishment of the avoidance system for Party and government cadres. It started with position avoidance, meaning that the spouses, children, and relatives of cadres who held leading and deputy leadership positions in Party committees, government, and discipline committees, or public security, courts, and prosecution should not have direct relations with the leading cadres or hold the leading posts of the general office, organization, personnel, supervision department, and discipline inspection organ at the same level of the leading cadre's office. It went on to implement official duties avoidance. The leading cadres of the Party and government were not allowed to participate in the appointment, removal, file management, and transmission of themselves or to instruct or hint to others to exert influence and intervene. In the work of appointing and dismissing cadres, adjusting wages, joining the Party, evaluating and appointing professional and technical posts, investigating and dealing with cases of violation of laws and regulations, selecting and dispatching out-of-country personnel, recruiting cadres, distributing graduates from colleges and universities, and resettling cadres transferred from the army, the leading cadres should take the initiative to explain to the organizations and avoid taking part in the examination, investigation, and discussion. When discussing, examining, and approving, no other person should be instructed or suggested to intervene. Leading cadres' spouses, children, relatives, and other staff members should not participate in the aforementioned evasive duties in the name of leading cadres or for the convenience of their work. Finally, it insisted on regional avoidance. The positions of county (city) Party committee secretary, county (city) mayor, county (city) discipline committee secretary, organization minister, personnel director, public security director, court president, and prosecutor general were not to be taken by the local cadres. If a local cadre held any of these posts, he or she would not be allowed to continue to hold his or her original post once his or her term of office had expired.

The unhealthy trend of cadres going abroad was a special corruption phenomenon in the process of China's Reform and Opening Up. Since the beginning of Reform and Opening Up, the number of private expatriates in China had increased dramatically. However, there had also been unhealthy tendencies related to going abroad, which were mainly manifested in several ways, such as excessive organization of Party and government cadres abroad, repeated visits, alternate visits abroad, and the substitution of Party and government cadres for professional cadres abroad. Some Party and government cadres, in the name of visits, had gone abroad for sightseeing and tourism, which led to the increase of foreign exchange expenditure and serious waste and caused adverse effects in China and abroad.

In order to curb this unhealthy trend, on July 4, 1987, the Central Committee of the Communist Party of China and the State Council issued Several Provisions on Strict Control of the Exit of Cadres of Party and Government Organs, declaring that cadres of Party and Government Organs who were not directly related to the task of going abroad and who were not in charge of the relevant business should not visit the country based on any excuses. Cadres of Party and government organs must not participate in the tasks that could be accomplished by professionals, and Party and government organs and other competent cadres in charge of business should not publicly or implicitly request to join overseas league groups of enterprises or institutions on the grounds of superior-inferior relations or some kind of working relations. The state delegations sent by enterprises and institutions should not invite cadres of Party and government organs and other competent departments who had no direct relationship with the task of going abroad to take part in the work for the purpose of "caring for the relationship" or achieving some purpose. Provisions required that local people's governments and departments of central and state organs with the power to go abroad for examination and approval, when examining and approving the affairs of Party and government cadres going abroad, carry out strict and careful examination of the delegation groups going abroad in accordance with the relevant provisions of the Central Committee and the State Council. Those who did not conform to the provisions were required to adhere to the principles and would not be approved. For those who had been approved to leave the country, if any irregularities were found before departure, the higher examination and approval organ should promptly instruct the original examination and approval organ to rectify them and, if necessary, redeploy the case for re-approval. After the issuance of this document, the unhealthy trend of cadres going abroad was initially stopped.

The Central Committee of the Communist Party of China promoted the improvement of the Party's style of work by focusing on major cases. For instance, some enterprises in the Jinjiang area of Fujian Province manufactured a large number of counterfeit drugs and sold them to various places through bribery. On July 13, 1985, the Central Commission for Discipline sent an open letter to the Party Groups of the Jinjiang Prefectural Committee and the Administration, requesting them to investigate and deal with the case in accordance with Party discipline and report it to the Central Committee. On July 27, after hearing the reports of the Fujian Provincial Party Committee and Provincial Discipline Commission of the CPC, the Commission handled the parties according to law and decided to remove the Standing Committee and Secretary of the Discipline Commission of Jinjiang County, who participated in the manufacture and sale of counterfeit medicines for profit.

From the beginning of 1986 to April 1989, a few leading cadres of the Ministry of Railways and Zhengzhou Railway Administration took the opportunity when the railway capacity failed to meet the needs of the traffic volume and there was a shortage of cars to, with various measures, seek personal gains by car and corrupt and accept bribes by taking advantage of their functions and powers. Later, it was found that the case involved 48 cadres at or above the section level of Zhengzhou Railway Bureau of the Ministry of Railways, one vice-minister of the Ministry of Railways, fifteen cadres at the bureau level, and nineteen cadres at the department level. The crimes involved more than 960,000 yuan. The Transportation Bureau of the Ministry of Railways had illegally demanded and received more than 760,000 yuan from cargo owners or subordinate units in various names, in violation of the regulations. The Central Commission for Discipline dealt with this case seriously. The State Council revoked Luo Yunguang, Vice Minister of the Ministry of Railways, who was responsible for offering and soliciting bribes from his subordinates. The prosecutorial organs investigated Luo Yunguang for bribery. At the same time, the Central Discipline Commission decided to dismiss Xu Jun, former director of the Transportation Bureau of the Ministry of Railways, Jia Shuang, Hu Jun, assistant director Wei Guofan, Ma Mingshan, former director of the dispatching office, He Zhigui, Liu Demin, deputy director of the Zhengzhou Railway Bureau, and Pan Keming, who had violated the criminal law and were tried by the relevant judicial organs.

From May 6 to June 2, 1987, a huge forest fire broke out in the Daxing'an Mountains, causing great losses to national property and people's lives, some of which could not be calculated in terms of money. Yang Zhong, Minister of Forestry, had seriously lost the party spirit principle that Party members and leading cadres should possess, lacked a high sense of political responsibility for the cause of the Party and the people, and was guilty of serious bureaucratic errors and dereliction of duty. Dong Zhiyong, deputy minister in charge of forest protection and fire prevention work, lacked a due sense of responsibility in forest protection and fire prevention work, and was guilty of serious bureaucratic errors and dereliction of duty, and also bore great responsibility for forest fire accidents in the Daxing'an Mountains. With the approval of the Central Committee of the CPC, the Central Commission for Discipline made a decision to revoke the post of Secretary of the Party Group of the Ministry of Forestry of Yang Zhong. The State Council asked the Standing Committee of the National People's Congress to approve the abolition of Yang Zhong as Minister of Forestry and Dong Zhiyong as Vice-Minister of Forestry, and instructed the Heilongjiang Provincial Government to conduct an in-depth inspection.

The Central Committee of the Communist Party of China educated the whole Party by grasping major cases, so that the entire Party could receive in-depth education in the Party's style of work and promote the formation of a situation in which the whole Party jointly grasped and administered the issue of this style of work. However, the struggle against corruption, upholding honesty, and rectifying unhealthy tendencies was a long-term one, which ran through the whole process of reform, opening up, and modernization. At that point, this work still had a long way to go.

CHAPTER 6

The Formation of the Third Generation of Central Collective Leadership and the Initial Establishment of the Guiding Role of Deng Xiaoping Theory

I

Comprehensive Governance and Rectification and a Series of Principles for Balanced Development

After the Thirteenth National Congress of the CPC, the Party led all the people of the country to continue to advance along the road of socialism with Chinese characteristics. Great achievements had been made in economic construction since the beginning of Reform and Opening Up, mainly in the areas of sustained and stable growth of the national economy, roughly doubling the gross national product, national fiscal revenue, and the average income of urban and rural residents in the previous ten years. Some serious economic and social problems that had plagued China for a long time had been settled, or were on the way to being settled, the basic needs of the vast majority of China's 1 billion people had been met, some areas were moving toward prosperity, and some areas that had not yet fully solved the basic necessities of food and clothing had still improved their people's lives. Market supply had also greatly improved, basically reversing the long-term serious shortage of consumer goods in the past. From 1984 to 1988, the GNP increased from 717.1 billion yuan to 1.4928 trillion yuan, indicating a vibrant situation in which agriculture and industry, rural areas and cities, reform and development mutually promoted each other, and the overall national strength had reached a new level.

1. Overall Development of Governance and Rectification

With the deepening of reform and the rapid development of the economy, some deep-seated contradictions in the economic system were gradually exposed. At the same time, in the process of reform and construction, there was a tendency to pursue only speed while ignoring objective conditions. In August 1988, amid a macroeconomic environment that was not relaxed, it was decided that price reform would be conducted to enable a breakthrough, triggering a mass purchasing rush and causing social shockwaves. A series of unstable and uncoordinated contradictions appeared in economic operations. Its manifestation was the "Four Excesses and One Chaos," which referred to excessive social demand, excessive speed of industrial development, excessive credit and monetary investment, excessive price rises, and a chaotic economic order. In response to these problems, the Central Committee made timely policy decisions to rectify and deepen reform, including restraining economic overheating, curbing inflation, conscientiously adjusting the economic structure so as to increase the output of grain, cotton, oil, and other major agricultural products, establishing and improving the necessary economic laws and regulations, as well as macro-control and supervision systems, and actively promoting the construction of a new order of the socialist commodity economy. After approximately a year of rectification, the over-rapid trend of economic development and the chaotic phenomenon in the economic field were rectified.

With the deepening of Reform and Opening Up, while the contradictions in the economic system were highlighted, social fashion also presented many new situations and problems. Under these circumstances, the Central Committee clearly put forward the policy of "grasping with both hands," or balanced development.

2. Requirements of the Balanced Development Policy

In the process of socialist modernization, why was it necessary to adhere to the principle of "grasping with both hands"? This was not the result of subjective assumptions, but the reflection of the objective law of China's socialist modernization.

The report of the Thirteenth National Congress of the Communist Party of China clearly pointed out that "grasping with both hands" was the strategic policy of building socialism with Chinese characteristics. This strategic policy had two meanings. First, in terms of importance, it meant that the two civilizations should be built together, which was related to the fundamental direction and the overall issue of the fundamental path with Chinese characteristics, because only by "grasping with both hands" could the material and spiritual civilizations be simultaneously developed in an all-round way, so as to improve China's comprehensive national strength. Second, in the long run, it meant that China should stick to both civilizations throughout the primary stage of socialism, not just for a while or for a certain period of time. If the Party's basic line at the primary stage of socialism remained unchanged for a hundred years, then the principle of "grasping with both hands" must also remain unchanged for that period. Adhering to "grasping with both hands" was a profound summary of the experience and lessons of Reform and Opening Up. In order to promote the development of social productive forces, it was crucial to speed up the pace of reform. This revolution would unfold in a wide range of fields and at considerable depth. It concerned the future of socialism and the interests of hundreds of millions of people. It was an extremely complex and mass exploration and innovation that would lead not only to great changes in people's economic and political life, but also tremendous changes in people's way of life, thinking, and state of mind. Therefore, some problems and negative phenomena would inevitably arise.

From the perspective of the practice of Reform and Opening Up, China was facing three general types of problems. The first was that some new contradictions and problems inevitably arose in the process of transformation of the old and new systems. The second was that the reformers' understanding of the central principles and policies was inaccurate and incomplete, or for lack of experience and thoughtful consideration, some biases emerged in their bold explorations. The final problem was that some people, under the banner of reform, exploited the loopholes of reform to "make huge profits," engage in "official and private trafficking," or other unhealthy practices, even breaking the law or discipline to commit economic crimes and engage in other criminal activities. In the first two situations, it was important to be careful to raise the awareness of the people, especially Party members and cadres, and ensure the healthy implementation of Reform and Opening Up through education. As for the third case, China needed to resolutely deal with those issues in accordance with Party, political, and legal disciplines, especially those serious economic crimes and other criminal activities. It was necessary to punish them severely according to law, strike them resolutely, and never be soft-handed. Practice had proven that the deeper the reform was, the more the Party should stick to "grasping with both hands." Otherwise, reform would not be carried on.

In the process of opening up to the outside world, on the one hand, advanced technology, equipment, and managerial expertise and methods conforming to large-scale socialized production had been introduced. On the other hand, it was also difficult to avoid side effects. The decadent things and lifestyles of foreign capitalism, as well as some reactionary political views and social theories of the bourgeoisie, would also infiltrate into Chinese society and people's spiritual world, and even flow in in large quantities, bringing serious harm to China's social life and the people's spiritual world. For example, in politics, the political viewpoints of the western bourgeoisie such as "liberalization," "democratization," and the "multi-party system" might infiltrate and lead to bourgeois liberalization of thought. In the economy, the values of the Western bourgeoisie, such as profit-seeking, self-interest, money worship, deception, fraudulent activities, drug trafficking and smuggling, bribery, speculation, and other acts, might flood in, which could lead to economic crimes and other criminal activities. In ideology and culture, obscene videos, photographs, movies, pornographic literature and art, books, music, and toxic social doctrines from abroad might be introduced, which would pollute the people's spiritual world and corrode their souls. Deng Xiaoping had foreseen this situation and said that when China opened to the outside world, it was opening windows to let in fresh air, but mosquitoes and flies would follow as well. What should it do to respond, then? Closing the door was obviously not possible. The only choice was to persist in Reform and Opening Up, while at the same time opposing bourgeois liberalization and cracking down on various criminal activities.

Therefore, in the historical process of intensifying the Reform and Opening Up, continuing to "grasp with both hands" was an important condition to ensure that the cause of Reform and Opening Up remained vigorous, and also an objective need to keep the reform and development on the right path.

3. Proposal and Elucidation of a Series of Balanced Development Policies

"Grasping with both hands" or balanced development, was an important experience in governing the country, which was summed up by the CPC in the process of Reform and Opening Up in the new era. The balanced development policy had several connotations at different levels. One was to grasp the construction of material and spiritual civilizations, and another was to grasp the Reform and Opening Up policy and Four Basic Principles. It also implied grasping the Reform and Opening Up policy and cracking down on economic crimes and other criminal activities as well as grasping the construction of two civilizations, democracy, and the legal system.

The policy of balanced development had emerged, developed, and been enriched in the practice of China's Reform and Opening Up. Deng Xiaoping, the chief architect of Reform and Opening Up, was the first leader in the Party to put forward and emphasize the principle of balanced development.

After the Third Plenary Session of the Eleventh Central Committee, while presiding over the formulation of the strategic principles of reform, opening up, and modernization, Deng Xiaoping began to pay attention to the issue of balanced development. On October 30, 1979, when he addressed the Fourth Congress of Chinese Literature and Art Workers on behalf of the Central Committee, he first proposed the idea that the two civilizations should be grasped together. He said, "Our country has entered a new period of socialist modernization. We should reform and improve the socialist economic and political system, develop a high degree of socialist democracy, and develop a complete socialist legal system while also greatly improving the social productive forces. While building a high level of material civilization, we should improve the scientific and cultural level of the whole nation, develop a noble and colorful cultural life, and build a high level of socialist spiritual civilization."[1]

On December 25, 1980, the Central Working Conference was held in Beijing. Deng Xiaoping made an important speech at the conference, systematically expounded the relationship between building material and spiritual civilization, and further put forward the idea of balanced development. He said, "We should build a socialist country, not only with a high level of material civilization, but also with a high level of spiritual civilization. The more the Party and the government carry out various policies of economic reform and opening up to the outside world, the more important it is for Party members, especially the senior responsible cadres of the Party, to attach great importance to and practice communist ideology and morality."[2]

On March 27, 1981, the head of the General Political Department of the Chinese PLA reported to Deng Xiaoping that the army adhered to the balanced development approach. Deng was very pleased. He said, "One thing that has been done well recently is the discussion of spiritual civilization. This has achieved results, and we should continue to do a good job in this area."[3]

With the development and deepening of Reform and Opening Up, criminal activities in the economic field started to develop and spread. In response to this situation, through investigation and research, the Central Committee of the Communist Party of China and the State Council, issued the Decision on Combating Serious Criminal Activities in the Economic Field (hereinafter referred to as the Decision) and began to investigate and punish economic criminal activities.

On April 10, 1982, the Politburo held a meeting to discuss the Decision. Deng Xiaoping made an important speech at the meeting, pointing out clearly that China should stick to balanced development in Reform and Opening Up. He said, "We should have two hands, one to adhere to the policy of opening up and invigorating the economy at home, the other to resolutely fight against economic crime. Without the crackdown on economic crime, the policy of opening up to the outside world will surely fail, as will the policy of invigorating the economy at home. With the fight against economic crime, opening up to the outside world and invigorating the economy at home can go in the right direction."[4]

It is evident that Deng's notion of balanced development had led to new progress. He not only referred to grasping the two civilizations together, but also included Reform and Opening Up and the fight against economic crime, because these issues were related to the success of the Reform and Opening Up policy.

In order to help the whole Party more thoroughly understand the importance, necessity, and urgency of balanced development, Deng emphasized the policy on many occasions.

On July 4, 1982, the Central Military Commission held a symposium. In his speech, Deng put forward four guarantees for adhering to the socialist system and doing a thorough job of modernization construction. These included system reform, building a socialist spiritual civilization, resolutely cracking down on criminal activities in the economic field, and doing a thorough job of party building and rectifying the Party's organization and style. He emphasized, "We must persist in opening up to the outside world and invigorating the economy at home. However, in order to ensure that this policy is really conducive to the construction of the Four Modernizations and not divorced from the socialist orientation in the implementation process, we must also have another hand, that is, to combat economic crime. Without this hand, there will be no restriction… The four guarantees should not be carried out for only a short time, then abandoned. We do not simply launch campaigns, but with the progress of the Four Modernizations, we must adhere to the four guarantees and not deviate from them even for a day. We must turn them into our regular work and struggle."[5]

At the Twelfth National Congress of the CPC held in October 1982, under the guidance of Deng Xiaoping's balanced development ideology, the two civilizations were clearly grasped together as the strategic policy for socialist modernization construction, so as to guide the work of the entire Party. According to the principle of balanced development, the Party had not only grasped the construction of the material civilization, but also strengthened the construction of the spiritual civilization, making some advancements.

However, due to various subjective and objective reasons, the construction of China's spiritual civilization had not achieved the desired results, even leading to the deterioration of the building of the spiritual civilization because of the practice of "one soft hand and one hard hand." The specific manifestations of this included:

1) *Corruption as a serious phenomenon, and the continued spread of unhealthy tendencies within the Party.* The Central Committee had taken measures to investigate and deal with major cases and had achieved certain results, which had not yet been consolidated. In addition, the situation of incompatible

reforms had not changed, and the ideological and political work had been weakened. As a result, the phenomenon of illegal activities and those that went against discipline by some party and government officials who traded power for money and sought personal gains had increased significantly. The phenomenon of overeating, drinking, and soliciting and accepting bribes had increased, and those of favoritism, backdoor smuggling, and cronyism had increased. As a result, many Party members forgot the purpose of serving the people wholeheartedly, provoking strong public discontent.

2) *The continued decline of social morality, and many members losing heart and mind.* Unhealthy tendencies and corruption within the Party could not be effectively curbed, seriously affecting the prestige and cohesion of the Party and the government among the masses. Feudal superstition in some areas had not been addressed, the phenomena of gathering, gambling, and prostitution had not been effectively handled, and in particular, the proliferation of pornographic videos and publications had caused serious harm to the minds and souls of young people.

3) *Worrying situations in education and science and technology.* Due to the difficulties and problems encountered in the reform of education and the science and technology system in practice and to the insufficient financial support from the government for education and science and technology, the income of the majority of educators and science and technology workers had been on the low end for years, the imbalance between manual and mental work remained unchanged, and even tended to increase, and the conditions of education and scientific research had not been properly improved, which had seriously affected the enthusiasm of the majority of intellectuals. There was an increasing outflow of intellectuals and job-hopping in some regions. Affected by this situation, the enthusiasm of students in school declined. "It is enough to achieve a passing score of 60 points" had become the mantra of some students. In rural areas, students dropped out of school before finishing. China's education and scientific and technological undertakings were once again facing serious challenges.

The Central Committee soon became aware of this one-hard-handed and one-soft-handed situation. On September 23, 1985, Deng Xiaoping sharply criticized this mistake at the National Congress. He said, "The construction of socialist spiritual civilization was put forward very early. The Central Committee, the local government, and the army have done much work. In particular, a large number of model workers among the masses has emerged, which has had a very good impact. However, as far as the whole country is concerned, the effect is still not satisfactory. The main reason is that the whole Party has not paid serious attention to it… Production has gone up in recent years, but the pernicious effects of capitalism and feudalism have not been reduced to the lowest possible level, and we are even seeing the revival of some bad elements that have been extinct since liberation. How can the superiority of socialism be brought into full play without our great determination to change this situation as early as possible? How can we fully and effectively educate our people and future generations? Without strengthening the construction of our spiritual civilization, the construction of our material civilization will also be destroyed, and detours will be taken. It is impossible for us to succeed in our revolution and construction based solely on material conditions."[6]

In order to garner the attention of the whole Party, especially the leading comrades of the Central Committee, Deng Xiaoping once again addressed the issue of balanced development at the Standing Committee of the Politburo of the Central Committee on January 17, 1986, pointing out that there must be a two-handed grasp of the Four Modernizations, and that a merely one-handed grasp was not feasible. The "two-handed grasp" involved one-handed economic construction and one-handed legal system building. Considerable achievements had been made in economic construction, and the situation was encouraging. This was China's success. But what was the point of economic success if morality declined? It would deteriorate and develop into a world of corruption, theft, and bribery. Therefore, it was important to discuss the Four Perseverances and dictatorship, which could ensure the smooth progress of the drive toward socialist modernization and effectively deal with those who undermined construction. He emphasized that the construction of a spiritual civilization and the improvement of Party and social conduct should start with specific events, and emphasized that the closer one's relationship to senior cadres, the more senior the cadres, and the more celebrated the figure, the more urgently they should be investigated and punished for their violations, being used as typical cases to warn others. Because these people's crimes were harmful, they had been caught and dealt with, and the effect of this crackdown had been great, indicating that the Party was determined to overcome all obstacles and grasp the construction of spiritual civilization. He believed that if the Party did this well, it could really promote reform and construction. If it was determined to do so, it was important to strive for at least ten years before the Party's and social conduct could be restored to that of the best period of the 1950s.

As is evident from this situation, Deng Xiaoping made great contributions to the formation of the Party's strategic policy of balanced development. In order to unswervingly adhere to his balanced development policy, he fought against various wrong ideas over a long period of time and never compromised or conceded on this major principle. In the process of struggling against wrong ideas, Deng also enriched and developed the strategic thought of balanced development.

4. The Balanced Development Policy Gradually Promoted through Practice

With the deepening of Reform and Opening Up, the Party's idea of balanced development had been advancing through practice. While concentrating on promoting economic construction, the entire country had also begun to strengthen the "other hand" in the ideological, cultural, and other fields.

a. Developing a Socialist Spiritual Civilization

After the Third Plenary Session of the Eleventh Central Committee, with the start of Reform and Opening Up and the full development of socialist modernization, the Party Central Committee gradually began to put the task of building a socialist spiritual civilization on the agenda.

1) *Proposing the thought of building a spiritual civilization.* In his speech "Adhering to the Four Basic Principles," delivered at the Party's theoretical work meeting in March 1979, Deng Xiaoping raised issues such as maintaining lofty revolutionary ideals, improving the moral standards of all the people, transforming the social atmosphere, and rectifying the Party's style. In fact, this included the basic requirements for building a socialist spiritual civilization. In September, Ye Jianying raised the concept of a socialist spiritual civilization for the first time in his speech at the Congress celebrating the 30th anniversary of the founding of the People's Republic of China. He said, "While building a high level of material civilization, we should improve the level of education, science, culture, and health

throughout the nation, set up lofty revolutionary ideals and revolutionary morality, develop a noble and colorful cultural life, and build a high level of socialist spiritual civilization. These are the important objectives of our socialist modernization and the necessary conditions for realizing the Four Modernizations."[7] This exposition not only clearly put forward the concept of a spiritual civilization, but also outlined the contents of a socialist spiritual civilization, including education, science, health, revolutionary ideals, revolutionary moral customs, and cultural life, clearly advancing the construction of building a socialist spiritual civilization as an important goal and necessary condition for China's modernization.

On December 20, 1980, at the Central Working Conference, one of the leaders of the Chinese Academy of Social Sciences at that time, Li Chang wrote a letter to Deng Xiaoping specifically calling for strengthening the construction of the socialist spiritual civilization. Deng Xiaoping wrote in his reply that the questions Li Chang raised in this letter deserved consideration. It also proposed that this letter be published and read to Party members attending the Central Working Conference. On December 25, in his speech at the conference, Deng accepted Li Chang's suggestion and discussed the issue of building a socialist spiritual civilization as an important topic, emphasizing once again its importance. He said, "The idea of a spiritual civilization refers not only to education, science, and culture (which are absolutely necessary), but also to communist ideas, ideals, beliefs, morals, discipline, revolutionary positions and principles, comrade-like relations between people, and so on."[8] The construction of a socialist spiritual civilization was summarized here in two basic aspects, namely, the construction of science and culture and the construction of ideology and morality, clarifying the connotation of the construction of a spiritual civilization.

In June 1981, the Sixth Plenary Session of the Eleventh Central Committee of the Communist Party of China adopted the Resolution on Several Historical Issues of the Party since the Founding of the People's Republic, which regarded spiritual civilization as one of the ten basic points in China's socialist modernization construction. For the first time, in the form of the resolution of the Central Plenary Session of the Party, the construction of a "modernized, highly democratic, and highly civilized, powerful socialist country"[9] was defined as essential to the Party's program of struggle in the new historical period.

2) *The gradual development of a socialist spiritual civilization.* In February 1981, nine units, including the National Federation of Trade Unions, the Central

Committee of the Communist Youth League, and the All-China Women's Federation, jointly issued the Initiative on Developing Civilized and Courtesy Activities in response to the Central Committee's call for strengthening the construction of a spiritual civilization. They proposed to carry out activities stressing civility, courtesy, hygiene, orderliness, morality, and beauty in mentality, language, behavior, and environment among the people throughout the country, especially among young people, activities aimed at what was called the "Five Emphases and Four Beauties." On February 28, the Ministry of Publicity, the Ministry of Education, the Ministry of Culture, the Ministry of Health, and the Ministry of Public Security jointly issued the Notice on Civil and Courteous Activities. According to the notice, civilized and courtesy propaganda and education activities, with the Five Emphases and Four Beauties making up the main substance, were carried out all over the country.

At the beginning of 1982, the General Office of the Central Committee of the Communist Party of China forwarded the Report of the Ministry of Propaganda on Deeply Developing the Activities of the Five Emphases and Four Beauties. That spring, according to the plan of the Central Secretariat, the National Civilization and Politeness Month was launched throughout the country, focusing on environmental hygiene and solving "dirty," "disorderly," and "poor" environmental problems. In January 1983, more than twenty departments, such as the Ministry of Publicity and Propaganda, suggested that educational activities of "loving the motherland, socialism, and the people" be carried out in the activities of the Five Emphases and Four Beauties, so as to enrich activities aimed at building a spiritual civilization.

In September 1982, the Twelfth National Congress of the Communist Party of China summarized the achievements of the Party's understanding of the construction of a socialist spiritual civilization after the Third Plenary Session of the Eleventh Central Committee, focusing on the theoretical elaboration of the construction of a high degree of socialist spiritual civilization. The report of the Twelfth National Congress put forward that a "socialist spiritual civilization is an important feature of socialism and an important manifestation of the superiority of the socialist system." While building a high level of socialist material civilization, it was important to strive to build a high level of socialist spiritual civilization, which was defined as a strategic policy for China's socialist modernization. In March 1983, in order to strengthen the leadership of the Five Emphases, Four

Beauties, and Three Loves, the Central Committee and State Council decided to establish the Five Emphases, Four Beauties, and Three Loves activity committees at the central, provincial, regional or municipal level and set up corresponding offices. That year, the activity of "building a model city" began to rise in Sanming City, Fujian Province. In Baoding, Hebei, and other places, model villages and towns and model neighborhoods were also built by the army and the people. In the second year, the relevant departments of the Central Government held a national working conference on the Five Emphases, Four Beauties, and Three Loves in Sanming City, Fujian Province. They summarized the experience of the campaign in large and medium-sized cities throughout the country, especially in Sanming City, and asked the whole country to learn from its example to promote the construction of urban spiritual civilization. After that, the activities of Five Emphases, Four Beauties, and Three Loves were organized and conducted widely in urban and rural areas in China, focusing on creating a beautiful environment, establishing good order, doing a thorough job of quality services, and building model units.

3) *The formulation of the first guiding principle for the construction of a spiritual civilization.* After 1984, with the full implementation of China's Reform and Opening Up, a large number of new contradictions and problems emerged in the social field, and the task of building a spiritual civilization became more prominent than before. In October 1984, the Third Plenary Session of the Twelfth Central Committee of the Communist Party of China adopted the Decision of the Central Committee of the Communist Party of China on Economic System Reform, which also put forward corresponding requirements for the construction of spiritual civilization. At the National Congress held in September 1985, it was noted that "while promoting the construction of material civilization, it is also important to vigorously strengthen the construction of socialist spiritual civilization," a point that became one of the basic guiding principles for national economic and social development during the Seventh Five-Year Plan period.[10] This was the first time that the construction of a spiritual civilization was included in the national economic and social development plan, indicating that the Party had considered the construction of spiritual civilization from the perspective of development strategy and guiding ideology. On this basis, the Sixth Plenary Session of the Twelfth Central Committee of the Communist Party of China held in September 1986 deliberated and adopted the Resolution of the

Central Committee of the Communist Party of China on the Guidelines for the Construction of Socialist Spiritual Civilization (hereinafter referred to as the Resolution). This was the first programmatic document formulated by the Party on the construction of a socialist spiritual civilization. From the strategic height of comprehensively building socialism and from the overall layout of China's modernization drive, the Resolution clearly stipulated the guiding principles and fundamental tasks for the construction of spiritual civilization.

First, the Party needed to clarify the position and role of the construction of a spiritual civilization in the overall layout of socialist modernization in China. The Resolution pointed out that the overall layout of China's socialist modernization construction was to take economic construction as the center, unswervingly carry out the reform of economic and political systems, and firmly strengthen the construction of the spiritual civilization, so as to coordinate and promote these various aspects.

In addition, it proposed guidelines and fundamental tasks for the construction of the spiritual civilization. Its guiding principles were that the construction of the spiritual civilization should promote socialist modernization, promote comprehensive reform and opening to the outside world, and adhere to the four basic principles. Its basic task was to meet the needs of socialist modernization, train socialist citizens with ideals, morality, culture, and discipline, and improve the ideological and moral quality and scientific and cultural quality of the entire Chinese nation.

Further, the specific content of the construction of spiritual civilization was more realistically elaborated. The Resolution proposed to mobilize and unite the people of all ethnicities with the common ideal of building socialism with Chinese characteristics, clarified the relationship between the highest ideal of the Party and the common ideal of all nationalities at the present stage, dialectically combined the requirement of advancement with the requirement of universality, put forward the basic requirement of socialist moral construction, and emphasized the need to advance among all the people the education of socialist democracy, the legal system, and discipline. This clearly reflected that the socialist spiritual civilization the Party aimed for was the unity of the revolutionary, democratic, and scientific spirit, and emphasized that effort should be made to promote the popularization and improvement of educational science and culture in a tangible way nationwide.

The Resolution also clarified the guiding role of Marxism in the construction of a spiritual civilization and clarified the responsibilities of Party organizations and Party members in the construction of that spiritual civilization.[11] The Resolution upheld the basic viewpoint on the construction of a socialist spiritual civilization put forward by the Party since the Third Plenary Session of the Eleventh Central Committee. At the same time, new developments had taken place in many areas, marking the preliminary formation of the theory of the construction of a socialist spiritual civilization with Chinese characteristics. This Resolution was significant for guiding and promoting the construction of the socialist spiritual civilization and ensuring the smooth development of socialist modernization.

b. Eliminating spiritual pollution in the ideological field and opposing bourgeois liberalization.

In the theoretical circles in the early 1980s, some people created confusion regarding humanitarian and alienation issues, blaming the socialist system and the leadership of the Communist Party for all the problems in society. In the press, some opposed the Party and the people, and in literary and arts circles, some denied Mao Zedong's literary and artistic thought and showed indifference to the slogan advanced by the Central Committee of the Communist Party of China which stated that literature and art should serve the people and socialist society. They were "eager to present the dark and gray things, even to fabricate and distort the history and reality of the revolution."[12] As a result, some works with serious erroneous tendencies and even vulgar, pornographic books and periodicals appeared on the screen, on the stage, and in bookstores.

In response to this situation, at the Second Plenary Session of the Twelfth Central Committee of the Communist Party of China, held in October 1983, Deng Xiaoping made a speech in which he stated that "the ideological front should not engage in spiritual pollution. The essence of spiritual pollution is to disseminate decadent, declining ideas of various bourgeois and other exploiting classes, and to disseminate distrust of socialism, communism, and the leadership of the Communist Party... In the long run, this issue concerns which generation will take over our cause and the fate and future of the Party and the country."[13] For this reason, it was necessary to criticize and correct it.

In accordance with the spirit of the conference, struggles against spiritual pollution and bourgeois liberalization were carried out in various regions. After a series of work, the spread of bourgeois liberalization was basically stopped, and the leadership of the Communist Party of China on the ideological front was strengthened. However, the exclusion of one interference did not mean that the interference of bourgeois liberalization would no longer occur.

In 1986, Fang Lizhi, Liu Binyan, Wang Ruowang, and others, taking the opportunity of studying political system reform, wantonly attacked the leadership of the Communist Party of China and the socialist system, which attracted the attention of some senior leaders of the Communist Party of China, especially Deng Xiaoping. In September 1986, at the Sixth Plenary Session of the Twelfth Central Committee of the Communist Party of China, Deng made it clear that he spoke "most about opposing bourgeois liberalization, sticking to it most firmly… What is liberalization? In fact, it is to guide our current policy towards capitalism… Liberalization itself is bourgeois, and there is no proletarian or socialist liberalization. Liberalization itself is a confrontation with our current policies and systems, or an opposition or a revision… It seems that opposing liberalization is not only about our times, but also about ten or twenty years in the future."[14]

However, Deng's warning did not attract sufficient attention, especially from the leading comrades who presided over the central work at that time. In the second half of 1986, the trend of liberalization was once again rampant. Fang Lizhi, Wang Ruowang, and Liu Binyan were more active. They pointed fingers at China's political system, claiming that the socialist cause since the founding of New China and the Communist movement had failed for more than thirty years. They totally denied the leadership of the Communist Party of China, advocating the implementation of a multi-party system and attacking the leadership of the Communist Party of China as the continuation of feudal rule and a one-party dictatorship, beautifying bourgeois democracy, advocating the abandonment of the people's democratic dictatorship, and degrading time and again the guiding position of Marxism in China's revolution and construction.

Under these circumstances, the propaganda of Party newspapers and periodicals did not take strong resistance measures, and there was an erroneous orientation, which enabled the trend of bourgeois liberalization to spread widely.

In the second half of 1986, various liberalization trends of thought flowed into the forums of colleges and universities. According to preliminary statistics, from October to late December 1986, Beijing University, Tsinghua University, and Beijing Normal University hosted more than twenty speeches and seminars attended by these people. These reports had a great impact on the thinking of some college students.

In January 1987, several young ideological and political workers surveyed the ideological status of college students in several key universities in Beijing and found that college students were involved in discussion of political system reform and cultural reflection, to varying degrees. According to the survey, college students were dissatisfied in four areas. First, they were dissatisfied with the speed of reform and thought that the progress of reform was too slow with too much resistance and too little effect. Second, they were dissatisfied with democratic rights and thought that workers, farmers, and intellectuals could not exercise enough democratic rights. Third, they were dissatisfied with the unhealthy Party conduct and thought that although major cases were dealt with, people were still indignant about the phenomenon of abusing power to seek personal gain. Finally, they were dissatisfied with the implementation of the intellectual policy, believing that "the thunder is loud but the rain is small." These four areas of dissatisfaction led to four reflections by college students. The first was on the fundamental lessons of the Chinese revolution, the second on the comparison between the two social systems, the third on the traditional culture of the Chinese nation, and the fourth on Marxism.[15]

"Reflection" produced many negative results, coupled with the changes in the international political arena in 1986, such as the flight of former Philippine President Marcos, the collapse of Haiti's dictatorship, and a series of other major events, all of which were constantly impacting the students' values. They were no longer satisfied with the change of ideas and theoretical talk. Many students' emotions shifted from uneasiness to discontent with an implied impulsiveness, which indicated a strong sense of participation. In the second half of 1986, marches and demonstrations of different scales took place in many cities.

In response to the above-mentioned phenomena, Deng Xiaoping met with Hu Yaobang and other leading comrades of the Central Committee on December 30, 1986. In his talk, Deng pointed out that adhering to the four basic principles and opposing bourgeois liberalization were of great importance to maintaining and developing a stable, united situation, persisting in Reform and Opening Up, and promoting socialist modernization. He correctly expounded the Central Government's current policy of handling of student disturbances. The core was "to uphold the Four Basic Principles… and people's democratic dictatorship… China has no future without the leadership of the Communist Party and socialism… Democracy can only be gradually liberalized and cannot merely be copied from the Western system." Only by resolutely "opposing bourgeois liberalization" could "China have hope." Deng Xiaoping's remarks further strengthened the determination of the Communist Party of China to oppose bourgeois liberalization. On January 6, 1987, universities in Beijing conveyed Deng Xiaoping's remarks to all the students, quickly dealing with the troubles caused by a few college students.

On January 12, the Central Committee of the Communist Party of China and the State Council decided to reorganize the leading group of China University of Science and Technology. On January 13, 17, and 23, the Shanghai Discipline Commission, Anhui Discipline Commission and the Discipline Commission of the *People's Daily* of the Communist Party of China decided to expel Wang Ruowang, Fang Lizhi, and Liu Binyan from the Party.

After a series of work, the Party and the government calmed the academic tide at the end of 1986, adhered to the correct leadership of the Party in the reform, opening up, and socialist modernization, and guaranteed the healthy development of the cause of socialism with Chinese characteristics.

c. Strictly cracking down on criminal activities in the economic field

After the Third Plenary Session of the Eleventh Central Committee of the Communist Party of China, the Party and state established and implemented the principles and policies of taking economic construction as the center, opening up to the outside world, and invigorating the economy at home, which allowed the economic construction of China to develop rapidly. However, the process of Reform and Opening Up would inevitably bring in some unhealthy factors. Because some necessary management measures failed to keep up with the times, the attention paid to economic crimes was insufficient, and the prevention and crackdown was not effective, leading to an increase in economic criminal activities. Some staff members of state organs had been corrupted in their thinking. By taking advantage of their powers or loopholes in economic management, they arbitrarily embezzled, stole, and defrauded state property, thus forming a trend of economic crime. Along with the serious development of other criminal offences, smuggling, speculation, corruption, theft, market disruption, and other economic criminal activities were also growing.

The above-mentioned criminal activities in the economic field attracted great attention from the Central Government. In January 1982, the Central Committee issued an urgent notice on combating serious economic crimes, pointing out that this was a major issue concerning the Four Modernizations and China's survival. On March 8, at the Twenty-Second Meeting of the Standing Committee of the Fifth National People's Congress, the Decision on Severe Punishment of Criminals Who Seriously Destroy the Economy was adopted, which increased the penalties for serious economic crimes, including the death penalty for economic criminals whose crimes were particularly serious in nature or circumstances. On April 10, Deng Xiaoping pointed out at the meeting of the Politburo in his report "Combating Serious Criminal Activities in the Economic Field" that fighting economic crimes was a long-term, ongoing struggle accompanied by the Four Modernizations. He said, "We should have two hands. One is to adhere to the policy of opening up and invigorating the economy at home, and the other is to firmly combat economic crimes. Without a crackdown on economic crime, the policy of opening to the outside world will surely fail, as will the policy of invigorating the economy at home. With the fight against economic crime, opening up to the outside world and invigorating the economy at home can go in the right direction… This trend has become quite strong. If we do not pay serious attention to it and resolutely stop it, then our Party and our country will have to face the question of whether 'their outlook' will change."[16]

On April 13, 1982, the Central Committee and the State Council promulgated the Decision on Combating Serious Criminal Activities in the Economic Field, pointing out sharply that combating serious criminal activities in the economic field and fighting against corruption and deterioration were related to the success of China's socialist modernization construction and the prosperity of the Party and the country, and that this struggle was bound to be long-term and enduring.

According to the requirements of the Central Committee, the whole country carried out a vigorous campaign against criminal activities in the economic field. According to the Report on Combating Serious Criminal Activities in the Economic Field, submitted by the Disciplinary Inspection Committee of the Central Committee of the Communist Party of China to the Standing Committee of the Sixth National People's Congress in July 1983, from January 1982 to the end of April 1983, there were more than 190,000 cases of economic crimes, involving more than 71,000 Party members, and more than 131,000 cases were closed. It sentenced nearly 30,000 people according to law and expelled more than 8,500 Party members involved in the case. Another 24,400 people confessed to various economic crimes, and more than 410 million yuan of stolen money and goods was recovered.[17] On May 31, Wan Li addressed the meeting of responsible cadres of the Central Party, government, and military organs convened by the Central Commission of Discipline, demanding that all units resolutely carry out the fight against serious criminal activities in the economic field. One hundred fifty-one cadres at or above the bureau level were assigned by the Central Commission of Discipline to various places to reinforce and strengthen the handling of criminal cases in the economic field, and directly participate in the investigation and handling of major cases.

According to the Central Committee's deployment, the Central Discipline Inspection Commission resolutely investigated and dealt with some major cases of violation of Party discipline and severe influences. At that time, the major influential cases were the Jinjiang counterfeit drugs case in Fujian Province and the Hainan Island reselling of imported automobiles incident.

In order to open up the market of a white fungus beverage, some people in Chendai Town, Jinjiang County, Jinjiang Region (now Quanzhou City) said it was a cold granule, with printed words "nourishing Yin and moistening the lungs, a cure for asthenia, fatigue, and cough," and imitated the approval number of the pharmaceutical department to sell it both inside and outside the province. From September 1982 to April 1985, there were more than 170 forged approval numbers of the health administrative departments in 59 township enterprises. Among them, 62 were used frequently and more than 100 varieties of counterfeit medicines were manufactured, with the total output of more than 100,000 boxes and an output value of about 40 million yuan. These counterfeit medicines were sold to

28 provinces or regions in the country, causing great shock throughout the nation and attracting the attention of high-level leaders in the Central Government. On July 13, 1985, the Central Discipline Commission issued an open letter to the Party Group of Jinjiang Prefectural Committee and Administration of Fujian Province, requesting an investigation and punishment according to the law, and reporting to the Central Committee in cases of large-scale manufacturing of counterfeit drugs by enterprises in the Jinjiang region and selling them to various places by bribery. On July 27, after hearing the reports of the Fujian Provincial Party Committee and the Provincial Discipline Commission of the Communist Party of China, the Standing Committee of the Central Discipline Inspection Commission handled the individuals involved according to the law and decided to remove from their positions the standing committee members of Jinjiang County Party Committee and the Secretary of the Discipline Inspection Commission, who had participated in the manufacture and sale of counterfeit drugs and profited from them. In September 1986, the Fujian Provincial Higher People's Court and Quanzhou Intermediate People's Court sentenced the criminals involved in manufacturing and selling counterfeit drugs according to the law. Three of the criminals were sentenced to fixed-term imprisonment of more than ten years, seven to fixed-term imprisonment of one and a half years to eight years, four to probation or fixed-term imprisonment, and three exempted from criminal punishment. The handling of the Jinjiang counterfeit drug case cracked down severely on the illegal acts of various elements in the economic field.

From January 1, 1984, to March 5, 1985, leading comrades of Party committees and district governments of Hainan District violated Party discipline and relevant state regulations and used the autonomy granted by the Central Committee to import a large number of goods controlled by the State for reselling and making money. More than 10,000 imported cars were sold to places outside the island. Most of the other imports were likewise sold outside the district. In order to import automobiles and other materials, in violation of the state regulations on foreign exchange control, the relevant cadres in Hainan Island illegally purchased foreign exchange at a high price of $570 million from outside the island, which was ten times the amount allowed by the state for retention of foreign exchange in Hainan. At the same time, loans for importing automobiles and other materials amounted to 4.21 billion yuan, 1 billion yuan more than Hainan's total industrial and agricultural output value in 1984. Many loans were actually insolvent, and 2.01 billion yuan remained outstanding at the time of the incident.[18] These practices not only violated the relevant provisions of the state, impacted the national plan and the market, and destroyed the credit policy, but also frustrated Hainan's newly emerging large-scale development and construction. After the automobile incident, following a two-month investigation, a joint investigation team composed of the China Discipline Commission, the State Audit Administration, the State Economic Commission, the Ministry of Economy and Trade, the Office of the Special Administrative Region of the State Council, the State Administration of Materials, the Guangdong Provincial Committee of the Communist Party of China, and the People's Government of Guangdong Province wrote an investigation report on the import and reselling of automobiles and other materials in Hainan. On July 31, the Central Committee and the State Council approved the investigation report. The Commission agreed that the Guangdong Provincial Committee and the provincial government should impose Party discipline on those involved in this case. The Guangdong Provincial Committee and the provincial government also carried out inspections.

The investigation and punishment of the aforementioned economic crimes effectively safeguarded the Party's discipline and the seriousness of national laws, and to a certain extent ensured the healthy development of the cause of reform, opening up, and modernization.

11

The 1989 Political Storm and the Formation of the Third Generation of the Central Leadership Collective

At a time when the work of managing the economic environment and rectifying the economic order needed to be carried out in depth, political disturbances occurred in Beijing and other places in the spring and summer of 1989. The Party Central Committee took firm measures to resolutely calm the storm. For a long time, the political forces of some Western countries had been infiltrating socialist countries through diverse channels to support various anti-Communist and anti-socialist activities. After the turmoil in some socialist countries in Eastern Europe, some Western countries aimed to step up the peaceful evolution of China through various channels. In addition, in the course of promoting Reform and Opening Up and developing the commodity economy, a few leading comrades in the Party lacked consistency in adhering to the Four Basic Principles and neglected ideological and political work, and serious corruption among a few cadres damaged the image of the Party among the people. During the spring and summer of 1989, a small number of people took advantage of the problems existing in the Party's work and the people's dissatisfaction with rising prices, and especially with the corruption of some cadres, to incite activities against the leadership of the Communist Party and the socialist system. They took the opportunity of the masses mourning Hu Yaobang to spread rumors, set off a planned, organized and premeditated anti-Party and anti-socialist upheaval, and incited some people who did not know the truth to occupy Tiananmen Square in Beijing, taking aim at key departments of Party and government leaders. With the resolute and strong support of Deng Xiaoping and other older revolutionaries, the Politburo of the Central Committee, relying on the people, clearly opposed the unrest, pacified the political disturbance, and safeguarded the political power of the socialist nation and the fundamental interests of the people.

This political storm greatly educated the Party and the people. On June 9, 1989, Deng Xiaoping made a speech pointing out that the nature of this incident was the opposition between bourgeois liberalization and adherence to the Four Basic Principles. Sooner or later, the storm was bound to come. It was decided by the international climate and China's own microclimate, and it would not be transferred by the people's will. The outbreak of this incident was worth thinking about, prompting the Party to think clearly about the past and the future. He raised two questions that required serious consideration. First, were the line, policy, and principles formulated at the Third Plenary Session of the Eleventh Central Committee correct or incorrect, including the development strategy of the "three step" development? Was it because of this turmoil that the correctness of the lines, principles, and policies formulated had been questioned? Should the Party continue to take them as the goal of its future struggle? Further, was the idea of "one center, two basic points" roughly included in the Thirteenth Party Congress correct? Was it wrong to adhere to the four principles of Reform and Opening Up?

To these questions, he categorically answered that the line, principles, and policies formulated by the Third Plenary Session of the Eleventh Central Committee of the Communist Party, including the "three step" development strategy, were not wrong. It was not right to say that the Party's strategic objectives were wrong because of this incident. The route of "one center, two basic points" was correct. The Four Perseverances were not wrong in themselves, and the basic point of Reform and Opening Up was not wrong.

The basic line, principles, and policies the Party had formulated should be carried out steadfastly. He noted, "If there is a mistake, it is that we are not consistent enough to adhere to the Four Basic Principles... If we are not consistent enough, it is because the Reform and Opening Up has not been sufficiently carried out."[19]

This disturbance seriously interfered with the process of reform, opening up, and modernization. At the same time, it exposed the problems existing in the leadership of the Central Committee, which needed to be restructured. Even before the storm subsided, Deng Xiaoping proposed the need to change the central leadership, saying that the new central leadership should present to the people a new look as a promising leading group to carry out reform. It was important to select leaders who were recognized by the people as adhering to the line of Reform and Opening Up and who had made achievements in political work, forming a promising collective leadership to carry out the reform. It was crucial to win the trust of the people and make the Party and the people trustworthy. According to Deng Xiaoping, after full deliberation, Jiang Zemin, a member of the Politburo and Secretary of the Shanghai Municipal Party Committee of the Communist Party of China, had become the leading candidate for the new generation of the central leadership core. The Fourth Plenary Session of the Thirteenth Central Committee of the CPC, held in late June 1989, analyzed the nature and causes of the political turmoil in China over the previous two months, preliminarily summed up the experience and lessons, and clarified the Party's policies and tasks at that time and in the subsequent period.

In view of the serious mistakes made by Zhao Ziyang at the crucial moment of stopping the unrest, the plenary decided to abolish all his leading posts in the Party and to adjust some members of the central leading bodies. Jiang Zemin was elected General Secretary of the Central Committee at the plenary session, forming a new Standing Committee of the Politburo of the Central Committee. The plenary emphasized that the Party should continue to resolutely implement its line, principles, and policies established after the Third Plenary Session of the Eleventh Central Committee, resolutely implement the basic line of "one center, two basic points" determined by the Thirteenth National Congress, and clearly declare that this basic line and the decision-making of the Thirteenth National Congress would not be shaken by political turmoil, enabling the Party to adhere to the correct course of the socialist cause with Chinese characteristics through the turbulent waves. Pacifying domestic turbulence was China's internal affair. However, some Western countries had taken the opportunity to impose sanctions on China in an attempt to force it to change the direction of its socialist development. At a critical historical juncture, facing tremendous pressure in China and abroad, the central leadership, with Jiang Zemin as its core, shouldered the heavy responsibility of leading the Party and the country, guiding the Party and the people of all ethnicities to withstand the pressure and firmly adhere to the Party's basic line at the primary stage of socialism. The Party Central Committee took a series of important measures to quickly restore normal production and social order in Beijing and other places and maintain the stability of the political situation throughout the country. It was important to investigate and deal with some major cases and promptly punish corruption. In order to overcome the phenomenon of 'one hard hand and one soft hand,' the Party organizations at all levels needed to concentrate on Party building and strengthen their leadership in propaganda and ideological work. The Party would continue to implement the policy of governance and rectification, promote reform, opening up, and economic development, and gradually improve the national economic situation.

In view of the effective work of the new central leadership, Deng Xiaoping submitted to the Politburo his request to resign as Chairman of the Military Commission of the Central Committee of the Communist Party of China. Deng's request was approved at the Fifth Plenary Session of the Thirteenth Central Committee, held in November 1989. The plenary session expressed high respect for Deng's example of abolishing cadres' life-long leading posts by resigning from his current post in the fundamental interests of the Party and the state. It also emphasized that a series of viewpoints and theories put forward by Deng on the basis of the principle of combining Marxism-Leninism with China's actual situation, especially the basic theory of building socialism with Chinese characteristics, were an important part of Mao Zedong Thought, an inheritance and development of it under the new historical conditions, and a valuable spiritual treasure of the Communist Party of China and the Chinese people."[20] The whole Party needed to earnestly study Deng's works and incorporate them into an important guiding role in the great process of socialist modernization in China.

From the Fourth Plenary Session of the Thirteenth Central Committee to the Fifth Plenary Session of the Central Committee, the transition from the second-generation central leadership group, with Deng Xiaoping as its core, to the third-generation central leadership group, with Jiang Zemin as its core, was successfully completed, guaranteeing the stability of the Party's policies and continuity and the stability of the country, while enabling Reform and Opening Up and the drive toward socialist modernization to continue. This fully demonstrated the Party's political maturity and organizational strength, but also provided the most important political and organizational guarantee for maintaining the country's long-term stability and pushing the great cause of socialism with Chinese characteristics into the 21st century.

III

The Publication of Deng Xiaoping's Southern Talks and the Initial Establishment of the Guiding Role of Deng Xiaoping Theory

The theoretical literature of the socialist experience entered the 1990s, just as socialist countries in Eastern Europe changed dramatically. The Soviet Union declared its disintegration. Some countries and regions around China, especially in Southeast Asia, witnessed accelerated economic development. The world pattern indicated a trend of political multipolarization and economic globalization. This was not only a serious challenge to China, but also a new development opportunity.

Although great achievements had been made in stabilizing the economy since 1988, the speed of economic development had slowed down. China's economic growth rate was 4.1% in 1989, and 3.8% in 1990. Deng Xiaoping was extremely concerned about this. On March 3, 1990, in a talk with the head of the Central Committee, he pointed out that special attention should be paid to the problem of the decline in the speed of economic development. "It's not just an economic issue, but actually a political one."[21] Whether China could withstand the pressure of hegemony and power politics and adhere to its socialist system depended on whether it could compete for a faster growth rate and realize its development strategy.[22] Faced with a complex situation both in China and abroad, some people were confused, doubtful about China's Reform and Opening Up, and lacking confidence in the future of socialism.

1. Publication of Deng Xiaoping's Southern Talk

From January 18 to February 21, 1992, Deng Xiaoping, at age 88, visited Wuchang, Shenzhen, Zhuhai, and Shanghai, where he made very important remarks. He summarized the experience of the Party in leading the people to explore the path of socialism with Chinese characteristics since the Third Plenary Session of the Eleventh Central Committee of the Communist Party of China, giving a clear answer regarding the reform. Since the opening up, many important theoretical and policy issues had often puzzled and constrained people's thinking. The Southern Talk illustrated ten important points.

1) It was necessary to unswervingly adhere to the basic line of 100-year management and propose that reform was also the liberation of productive forces. Deng Xiaoping pointed out that revolution was the liberation of productive forces, and reform was also the liberation of productive forces. In the past, it was insufficient to talk only about developing productive forces under socialist conditions and not about emancipating productive forces through reform. The liberation and development of productive forces should be fully discussed. He emphasized that the key to upholding the Party's line, principles, and policies after the Third Plenary Session of the Eleventh Central Committee was to adhere to "one center and two basic points." He noted, "Not adhering to socialism, not carrying out Reform and Opening Up, not developing the economy, and not improving people's lives will only lead to a dead end. The basic line should be managed for a hundred years and not shaken. Only by sticking to this line will the people's belief and support be won. Whoever wants to change the line, principles, and policies established since the Third Plenary Session of the Central Committee will be overthrown if the people do not agree to them."[23]

2) The Party put forward the criteria of "Three Benefits" to judge whether Reform and Opening Up was correct or not. The Thirteenth National Congress of the Communist Party of China, based on Mao Zedong's thought in *On the*

United Government, had played an important role in adhering to the Party's basic line, centering on economic construction. In order to continue to dispel people's doubts about Reform and Opening Up, Deng Xiaoping further pointed out in his Southern Talk that Reform and Opening Up should be bolder and more experimental. If the Party was sure of this, it should try boldly to make serious progress. The important experience of Shenzhen was its daring to break through. Who dared to say with 100% certainty what to do or that avoiding risks was necessary? Reform and Opening Up that failed to make progress or take risks was, to say the least, afraid of capitalist things or of taking the road of capitalism. The key was whether it was of the "capital" or "socialist" family. In response to the controversy over the establishment of special economic zones over a period of time, he clearly said, "The criteria for judging should mainly depend on whether it is conducive to the development of productive forces in a socialist society, whether it is conducive to the enhancement of the comprehensive national strength of socialist countries, and whether it is conducive to the improvement of people's living standards [...] The family name of the Special Administrative Region is 'socialist' and not 'capital.'"[24] He also said that there were different opinions on the Reform and Opening Up policy. Those should be made visible, but without controversy. Otherwise, the Party would waste all its time and nothing could be done.

3) It was pointed out that the planned and market economies were not the essential difference between socialism and capitalism. Socialism could develop a market economy. As early as 1979, Deng Xiaoping pointed out that the market economy could not be said to exist only in a capitalist society. Socialism could also develop a market economy. Since then, he had been paying attention to and studying this issue. He had discussed it on more than ten occasions. He believed that there was no fundamental contradiction between socialism and the market economy. "Don't think that a market economy is the path of capitalism – that's not the case."[25] He noted, "When it serves socialism, it's socialism."[26] In his talk in the South, he emphasized once again, "A more planned or market economy – that is not the essential difference between socialism and capitalism. A planned economy is not equal to socialism, as capitalism also has a plan. A market economy is not equal to capitalism, as socialism also has a market. Plans and markets are economic instruments."[27] It also required that socialism should boldly absorb and draw lessons from all the advanced management methods and styles reflecting

the law of modern socialized production in all countries of the world, including developed capitalist countries. This point of view formally put forward the theory of the socialist market economy to the Fourteenth National Congress of the CPC, which had a decisive influence on the ultimate realization of the transformation from a planned economy to a socialist market economy in China.

4) For the first time, the issue of the essence of socialism had been clearly raised to correct the unscientific understanding of the essence of socialism. What was the essence of socialism? In the 160 years from utopian socialism to scientific socialism, the communists had always pursued socialism as their ideal, but they had never raised such a question, nor had the "theoretical books" of Marxist-Leninist works defined it. People were just accustomed to thinking that socialism involved public ownership, distribution according to work, a planned economy, the dictatorship of the proletariat, guidance by Marxism, and so on. These elements were undoubtedly important for the construction of socialism, but it was not scientific to regard them as the understanding of the essence of socialism, because it did not fit with the general principle of historical materialism to define social form from two aspects of conflicting movement of productive forces and productive relations. It also deviated from the understanding of the basic contradiction of socialist society, that is, the contradiction between productive relations and productive forces, and that between the superstructure and economic foundation. These elements, which were vaguely regarded as the essence of socialism, were the substance of production relations and superstructure, and completely dispensed with the requirement of developing productive forces. This was an epistemological source of errors made in exploring socialism in the past. When Deng Xiaoping reflected on the lessons of building socialism in China in the mid-1980s, he pointed out with great emphasis that "although we are now engaged in socialism, we are not in fact qualified."[28]

An important reason for this lay in the fact that the fundamental task of socialism was not to concentrate on the development of productive forces. With such painful lessons, Deng Xiaoping first raised the issue of the essence of socialism in his talks in the South. He pointed out that "the essence of socialism is to liberate and develop productive forces, eliminate exploitation and polarization, and ultimately achieve common prosperity."[29] The new definition of the essence of socialism highlighted the ultimate decisive role of productivity and the contradictory movement between productivity and production relations, and between the economic basis and superstructure, thus laying a theoretical foundation for the basic task theory and the top theory of socialism put forward by the Party.

5) It emphasized that the key to seizing the opportunity and developing oneself was to develop the economy, and it put forward the important idea that "development is the absolute principle." Deng Xiaoping repeatedly emphasized that at that time, the economic development of some neighboring countries and regions was faster than China's. If China did not develop or developed too slowly, the common people would lag behind in comparison to China's neighbors. Therefore, if possible, China should not hinder development. Where conditions permitted, the Party should undertake it as quickly as possible. As long as it focused on efficiency, quality, and an export-oriented economy, there was nothing to worry about. It was important to seize the opportunity. China's economic development must strive to reach a higher level every few years. Apparently, it was not enough to encourage unrealistic high-speed development, but to develop steadily and coordinately with a solid foundation and an efficiency-oriented approach. He pointed out clearly, "For a big developing country like ours, if we want to develop faster, we cannot always stay at ease and completely undisturbed. We should pay attention to steady, coordinated economic development, but stability and coordination are relative and not absolute. Development is the absolute principle."[30] To develop the economy, it was important not only to seize opportunities, but also to rely on science, technology, and education. Science was the only way to promote science.

6) It proposed the strategic estimation that China should be vigilant against the Right, but also mainly prevent the Left. Since Reform and Opening Up, Deng Xiaoping had been fighting on two fronts, opposing the wrong tendencies of both Left and Right, but he had repeatedly pointed out that the main thing was to oppose Left. In this Southern conversation, he clarified, "Now, there are things on the Right that affect us, and things on the Left that affect us, but what is deeply rooted is still something on the Left. Some theorists and politicians scare people with big labels, which is not a rightist, but a leftist problem. The Left is revolutionary, giving the impression that the more Left, the more revolutionary. The Left has been terrible in the history of our Party, though, and could destroy a good thing in no time. The Right may bury socialism, and the Left may do the same. China should be vigilant against the Right, but mainly prevent the

Left."³¹ This striking conclusion was a profound summary of the Party's historical experience and that of other socialist countries, as well as the fresh experience of the main tendencies since Reform and Opening Up. It was of important guiding significance for the Party to adhere to the basic line for 100 years and keep a clear mind in strategic estimation.

7) It proposed that the Party should adhere to the principle of "grasping with both hands," and that both hands should be firm. In view of the lessons of the political turmoil in the 1980s, Deng Xiaoping clearly pointed out that "we should stick to a two-handed grasp, one hand grasping Reform and Opening Up, and one grasping the crackdown on various criminal activities. Both hands should be firm. Fighting against various criminal activities and eliminating various ugly phenomena, we must not be soft-handed."³² In view of the goal of Guangdong Province catching up with the "Four Little Dragons" in Asia within twenty years, he warned Guangdong's Party members that not only the economy, but also the social order and ethos should be improved. "Both civilizations should surpass them, which is socialism with Chinese characteristics."³³ He emphasized that corruption should be opposed throughout the process of Reform and Opening Up. For cadres and members of the Communist Party, the construction of an honest, clean government should be taken as a major task. It was still necessary to rely on the legal system, which was more reliable. As long as the Party developed its productive forces, maintained a certain rate of economic growth, and stuck to both hands, it could build a socialist spiritual civilization.

8) It emphasized that the correct political line should be guaranteed by the correct organizational line. The key to the long-term stability of the country was to do a good job within the Communist Party. Deng Xiaoping emphasized that in realizing the handover of the new and old leading collectives of the Party, "the key to China's issue is that the Communist Party should have a good Politburo, especially a good Standing Committee of the Politburo." As long as there was no problem in this area, China would be as stable as Mount Tai. "What matters most is a united leadership core. If we can stay this way for fifty or sixty years, socialist China will be invincible."³⁴ In his talks in the South, he further discussed the issue of the relationship between political and organizational lines, pointing out that "the key to success in China's affairs, whether socialism and Reform and Opening Up can be maintained, whether the economy can develop faster, and whether the country can maintain long-term stability, in a sense, lies in the people." Attention

had to be paid to training people, and according to the standards of "revolutionary, younger, knowledgeable, and professional," people with both ability and morality should be selected to join the team. Imperialism pursued peaceful evolution and pinned its hopes on future generations. Therefore, it was important to educate the army, the dictatorship organs, Party members, the people, and the young. "Whether China is going to have problems or not lies within the Communist Party. We should remain alert about this... We say that the Party's basic line should govern for a hundred years, and that this is the only way to ensure long-term stability."[35]

9) It emphasized that the consolidation and development of the socialist system required a long historical stage. Socialist society had a short transitional stage and a long historical period. This was a problem that had not been solved by anyone from Marx to Lenin, nor had Mao Zedong really solved it. According to the previous point of view, although socialism was also said to be a low-level stage of communism, this was for lack of awareness of the long-term nature of communism, as socialism was more concerned with its transitional nature. This was the theoretical root of the mistakes made by all socialist countries' due to over-eagerness for achievements. After three years of the Great Leap Forward in China, Mao Zedong said that socialism was a rather long historical period, but he mainly talked about it from the perspective of class struggle. Deng Xiaoping summed up the historical lessons of socialist development and warned the whole Party with a statesman's strategic thinking and a historian's profound vision, saying, "We have only been building socialism for decades and are still in the initial stage. To consolidate and develop the socialist system, we still need a long historical stage. We need generations, even dozens of generations, to work tirelessly and unremittingly. We must not take it lightly."[36]

10) A scientific summary of the essence of Marxism was made, emphasizing the importance of resorting to historical materialism to educate young people to understand the law of human social development. Although Deng Xiaoping said that he did not read many books, he had rich political wisdom and high theoretical insight, and he thus made a scientific summary of the essence of Marxism. He pointed out, "Seeking truth from facts is the essence of Marxism. We should advocate this, not mere dogmatism. The success of our Reform and Opening Up depends not on dogmatism, but on practice and seeking truth from facts... We have talked about Marxism for a lifetime. In fact, Marxism is

not mysterious. It is a very simple thing, a very simple truth."[37] On this basis, he proposed that "we should learn what is essential and practical in Marxism and Leninism." He emphasized that Marxism was a science, and that historical materialism revealed the law of human social development. There would be more people in favor of Marxism in the world over time. Socialism would inevitably replace capitalism after a long process of development, an irreversible overall trend of social and historical development. Severe twists and turns had taken place in some countries, seemingly weakening socialism. However, the people had been trained to learn from these trials, which would promote the development of socialism in a healthier direction. It was important to continue to advance on the path of building socialism with Chinese characteristics. Deng noted, "If, from the founding of the People's Republic, we can build our country into a developed country of a medium level in a hundred years, it would be a great achievement. From now to the middle of the next century will be a key stage, and we must work hard. We have a heavy burden on our shoulders and a great responsibility."[38]

Deng Xiaoping's Southern Talk was very rich in content. In a sense, it was not only a concentrated reflection of Deng's thinking on Reform and Opening Up, but also a symbol of the development of his ideology and theory to a new height. This was mainly manifested in two aspects. On the one hand, the Southern Talks were systematic writings, which not only had a systematic structure to their content, but also answered many important questions, such as those regarding the nature and definition of socialism and how to build socialism in a more comprehensive way. Compared with his other works, it was a comprehensive theoretical document that formed a more complete system of individual thought. On the other hand, the Southern Talks endowed the theory of socialism with Chinese characteristics with many new ideas. The above viewpoints not only represented the new development of the theory of socialism with Chinese characteristics, but also reflected the new realm it had reached. Not only did it have a profound, incisive thought and a dignified theoretical strength, but its language was vivid and thorough, with a fascinating sense of novelty. The Southern Talk was an important part of Deng's theory of enriching and developing socialism with Chinese characteristics in his later years. It is also "another declaration of emancipating the mind and seeking truth from facts to push reform, opening up, and modernization construction to a new stage."[39]

2. The Formation of Deng Xiaoping's Theory and the Preliminary Establishment of Its Guiding Position

The Fourteenth National Congress of the CPC was held in mid-October 1992. The main tasks of the Congress included the comprehensive summary of the great practice and basic experience in the previous fourteen years of Reform and Opening Up, determining the strategic plan for the next period, seizing the favorable opportunity, accelerating the pace of reform, opening up, and modernization, and winning greater victories in the cause of socialism with Chinese characteristics. All of this was to be achieved under the guidance of Deng's theory of building socialism with Chinese characteristics. The conference made three decisions of far-reaching historical significance. First, it preliminarily established the guiding position of Deng's theory of building socialism with Chinese characteristics throughout the Party. Second, it made clear that the goal of China's economic system reform was to establish a socialist market economic system. Third, it was noted that the Party should seize the opportunity, accelerate development, and concentrate on economic construction. Marked by Deng's Southern Talks and the Fourteenth National Congress of the Party, the cause of socialist reform, opening up, and modernization had reached a new stage of development.

Since the Third Plenary Session of the Eleventh Central Committee of the Communist Party of China, the Party had continuously enriched its understanding of the socialist path with Chinese characteristics in the practice of Reform and Opening Up, gradually forming the theory of socialism with Chinese characteristics. The formation of this theory had mainly gone through three stages of development.

The first stage was from the Third Plenary Session of the Eleventh Central Committee at the end of 1978 to the Twelfth Congress in 1982. In the process of settling the chaos and starting the reform, Deng Xiaoping's theory of building socialism with Chinese characteristics had gradually taken shape. Starting from the Third Plenary Session of the Eleventh Central Committee, the CPC had conscientiously cleaned up and corrected the past leftist mistakes, successfully completed the rectification of the disorder in the guiding ideology, and through the summary of historical experience and the practice of Reform and Opening Up, once again carried out the correct combination of the basic principles of Marxism with the practice of socialist construction in China. In this process, under the guidance of Deng Xiaoping, the Party put forward a series of new principles and policies concerning China's socialist construction, forming a number of new understandings about what socialism was and how to build it. In 1981, the Resolution on Several Historical Issues of the Party since the Founding of the People's Republic summarized these new achievements as ten main points of view, which could be regarded as the rudiment of Deng Xiaoping's theory of building socialism with Chinese characteristics. At the Twelfth National Congress, Deng put forward the idea of "building socialism with Chinese characteristics," which launched the Party's second historic leap in realizing the localization of Marxism, and the theoretical achievements of this leap had a distinct theme.

The second stage was from the Twelfth National Congress in 1982 to the Thirteenth National Congress in 1987. Deng Xiaoping's theory of building socialism with Chinese characteristics formed a basic outline in the process of thoroughly carrying out Reform and Opening Up. Reform and Opening Up was carried out comprehensively, an example of a magnificent development process from rural reform to urban reform, from economic system reform to all aspects of system reform, and from domestic revitalization to opening up. The deepening of reform urgently required theoretical guidance. During this period, Deng repeatedly raised the primary basic theoretical question of "what is socialism and how to build it." In October 1984, the Third Plenary Session of the Twelfth Central Committee of the Communist Party of China adopted the Decision on Economic System Reform, which suggested that the socialist economy was a planned commodity economy on the basis of public ownership, breaking through the traditional idea of confronting the planned economy with a commodity economy. In 1987, the Thirteenth National Congress of the Communist Party of China systematically expounded the theory of the primary stage of socialism. Together with the theory of the socialist commodity economy, it formed two new achievements in the process of localization of Marxism, which provided powerful theoretical guidance for Reform and Opening Up. The Thirteenth National Congress highly appraised the great significance of opening up the road of building socialism with Chinese characteristics after the Third Plenary Session of the Eleventh Central Committee. It called it the second historic leap of combining Marxism with Chinese practice, and called the theoretical achievements of this leap "the theory of building socialism with Chinese characteristics." The Thirteenth National Congress of the Communist Party of China listed twelve main points of view of this theory. These included 1) emancipating the mind, seeking truth from facts, and taking practice as the sole criterion for testing truth, 2) that building socialism must follow its own path in accordance with its own national conditions, 3) the long period required for the initial stage of socialism based on the condition of a backward economy and culture, 4) developing productive forces and concentrating on modernization as the fundamental task of socialist society, 5) the socialist economy as a planned commodity economy, 6) reform as an important driving force for the development of socialist society and opening to the outside world as a necessary condition for the realization of socialist modernization, 7) socialist democratic politics and socialist spiritual civilization as important features of socialism, 8) adhering to the four basic principles and the general policy of Reform and Opening Up as mutually integrated and indispensable, 9) realizing national unity with "one country, two systems," 10) the style of the ruling party determining the Party's life and death, 11) developing relations with foreign Communist Parties and other political parties in accordance with the principles of independence, full equality, mutual respect, and non-interference in internal affairs, and 12) peace and development as the themes of the contemporary world. It was noted that "these views constitute the outline of the theory of building socialism with Chinese characteristics, initially answering the basic questions of the stage, task, motive, condition, layout, and international environment of our socialist construction, and mapping out the scientific track of our progress."[40]

The third stage lasted from the Thirteenth National Congress to the Fourteenth National Congress. During this stage, Deng Xiaoping's theory of building socialism with Chinese characteristics matured and a scientific system was formed. At the end of 1980s and the beginning of 1990s, China's reform entered a critical stage, while serious political disturbances occurred in China and abroad. At this critical historical juncture, the Communist Party of China firmly depended on the people, firmly adhered to the Four Basic Principles, safeguarded the independence, security, and stability of the country, unswervingly adhered to economic construction as the center, and firmly promoted Reform and Opening Up. The cause of building socialism with Chinese characteristics not only successfully withstood the severe tests, but also perfected Deng Xiaoping's theory of building socialism with Chinese characteristics.

In 1990, the Seventh Plenary Session of the Thirteenth Central Committee of the Communist Party of China adopted the Suggestions on Formulating the Ten-Year Plan for National Economic and Social Development and the Eighth Five-Year Plan, which summarized the basic theory and practice of building socialism with Chinese characteristics after the Third Plenary Session of the Eleventh Central Committee of the Communist Party of China into twelve principles. These twelve principles included 1) adhering to the people's democratic dictatorship system led by the working class and based on the alliance of workers and peasants, 2) adhering to the development of social productive forces as the fundamental task of socialism, 3) constantly improving the socialist economic, political, and other fields of management systems through reform, 4) adopting the development of foreign economic and trade relations, the utilization and introduction of foreign capital and continuing to open up to the outside world in various forms, such as advanced technology, 5) adhering to the ownership structure in which socialist public ownership coexisted with various economic components, 6) actively developing the socialist planned commodity economy, 7) implementing a distribution system with distribution according to work as the main body and supplemented by other modes of distribution, 8) adhering to Marxist-Leninist and Mao Zedong Thought and continuously improving the ideological, moral, scientific, and cultural quality of the nation while building a socialist spiritual civilization, 9) establishing and developing socialist national relations of equality, mutual assistance, unity, cooperation, and common prosperity, and adhering to and improving the system of regional national autonomy, 10) promoting the gradual realization of the great cause of reunification of the motherland in accordance with the concept and practice of "one country, two systems," 11) upholding the independent foreign policy of peace and developing friendly relations with all countries on the basis of the Five Principles of Peaceful Coexistence, and 12) upholding the leadership of the Communist Party and constantly improving the Party's leadership system, style, and methods so as to make the Party a strong leading core of the socialist cause. Some of these had been adhered to by the Party for decades and developed under new historical conditions, while others summarized the fresh experience of modernization and Reform and Opening Up over the previous ten years, which condensed Deng Xiaoping's outstanding contributions to inheriting and developing Mao Zedong Thought under the new historical conditions. The generalization of these twelve principles was a further deepening of the understanding of socialism with Chinese characteristics.

In 1991, in his speech at the 70th Anniversary Congress of the Party, Jiang Zemin summarized the main content of the theory of building socialism with Chinese characteristics from three aspects, the economy, politics, and culture. At the beginning of 1992, Deng Xiaoping's Southern Talk offered a further summary of the basic experience since the Third Plenary Session of the Eleventh Central Committee of the Communist Party of China and answered many important questions that had puzzled and restrained people's theoretical thinking for some time. It not only marked the elevation of Deng Xiaoping's thought to a new height, but also brought the Party's understanding of the theory of building socialism with Chinese characteristics to a new level. In view of this, on the basis of the above theoretical advancements, the Fourteenth National Congress offered a new summary of the content of the theory of building socialism with Chinese characteristics, and for the first time used the term "Comrade Deng Xiaoping's theory of building socialism with Chinese characteristics."

The nine aspects of Deng Xiaoping's theory of building socialism with Chinese characteristics summarized in the Fourteenth National Congress of the Communist Party of China included:

1) On the path of socialist development, it was important to emphasize the Party's own way, rather than take books as dogma or copy foreign models. The Party should take Marxism as guidance and practice as the sole criterion for testing truth, emancipating minds, seeking truth from facts, respecting the initiative spirit of the masses, and building socialism with Chinese characteristics.
2) On the issue of the stage of development, the Party had made a scientific conclusion that China was still at the primary stage of socialism, emphasizing that this was a long historical period of at least a hundred years, and that all policies and principles must be formulated on the basis of this basic national situation, not divorced from reality or going beyond the present stage.
3) On the fundamental task of socialism, it was pointed out that the essence of socialism was to liberate and develop productive forces, eliminate exploitation and polarization, and ultimately achieve common prosperity. The Party needed to put the development of productive forces as its top

priority, take economic construction as the center, and promote all-round social progress. To judge the merits and demerits of all aspects of work, in the final analysis, the criterion was the "three benefits."

4) On the driving force of socialist development, the Party emphasized that reform was a revolution and the only way to liberate productive forces and realize China's modernization. At the same time, it emphasized that opening up was an indispensable means of reform and construction. The Party should absorb and utilize all the advanced civilized achievements created by all countries in the world, including capitalist countries, to develop socialism.

5) On the issue of external conditions for socialist construction, it was pointed out that peace and development were the two major themes of the contemporary world. The Party must adhere to an independent foreign policy of peace and strive for a favorable international environment for China's drive toward modernization.

6) On the issue of political guarantees for socialist construction, the Party emphasized that it must adhere to the four basic principles, not only guaranteeing the healthy development of reform, opening up, and modernization, but also obtaining material from reform, opening up, and modernization for the new era.

7) On the issue of strategic steps, it was proposed that basic modernization should be carried out in three steps. Some people in some regions must be allowed and encouraged to become prosperous first, through hard work, so as to promote more regions and people systematically achieving common prosperity.

8) On the issue of leadership and strength, it was emphasized that the Communist Party was the core of leadership in the cause of socialism. The Party must adapt to the needs of reform, opening up, and modernization, constantly improve and strengthen its leadership in all aspects of work, and improve and strengthen its own construction. It needed to rely on the broad masses of workers, peasants, and intellectuals, on the unity of the people of all ethnicities, on the broadest united front of all socialist workers, patriots who supported socialism, and patriots who supported the reunification of the motherland.

9) On the issue of the reunification of the motherland, the creative concept of "one country, two systems" was put forward to promote the great cause of peaceful reunification of the motherland. The summary of the above nine aspects indicated that Deng Xiaoping's theory of building socialism with Chinese characteristics formed a relatively complete scientific system. The Report of the Fourteenth National Congress of the Communist Party of China had pointed out that this scientific theoretical system gradually formed and developed on the basis of summing up the historical experience of China's socialist victories and setbacks, drawing lessons from the historical experience of other socialist countries in the process of China's reform, opening up, and socialist modernization under the historical condition that peace and development had become the themes of the times. The report highly appraised the great significance of this theory, pointing out that it had "for the first time systematically and preliminarily answered a series of basic questions about how to build socialism and how to consolidate and develop socialism in a country with a relatively backward economy and culture, and inherited and developed Marxism with new ideas and viewpoints." This was the basic and proper principle of Marxism-Leninism. The product of the combination of contemporary China's reality and the characteristics of the times was the inheritance and development of Mao Zedong Thought, which was "Marxism in contemporary China and a powerful ideological weapon guiding us to achieve new historical tasks."[41]

In view of the theoretical significance and guiding role of "Comrade Deng Xiaoping's theory of building socialism with Chinese characteristics," the Fourteenth National Congress of the Communist Party of China put forward the strategic task of arming the whole Party with this theory. "When we study Mao Zedong Thought and Marxism-Leninism, the central aim is to study the theory of building socialism with Chinese characteristics." The great significance of Deng Xiaoping's theory of building socialism with Chinese characteristics was written in the revised Party Constitution of the Fourteenth National Congress, which had initially established its guiding position throughout the Party. Deng Xiaoping's theory of building socialism with Chinese characteristics, summarized and named in the Fourteenth Party Congress, was the first great theoretical achievement of the second historic leap of combining Marxism with Chinese practice and the latest achievement in exploring the localization of Marxism since Reform and Opening Up. With this as its source and through constant summing up of the new experience of reform, opening up, and modernization, the CPC achieved great theoretical innovation time after time and saw many new achievements in the new century.

CHAPTER 7

The Socialist Market Economic System and the Basic Program of the Initial Stage of Socialism

I

The Ultimate Goal of the Reform of the Market Economic System and the Formulation of the Program of Action

How should China's economic system be reformed? Was it enough to mend it within the framework of the original planned economic system, or was it necessary to set up a new market economic system as the goal, accompanied by the comprehensive process of Reform and Opening Up? This was not only an economic issue, but also a political one, which was related to the overall situation of socialist modernization. The Party had tirelessly explored this issue and had undergone a process of emancipating the mind and gradually defining the Party's understanding. The previous discussion on the decision of the Third Plenary Session of the Twelfth Central Committee of the Communist Party of China on economic restructuring had partially touched on this issue. Here, a systematic review is offered, from the perspective of an ideological understanding of the central decision-making groups.

As early as July to September 1978, at a meeting of the State Council, some people proposed the idea that the Party should give more emphasis to the role of the law of value. In December 1978, Deng Xiaoping wrote in the outline of his speech "Emancipating the Mind, Seeking Truth from Facts, and Looking Forward Together" that "the contradiction between autonomy and national plans is mainly regulated by the law of value and the relationship between supply and demand (product quality)."[1] That is to say, it was regulated by the market. This was the preliminary expression of Deng Xiaoping's thought on regulating economic activity through the market.

In March 1979, Chen Yun suggested in the Outline of Planning and Market Issues, "There must be two kinds of economy during the whole socialist period, the planned economy (planned and proportionate part) and the market regulation (that is, production based not on plans but only on the changes of market supply and demand, or, the part with unplanned regulation). The first part is basic and primary, while the second part is subordinate and necessary."[2] He also pointed out that "in the future economic adjustment and institutional reform, the adjustment of the proportion of the planned economy to the market economy will actually account for a large proportion. It is not necessarily true that the more the planned economy increases, the smaller the absolute amount of the market economy will be, but more likely, both will increase accordingly."[3] After this, Chen Yun's prediction was proven by the process of launching and developing the reform. China's economic system reform had not initially broken the planned system framework, but on the one hand, in the planned system, China was to give play to the role of the market and the law of value, appropriately reducing the proportion of mandatory plans and increasing the proportion of guiding plans. On the other hand, it aimed to pay attention to exerting and expanding the scope of market regulation outside the planned system. In this way, the guiding plan in the planning system and the market regulation outside the planning system were increased, and the law of the market was reflected both inside and outside the planning system. Practice affirmed that the importance of the market in economic development could not be ignored, and the socialist economy could not do without the role of market regulation. In this regard, Deng Xiaoping made a clearer exposition, first linking the market economy with socialism.

In November 1979, when meeting with foreign guests, Deng Xiaoping pointed out, "It is certainly incorrect to say that the market economy exists only in a capitalist society, and that there is only a capitalist market economy. Why can't socialism develop the market economy? This can't be said to be capitalism. We take the planned economy as the core, complemented by the market economy, but this is a socialist market economy."[4] Here, Deng Xiaoping explicitly used the term "socialist market economy." In June 1981, the Sixth Plenary Session of the Eleventh Central Committee of the Communist Party of China adopted the Resolution on Some Historical Issues of the Party since the Founding of the People's Republic of China. In summarizing the path of socialist modernization in China, it was proposed that "the auxiliary role of market regulation should be brought into play." This formulation was confirmed in the report of the Twelfth National Congress of the Communist Party of China as the principle of "giving priority to the planned economy and supplementing it with market regulation." This reflected the level of recognition and understanding of this issue at that time.

The Decision on Economic System Reform, adopted at the Third Plenary Session of the Twelfth Central Committee in 1984, made a significant contribution to the resolution of the issue of the unification of socialism and the commodity economy. The drawback was that the problem of the unification of socialism and the market economy was not yet resolved. The traditional idea that socialism could not develop a market economy still held considerable sway. However, when the Decision on Economic System Reform proposed that the socialist economy was a planned commodity economy on the basis of public ownership, it pointed out that implementing a planned economy did not mean giving priority to mandatory plans, and that guiding plans were also a specific form of plans. This provided a theoretical basis for gradually narrowing the scope of mandatory plans, expanding the scope of market regulation, and promoting the reform of market orientation. The Thirteenth National Congress further pointed out that the new system of the socialist planned commodity economy should be a system of internal unity of planning and market. From that time on, the central document no longer stated that "the planned economy is the main factor." After the Fourth Plenary Session of the Thirteenth Central Committee of the Communist Party of China, it was proposed that an economic system and operational mechanism that combined the planned economy with market regulation to adapt to the development of the planned commodity economy be established.

After the Third Plenary Session of the Twelfth Central Committee, various regions vigorously developed the commodity economy, and market-oriented reforms were expanded and deepened. At the same time, in theory, there was also a series of debates about the nature of the market economy and whether China should implement a market economy. The focus of the debate was whether to develop the market economy under the name of "socialism" or "capitalism." In this regard, Deng made a clear statement, expounding on many occasions the view that there was no fundamental contradiction between socialism and the market economy,[5] emphasizing the theoretical understanding that the difference between capitalism and socialism did not lie in the issue of whether the economy was planned or market based. This article combed through Deng's many expositions on the market economy. In addition to the above-mentioned expositions in November 1979, the second came in January 1980, when he talked about seeking a way to develop the economy in line with China's actual situation, proposing that "the combination of planned and market regulations" could be adopted. The third was a talk with the head of the State Planning Commission in July 1982, where he stated, "Compared with capitalism, socialism has the advantage of being able to take the entire nation as one chessboard, concentrating its efforts and ensuring its focus. The disadvantage is that the market is not well explored and the economy is not active enough. How do we handle the relationship between the planned and market economy then? If we settle it well, it will be beneficial to economic development. If we fail to do so, it will be worse."

The fourth and fifth occasions were both in relation to the evaluation of the Decision on Economic System Reform (hereinafter referred to as the Decision) of the Third Plenary Session of the Twelfth Central Committee of the Communist Party of China. The fourth time was an impromptu speech on October 20, 1984, when the Decision was adopted at the plenary session. It stated that the Decision was political economics that combined the basic principles of Marxism with the practice of socialism in China. The fifth was a speech delivered by the Central Advisory Commission two days later, saying that the Decision turned to expressions that the Party's predecessors had never used. The sixth time was a talk with the American entrepreneur delegation in October 1985, which clearly pointed out, "There is no fundamental contradiction between socialism and the market economy. The question is how to develop social productive forces more effectively. We have been engaged in a planned economy in the past, but years of practice have proven that, in a sense, a planned economy alone will restrain the development of productive forces. Combining a planned economy with a market economy will liberate productivity and accelerate economic development.[6] The seventh time came in February 1987, when Deng spoke with several leaders of the Central Committee. He said, "Why is it capitalism whenever we talk about the market, while only planning is socialism?" He went on to say that planned and market regulations were both means to an end. As long as it was good for the development of productive forces, it could be used. If it served socialism, it was socialist, while if it served capitalism, it was capitalist. It was wrong to say that planning was socialism. There was a planning office in Japan, and there were plans in the United States. China needed to learn from the Soviet Union and develop a planned economy. Later, the Party talked about the planned economy, but now it should stop talking about it.[7]

The eighth time, in September 1988 occurred, when Deng was listening to a report on economic work. He said that macro-management should be reflected in the Central Government's fulfillment of its commitment, and now it was the time for macro-management moving toward a moderately well-off society. There was no direct mention here of the issue of a planned or market economy, but it was based on the implementation of a socialist market economy. It was important authoritative evidence for later emphasizing the central macro-control under the condition of a socialist market economy.

The ninth speech was delivered on June 9, 1989, where he said, "We must continue to adhere to the combination of a planned economy and market regulation, which cannot be changed. In practical work, during the period of adjustment, we can strengthen or make more plans, while at another time, we can make more market adjustments and be more flexible."[8]

The tenth time was in December 1990, when he said to several leaders of the Central Committee, "We must understand theoretically that the distinction between capitalism and socialism does not lie in the issue of a planned or market economy. Socialism also has a market economy, and capitalism also has planned management. We should not assume that a market economy is the path of capitalism – that is not the case."[9]

The eleventh occasion was the talk on inspecting Shanghai at the beginning of 1991, where he said, "We should not think that the planned economy is socialism and the market economy is capitalism. That's not the case. Both are means, and the market can also serve socialism."[10]

The twelfth time was the Southern Talk. In the 1992 Southern Talk, especially in response to the controversy on the nature of planned and market economy being "socialist" or "capitalist," Deng Xiaoping pointed out that "more plan or more market" was not the essential difference between socialism and capitalism. The planned economy was not equal to socialism, as capitalism also had a plan, while the market economy was not equal to capitalism, as socialism also had a market. Planning and markets were both economic instruments. This gave a thorough, penetrating answer to the long-debated and important theoretical question of whether socialism could develop a market economy or not, fundamentally removing the ideological shackles that took the planned economy as the basic characteristic of socialism and laying an ideological and theoretical foundation for the establishment of the goal of a socialist market economic system.

In the process of preparing for the Fourteenth National Congress of the CPC, the Central Committee repeatedly studied this issue before deciding on the establishment of the target model of economic system reform. On June 9, 1992, Jiang Zemin made a report to the Central Party School, proposing the idea of establishing a socialist market economic system. He first elaborated Deng Xiaoping's thought that "socialism also has a market."Through more than ten years of Reform and Opening Up, the Party had developed a deeper understanding. In the past, it often only saw the negative effects brought by the spontaneity of the market, seldom noting the positive role of the market in stimulating competition among enterprises and promoting economic development. In particular, it could not see that the market was also a way of allocating resources, nor could it see its role in optimizing the allocation of resources. This was a one-sided understanding. Clearly, emphasizing the advantages of the market did not mean that the market was comprehensive and omnipotent, and the market had obvious limitations. Therefore, it was necessary to give full play to the advantages of planned regulation to compensate for and resist the negative role of market regulation, if the overall development of the economy was to be ensured. He also pointed out that it was imperative to fundamentally reform the highly centralized planned economic system. Otherwise, it was impossible to realize the modernization of China. How should reform be carried out, and what was the goal? He said that there were three ways to establish a new economic system. One was to establish a socialist commodity economic system combining planning with the market, while the second was to establish a socialist planned market economic system, and the third was to establish a socialist market economic system. After consulting opinions from various angles and weighing and comparing on many occasions, the Central Government preferred to opt for the socialist market economic system." On June 12, Jiang Zemin told Deng Xiaoping what he thought. Deng immediately expressed his support for this formulation.[12] He said that, in fact, the Party had been practicing this, as was evidenced in Shenzhen as a model of the socialist market economy. Since that time, the Party committees of thirty provinces, autonomous regions, and municipalities directly under the Central Government agreed to the socialist market economy.

In the autumn of 1992, the Fourteenth National Congress officially put forward the reform goal of establishing a socialist market economic system. Jiang Zemin pointed out in the Report of the Fourteenth National People's Congress that the goal of China's economic system reform was to establish a socialist market economic system in order to further liberate and develop productive forces. The socialist market economic system to be established in China was meant to make the market play a fundamental role in the allocation of resources under the macro-control of the socialist country, to make economic activities follow the requirements of the law of value and to adapt to the changes of supply and demand relations, to allocate resources to the sectors with better benefits through the functions of price leverage and competition mechanism, and to give pressure and motivation to enterprises. The advantages of market sensitivity to various economic signals were used to promote timely coordination of production and demand. At the same time, it was important to see that the market had its own weaknesses and negative aspects, and it was necessary to strengthen and improve the state's macro-economic regulation and management. The report also pointed out that the socialist market economic system was integrated with the basic socialist economic system. In the ownership structure, public ownership, including ownership by the whole people and collective ownership, was the main body, while individual, private, and foreign capital economy were the supplements. Various economic components developed together over a long period, which could voluntarily carry out various forms of joint operations. State-owned collective enterprises and other enterprises all entered the market, and the state-owned enterprises played the leading role through equal competition. In the distribution system, distribution according to work was the main body, and other distribution modes were supplementary, giving consideration to efficiency and fairness. In terms of macro-control, the Party aimed to combine the current interests of the people with long-term interests, and local control with overall interests, giving fuller play to the advantages of both planning and market means. In March 1993, the First Session of the Eighth National People's Congress amended the Constitution, replacing "the state implements a socialist planned economy" with "the state implements a socialist market economy." The socialist market economy was thus written into the Constitution.

The establishment of the goal of the socialist market economic system marked a new leap in the Party's understanding of the theory of scientific socialism and the practice of Reform and Opening Up. It had been fourteen years since the reform started with the idea of giving full play to the auxiliary role of market regulation and the establishment of the socialist market economic system at the Fourteenth National Congress of the Communist Party of China. The final establishment of this goal was an important achievement of the Party's arduous exploration in the practice of reform, opening up, and modernization, as well as an inevitable result of the in-depth development of the cause of socialism with Chinese characteristics. This new decision made the direction of China's economic system reform and socialist modernization clearer.

According to the decisions of the Fourteenth National Congress, while speeding up the implementation of various reforms, the Central Committee and the State Council had made an overall plan for the establishment of a socialist market economic system. In November 1993, the Third Plenary Session of the Fourteenth Central Committee of the CPC adopted the Decision of the CPC Central Committee on Several Issues Concerning the Establishment of a Socialist Market Economy System (hereinafter referred to as the Decision), and put forward a relatively complete idea and plan for how to establish a socialist market economic system. The Decision pointed out that the establishment of a socialist market economic system was meant to make the market play a fundamental role in the allocation of resources under the macro-control of the state, to liberate and develop the productive forces to the maximum extent, to enhance the comprehensive national strength of the country, to improve people's living standards more rapidly, and to give full play to the superiority of the socialist system.

To achieve this goal, the Decision set forth five main parts in the establishment of a socialist market economic system. First, it was important to adhere to the principle of public ownership as the main body and common development of various economic components, further transform the operating mechanism of state-owned enterprises, establish a modern enterprise system that would meet the requirements of the market economy, and have clear property rights and responsibilities, with separation of government and enterprise, and with scientific management. Second, it was important to establish a unified, open market system throughout the country, to achieve close integration of urban and rural markets, to link up domestic with international markets, and to promote the optimal allocation of resources. Third, it was necessary to change the functions of the government in managing the economy and establish a sound macro-control system with indirect means as the main approach to ensure the healthy operation of the national economy. Fourth, it was important to establish an income distribution system with distribution according to work as the main body, giving priority to efficiency and giving consideration to fairness, and encouraging some people in some areas to get rich first and take the path of common prosperity. Fifth, it was necessary to establish a multi-level social security system to provide urban and rural residents with social security suited to China's national conditions and promote economic development and social stability. These five items were the basic components in the initial construction of the socialist market economic system. They were an interrelated, interdependent, organic whole. There were fifty articles in the Decision, forming the overall framework of comprehensive reform with the reform of the socialist market economic system as the core.

At the closing meeting of the plenary session, Jiang Zemin pointed out that the Decision was based on Deng Xiaoping's theory of building socialism with Chinese characteristics and the spirit of the Fourteenth National Congress. It embodied the objectives and basic principles of the proposed economic system reform and further developed it in some aspects. It was the Party's action program for economic system reform in the 1990s. The Decision had initially solved the problems of how to combine the basic socialist system with the market economic system and how to transform the old system into a new one. It would vigorously promote the reform of the socialist market economic system and become a guideline for the planned and systematic establishment of a new socialist market economic system. It would also help lay a solid foundation in the economic system to enable China to catch up with the economic level of developed countries by the middle of the 21st century.

II

The Overall Development of Reform of the Socialist Market Economy System

With the establishment of the objectives of the reform of the socialist market economic system at the Fourteenth National Congress of the CPC and the Third Plenary Session of the Fourteenth Central Committee, China's Reform and Opening Up had reached a new stage of transformation from the planned economy to the market economy overall. After the Third Plenary Session of the Fourteenth Central Committee, the Central Leading Group, with Jiang Zemin as its core, continued to explore ways to deepen reform around the above-mentioned basic components of the socialist market economic system, putting forward some important ideas and policies while actively, steadily, and comprehensively promoting the reform of the market economic system. The most important aspects were:

1) *Actively promoting the reform of state-owned enterprises and establishing a modern enterprise system.* State-owned enterprises were the main body of China's national economy. The reform of state-owned enterprises was the central link of economic system reform. The modern enterprise system with public ownership as the main body was the foundation of the socialist market economy.

The Third Plenary Session of the Fourteenth Central Committee had determined that the direction of state-owned enterprise reform was to establish a modern enterprise system. This was an inevitable requirement for the development of large-scale socialized production and the socialist market economy and an effective form of realizing the combination of public ownership and the market economy. It indicated that the reform of China's economic system had entered a stage of institutional innovation with the realization of public ownership at its core, from the past policy adjustment with the content of decentralization and transfer of power, interest to tax, separation of powers, and so on. This was a tremendous change in thinking on reform, and also an important manifestation of the deep-seated reform. To this end, the Central Government made a decision to concentrate its efforts on large and medium-sized enterprises, while also liberalizing and invigorating small and medium-sized state-owned enterprises and promoting the optimization and reorganization of state-owned assets by intensifying the efforts of enterprise alliance, reorganization, mergers, and bankruptcy. Since 1994, the State Council had successively determined that 1) 100 large and medium-sized state-owned enterprises should carry out pilot projects to establish a modern enterprise system, and pilot projects to optimize capital structure and asset restructuring in 18 cities, 2) efforts would be concentrated on 1,000 key state-owned backbone enterprises related to the national economy and people's livelihood, and 3) cross-regional and cross-industry conglomerates would be developed, integrating industry, technology and trade, starting with 56 enterprise groups. The reform of the corporate system and shareholding system was carried out extensively in pilot enterprises. Through the transformation of the operation mechanism, the adjustment of industrial structure, and the reorganization of assets, much experience was accumulated in the establishment of the modern enterprise system in large and medium-sized state-owned enterprises. Small state-owned enterprises adopted diversified management and organizational forms that were open and vibrant. By the end of 1993, nearly 4,000 enterprises had carried out joint share holding pilot projects in accordance with the requirements of standardization. The laws and regulations concerning the joint share holding system were also gradually established. The share holding system was an effective way to change the operation mechanism of enterprises and establish a modern enterprise system.

2) *Cultivate and develop the market system and vigorously promote the reform of the financial and price systems.* The key to the establishment of the socialist market economic system was to give full play to the basic role of the market mechanism in the allocation of resources, which required the cultivation and development of the market system. While continuing to develop the commodity market, it was important to vigorously develop the production market, actively cultivate the financial market including bonds, stocks, and other securities, develop the technology, labor, information, and real estate markets, and form a unified and open market system as soon as possible. A major breakthrough in the Decision of the Central Committee of the Communist Party of China on Several Issues Concerning the Establishment of a Socialist Market Economy System (hereinafter referred to as the Decision) adopted at the Third Plenary Session of the Fourteenth Central Committee was the first time that the "labor market" had been put forward. According to Marx's *Das Kapital*, only under the capitalist system could labor become a commodity. The practice of Reform and Opening

Up demonstrated that in the primary stage of socialism, due to the existence of multiple ownership economies, the labor force still had commodity attributes and would create surplus value. For instance, a large number of migrant workers pouring into urban employment created a huge labor market. Recognizing the objective reality of the labor market could not only protect the legitimate rights and interests of workers through labor law, but also promote the optimal allocation of labor resources. In the Decision, it was a great emancipation of the mind to change the "labor-export market," which had been commonly used before, into the "labor market." The financial market played a central role in developing the market economy.

Shortly after Deng Xiaoping adopted the Decision on Economic System Reform at the Third Plenary Session of the Twelfth Central Committee, he pointed out that China's banks had previously functioned as money issuing companies or treasuries, not real banks. He noted, "The pace of financial reform should be greater. We need to make banks real banks."[13] In the early 1990s, when it came to the development of Pudong in Shanghai, he pointed out, "Finance is very important and the core of a modern economy. If finance is done well, the whole chess game will be enlivened with one dynamic move. Shanghai was formerly a financial center and a place where currencies could be freely converted. It should remain the same in the future."[14] In November 1990 and July 1992, with the authorization of the State Council and the approval of the People's Bank of China, the Shanghai and Shenzhen Stock Exchanges were established, realizing the centralized trading of stocks and forming the national stock exchange market, which also became an important symbol of the formation of China's capital market and the reform of the financial system. Since 1994, China gradually established a central bank macro-control system under the leadership of the State Council, which independently implemented a monetary policy. In the initial stage, the basic program was to separate policy-based finances from commercial finance, to establish a financial organization system with state-owned commercial banks as the main body and coexistence of various financial institutions, and to unify open, orderly competition and strict management of financial markets. From that time, a single floating exchange rate system with management based on market supply and demand was established, linking the RMB price with the market price of foreign exchange adjustments and the free convertibility of foreign exchange under the current account. It played an important role in further communicating domestic and foreign markets, improving the external economic environment, further attracting foreign investment, and developing an open economy.

The reform of the price management system was not only one of the earliest reforms initiated by the reform of the economic system, but also one of the reforms that constantly increased the intensity of adjustment. With the successive harvest of agriculture and the increasing supply of agricultural products, by 1993, the price and operation of the vast majority of agricultural products, including grain, had been liberalized. The original ration of grain had been transformed into market supply, and the ration coupons and principal of urban residents had been abolished. Most of the prices of means of production were merged into a single market price by a "two-track" system. The proportion of the market price in total retail sales of social commodities rose from 50.3% before 1991 to 93.8% in 1993, establishing the dominant position of market price in the price system. In the meantime, the system of price regulation and control with economic, legal, and necessary administrative means was established. This marked the smooth passage of price reform, which was considered the area most prone to social shocks. This was another major achievement of Reform and Opening Up.

3) *Establish and improve the macro-control system and actively promote reform of the fiscal and taxation system and the investment system.* The socialist market economic system established in China was meant to better combine planning with market forces. The main task of macro-control was to maintain the basic balance of total economic output, promote the optimization of economic structure, guide the sustained, rapid, and healthy development of the national economy, and promote the overall progress of society. The main economic measures adopted were to establish a mechanism of coordination and restriction among planning, finance, and financial management, and to strengthen the comprehensive coordination of economic operations.

Actively promoting the reform of the fiscal and taxation system was a key point in establishing and improving the macro-control system after the Third Plenary Session of the Twelfth Central Committee of the Communist Party of China. In December 1993, the State Council decided to implement a tax-sharing system, which divided various incomes into fixed central revenue, fixed local revenue, and shared central and local revenue. Accordingly, the tax collection and management system needed to be adjusted to establish a standardized distribution relationship between the central and local governments, so as to systematically guarantee the unity of financial and administrative powers of governments at all levels and gradually increase fiscal revenue to account for the gross national product. The proportion of value should be increased appropriately to enhance the ability of central macro-control. At the same time, on the basis of a unified tax law, a fair tax burden, a simplified tax system, and a reasonable decentralization principle, it was important to focus on the implementation of the turnover tax system with VAT as the main body, change product tax into consumption tax, levy business taxes in the service industry, and adopt the method of excess progressive tax on the individual income tax in order to gradually form a fair competition environment. After 1997, the tax policy of the financial and insurance industry was further adjusted, and China's tax system was gradually brought in line with international rules.

Another important measure to strengthen the macro-control system was to actively promote the reform of the investment and financing system. This was mainly to further strengthen the dominant position of enterprises in investment and financing, and to introduce more market competition mechanisms in the field of investment and financing. To try out the capital system for various operational fixed assets investment projects, investment projects needed to implement capital before they could be constructed. Various financing modes had been introduced into infrastructure, basic industries, and public utilities, and funds from all walks of life had been widely absorbed to promote investment and financing to maximize economic and social benefits.

4) *Deepening the reform of the foreign trade system and establishing an operating mechanism to adapt to the current rules of the international economy.* To establish a socialist market economic system, it was necessary to make full use of both international and domestic markets and resources. This required standardizing foreign economic activities and deepening the reform of the foreign trade system. Three measures were taken at that time. One was to cancel the directive plan for foreign trade imports and change it into a domestic plan. For domestic production construction and commodities required by the market, enterprises needed to organize imports on their own according to market demand, reduce the quantity of quota commodities under management, and standardize the measures for the management of import quota commodities. The second was to give qualified enterprises the right to import and export business, change the lagging state of foreign trade enterprises' business mechanism transformation, improve their adaptability to the increasingly fierce international market competition,

and cultivate and strengthen a number of large foreign trade enterprises with international competitiveness. Third, it was important to improve foreign trade laws and regulations in line with international practices, speed up the integration of the foreign trade system with international practices, and at the same time reduce the overall level of tariffs. Since April 1, 1996, the total level of import duties on more than 4,000 commodities had dropped to 23%, and to about 17% by October 1, 1997. These measures not only helped more competitive foreign goods enter the Chinese market, but also promoted China's economic development and sped up China's entry into the World Trade Organization. The transition from the planned economy to the socialist market economy was typical of "crossing the river by feeling the stones." It was beyond reproach. Without experience, the Party could only open up its path in this way. This was the practical epistemology of Marxism. Through the above and other reforms, this difficult transition was basically realized. The degree of marketization and socialization of the national economy was markedly improved, and economic vitality was significantly enhanced. All these created favorable conditions for the continuous improvement and perfection of the socialist market economic system.

III

The Important Juncture of Historical Development and the Great Banner of Deng Xiaoping Theory

On February 19, 1997, after Deng Xiaoping's death, whether the Communist Party of China could continue to hold high the great banner of Deng Xiaoping's theory and whether China's Reform and Opening Up and modernization construction could continue to advance along the path of socialism with Chinese characteristics initiated by Deng Xiaoping had become a major concern of the whole Party, the people, and the world. The Central Committee, under Jiang Zemin's leadership, gave a clear answer to this key issue concerning the overall situation of China's development. It stated that it would inherit Deng Xiaoping's legacy, uphold the great banner of Deng Xiaoping's theory, and unswervingly follow Deng Xiaoping's path of building socialism with Chinese characteristics.

The Central Committee's Letter to the Party, the Army, and the People of

All Ethnic Groups and Jiang Zemin's mourning speech at the Deng Xiaoping Memorial Conference highly appraised Deng's outstanding revolutionary career of the previous seventy years and his enduring merits for the independence and liberation of the Chinese nation and the cause of socialist modernization in China. The eulogy emphasized that Deng Xiaoping's most precious gift to the Chinese nation was his theory of building socialism with Chinese characteristics and the basic line of the Party in the primary stage of socialism formulated under the guidance of this theory. This was a guide to action that must be followed. On the journey across the new century, raising the great banner of Deng Xiaoping's theory of building socialism with Chinese characteristics and better implementing the Party's basic line were the unswerving determination and belief of the leading collective of the Central Committee and the consensus and aspiration of the entire Party, army, and Chinese people of all ethnicities.

On May 29, Jiang Zemin delivered a speech at the graduation ceremony of the provincial and ministerial advanced courses in the Central Party School, stressing once again the need to hold high the banner of Deng Xiaoping Theory. He said that in the new era of socialist reform, opening up, and modernization, and on the journey across the new century, it was important to hold high the great banner of Deng Xiaoping's theory of building socialism with Chinese characteristics and use this theory to guide the Party's entire cause and work, which was the unshakable conclusion drawn by the Party from history and reality. The issue of flags was of paramount importance. The flag was the direction, and the flag was the image. The Party should have a high degree of consciousness and determination on this issue. No matter what difficulties or risks it encountered, it should not waver.

In September 1997, when the Fifteenth National Congress was held, Jiang Zemin wrote a report entitled "Raising the Great Banner of Deng Xiaoping Theory and Pushing the Cause of Comprehensive Building of Socialism with Chinese Characteristics into the 21st Century." Standing at the height of the times, the report reviewed the great changes of the Chinese nation over the previous hundred years, pointing out that China had undergone three tremendous historic changes since the 20th century, resulting in three great men being at the forefront of the times: Sun Yat-sen, who led the 1911 Revolution and overthrew the autocratic system that had ruled China for thousands of years; Mao Zedong, who led the new democratic revolution to victory and founded New China and the socialist system; and Deng Xiaoping, who led the Reform and Opening Up of the new great revolution and the socialist drive toward modernization. The third great historic change had successfully opened up a new path for building socialism with Chinese characteristics, realizing national rejuvenation, national prosperity, and the people's wellbeing. Socialism had shown its vigor and vitality in China and attracted worldwide attention. Deng Xiaoping's great contribution to China and the world had won the heartfelt respect and love of the Chinese people and the people of the world.

The report of the Fifteenth National Congress of the Communist Party of China further expounded the historical position of Deng Xiaoping's theory of building socialism with Chinese characteristics, and for the first time used the term "Deng Xiaoping Theory." Jiang Zemin pointed out that the Communist Party of China attached great importance to theoretical guidance. Guided by Marxism-Leninism, the Communist Party of China integrated it with China's actual situation, attaining two historic leaps with two theoretical achievements. Mao Zedong was the main founder of the theoretical achievements of the first leap. The Party called this Mao Zedong Thought, noting, "The main founder of the theoretical achievements of the second leap is the theory of building socialism with Chinese characteristics. Its main founder is Deng Xiaoping. The Party calls it Deng Xiaoping Theory." In evaluating the historical status of Deng Xiaoping's theory, the report of the Fifteenth National Congress of the Communist Party of China pointed out that Deng's theory was the correct theory to guide the Chinese people to achieve socialist modernization in the process of Reform and Opening Up. In contemporary China, only Deng Xiaoping's theory, which combined Marxism with contemporary Chinese practice and the characteristics of the times, could solve the problem of the future and destiny of socialism. Deng Xiaoping Theory was the Marxism of contemporary China and a new stage of development for Chinese Marxism.[15]

The report points out that the reason Deng Xiaoping Theory could initiate a new stage of Marxist development in China was primarily that Deng Xiaoping Theory adhered to emancipating the mind and seeking truth from facts, inherited predecessors on the basis of new practice, and broke through the stereotypes and opened up a new realm of Marxism. In addition, Deng Xiaoping Theory adhered to the basic achievements of scientific socialism theory and practice, grasped the fundamental issue of "what is socialism and how to build it," profoundly revealed the essence of socialism, and raised the understanding of socialism to a new scientific level. Further, Deng Xiaoping's theory stuck to observing the world from the broad perspective of Marxism, making a correct analysis and a new scientific judgment on the characteristics of the present era and the overall international situation, the success or failure of other socialist countries in the world, the gains and losses of developing countries in their pursuit of development, and the development situation and contradictions of developed countries. Finally, Deng Xiaoping Theory was a branch of the theory of building socialism with Chinese characteristics gradually formed and developed under the historical condition in which peace and development had become the theme of the times, in the practice of China's reform, opening up, and modernization, on the basis of summing up the historical experience of the successes and frustrations of China's socialist construction and drawing lessons from the historical experience of the rise and fall of other socialist countries. For the first time, this theory had systematically and preliminarily answered a series of basic questions about the development path, stage, fundamental task, driving force, external conditions, political guarantee, strategic steps, Party leadership and reliance, and the reunification of the motherland of China, and guided the CPC to formulate a basic line in the first stage of socialism. It ran through the fields of philosophy, political economy, and scientific socialism, and covered a relatively complete scientific system in the fields of economy, politics, science and technology, education, culture, nation-building, military affairs, diplomacy, the united front, and Party building. Therefore, Jiang Zemin said that the soul of the conference was to hold high the great banner of Deng Xiaoping Theory, noting, "In contemporary China, Marxism-Leninism, Mao Zedong Thought, and Deng Xiaoping Theory are the unified scientific systems that come down in one continuous line. To adhere to Deng Xiaoping Theory is to truly adhere to Marxism-Leninism and Mao Zedong Thought, and to hold high the banner of Deng Xiaoping Theory is to truly hold high the banner of Marxism-Leninism and Mao Zedong Thought."[16] The amendment to the Party Constitution adopted by the General Assembly further established Deng Xiaoping Theory as the guiding ideology of the Party and clearly stipulated that the Communist Party of China took Marxism-Leninism, Mao Zedong Thought, and Deng Xiaoping Theory as its own guideline for action.

The Congress also gave a new explanation and generalization of the theory of the primary stage of socialism, which was regarded as the foundation of Deng Xiaoping's theory, thus enriching and developing the theory first expounded at the Thirteenth National Congress of the Communist Party of China.

For the first time, this explanation clearly pointed out that China's greatest reality was that it would remain at the primary stage of socialism for a long period. As the comprehensive reform entered the critical stage, many contradictions and difficulties arose, and some new doubts needed to be clarified. This was to further understand China's national conditions and firmly believe in the Party's basic line and policies at this stage. Only when China had a correct understanding of the basic national conditions could it firmly understand why it must carry out the current line and policy instead of other ones. The report clearly pointed out, "We say that every move should be based on reality. The biggest reality is that China is now and will remain at the primary stage of socialism for a long time. We note that if we are to make clear what socialism is and how it may be built, we must make clear what socialism is at the primary stage and how to build socialism at the primary stage." That is why the Fifteenth National Congress emphasized the primary stage of socialism and reinterpreted this theory.

At the new height of exploring "what socialism is and how to build it," the connotation and characteristics of the primary stage of socialism were defined. "What socialism is and how to build it" was a fundamental issue that Deng Xiaoping had constantly talked about in summing up China's historical experience. After the publication of Volume 3 of *Selected Works of Deng Xiaoping* in November 1993, the entire Party began to study and discuss this fundamental issue, which raised the awareness of socialism to a new level. The Fifteenth National Congress of the Communist Party of China stressed an important feature of the primary stage of socialism, that is, to stand at this high level and analyze problems, and to have a richer understanding of them. This paper analyzed the connotation and characteristics of the primary stage of socialism, stressed that it was a continuous development process from one state to another, and highlighted the dynamic nature of its basic characteristics. The Thirteenth National Congress made five points about the basic characteristics of the primary stage. According to new experience, the Fifteenth National Congress re-examined it and expanded it into nine parts, including the general characteristics, the development characteristics of material civilization, the development characteristics of spiritual civilization, and the development characteristics of political civilization. The Fifteenth National Congress summarized the basic characteristics of the primary stage of socialism. 1) It was the historical stage of gradual breaking away from underdevelopment and basically realizing socialist modernization. 2) It was the historical stage of an agricultural country largely made up of an agricultural population and mainly relying on manual labor, which gradually transformed into an industrialized country with a majority of non-agricultural population and modern agriculture and modern service industries. 3) It was largely a semi-natural economy and had gradually transformed into a historical stage with a high degree of market-oriented economy, a historical stage in which illiterate and semi-illiterate people accounted for a large proportion, science and technology education and culture lagged behind, and science and technology education and culture were relatively developed. While poor people accounted for a large proportion, and their living standards were relatively low, some people were relatively wealthy, and the economy and culture of the region were very rich. Unbalanced development was the historical stage in which the gap was gradually narrowed through successive development. Through reform and exploration, a more mature and dynamic socialist market economy system, socialist democratic political system, and other aspects of the system were established and perfected. It was the historical stage in which the broad masses of the people firmly established the common ideal of building socialism with Chinese characteristics and constantly strove for self-improvement. Enterprising, arduous struggle, and industrious and thrifty nation-building in conjunction with building the material civilization and striving to build spiritual civilization, were characteristics of the historical stage of gradually narrowing the gap with the world's most advanced level and realizing the great rejuvenation of the Chinese nation on the basis of socialism.[17]

According to the spirit of Deng Xiaoping's Southern Talk, it would take at least 100 years to further affirm the primary stage of socialism. The contradiction between the increasing material and cultural needs of the people as the main social contradiction and the backward social productive forces would "run through the whole process of the primary stage of socialism and all aspects of social life in our country," and only by firmly grasping this major contradiction could China clearly observe and grasp the overall situation of social contradictions and effectively promote the resolution of various social contradictions, thus providing a more solid foundation for "development as the absolute principle, with the key to solving all problems in China being to rely on its own development."[18]

For the first time, the relationship of "reform, development, and stability" put forward after the Fourteenth National Congress of the Communist Party was brought into the historical framework of the primary stage of socialism and emphasized. Not only were the strategic position of the three relations in the overall situation of socialist modernization construction more clearly handled, but it was further determined that it was a long-term basic policy applicable to the whole primary stage of socialism. This not only enhanced the understanding of the status of the relationship among reform, development, and stability, but also enriched the basic issues that should be grasped in the primary stage of socialism.

The reinterpretation of the theory of the primary stage of socialism at the Fifteenth National Congress of the CPC not only made Deng Xiaoping's basic theory more epochal, but also made it the theoretical basis for the third generation of leading collectives to put forward the basic program of the primary stage of socialism.

IV

Formation of the Basic Program for the Primary Stage of Socialism

According to Deng Xiaoping's theory and the Party's basic line, the Fifteenth National Congress of the Communist Party of China put forward the Party's basic program in the primary stage of socialism for the first time, focusing on the goal of building a prosperous, democratic, civilized socialist modern country. If it was a great theoretical contribution to the Thirteenth National Congress to clearly summarize the Party's basic line after the first exposition of the theory of the primary stage of socialism, then it was a great theoretical contribution to the Fifteenth National Congress to clearly put forward the Party's basic program in this period when reinterpreting the issue of the primary stage of socialism at a new height.

The Party's understanding of the basic program of the primary stage of socialism had also undergone a process of exploration. As early as 1979, Ye Jianying, on behalf of the Central Committee of the CPC, put forward the program of comprehensively realizing modernization in his speech commemorating the 30th anniversary of the founding of New China. This was what Deng Xiaoping reiterated in his subsequent speech, saying, "Our country has entered a new period of socialist modernization construction." It should reform and improve the socialist economic and political system and develop a high degree of socialist democracy and a complete socialist legal system, while greatly improving the social productive forces. While building a high level of material civilization, we should improve the scientific and cultural level of the whole nation, develop a noble and colorful cultural life, and build a high level of socialist spiritual civilization."[19] After that, Deng Xiaoping repeatedly emphasized that there were many tasks involved in building socialism with Chinese characteristics. It was important to adhere to the comprehensive development and progress of socialist society on the premise of economic construction, and not to ignore one thing or the other. For this reason, he put forward a series of strategic ideas and policies of "grasping with both hands," requiring that in the whole process of Reform and Opening Up and the construction of modernization, the Party should grasp Reform and Opening Up while also cracking down on crime. It was also important to conduct economic construction and build democracy and the legal system at the same time and to focus on building the material and spiritual civilizations at the same time. He emphasized the need to adhere to "grasping with both hands, and both hands must be firm." Therefore, Deng Xiaoping's theory was the theory of comprehensive economic, political, and cultural construction and the all-round development of socialism with Chinese characteristics.

At the Fourth Plenary Session of the Thirteenth Central Committee, Jiang Zemin pointed out that when it came to the line and a series of basic policies after the Third Plenary Session of the Eleventh Central Committee, the Party should first be firm and unswerving. Further, it should implement them consistently and comprehensively. In December 1990, the Seventh Plenary Session of the Thirteenth Central Committee of the Communist Party of China adopted the Recommendations of the Central Committee of the Communist Party of China on Formulating the Ten-Year Plan for National Economic and Social Development and the Eighth Five-Year Plan. Several principles for building socialism with Chinese characteristics were related to economic, political, and cultural aspects. On July 1, 1991, in his speech at the Congress celebrating the 70th anniversary of the founding of the Party, Jiang Zemin systematically summarized the basic content of the economy, politics, and culture of socialism with Chinese characteristics in accordance with Mao Zedong's ideas on the new democracy. He noted that:

1) To build a socialist economy with Chinese characteristics, it was necessary to adhere to the socialist public ownership of the means of production as the main body, while permitting and encouraging the appropriate development of other economic components. The Party must not deviate from the development level of productive forces to establish a single public ownership, nor shake the dominant position of the public ownership economy, nor engage in privatization. Rather, it must take distribution according to work as the main body and other modes of distribution as the supplement. The supplementary distribution system should not only overcome equalitarianism, but also prevent polarization and gradually realize the common prosperity of all the people. It was necessary to establish an economic system and operation mechanism that adapted to the development of the socialist planned commodity economy and combined the planned economy with market regulation, and played an active role in market regulation under the guidance of national laws, regulations, and plans, so as to overcome the disadvantages of over-centralization and over-management without overly decentralizing or weakening macro-control.[20]

2) To build socialism with Chinese characteristics, it was important to adhere to the people's democratic dictatorship led by the working class and based on the alliance of workers and peasants, not weaken or abandon the people's democratic dictatorship. It was important to adhere to and improve the people's congress system, not the parliamentary system of the West. It was also necessary to adhere to and improve the multi-party cooperation and political consultation system led by the CPC, and not to abandon it. The Party should not weaken and negate its leadership, nor should it carry out the multi-party system of the West.[21]

3) To build a socialist culture with Chinese characteristics, it was necessary to be guided by Marxism-Leninism and Mao Zedong Thought, and not to diversify the Party's guiding ideology. The Party must adhere to the principle of serving the people and socialism and of letting a hundred flowers bloom and a hundred schools of thought contend, prosper, and develop socialist culture, not allowing things to spread that would poison people's mind nor impair or go against socialism. It was important to inherit and carry forward the excellent national cultural traditions and fully embody the spirit of the socialist era, base the Party on its country and fully absorb the excellent achievements of world culture, not allowing national nihilism or overall Westernization.[22] Jiang Zemin emphasized that "the economy, politics, and culture of socialism with Chinese characteristics

are an organic unity and an inseparable whole," and the Party should firmly grasp these basic requirements of the economy, politics, and culture of socialism with Chinese characteristics.[23]

After Deng Xiaoping's Southern Talk in 1992 and the Fourteenth National Congress of the Communist Party of China, new and significant achievements had been made in the economic, political, and cultural construction of China, and the contents of the economic, political, and cultural construction of socialism with Chinese characteristics were more abundant. On this basis, based on Deng Xiaoping's theory of building socialism with Chinese characteristics summarized in the Fourteenth National Congress, the Fifteenth National Congress further summarized the experience in economic, political, and cultural aspects of building socialism with Chinese characteristics, defining the economy, politics, and culture of socialism with Chinese characteristics at the primary stage of socialism, and determining how to build such an economic and political system. Governance and culture had made more incisive expositions and formally put forward the Party's basic program in the primary stage of socialism. This basic program, centering on the Party's basic line and the goal of socialist modernization, put forward the requirements and tasks in the areas of the economy, politics, and culture.

1) *"Building a socialist economy with Chinese characteristics" meant developing a market economy under socialist conditions and continuously liberating and developing productive forces.* This required adhering to and improving the basic economic system in which socialist public ownership was the main body and the multi-ownership economy developed together, adhering to and perfecting the socialist market economic system so that the market played a fundamental role in the allocation of resources under the macro-control of the state, adhering to and perfecting the various distribution modes with distribution according to work as the main body, while allowing some regions and some people to get rich first and driving them to do so. The Party should help the latter become wealthy and gradually move toward common prosperity, adhere to and improve opening up, actively participate in international economic cooperation and competition, ensure the sustained, rapid and healthy development of the national economy, and share the fruits of economic prosperity. "Developing the market economy and continuously emancipating and developing productive forces under socialist conditions" was a new addition to Deng Xiaoping's Southern Talk, which was regarded as the basic feature of building a socialist economy with Chinese characteristics, highlighting

a new understanding of the essential requirements of socialism and a new way to realize them, and was helpful to grasping the essence of constructing the socialist economy with Chinese characteristics. As for how to build such an economy, the four areas of the basic economic system, the market economic system, various distribution modes, and opening up in the primary stage of socialism discussed in the report were also clearer and more comprehensive. In fact, what the report said about the strategy of economic system reform and development was the concrete development of building a socialist economy with Chinese characteristics. It broke through long-standing, traditional ideas on a series of issues and further embodied the requirements of developing the economy during the primary stage of socialism.

2) *"Building the politics of socialism with Chinese characteristics" meant ruling the country according to law and developing socialist democratic politics under the leadership of the Communist Party of China and on the basis of the people being the shapers of the country.* This required upholding and improving the people's democratic dictatorship led by the working class and based on the alliance of workers and peasants, upholding and improving the system of the people's congress and the multi-party cooperation, political consultation, and regional national autonomy led by the Communist Party, developing democracy, improving the legal system, and building a socialist country ruled by law. It aimed to achieve social stability, clean and efficient government, unity and harmony among the people of all ethnic groups, and a lively political situation. Compared with the speech in July 1991, the general requirement of "administering the country according to law and developing socialist democratic politics" was highlighted here. Among the basic political systems listed, the system of regional ethnic autonomy had been added, which was very necessary and in line with the characteristics of China's multi-ethnic population in terms of political system. Since then, the Party's literature said that the basic political system of China at the present stage included this article. The requirements of "building a socialist country ruled by law" and "honest and efficient government" were also added here, which not only reflected the wishes of the masses, but also expressed the Party's efforts to achieve the goal of democratic politics. Taking these two points as the content of building socialist politics with Chinese characteristics reflected the great progress of the Party's democratic and legal thought.

3) *"Building a culture of socialism with Chinese characteristics" meant developing*

a modern, world-oriented, future-oriented, national, scientific, and popular socialist culture under the guidance of Marxism, aiming at cultivating citizens with ideals, morality, culture, and discipline. This required the Party to persist in arming all its members and educating the people with Deng Xiaoping Theory, striving to improve the ideological and moral quality of the whole nation and the level of education, science, and culture, adhering to the direction of serving the people and socialism, and the policy of letting different schools of thought flourish while focusing on construction and prospering academia and art. It was important to build a socialist spiritual civilization based on China's actual situation, inherit the excellent traditions of history and culture, and absorb the beneficial achievements of foreign cultures. The content here was based on the speech in July 1991 and absorbed the new achievements of the Sixth Plenary Session of the Fourteenth Central Committee of the Communist Party of China in October 1996, the Resolution on Several Important Issues in Strengthening the Construction of Socialist Spiritual Civilization, so as to raise awareness. In order to define concisely and completely the culture of socialism with Chinese characteristics, the above-mentioned phrase, "guided by Marxism, aiming at cultivating citizens with ideals, morality, culture, and discipline, and developing a modern, world-oriented, future-oriented, national, and scientific mass socialist culture" integrated Deng Xiaoping's thought and covered many aspects of it. The requirements of these aspects highlighted the characteristics of keeping pace with the times. In order to achieve this goal, the points mentioned at the level of "how to construct it" included the requirements of building a socialist culture with Chinese characteristics for the construction of a spiritual civilization.

The above basic goals and policies for building socialism with Chinese characteristics constituted the basic program of the Party in the primary stage of socialism. Jiang Zemin pointed out in the report of the Fifteenth National Congress of the Communist Party of China that "this program is an important part of Deng Xiaoping's theory, an expansion of the Party's basic line in economic, political, and cultural areas, and a scientific summary of the most important experience in recent years."[24] The proposal of this basic program had important guiding significance for the unification of the Party's ideology and the struggle of the people of all ethnicities for the cause of building socialism with Chinese characteristics.

CHAPTER 8

The Development of Socialist Democracy with Chinese Characteristics and the Socialist Spiritual Civilization

I

Active Promotion of the Construction of Socialist Democratic Politics

Democratic political construction was an important part of building socialism with Chinese characteristics. After entering the new stage of Reform and Opening Up, the Central Committee, led by Jiang Zemin, took more practical measures to promote the reform of the political system and build socialist democratic politics with Chinese characteristics, in accordance with the deep understanding of China's national conditions and the need for changes in the situation. These measures achieved fruitful results in many areas, including system construction.

1. **Proposal of the Policy of "Actively and Steadily Promoting the Reform of the Political System"**

Deng Xiaoping was the chief architect of reform, opening up, and modernization, as well as of political system reform. His many speeches clearly defined the fundamental objectives and overall framework of China's political system reform. After the Fourth Plenary Session of the Thirteenth Central Committee of the CPC, the Central Committee, under Jiang's leadership, consistently adhered to Deng Xiaoping's theory on political system reform and further put forward the policy of "actively and steadily promoting political system reform." In July 1995, Jiang Zemin pointed out, "While carrying out economic system reform, we should actively and steadily promote political system reform and strive to build a socialist democracy with Chinese characteristics."[1] In his speech to commemorate the 20th anniversary of the Third Plenary Session of the Eleventh Central Committee in December 1998, he went on to point out, "To actively and steadily promote the reform of the political system is the inherent requirement for the self-improvement and development of the socialist political system in China, and is also an important decision made by our Party in summing up our historical and practical experience."[2] This decision-making was a basic guideline with long-term guiding significance in the development of China's political system reform.

The policy of "actively and steadily promoting the reform of the political system" had two meanings. First, the reform of the political system continued without being interrupted by political disturbances, contrary to what some people overseas reported. As stated in the report of the Fourteenth National Congress, "We should actively promote the reform of the political system so as to achieve a greater development in socialist democracy and the construction of the legal system." Since that time, the Communist Party of China had made great efforts in strengthening China's basic political system, improving democratic centralism, improving the scientific and democratic mechanism of decision making, and strengthening grassroots democratic construction. Therefore, those propositions about the stagnation of China's political system reform were unfounded. Secondly, the basic principle of promoting the reform of the political system was to be "positive and stable." Being positive meant that the reform of the political system could not be stopped and had to be carried forward with a positive attitude. In particular, when economic system reform entered a critical stage and the socialist market economic system needed to be further improved, the political system reform had to be adapted. With the deepening of economic system reform, the defects of some specific leadership systems and working mechanisms would constitute institutional obstacles to economic and social development. Jiang Zemin pointed out in June 2000 that, in order to make the new socialist market economic system much better, a series of deep-seated problems needed to be addressed, including "the management system and operation mechanism of the government and the leadership system of the Party and the state, all of which needed to be further improved and perfected through deepening reform." In terms of system innovation, "it is necessary to constantly improve systems in all aspects adapted to the requirements of developing socialist market economy and of building socialism with Chinese characteristics in an all-round way."[3] Being "prudent" was vital because the reform of the political system was an extremely complex, systematic project, which was very difficult. According to Deng Xiaoping, until the mid-1980s, there was "no clear clue."[4] He said, "This problem is too difficult. Every reform involves a wide range of people and things. It touches on the interests of many people and encounters many obstacles. It needs to be carefully carried out... The country is big, the situation is complicated, and the reform is not easy, so the decision-making must be prudent."[5] Jiang Zemin pointed out in the report of the Fifteenth National Congress that "the construction of socialist democracy is a historical process of gradual development, which needs to proceed from our national conditions and advance step by step and in an orderly manner under the leadership of the Communist Party." Therefore, it would take time to reform the political system, and the Party could only adopt a "positive and stable" policy.[6]

According to Deng Xiaoping's overall goal of political system reform and the specific requirements of "sorting out a clue," it was necessary to further integrate and promote the idea of political system reform. Jiang Zemin pointed out in the report of the Fifteenth National Congress of the Communist Party of China, "At present and in the future, the main tasks of the political system reform are to develop democracy, strengthen the legal system, separate government from enterprises, streamline institutions, improve the democratic supervision system, and maintain stability and unity."[7] In April 2001, he put forward six principles to promote the reform of the political system. These were:

1) To reform the leadership system of the Party and the state is not to weaken the leadership of the Party, but to strengthen and improve it. It should be conducive to consolidating the socialist system and the leadership of the Party, and to developing social productive forces under the leadership of the Party and the socialist system.

2) The goal of the reform is to maintain the vitality of the Party and the state, overcome bureaucracy, improve work efficiency, expand grassroots democracy, and mobilize the enthusiasm of grassroots workers, farmers, and intellectuals.
3) The aim of strengthening and improving intra-Party democracy is to continuously promote the development of the people's democracy.
4) The success of the reform depends on the stability of the political situation of the country, the unity of the people of all ethnic groups, the improvement of their lives, and the sustainable development of their productive forces.
5) We must not lose the superiority of our socialist system or turn to the so-called democracy of the West. We must decide on the content and steps of the reform according to our own practice and situation.
6) The reform of the political system is very complicated. Every measure involves the interests of tens of millions of people. It should be carried out systematically under good leadership and in an orderly manner.[8]

These principles made the reform of the political system firmer and clearer, following a positive and stable direction.

2. Perfecting the System of Multi-party Cooperation and Political Consultation Under the Leadership of the Communist Party of China

The system of multi-party cooperation and political consultation led by the CPC was a basic political system in China and an important aspect of political system reform. In 1987, when the Thirteenth National Congress put forward the task of reforming the political system, it proposed to improve "the system of multi-party cooperation and political consultation under the leadership of the Communist Party."

After the Thirteenth National Congress of the Communist Party of China, some members of democratic parties and non-Party personages in Beijing put forward their views and opinions on the issue of "multi-party cooperation." At the beginning of January 1989, Deng Xiaoping read the instructions and said, "We can organize a special group (members of which should be from democratic parties) to formulate a plan for members of democratic parties to participate in politics and perform their supervisory duties, which will be completed within one year and implemented next year."⁹ According to Deng Xiaoping's instructions, the special group would be led by democratic parties and heads of relevant departments such as the Standing Committee of the National People's Congress, the State Council, the National Political Consultative Conference, the Central Organizational Department, the Central Propaganda Department, and the United Front Department. After more than a year of work, the draft work was completed. In February 1990, the *People's Daily* published the Opinions of the Central Committee of the Communist Party of China on Adhering to and Improving the System of Multi-Party Cooperation and Political Consultation under the leadership of the Communist Party (referred to as Opinions), which stipulated various issues.

1) *On the forms of political consultation.* The Opinion summarized the effective experience between the CPC and the democratic parties after the founding of New China. It held that the several forms of consultation should be adopted. First, based on the needs of the situation, the main leaders of the Central Committee should invite the main leaders of the democratic parties and representatives of non-Communist parties to hold high-level and small-scale open talks periodically so as to freely discuss issues, communicate ideas, and seek opinions on areas of common concern. Second, the Communist Party of China should hold seminars for democratic parties and non-Party personages to inform or exchange important information, convey important documents, and listen to policy suggestions or discuss certain topics put forward by democratic parties and non-Party personages. Third, in addition to consultation at the meeting, democratic parties and non-Party personages could make written policy recommendations to the Central Committee on major issues of state policies, principles, and modernization construction, or invite the leaders of the Central Committee to talk directly.

2) *On the role of democratic parties in the National People's Congress.* The Opinions stipulated that members of democratic parties and non-Party personages constituted an appropriate proportion among the deputies to the National People's Congress, members of the Standing Committee of the National People's Congress, and members of the Standing Special Committee of the National People's Congress, and that members of democratic parties and non-Party personages with corresponding expertise could be employed as advisors to the Special Committee. The people's congresses of provinces, autonomous regions, and municipalities directly under the Central Government would ensure

that members of democratic parties and non-Party people accounted for an appropriate proportion. In the municipal, state, and county people's congresses, the proportion of non-Party participants should be guaranteed. Cities, prefectures, and counties with democratic parties should ensure that members of democratic parties accounted for an appropriate proportion of the population.

3) *On members of democratic parties and non-Party personages holding leading positions in governments and judicial organs at all levels.* The Opinion held that practical measures should be taken to appoint members of democratic parties and non-Party personages to the leading posts of the State Council, its relevant ministries, local governments at or above the county level, and relevant departments. Members of qualified democratic parties and personages without party affiliation were to be elected to lead prosecutorial and judicial organs. A group of qualified and knowledgeable members of democratic parties and non-Party personages would be employed as special inspectors, prosecutors, auditors, and educational supervisors. The investigation of major cases organized by government departments such as supervision, auditing, industry and commerce, and tax inspections could involve members of democratic parties and non-Party people.

4) *On the role of democratic parties in the CPPCC.* The CPPCC was to become an important place for all parties, people's organizations, and representatives from all walks of life to unite, cooperate, and participate in politics and deliberation. The Opinion clearly stipulated that at various meetings of the CPPCC, members of the CPPCC would be guaranteed the freedom to criticize and to express differing opinions. It was crucial to ensure that democratic parties and non-Party personages accounted for a certain proportion of the standing committees of the CPPCC and the leading members of the CPPCC. The special committees of the CPPCC should have the participation of democratic parties and non-Party personages. A certain number of democratic parties and non-Party personages should serve as full-time leading cadres in the organs of the CPPCC and truly exercise their duties, powers, and responsibilities.

The purpose of this Opinion formulated by the Central Committee was to give further play to the role of democratic parties in politics, deliberation, and democratic supervision. According to this requirement, the Opinion clearly stipulated a series of issues concerning the participation of democratic parties in political affairs and deliberations. First, it clearly put forward the purpose of participating in political affairs. Second, it clearly pointed out the differences between multi-party cooperation and the political consultation system led by the Communist Party of China and the Western multi-party system. Third, it clearly defined the relationship between the CPC and other democratic parties. Fourth, it further clarified China's political consultation and the basic principles of cooperation between the CPC and democratic parties. Fifth, it pointed out the basic points for the participation of democratic parties in politics. Sixth, it stipulated the general principles for giving full play to the supervising role of the democratic parties. And seventh, it stipulated the guidelines for the activities of democratic parties.

This Opinion was a summary of the positive and negative experiences of multi-party cooperation and the political consultation system led by the CPC after a long period of revolution and construction. Practically speaking, it was a sign that the system of multi-party cooperation and political consultation led by the CPC was gradually becoming institutionalized and standardized. Theoretically, it enriched and developed the theory of Marxist party relations by summing up the practical experience of decades of long-term cooperation between the CPC and various democratic parties. The formulation and implementation of the Opinions was an important step in promoting the reform of the political system and strengthening the construction of socialist democratic politics. It was of great, far-reaching significance to allowing the advantages of the socialist system led by the CPC to work to their fullest and developing socialist democratic politics.

In December 2000, speaking at the National United Front Work Conference, Jiang Zemin pointed out, "The system of multi-party cooperation and political consultation led by the Communist Party is the crystallization of the political experience and wisdom of the Chinese people. The prominent features of our political system lie in the leadership of the Communist Party, multi-party cooperation, the rule of the Communist Party, and multi-party participation in politics. The democratic parties are not parties out of power or opposition parties, but friendly parties and participating parties that cooperate closely with the Communist Party. The Communist Party and the democratic parties conduct democratic consultation and scientific decision-making, and they concentrate their efforts on major national issues. The Communist Party and the democratic parties also concentrate on major affairs. They should supervise each other, promote the improvement of the leadership of the Communist Party, and strengthen the construction of political parties. This not only avoids the political turbulence caused by multi-party competition and mutual strife, but also avoids a variety of unhealthy practices caused by one-party autocracy and lack of supervision. The great advantage of our political party system lies in this, as well as in the fundamental difference from the foreign one-party system and multi-party system."[10] This speech was a profound summary of the political advantages of this basic political system, and it enriched the theory of democratic political construction in the localization of Marxism in China.

3. Developing Grassroots Autonomy and Expanding Grassroots Democracy

There was a remarkable change in the general idea of political system reform around the time of the Fourteenth National Congress. Before the Fourteenth National Congress, the Party mainly adopted a top-down approach. The Fourteenth National Congress focused on promoting the construction of a democratic political system at the grassroots level through the combination of bottom-up and top-down approaches, according to the idea of moving "from the easy to the difficult," positioning it as one of the socialist democratic systems that must be adhered to and perfected.

The main points of democratic political construction at the grassroots level were first, strengthening villagers' autonomy in rural areas and establishing and improving villagers' committees. Second, the Party promoted and improved the construction of residents' autonomy systems in urban communities. Third, the Party aimed to give full play to the role of workers' congresses in enterprises so as to institutionalize workers' participation in democratic management of those enterprises. With regard to rural villagers' autonomy, after the Constitution adopted in 1982 established the legal status of villagers' committees as grassroots mass autonomous organizations in rural areas, the Organic Law of the People's Republic of China on Villagers' Committees (for trial implementation), adopted by the Standing Committee of the Sixth National People's Congress in November 1987, clearly stipulated the nature, functions, and related issues of villagers' committees. In November 1994, the Central Committee issued a circular requiring all localities to conscientiously implement this law when strengthening the construction of grassroots Party organizations in rural areas, improve villagers' committees and groups, improve the system of villagers' autonomy, and better play the role of self-management, self-education, and self-service of grassroots mass autonomous organizations. With regard to the construction of urban community residents' autonomy systems, after the system of residents' committees was written into the Constitution of the People's Republic of China in 1982, the Standing Committee of the National People's Congress enacted the Organization Law of Urban Residents' Committees in 1989, which provided legal guarantees for the development of urban residents' committees. As the basic system of democratic political construction and democratic management at the grassroots level, the Workers' Congress increasingly emphasized its irreplaceable role in implementing democratic management, coordinating labor relations, safeguarding the legitimate rights and interests of workers, and promoting the reform, development, and stability of enterprises.

The Fifteenth National Congress fully affirmed the practice of expanding democracy at the grassroots level and guaranteeing the people's direct exercise of democratic rights as the most extensive practice of socialist democracy. At the same time, it further demanded that both urban and rural grassroots political power and grassroots mass self-governing organizations should improve the democratic electoral system, implement open government and finance, and allow the masses to participate in discussions and decisions on grassroots public affairs. In public service and public welfare undertakings, cadres were to be subject to democratic supervision. The democratic management system of enterprises and undertakings, which took the workers' congresses as its basic form, were to continue to be upheld and improved, staff members were to be organized to participate in reform and management, and their legitimate rights and interests were to be safeguarded. Any erroneous acts, such as suppressing democracy or forcing compliance with orders, would be resolutely corrected. According to this requirement, in April 1998, the General Office of the Central Committee of the Communist Party of China and the General Office of the State Council issued the Notice on the Universal Implementation of the System of Open Rural Affairs and Democratic Management in Rural Areas, which put forward more specific requirements for the improvement of democratic elections, democratic decision-making, democratic management, and democratic supervision. That June, the Organization Law of the Villagers' Committee of the People's Republic of China (Revised Draft), drafted by the State Council, was deliberated, and was then adopted at the fifth meeting of the Standing Committee of the Ninth National

People's Congress that November. Subsequently, the work of democratically electing members of villagers' committees was carried out in the vast rural areas throughout the country, and the villagers' autonomy system was gradually improved. By the end of 2004, 644,000 villagers' committees had been set up in the countryside. Most provinces, autonomous regions, and municipalities directly under the Central Government had generally completed five or six sessions of the village committee election.

In 1999, the Ministry of Civil Affairs of the People's Republic of China piloted community construction in twenty-six urban areas, strengthened the construction of residents' committees, and carried out democratic elections, decision-making, management, and supervision. By the end of 2004, 71,375 residential committees had been established throughout the country. As of September 2004, there were 595,000 workers' congresses in enterprises and institutions, covering 78,364,000 workers, accounting for 58.5% of the workforce.

With the deepening of economic system reform, the Central Government put more emphasis on the positive role of democratic management and supervision in the workers' Congress of state-owned enterprises. In October 1998, Jiang Zemin pointed out that "the implementation of democratic management of workers and masses in state-owned enterprises, like the implementation of villagers' autonomy in rural areas, is an important creation in building socialist democracy with Chinese characteristics. In carrying out different work in enterprises, the democratic management of the workers and masses can only be strengthened. It cannot be weakened in any way. The more important issues concerning enterprise reform, development, and the vital interests of the masses are involved, the more important it is to listen carefully and fully to the opinions of the broad masses of workers through staff congresses and other forms, so as to truly achieve collective efforts and work together to improve the management and efficiency of enterprises."[111] The workers' congresses of many enterprises played an active role in promoting the democratic political construction at the grassroots level and the reform and development of enterprises.

II

Implementation of the Basic Strategy of the Rule of Law in the Country

The development of socialist democracy had to be closely integrated with the improvement of the socialist legal system, which was an important task and inevitable requirement for the development of socialist democratic politics. An important aspect of promoting the reform of the political system was to continuously strengthen the socialist legal system. When the Thirteenth National Congress discussed the reform of the political system, it made a new exploration of strengthening construction of the socialist legal system and systematically moved China's socialist democratic politics toward institutionalization and legalization. Under the guidance of this ideology, the construction of the legal system and other systems in China was steadily promoted. In April 1990, the Central Committee's Circular on Maintaining Social Stability and Strengthening Political and Legal Work pointed out that "strengthening the construction of socialist democracy and the legal system is an important aspect of improving the socialist system and an important guarantee for maintaining social stability." In order to strengthen the leadership of political and legal work, political and legal committees were restored at the central and local levels.

In 1992, the Fourteenth National Congress of the Communist Party of China set new requirements for perfecting the socialist legal system while establishing the reform objectives of the socialist market economic system. Jiang Zemin pointed out that "strengthening legislative work is an urgent requirement for the establishment of a socialist market economic system, especially formulating and improving laws and regulations to guarantee Reform and Opening Up, strengthening macroeconomic management, and standardizing micro economic behavior."[12] After the Fourteenth National Congress, in the practice of establishing the socialist market economic system, the Central Committee repeatedly emphasized that the establishment and perfection of the socialist market economic system needed to be regulated and guaranteed by complete laws, and that it was important to learn to use legal means to manage the economy, so as to achieve the unity of Reform and Opening Up and legal construction. For this reason, the Decision on Several Issues Concerning the Establishment of a Socialist Market Economy

System in 1993, clearly set forth the goal of construction of the legal system, particularly in following the principles stipulated in the Constitution, speeding up economic legislation, further improving civil, commercial, and criminal laws, relevant state institutions, and administrative laws, and initially establishing laws adapted to the socialist market economy by the end of the 20th century. It was further necessary to reform and improve the judicial system and administrative law enforcement mechanism and improve the level of judicial and administrative law enforcement. Finally, it was important to establish and improve the law enforcement supervision mechanism and legal service institutions, carry out in-depth legal education, and improve the public legal awareness and concepts of the rule of law. The establishment of these goals reflected the need to develop the socialist market economy and the requirements of governing the country by law.

After December 1994, the Central Committee held regular legal lectures in Huairen Hall, Zhongnanhai. Leading members of the Politburo of the Central Committee, the Secretariat of the Central Committee, and the State Council took the lead in participating in the study of the law, thus promoting the formation of a culture of conscious learning of legal usage and enhancing the awareness of the legal system throughout the Party and the entire society. In February 1996, when the third Legislative Law Lecture was held by the Central Committee, Jiang Zemin put forward the idea of "governing the country by law." In his concluding remarks, he said that strengthening the socialist legal system and governing the country according to law were an important part of Deng Xiaoping's theory of building socialism with Chinese characteristics and an important policy for the Party and government to manage state and social affairs. Achieving and adhering to the rule of law meant gradually legalizing and standardizing all the work of the state. In other words, under the leadership of the Party and in accordance with the provisions of the Constitution and law, the broad masses of the people participated in the management of state, economic, and cultural undertakings and social affairs through various channels and forms. This was the path to gradually realizing the institutionalization and legalization of socialist democracy. Realizing and adhering to the rule of law was of great significance for promoting sustained, rapid, and healthy economic development and overall social progress and guaranteeing the long-term stability of the country. That March, the Fourth Session of the Eighth National People's Congress took "ruling the country by law" as the goal and direction of the political system reform, and wrote the Ninth

Five-Year Plan for National Economic and Social Development and the Outline of the Vision Target for 2010, which were approved by the Conference.

In 1997, when the Fifteenth National Congress made a strategic plan for cross-century development, it put "governing the country by law" in a more prominent position as a strategy for governing the country. The report of the Fifteenth National Congress pointed out that the development of democracy must be closely combined with the improvement of the legal system and the rule of law. Ruling the country by law and building a socialist country ruled by law were the basic strategy for the Party to lead the people and govern the country, the objective need for the development of a socialist market economy, an important symbol of social civilization and progress, and an important guarantee for the long-term stability of the state. In March 1999, the amendment to the Constitution adopted at the second session of the Ninth National People's Congress added the idea of "administering the country according to law and building a socialist country ruled by law," fixing it in the form of a fundamental national law.

After the Third Plenary Session of the Eleventh Central Committee, great achievements were made in the construction of the socialist legal system. In terms of legislation, in addition to amending the Constitution and four amendments to the Constitution, by the end of 2002, the NPC and its Standing Committee had formulated 297 laws and passed 125 decisions on relevant legal issues. The State Council had also formulated 933 administrative regulations. China's socialist legal system had taken its initial form. After the Fifteenth National Congress, under the guidance of the basic strategy of "governing the country according to law and building a socialist country ruled by law," further legislative efforts were made to promote the reform of the judicial system and strive for the goal of forming a socialist legal system with Chinese characteristics by 2010.

III

Practical Enrichment and Development of Socialist Spiritual Civilization

While promoting Reform and Opening Up and concentrating on economic development, the CPC had gradually enriched the ideology of building a socialist spiritual civilization. The Resolution on Guidelines for the Construction of a Socialist Spiritual Civilization in September 1986 had played an important role in the practice of the construction of a spiritual civilization. At the beginning of 1992, Deng Xiaoping's Southern Talks raised the construction of a spiritual civilization to a new height, emphasizing that the Party should stick to "grasping with both hands," that both hands should be firm, and that the construction of both civilizations should surpass capitalism. The Fourteenth National Congress of the Communist Party of China clearly pointed out that "socialism with Chinese characteristics can only be achieved if both the material and spiritual civilizations are well developed," and listed the construction of the socialist spiritual civilization as the driving force for the development of socialism with Chinese characteristics, along with the development of a socialist market economy and socialist democratic politics, emphasizing that the construction of the spiritual civilization should be highlighted. These expositions not only further clarified the important position of the construction of the spiritual civilization in the construction of socialism with Chinese characteristics, but also further clarified the basic principles of the construction of that spiritual civilization. The policy of "building a spiritual civilization" was a scientific conclusion drawn by summing up the historical lessons of the past. It required persistent discussion, reasoning, education, and guidance to resolve ideological issues. Only in this way could the Party fully mobilize the enthusiasm and creativity of the broad masses of the people in building socialism and build a socialism with Chinese characteristics that was full of vigor and vitality. This was a great step in the guiding principle of building a socialist spiritual civilization.

Promoted by the Southern Talks and the Spirit of the Fourteenth National Congress, the Central Committee made new explorations into the theory and practice of the construction of a spiritual civilization and made new progress in strengthening ideological and moral construction and developing education, science, and cultural undertakings.

In the area of strengthening ideological and moral construction, the Fourteenth National Congress emphasized that among the people of all ethnicities, especially young people, the Party should vigorously carry out education on its basic line, patriotism, and collectivism, and socialist ideological education, and establish correct ideals, beliefs, and values. After the meeting, various forms of patriotism, collectivism, and socialist education activities were widely carried out throughout society. On August 23, 1994, the Central Committee promulgated the Outline for the Implementation of Patriotic Education, which clearly stipulated and deployed the guiding principles, main content, and work priorities for the development of patriotic education, requiring relevant departments at all levels to take patriotism as a basic project for strengthening the construction of socialist spiritual civilization. On August 30, the Central Committee of the Communist Party of China promulgated Several Opinions on Further Strengthening and Improving Schools' Moral Education, which required that the educational front must stand at a historical height and recognize the importance of schools' moral education in the new period from a strategic perspective. In accordance with the requirements of the Central Committee, Party committees at all levels generally planned and deployed patriotic education, focusing on building patriotic education bases and creating a social atmosphere for patriotic education.

In terms of publicity and ideological work, Jiang Zemin proposed in his speech at the National Conference on publicity and ideological work in January 1994, that publicity and ideological work must arm people with scientific theories, guide them with correct public opinions, shape them with a noble spirit, inspire them with excellent works, and constantly cultivate and bring up new generations of socialism with ideals, morality, culture, and discipline, so as to play a powerful role in ideological and public opinion support in the great cause of building socialism with Chinese characteristics. This was not only the guiding principle of cultural propaganda in the new era, but also played a key guiding role in improving the effectiveness of various measures for the construction of a spiritual civilization.

In the development of education, the Fourteenth National Congress further emphasized that education must be given priority to the strategic position of development and strive to improve the ideological, moral, scientific, and cultural level of the whole nation, which was the fundamental plan for realizing China's modernization. To this end, the Fourteenth National Congress solemnly declared that by the end of the 20th century, illiteracy among young and middle-aged people would be basically eradicated and nine-year compulsory education would be basically realized. In October 1989, the China Youth Development Foundation launched the Hope Project through social fund-raising, which aimed at helping out-of-school teenagers and financing schools in poverty stricken areas. Immediately after the project was implemented, it received wide support from people of all walks of life. In May 1990, the first Hope Primary School was founded in Jinzhai County, Anhui Province. The initiation of the Hope Project was like the construction of a bridge leading poor teenagers to school, which effectively promoted the development of education.

In the development of cultural undertakings, emphasis was laid on promoting the theme of the times. In 1991, initiated by the Central Committee, the Ministry of Propaganda organized and implemented the Five-One Project, aimed at promoting the theme of the times and excellent traditional culture in the construction of the spiritual civilization. Taking provinces, autonomous regions, municipalities directly under the Central Government, and other state organs as the evaluation units, a good book, a good play, an excellent film, an excellent TV show, and a good theoretical article were produced every year. (Later, a good song, a good radio play, a good theoretical monograph, and other similar items were added.) After the implementation of this project, excellent works emerged, which highlighted the theme of the times, enthusiastically eulogized Reform and Opening Up and socialist modernization, and strove to answer important real-life theoretical and practical questions.

With the gradual implementation of various measures for the construction of the spiritual civilization, the relationship between the construction of a spiritual civilization and economic and social development had become increasingly close. In September 1995, the Fifth Plenary Session of the Fourteenth Central Committee and the Resolution on the Ninth Five-Year Plan for National Economic and Social Development, the Outline of Vision for 2010, and the Report on the Outline adopted by the Fourth Session of the Eighth National People's Congress in March 1996, brought the construction of the spiritual civilization into the planning of economic and social development.

In order to strengthen the Party's guidance in the construction of the spiritual civilization under the conditions of the socialist market economic system, the Sixth Plenary Session of the Fourteenth Central Committee adopted the Resolution of the Central Committee of the Communist Party of China on Several Important Questions Concerning the Strengthening of the Construction of Socialist Spiritual Civilization in October 1996 (referred to as the Resolution). This was the second resolution made by the Party Central Committee in ten years that targeted the strengthening of construction of the socialist spiritual civilization. This resolution focused on the grand goal of China's cross-century development and further clarified the guiding ideology, general requirements, and the main objectives of the construction of the socialist spiritual civilization over the next fifteen years. The Resolution pointed out that the guiding ideology and general requirements for the construction of the spiritual civilization were guided by Marxism-Leninism, Mao Zedong Thought, and Deng Xiaoping's theory of building socialism with Chinese characteristics, adhering to the Party's basic line and principles, strengthening ideological and moral construction, developing educational science and culture, arming people with scientific theories, guiding them with correct public opinion, shaping them with a noble spirit, inspiring them with excellent works so as to nurture socialist citizens with ideals, morality, culture, and discipline, improving the ideological and moral quality and scientific and cultural quality of the entire nation, and uniting and mobilizing people of all ethnicities to build China into a prosperous, democratic, and civilized modern socialist country.

With regard to the main objectives of the construction of the socialist spiritual civilization in the fifteen years from 1996 to 2010, the Resolution stipulated that the common ideal of building socialism with Chinese characteristics should be firmly established throughout the nation, the commitment to adhering to the Party's basic line should be firmly established, and the remarkable improvement in the quality of citizens with ideological and moral cultivation, scientific education level, and democratic and legal concepts as the main substance should be realized. The Party would substantially improve the quality of cultural life, which mainly featured positive, healthy, rich, and diversified life and service for the people, and it would raise the degree of urban and rural civilization, marked by a social atmosphere, public order, and living environment, and form a good environment for the coordinated development of the construction of the material and spiritual civilization throughout the country.

The Resolution offered a preliminary summary of the experience of the construction of the spiritual civilization under the new situation of the socialist market economy, fully affirmed that the development of the socialist market economy was conducive to enhancing people's consciousness of self-reliance, competition, efficiency, democracy, the legal system, and a pioneering and innovative spirit, and clearly pointed out that the weaknesses and negative aspects of the market itself could also be reflected in the nation's spiritual life. In order to strengthen the construction of a spiritual civilization, it was necessary to guide people to correctly handle the relationships between competition and cooperation, autonomy and supervision, efficiency and fairness, wealth first and more wealth later, and economic and social benefits, and also to advocate putting the interests of the state and the people first, to fully respect the legitimate interests of citizens and individuals, and to strictly prevent the introduction of the principle of commodity exchange in economic activities into the political life of the Party and the administrative activities of the government organs. These experiences reflected the Party's new thinking on the construction of the spiritual civilization under the conditions of the market economy. The Resolution adopted at the Sixth Plenary Session of the Fourteenth Central Committee indicated that the Party's understanding of the construction of a spiritual civilization had been raised to a new level.

After the Sixth Plenary Session of the Fourteenth Central Committee, in order to implement the spirit of the Plenary Session, all regions and departments had taken increasing investment in the construction of a spiritual civilization and carrying out mass activities to create a spiritual civilization as important parts of formulating development plans and long-term goals. In order to ensure the implementation of the Resolution, in May 1997, the Central Committee decided to set up a Central Steering Committee for the Construction of a Spiritual Civilization as a deliberative body for the Central Committee to guide the construction of a national spiritual civilization. Subsequently, the provinces, autonomous regions, and municipalities directly under the Central Government established corresponding institutions to strengthen the construction of a spiritual civilization. Mass activities with the main aim of creating model cities, villages, towns, and industries were vigorously carried out throughout the country, presenting a vivid scene of joint effort and active participation among the broad masses, creating a positive atmosphere for reform, opening up, and economic construction.

IV

Development of Advanced Socialist Culture with Chinese Characteristics

Developing the advanced culture of socialism with Chinese characteristics was an inevitable requirement for comprehensively promoting the cause of socialism with Chinese characteristics, and was also the goal of the construction of the socialist spiritual civilization. The central leading group, with Jiang Zemin as its leader, strove to explore the correct way to develop the advanced socialist culture with Chinese characteristics.

In his speech celebrating the 40th anniversary of the founding of New China in 1989, Jiang Zemin pointed out that in the final analysis, the construction of the spiritual civilization was meant to improve the quality of the whole nation and foster a new generation with "four haves." He said, "It is impossible to imagine that a nation without strong spiritual pillars can stand on its own among the nations of the world." He emphasized that China should actively absorb all the outstanding achievements of its historical culture as well as foreign culture and "oppose the national nihilism which negates Chinese traditional culture and the idea of worshipping and flattering foreign countries."[13]

In his speech commemorating the 70th anniversary of the founding of the Communist Party in 1991, Jiang expounded the guiding ideology, basic elements, and development direction of socialist cultural construction while discussing "the culture of socialism with Chinese characteristics." He pointed out that China should "resist and eliminate all backward and decadent ideological and cultural influences and constantly create an advanced and healthy new socialist culture [...] Only by being deeply rooted in China and relying on the strength of the people, facing modernization, the world, and the future can we create a socialist culture worthy of this great era."[14] Here, the ideological seeds of developing an advanced culture of socialism with Chinese characteristics had sprouted.

In 1997, the report of the Fifteenth National Congress elaborated on the program of building a socialist culture with Chinese characteristics. Compared with the previous documents, it added the requirement of developing the "scientific and popular socialist culture of all ethnicities," emphasizing the importance of "building a socialist spiritual civilization based on Chinese reality, inheriting the excellent cultural traditions of history, and absorbing the beneficial achievements of foreign cultures." The new generalization of "building a socialist culture with Chinese characteristics" at the Fifteenth National Congress not only highlighted its "cultural" color, but also linked up with the connotation of the socialist spiritual civilization in fundamental ways. Jiang pointed out, "The culture of socialism with Chinese characteristics is consistent with the socialist spiritual civilization that we have been advocating since the adoption of the Reform and Opening Up policy. Culture is relative to economics and politics. A spiritual civilization is relative to the material civilization. Only with the coordinated development of the economy, politics, and culture and the well-being of both civilizations can socialism with Chinese characteristics be presented."[15] Here, the corresponding relations between "civilization" and "culture" are clearly illustrated. It was precisely based on this understanding that, in order to gradually improve their corresponding relations, starting from the Fifteenth National Congress of the Communist Party of China, this new expression of changing the perspective of understanding had become a symbol of the transformation of the socialist spiritual civilization construction theory to the development of advanced socialist cultural ideas with Chinese characteristics.

In February 2000, when Jiang Zemin delivered his "Three Represents" speech, the idea of developing an advanced socialist culture with Chinese characteristics became more prominent. In the important thought of the "Three Represents," the concept of "advanced culture" was not only particularly noticeable, but also linked closely the development of advanced culture with the construction of the Party. Jiang said, "Because the Party represents the direction of advanced culture, all Party members must adhere to the guidance of Marxism, strive to inherit and develop all the fine cultural traditions of the Chinese nation, and strive to learn and absorb all the excellent cultural achievements from foreign countries, so as to continuously create and promote socialist culture with Chinese characteristics and facilitate the comprehensive, coordinated development of socialist material and spiritual civilizations and the social progress."[16]

In his speech on July 1, 2001, Jiang Zemin not only reviewed the historical direction of the CPC's representative of advanced culture and promoted the historical process and great achievements of the socialist cultural construction, but also expounded the theoretical and practical principles of the CPC's continuing representative of the direction of the advanced culture of China from the realistic point of view. He pointed out, "If our Party intends to always represent the direction of China's advanced culture, that is, the Party's theory, line, program, policy, principles, and different work, it must strive to embody the requirements of developing a modern, global-oriented, and future-oriented socialist culture of the scientific masses of the nation and promote the continuous improvement of the ideological, moral, scientific, and cultural qualities of the entire nation to provide spiritual impetus and intellectual support for China's economic development and social progress."[17] He also stated, "In contemporary China, the development of advanced culture means the development of a socialist culture with Chinese characteristics and the construction of a socialist spiritual civilization."[18] In this way, the relationship between the three concepts of "advanced culture," "socialist culture with Chinese characteristics," and a "socialist spiritual civilization" was clear at a glance, and their connotations were the same. The speech also discussed the dialectical relationship between the two civilizations, the development trend and requirements of China's advanced culture, the fundamental task of developing socialist culture, the development of socialist culture, the inheritance and development of all excellent cultures, and the full expression of the relationship between the spirit of the times and the spirit of creativity. Thus, the main frame of developing an advanced socialist culture with Chinese characteristics was basically constructed. By 2002, the report of the Sixteenth National Congress of the Communist Party of China further elaborated its chapter structure from "economic construction and reform of the economic system," "political construction and reform of political system," and "cultural construction and reform of the cultural system." In the chapter "Cultural Construction and Reform of the Cultural System," the notion of advanced socialist culture with Chinese characteristics was discussed comprehensively, and the general requirements for developing an advanced socialist culture with Chinese characteristics in the new century were put forward. According to Jiang Zemin's exposition, the development of an advanced culture of socialism with Chinese characteristics generally included such basic principles.

Primarily, it was important to adhere to the guidance of Marxism. Jiang pointed out that "what kind of cultural orientation to adhere to and what kind of culture to promote the construction of is the ideological and spiritual banner of a political party."[19] Adhering to the guiding position of Marxism and never allowing pluralism in the guiding ideology were the fundamental principles for building a socialist culture with Chinese characteristics.

Further, it was necessary to adhere to the fundamental task of cultivating a new people of "Four Haves" to build an advanced socialist culture with Chinese characteristics. He noted, "The fundamental task of developing a socialist culture is to train generation after generation of citizens to have ideals, morality, culture, and discipline."[20] This was a comprehensive requirement for the quality of all citizens. Whether discussing the construction of a socialist spiritual civilization or developing an advanced socialist culture with Chinese characteristics, it was necessary to undertake this task. It was the fundamental driving force for advancing the cause of socialism with Chinese characteristics.

It was essential to adhere to the "two serving" direction and the "double hundred" policy. Serving the people and serving socialism was the fundamental purpose of developing socialist culture, while the idea that "let a hundred flowers bloom and a hundred schools of thought contend" was the basic principle of building socialist culture. After the Third Plenary Session of the Eleventh Central Committee, Deng Xiaoping and Jiang Zemin stressed on many occasions that the "double hundred" policy could not be changed or lost, but must be persistently upheld. The "double hundred" policy reflected the characteristics and laws of the development of cultural undertakings and was the basic policy for promoting the prosperity and development of the advanced culture of socialism with Chinese characteristics.

Further, it was necessary to adhere to the development direction of "orientations for modernization, the world, and the future." These Three Orientations were the guarantee that socialist culture with Chinese characteristics would have the distinct characteristics of the times. To achieve the Three Orientations, the Party needed to adhere to the policy of "making the past serve the present and making foreign things serve China." Further, "the essence of the traditional national culture should be preserved while the dregs should be removed, and the characteristics of the times should be combined to develop it, weeding out the old and bringing forth the new, so as to make it continue to develop and flourish. It is also necessary to actively absorb all the excellent cultural achievements created by humankind and integrate these into the culture of socialism with Chinese characteristics. Only by remaining deeply rooted in China, relying on the strength of the people, and oriented toward modernization, the world, and the future, can we create a socialist culture worthy of this great era."[21]

Finally, the CPC needed to adhere to the connotation and traits of the socialist culture with Chinese characteristics, which was "national, scientific, and popular culture." Its "national character" lay in its origin in Chinese civilization's five thousand years of history and in the practice of socialism with Chinese characteristics. It had not only the national form popular among the people, but also rich content that reflected the people's modern lifestyle, thinking, moral sentiment, aesthetic taste, and customs. Its "scientific nature" lay in its advocacy of science, its opposition to superstition, and its resolute struggle against all feudal ignorance and the decadent ideological culture of pseudoscience. Its "popularity" lay in that it originated from the people, served them, educated them, and was enjoyed by them.

To sum up, the construction of the advanced socialist culture with Chinese characteristics meant vigorously developing advanced culture, supporting healthy and beneficial culture, striving to transform backward culture, resolutely resisting decadent culture, constantly enriching the people's spiritual world, constantly strengthening the people's spiritual might, and striving to form the theoretical guidance, the power of public opinion, the spiritual pillars, and the cultural conditions to reflect the development requirements of China's advanced productive forces, the direction of China's advanced culture, and the fundamental interests of the vast majority of the nation's people.

While the theoretical understanding of the advanced culture of socialism with Chinese characteristics was constantly enriched and improved, the Central Committee also emphasized several important aspects in the concrete implementation of the development of the advanced culture of socialism with Chinese characteristics and increased its input in improvement and reform.

First, the Party should promote the healthy development of social and cultural undertakings and the socialist market economy by strengthening ideological and moral construction. Ideological and political work was an important political advantage of the Communist Party of China. Jiang Zemin pointed out that the more the Party developed the economy and Reform and Opening Up, the more it should attach importance to ideological and political work. He noted, "Strengthening socialist ideological and moral construction is an important part of and central link in the development of advanced culture."[22] In September 2001, on the basis of summing up years of practical experience, the Central Committee promulgated the Outline for the Implementation of Civil Morality Construction. The Outline suggested that the common ideal of building socialism with Chinese characteristics and a correct world outlook, outlook on life, and values should be firmly established throughout the nation. In addition, the basic moral norms of "patriotism, obedience to the law, courtesy, integrity, unity, friendliness, diligence, thrift, self-reliance, and dedication" should be vigorously advocated throughout the society. Further, the socialist ideological and moral system should be established in accordance with the socialist market economy, the legal norms of justice, and inheriting the traditional virtues of the Chinese nation.

Second, the Party should carry forward and cultivate the great national spirit. National spirit was the spiritual support for any nation's survival and development. A nation could not stand on its own in the forest of the nations without inspiring spirit and noble character. Jiang Zemin pointed out that over the past five thousand years of development, the Chinese nation had formed a great national spirit of unity, love of peace, diligence, courage, and self-improvement, with patriotism at its core.[23] This national spirit, broad and profound as it was, had a long history and was an indivisible, important component of the life of the Chinese nation. This national spirit, combined with the fine tradition and the spirit of the times formed by the Party through its leadership of the people in the long-term revolution, construction, and reform, was a powerful driving spiritual force for the Chinese nation's endless progress and prosperity.

Third, through the development of education and science, the Party could fundamentally promote the development of cultural undertakings. Education was the foundation of a century-long plan, and the rise and fall of national fortunes depended on education. Education was the basis for the development of science and technology and the nurturing of talent. It played an overarching, leading role in the construction of modernization and must be placed in a strategic position of priority development. Deng Xiaoping pointed out, "We should do everything possible to be patient in other areas, even at the expense of speed, and resolve the issue of education."[24] Jiang Zemin stressed that in the process of socialist modernization, the strategic position of giving priority to the development of education must always be upheld and remain unshakable.

If the Party did not maintain this understanding of education, it would lose the opportunity and delay major events, making historic mistakes. In view of the fact that philosophy and social sciences had not received due attention in society, Jiang Zemin pointed out that philosophy and social sciences were an important tool for people to understand and transform the world, and an important force for promoting historical development and social progress. "In the process of understanding and transforming the world, philosophy and social sciences are as important as natural sciences. It is as important to train high-level philosophical and social scientists as it is to train high-level natural scientists. It is as important to improve the quality of philosophy and the social sciences throughout the nation as to improve the quality of natural sciences, and it is also important to appoint individuals talented in philosophy and the social sciences and give full play to their roles."[25] It was necessary to correct the bias of some regions and departments that did not attach importance to philosophy and the social sciences.

Fourth, it was necessary to vigorously promote the reform of the cultural system. Since the Fourth Plenary Session of the Thirteenth Central Committee, the Central Committee had vigorously promoted the reform of the management system of cultural undertakings in order to meet the requirements of the development of the socialist market economy in accordance with the characteristics and laws of the construction of a socialist spiritual civilization. The National Conference on propaganda and ideological work, held in January 1994, further clarified the principles of promoting the main theme and advocating diversified cultural construction. In cultural construction, all regions and departments needed to adhere to the principles of orientation, total quantity, structure, and efficiency, and actively cultivate the socialist cultural market so as to make it develop healthily. On this basis, the Sixth Plenary Session of the Fourteenth Central Committee of the Communist Party of China, held in 1996, made a detailed plan for the development of socialist cultural undertakings in the new century. The plenary session pointed out that the primary task of prospering literature and art was to produce more excellent works with unified ideological and artistic qualities and a strong appeal under the guidance of correct guidelines. Journalism and propaganda needed to adhere to the principle of Party spirit, to the principle of seeking truth from facts, to unity, stability, and encouragement, and to give priority to positive propaganda, while firmly grasping the correct direction for public opinion. Philosophy and the social sciences must be firm. Guided by Marxism-Leninism, Mao Zedong Thought, and Deng Xiaoping's theory of building socialism with Chinese characteristics, it was important to adhere to the principle of integrating theory with practice, serve the decision-making of the Party and the government, and serve the construction of the two civilizations. The cultural market should focus on prosperity and management at the same time, vigorously support healthy cultural products, and advocate beneficial cultural and recreational activities suitable for the consumption level of the masses to promote the healthy development of the cultural market. In order to achieve the above goals, it was necessary to continue to deepen the reform of the management system of cultural undertakings and quickly form a development pattern in which the state guaranteed priority and encouraged society to set up cultural undertakings.

Under the guidance of these ideas, the reform of the management system and operation mechanism of cultural undertakings had gradually deepened. In terms of ownership, it had changed the long-standing practice of state-sponsored cultural undertakings and allowed the development of cultural industries in various forms of ownership. In terms of administrative management, it was necessary to establish the management system of cultural undertakings with classified guidance and management, reform the personnel and distribution systems within cultural undertakings, to support the undertakings rather than the people, as was done in the past, and to fully stimulate the vitality of cultural undertakings.

After the Sixth Plenary Session of the Fourteenth Central Committee and the Fifteenth National Congress of the CPC, the construction of cultural undertakings had taken "excellent project strategy" as its core, and under the impetus of strengthening management and deepening reform, a new situation of prosperity and development had emerged. In addition to continuing to conscientiously organize and implement the Five-One Project for the construction of spiritual civilization, departments and regions had also strengthened the management of the production of spiritual products and the cultural market. The state had successively formulated and improved relevant policies and regulations such as Publishing Management Regulations, Printing Industry Management Regulations, Audiovisual Products Management Regulations, Business Performance Management Regulations, and Radio and Television Management Regulations to provide the necessary legal and policy support for the entry of cultural products into the market, so that healthy cultural products firmly occupied a dominant position in the cultural market. By the end of 2000, national radio and television coverage reached 92.1% and 93.4% respectively, which were 13.4% and 8.9% higher than in 1995. Excellent works reflecting the spirit of the times and closer to people's daily lives were constantly emerging. Through organizing the exhibition and broadcasting and distribution of the award-winning works of the Five-One Project, the exemplary role of excellent works was brought into full play. Socialist cultural positions were consolidated and a healthy, upward environment of public opinion, a civilized and harmonious social atmosphere, and a rich, diverse cultural life were formed.

After the Fourth Plenary Session of the Thirteenth Central Committee of the Communist Party of China, the relatively complete and systematic theory of building an advanced socialist culture with Chinese characteristics was a new development of the Party's thought on Marxist cultural construction under the new historical conditions, and also a new achievement on the path of exploring the localization of Marxism in China.

CHAPTER 9

The Cross-Century Development Strategy of Reform and Opening Up and the Development of Socialism with Chinese Characteristics

Beginning in the 1990s, when the CPC Central Committee, led by Jiang Zemin, pushed forward the cause of socialism with Chinese characteristics, it made a comprehensive arrangement and deployment on how to move into the new century in the areas of development strategy, diplomacy, national defense, and the reunification of the motherland. On these issues, it fully reflected the third generation of central leadership's theoretical development and practical innovation to Marxism in the light of the global situation and the national conditions facing China.

I

Formulation of the Strategy for Reform, Opening Up, and Modernization in the New Century

After the 1990s, with the advanced realization of the strategic objectives of "the first step" and "the second step" in China's social development, the third generation of the Party's leading group, under Jiang's leadership, made new plans for the realization of the strategic objectives of "the third step." On this basis, it put forward "revitalizing the country through science and education," "sustainable development," and "combining introduction with reaching out." A series of strategic deployments further enriched and developed the modernization development strategy with Chinese characteristics.

1. Strategy of Rejuvenating the Nation through Science, Education, and Sustainable Development

The strategy of rejuvenating the country through science, education, and sustainable development was an important strategic decision put forward by the Central Committee to realize the grand goal of "three steps" by proceeding from Deng Xiaoping's theory and the Party's basic line, proceeding from China's national conditions, and scientifically analyzing the trend of global economic and social development.

From the late 1970s to the early 1990s, Deng Xiaoping emphasized many times that "science and technology are the key to realizing the Four Modernizations, and education is the basis… In the long run, education and science and technology should be given attention… Science and technology are the primary productive forces," and other similar ideas.

In the 1990s, on the basis of inheriting Deng Xiaoping's theory, the Jiang-led central leading group further put forward the strategic thought of rejuvenating the country through science and education, listing it as the basic national policy. In 1992, at the Fourteenth Party Congress, Jiang pointed out that "economic construction must be transferred to the track of relying on scientific and technological progress and improving the quality of workers." The Decision of the State Council of the Central Committee of the Communist Party of China on Accelerating the Progress of Science and Technology promulgated on May 6, 1995, was the first time implementation of the strategy of rejuvenating the country through science and education was undertaken. Jiang pointed out that "rejuvenating the country through science and education means fully implementing the idea that science and technology are the first productive force, adhering to education as the basis, placing science and technology and education in an important position for economic and social development, enhancing the country's scientific and technological strength and the ability to realize the transformation of productive forces, and improving the scientific and technological and cultural quality of the entire nation." In the same year, in its recommendations on the Ninth Five-Year Plan for National Economic and Social Development and the long-term goal for 2010, the Fifth Plenary Session of the Fourteenth Central Committee listed the implementation of the strategy of rejuvenating the country through science and education as one of the important policies for accelerating socialist modernization in China over the next fifteen years and into the 21st century. In 1996, the Fourth Session of the Eighth National People's Congress officially adopted the Ninth Five-Year Plan for National Economic and Social Development and the Vision Target for 2010, in which "rejuvenating the nation through science and education" became the basic national policy.

The purpose of rejuvenating the country through science and education was not only to promote the rapid development of economic construction, but also to promote the coordinated development of the economy and society. To achieve rapid and coordinated development, it was necessary to fully consider the sustainability of development, make the scale and speed of development adapt to the basic national conditions, and conform to the objective laws of economic and social development. Therefore, after the rapid development of China's economic construction in the 1980s, the Central Committee began to pay more attention to China's sustainable development. On the basis of summing up China's historical experience, drawing lessons from the development of industrialized countries, and constantly recognizing the laws of economic development, the Central Committee put forward the strategy of sustainable development.

In October 1993, according to Deng Xiaoping's thought on coordinated development of the population, environment, and resources and China's actual situation, the Party Central Committee and the State Council put forward the idea of implementing a sustainable development strategy in China. In 1994, the Chinese government formulated, completed, approved, and adopted China's Agenda for the 21st Century – China's White Paper on the Population, Environment, and Development in the 21st Century, which established the overall strategic framework for China's sustainable development in the 21st century and the main objectives in various fields. In March 1996, the Ninth Five-Year Plan for National Economic and Social Development and the Outline of Vision Targets for 2010, approved by the Fourth Session of the Eighth National People's

Congress, regarded sustainable development as an important guiding principle and strategic objective, clarifying the major decision for China to implement a sustainable development strategy in its future economic and social development. The Fifteenth National Congress of the Communist Party of China reiterated this strategic decision, emphasizing that China was a country with a large population and relatively insufficient resources. In the process of modernization, it was important to implement a strategy of sustainable development.

A sustainable development strategy was a major breakthrough in the traditional concept of development. Approaching the issue from a new angle, it fully expounded the major problem of how China would develop in the future, put forward a series of basic ideas on how to build socialism in a country with a backward economy and culture and an unbalanced level of development in its productive forces, and how to promote economic growth and the all-round development of society, pointing out the correct development path for the cause of building socialism with Chinese characteristics.

2. Development Strategy of the Western Regions

Implementing the strategy of developing the western regions to accelerate the development of the central and western regions was an important decision made by the leading group of the Central Committee in the late 1990s, under Jiang Zemin's leadership and in accordance with Deng Xiaoping's strategic thought on the "two overall situations" of China's modernization construction, with a far-sighted view, commanding the overall situation, and oriented for the 21st century.

In 1988, Deng Xiaoping proposed the strategic thought of "two overall situations" when the reform, opening up, and modernization were carried out. He said, "It is a matter of great importance for the overall situation that coastal areas should speed up their opening to the outside world, so that this vast area with 200 million people can develop faster and better, so as to promote the better development of the Mainland. The Mainland should take into account this overall situation. On the other hand, when they develop to a certain extent, the coastal areas are required to make more effort to help the development of the hinterland, in line with the overall situation. At that time, the coastal areas should be subject to the overall situation."[1] He also envisaged that by the end of the 20th century, when the whole country reached a moderately well-off level, more effort should be made to help the central and western regions accelerate their development.

After 1995, because the realization of the second development goal of China's modernization strategy was ahead of schedule, the Central Committee began to give more consideration to Deng Xiaoping's second overall development situation. In formulating the Ninth Five-Year Plan and the outline of the 2010 long-term goals, it took gradually narrowing the regional development gap and promoting the coordinated development of the regional economy as an important policy. At the Fifteenth National Congress in 1997, it was clearly pointed out that the Party should promote the rational distribution and coordinated development of the regional economy and gradually narrow the gap of regional economic development. According to the general principle of "overall planning, adapting measures to local conditions, giving full play to advantages, division of labor, cooperation, and coordinating development," the Central Government made a new overall arrangement for the healthy development of the regional economy in China.

On June 17, 1999, Jiang Zemin hosted a symposium in Xi'an on the reform and development of the five northwest provinces and regions. He proposed that China should lose no time in implementing the strategy of developing the western region to accelerate the growth of the central and western regions. He pointed out that speeding up the development of the western region was a strategy of overall development, which was not only of great economic significance, but also of great political and social significance. The conditions for speeding up the development of the central and western regions were basically in place and the time was ripe. From then on, China should take this as a major strategic task of the Party and the state and put it in a more prominent position.

After a series of deliberations, in October 2000, the Fifth Plenary Session of the Fifteenth Central Committee of the Communist Party of China adopted the Recommendations of the Central Committee of the Communist Party of China on Formulating the Tenth Five-Year Plan for National Economic and Social Development, which formally put forward the strategy for the development of the western region. It pointed out that the implementation of the strategy of developing the western region, accelerating the development of the central and western region, relating to economic development, national unity, social stability, coordinated development of the regions, and ultimately achieving common prosperity were important measures in achieving the third strategic goal. From that time, the strategy of western development was rapidly put into practice and achieved remarkable results.

3. Combination Strategy of "Letting In" and "Reaching Out"

According to the new trend of worldwide economic globalization and the development process of China's Reform and Opening Up, at the turn of the century, the Central Committee put forward and implemented the strategy of combining "letting in" and "reaching out" to open up to the outside world in a timely manner, so as to further form a new pattern of multi-directional, multi-level, and wide-ranging development.

In February 1998, at the Second Plenary Session of the Fifteenth Central Committee, Jiang Zemin elaborated on the policy of dealing with the Asian financial crisis, pointing out that while actively expanding exports, leaders should systematically organize and support a number of powerful, advantageous state-owned enterprises to invest and set up factories abroad, which required both "introduction" and "going out." These were two interrelated and mutually reinforcing aspects of opening up, both of which were indispensable. In October 2000, the Fifth Plenary Session of the Fifteenth Central Committee officially put forward the need to seize opportunities, meet challenges, seek advantages and avoid disadvantages, promote all-round, multi-level, and wide-ranging opening up, develop an open economy, implement the "reaching out" strategy, and strive to make new breakthroughs in the utilization of both domestic and foreign resources and both markets.

In March 2001, the Outline of the Tenth Five-Year Plan for National Economic and Social Development of the People's Republic of China, adopted at the Fourth Session of the Ninth National People's Congress, further proposed the deployment of the strategy of "going global" in opening up. According to this arrangement, China's opening up had developed from focusing mainly on imports to combining "letting in" with "reaching out," actively participating in international cooperation, making the field of opening up wider and more proactive, and had achieved remarkable results in a very short time. By the end of 2001, China had participated in 195 overseas resource cooperation projects, with a total investment of 4.6 billion US dollars; established 6,610 overseas enterprises with a total investment of 12.3 billion US dollars, of which the Chinese side had invested 8.4 billion US dollars; signed a total of 99.7 billion US dollars contract for foreign contracted projects, completed a turnover of 71.5 billion US dollars, and promoted exports by nearly 6 billion US dollars; and signed a total of 26.8 billion US dollars of contracts for foreign labor services. The turnover was 20.7 billion US dollars, and 2.52 million people were sent out. Various forms of foreign economic cooperation projects continued to grow steadily. In 2001, fifteen new large-scale projects involving power, transportation, construction, petrochemical, and other industries were signed. The average investment of overseas projects reached US$252,000, which was nearly 30% higher than the previous year. A number of large backbone enterprises, such as CNPC and the Haier Group, played a leading role in the implementation of this overseas investment strategy and had begun to take shape as transnational corporations.

The opening strategy of "letting in" and "reaching out" effectively promoted the development of an open economy and made the opening pattern of all-round, multi-level, and wide-ranging areas clearer. China's economy further integrated into the process of economic globalization and gained a broader space for development. This was another far-sighted decision made by the Central Committee on the road of cross-century development.

The proposition and implementation of the above development strategy reflected the objective process and law of China's modernization construction. It not only had Chinese characteristics, but also reflected the great tradition of the Chinese Communists who excelled at combining the basic principles of Marxism with China's actual situation.

II

The Deepening of the Reform of State-owned Enterprises

At that time, state-owned enterprises were the pillar of China's national economy and had made great contributions to the country's construction and development for many years. However, due to the long-term operation under the planned economic system, the state had too much control over enterprises, a rigid management mechanism, and neglect of the role of the market, so the task of reform was also the most arduous.

1. Achieving the Three-year Goal of Escaping Difficulties and Establishing a Modern Enterprise System

After 1994, the reform of state-owned enterprises entered a stage of transforming the operation mechanism and establishing a modern enterprise system. With the transformation of the system and the drastic change of the market environment, many contradictions and problems that had accumulated in state-owned enterprises under the planning system were also exposed, mainly manifested in inactive mechanisms, and quite a number of enterprises did not meet the requirements of the market economy. As a result, in the fierce market competition, it found itself in an unprecedented predicament. In the first quarter of 1996, the first net loss since the founding of New China appeared after the offset of profits and losses of 688,800 independent state-owned industrial enterprises in China.

In view of this situation, the Central Committee believed that the only way for state-owned enterprises to eliminate this problem was to adapt to the needs of the developing socialist market economy, continue to accelerate and deepen reform, and establish a modern enterprise system. The Fifteenth National Congress therefore further clarified the direction of the reform of state-owned enterprises and put forward the goal of striving to establish a modern enterprise system for the majority of large and medium-sized state-owned backbone enterprises by the end of the 20th century, improving their operating conditions and creating a new situation for the reform and development of state-owned enterprises, so as to push the reform of state-owned enterprises to a critical stage.

The difficulties in the operations of state-owned enterprises lay not only in the inactive mechanism, but also in the unreasonable layout and structure of the state-owned economy, the long and dispersed front, the small scale of enterprises, and the low quality of enterprises. This was a major reason for high input, low output, high consumption, and low benefit. Without changing the layout and structure, the reform of individual enterprises would be difficult to advance. Therefore, the Fifteenth National Congress also proposed that the state-owned economy should be strategically adjusted, and that the state-owned economy must take a dominant position in the important industries and key areas related to the lifeline of the national economy. In other areas, it was possible to strengthen the focus and improve the overall quality of state-owned assets through asset restructuring and structural adjustment. It was necessary to combine the reform of state-owned enterprises with restructuring, transforming and strengthening management, focusing on improving the whole state-owned economy, grasping the big ones and letting the small ones live, and carrying out strategic restructuring of state-owned enterprises.

The First Plenary Session of the Fifteenth Central Committee clearly pointed out that it would take about three years for most large and medium-sized state-owned loss-making enterprises to escape the predicament through reform, reorganization, transformation, and strengthening management, and to strive to make the majority of large and medium-sized state-owned backbone enterprises initially establish a modern enterprise system by the end of the 20th century.

After the Fifteenth National Congress, the reform focused on the establishment of a modern enterprise system was comprehensively carried out. The pilot project of establishing a modern enterprise system started in 1994 was greatly expanded beginning in 1997. The pilot cities "optimizing capital structure" increased from 18 to 111, and the pilot cities establishing enterprise groups expanded from 56 to 120. Through these pilot projects, according to the requirements of the developing socialist market economy, all state-owned enterprises were strategically restructured and a new management system was established.

China Petroleum and Natural Gas Corporation, China Petrochemical Group Corporation, Shanghai Xinbao Steel Group Company, ten national defense industry groups, three non-ferrous metals groups, and four information industry groups were formed. These large-scale enterprise groups operated according to market requirements, no longer assuming administrative functions, and were authorized by the government to operate state-owned assets, thus enhancing their ability in self-development and participation in international competition.

By encouraging mergers and acquisitions, regulating bankruptcy, diverting laid-off workers, reducing staff, and increasing efficiency, the pilot cities of "optimizing capital structure" had begun to form a competitive mechanism of eliminating the fittest. Small state-owned enterprises needed to be reorganized, united, merged, leased, contracted, put under a joint-stock cooperative system, and sold, and some key links in the sale of small enterprises needed to be standardized.

The basic characteristic of the modern enterprise system was a corporation system, and the typical form of the company system was the joint stock limited company and the limited liability company. Its prominent feature was that small capital was combined into legal entity capital in the form of shareholding, in order to meet the needs of large-scale social production and pursuit of greater value-added capital. This was a typical form of enterprise organization in modern economic society. China's share-holding system reform began gradually in the mid and late 1980s. By the early 1990s, a large number of pilot joint-stock enterprises had appeared all over the country.

With the approval of the State Council, the Shanghai Stock Exchange opened on December 19, 1990, and the Shenzhen Stock Exchange opened on July 3, 1991. After 1992, inspired by the spirit of Deng Xiaoping's Southern Talks, the joint-stock reform entered a new stage of development. That March, the relevant departments of the State Council jointly formulated eleven laws and regulations, such as the Pilot Measures for Joint-stock Enterprises, to further standardize and promote the reform of the joint-stock system.

After 1998, according to the requirement of establishing the modern enterprise system, a large number of state-owned enterprises carried out the reform of the company and joint-stock systems. Many large enterprises and conglomerates were successfully listed in the capital market both in China and abroad after asset reorganization to align with international practice. They not only raised a large amount of social funds and improved the asset structure and operating conditions of the socialist cause, but also established a modern enterprise system, promoted the formation of a diversified investment and financing system, expanded the country's financial revenue channels, and improved the economy. Economic efficiency played an important role.

By the end of 2000, there were 1,088 listed companies in the Shanghai and Shenzhen Stock Exchanges, 1,257 listed securities, 58.01 million investors in the stock market, and the total market value of stocks was 4.8091 trillion yuan, accounting for more than 50% of GDP.[2] In a period of just ten years, China's joint-stock economy had gone through the road that Western developed countries required a century to complete. This played a decisive role in national economic life and played an increasingly obvious role in promoting economic development and reform.

In order to reverse the losses of state-owned enterprises, the Party first chose the textile industry, which suffered the most serious losses, as the breakthrough point. Starting from "reducing ingots, reducing staff, and increasing efficiency," textile industry assets were restructured, the production structure was adjusted, and the operation mechanism was changed according to market requirements.

In 1998, 5.12 million cotton spindles were compressed and backward, 660,000 laid-off workers were diverted and laid off, and a loss of 2.6 billion yuan was seen. This was an important step towards realizing the goal of turning losses into profits throughout the industry in just three years. The coal industry also adopted such measures as "decentralization, well-shutdown, and production reduction" to reduce excess production capacity, eliminate backward enterprises, and begin to reverse losses.

In order to ensure the overall realization of the goal of three-year reform and extrication from difficulties for state-owned enterprises, the Central Committee and the State Council also decided to establish the system of inspectors commissioned by the State Council. State-owned enterprise inspectors were appointed by cadres at or above the Deputy ministerial level. The State planned to gradually send inspectors to 1,000 large enterprises and enterprise groups, and to 500 enterprises in 1998. Its main task was to check the accounts, check the profits and losses of enterprises, and check assets and liabilities. At the same time, it was to evaluate the financial situation of enterprises and the performance of the main leading members, then report to the State Council after examination and verification by relevant departments. Local governments dispatched supervisory board personnel to state-owned enterprises or wholly state-owned companies or state-owned holding companies under a division of labor supervision.

On April 28, 1998, the first batch of twenty-one inspectors and eighty assistants began training. In order to ensure that the commissioners effectively performed their duties, the State Council formulated and promulgated the Regulations on Inspection Commissioners. The Ombudsman exercised supervision power on behalf of the state and strengthened the government's supervision over enterprises while separating the real administration from the enterprises and letting them operate independently. Through financial supervision and inspection of business results, it evaluated the implementation of the Party's principles and policies, state laws and regulations, and business performance of the main leaders of various enterprises. According to the inspection conclusion, the State Council rewarded, punished, appointed, and dismissed the main leaders of enterprises through personnel departments. The implementation of this system played a powerful role in promoting the construction of the leading group of state-owned enterprises and the implementation of various reform measures.

2. Implementing the Reemployment Project for Laid-off Workers in State-owned Enterprises

Ensuring the basic living security and reemployment of laid-off workers in state-owned enterprises was an important part of the success of the reform of state-owned enterprises. It was understood that "the way to govern is to offer security to the people, which in turn involves feeling their suffering." The Central Committee paid great attention to the temporary difficulties encountered by some laid-off workers. Jiang Zemin emphasized on many occasions that the vast number of employees in state-owned enterprises had made significant contributions to national economic construction, Reform and Opening Up, and the development and growth of state-owned enterprises in previous decades. Party committees and governments at all levels should therefore always be concerned about them and earnestly safeguard their interests.

From May 14–17, 1998, the Central Committee of the Party and the State Council held a conference on the life security and reemployment of laid-off workers in Beijing to formulate measures for the diversion of laid-off workers from enterprises and the implementation of reemployment projects. Jiang pointed out at the meeting that this work was not only a major economic issue, but also a major political issue. Further, it was not only a pressing realistic issue, but also a long-term strategic issue. Party committees and governments at all levels needed to make proper execution of this task a top priority. The meeting put forward that the basic living expenses of laid-off workers must be guaranteed. Funds were shared by the government, enterprises, and other sectors of society. The basic living expenses were to be paid to every laid-off worker on time. They should not be delayed, misappropriated, or withheld. Otherwise, those in charge would be held accountable. The most important thing was to help laid-off workers with re-employment. This work was related to the success of the reform of state-owned enterprises, the vital interests of employees, the insurmountable stage in the process of reform, and the overall major undertakings and important tasks.

In June, the Central Committee and the State Council issued the Notice on Effectively Improving the Basic Living Security and Re-employment of Laid-off Workers in State-owned Enterprises, pointing out that in the coming period, in order to ensure the realization of the reform objectives of state-owned enterprises put forward by the Fifteenth National Congress of the Communist Party of

China and complete the strategic adjustment of the state-owned economy, it was necessary to ensure that the number of re-employed workers was greater than that of laid-off workers. In 1998, more than 50% of previously laid-off workers and those made redundant that year were re-employed. This meant that it would take about five years to establish a preliminary social security system and employment mechanism to meet the requirements of the socialist market economic system.

Central leaders also went to the grassroots level many times to investigate and study the employment and livelihood of laid-off workers and to console the people living in difficult circumstances. Local governments established three guarantee lines for laid-off workers in accordance with the Central Government's deployment. First, a basic living allowance was offered to laid-off workers. Second, people still unemployed after three years would be entitled to unemployment insurance. And third, those who had not been employed for two years could enjoy a minimum living allowance for urban residents, according to regulations. Meanwhile, governments at all levels strengthened various forms of vocational training, broadened employment channels, established re-employment service centers, guided workers to change their concept of career choice, and vigorously promoted the re-employment projects for laid-off workers. From 1998 to 2000, 21 million laid-off workers from state-owned enterprises entered reemployment service centers nationwide, of which 13 million were reemployed, providing a strong guarantee for the smooth progress of the reform of state-owned enterprises.

3. Strengthening the Party's Leadership Over Large State-Owned Enterprises

In order to strengthen the leadership of large and medium-sized state-owned enterprises, on July 9, 1998, with the approval of the Central Committee, the Central Working Committee on Large and Medium-sized Enterprises was established, with Wu Bangguo, a member of the Politburo of the Central Committee and Vice Premier of the State Council, as secretary. Its duties were to manage the leading positions of the Party in large state-owned enterprises and state-holding enterprises under the supervision of the State Council, so as to promote the implementation of the Party's line, policy, and related spirit of the Party Central Committee and the State Council in large state-owned enterprises, to study, explore, reform, and strengthen the leadership of the Party in large state-owned enterprises in accordance with the requirements of the socialist market economic system and the establishment of a modern enterprise system team building, and to complete other related work assigned by the Central Committee. The State Council also stipulated that government organs were strictly prohibited from providing guarantees for enterprises' economic activities. The implementation of these supporting measures accelerated the pace at which state-owned enterprises were reformed.

During this period, the Party Central Committee strengthened the investigation of state-owned enterprises, and the leaders of the Central Committee went to the front line many times to give concrete guidance to the reform. From April to August 1999, Jiang Zemin visited Chengdu, Wuhan, Xi'an, Qingdao, and Dalian, hosted a series of symposiums, and made important comments on the reform and development of state-owned enterprises. He pointed out that promoting the comprehensive reform and development of state-owned enterprises was an indispensable and insurmountable barrier. Fighting this battle well was not only related to the success of the reform of state-owned enterprises, but also to the success of the reform of the entire economic system. It was important to seize the opportunity, put forth great determination and effort to resolve the deep-seated contradictions and problems faced by state-owned enterprises, and further enhance the vitality of state-owned enterprises. The state should concentrate its efforts on developing a number of large enterprises and large enterprise groups in important industries and key areas that were closely related to the lifeline of the national economy, so as to make them the main force of the national economy. State-owned small and medium-sized enterprises should adopt various forms to be liberalized and invigorated, and they should be encouraged to adopt more flexible management methods and accelerate their development. A modern enterprise system was the basic system for developing enterprises under the condition of a socialist market economy. Without the establishment of an effective mechanism for enterprise management and market operations, the socialist market economic system could not be established, and the organic combination of public ownership and the market economy was unlikely to ever be realized. In the reform of state-owned enterprises, it was important to pay attention to strengthening the leadership of the Party. These important speeches further pointed out the direction for the reform of state-owned enterprises.

In September 1999, the Fourth Plenary Session of the Fifteenth Central

Committee of the Communist Party of China further discussed the reform and development of state-owned enterprises, adopted the Decision of the Central Committee of the Communist Party of China on Several Major Issues Concerning the Reform and Development of State-owned Enterprises (hereinafter referred to as the Decision), and set the goal for the reform and development of the state. The Decision pointed out that the reform of state-owned enterprises was a broad and profound change. To enhance the economic strength, national defense strength, and national cohesion of the country, it was necessary to constantly promote the development and growth of the state-owned economy and generally enhance the vitality of state-owned enterprises and the control of the state-owned economy. This was of great significance to the establishment of a socialist market economic system, the promotion of sustained, rapid, and healthy economic development, the improvement of people's living standards, the maintenance of a stable and united political situation, and the consolidation of the socialist system. To promote the reform and development of state-owned enterprises, it was necessary to put forth maximum effort to achieve the goals set by the Fifteenth National Congress and the First Plenary Session of the Fifteenth Central Committee. By 2010, in order to meet the requirements for two fundamental changes in the economic system and the mode of economic growth and to expand opening up, it was important to basically complete the strategic adjustment and reorganization of state-owned enterprises, form a more reasonable layout and structure of the state-owned economy, establish a relatively perfect modern enterprise system, and significantly improve the economic benefits, as well as the ability to develop science and technology to compete in the market and to endure risks, so that the state-owned economy would play a better leading role in the national economy. The Decision also put forward a series of important policy measures, including adjusting the layout of the state-owned economy strategically, combining with the optimization and upgrading of the industrial structure and the adjustment of ownership, sticking to making progress rationally and being selective about what to do; differentiating different situations, continuing to implement strategic restructuring of state-owned enterprises; stressing the separation of government and enterprises; and exploring the effective form of state-owned assets management. It was important to establish and improve a modern enterprise system through standardized reform of the company system and transformation of the operation mechanism, gradually solve the problems of excessive debt ratio, insufficient capital, and the heavy social burden of state-owned enterprises, do well in reducing staff and increasing efficiency, re-employment, and social security, speed up technological progress and industrial upgrading, strengthen the leadership of the Party in the reform and development of state-owned enterprises, and engage in other similar endeavors.

The above goals, policies, and measures clarified the overall thinking and the policy of the reform of state-owned enterprises. They not only had guiding significance for the three-year goal of reform and extrication from difficulties, but also for the cross-century development of state-owned enterprises.

Under the guidance of the spirit of the Fourth Plenary Session of the Fifteenth Central Committee, state-owned enterprises continued to make great strides in pushing forward the in-depth reform and tackling the key problems at multiple levels. From 1998 to 2000, more than 2,700 pilot enterprises with a modern enterprise system established by the Central Government and selected by various localities mostly carried out the reform of the company and joint-share-holding systems. Of the 520 state-owned and state-owned holding enterprises listed in state-owned key enterprises, 430 (83.7%) carried out reform of the company system. By the end of 2000, 6,599 large and medium-sized state-owned and state-holding enterprises, which lost money in 1997, had been reduced by more than 70%. The profits of state-owned and state-controlled industrial enterprises had reached 239.2 billion yuan, an increase of 197 times over that of 80.6 billion yuan in 1997. The profits of small and medium-sized state-owned enterprises had also reached 4.81 billion yuan, ending the trend of net loss that had prevailed for the previous six consecutive years.[3] Many state-owned enterprises, which had been in difficulty for a long time, entered a period of reform and development of state-owned enterprises, basically achieving the three-year goal of the reform of large and medium-sized state-owned enterprises put forward by the Fifteenth National Congress. This was the result of the Central Committee seizing the opportunity and making correct decisions at the critical stage of reform and development. It was also a great contribution made by the working class and the Party to the country's economic construction and reform.

III

Adherence to "One Country, Two Systems" for the Great Cause of National Reunification

The great undertaking of adherence to the principle of "one country, two systems" and promoting the reunification of the motherland was launched in the 1980s, achieving positive results. In the 1990s, great progress was made in this undertaking.

1. Eight Proposals for Developing Cross-Strait Relations

After the 1980s, with the proposal of the CPC's "one country, two systems" policy and the historic and significant changes taking place in the Mainland, the Kuomintang authorities in Taiwan were forced to adjust their Mainland policy. In 1987, Chiang Ching-kuo declared that martial law in Taiwan would be lifted from July 15. He then opened up channels for Taiwanese compatriots to visit relatives in the Mainland. After this, the long-term isolation of compatriots on both sides of the Straits was finally broken. Taiwanese compatriots came to the Mainland in large numbers to visit relatives, travel, and do business, and the economic and trade relations between the two sides of the Taiwan Strait expanded rapidly.

The Central Committee of the Communist Party of China attached great importance to this new change in cross-strait relations and actively promoted the further development of cross-strait relations. In December 1990, the Central Committee of the Communist Party of China convened a national working conference on Taiwan. It pointed out that the top priority for Taiwan work was to strengthen cross-strait ties, further expand personnel and various exchanges, especially economic and trade exchanges, and achieve two-way and direct "three links." On March 5, 1994, the Sixth Session of the Standing Committee of the Eighth National People's Congress passed the Law of the People's Republic of China on the Protection of Taiwanese Compatriots' Investment, bringing the protection of Taiwanese businessmen's investments onto a legal track and further promoting the development of cross-strait economic relations. In April 1994, the Central Committee of the Communist Party of China and the State Council held a special conference on Taiwan's economic work, comprehensively summarized the successful experience of the development of cross-strait economic relations, and put forward the principle of "giving equal priority to and appropriately relaxing" the areas and projects in which Taiwanese businessmen had invested. All regions and departments were to attach great importance to the economic work against Taiwan, take effective measures to protect the legitimate rights and interests of Taiwanese businessmen in the Mainland, and improve the investment environment of Taiwanese businessmen in the Mainland.

In order to facilitate substantive progress in cross-strait relations and establish channels for cross-strait communication, on December 16, 1991, the Mainland established the Association for Cross-Strait Relations. This was a non-governmental organization aimed at promoting cross-strait exchanges, developing cross-strait relations, and achieving peaceful reunification of the motherland. In March 1992, the Association for Cross-Strait Relations and the Taiwan Strait Exchange Foundation began business talks. In order to clearly adhere to the one-China principle, Tang Shubei, the executive vice-president of the Shanghai Association, made a further elaboration on the attitude of adherence to the one-China principle in cross-strait business negotiations after the first working talks ended in March 1992. In this regard, the Taiwan side had to express its position of "adhering to the one-China principle" and recognize the fact that Taiwan was part of China's territory. After many consultations, the two sessions reached their "1992 Consensus" of verbally expressing "both sides adhere to the one-China principle."

On August 4, 1992, President Wang Daohan of the Association for Relations Across the Taiwan Straits (ARATS) sent a letter to Gu Zhenfu, chairman of the Straits Exchange Foundation (SEF), hoping to hold talks on cross-strait economic development and conference affairs for the two sessions. On the 22nd, the SEF responded by accepting the invitation. After many preparatory consultations, from April 27–28, 1993, Wang Daohan, President of ARATS, held his first meeting with Gu Zhenfu, Chairman of the SEF, in Singapore. Although the talks were merely non-official, economic, transactional, and functional, they were of great significance and attracted worldwide attention. The two sides reached the Wang-Gu Talks Common Agreement, the Agreement on Liaison and Talks between the Two Conferences, and other documents. From that time, in order to implement the agreements reached during the Wang-Gu Talks, from August 1993 to January 1995, the ARATS and the SEF held six working talks at the level of Under Secretary General in Beijing, Taipei, and Nanjing. Tang Shubei, the executive vice-president of the Association, also went to Taiwan for discussions with Jiao

Ren, vice-chairman and secretary-general of the SEF, to reach specific consensus on the settlement of cross-strait maritime fishing disputes, on the repatriation of aircraft hijackers, and on repatriation of people entering the other party's area in violation of relevant provisions and related issues. The two sides believed that strengthening multi-level communication between the two sessions was conducive to further enhancing understanding, eliminating misunderstandings, narrowing differences, and fostering mutual trust.

In order to clarify the principles and policies of the Chinese government on the Taiwan issue in China and abroad, on January 30, 1995, on behalf of the Communist Party of China and the Chinese government, Jiang Zemin delivered an important speech entitled "Continuing to Struggle for the Completion of the Great Cause of the Reunification of the Motherland." He put forward eight proposals for developing cross-strait relations at this stage and promoting the process of peaceful reunification of the motherland. These included 1) adhering to the one-China principle as the basis and prerequisite for achieving peaceful reunification, 2) systematically conducting negotiations on peaceful reunification across the Taiwan Strait, 3) making efforts to achieve peaceful reunification without a commitment to abandon the use of force, 4) vigorous development of cross-strait economic exchanges and cooperation in the 21st century, 5) compatriots on both sides jointly inheriting and developing the fine traditions of Chinese culture, 6) further hope put on Taiwan compatriots, 7) welcoming all parties and people from all walks of life in Taiwan to exchange views with the Mainland on cross-strait relations and peaceful reunification, and 8) leaders of the two sides exchanging visits in appropriate capacities. The eight propositions put forward by Jiang Zemin further promoted the nine principles put forward by Ye Jianying in 1981, which made Deng Xiaoping's thought of "peaceful reunification of one country with two systems" more specific in terms of premises, principles, methods, and steps. These eight propositions embodied not only the consistency and continuity of the principles and policies of the Communist Party of China and the Chinese government toward Taiwan, but also the firm determination and great sincerity of the CPC and the Chinese government in developing cross-strait relations and realizing the peaceful reunification of the motherland. They were programmatic documents for resolving the Taiwan issue in the new period and had strong practical and far-reaching historical significance.

2. Successful Resolution of the Return of Hong Kong and Macao to the Motherland

With the smooth development of cross-strait relations, the countdown to the return of Hong Kong and Macao began. Although there were many reasons for the continuous development of relations between Taiwan, Hong Kong, Macao, and the Mainland, the most fundamental one was the policy of "one country, two systems." Although the concept of "one country, two systems" was initially put forward to solve the Taiwan issue, it was first successfully applied to the Hong Kong and Macao issues.

The Hong Kong situation was a lingering historical issue of British colonial aggression against China. Hong Kong included three parts, Hong Kong Island, Kowloon, and the New Territories, which had been Chinese territory since ancient times. After the Opium War in 1840, Britain forced the Qing government to sign three unequal treaties, namely the Nanjing Treaty, the Beijing Treaty, and the Special Article on the Development of Hong Kong Border Sites, then occupied Hong Kong, Kowloon, and the New Territories, plunging Hong Kong into a period of British colonial rule. None of the previous Chinese governments after the 1911 Revolution recognized the above-mentioned unequal treaties, and they had many negotiations with Britain to restore Hong Kong. On the eve of the founding of New China, due to the special internal and external environments, the Central Committee and Mao Zedong decided to "temporarily leave Hong Kong alone." After the founding of the People's Republic of China in 1949, the Chinese government adopted the policy of "long-term planning and full utilization" towards Hong Kong. It did not recognize the three unequal treaties imposed on China by imperialism. However, considering the historical circumstances, it temporarily maintained the status quo of Hong Kong and decided to settle the issue peacefully through negotiations at an appropriate time.

After entering the new period of Reform and Opening Up, with the approach of Hong Kong's "lease" period, the Communist Party of China began to consider the issue of restoring Hong Kong's sovereignty under the policy of "one country, two systems." Since October 1982, after twenty-two rounds of arduous negotiations in three stages, the heads of state of China and Britain signed the Joint Statement on Hong Kong on December 19, 1984. The statement declared that the Chinese government would resume the exercise of sovereignty over Hong Kong on July 1,

1997, and that the British government would return Hong Kong to China on the same day. In accordance with the relevant provisions of the joint statement, the handover ceremony between China, Britain, and Hong Kong was held in Hong Kong from midnight on June 30 to early morning on July 1, 1997. The successful return of Hong Kong was the result of the successful implementation of the concept of "one country, two systems." It symbolized that the Chinese people had washed away the century-old national shame of Hong Kong's occupation and that Hong Kong's development had entered a new era.

When the process of Hong Kong's return started, the issue of Macao's return was put on the agenda. In 1974, the Portuguese government announced that it would abandon all its overseas colonies and recognized that Macao was not a colony but a Chinese territory. In February 1979, China and Portugal established diplomatic relations. The two sides reached an understanding on the Macao issue, and the Portuguese government recognized Macao as China's territory. The two sides agreed to resolve the issue through negotiations between the two governments at an appropriate time. In June 1986, the Chinese and Portuguese governments began negotiations on Macao. On April 13, 1987, the Prime Ministers of the Chinese and Portuguese governments formally signed the Joint Statement on Macao between the government of the People's Republic of China and the government of the Portuguese Republic in Beijing, which announced that Macao was China's territory, and the government of the People's Republic of China would resume the exercise of sovereignty over Macao on December 20, 1999. From midnight on December 19 to early morning on December 20, 1999, with the participation of the country's top leaders, the government delegations of China and Portugal held a grand ceremony of regime transfer in Macao. President Jiang Zemin solemnly declared that the Chinese government would resume the exercise of sovereignty over Macao.

The smooth return of Hong Kong and Macao ushered in a new era of common development between Hong Kong, Macao, and the Mainland. Resolving the issues of Hong Kong and Macao's return through diplomatic negotiation and "one country, two systems" was a great pioneering work of the CPC on the path of the localization of Marxism and a great contribution made by the Chinese people to the cause of peaceful world development and progress. The successful practice after the return of Hong Kong and Macao proved that "one country, two systems" was not only the most realistic way to realize the reunification of the motherland, but also the most important institutional guarantee for the stability, prosperity, and development of the returned areas.

3. Promoting an Early Settlement of the Taiwan Issue in Accordance with the "One Country, Two Systems" Policy

In the late 1980s, great changes took place in Taiwan's internal affairs. With the lifting of martial law and the localization of real administrative power, the forces of "Taiwan independence" grew more active. From the beginning of 1988, when Lee Teng-hui came to power, to 2000, he purged dissidents and consolidated his position through various conspiracies. He gradually abandoned the one-China principle and pursued the policy of division to create "two Chinas." After 1993, Taiwanese authorities stepped up their actions, such as seeking to "participate in the United Nations" and engaging in so-called "holiday diplomacy" and "money diplomacy," deliberately creating "two Chinas" and "one China, one Taiwan" in the international community. In particular, in June 1995, with the permission of the American government, Lee Teng-hui visited the United States and made a public political speech at Cornell University, repeatedly emphasizing the "Republic of China in Taiwan" and stepping up the activities of "two Chinas" in the international arena. At the same time, Taiwan held successive "military drills" against the Mainland, creating tension between the two sides.

The Chinese government and people had always remained vigilant against the growing separatist activities of Taiwanese authorities and had waged resolute anti-secession and anti-Taiwanese independence struggles from the political, military, diplomatic, and public opinions perspectives. The Chinese people's struggle against separatism and "Taiwanese independence" had effectively attacked the separatist forces advocating "Taiwanese independence" in Taiwan, made the international community further understand the harmfulness of "Taiwanese independence," and made the broad masses of Taiwanese people further realize that "Taiwanese independence" was a dead end. The United States government also made a commitment to continue to pursue the "one-China" policy and expressed its non-support for Taiwan's independence. Under various pressures, Taiwan's leaders had to say that there was no need and would not be an immediate declaration of "Taiwanese independence."

Due to Lee Teng-hui's visit to the United States, the second Wang-Gu Talks could not proceed as planned, and the talks at all levels of the two sessions had to be completely suspended. In order to ease and improve cross-strait relations, the Taiwan Affairs Office of the Central Committee of the CPC, the Taiwan Affairs Office of the State Council, and the Maritime Association expressed their willingness to resume negotiations under the one-China principle. In September 1997, in the report of the Fifteenth National Congress of the Communist Party of China, Jiang Zemin once again solemnly appealed to the Taiwan authorities to hold political negotiations with the CPC as early as possible. After many consultations, from October 14-19, 1998, Gu Zhenfu led a delegation of Taiwan's SEF to visit the Mainland. Jiang Zemin met with Gu Zhenfu and his wife. Wang Daohan and Gu Zhenfu met twice, reaching four consensus points, initiating the prelude of cross-strait political dialogue and improving the atmosphere of cross-strait relations.

However, while insightful people in the Mainland and Taiwan actively promoted the development of cross-strait relations, Taiwanese authorities chose the path of continued destruction and confrontation. On July 9, 1999, Lee Teng-hui publicly put forward the "two-state theory," claiming that cross-strait relations were "state-to-state, or at least special state-to-state relations." In March 2000, in Taiwan's elections, the Kuomintang was defeated, and Chen Shui-bian, leader of the Democratic Progressive Party, was elected as Taiwan's new leader. Although at the beginning of his presidency, he repeatedly advocated the "sincerity" and "goodwill" of reopening the two dialogue sessions and improving cross-strait relations, he nevertheless adopted an evasive, vague, and resistant attitude toward the key issue of accepting the one-China principle. From that time, he not only denied the existence of the 1992 Consensus and deliberately obstructed the resumption of cross-strait negotiations, but also used various means to gradually implement the Taiwan Independence Program. On August 3, 2002, Chen Shui-bian delivered a televised speech at the 29th Annual Conference of the World Federation of Taiwan Fellow Citizens, held in Tokyo, Japan. He publicly claimed that "Taiwan is one country on the other side of China" and advocated a "referendum" to determine "Taiwan's future, destiny, and present situation," which exposed the essence of his stubborn adherence to "Taiwanese independence."

Both the "two-state theory" and the "one-side-one-country theory" were statements that led Taiwan to disaster rather than to the well-being of the people of Taiwan. As soon as these remarks were disseminated, they were firmly opposed by all the Chinese people, including Taiwanese compatriots. People from all walks of life throughout the country, as well as Mainlanders and ethnic Chinese living overseas, strongly condemned the statements and actions of the Taiwan authorities in splitting the motherland.

Although Taiwanese authorities restricted and obstructed the further development of cross-strait relations with numerous divisive activities, the various exchanges and cooperation between the two sides were irresistible. With the increase of people-to-people exchanges between the two sides of the Taiwan Strait, Taiwanese compatriots gained a better understanding of the situation in the motherland and the Mainland. More people realized that Taiwan's development and future could not be separated from the motherland and the Mainland. Economic and trade exchanges were the most active and vibrant factors in cross-strait relations. As of October 2002, Taiwanese businessmen had invested more than 55,000 yuan in the Chinese Mainland, with a contract capital of more than 60 billion US dollars. The total trade volume between the two sides reached more than 260 billion US dollars.[4] Under such circumstances, the Taiwanese people urgently demanded the realization of direct "three links." With the Mainland and Taiwan both joining the WTO, the Mainland had established closer economic relations with Taiwan, Hong Kong, and Macao. This trend would undoubtedly further increase the common economic interests of the people on both sides of the Strait, promote the common economic development and prosperity of the two sides, and become an important force in maintaining and promoting cross-strait relations and realizing the reunification of the motherland.

The progress of the CPC in promoting the great cause of the reunification of the motherland clearly indicated that "peaceful reunification of one country with two systems" was the basic principle of reunification, and it was a creative development in Marxist strategic thinking by the CPC on how to achieve the reunification of the country. The efforts of the CPC toward promoting the peaceful reunification of the motherland represented the common desire and interests of all the people of the country and compatriots in China and abroad. Adherence to this basic principle and realization of the complete reunification of the motherland at an early date was an unshakable conviction of all Chinese people and the irreversible trend of historical development.

IV

Forging a Comprehensive Pattern for Foreign Relations in the New Century

Adhering to and developing the thought of peaceful, independent diplomacy was a new contribution of the CPC to the treasure house of Marxist thought on diplomacy in the 20th century. This idea further strengthened the ability of the CPC to deal with international affairs in its diplomatic contacts. The construction of an all-round, multi-level diplomatic relationship pattern, the rapid development of various partnerships, and frequent diplomatic activities of the leaders were all manifestations of the enhancement of the ability of the CPC to deal with international affairs. All of these reflected the promotion and development of Marxist diplomatic thought by the CPC in a "newer" sense.

From a practical point of view, since the mid-1990s, China's diplomatic work mainly faced three tasks. The first was to cope with the changes in international relations brought about by the trend of multi-polarization and to establish a comprehensive and multi-level pattern of foreign relations for the 21st century. The second was to oppose various expressions of hegemony and power politics, to maintain world peace, and to promote the establishment of a more just and rational country. The new international political and economic order aimed to safeguard the rights and interests of all countries in the world, especially developing countries. Finally, the third was that the CPC should deal with the impact of the trend of economic globalization and the rapid development of high technology on China.

Under the leadership of the Central Committee, led by Jiang Zemin, China fully implemented the established basic foreign policies and enriched and developed its ideological connotation in accordance with the changes of the international situation and new practice. China's diplomatic independence and autonomy were more distinct. Its prominent manifestations were first, from national interests, it was important to always put the sovereignty and security of the country in the primary position and never allow any country to interfere in China's internal affairs. Second, it was necessary to adhere to the principle of independent decision-making on the areas and speed of opening up according to national conditions. The CPC should not only stick to opening up and make full use of the favorable conditions and opportunities brought about by economic globalization, but also keep a clear understanding of the risks that may be encountered, reinforce prevention, and earnestly safeguard national economic security. Third, the Party should stick to true non-alignment. Not only did China refrain from forming alliances with any other country, but it also did not carry the flag of the world socialist movement or take the lead in developing countries. Fourth, China should respect the diversity of the world, handle international affairs in a spirit of mutual respect and seeking common ground while shelving differences, and promote the democratization of international relations.

China's diplomacy also indicated some new features in its form. For one, summit diplomacy had played an unprecedented and irreplaceable role. The frequent appearance of Chinese leaders on important international occasions had expanded China's international influence and demonstrated the improvement of China's international status. In addition, in China's partnership and cooperation with other countries and regional organizations, regular meetings, consultations, and dialogues at different levels had been generally established. This new mechanism not only improved the effectiveness of bilateral and multilateral cooperation, but also contributed to the stability and further development of relations between all parties. Finally, the Communist Party of China paid attention to practical results and extensively exchanged and cooperated with the ruling parties and legitimate opposition parties in various countries in the world, so that the relationship between the parties served the national development strategy and overall foreign diplomacy, and provided an important guarantee for the long-term stability and healthy development of national relations.

At the turn of the century, China had basically established an all-round, multi-level pattern of diplomatic relations. Since Reform and Opening Up, China's diplomacy had been developing in this direction, and in the second half of the 1990s, great progress was made in this work. In constructing the pattern of foreign relations facing the 21st century, China had taken into account not only the relations with major powers and developed countries, but also with neighboring countries and developing countries as well. It attached great importance to the bilateral relations between countries and actively carried out multilateral diplomatic activities. It also attached importance to the relations with governments of various countries, as well as the relations between the Communist

Party of China and political parties of all countries in the world. It also paid attention to various forms of non-governmental diplomacy.

Stabilization and development of relations with major and developed countries were of great significance to China's socialist modernization and the maintenance of world peace and development. In the mid-1990s, China's leaders proposed that China should actively devote itself to the development of a new type of big power relations characterized by non-alignment, non-confrontation, and non-targeting of third parties. According to this principle, China established and developed the basic framework of bilateral relations facing the 21st century with Russia, the United States, France, Britain, Japan, Canada, and the European Union.

China was the largest developing country in the world and the United States the largest developed country in the world. There were always some contradictions and differences between the two, some of which would be difficult to eliminate even over a long time. However, on major issues related to world peace and development, the two countries shared common interests. Because of this, although Sino-US relations had ups and downs, the general trend was to continue to move forward. China's leaders had always looked at Sino-US relations from a strategic, long-term perspective, adhered to the three Sino-US joint communiqués as the basis for the development of bilateral relations, advocated that the differences between the two countries should be correctly handled in the spirit of mutual respect, equal consultation, and seeking common ground while reserving differences, and actively sought the convergence of common interests. In October 1997, President Jiang Zemin paid a state visit to the United States. Both sides announced that they would work together to establish a constructive strategic partnership for the 21st century. Maintaining and developing healthy and stable relations between China and the United States was not only in the fundamental interests of the two peoples, but also conducive to peace, stability, and development in the Asia-Pacific region and the whole world.

China and Russia were each other's largest neighboring countries. In 1991, when the Soviet Union disintegrated, China and Russia immediately established diplomatic relations, thus achieving a smooth transition between China and the Soviet Union in relation to Sino-Russian relations. From that time, bilateral relations entered a new stage of mutual respect, good-neighborliness, and friendship. In the latter half of the 1990s, Sino-Russian relations made more obvious progress. In April 1996, President Boris Yeltsin paid a state visit to China. China and Russia signed a Joint Statement, declaring that they were "determined to develop a strategic partnership of cooperation oriented to the 21st century with equality and trust." In April 1997, President Jiang Zemin paid a state visit to Russia. The two countries signed the Joint Statement on World Multi-polarization and the Establishment of a New International Order, expressing their willingness to work together for the establishment of a peaceful, stable, just, and rational new international political and economic order. President Jiang Zemin paid a state visit to Russia in July 2001. The two heads of state officially signed the Treaty of Good-Neighborliness, Friendship, and Cooperation between China and Russia, an important milestone in bilateral relations. China and Russia became good neighbors with a friendly coexistence, and their exchanges and cooperation in many fields had broad prospects for development.

China's relations with Western Europe basically returned to normal after 1991 and entered a stage of steady development. Frequent exchanges of visits between China and European heads of state had strongly promoted the development of bilateral relations. During his visit to France in September 1994, President Jiang Zemin put forward four principles of China-Western Europe relations and expressed his willingness to face the 21st century and develop long-term and stable friendly cooperative relations. In 1997 and 1998, China established comprehensive partnerships with France and Britain. As an important regional organization, the EU had taken a series of measures which were conducive to the development of China-EU relations. In 1998, the first meeting between leaders of China and the European Union was held in London. The two sides issued a joint statement emphasizing their willingness to establish a long-term, stable constructive partnership for the 21st century. Subsequently, the EU decided to elevate its relations with China to the same level as those of the United States, Japan, and Russia. With the joint efforts of both sides, China's cooperation with European countries in various fields showed good prospects.

China and Japan were neighbors with only a strip of water separating them. Since the normalization of diplomatic relations in 1972 and the signing of the Treaty of Peace and Friendship in 1978, Sino-Japanese relations had entered a new era of comprehensive development, and bilateral relations had made progress in various fields. In 1998, President Jiang Zemin paid a state visit to Japan. The two sides issued the Sino-Japanese Joint Declaration, announcing that China and Japan would establish "friendly cooperative relations committed to peace and development." At the same time, for the first time, Japan acknowledged its aggression against China, expressed profound reflection and apology, and jointly confirmed with China that a correct understanding and treatment of history was an important basis for the development of Sino-Japanese relations. As a result, the overall development of Sino-Japanese relations was smooth. The friendly exchanges and mutually beneficial cooperation between the two sides in various fields made continuous progress, bringing important benefits to the two countries and making positive contributions to peace, stability, and development in the region and the world.

Actively developing good-neighborly and friendly relations with neighboring countries, maintaining peace and stability, and promoting common development was one of the important objectives of China's diplomacy. In the early 1990s, China normalized its relations with all neighboring countries. From that time, China's relations with its neighboring countries continued to develop. China established diplomatic relations with Central Asian countries and the "Shanghai Five Nations" mechanism, as well as the "Shanghai Cooperation Organization" of China, Russia, Kazakhstan, Kyrgyzstan, and Tajikistan, plus Uzbekistan, and participated in the six-party talks aimed at establishing a peace mechanism on the Korean Peninsula, which made positive contributions to maintaining peace and stability on the Korean Peninsula and in Northeast Asia.

The relationship between China and ASEAN attracted great attention. In 1996, China became a partner of ASEAN's comprehensive dialogue. At the end of 1997, the two sides issued the Joint Statement of the China-ASEAN Summit, which defined the goal of establishing a good-neighborly and mutual trust partnership facing the 21st century and the principles guiding bilateral relations. On disputed issues such as the South China Sea, China made it clear that it was willing to properly resolve disputes with relevant countries through peaceful negotiations in accordance with recognized international law and other principles and legal systems. After the outbreak of the Asian financial crisis, China provided assistance to the countries concerned through bilateral and multilateral channels and fulfilled its promise of non-devaluation of the RMB, which was widely praised by the international community. After entering the 21st century, the mutually beneficial cooperation between China and ASEAN countries in various fields expanded and played an important role in promoting regional peace and stability.

Consolidating and developing friendly and cooperative relations with South Asian countries was an important component of China's stability around the world. In November 1996, President Jiang Zemin paid a state visit to India. During his visit to India, President Jiang put forward five propositions for building long-term and stable good-neighborly relations between China and South Asian countries for the future. The two countries decided to establish a constructive partnership of cooperation for the future on the basis of the Five Principles of Peaceful Coexistence. Subsequently, China and Pakistan also announced the establishment of a comprehensive partnership for the 21st century. At the beginning of 2002, the new Afghan government was established, and the Chinese government immediately recognized and supported it. The improvement and development of China's relations with other countries in South Asia played an important role in maintaining peace and stability in the region.

Active multilateral diplomacy was a prominent feature of China's diplomacy at the turn of the century. In 1971, after resuming its legitimate seat in the United Nations, China began to gradually participate in various fields of multilateral diplomacy centering around the United Nations. In the mid-1980s, China clearly listed multilateral diplomacy as a major part of its independent and peaceful foreign policy. In the 1990s, China became more active in the field of multilateral diplomacy and made remarkable achievements.

Opposing hegemony and power politics and safeguarding the rights and interests of developing countries were important principles that China followed in multilateral diplomatic activities. After the end of the Cold War, in the face of Western countries' interference in the internal affairs of developing countries under various pretexts in the field of multilateral diplomacy, China always adhered to the principles of respecting national sovereignty and independence, non-interference in internal affairs, equality, and mutual benefit, working closely with developing countries and supporting each other while effectively resisting and fighting against various hegemonic acts in international relations. Since 1990, with the support of Third World countries, China defeated the anti-China proposals put forward by Western countries ten times in succession at the UN Human Rights Commission. China supported and actively participated in a series of useful work of the United Nations and other organizations aimed at promoting North-South dialogue and strengthening South-South cooperation. China established effective cooperation with the Group of 77 nations and participated in the Non-Aligned Movement as an observer.

The establishment of a new international political and economic order was a major issue in contemporary international relations. As early as the late 1980s, Deng Xiaoping put forward the idea of establishing a new international political and economic order on the basis of the Five Principles of Peaceful Coexistence. After the end of the Cold War, this problem became even more prominent. The Chinese government believed that the new international political and economic order should guarantee the rights of all countries to sovereign equality and non-interference in their internal affairs, equal participation in international affairs, and equal rights to development, especially those of developing countries. China held that the Five Principles of Peaceful Coexistence, the purposes and principles of the Charter of the United Nations, and other generally recognized norms of international law should be the political basis of the new international order. In March 1999, President Jiang Zemin gave a speech during his visit to Switzerland, comprehensively expounding China's basic proposals for establishing a new international political and economic order.

In the 1990s, an important part of China's multilateral diplomacy was the negotiation of accession to the World Trade Organization. For historical reasons, New China did not participate in GATT for some time after its founding. After China's Reform and Opening Up, in order to meet the needs of the development of the situation, in July 1986, the Central Committee of the Party made a decision to apply for the restoration of the status of the contracting parties to the GATT, then set up a specialized agency to organize foreign negotiations in a unified way. Negotiations on China's "customs clearance" and accession to the WTO were conducted under the leadership of the Central Committee of the Communist Party of China. During the 15-year negotiation process, China always adhered to three principles: 1) as an international organization, the WTO was incomplete without the participation of China, the largest developing country, 2) China could only participate as a developing country, and 3) China's accession to the WTO required a balance of rights and obligations. After continuous effort and difficult negotiations, China finally reached an agreement with all parties concerned. On November 10, 2001, the Fourth Ministerial Conference of the World Trade Organization, held in Doha, Qatar, deliberated and adopted by consensus the decision of China's accession to the WTO. China's accession to the WTO was a great step toward it becoming a truly global trade organization and exerted a great influence on China's economic system reform and economic development.

In the 1990s, China initiated and participated in a series of regional multilateral organizations with an open attitude. China clearly supported multi-form, multi-level, and multi-channel regional dialogue and cooperation on the basis of equal participation consensus, seeking common ground while shelving differences, making steady progress, and actively promoting multilateral confidence-building measures with neighboring countries, safeguarded regional security and stability, and promoted regional economic development. In October 2001, the ninth APEC Leaders' Informal Meeting was held in Shanghai. This was the highest-level and largest international conference ever held in China. The successful hosting of this conference played a positive role in promoting economic recovery and development in the Asia-Pacific region.

At the beginning of the 21st century, although the international situation was changing, the general trend of development had not changed. The Sixteenth National Congress of the Communist Party of China, held in November 2002, pointed out that peace and development were still the themes of the present era. Maintaining world peace and promoting common development were the common aspirations of all peoples and irresistible historical trends. The trend of world multi-polarization and economic globalization had brought opportunities and favorable conditions for world peace and development. A new world war would not be possible in the foreseeable future. It was possible to strive for a long period of peace in the international environment and a good surrounding environment. China would unswervingly pursue an independent foreign policy of peace with the purpose of safeguarding world peace and promoting common development.

V

Forging Ahead with Military Revolution with Chinese Characteristics

A new military strategy established by the Central Committee of the Communist Party of China in the 1990s and after entering the new century saw China's army base its preparations for military struggle on winning local wars through high technology and information technology, and strengthening the quality of army building accordingly. This strategic policy, further developed on the basis of that in the 1980s, was more in line with the scientific and technological background of the 1990s and the requirements of strategic military development.

1. Establishing China's Strategic Military Policy in a High-Tech Environment

In the early 1990s, two remarkable changes took place in the world military situation. The first was the end of the Cold War and the collapse of Warsaw Treaty Organization, one of the two major military groups, and the second was the revolutionary development of the application of advanced technology in the military field represented by microelectronics and information science. The first change made large-scale wars more impossible and local wars more likely. The second change would lead to ongoing military revolution. The military mode of the big industrial era, characterized by the dumping of steel, would become a thing of the past, while the arms competition between advanced and information technology was ascendant. Following this trend, countries all over the world accelerated military reform and strove to build a high-quality, low-quantity, reasonable, and competent armed force.

Faced with the new situation, the new Central Military Commission, under the leadership of Jiang Zemin, made another timely major adjustment to China's national defense strategy. At the enlarged meeting of the Military Commission held in early 1993, it was decided that the Chinese army's strategic principle should be based on winning local wars under the conditions of modern technology, especially high technology, so as to speed up the quality construction of the PLA and improve its emergency combat capabilities. In order to implement the new strategic policy, the CMC also put forward two fundamental changes centering on the idea of "strengthening the army by science and technology." This included the transformation from dealing with local wars under general conditions to winning local wars with modern technology, especially high-tech conditions, and the transformation from quantity-scale to quality-efficiency and manpower-intensive to technology-intensive military construction. This was the second adjustment of China's national defense strategy since the 1990s.

High-tech required high investment for strong backing, while national construction required that "the army should be patient" and "live a few years of a tight life." In response to this contradiction, China's defense research and equipment took a circuitous route to concentrating limited financial and material resources in the main area, so as to ensure that once something happened, there would be a "counter-attack" against any powerful enemy. However, the cost of doing so slowed down the pace of developing military equipment once again at the overall level, further widening the distance from the equipment level of developed countries in the world.

After Jiang Zemin assumed the chairmanship of the Military Commission, the direct problem he faced was how to build the army according to higher standards so as to speed up the pace of military construction and adjust the military strategy to adapt to the new, changing situations and tasks.

In December 1990, shortly after Jiang Zemin assumed the chairmanship of the Central Military Commission, at an important military working meeting held by the General Staff, he put forward the general requirements for military construction under the new situation, namely, "political qualifications, military excellence, strict discipline, strong support, and a good style of work." These five phrases constituted the fundamental direction of military construction in the new era, and also covered the basic content of military construction. This was the inheritance and development of Deng Xiaoping's general policy and task of "building a strong, modern, regular revolutionary army" in 1981.

After the formulation of the general requirements for military construction, the major issue to be solved was how to put forward the military strategic policy under the new situation. In response, Jiang Zemin, as chairman of the Military Commission, soon put forward that military strategy was ultimately the way to govern the country. To survive and develop a country or a nation, and to gain a firm foothold in the fierce international competition, it was necessary to have a proper strategic military policy.

So, in what direction was the new military strategy to be adjusted? This was a direct issue facing the new Military Commission. On November 9, 1992, Jiang Zemin made it clear at a military working conference that the international situation was developing rapidly. It was important to closely watch and grasp the development and changes of the situation and correctly determine China's strategic military policy.

Following Jiang Zemin's way of thinking, the Military Commission held a symposium on military strategy in December of that year. After thorough deliberation and discussion, General Zhang Zhen, Vice-Chairman of the Military Commission, made a preliminary summary of the new strategic military principles in his concluding speech at the symposium, saying that China should base itself on winning a local war through high-tech means. After the symposium, the General Staff Department organized many investigations according to the intention of the Military Commission. The Standing Committee of the Military Commission also held numerous discussions, ultimately unifying its understanding.

At the beginning of 1993, the enlarged meeting of the Central Military Commission was held. At the meeting, on behalf of the Central Military Commission, Jiang Zemin formally proposed the strategic military policy of China's army under the new situation, that is, "to prepare for military struggle on the basis of winning wars through modern technology, especially approaching local wars with high technology."

2. Promoting Military Reform Under the New Situation in the Direction of "Winning" and "Not Deteriorating"

Guided by the general requirements for military construction and the general principles of military strategy in the 1990s, the CMC led the entire army to carry out continuous, in-depth reform in all aspects of military and national defense construction, taking "winning" and "no deterioration" as the orientation and aiming at building up a competent army and strengthening it with science and technology.

1) *Further strengthening the ideological and political construction of the army.* The most important link in implementing the general requirement of building the

army in the new period was to persevere in the absolute leadership of the Party over the army and put ideological and political work at the top of all of the army's work.

After the Fourteenth National Congress of the CPC, the first decision made by the Central Military Commission was to reiterate and carry forward the tradition of the old Red Army and adhere to the principle of the Party's leadership in the army. The idea of adhering to the Party's absolute leadership in the army was extensively taught and thoroughly carried out throughout the army, so that the officers and soldiers strengthened their consciousness and firmness in obeying the Party's absolute leadership and adhering to the Party's basic line.

After the Fifteenth National Congress of the CPC, according to the unified deployment of the Central Committee, the entire army carried out learning and education activities from top to bottom, in stages and batches, with "emphasizing learning, politics, and righteousness" as the main topics, and carried out extensive educational activities to learn and practice the important thought of the "Three Represents." The Military Commission and the General Political Department also formulated a series of pertinent decisions, such as the Opinions of the General Political Department on Strengthening the Education and Management of Midlevel and Senior Military Cadres, the Opinions on Implementing the Decision of the CPC Central Committee on Strengthening and Improving the Party's Style of Work, and the Decision on Issues Concerning the Political and Ideological Construction of the Army Under the Conditions of Reform, Opening Up, and Development of the Socialist Market Economy. It was agreed and stipulated that the ideological and political work of the entire army was closely centered on the theme of ensuring the Party's ideological and political mastery of the army and constantly enhancing its self-awareness and firmness in following the Party's words. It was important to further enhance the education of theoretical armed forces and patriotic dedication, a revolutionary outlook on life, respect for cadres and soldiers, and an arduous struggle. It was important to fully implement the Outline of Military Grassroots Construction and strive to lay a solid foundation for military construction.

From 1992 to 2001, nearly 10,000 theoretical classes were held in the army, and 85% of cadres above regiment level received rotational training. The initiative of grassroots officers and soldiers in striving for excellence had been greatly enhanced. In the campaign of "striving for advanced companies and for excellent soldiers,"

60,000 advanced companies and 3.6 million excellent soldiers had emerged. Strong ideological and political work ensured the coordinated development and overall progress of military construction.

2) *Reforming the commander-in-chief organization of the Chinese People's Liberation Army.* The reform of the army in the 1990s was multifaceted, marked by the establishment of the General Equipment Department, and all the reforms were comprehensively carried forward. These reforms included the reform of the military commander-in-chief organization marked by the establishment of the general equipment department, the reform of the education and training system aimed at "winning," and the reform of the logistics support system marked by the joint logistics of the three forces.

On April 5, 1998, the General Equipment Department of the Chinese People's Liberation Army (PLA) was formally established, which was a major reform of the structure of the commanding organs of China's army. For a long time, the structure of the commanding organs of China's military had changed from three to four headquarters. The formation of "general equipment sector" meant that under the guidance of the new military strategy, the PLA would pay more attention to the development and improvement of weapons and equipment than ever before. Weapons and equipment were the material basis of "winning" and the establishment of a "general equipment sector" was of great significance for strengthening the leadership of research and production, unified management, and overall operations of weapons and equipment.

In order to solve the contradiction between the actual needs of the army and obedience to the overall situation of national economic construction, Jiang Zemin, Chairman of the Military Commission, put forward a very penetrating idea, which was to highlight the key points, be selective in determining what to do and in what areas to catch up, and to speed up the development of several "ace weapons" that would frighten any enemy. Under the guidance of this idea, after ten years of hard work, the army achieved renewal and the replacement of the main weapons such as battle tanks, naval vessels, and combat aircraft. It formed its own unique characteristics in some missile and anti-stealth technologies, and also made remarkable achievements in the field of aerospace.

3) *To improve the education and training system of the army and to again reduce its posts.* The fundamental factor determining victory or defeat in war was humans. The quality of humans was very important to victory or defeat in war under the

condition of modernization, especially in a local high-tech war. From the 1990s, the whole army carried out many powerful reforms in the education and training system for military personnel.

In order to train important military personnel, the Central Military Commission made major adjustments to the military academy system. In order to meet the needs of winning local high-tech wars and fostering human resources who could strengthen the army with science and technology, five comprehensive universities were newly established, including the National University of Defense Science and Technology, the Information Engineering College, the Polytechnic University, the Naval Engineering University, and the Air Force Engineering University. The training of military personnel also phased out the previous one dimensional mode and gradually turned to a parallel model of self-training and relying on national education. More than fifty colleges and universities, such as Peking University and Tsinghua University, had undertaken the task of training cadres for the army, producing a large number of outstanding individuals for the army each year.

According 2002 statistics, the army had more than 30,000 cadres with doctoral and master's degrees. The proportion of military, divisional, and regimental leaders with college education or above was 88%, 90%, and 75% respectively, and the proportion of military officers with college education or above was 71.8%.[5]

Another important measure for building up a competent army and strengthening the military with science and technology was to reduce military posts and take the path of training elite troops with Chinese characteristics. In September 1997, at the Fifteenth National Congress of the Communist Party of China, Jiang Zemin announced that, on the basis of the reduction of 1 million military posts in the 1980s, China would reduce another 500,000 military posts in three years. This important strategic decision was made in accordance with the new changes in the international situation and the internal laws of the army's own construction.

After broad disarmament since 1985, the PLA still had a total force of more than 3 million (including civilian personnel). Obviously, this amount was still on the high side, but large-scale disarmament was restricted by various factors inside and outside the army. It could not be accomplished overnight, but could only be carried out in a planned, systematic way. Disarmament of 500,000 yuan worth of equipment was a concrete arrangement for steadfastly and steadily reducing the number of troops and improving their quality. Its aftereffect would not only be a simple reduction in quantity, but also a new step in the army's system and quality construction along with the deepening of reform, and the overall combat effectiveness would inevitably be strengthened. By 2002, the total posts of the People's Liberation Army (including active and reserve forces) had remained below 2.5 million.[6]

4) *To abolish all business activities of the armed forces and the armed police forces.* Since Reform and Opening Up, the army had been living a tight life, subordinating itself to the overall situation of the country, with economic construction at the center. In order to solve its economic difficulties, for a period of time, the armed forces and armed police forces generally carried out operational production and business activities. Most of the funds generated were spent on improving the living, working, and training conditions of the army. However, with the passage of time, some negative effects were gradually exposed, mainly the distraction of leaders at all levels and promotion of unhealthy tendencies. Jiang Zemin pointed out shortly after he became chairman of the Military Commission that the army should take "imperial grain." To this end, the Military Commission took measures to gradually shrink and clean up the production and operation activities of the army, and eventually, in accordance with the unified deployment, stopped all business activities in July 1998. Within the prescribed time limit, the army and the armed police force would transfer or revoke thousands of business enterprises and economic and trade companies. All units had implemented the orders of the Military Commission to the letter, reflecting the army's consistent good style of obeying the overall situation and prohibiting orders and actions.

After the cessation of all business activities by the armed forces and the armed police forces, the state had allocated a large amount of special funds for this purpose in order to ensure that the life of the army, especially the life of the grassroots officers and soldiers, would not be affected, creating good conditions for them to serve in peace and devote themselves to national defense. Since the 1990s, more than 1.6 billion yuan had been invested in supporting the management of living facilities for the troops stationed in remote and difficult areas. Many border guard posts and plateau and island troops had settled in standard barracks, eaten fresh vegetables, bathed in hot water, and watched TV. In the implementation of the "vegetable basket" project, the self-sufficiency rate of the main non-commercial agricultural and sideline food supply in more than half of the company reached

70%, and a considerable number of units basically realized self-sufficiency in food supplies. In order to improve the cultural life of grassroots officers and soldiers, headquarters also allocated funds to improve grassroots cultural facilities and promote the development of grassroots cultural activities.

5) *Strengthening the rule of law.* In view of the new situation and problems brought about by the development of the social environment of the socialist market economy to military construction, the CMC emphasized the importance of administering the army according to law in the reform of the 1990s. In addition to the revision of the three traditional decrees (i.e. internal affairs decrees, discipline decrees, and combat decrees) according to the development of the situation, the National People's Congress, the State Council, and the CMC had formulated and promulgated a series of laws, regulations, and decrees successively, including the National Defense Law, Military Service Law, Active Military Officers Law, Military Facilities Protection Law, and other special laws related to the army and national defense construction, and formulated more than 1,000 military regulations, such as the draft work regulations, national defense traffic regulations, headquarters regulations, Ministry of Political Affairs work regulations, logistics regulations, and weapons and equipment management regulations. More than 2,000 rules and regulations had been formulated by the four headquarters, the various armed services, and the major military regions.

After three consecutive five-year stints of planning the popularization of the law, the army launched the fourth five-year education of law popularization in 2001. In the education of law popularization, the whole army made extensive study of common sense of law, focusing on military laws and regulations. In the process of popularizing the law, many grassroots units of the army also carried out legal consultation activities to help officers and soldiers resolve the legal problems encountered in daily life, learn to use legal means to safeguard the legitimate rights and interests of soldiers and their families, and consciously enhance the concept of the legal system in the process of learning, maintaining, and using the law. At the turn of the century, the construction of the army and national defense had basically been carried out in accordance with laws and regulations. Military construction had been brought into the orbit of legalization, which had effectively guaranteed and promoted the modernization and regularization of the army.

In addition to these reforms, the PLA also carried out a series of reforms, such as the military service system, the officer service system, the military housing system, the military insurance system, and the combat command system. Through various reforms, the overall military and political quality of the army had greatly improved.

3. The Path of Training Elite Forces with Chinese Characteristics Amidst Informationization

In the 21st century, a series of new changes had taken place in the international and domestic environment. Informationization occupied an increasingly prominent position in the high-tech fields, which was the prominent feature of this change. According to this change, the Central Military Commission made timely adjustments to its military strategic policy, transforming the winning of local wars under the conditions of modernization, especially under high-tech conditions, into winning local wars under the conditions of information technology. At the same time, it also put forward the development goal of "three offers, one role-play." This further realized the advancement of the CPC's strategic military thought with the times and formed the latest achievements of Marxist military thought, thus pushing this thought to a new height in the new century and new stage.

Since the dramatic changes in the Soviet Union and East Asia in the 1990s, American foreign policy had been attempting to dominate the world by itself, which was in sharp conflict with the efforts of many countries, including China, who advocated world multi-polarization. For a period of time, because of the lack of strong restrictions on the United States in the world, the US almost acted in any way it wished. According to statistics, during this period, the United States used force to interfere in the internal affairs of other countries twice as often as during the Cold War. The enhancement of its soft power had also greatly exceeded the level it had known during the period of the US-Soviet struggle for hegemony.

In recent years, with the rapid development of China, the United States had increasingly strengthened its siege and suppression of China in all areas. There were contacts, cooperation, struggles, and compromises between China and the United States. The game between them extended to political, economic, military, diplomatic, and other areas.

Since Reform and Opening Up, the rapid development of China's economy had not only brought tremendous progress to China, but also contributed greatly to the development of the world economy, as is the consensus of most countries today. However, not all were happy about this. Some hostile forces always tried their best to obstruct China's development and set up many obstacles, both overtly and covertly. At the same time, with the development of the trend of economic globalization, the economic integration of various countries was accelerating day by day. In the field of industry and commerce, the idea of interconnectedness had become the global trend. With the great development of the economy and science and technology, the extension of national interests was also expanding. In the agricultural age, the frontier of national interests ended with the land, while in the industrial age, it expanded to the ocean, then spread to the sky after World War II. In the high-tech era, the collision of national interests extended to space, while in the information age, it went beyond, into the electromagnetic field. The expansion of the frontier of national interests required that the functions of the army should also be extended to provide a strong security guarantee and strong strategic support for the maximization of national interests.

The development and change of the international and military situations soon aroused great concern in the military. On January 1, 2002, the PLA newspaper wrote that "in the new year, we will continue to pay attention to the problem of joint operations in the information age, focusing on the basic theory of joint operations, especially the theory and practice of joint operations of foreign forces, and focusing on reflecting the general law of joint operations and concluding them. In accordance with our army's actual situation, measures are put forward in the training of joint combat personnel and joint combat training, so as to improve the joint combat capability of all branches of our army."[7] From the historical task of national reunification, after entering the new century, the situation of national reunification in China was still not optimistic. The activities of Taiwanese independence forces in the island were rampant, constantly provoking the bottom line of the peaceful reunification of China. While the CPC was trying its best to achieve peaceful reunification of the motherland, it also had to be ready for military struggle at all times.

These new characteristics of the times meant higher requirements for the functions of the army. At the enlarged meeting of the Central Military Commission on September 20, 2004, Jiang Zemin, the outgoing Chairman of the CMC, pointed out, "We must have a broad, forward-looking vision, adhere to innovation, re-innovation, and more innovation, actively meet the severe challenges of the new world military reform, and push forward the military reform with Chinese characteristics with a sense of urgency, striving to complete the dual history of mechanization and information construction while unswervingly achieving the strategic objectives of building an information-based army and winning the information-based war."

At the same meeting, Hu Jintao, who had just taken over the post of Chairman of the Military Commission, asked the whole army to "continuously strengthen the ideological and political construction of the army, grasp the ability of the correct direction of the military construction, constantly improve our ability in leading the preparation for military struggle, leading the army to complete the combat tasks under the condition of informationization, and constantly improving the cost of advancing the military reform with Chinese characteristics and advancing the mechanized informationization construction of the army. We should constantly improve our ability to strictly administer the army according to law and to strengthen the regularization of the army."[8]

In 2004, the white paper on National Defense issued by China officially announced to the outside world, "The PLA bases itself on winning local wars under the condition of informatization and emphasizes strengthening the construction of weaponry and equipment, joint operation capabilities, and battlefield construction. We should adhere to the ideology of a people's war and develop the strategy and tactics of the people's war. To meet the requirements of integrated joint operations, we should establish a modern operational system that can give full play to the overall effectiveness of the armed forces and the military potential of the country."[9] At this point, the army began the Third Military Strategy Transformation in the new era, that is, moving from winning local wars through modern technology, especially high technology, to winning local wars under the condition of information technology.

In accordance with the requirements of this new military strategy, Military Commission President Hu Jintao, on behalf of the Central Military Commission, made timely new adjustments to the historical mission of the army. On March 13, 2005, President Hu Jintao delivered an important speech at the plenary meeting of the PLA delegation at the Third Session of the Tenth National People's Congress, demanding that the army "provide an important strength guarantee for the Party to consolidate its ruling position, provide a strong security guarantee for safeguarding the country's important strategic opportunities, provide a strong strategic support for safeguarding the country's interests, and play a key role in safeguarding world peace and driving common development."[10] This "three provides and one role-play" reflected the new requirements of the Party's historical tasks for the army, adapted to the new changes in the security situation in China, reflected the new needs of the national development strategy, conformed to the new trend of world military development, seized the major issues with overall and fundamental significance in military construction, further expanded the functions and tasks of the army, and clarified the national defense and military construction. The development goals set had raised the standards for preparing for military struggle and enriched the guiding principles for the use of military forces. Hu Jintao's important exposition, which was in line with Mao Zedong, Deng Xiaoping, and Jiang Zemin's important thoughts on the historical mission of the army and kept pace with the times, was an important innovation of the Party's guiding military theory, and it indicated that the Party's understanding of the law of national defense and army construction in the new century had reached a new level.

The new mission entrusted to the PLA by the Party Central Committee and the CMC was of epoch-making significance. In the past, the Communist Party of China had a relatively general understanding of the historical mission of the People's Army. It was generally believed that the army was the "strong pillar" of the people's democratic dictatorship and the "Great Wall of Steel" to defend the motherland. The new historical mission was no longer just a political conviction, it had been based on the commanding height of the times, starting from the broader and deeper needs of the times, to comprehensively examine the functions of the contemporary Chinese armed forces.

Although the four aspects covered by the new historical mission were not completely new arguments being put forward for the first time, it was the first time in history that the four important arguments were linked together to form a tightly integrated logical relationship. The Party's leadership in the army was the basic principle of the People's Army's military construction, and Marxist state theory held that the army was the main component of the country. According to these two basic principles, in a country under the people's democratic dictatorship, the armed forces must firmly grasp the hands of the ruling working class political parties and play an important role in their effective governance. Experiences and lessons from both positive and negative aspects had repeatedly proved that if the Party firmly grasped these two points, the cause of socialism would move forward.

By contrast, under the attack and lure of hostile forces in China and abroad, the cause of the Party and the state could be overthrown and the interests of the people would be greatly harmed if they were not grasped. When facing the complicated international environment and a domestic situation with frequent contradictions, it became particularly important for the army to provide an important strength guarantee for the Party to consolidate its ruling position.

China's modernization could not be separated from a positive international environment. In particular, in an increasingly intensified trend of world economic globalization, safeguarding world peace meant safeguarding its own development. In the past, China's comprehensive national strength had been insufficient, so it was particularly emphasized that it should seize the opportunity available in peacetime to develop itself. Now, China had a certain foundation, ability, and necessity to create a peaceful, harmonious international environment with its own strength, alongside all the world's peace-loving and peace-keeping forces. The Central Military Commission's endowment of the army's function of "playing an important role in safeguarding world peace and promoting common development" was quite timely.

CHAPTER 10

The Advancement of the New Great Project of Party Building and the Formation of the Important Concept of the "Three Represents"

The Party Central Committee, under Jiang Zemin's leadership, had gradually formed the important concept of the "Three Represents" by summarizing the experience of socialist modernization construction and Party building in the process of vigorously promoting the building of socialist modernization and continuously promoting the great new project of party building. The important concept of the "Three Represents" was the further enrichment and development of Marxist socialist construction and party building theory under the new historical conditions. The "Three Represents" was another important achievement of the CPC in the process of the localization of Marxism. This important thought fully reflected new changes in international and domestic historical development and the new requirements of the development of the times, playing an extremely important guiding role in the development of all aspects of contemporary China. It was for this reason that the Sixteenth National Congress of the Communist Party of China formally established it as the guiding ideology of the Party.

I

Further Clarification of the General Objectives and Tasks of Party Building and the Continuation of the New Great Project

In the 1990s, the Communist Party of China encountered a new situation of the socialist market economy in the process of reform and development. Under the condition of the socialist market economy, what kind of party should be built, how to build it and what kind of goals to achieve in building the party had become the new topic of the CPC's self-construction. In this regard, the third generation of the central leadership group with Jiang Zemin as its leader creatively put forward the general objectives and tasks of party building under the conditions of the socialist market, based on the principle of Marxist party building and the actual situation in China.

1. New Requirements of Reform and Opening Up and Development of the Market Economy for Party Building

Combining the socialist system with the market economy was not only a great innovation, but also a new subject and a difficult problem. Under the conditions of the socialist market economy, determining how to strengthen the Party's construction was an unprecedented cause and undoubtedly a new challenge for the CPC.

To develop the socialist market economy, the fundamental problem to be solved was how to change from a planned to a market-oriented economy. This change would inevitably lead to profound changes in all areas of society, including the positive and negative effects on the Party's construction.

The positive influence of the market economy on the Party's construction was mainly manifested in several ways. First, the basic law followed by the market economy was the law of value, which emphasized the principle of material interests and insisted on taking benefits as the focus. To act in accordance with this law would help Party organizations and Party members further establish a realistic ideology and work style and overcome the unhealthy tendency of formalism, fraud, and a disconnect from the actual situation. Second, the diversification of market participants and of trading methods, and the value orientation of giving priority to efficiency and giving consideration to fairness were conducive to the Party organizations and the broad masses of Party members maintaining and developing a positive mental state for striving toward progress and tenacity, and overcoming the old-fashioned and complacent ideological style. Third, the openness and fairness of market competition were conducive to strengthening the democratic consciousness of Party organizations and the general membership, overcoming such erroneous practices as "only one authoritative voice" and acting according to the subjective will. Fourth, the unity and openness of the market system was conducive to Party organizations and Party members learning from foreign beneficial experiences, overcoming closed conservative ideas, and enhancing the sense of openness. Fifth, the market economy was an economy ruled by law. A variety of market behaviors and the relationship between responsibilities and rights of market subjects had to be regulated by laws and regulations. This kind of norm was conducive to strengthening the concept of system construction of Party organizations and members, and overcoming the wrong tendency of not handling affairs based on the rules and regulations, and not abiding by the disciplines of the Party. Sixth, the market economy was mainly regulated indirectly through the market, without emphasizing direct administrative intervention. This was conducive to correctly handling the relationship between the Party and the government and overcoming the substitution of the Party for the government.

The negative effects of the socialist market economy on Party building were mainly manifested in several areas. First, the market economy emphasized material interests. Driven by material interests, people's world view, outlook on life, and values were prone to some distortions, which generated money worship, hedonism, and individualism. Some people even lost the Party principle and conducted power and money transactions, thus undermining the Party's image. This meant education in the Party's ideals and beliefs, world view, outlook on life, and values needed to be more arduous in a society that embraced the market economy. Second, the prominent feature of the market economy in terms of activity mode was the horizontal connection between market subjects, which had strong spontaneity and decentralization. It was easy to dilute the Party members' overall organizational concepts, breed decentralism and anarchism, and make the Party members' organizational management more difficult. Third, the market economy was an open economy. This openness was not only manifested in opening to the outside world, but also in connecting domestic and international markets, participating in the international division of labor and international competition as much as possible, so as to achieve the goal of more effective allocation of domestic resources and the utilization of international resources. On the one hand, this kind of openness would promote the acceleration of population flow, while on the other, it was easy to spread foreign ideas and cultures with the expansion of opening to the outside world. This made the teams of Party members unstable and brought difficulties to the work of unifying Party members' ideas.

The socialist market economy was a double-edged sword for Party building, which had both opportunities and challenges. Faced with such opportunities and challenges, the Communist Party of China had to adapt to the new requirements of the changing situation and clearly put forward in practice the general objectives and tasks of the Party's construction that were suitable for the requirements of the socialist market economy, so as to enable the Party to continuously strengthen its own construction with the development of the times and improve its ability to manage the market economy and consolidate its ruling position.

2. Further Clarifying the General Objectives and Tasks of Party Building

Clarifying the general objectives and tasks of the Party's construction was the primary issue of the construction of the ruling party. After the Communist Party of China came into power, it made a long-term exploration in its efforts to establish the correct goal of Party building. After the Third Plenary Session of the Eleventh Central Committee, with the shift of the focus of the Party's work, it was proposed that Party building should become a strong core leading the cause of socialist modernization, thus clarifying the direction of party building throughout the socialist historical period. After the Fourth Plenary Session of the Thirteenth Central Committee of the CPC, the Central Committee, under the leadership of Jiang Zemin, conscientiously summarized the experience and lessons of the Party's construction since Reform and Opening Up, actively explored new ways to strengthen the Party's construction in the developing socialist market economy, and clearly put forward the general objectives and tasks of the Party's construction in accordance with Deng Xiaoping's political account of "focusing on the Party's construction."

The general goal and task of party building were gradually formed in the practice of strengthening and improving party building by the central leading collective, with Jiang Zemin as its core. In August 1989, the Central Committee issued a circular on strengthening party building, requiring Party committees at all levels to resolve urgent problems in party building in accordance with the requirements of the Party's basic line, so as to enable the CPC to withstand the test of ruling, Reform and Opening Up, the development of the commodity economy, and the test of opposing peaceful evolution under new historical conditions. In March 1990, the Sixth Plenary Session of the Thirteenth Central Committee of the Communist Party of China adopted the Decision of the Central Committee of the Communist Party of China on Strengthening the Relations between the Party and the People, which emphasized that the Party and the country were in a critical period of historical development. The relationships between the Party and the masses and between cadres and the masses were generally good, but in recent years, some Party members and cadres had also been engaged in serious corruption and been distanced from the masses, a matter concerning which all the Party members needed to remain alert and constantly fight against such unhealthy tendencies. In 1992, in accordance with the needs of developing the socialist market economy and from the perspective of strengthening the Party's construction, the Fourteenth National Congress highlighted the importance of learning Deng Xiaoping's theory of building socialism with Chinese characteristics, strengthening the Party's construction, tightening the relationship between the Party and the masses, reinforcing the construction of grassroots organizations, and establishing and improving democratic centralization.

In order to carry out the tasks of Party building put forward by the Fourteenth National Congress and to adapt Party building to the reform of the socialist market economic system, the Fourth Plenary Session of the Fourteenth Central Committee held in September 1994 made the Decision on Several Major Issues Concerning Strengthening Party Building (hereinafter referred to as the Decision). The Decision clearly put forward the general goal and task of the new great project of Party building, that is, "to build the Party into a Marxist party armed with the theory of building socialism with Chinese characteristics, serving the people wholeheartedly, fully consolidated ideologically and politically, able to withstand various risks, and always at the forefront of the times." According to this general objective and task, the Decision required that while continuing to implement the Central Government's plan for ideological and style construction, it was necessary to focus on settling the central issue of the Party's organizational construction, especially regarding three issues. The first was upholding and improving democratic centralization and paying special attention to system construction. The second was strengthening and improving the Party's grassroots organizational construction. The third was training and selecting leading cadres with both ability and integrity, especially young cadres. Focusing on institutional development was an important feature of the Decision adopted at the Conference.

In September 1997, the Fifteenth National Congress summarized the new experience of Party building and further summarized the general objectives and tasks of Party building put forward at the Fourth Plenary Session of the Fourteenth Central Committee, emphasizing "building the Party into a Marxist political party armed with Deng Xiaoping Theory, serving the people wholeheartedly, consolidated ideologically and politically, able to withstand various risks, constantly at the forefront of the times, and leading all the people of the nation to build socialism with Chinese characteristics." The Congress called on the entire Party to engage in overall strengthening of the Party's construction ideologically, organizationally, and in terms of style, in accordance with the general objective of the new great project of Party building, to continuously improve its leadership, to constantly enhance its ability to resist corruption, change, and risk, and to lead the people to accomplish new historical tasks with a new look and a stronger fighting capacity.

3. Preliminary Implementation of the General Objectives and Tasks of the Party's Construction

After the Fourth Plenary Session of the Fourteenth Central Committee, the Party's construction was gradually pushed forward in terms of ideology, politics, and organization, in accordance with the requirements of the general objectives and tasks.

In terms of ideological construction, the Fourteenth National Congress of the Party established Deng Xiaoping's guiding position in building socialism with Chinese characteristics throughout the Party, putting forward the strategic task of arming the entire Party with this theory. In 1993 and 1994, after the first, second, and third volumes of *Deng Xiaoping's Selected Works* were published, the Central Committee immediately issued a circular requesting the entire Party to organize the material and study it conscientiously. From the end of 1993 to May 1994, the

Central Committee organized 175 leading cadres and some experts and scholars from various departments of the Party, the government, and the military. They went to the Central Party School in four batches to attend a seminar on the theory of leading cadres at the provincial and ministerial levels, carefully studying *Deng Xiaoping's Selected Works*. In order to further promote cadre training, in May 1996, the Central Committee formulated the National Plan for Cadre Education and Training (1996–2000), which formulated a comprehensive plan for strengthening cadres' ideological and theoretical education.

In the process of carrying out theoretical study throughout the Party, a set of learning systems was gradually established. For example, members of Party committees at or above the county level regularly participated in Party school training and the learning system of the central group of Party committees. In addition, organizations at all levels also adopted various forms, such as organizing lecture groups for counseling and holding theoretical seminars to promote the extensive development of learning. These measures stimulated the enthusiasm of the majority of Party members and cadres to study theory, and promoted the improvement of the ideological and theoretical level of the whole Party.

In terms of improving democratic centralization, after the Fourteenth National Congress, the Central Committee gradually intensified its efforts to build democratic centralization in view of the problems of insufficient democracy and centralization in the Party. In terms of guaranteeing the democratic rights of Party members, the channels of democracy within the Party had been opened up and broadened so that Party members could participate more fully in Party affairs. By establishing an effective mechanism to ensure that grassroots Party members made timely reflection of their views to the higher Party organizations through the lower Party organizations, and on the basis of fully listening to the views of the Party members and the subordinate Party organizations, they could draw on different ideas and constantly promote the scientific nature and democratization of decision-making. In terms of decision-making procedures, the CPC should further improve the deliberation and decision-making mechanism within the Party Committee in accordance with the principles of "collective leadership, democratic centralization, individual thinking, and conference decision." In terms of leadership and governance, it was emphasized that the Party's leadership system should be further strengthened and improved in accordance with the principle of the overall situation and coordination of all parties, so as to ensure the core role of the Party Committee in leadership and give full play to the role of the NPC, the government, the CPPCC, the people's organizations, and other aspects. The implementation of these measures gradually institutionalized and standardized the construction of the Party's democratic centralization.

In terms of organizational construction of the rural grassroots Party, the Central Organizational Department held a meeting in Laixi, Shandong Province, in 1990 to determine the core leadership position of the Party branch in village-level organizations. In 1992, the Central Organizational Department held a meeting in Zhangqiu, Shandong Province, focusing on summing up and promoting the experience of "building a system according to law, governing villages by system, and democratic management," and promoting the rural grassroots organizations with the Party branch as the core to embark on the track of institutionalization and standardization. In 1994, under the guidance of the Party's spirit of grassroots organization construction at the Fourth Plenary Session of the Fourteenth Central Committee of the Communist Party of China, the Central Committee of the Communist Party of China held a national conference on grassroots organization construction from October 26-29 in rural areas in Beijing. On November 5, the Central Committee issued the Notice on Strengthening the Construction of Rural Grassroots Organizations, which clearly put forward "five goods" as requirements for the construction of rural grassroots Party organizations, namely building a good leadership team, training a good team, selecting a good way to develop the economy, improving a good operating mechanism, and improving a good management system. Accordingly, the responsibility system for Party building and the contact working spot system of leading cadres was established and implemented throughout the country. Since 1994, the Party's organizational departments rectified 282,000 weak and scattered Party branches in the countryside in stages and batches and carried out rotational training for Party members and cadres in the countryside, which improved about 80% of the village-level Party organizations to varying degrees.

In the construction of grassroots Party organizations in state-owned enterprises, in December 1996, the Central Organization Department of the CPC, the Central Policy Research Office, the State Economic and Trade Commission, the State Commission for Reform of Sports and Physical Education, and the National Federation of Trade Unions jointly convened a working conference on party building in state-owned enterprises in Beijing. In January 1997, the Central

Committee issued the Notice on Further Strengthening and Improving Party Construction in State-owned Enterprises, which clearly stipulated the objectives, policies, and principles of Party organization construction in state-owned enterprises. According to the spirit of the document, in the process of establishing a modern enterprise system, Party committees at all levels adhered to the Party's political leadership over enterprises, gave full play to the political core role of Party organizations in enterprises, adhered to the principle of wholeheartedly relying on the working class, explored new ways and methods of Party building around enterprise reform and development, and achieved remarkable results and accumulated new experience.

In terms of neighborhood party building in urban areas, some neighborhood cadres from sixteen provinces and cities in China discussed in June 1995 in Tianjin how they might best strengthen the construction of grassroots party organizations, and summarized and exchanged experiences. A year later, on the basis of coordinating all aspects of the situation, the Central Organizational Department issued the Opinions on Strengthening the Construction of the Neighborhood Party on September 3, 1996, requesting that the construction of the Neighborhood Party should proceed from the characteristics and actual situation of the urban work under the new situation, focusing on improving urban management and social services, maintaining social stability and developing the neighborhood economy, focusing on strengthening the construction of the leading group, and improving the quality of cadres, so as to strengthen the cohesion and fighting capacity of Party organizations and give full play to the vanguard and exemplary role of Party members, which in turn would contribute to the healthy development of the construction of the socialist material and spiritual civilizations in cities. According to this spirit, cities in different areas gradually established the working network of Party organizations in the communities, so that the Party organizations in the communities played an increasingly important role in strengthening the construction of the spiritual civilization and the ideological and political work of the masses, doing a thorough job of the comprehensive management of social security, closely linking the Party with the masses and improving the quality of the residents and the degree of urban civilization. In non-public economic organizations, Party building was further strengthened during this period.

In the developed areas of the non-public ownership economy, the Party's organizations were established in some foreign-invested enterprises and private enterprises. The cohesion of the Party's organizations and the vanguard and exemplary role of Party members were also well reflected in these enterprises. In September 2000, on the basis of extensive investigation, research, and summary of practical experience in various places, the Central Organizational Department issued the Opinions on Strengthening Party Construction in Non-public Economic Organizations, such as Individuals and Private Sectors (Trial Implementation). According to the requirements of this document, by June 2001, 44,000 Party organizations had been established in non-public enterprises throughout the country.

At the same time, the Central Committee also put forward a series of new ideas and requirements for Party building in departments such as government organs, schools, and scientific research institutes, which generally strengthened the Party's grassroots organization construction under the new historical conditions.

While strengthening the construction of the Party's grassroots organizations, Party organizations at all levels also generally strengthened the construction of the teams of Party members. In accordance with the policy of "adhering to standards, improving structure, prudent development, and guaranteeing quality," advanced elements from all fronts were constantly enriched into the teams of Party members, adding fresh blood to the Party's organizations. The cohesion and creativity of Party organizations was continuously strengthened.

4. Adhering to and Improving Democratic Centralization and Strengthening the Construction of the Democratic System Within the Party

Democratic centralization was a system that combined centralization on the basis of democracy, with democracy remaining firmly under the guidance of centralization. It was also the application of Marxist epistemology and the mass line in the Party's life and organizational construction. The democracy of democratic centralization pointed to the full expression of the wishes and opinions of Party members and organizations and the full expression of their initiative and creativity, while centralization pointed to the cohesion of the will and wisdom of the whole Party and the consistency of its actions.

According to the tasks and requirements put forward at the Fourth Plenary Session of the Fourteenth Central Committee, the Central Committee took a series of measures to strengthen and improve the democratic centralization of the Party in view of the problems of insufficient democracy and centralization in the Party. On the one hand, it was important to adhere to the goal of realizing the Party's program, taking guidance, protection, and initiative as the starting point and actively opening up and broadening the democratic channels within the Party, so that Party members could have more understanding and participation in the affairs within the Party and be required to participate in the discussion of policy issues from the Central Committee to each branch, from the decision-making of the leading organs to the meetings of the Party and the Party's newspapers and periodicals, and within the Party. Democracy was to be fully promoted when leading cadres were elected for evaluation and supervision.[1] In order to protect the democratic rights of Party members, in December 1994, the Central Committee of the Party formulated and promulgated the Regulations on the Protection of the Rights of Party Members (for trial implementation), which clearly stipulated the principles for Party members to exercise their rights correctly and the measures for guaranteeing Party members to exercise their rights.

On the other hand, it was important to focus on the overall situation of the Party's work, reiterating the provisions of the Party Constitution, emphasizing the "Four Obediences," ensuring the smooth passage of the Central Committee's decrees, and maintaining consistency with the Central Committee on the Party's basic line and general principles, policies, objectives, and major issues related to the overall situation. In order to strengthen and improve the Party's leadership, the Central Committee also proposed that, in accordance with the principles of "collective leadership, democratic centralization, individual deliberation, and decision-making at meetings," the deliberation and decision-making mechanism within the Party committee should be further improved, the decision-making mechanism combining leadership, experts, and the masses should be established and perfected, and the democratic and scientific decision-making system should be gradually improved. Further, the combination of collective leadership and individual division of labor and responsibility should be upheld and perfected. Regulations on the work of central and local Party committees needed to be formulated to further clarify and standardize the scope of responsibilities, rules of procedure, and decision-making procedures of Party committees and their standing committees, and the system of Party congresses needed to be perfected in order to further play the role of plenary sessions of Party committees at central and local levels. Improvement needed to be made in the system of organizing life associations, democratic life associations of Party members and leading cadres, and political life within the Party. It was important to improve the internal supervision of the Party, strictly enforce the Party's discipline, formulate regulations on internal supervision, improve the internal supervision system of the Party, and combine internal supervision with mass supervision, public opinion supervision, supervision by democratic parties and non-party personages, and combine top-down and bottom-up supervision to gradually form a strong supervision system. Finally, it was necessary to coordinate all parties in accordance with the overall situation. In principle, the CPC should further strengthen and improve the Party's leadership system, not only to ensure the central role of the Party committee, but also to give full play to the role of the People's Congress, the government, the CPPCC, the people's organizations, and other organizations.

The implementation of these principles gradually institutionalized and standardized the construction of the Party's democratic centralization.

5. Developing Education in the "Three Advocates" and Exploring New Ways to Strengthen the Party's Construction

As it entered the new century, faced with the new situation and new tasks of deepening Reform and Opening Up, the Party Central Committee under Jiang Zemin's leadership created a new form of Party spirit education with the spirit of rectification, with the main content being the "Three Advocates" (advocating learning, politics, and integrity) on the basis of an in-depth summary of the Party's historical experience. This achieved remarkable results.

In 1995, Jiang Zemin pointed out that some cadres did not pay attention to learning and self-transformation under the new situation of the developing market economy, and had thus lost their direction in the increasingly complex struggle and embarked on the road of corruption and degeneration. He repeatedly mentioned that they should be educated in learning, politics, and integrity. This requirement immediately attracted the attention of Party committees at all levels, and the Three Advocates gradually became an important part of education for Party members and cadres. In 1998, the Central Organizational Department, together with relevant departments, drew up the implementation plan for education in the Three Advocates after repeated investigation and consultation.

On November 21, the Central Committee issued the Opinions on Intensive Development of Party Style Education Among Party and Government Leading Groups and Leading Cadres at or Above the County Level, with "Learning, Politics, and Integrity," making comprehensive arrangements for carrying out education in the Three Advocates. From that time, education in the Three Advocates began to be comprehensively carried out in stages and batches.

This education in the Three Advocates adopted a top-down approach. First, pilot projects were carried out by directly affiliated organs of the Central Government, the central state organs, the provinces, autonomous regions, and municipalities directly under the Central Government, and the directly affiliated organs, and then at the local, municipal, and county levels. On December 5, 1998, the Central Committee convened a national teleconference, at which Hu Jintao delivered a speech on mobilization of education on the Three Advocates. From that time, the Central Government carried out pilot projects in Shandong, Guangxi, Inner Mongolia, the Ministry of Land and Resources, the Ministry of Education, the General Administration of Radio and Television, and the Central Committee of the League. From the start of the pilot project, the Three Advocates of each unit were launched in four steps: 1) ideological initiation, learning, and improvement, 2) self-analysis, listening to opinions, exchange of ideas, criticism, and self-criticism, 3) conscientious rectification, and 4) consolidation of achievements.

On March 19, 1999, in order to summarize and exchange the situation and experience of the Three Advocates education pilot project and to study and deploy the next step, the Central Committee convened the first national Three Advocates Education Work Conference. The meeting heard the experience of the pilot units and deployed the first Three Advocates education project. It was decided that the Three Advocates of the provincial and ministerial units should be carried out in two batches. In the first batch, seventy central and state organs, ministries, and bureaus, including sixteen provinces, districts, municipalities, and the Supreme People's Procuratorate, were listed in Beijing and Hubei. In the second batch, sixty ministries and bureaus, including twelve provinces, such as Zhejiang and Ningxia, and the Ministry of Finance were listed.

The Standing Committee of the Politburo attached great importance to education in the Three Advocates. At the end of 1999, it devoted special time to study of the Three Advocates. It made a careful review and summary of the ten years of work and basic experience since the Fourth Plenary Session of the Thirteenth

Central Committee, and made a thorough reflection on some important strategic issues in future reform and development. Members of the Standing Committee, in line with their attitude of being highly responsible to the Party, the country, and the people, took the lead in discovering shortcomings in their work, carrying out criticism and self-criticism, and putting forward improvement measures, effectively promoting the in-depth development of the education in the Three Advocates.

Following the first Three Advocates Education Working Conference, the Central Committee held the Second and Third national Three Advocates Education Working Conference in June 1999 and January 2000, and deployed the Three Advocates work at all stages. According to these arrangements, the Central Committee sent a number of inspection teams to various provinces, autonomous regions, and municipalities directly under the Central Government and ministries and commissions of central and state organs to learn about the situation and to strengthen the guidance, inspection, and supervision of the Three Advocates education work. After centralized education in the Three Advocates was completed, local governments and units, in accordance with the central requirements, did a thorough job of ideological education and implemented rectification measures. At the same time, they organized and carried out "review" activities to see whether the consciousness of "emphasizing learning, politics, and integrity" had really been improved and whether the outstanding problems reflected by the masses had been resolved. They asked whether there had been any obvious improvements in the work, in order to consolidate and expand the achievements of education in the Three Advocates.

According to the Central Government's deployment, education in the Three Advocates education at the county (city) level was also launched. In order to do a thorough job, the Standing Committee of the Politburo went to seven counties (cities) to conduct in-depth investigation and research and give specific guidance. On February 20, 2000, Jiang Zemin personally attended the Three Advocates Education Conference for Leading Cadres in Gaozhou City, Guangdong Province, delivering a mobilization speech. These measures further reflected the Central Committee's great attention to education in the Three Advocates and greatly promoted these education programs at the county (city) level. By the end of September 2000, the Three Advocates education work of Party and government leading groups and leading cadres at or above the county level had basically come to an end, and it began to enter the stage of summary, improvement, and in-depth rectification.

From 1998 to the end of 2000, a total of 700,000 leading cadres of the Party participated in the Three Advocates education work. Cadres and the masses inside and outside the Party were very concerned about this educational activity and showed great enthusiasm for participation. More than 5 million people had directly listened to mobilization reports, participated in democratic evaluation, and helped rectify it. The majority of cadres had generally received a profound Marxist education, undergone a rigorous exercise in democratic life within the Party, and had made remarkable progress in adhering to the mass line and the democratic centralization of the Party. Practice indicated that the education in the Three Advocates was a creative exploration and successful practice to strengthen the Party's construction under the new situation, especially the ideological and political construction of leading groups and cadres. It enriched and developed the spirit of the Yan'an Rectification Movement and the Party's "three work styles" in the new historical period.

11

The Training and Selecting of Leading Cadres with Competence and Integrity to Build a Qualified Team

After the political line had been determined, cadres were the decisive factor. To train and select leading cadres with both ability and integrity was the fundamental strategy enabling the Party and the state to maintain long-term stability. The work of building a contingent of high-quality cadres started in the 1980s and accelerated further in the 1990s.

In 1991, the Central Committee issued the Decision of the Central Committee of the Communist Party of China on Accelerating the Training and Education of Young Cadres. It clearly put forward that the Party should strengthen the strict requirements and management of young cadres, strengthen their ideological and theoretical education, and enable them to undergo practical training by means of exchanges and rotations. In October 1992, the Fourteenth National Congress of the Communist Party of China clearly proposed that the CPC should train and select successors to the cause of socialism in accordance with the principle of the Four Modernizations of the cadres and the principle of combining virtue with ability. In September 1994, the Fourth Plenary Session of the Fourteenth Central Committee put forward the training and selection of leading cadres with both ability and integrity as two major strategic tasks. At the same time, it clearly put forward four requirements for the reform of the cadre system. First, it was important to expand democracy in the selection and appointment of leading cadres. In selecting, employing or appointing leading cadres, it was necessary to follow the mass line and let the masses participate more through democratic recommendation, public opinion polls, or democratic evaluation. Second, it was necessary to improve the assessment system of leading cadres and link it with the system of promotion, award, and punishment. Third, it was necessary to conscientiously implement the exchange system of leading cadres and combine it with the system of avoidance and the tenure system of leading groups at all levels. Fourth, it was necessary to strengthen supervision and inspection of the selection and appointment of leading cadres and resolutely prevent and correct unhealthy tendencies in employment. The principles put forward by the Fourteenth National Congress and the four reform requirements put forward by the Fourth Plenary Session of the Fourteenth Central Committee were the guiding opinions on the training and selection of leading cadres from the height of the 1990s. These principles and requirements had clear directions, fully reflected the characteristics of democracy and openness, were easy to operate, and had a strong guiding role.

In order to act upon the spirit of the Fourth and Fourteenth Plenary Sessions of the Fourteenth Central Committee, the National Organizational Working Conference was held in Beijing from November 30 to December 3, 1994. The conference focused on researching and deploying the work of training and selecting leading cadres with both ability and integrity, and strengthening the construction of leading groups at all levels. On November 30, Hu Jintao made a report entitled "Grasping the Task of Training and Selecting Leading Cadres with Both Ability and Moral Integrity, and Building Leading Groups at All Levels into Strong Leading Collectives to Implement the Party's Basic Line." He proposed that the quality of leading cadres at and above the county level should be improved overall as a key point of cadre work in the future. On December 2, Jiang Zemin emphasized in his speech at the meeting that at present and in the future, the construction of cadre contingents must focus on two strategic tasks.

One was to comprehensively improve the quality of existing leading cadres and build leading groups at and above the county level, and the other was to quickly train and select outstanding young cadres and strive to bring up a large number of leading talents capable of shouldering heavy responsibilities while moving into the new century. In their speeches, Jiang Zemin and Hu Jintao further clarified the key points of training and selecting leading cadres with both ability and moral integrity. In order to effectively grasp the work of training and selecting leading cadres, in January 1995, the Central Committee issued the Circular of the Central Committee of the Communist Party of China on Accelerating the Training and Selection of Excellent Young Cadres, requiring organizations at all levels to improve and strengthen the work of reserve cadres so as to provide sufficient reserve candidates for leading groups at all levels, intensify training efforts, and improve the quality of young cadres in an all-round way. To promote young cadres, it was necessary to focus on the healthy growth of a generation. In accordance with these spiritual requirements, Party committees across the central and local levels had generally strengthened cadre training and education.

While strengthening the training and education of cadres, the rational selection of cadres was put on the agenda. In January 1995, the Central Committee issued a circular on the training and selection of outstanding young cadres, clearly putting forward the objectives, principles, and requirements for the selection of young cadres. In February 1995, the Central Committee issued the Provisional Regulations on the Selection and Appointment of Leading Party and Government Cadres, which clearly stipulated the principles, conditions, procedures, and methods for the selection and appointment of cadres in the form of laws and regulations. On June 21, 1996, Jiang Zemin delivered an important speech entitled "Efforts to Build a Contingent of High-Quality Cadres" at the symposium commemorating the 75th anniversary of the founding of the CPC. He further proposed five criteria to improve the political and professional qualities of Party cadres. The first was to have a lofty communist ideal, adhere to the correct political direction, and firmly follow the path of building socialism with Chinese characteristics, resolutely following and implementing the Party's basic theory, line, and policies. The second was to strive to practice the Party's purpose of serving the people wholeheartedly, closely linked with the masses, especially the workers and peasants, and resolutely safeguarding the interests of the people. The third was to emancipate the mind, seek truth from facts, proceed from reality, be good at pioneering and advancing, and have a materialistic and dialectical way of thinking. The fourth was to be the role models for abiding by discipline and law, maintaining integrity, carrying forward the spirit of persistent struggle to consciously resist corruption and downward change, and resolutely opposing negative corruption. The final criteria was to study hard, work diligently, and continuously strengthen the acquisition of knowledge and experience, and possess the professional knowledge and ability to do their jobs well.[2]

After 1996, with the concerted efforts of the Central Committee and Party committees at all levels, the work of cadre selection and appointment gradually moved towards institutionalization and standardization. In August 2000, the Central Committee issued the Outline On Intensive Reform of the Cadre and Personnel System, which clearly stipulated the basic objectives, principles, party and government cadre system reform, and personnel system reform of state-owned enterprises. In July 2002, in accordance with the requirements for the new century, new stage, and new tasks, and on the basis of absorbing the achievements of the reform of the cadre and personnel system after 1995, the Central Committee revised and improved the Provisional Regulations on the Selection and Appointment of Leading Cadres of the Party and Government and promulgated the Regulations on the Selection and Appointment of Leading Cadres of the Party and Government, setting more scientific, standard, and strict regulations on the basic principles, procedures, and methods for the selection and appointment of cadres and for expanding democracy and strengthening supervision, which provided basic rules and guarantees for preventing and curbing unhealthy tendencies in employment in the very beginning and promoting the scientific, democratic, and institutionalized work of cadres. In 2004, the Central Government further strengthened the reform of the cadre and personnel systems. The Central Government promulgated five documents, including the Initial Provisions for the Open Selection of Leading Party and Government Cadres and the Initial Provisions for Competition for Employment in Party and Government Organs. In addition, with the prior approval of the Central Government, in early 2004, the Central Discipline Commission and the Central Organizational Department jointly issued the Notice for Cleaning Up Part-time Employment of Leading Party and Government Cadres in Enterprises. These were collectively referred to as the "5 + 1" documents. These documents and the Civil Servants Law of the People's Republic of China, promulgated in 2005, focused on the selection and appointment of leading cadres and made clear, systematic provisions. The promulgation of these policies and regulations further perfected the system of selecting and appointing leading cadres, and the work of selecting and appointing leading cadres systematically stepped onto the path of institutionalization and standardization, thus effectively guaranteeing that outstanding personnel would stand out and that the cooperation and alternation between the old and the new among leading cadres at all levels would be managed in a timely way.

III

Strengthening the Party's Work Style and the In-depth and Persistent Struggle Against Corruption

How a political party might always maintain a healthy body was a long-standing issue for which Marxist thinkers of all ages had been striving. Since the 1990s, with the development and change of the social situation, the Communist Party of China had gradually put forward and formed a set of systems and ideas in the practice of anti-corruption. These systems and ideas were more embodied in the original development and creation of the CPC through the process of the localization of Marxism.

In the new stage of Reform and Opening Up, in the process of China's transition from a planned economy to a socialist market economy, some weak links still existed in supervision and management, and some local and departmental organs neglected ideological and political work, due mainly to the shortcomings of the old system and imperfect legal system. As a result, corruption had spread and grown in some Party and government organs and law enforcement departments.

In view of the serious situation in the fight against corruption, the Central Committee and the State Council had actively taken pertinent measures. As early as the beginning of Reform and Opening Up, the Party began to pay attention to the problem of opposing unhealthy tendencies. In 1987, the Thirteenth National Congress of the Party formally put forward the policy of "strictly administering the Party." After the Thirteenth National Congress, some measures for building an honest, clean government were introduced one after another. From August 20–25, 1993, the Chinese Commission for Discipline held its second plenary meeting in

Beijing. At the meeting, Jiang Zemin proposed that anti-corruption work should be carried out from three aspects. First, leading cadres at all levels of the Party and government should take the lead in practicing honesty and self-discipline. Second, the Party should concentrate its efforts on investigating and handling a number of major cases, focusing on cases that occurred in the leading organs of the Party and government, judicial departments, administrative law enforcement departments, and staff of economic management departments. Third, the Party should firmly grasp the prominent problems in its region, departments, and units and deal with the masses' greatest areas of dissatisfaction.[3] These three requirements directly point to the "three organs and one department" for large, major cases – leading organs of the Party and government, leading cadres and judicial organs, administrative law enforcement organs, economic management departments, and the staff. According to the spirit of Jiang Zemin's speech and the needs of the anti-corruption work, the plenary session made five provisions in the fight against corruption among leading cadres at or above the county (department) level. First, for those leaders, no business enterprises, no paid intermediary activities, and no preferential conditions for spouses, children, and relatives or friends to run business enterprises were allowed. Second, it was forbidden to take part-time jobs (including honorary positions) in various economic entities or to receive any remuneration on the basis of individual approval, and it was forbidden to reimburse subordinate units and other enterprises and institutions for various expenses that should be paid by individuals. Third, no trading in stocks was allowed. Fourth, no gifts or securities were allowed in official activities, no credit cards given by subordinate units or other institutions were allowed, and no credit cards handled by the units with public funds were allowed to be used by individuals. Fifth, it was forbidden to use public funds to obtain various forms of club membership and to participate in high-consumption recreational activities.

On October 5, 1993, the Central Committee and the State Council issued the Decision on Several Recent Works in the Fight Against Corruption, which reiterated the three tasks in the fight against corruption proposed by the Second Plenary Session of the Central Commission for Discipline and the "Five Provisions" for leading cadres. In February 1994, the Third Plenary Session of the Disciplinary Inspection Committee of the Central Committee held in Beijing, on the basis of the "Five Provisions" put forward by the Second Plenary Session, put forward and reiterated several requirements. First, there was to be no purchase or upgrade of imported luxury cars in violation of the provisions, no use of the functions and powers to upgrade or borrow cars and put cost of car-purchase onto enterprises or subordinate units, no use of loans, raised funds, and special funds to purchase cars for the use of leading cadres, and county (city) Party and government leading organs and units were not allowed to buy cars for workers whose wages were in arrears. Second, it was forbidden to buy houses at a reduced price in violation of the provisions of the State Council on housing system reform, to use authority to provide preferential conditions for the purchase of houses for oneself, or one's children or relatives, and to use public funds to decorate houses for individuals beyond the accepted standard. Third, leading cadres should be light and obedient in official domestic activities, and accommodation should not exceed local reception standards, and special events for leading cadres should not be held. Fourth, it was forbidden to make use of such opportunities as marriages, funerals, weddings, job transfers, birthdays, or relocation to make extravagant or wasteful use of public funds and public property, or to borrow money. Fifth, it was forbidden to use public funds to buy houses, build private houses, and engage in profit-making activities for individuals and their relatives and friends. In May, the Central Commission for Discipline formulated the implementation proposition of the "New Five Provisions" on the integrity and self-discipline of leading cadres.

In June 1994, the Central Committee decided to organize twenty investigation teams to supervise and inspect anti-corruption work in twenty-four ministries and commissions of central state organs and twenty-four provinces, autonomous regions, and municipalities directly under the Central Government in early July. On the basis of investigation and research, in January 1995, the Fifth Plenary Session of the Central Discipline Inspection Commission instituted four supplementary provisions on the integrity and self-discipline of leading cadres. First, discounts, intermediary fees, and gifts collected in business and management activities were not allowed to be owned by individuals, and wages and bonuses for part-time positions were not allowed to be collected in violation of the provisions. Second, individuals were not allowed to do business privately, and their families and friends were not allowed to use their powers to provide various conveniences for doing business. Third, it was forbidden to occupy additional houses in violation of regulations, and to purchase or construct super-standard houses with public funds. Fourth, it was forbidden to buy cars during the period of non-policy losses of enterprises, arrears of salaries of employees and teachers, or to buy imported luxury cars such as Mercedes-Benz, Lincolns, Cadillacs, and Dukes. The integrity and self-discipline of leading cadres in public institutions was to be carried out with reference to the provisions of the integrity and self-discipline of leading cadres in state-owned enterprises.

In April, the Central Discipline Inspection Commission formulated, implemented and handled the "supplementary provisions" concerning the integrity and self-discipline of leading cadres, which included no building private houses in violation of regulations; no participating in fund-raising and building houses in violation of regulations; no use of military and police vehicle number plates and foreign vehicle number plates in violation of regulations; no use of public funds and unit vehicles to learn driving skills without approval; no participating in entertainment activities such as business song halls, dance halls, nightclubs paid with public funds; and no accepting of banquets that may have an impact on the fair execution of official duties in contact with domestic units and individuals.

These provisions and opinions put forward clear requirements for the integrity and self-discipline of leading cadres, which made anti-corruption work basically rule-based. On this basis, in January 1996, the Sixth Plenary Session of the Central Discipline Inspection Commission made it clear that the construction of clean, honest Party conduct and the struggle against corruption should be continuously deepened in accordance with the three working patterns of leading cadres' honesty and self-discipline, investigation and punishment of cases of violations of law and discipline, and correction of the unhealthy tendencies of departments and industries. In particular, the meeting called on leading cadres at provincial and ministerial levels to abide by the provisions of honesty, self-discipline, Party discipline, and state law, and required their subordinates to do so, to forbid others to do so, and to resolutely refrain from doing so. The meeting put forward the responsibility system for anti-corruption work, and the leaders were to be held accountable for serious corruption problems in their regions, departments, families, and relatives.

In order to ensure the implementation of the relevant provisions on the integrity and self-discipline of leading cadres, the Central Discipline Commission also took a series of specific measures. First, it appointed ministerial cadres to inspect local and departmental areas and take responsibility for understanding the implementation of the Party's line, principles, and policies by provincial and ministerial leading groups and their members, reporting directly to the Central

Discipline Commission and reporting to the Party Central Committee in a timely manner. The second was to stipulate that the local and departmental disciplines commissions (discipline inspection teams) of the Party would have the right to conduct preliminary verification if they found that the Party committees (Party groups) or their members at the same level had violated Party discipline, and to report directly to the higher discipline inspection committees. No organization or individual would interfere with or obstruct them. The third was to require the local and departmental discipline commissions (discipline inspection teams) of the Party to receive members of Party committees (Party groups) at the same level. The prosecution and accusation must be reported to the Party committees (Party groups) at the same level and to the discipline inspection committees at the next higher level. No one had the right to withhold such reports.

At the same time, the Central Committee and the State Council further improved the relevant institutions and the relevant systems and mechanisms. In terms of system construction, after the Sixteenth National Congress, the Central Committee, under the leadership of Hu Jintao, attached great importance to the construction and innovation of the anti-corruption system and focused on preventing and solving corruption problems from the source. The Third Plenary Session of the Sixteenth Central Committee put forward for the first time that the CPC should establish and improve a system of punishment and prevention of corruption that was compatible with the socialist market economic system, paying equal attention to education, supervision, and system. After this, the Fourth Plenary Session of the Sixteenth Central Committee put forward the Sixteen-Character Principle of Party Conduct and Clean Government Construction and Anti-Corruption Struggle under the new situation, that is, to "treat both root causes and symptoms with comprehensive governance, simultaneously punishing and preventing, with focus on prevention," and called for the establishment of a system of punishment and prevention of corruption with equal emphasis on education, system, and supervision. In December 2004, the Politburo of the Central Committee considered and adopted the Outline for Implementing the System of Punishment and Prevention of Corruption, with Equal Emphasis on Education, Institution, and Supervision (referred to as the Outline), and clarified the guiding ideology, main objectives, and working principles for the establishment of a system of punishment and prevention of corruption. The Outline put forward that the main objectives of establishing and improving the system of punishing and preventing corruption were to establish the basic framework of the system of punishing and preventing corruption by 2010, and to establish a long-term mechanism of ideological and moral education, a system of combating corruption and promoting honesty, a monitoring mechanism of power operation, and a perfect system of punishing and preventing corruption after a period of efforts. The working principles were 1) adhering to and perfecting the socialist market economic system, developing socialist democratic politics, building an advanced socialist culture, and building a harmonious socialist society, 2) adhering to equal emphasis on education, institution, and supervision, 3) adhering to the unity of being scientific, systematic, and feasible, and 4) adhering to the combination of inheritance and innovation. The Outline was a guiding document for the further development of the Party's style of work and the work of combating corruption and promoting honesty at present and in the future. In January 2005, the Central Committee issued the Outline nationwide, requiring Party committees and governments at all levels to effectively carry out all aspects of anti-corruption work.

In the process of promoting the construction of the anti-corruption and honesty system, the Party and the state issued a series of laws and regulations to continuously enrich and improve the content of the anti-corruption and honesty system. In December 2003, the Central Committee promulgated the Regulations on Supervision within the Party (for trial implementation). For the first time, it comprehensively stipulated the key points, ways, and methods of supervision within the Party in the form of Party regulations. It clearly pointed out that the key objects of supervision within the Party were the leading organs and cadres at all levels, especially the principal leaders of leading groups at all levels. In December 2003, the Central Committee issued the revised Regulations on Disciplinary Punishment of the Communist Party of China, which made a comprehensive and specific provision for the handling of various violations of discipline by Party members under the new situation. In accordance with the goal of establishing a rational structure, scientific allocation, rigorous procedures, and an effective power operation mechanism, the CPC combined the strengthening of the system construction of power restriction with the effective supervision of cadres. In September 2004, the Central Committee promulgated and implemented the Regulations on the Protection of the Rights of Party Members. The General Office of the Central Committee also issued regulations such as the

Measures for Supervision and Inspection of the Selection and Appointment of Leading Party and Government Cadres (Trial Implementation) and the Initial Provisions for the Open Selection of Leading Party and Government Cadres. In July 2005, the Central Discipline Commission discussed and adopted the Provisions on the Discipline Commission's Assistance to the Party Committee in Organizing and Coordinating Anti-Corruption Work (Trial Implementation). In April 2007, the State Council promulgated the Regulations on the Disposal of Civil Servants in Administrative Organs. In addition, the Central Discipline Inspection Commission, together with relevant departments, formulated a series of supporting provisions, such as the Interim Provisions on the Inspection Work of the Discipline Inspection Commission of the Central Committee of the Communist Party of China and the Organizational Department of the Central Committee of the Communist Party of China, and the Opinions on the Discipline Inspection Unit of the Central Committee of the Communist Party of China to perform its supervisory duties. The promulgation of these laws and regulations had initially formed a system of internal supervision laws and regulations with the Party Constitution as the core, the supervision regulations as the main body, and a series of supporting provisions as an important supplement.

Establishing and improving the system of punishing and preventing corruption was an important decision made by the Central Committee on the basis of summing up historical experience and judging the situation scientifically. It was also a further deepening of the Party's understanding of the ruling law and the working law of fighting corruption and promoting honesty. The establishment and gradual improvement of this system and the education activities to maintain the advanced nature of Communist Party members promoted each other, effectively strengthened the Party's ruling capacity and advanced nature construction, and strengthened the Party's ability to resist corruption and change and to resist risks under the conditions of developing the socialist market economy.

IV

The Formation of the Important Concept of the "Three Represents" and the Establishment of Its Leading Position

Since the Fourth Plenary Session of the Thirteenth Central Committee, the leading collective of the Central Committee led by Jiang Zemin had held high the great banner of Deng Xiaoping Theory, accurately grasped the characteristics of the times, scientifically judged the historical orientation of the Party, focused on the theme of building socialism with Chinese characteristics, collected the wisdom of the entire Party, carried out theoretical innovation with the great courage of Marxism, and advanced the importance of the "Three Represents." After the important concept of the "Three Represents" was put forward and further enriched and developed, it was formally established as the guiding ideology of the Party at the Sixteenth National Congress of the Party in 2002.

1. Formation of the Important Concept of the "Three Represents"

By constantly summing up the Party's historical and practical experience since the Fourth Plenary Session of the Thirteenth Central Committee, the Central Committee, led by Jiang Zemin was increasingly concerned with what socialism was, how to build it, and what kind of Party should be built and how to build it. This laid the foundation for clearly putting forward the important concept of the "Three Represents." On this basis, on February 20, 2000, Jiang Zemin, at the Three Advocates Education Conference for Leading Cadres in Gaozhou District, Maoming City, Guangdong Province, put forward the requirement of the "Five Always." That is, "We should ensure the Party always maintains the nature of the working class vanguard, always represents the interests of the overwhelming majority of the people, always becomes the representative of the advanced productive forces of society, and always leads the people of all ethnicities to promote social life. The development of productive forces would always play a strong and effective role as the core of leadership, and we must further improve the Party's ideological, organizational, and style of work in the light of new historical conditions."[4] After attending the Three Advocates conference in Gaozhou, Jiang Zemin visited Shenzhen, Shunde, and Guangzhou from February 21–25. On the

24th, he chaired a symposium on party building in Guangzhou, further putting forward the idea of the "Three Represents." At the meeting, Jiang Zemin said, "Summarizing the history of our Party for more than seventy years, we can draw an important conclusion. That is, our Party has won the support of the people because it always represents the development requirements of China's advanced social productive forces, the direction of China's advanced culture, and China itself in all historical periods of revolution, construction, and reform. Focused on the fundamental interests of the overwhelming majority of the people, and through the formulation of the correct line, principles, and policies, we unremittingly strive for the realization of the fundamental interests of the country and the people." Under the new historical conditions, "all Communist Party members and leading cadres should have a deep understanding and firm grasp of the "Three Represents" to guide their thoughts and actions, so that they can truly become a qualified Party member and leading cadre of the Party."[5] This was Jiang Zemin's creative answer to the important question of what kind of party to build and how to build it at the turn of the century, following the Fourth Plenary Session of the Fourteenth Central Committee and the Fifteenth National Congress, in accordance with the new changes in the international and domestic situation. This answer made the general goal, task, and direction of party building clearer.

The important concept of the "Three Represents" had strong repercussions both inside and outside the Party and in China and abroad. The entire Party and the whole country carried out studies with great enthusiasm, deepening their understanding of this important idea. On this basis, Jiang Zemin also discussed how to strengthen and improve the Party's leadership under the new situation from different perspectives, at the economic work conference, the United Front Work Conference, and the meeting of the Commission of Intermediate Discipline held by the Central Committee, so as to enrich and improve the important concept of the "Three Represents."

After the important idea of the "Three Represents" was put forward, in order to carry out this important thought, the Central Committee focused on two aspects of work. The first was that the Party should carry out study and education activities on the important concept of the "Three Represents." On November 30, 2000, the General Office of the Central Committee formulated the Opinions on Important Thought Study and Education Activities of the "Three Represents" in the Rural Areas. It required that, starting from the winter of 2000 and the spring of 2001, the leading groups and grassroots cadres of county (city) departments, towns, and villages throughout the country should study the important concept of the "Three Represents" in a planned and systematic manner in roughly two years. Party committees and governments at all levels soon worked out implementation plans. The leaders of many provinces, prefectures (cities), and counties also implemented the responsibility system, identified contact points, conducted in-depth investigations and studies at the grassroots level, and guided work face to face. Through the development of this activity, the ideological and working styles of grassroots cadres in rural areas was significantly improved, thus further promoting the development of the rural economy and the improvement of farmers' lives, so that this activity received the effect of "cadres being educated and farmers gaining the benefits."

Second, the Party's construction had to be taken as a key subject, and special investigation needed to be carried out extensively. Relevant departments of the Central Committee formed task groups to conduct investigations and studies, listen widely to opinions, and understand various aspects of the situation. In addition, various forms of research were carried out in various places and departments, which provided plenty of valuable materials for considering and addressing the problems of Party building under the new situation. Through research and discussion, all Party members achieved some results and consensus, but they also deeply felt that there were still many problems to be studied and solved. In response, Jiang Zemin stated at the Fifth Plenary Session of the Fifteenth Central Committee held in October 2000, "There is still a lot of work to be done to make all Party members deeply understand and fully and correctly grasp the requirements of the thought behind the "Three Represents." First of all, further research should be made on the combination of theory and practice in order to form a consensus and give an answer."[6] In January 2001, Jiang Zemin emphasized in his Speech at the National Conference of Propaganda Ministers that in commemorating the 80th anniversary of the founding of the Communist Party of China, it was important to "carry out in-depth propaganda and education in the 'Three Represents' throughout the Party" and "strive to study, publicize and implement the requirements of the 'Three Represents.'"[7]

On July 1, 2001, the Central Committee held a grand congress in Beijing to celebrate the 80th anniversary of the founding of the Communist Party of China. Jiang Zemin delivered an important speech at the meeting, which systematically expounded the scientific connotation of the important concept of the "Three Represents." Jiang Zemin pointed out that if the Party wanted to always represent the development requirements of China's advanced productive forces, that is, the Party's theory, line, program, principle, policy, and various work, it must strive to conform to the law of the development of productive forces, reflect the requirements of constantly promoting the emancipation and development of social productive forces, especially the requirements of promoting the development of advanced productive forces, and constantly improve the people through the development of productive forces. The Party should always represent the orientation of advanced Chinese culture, that is, the Party's theory, line, program, policy, principles, and various work. It must strive to embody the requirements of developing a modern, world-oriented, and future-oriented socialist culture of the scientific masses of the nation, and promote the ideological, moral, and scientific and cultural qualities of the whole nation. To continuously improve and provide spiritual impetus and intellectual support for China's economic development and social progress, the Party must always represent the fundamental interests of the overwhelming majority of the Chinese people, that is, the Party's theory, line, program, principle, policy, and various work. It needed to persist in taking the fundamental interests of the people as the starting point and destination, and give full play to the enthusiasm, initiative, and creativity of the people. On the basis of the continuous development and progress of the society, the people would continue to obtain tangible economic, political, and cultural benefits.

In the July 1st Speech, Jiang Zemin not only comprehensively explained the scientific connotation and basic content of the important concept of the "Three Represents," but also clearly pointed out how to implement it. After the July 1st Speech was delivered, a series of theoretical seminars were held by the central and local governments to discuss the spirit of Jiang Zemin's July 1st Speech. The Central Ministry of Propaganda mobilized the responsible comrades and theoretical workers from relevant departments to form an important speech mission on July 1, which was sent to the central state organs and all parts of the country to disseminate the spirit of the speech on July 1, achieving positive results. The Central Organizational Department organized relevant departments to set up task groups and continued to carry out a series of special investigations around the Party's construction under the new situation. There was a general upsurge of learning and practicing the "Three Represents" across the country.

With the deepening of the study and practice of the "Three Represents," the people gained a deeper understanding of how to build the Party in accordance with the requirements of the "Three Represents."

On May 31, 2002, Jiang Zemin delivered an important speech at the graduation ceremony of the provincial and ministerial cadres' study seminar of the Central Party School. Focusing on the situation, tasks and working principles facing the Party at the new stage of the new century, he further elaborated the guiding significance and spiritual essence of the important concept of the "Three Represents." He pointed out that in order to create a new situation of socialism with Chinese characteristics, it was important to hold high the great banner of Deng Xiaoping Theory and fully implement the requirements of the "Three Represents." The "Three Represents" were in line with Marxism-Leninism, Mao Zedong Thought, and Deng Xiaoping Theory, reflecting the new requirements of the development of the contemporary world and China for the work of the Party and the state. The "Three Represents" was the foundation of the Party's founding, governing, and power source. It was also a powerful theoretical tool for strengthening and improving the Party's construction and promoting the self-improvement and development of China's socialist system.

He emphasized that the key to the implementation of the "Three Represents" was to keep pace with the times, to maintain the advanced nature of the Party, and to uphold the essence of governing for the people. All Party members needed to firmly grasp this fundamental requirement and constantly strengthen their consciousness and firmness in implementing the requirements of the "Three Represents." At the same time, he profoundly expounded the importance of adhering to the Party's ideological line and promoting the Party's theoretical innovation. He emphasized that adhering to the ideological line of emancipating the mind, seeking truth from facts, and carrying forward the spirit of keeping pace with the times were the decisive factors for the Party to maintain its advanced nature and creativity as it was the long-term ruling Party. Whether the Party could always do this would determine the future and destiny of China's development.

This speech further unified the Party's ideology and made full preparations for the convening of the Sixteenth National Congress and the establishment of the guiding position of the important concept of the "Three Represents" in the Party.

From November 8–14, 2002, the Sixteenth National Congress of the Communist Party of China was held in Beijing. The Congress formally established the important concept of the "Three Represents" as the guiding ideology of the Party. After summing up the valuable experience accumulated by the Party over the previous thirteen years, the report of the General Assembly clearly pointed out, "These experiences, in connection with the historical experience since the founding of the Party, come to a conclusion that the Party must always represent the development requirements of China's advanced productive forces, the direction of China's advanced culture, and the fundamental interests of the overwhelming majority of the Chinese people."

The important concept of the "Three Represents" was formed on the basis of scientifically judging the historical position of the Party. To carry out the "Three Represents," it was necessary to ensure the whole Party in the spirit of keeping pace with the times and constantly open up a new realm for the development of Marxist theory. It was important to regard development as the top priority of the Party's rule and rejuvenation of the country and constantly create a new situation for modernization. It was also crucial to mobilize all the positive factors in the broadest and fullest way to continuously add new force to the great rejuvenation of the Chinese nation and to promote the Party's construction in the spirit of reform and constantly inject new vitality into the Party's body. In brief, the "Three Represents" were constantly developing and advancing. The whole Party had to constantly emancipate its mind, develop its theory, and create new ideas in practice. The "Three Represents" were to be carried out in all fields of socialist modernization and embodied in all aspects of Party building, so as to keep pace with the development of the times and share the destiny of the people.

Through a series of elaborations, the report summarized the background, historical position, scientific connotation, spiritual essence, and guiding significance of the "Three Represents." Generally speaking, the "Three Represents" aimed to continue to explore what socialism was and how it should be built by creatively applying Marxism-Leninism and Mao Zedong Thought, and especially Deng Xiaoping Theory, while closely combining these with the new situation of the times, the new requirements of the vast majority of the people, and the new practice of China's reform, opening up, and modernization. Regarding the issue of what socialism was and how to build it, the Party needed to shift from adhering to and perfecting the basic economic system with socialist public ownership as the main body and the multi-ownership economy developing together to adhering to and perfecting the distribution system with distribution according to work as the main body and coexistence of various distribution modes, from establishing the socialist market economic system to promoting the strategic adjustment of economic structure and the transformation of the mode of economic growth, from promoting the development of the western region and promoting the coordinated development of the region to implementing the opening strategy of combining "letting in" with "reaching out," from developing socialist democratic politics to building a socialist country ruled by law, from developing advanced socialist culture to promoting the coordinated development of socialist material, political, and spiritual civilization, and from promoting multi-polarization of the world and democratization of international relations to correctly coping with and responding to economic globalization and promoting the Communist Party. A series of other innovative theoretical achievements were made as well. On the question of how to build the Party and what kind of party to build, it was important to persist in examining the CPC itself in light of the requirements of the development of the times, to strengthen and improve itself with the spirit of reform and settle the two historic issues of improving the Party's leadership, ruling competence, and ability to resist corruption and risks so as to promote the new great project of party building comprehensively, which constituted a new understanding of party building.

It was precisely because the "Three Represents" had generated a whole set of new theoretical achievements that the Sixteenth National Congress established the "Three Represents" as the guiding ideology of the Party, along with Marxism-Leninism, Mao Zedong Thought, and Deng Xiaoping Theory. Establishing the "Three Represents" as the guiding ideology of the Party was a historic decision and contribution of the Congress. On the basis of a series of discussions at the Sixteenth National Congress, the amendments to the Party Constitution adopted by the Congress include the "Three Represents" alongside Marxism-Leninism, Mao Zedong Thought, and Deng Xiaoping Theory as the guideline for the action of the Communist Party of China, which clearly stipulated that the Communist Party of China was the vanguard of the Chinese working class, as well as of the Chinese people and the Chinese nation. The CPC took Marxism-Leninism, Mao Zedong Thought, Deng Xiaoping Theory, and the Important Concept of the "Three Represents" as its guide for action, demonstrating the importance of the "Three Represents." It formed part of the guiding ideology that the Party needed to adhere to over a long period. Just as the Seventh Congress of the Party established Mao Zedong Thought as the guiding ideology of the Party and the Fifteenth Congress of the Party established Deng Xiaoping Theory as the guiding ideology of the Party, which played an extremely important role in promoting the successful development of China's revolution and construction, the Sixteenth Congress established the "Three Represents" as the guiding ideology of the Party, which would also play an important role in comprehensively creating a new situation for the cause of socialism with Chinese characteristics.

After the "Three Represents" were written into the Party Constitution at the Sixteenth National Congress, on March 14, 2004, the Second Session of the Tenth National People's Congress adopted the Amendment to the Constitution of the People's Republic of China, which incorporated the "Three Represents" into the Constitution and established its guiding position in the political and social life of China. This was of great significance to the Party and state. In the new stage of the new century, the Communist Party of China needed to hold high the banner of Deng Xiaoping's theory and the "Three Represents," adhere to the socialist path with Chinese characteristics, and lead the people to strive for building a well-off society in an all-round way and fundamentally realize modernization.

2. The Historical Significance of the Establishment of the "Three Represents" as the Party's Guiding Thought

The establishment of the "Three Represents" in the guiding position for the Party was of great historical significance in the history of the development of Marxism, especially in the history of scientific socialism.

First, it was important to advance Marxism to a new era and theoretical level. The "Three Represents" was the product of China's Reform and Opening Up and the practice of socialist modernization. This important thought, standing at the height of the times of China's development and world development, further addressed the questions of "what is socialism and how to build it" and creatively answered the questions of "what kind of party should we build and how should we build it," greatly enriching the theoretical treasure house of Marxism and opening up a new realm of theoretical development in Marxism on the basis of inheriting the existing knowledge of it. The formation of the "Three Represents" and the establishment of its guiding position in the Party, especially its important practical guiding role in China's economy and society, indicated that the CPC's understanding of the ruling law of the Party, the law of socialist construction, and the law of human social development had reached a new theoretical level.

Second, it was important to endow Marxism with the new connotation of the times. The "Three Represents" were the inheritance and development of Marxism-Leninism, Mao Zedong Thought, and Deng Xiaoping Theory. This important thought, proceeding from the new reality of China and the world, through the continuous summary of practical experience and the theoretical summary of the spirit of the times and the requirements of practice, creatively combined the Party's construction with the development and changes of the contemporary world and the development trend of contemporary China, with the self-improvement and development of our socialist institution, and with the realization of the grand goals and objectives of socialism with Chinese characteristics. These tasks were closely combined, giving the Party's nature, purpose, guiding ideology, and historical tasks a distinct connotation and characteristics of the times. Therefore, this important thought reflected the new requirements of the development and change of the contemporary world and China for the work of the Party and the state. It was the latest achievement of the development of Marxism in China. It was a powerful theoretical weapon to strengthen and improve the Party's construction and promote the self-improvement and development of socialism in China. It was also the guiding ideology that the Party had to adhere to over a long period. It was the foundation of the Party's founding and governing, as well as the source of its strength.

Third, it creatively inherited and developed the basic views of Marxism. The "Three Represents" creatively developed basic Marxist viewpoints on the rule of the Party in power, the rule of socialist construction, and the rule of human social development, such as that the progress of human society is ultimately determined by productive forces, guided by advanced culture, and promoted by the masses of the people, which indicated that socialism with Chinese characteristics was a socialist market. The organic unity of economy, socialist democratic politics, and advanced socialist culture was a society in which the socialist material civilization, spiritual civilization, and political civilization developed in an all-round way. It profoundly clarified the internal relationship between the socialist modernization undertaking led by the Communist Party of China, the development and progress of Chinese society, the great rejuvenation of the Chinese nation, and the new great project of the Party's construction. These main viewpoints creatively developed the basic theory of Marxism on the basis of inheriting the existing knowledge of Marxism.

In conclusion, the "Three Represents" closely combined with the new conditions of the times, upheld and developed Marxism with great theoretical courage and the scientific spirit of seeking, gave it new vigor, and proved once again that the basic principles of Marxism remained the Party's sharp tool for recognizing and transforming the world and pushing forward the continuous development of social practice.

CHAPTER II

The Proposal of Building a Moderately Well-off Society in a Comprehensive Way and a Scientific Outlook on Development

Under the guidance of Deng Xiaoping's thought and the important theory of the "Three Represents," China's economic and social development and all aspects of the work developed by leaps and bounds. By the end of the 20th century, China initially built a new system of a socialist market, and people's life in general reached a reasonably prosperous level. On this basis, the Central Committee further set a new goal for building a prosperous society in an all-round way, according to the domestic and international situation and the basic conditions of China's economic and social development. To better guide the overall construction of a prosperous society and the smooth progress of economic and social development, the CPC raised the scientific view of development in the new century. With the aim of comprehensively building a moderately prosperous society and with the guidance of the scientific view of development, Chinese society further embarked on a new historical journey of socialist modernization.

I

The New Goal of Building a Moderately Well-off Society in a Comprehensive Way and the Reform Program for Improving the Market Economy

After the Fourteenth National Congress of the CPC in 1992, the Communist Party of China continued to increase the intensity of eliminating the old to make way for the new in accordance with the goal of reform aimed at establishing a system of socialist market economy, which resulted in great breakthroughs in many areas of reform, driving the fundamental transition from a traditional planned economy to a socialist market economy. The socialist market economic system had initially been established by 2000, and the people's livelihood had generally improved to a moderately prosperous level.

1. The Initial Establishment of a Socialist Market Economic System and the Overall Realization of a Prosperous Society

The initial establishment of the socialist market economic system was mainly manifested in the following aspects: the structure of ownership had been increasingly diversified, the vitality of the national economy at the micro-level had been enhanced, the market system had basically been established, market production factors had been built to a certain scale, the new macro-control system had been explored actively and functioned in an indirect way, the reform of income distribution had been gradually deepened, the construction of the social security system had been progressed steadily, the reform of government institutions and transformation of functions had accelerated, the marketization of the national economy significantly improved with the deepening of the reform, and the fundamental role of the allocation of market resources was gradually enhanced.

By the end of year 2000, China had initially set up the socialist market economic system, becoming a developing country with a market economy. This marked a fundamental change in the economic system in China, occurring over the two decades after the adoption of the Reform and Opening Up policy, particularly since the Fourteenth National Congress of the CPC. It not only greatly changed the institutional environment for China's economic development, but also had a profound influence on the social life and ideology of the Chinese people. It was a decisive factor for both China's reform and construction and the Party's theoretical development and innovation.

The Party observed that China had basically established a socialist market economic system. Meanwhile, the Party made another observation from the macro prospective, noting that China had generally built a moderately prosperous society, on which a new blueprint had been mapped out for future development in the new century.

The application of the concept of "a moderately prosperous society" in China had undergone a historical evolution in the new era. As early as in 1979, Deng Xiaoping raised the concept of "a moderately prosperous" society and set up the goal of reaching it by the end of the 20th century. Since then, he had elaborated the idea of "moderately prosperous" from different angles on many occasions, enriching the connotation of this concept.

In December 1990 at the Seventh Plenary Session of the Thirteenth Central Committee, the CPC adopted the proposals for Formulating the Ten-Year Plan for National Economic and Social Development and the Eighth Five-Year Plan, putting forward the goals of "improving people's lives from subsistence level to a moderately prosperous level, providing abundant consumer goods, optimizing the consumption structure, significantly improving living conditions, enriching cultural life, continuously improving social service, public health, and facilities."[1] All this was planned with concern for quality of life. The National Bureau of Statistics issued 16 indicators of "a moderately prosperous society" in 1991, including per capita GDP, Engels coefficient, per capita disposable income for urban and rural people, and per capita net income of farmers. According to this standard, the Chinese people's life had reached a "moderately prosperous" level by the year 2000.

At the Fifth Plenary Session of the Fourteenth Central Committee of the CPC in 1995, the Party set the goal of building a moderately prosperous society by the year 2000, as stated in the Central Committee's Proposals on the Formulation of the Ninth Five-Year Plan for National Economic and Social Development and the 2010 Vision. China planned to "basically eliminate poverty to improve people's lives to a moderately prosperous level by 2000."[2] Generally speaking, the definition of a prosperous life, similar to the international standard for quality of life, included conditions of living materials such as food, clothing, housing, and transportation; conditions of the living environment such as air, traffic, water quality, and green space; and conditions of the social environment such as social order, sense of security, and social morality.

After years of Reform and Opening Up, by 2000, China had attained the second strategic goal of socialist modernization and the overall moderately prosperous level. As a result, at the Fifth Plenary Session of the Fifteenth Central Committee in 2000, the Party announced that China had already accomplished the goal of building a moderately prosperous society in general, that "from the beginning of the new century, China will enter a new development stage of building a moderately prosperous society in an all-round way and speeding up socialist modernization," and that it would start the third step of the strategic deployment, which would be a new milestone in the history of the Chinese nation.[3] According to the proposal put forward at the Fifth Plenary Session of the Fifteenth Central Committee, the State Council formulated the Outline of the Tenth Five-Year Plan for National Economic and Social Development, approved at the Fourth Session of the Ninth National People's Congress in March 2001. The outline provided a blueprint for the economic and social development for the first five-year plan in the new century and specified the guiding principles and main tasks, serving as the action plan for the Chinese people of all ethnic groups to work together at the beginning of the new century. With the implementation of the Tenth Five-Year Plan, China entered a new development stage of building a moderately prosperous society in an all-round way and accelerating socialist modernization.

At the end of the twentieth century, Chinese people reached the level of a moderately prosperous life in general, which "is a new milestone in the history of the Chinese nation."[4] This laid a solid foundation for its further development in the new century.

2. The Sixteenth National Congress of the CPC and the Setting of the Goal of Building a Moderately Prosperous Society in an All-Round Way

Shortly after entering the new century, the Communist Party of China held the Sixteenth National Congress in Beijing from November 8–14, 2002. The Congress adopted Jiang Zemin's report "Building a Moderately Prosperous Society in an All-round Way to Create a New Scenario of Socialism with Chinese Characteristics" on behalf of the Fifteenth Central Committee. The Congress also approved the Constitution of the Communist Party of China (Amendment) and the work report of the Central Discipline Inspection Commission. It elected 198 members of the Central Committee and 158 alternate members to form the new Central Committee and the new Central Discipline Inspection Commission.

The theme of the Congress was to hold high the great banner of Deng Xiaoping Theory, carry out the important theory of the "Three Represents," draw on the past for the future, and keep pace with the times, so as to build a moderately prosperous society in an all-round way, speed up socialist modernization, and strive for a new situation centered on socialism with Chinese characteristics.

Centering around this theme, the reports of the Sixteenth National Congress made it clear to the world that the banner the CPC raised at the new stage in the new century were the banners of Mao Zedong Thought, Marxist-Leninist Thought, Deng Xiaoping Theory, and the "Three Represents." The path that the CPC took was the path of socialism with Chinese characteristics, which was initiated by Deng Xiaoping and held and developed by the Central Committee under Jiang Zemin's leadership. Under the leadership of the CPC, the Chinese people would achieve the goal of building a moderately prosperous society and achieve modernization in the first 50 years of the new century. These distinct and forceful answers reflected the determination of the Central Committee, the wishes of the people, and the requirements of the party and national development. It was of great significance for unifying the party and the people's thoughts, integrating manpower with one heart and one mind, and working hard amid difficulties to create a new scenario for the cause of socialism with Chinese characteristics.

The report reviewed the course of the Party's struggle and its basic experience over the previous thirteen years since the Fifteenth National Congress, especially since the Fourth Plenary Session of the Thirteenth Central Committee in 1989. The report pointed out that it was widely accepted that the previous thirteen years was a period in which China's overall national power had been significantly enhanced and the Chinese people gained the greatest benefit, a time when society sustained stability with proper administration and substantial harmony, and when China significantly enhanced its influence in the world and its national cohesiveness. Over the previous thirteen years, China acquired valuable experience and deepened its understanding of what socialism is, how to build it, what kind of party it was aiming for, and how to build the party. China's experience was

1) holding onto Deng Xiaoping Theory as the guideline to constantly facilitate theoretical innovation, 2) adhering to economic construction as the core to tackle problems along the way from the perspective of development, 3) adhering to the Reform and Opening Up policy to constantly improve the socialist market economic system, 4) adhering to the four cardinal principles to develop the socialist democratic politics, 5) adhering to the material and spiritual civilization to rule the country by both law and virtue, 6) adhering to the overriding principle of stability to properly balance the relations between reform, development, and stability, 7) adhering to the Party's absolute leadership over the army to build competent troops with Chinese characteristics, 8) uniting all the forces that could be united to consolidate the cohesiveness of the Chinese nation, 9) adhering to the independent foreign policy of peace to safeguard world peace and promote common development, and 10) adhering to strengthening and improving the Party's leadership to foster the new great project concerning Party building.

These ten principles represented the basic experience that the Party had grasped to lead the Chinese people in the building of socialism with Chinese characteristics. All this experience, together with the historical experience of the Party since its founding, boiled down to the "Three Represents." This was the essential requirement of upholding and developing socialism, and the inevitable conclusion of the Party's arduous exploration and great practice.

According to the requirements of creating a new situation for the cause of socialism with Chinese characteristics, the Sixteenth National Congress of the CPC decided on the goal of building a moderately prosperous society in an all-round way based on in-depth analysis of the new situation and the tasks the Party and the state were facing. Jiang Zemin pointed out in the report of the Sixteenth National Congress that, according to the proposal put forward at the Fifteenth National Congress, the development goal by 2010, at the 100th anniversary of the founding of the CPC and New China, "we will integrate our resources in the first twenty years of this century to build a moderately prosperous society at a higher level in an all-round way that benefits over one billion people, with a more developed economy, more robust democracy, more advanced science and education, more prosperous culture, more harmonious society, and more affluent lives for the people. This is an indispensable transitional stage of development to fulfill the third strategic goal of modernization construction, and a crucial stage to improve the socialist market economic system and further opening to the outside world. From this stage of construction onward, we will continue to strive for several decades to largely achieve modernization and to build China into a prosperous, democratic, and civilized socialist nation by the middle of this century."[5]

By the year 2020, China envisioned a bright future, which would be presented as follows:

1) *On the basis of optimizing the structure and improving efficiency, the GDP will be quadrupled in 2020 compared with that in 2000.* The overall national power and international competitiveness was to be substantially enhanced, and industrialization largely accomplished. A sound socialist market economic system and a more open and dynamic economic system would be built. The proportion of the urban population would be greatly increased, and the widening gap between the workers and farmers, between the urban and rural areas, and between different regions would be steadily narrowed. The social security system was to be relatively sound, with a moderately high rate of social employment, generally increased family property, and a more affluent life for the people.

2) *The socialist democracy and legal system will be improved, with a better rule of the socialist law, and people's political, economic, and cultural rights and interests well respected and protected.* Society would enjoy a sounder democracy at the grassroots level and a good social order, and its people would live and work in peace and contentment.

3) *The entire nation will enjoy clearly better ideology and morality, greater scientific and cultural competence, and improved health, with a sound modern national education system, scientific, technological, and cultural innovation system, and national fitness and medical health care system.* The people would enjoy equal opportunity for education, with high school education basically popularized and illiteracy eliminated. A society of lifetime learning would be formed for everyone to facilitate the overall development of the people.

4) *The nation will enjoy strikingly sustainable development, with a better ecological environment, optimized utilization of resources, and greater harmony between humans and nature, leading the whole of society onto the development path of civilization, featuring higher productivity, an affluent life, and a sound ecosystem.*

The goal set at the Sixteenth National Congress, that of building a moderately prosperous society in an all-round way, was more profound in content and in meaning, though the statement had only added the term "in an all-round way."

The goal of "building a moderately prosperous society in an all-round way" was put forward, targeting the "prosperous" state reached at the end of the 20th century which was low-level, not comprehensive, and unbalanced. Therefore, the building of a moderately prosperous society in an all-round way could be summarized, in terms of its fundamental concept and development indicators, as three "mores," i.e., "a more balanced development at a higher level" and "beneficial to more people."

The goal of building a moderately prosperous society in an all-round way set at the Sixteenth National Congress was a goal of overall economic, political, cultural, and social development for socialism with Chinese characteristics. It was also the further enrichment and development of the three-step strategic concept of China's socialist modernization.

1) The notion of building a moderately prosperous society in an all-round way brought the concept of social development to a new height. Development was the Party's first priority in governing and rejuvenating the country. It was a remarkable achievement the Chinese people had made in social development under the leadership of the CPC to move from satisfying the basic needs of the people to building a moderately prosperous society. However, even with this great leap in development, there were still many challenges and problems to be settled in the nation. For instance, with productivity, science and technology, and education relatively underdeveloped, China still faced the pressure of developed countries' dominance in economy, science and technology, and other aspects. Further, the economic system and other management systems were not well developed, the binary economic structure of urban and rural areas had not yet been changed, and the widening gap between regions had not been fundamentally narrowed. There were people in certain regions who were not yet out of poverty, the total population continued to increase, with a growing proportion of the aging population, and the pressure on employment and social security was increasing. The conflicts between natural resources, ecological environment and socioeconomic development were becoming acute, and there were problems that could not be ignored in the construction of culture, democratic and legal systems, and morality. All this required overall planning and resolution. The initiation of the concept and goal of building a moderately prosperous society in an all-round way showed that the top decision-makers of the CPC had a thorough understanding of the situation, thus pushing the understanding of the overall development of China's socialist

modernization in economy, politics, culture, social construction, and other fields to a new stage.

2) The concept of building a moderately prosperous society in an all-round way had, in terms of consolidating and developing socialism, extended China's perspective from productivity to people's lives. In summarizing the basic experience over the previous thirteen years, the report of the Sixteenth National Congress clearly stated its goal of "solving the problems that are in progress from the perspective of development." In discussing how to solve the problem of development, classic Marxist writers pointed out that socialism was superior to capitalism primarily in that the former could generate a higher social productivity than the latter, which was undoubtedly a definite conclusion. However, given the positive and negative historical experience from home and abroad since the 1990s, people's recognition of a nation, a political party, or a society depended not only on social productivity, but on its ability to constantly improve people's living standards and quality of life, and to optimize the social and cultural environment. The initiation and formulation of the concept and goal of building a moderately prosperous society in an all-round way indicated the new understanding of and progress in Marxism concerning the liberation and development of social productivity forces.

3) The idea of building a moderately prosperous society in an all-round way reflected the practical value of the important theory of the "Three Represents." To build a moderately prosperous society in an all-round way was, in essence, to constantly liberate and develop social productivity and build an advanced socialist culture and improve people's living standards and quality of life, so as to accomplish political, economic, cultural, and social development. The top priority in carrying out the "Three Represents" was development, which embodied advanced productivity, advanced culture, and the fundamental interests of the overwhelming majority of the people. In terms of the essential requirements for social evolution, the implementation of the important theory of the "Three Represents" and the building of a moderately prosperous society in an all-round way shared historical and logical consistency.

4) Building a moderately prosperous society in an all-round way was an action plan that fully embodied the spirit of the times in the new century. To set a goal and an action plan consistent with the requirements of the times and indicative of the expectations of the people was the key for a political party to integrate

and mobilize all positive factors to work together for a common goal. From a historical point of view, the Party had put forward inspiring goals based on the development of the times and the requirements of social progress in different historical periods to unite the people around the Party to have won one victory after another in revolution, construction, and reform. The Party set the goal of building a moderately prosperous society in an all-round way at the Sixteenth National Congress, which undoubtedly conformed to the national conditions and the times, representing the fundamental interests of the people and the requirements of the times. A realistic and innovative goal, it constituted the action plan of facilitating the construction of socialist modernization in the new century.

3. Guidelines for Further Improving the Reform of the Socialist Market Economic System

The development of the socialist market economy was a great innovation that the CPC made in Marxist economic theory. To align with the direction of the reform of the socialist market economy, China not only steadily shifted to a socialist market economic system from a planned economic system, but also enriched and developed the guidelines of the reform of the socialist market economy through practice and exploration.

After the Third Plenary Session of the Eleventh Central Committee of the CPC, China launched the Reform and Opening Up policy. After more than ten years of practice and theoretical exploration, the relationship between planning and market was gradually identified, which laid the foundation for setting the goal for the reform of the socialist market economy. The Party set the goal of socialist market economic reform at the Fourteenth National Congress of the CPC in 1992. The Third Plenary Session of the Fourteenth Central Committee in 1993 adopted the Central Committee's Decision on the Key Issues to Establish a Socialist Market Economic System. The overall plan for reform of the socialist market economy was proposed, and its basic connotation and framework initially defined, constituting the guidelines for China's economic system reform in the 1990s. Armed with this summary of practical experience, the Party formed a better understanding of the socialist market economy at the subsequent Fifteenth and Sixteenth National Congresses, initially establishing the socialist market economic system. As a result, China's economic system reform made significant progress.

a. The pattern of the common development of the multi-ownership economy was basically formed, with public ownership as the main body.

With years of adjustment and improvement, the ownership structure of China was more rationalized. Public ownership shifted from singularity to diversity in form, with more appropriate national economic patterns. Most large and medium-sized state-owned enterprises established modern enterprise systems by the year 2000. The urban and rural collective economies gained new vitality in reform and restructuring, and some enterprises with solid foundations gained new momentum for development by adopting a market mechanism. Other non-state-owned economy like the self-employed, private sectors, joint ventures, and wholly foreign owned enterprises grew dramatically from weak to strong. Joint stock systems and the diversified ownership economy became increasingly important under the state policy. In accordance with market-oriented reform and adjustment of ownership structure, the distribution system was constantly improved, and a variety of modes of distribution coexisted with the major mode of "distribution of income based on one's performance." The incentive mechanism was gradually improved, and a new situation took shape where production factors like labor, capital, technology, and management were involved in distribution based on their respective contributions.

b. The socialist market economy system was initially established.

The fundamental economic system was set up and various market factors were constantly nurtured. As a result, the micro foundation of the socialist market economic system was built up. With the further expansion of the commodity market, the development of production market elements such as capital, labor, technology, and real estate were accelerated, and the basic role of the market in terms of resource allocation was enhanced. In promoting market-oriented reform, the nation dramatically boosted the reform of the macroeconomic management system and enhanced its ability to control the economy on the macro level. With coordination between national planning, financial policy, and monetary policy, as well as a variety of means of regulation, the nation steadily improved its macro-control policy.

c. China's economic and social development greatly improved.

China had already moved from the early stages to the middle stages of industrialization. The mode of economic growth had gradually transformed from extensive to intensive, and economic quality greatly improved with the expansion of the total economy. China's total economic output and total import and export trade ranked top in the world. People's living standards achieved two historic leaps, and the challenge of meeting the people's basic needs had been solved since the 1980s, with the second leap from "food and clothing" to "moderately prosperous," occurring in the 1990s. The issue of insufficient food supplies that plagued the Chinese people for thousands of years had been fundamentally solved under the leadership of the Communist Party of China, and the dream of living a prosperous life had come true. Alongside this period of rapid economic growth and social progress, education, science, culture, the population, the environment, and other social undertakings had obtained historic achievements, embarking on the road to sustainable development and social progress. This was the victory of the socialist system and a new milestone in the history of the development of the Chinese nation.

d. The social security system had been initially established and the social security policy continued to be improved, focusing on pension, unemployment, and medical insurance for urban workers.

Channels of social security funds had been diversified, and management services had been socialized. The Three Guarantees, (i.e. the basic livelihood guarantee system for laid-off workers in state-owned enterprises, the unemployment insurance system, and the minimum living security system for urban residents) was continuously improved and played a significant role in maintaining social stability.

Through a series of reforms over a set period of time, China's economic and social development made great progress under marketization, and achievement of astonishing scale. At the same time, it is noteworthy that despite such a series of achievements, some long-standing, deep-seated contradictions had not yet been fundamentally solved. In addition, new problems and contradictions had emerged in the economic and social fields. The key issues included an irrational economic structure, the development gap between urban and rural areas, the slow growth of farmers' income, the increasing numbers of unemployed workers, the contradiction of employment, the increasing pressures of resources, and the environment and the overall comparatively weak economic compctitiveness. There were many reasons for these problems. One key reason was that China's socialist market economic system was still not complete and was unable to adapt to the development of productive forces in many ways, especially the advanced productive forces. New demands arose at the same time, from both the positive and negative aspects of the situation, that deepened the reform of the socialist market economic system.

Reform was a powerful driving force for economic development and social progress. In order to adapt to the accelerating international environment of economic globalization and technological development, during the Third Plenary Session of the Sixteenth Central Committee in October 2003, the Party adopted the Decisions on Some Issues Concerning the Improvement of the Socialist Market Economic System (referred to as the Decision), putting forward the reform objectives and tasks and making decisions and deployment to address both present and future key institutional issues of the system.

The main goal was improving the socialist market economic system. It was pointed out in the Decision that in accordance with the overall coordination of urban and rural development, regional development, overall economic and social development, harmonious development between humans and nature, domestic development, and opening to the outside world, it was necessary to enhance the basic role of the market in resource allocation, to enhance the vitality and competitiveness of enterprises, to complete the national macro-control system, to improve the government's functions in social management and public services, and to provide strong system guarantees from comprehensive building of a moderately prosperous society.

The main tasks of the socialist market economic system was reform. It was clearly demonstrated in the Decision that the goal was to improve the basic economic system with public ownership as the main body and the common development of a multi-ownership economy, to establish a system conducive to gradual change of the binary economic structure of urban and rural areas, to form a mechanism by which to promote coordinated regional economic development, to build a unified, open, competitive, and orderly modern market economic system, to improve the macro-control system, administrative management system, and economic legal system, to improve employment, income distribution, and the social security system, and to establish a mechanism to promote sustainable economic and social development.

The guiding ideology and principles aimed at deepening the reform of the socialist market economic system. It was clearly demonstrated in the Decision that Deng Xiaoping's theory and the "Three Represents" would be the guiding principle for implementing the basic line, basic program, and basic experience of the Party to fully carry out the mandates of the Sixteenth Congress, to emancipate the mind, to seek truth from facts, and to keep pace with the times. It was imperative to stick to reform of the socialist market economy, paying attention to construction and innovation of systems. The people's creativity had to be respected and full play given to the initiatives of the central and local governments. It was necessary to adhere to correct handling of the relationship between reform, development, and stability, promoting reform in a focused, systematic manner. It was important for the Party to adhere to overall consideration and coordination of the various interests in the process of reform, and set up a people-oriented, holistic, balanced, and sustainable perspective of development, promoting the development of the economy, society, and the people. From the point of view of a guiding ideology of deepening reform of the socialist market economy, compared with the Central Committee's Decision on the Key Issues to Establish a Socialist Market Economic System in 1993, the Decision integrated the initiatives of the Party with an emphasis on reflecting the guiding ideology with the pace with the times.

The Decision embodied the Party's understanding of the economic and social development situation in China at the turn of the 21st century, which was characterized by its distinct inheritance and continuity. The document was of historical significance, serving as a link between the past and future. It also added some points in a systematic way that had been neglected ten years earlier. It served as a programmatic document for China to improve the socialist market economy in the new century, solidifying the guidelines for reform of the socialist market economy in three aspects.

Primarily, the Decision further developed Marxist economic theory. Since the Third Plenary Session of the Eleventh Central Committee, especially during the Fourteenth Party Congress and the Third Plenary Session of the Fourteenth Central Committee, with the gradual establishment and improvement of the socialist market economic system, there were some new features in the process of reform. The reform of China was no longer "wading through the river by touching the stones," as it was in the 1980s. Instead it was executed under the guidance of the overall reform program. The topics discussed between Party leaders and academic circles shifted from "shall we reform" to "how shall we reform." The theory of the socialist market economy developed and was continuously enhanced over time in the deepening of reform practice and theoretical debates.

After the basic consensus in favor of switching economic operations to a market system had been reached both inside and outside the Party, the focus of the theoretical debate shifted to the field of ownership. Thus, the argument of various points of view could be summarized in one question, whether the focus of the proposed reform was "public" or "private." The Party answered this question decisively in the Fifteenth National Congress. With regard to the understanding of the status of the non-public economy, on the basis of the fundamental realities in China during the primary stages of socialism, the report of the Fifteenth National Congress broke through the status quo of "important supplement" and "beneficial supplement" to emphasize the public economy. It was widely agreed that the common development of a multi-ownership economy with public ownership as the main body was a "basic economic system" in the primary stage of socialism in China. The non-public economy was an "important component" of the socialist market economy. In reference to the public ownership economy, the report emphasized that the public sector included not only the state-owned and collective economies, but also the mixed ownership of them. Public ownership should be diversified, and all modes of business operations and organizational forms that reflected laws of socialized production could be boldly applied. It was important to strive to seek actualized forms of public ownership that greatly stimulated the development of productive forces. In reference to the state-owned economy, the report stated that the leading role of the state-owned economy was to control the lifeline of the national economy nationwide. The leading role of the country's state-owned economy was mainly about the power to strategically adjust the layout of the state-owned economy. Taking into account the theory of the socialist market economy against the theoretical background of the primary stage of socialism, the Fifteenth National Congress clearly answered the question of the "public" or "private" ownership of reform and radically developed the theory of the socialist market economy.

In the mid and late 1990s, the second stage strategic goal of China's modernization was basically realized. At the beginning of the 21st century, the third stage strategic goals were launched in a timely manner. From the top down, people discussed the problems during the "period of strategic opportunity" and the "period of contradiction." The new leadership team of the Central Committee elected in the Sixteenth Congress put forward the Scientific View of Development, which was a "people-oriented," "comprehensive, coordinated, and sustainable" scientific view of development, catering to the new situation and new tasks in the Third Plenary Session of the Sixteenth Central Committee, and issued the Decision on Some Issues Concerning the Improvement of the Socialist Market Economic System (referred to as the Decision).

The Decision marked the first announcement of the goal of "vigorously developing the mixed-ownership economy of state-owned capital, collective capital, non-public capital, and other shares, diversifying the subjects of investment, and making the shareholding system the main form of public ownership." Prior to this, the idea that "the shareholding system was one of the forms of public ownership" had been raised. The report of the Sixteenth National Congress stated its goal of "actively implementing the shareholding system and developing the mixed ownership economy." The major changes regarding the formulation in the Decision were intended to accelerate the diversification of state-owned enterprises and provide more opportunities for private enterprises and foreign investors to invest in state-owned joint share companies. Regarding property rights, the Decision pointed out for the first time that "property rights are the core and main content of ownership, including real rights, creditor's rights, equity and intellectual property rights, and other property rights." The reform of enterprises shifted from the establishment of the modern enterprise system to the establishment of the modern property rights system, indicating that China's enterprise reform had entered a new stage, both theoretically and practically.

In addition, the Decisions deepened and improved the understanding of the reform goals of the socialist market economy. It is pointed out in the Decisions in the Third Plenary Session of the Sixteenth Central Committee of the CPC that, in accordance with the overall coordination of urban and rural development, regional development, overall economic and social development, harmonious development between humans and nature, domestic development and opening to the outside world, it was necessary to enhance the basic role of the market to a great extent in resource allocation, to enhance the vitality and competitiveness of enterprises, to complete the national macro-control system, to improve the government's function in social management and public services, and to provide a strong system guarantee for building a moderately prosperous society in an all-round way. According to this statement, it deepened and improved the connotation of reform goals of the socialist market economy in three areas. First, it determined the "Five Coordinations" as a foothold for deepening reform. This was one of the most critical reform theories proposed by the Party on the basis of the actual situation, reviewing historical experiences since the Third Plenary Session of the Eleventh Central Committee and looking forward to future trends in the domestic and international environment. This was a distinctive feature of the reform goals proposed in the Decision. Further, it reflected the unification of the phase and continuity of China's reform of its economic system. The Party proposed the reform goals in the Third Plenary Session of the Fourteenth Central Committee, which established that the socialist market economic system would play the basic role of macro control. After ten years of hard work in practice and exploration, the goals of reform had basically been achieved. On this basis, the Decision had further expanded the notion of enhancing the basic roles of marketization, vitality, and competitiveness of enterprises, completing the national macro-control system, and strengthening the government's function in public services, in connection with the ideas attached to development of the socialist market system that had been raised in the Third Plenary Session of the Fourteenth Central Committee. The combination of these ideas formed the key to deepening reform of the socialist market economic system. It not only enriched the concept of the reform goals of the socialist market economic system, but also reflected the unification of the phase and continuity of the reform of China's economic system. Finally, it integrated ideas contained in the security system. From the basic point of view of Marxism, society was an open system where urban and rural areas, regions, human beings, and nature were highly interdependent. The relationship between the economy and society was inseparable, and the internal conditions and external environment were correlative. Therefore, it was important to analyze the issues from multiple angles, including economic and social, urban and rural, human and natural, domestic and international, and developed and underdeveloped. Only then could the goals of reform be set and reform be carried out to promote the liberation and development of productive forces more effectively.

The Decision further specified historical tasks for deepening the reform of the socialist market economy. The Party illustrated seven tasks to further deepen the reform in the Decisions in the Third Plenary Session of the Sixteenth Central Committee. These were 1) to improve the basic economic system through common development of a multi-ownership economy, with the public ownership as the main body, 2) to establish a conducive system that gradually changed the binary economic structure of urban and rural areas, 3) to form a mechanism that promoted the coordinated development of the regional economy, 4) to set up a unified, open, competitive, and orderly modern market system, 5) to improve the macro-control system, administrative system, and economic legal system, 6) to enhance the employment, income distribution, and social security system, and 7) to establish a mechanism that promoted the sustainable development of the economy and society.

The Party proposed the establishment of the socialist market economic system in the Third Plenary Session of the Fourteenth Central Committee, and demonstrated the major tasks mainly in the fields of establishing a market system for state-owned enterprises, the construction of the macro-control system, and the establishment of the distribution and social security systems. Taking into account the historical conditions at that time, the Party emphasized the integrity of the market system when defining the tasks for reform during the Third Plenary Session of the Fourteenth Central Committee. Based on the Central Committee's Decisions on the Key Issues for Establishing a Socialist Market Economic System in the Third Plenary Session of the Fourteenth Central Committee, the Party determined the tasks for reform in the Decisions in the Third Plenary Session of the Sixteenth Central Committee, further targeting the actual situation so that the historical tasks of economic reform were clarified and made more specific. From the perspective of the actual situation, unless the problems in the area of effective actualization of public ownership were solved and orderly market competition and transformation of the government's public function established, it would be unable to sustain the healthy, rapid development of China's economy and difficult to improve the competitiveness of the industry and maintain the positive situation of opening up to the outside world. If there were no guarantee from the system and mechanism that the gap between the urban and rural areas and regions would be gradually narrowed and that the disharmonious issues between humans and nature would be resolved, it would be difficult to maintain lasting social stability and achieve the grand goal of building a moderately prosperous society in an all-round way. Aiming at these problems, the Decision proposed these seven clear and specific reform tasks, with a fundamental purpose of removing the institutional barriers that hindered the development of productive forces, providing a strong guarantee system for building a moderately prosperous society in an all-round way.

The above historical process fully reflected the development of the reform practice in China, the Party's efforts to combine the basic principles of Marxism with the practice of China's Reform and Opening Up, and the Party's deepened understanding of the law of development of the socialist market economy.

II

The New Situation of Deepening Reform and Development and the Proposal of a Scientific Outlook on Development

After entering a new stage in the new century, China's socio-economic development entered a critical period. As it faced this critical time, the Central Committee, under General Secretary Hu Jintao's leadership, inherited beneficial thoughts from previous generations, summed up the historical experience over the years, offered scientific analysis of the current situation, and proposed a timely scientific view of development.

1. China's Situation and Challenges in the Critical Period of Reform and Development

The proposal of a Scientific View of Development did not come about by accident, but was an inevitable development from the international and domestic situation that was in line with the latest general thinking in world development. From the international situation, in the current world, peace, development, and cooperation were the trends. The trend toward multi-polarization and economic globalization continued to develop, interdependence between nations was deepening, profound changes in relationships around the world were under way, and world power was continually shifting. Science and technology developed with each passing day, and scientific innovation and the proliferation of technology were accelerating. The restructuring of international industry and the transfer of production factors were speeding up, and regional economic integration into the world economy was in a new round of recovery and growth. In this global tide of development, the international community was generally optimistic about China's development potential. Valuing the role and impact of China greatly enhanced their willingness to cooperate with it. This was a positive side of the development for China. However, at the same time, it must be made clear that China faced some major development challenges. Some of the main challenges included hegemonism and power politics continuing to have a huge impact on world peace and the development of instability, uncertainties, world economic development, increased international competition for resources, markets, technology, and talent, an increase in trade barriers and friction, and the long-term dominant pressure in the economy, sciences, and technology from developed countries. While these had so far been conducive to the development of the country, it was possible the negative factors would continue to increase as well. Faced with an environment such as this, it was important to view China's development in light of the overall global situation so that it could mitigate weaknesses and avoid disadvantages while playing to its own strengths, maximizing its comparative advantage, grasping favorable conditions, seizing opportunities, responding to challenges, and striving to achieve development initiatives.

From the domestic situation, it was evident that the country had made remarkable achievement through unremitting effort since the founding of the People's Republic of China, particularly since the adoption of the Reform and Opening Up policy. Everything from productive forces to productive relations and from the economic base through the superstructure had undergone significant change. By the year 2000, China victoriously achieved the developmental goals of the second stage of the "three-step" strategy of modernization, and overall the people were generally living a prosperous life. According to the development goal proposed at the Fifteenth National Congress, attained by 2010 when the Party and New China had been established for 100 years, the Sixteenth National

Congress had clearly put forward a goal that would see comprehensive benefits that would allow China's more than 1 billion people to live a prosperous life by the end of the second decade of the 21st century. This was an essential transitional stage in development toward achieving the three-step goal of modernization, and it was also a critical period for improving the socialist market economic system and opening up further to the outside world.

The main features and challenges that characterized this period were that China's socio-economic development had entered a new stage, and reform and development were entering a critical period. Overall national strength faced fiercer competition in an increasingly complex, changeable external environment. China's industrialization and urbanization were accelerating, and its economic restructuring was speeding up as a large number of surplus agricultural laborers were transferring from rural to urban areas. Improvements in the marketized economy came rapidly, and deepening reform further touched on deep-seated contradictions and issues, preparing ground for the challenging stage of institutional innovation. As regional and socio-economic developments were uneven, closing the gap was an even more arduous task. China's economy depended on external factors to a greater degree, with the world economy increasingly impacting national economic and social development. The expanding demands of the material culture of the people and the interests of society became diverse and complex, making it difficult to address the various social needs. The people's awareness of the legal system continued to increase, and political participation continued to grow. The development of socialist democratic politics and the implementation of a basic strategy for the rule of law brought new expectations to the foreground, and the people were increasingly affected by a variety of ideas through a greater number of channels, their thinking becoming more independent, selective, and variable. For Hu Jintao as Secretary General of the Central Committee, it was a task of the new era to take great control of complex situations and to achieve solid and rapid development.

Seen from the perspective of global development, the economy developed to the level that the per capita GDP hit the 1,000 USD threshold, an important indicator that economic development had jumped to a new level. When a country hit this threshold, there were generally two potential future results. Some took off, while others hovered at this level. Accelerated development could only occur when the situation was handled properly. Some countries in East Asia and the region at large were doing a better job managing relations at this time and had achieved a continuous increase over a long period of time. In Latin America, some countries made a wrong move, spiraling into turmoil and stagnation, falling into the "Latin America trap."

By 2003, China's per capita GDP exceeded 1,000 USD. According to internationally recognized standards, this meant it had come out of the ranks of low-income countries. It was a monumental event in the history of the development of the Chinese nation, creating a new starting point to more effectively promote socialist modernization. When China's socio-economic development embarked from this new starting point, the question of how China could learn from the successful experience of foreign development and avoid its mistakes not only became a hot topic of discussion in ideological and academic circles, but also became the subject most often considered by the CPC's highest level of decision-makers in the new era.

2. The Scientific View of Development

The Central Committee led by Hu Jintao inherited a view of development derived from Marxism-Leninism, Mao Zedong Thought, Deng Xiaoping Theory, and the "Three Represents," drawing on the experience of long periods of development in various countries, learning from the useful achievements of foreign development theory, summarizing the long period of development and political experience in China, and offering a profound analysis and understanding of the characteristics of the stages of China's development. The Scientific View of Development was proposed on this foundation.

As early as March 1999, when Hu Jintao attended the Second Plenary Session of the Ninth National People's Congress, he deliberated a proposal made by the Fujian delegation, where it was mentioned that "it is necessary to firmly establish a scientific view of development." On April 15, 2003, on a visit to Guangdong Province, Hu made clear that "we insist on wholesale scientific development."[6] On July 28, at the National Prevention of SARS Work Conference, Hu pointed out that "through the fight against SARS, we realize more profoundly than ever that China's social and economic development and its urban and rural development are not sufficiently well-coordinated… We must attach great importance to the existing problem and take practical measures to resolve it to turn the campaign for the prevention and control of SARS into a vital opportunity to improve our work and boost our development cause."[7]

He said, "When we talk about development as the Party's first priority in governing and rejuvenating the country, this 'development' refers not just to economic growth, but also adheres to economic construction as the core, with economic development serving as the foundation for overall social development. We must adhere more closely to the idea of comprehensive, coordinated, and sustainable development and be more conscious in our adherence to the cultivation of coordinated development in socialist material, political, and spiritual civilization. We must adhere to the principle of socio-economic development as the basis for promoting the comprehensive development of humankind, and harmony between humanity and nature. Through the process of development, we should focus not only on economic indicators, but also on humanist indicators, as well as resources and environmental indicators. We should increase our input in boosting both economic growth and social progress, and in protecting our resources and environment as well."[8]

At the Third Plenary Session of the Sixteenth Congress of the Central Committee in October, in A Number of Issues Regarding the Party's Declaration on the Improvement of the Socialist Market Economic System, the guiding ideology and principles of deepening economic reform were laid out in these terms, "We must adhere to a people-oriented approach, establishing a comprehensive, coordinated, and sustainable concept of development so that we may promote socio-economic and human development." On October 14, at the Second Plenary Session of the Sixteenth Congress of the Central Committee, Hu Jintao further stated that "to establish and implement comprehensive, coordinated and sustained development through a scientific approach is of great significance in our adhering to the strategic thinking of 'development is of paramount importance.' To establish and implement a scientific view of development is a summary of our twenty years of experience in Reform and Opening Up practice. It is a critical message deriving from overcoming the SARS epidemic, and an urgent requirement for building a moderately prosperous society. This approach to development is in line with the objective laws of nature." This "people-oriented approach [to] establishing a comprehensive, coordinated, and sustainable approach to development" was what officially termed the "Scientific View of Development."⁹ In February 2004, the Central Committee held a meeting of leading cadres at provincial and ministerial level at the Central Party School "to establish and implement the Scientific View of Development." In this special study session, Wen Jiabao, Zeng Qinghong, Zeng Peiyan, and other leading comrades from the Central Government explained the significance of the Scientific View of Development, emphasizing that adherence to the people-oriented approach was the core and essence to the Scientific View of Development, and specifying the expectation that the Scientific View of Development be established and implemented at all levels of government. As a result, the phrase "the Scientific View of Development" came to be widely used among the central leadership.

On March 10, 2004, at the Central Work Forum on Population, Resources and Environment, Hu Jintao pointed to the significance of developing a profound, comprehensive interpretation of the concept of a Scientific View of Development as a guiding foundational principle. He pointed out that the concept of adhering to a people-oriented, comprehensive, and sustainable approach to development took Deng Xiaoping's thinking in the "Three Represents" as an important guide, just as it had served to guide the strategic thinking in the development of the Party and State Bureau since the beginning of the new century. The Scientific View of Development summarized the past twenty years of successful experience in Reform and Opening Up and modernization, and drew upon the lessons learnt from the development processes of other countries. It also summarized the important inspiration gained from overcoming the SARS epidemic and demonstrated the objective law of socio-economic development, reflecting the Party's new understanding of development issues. The entire Party needed to follow the important idea of the "Three Represents" and the spirit of the Sixteenth National Congress to elevate their strategy, developing a profound understanding of the establishment and implementation of the Scientific View of Development, and to unswervingly work toward this goal in order to better accomplish the historical task of moving into a new developmental stage in the new century. To establish and implement the scientific view of development, it was first necessary to grasp, fully and accurately, the basic internal requirements. Keeping the people-oriented approach as a basis meant that the goal was to achieve overall development as a people, with development growing out of the fundamental interests of the people. Development was promoted for the sake of continually meeting the needs of the people to improve their quality of life and meet their cultural needs, thereby protecting the people's economic and cultural rights and interests so that the results of development could benefit all. Comprehensive development meant making economic construction a central concern in the overall promotion of the economy, politics, governance, and cultural construction, in order to achieve economic development and social progress. Coordinated development involved coordinating development between urban and rural areas, between different regions, between social and economic development, and harmonious development between humans and nature. It also included coordinating domestic development and opening up to the outside world to promote coordination between productive forces and relations in production, between the economic basis and the superstructure. Sustainable development meant promoting harmony between humans and nature to achieve economic and human development in harmony with the environment and resources, while adhering to the development of production in a way that was prosperous and good for the development of an ecological civilization, so that it could be sustained for generations to come.[10] This elaboration deepened the understanding of the Scientific View of Development, clarifying its requirements, and strengthening the significance of it as a guiding principle.

At the Fifth Plenary Session of the Sixteenth National Congress in October 2005, it was proposed that the Scientific View of Development was an embodiment of a worldview and a methodology to guide the issue of global development. The Eleventh Five-Year Plan reviewed at the Plenary Session fully implemented the requirements of the Scientific View of Development. The Plan was reviewed and passed at the Fourth Plenary Session of the Tenth National People's Congress in 2006. This Plenary Session elevated the discussion of the Scientific View of Development to the level of a "global view and methodology," further clarifying the importance of the thinking as a guideline for the Party as a whole. From that time on, Hu Jintao continued to emphasize the concept of the Scientific View of Development on numerous occasions, highlighting its focus, basic content, and requirements. He issued several directives and instructions concerning the establishment and implementation of the Scientific View of Development throughout the Party, with the full consensus of the people, stating that the comprehensive construction of a stable society was the ambitious overarching goal. In 2007, the Seventeenth National Congress formally wrote the Scientific View of Development into the Party's constitution, elevating it as a guiding principle.

3. The Scientific View of Development and the Inheritance and Development of Marxism

The Scientific View of Development was a major strategic thought of the Party with Deng Xiaoping Theory and the "Three Represents" as the guiding principle. It demonstrated the Party's accurate grasp of global development trends and a serious summary of China's own experience of development based on an in-depth analysis of the characteristics of that particular stage in China's development. This major strategic thought was an inheritance and development of Marxist-Leninist Thought, Mao Zedong Thought, Deng Xiaoping Theory, and the "Three Represents," an embodiment of the Marxist worldview and methodology for global development, and a guideline to be adhered to long-term in order to achieve economic, political, social, and cultural construction.

Primarily, the Scientific View of Development inherited and developed the basic ideals of Marxist views of development. The Scientific View of Development adhered to the basic views of Marxism, in close connection with the real practice of socialism with Chinese characteristics, absorbing new achievements of human civilization and progress and standing at the height of human history. It focused on the rich connotations of development, innovative concepts of development, progressive ideas in development, and openness in development. Regarding the path to development, development models, development strategies, motivation for development, development goals, and the requirements for development, it further addressed the new situation with an eye to a series of major issues that had come up under China's new development situation. Building on the initial form of the Marxist theory of social development, the inheritance and development of Marxism-Leninism and Mao Zedong Thought, and the main content, connotations, and essence of Deng Xiaoping's "Three Represents" had been developed. To sum up, 1) continuous development was an eternal theme of human society, 2) the coordination and sustainability of development must always be emphasized, alongside a commitment to live harmoniously with nature, and 3) the ultimate goal of development was to achieve comprehensive social progress and the overall development of humankind. This concept of development demonstrated that the Party held onto a Marxist concept of development based on an understanding of the issues it faced in a new realm and that the laws of the development of human society, of socialist construction, and of the ruling Communist Party had been raised to a new level, enabling the Party to advance with the times in its development view.

In addition, the Scientific View of Development was a methodology focusing on the issues of the nature of development and how it could be produced. The Scientific View of Development revealed the correct path for China's socio-economic development, providing a guide for the promotion of the basic foundation of development. The Scientific View of Development required correct handling of socio-economic development, the speed and efficiency of development, market mechanisms and macro-control, stability of reform and development, and other factors related to the construction of socialist modernization. In order to achieve economic development and social progress, it was necessary to give attention to urban and rural development, regional development, socio-economic development, harmonious development between humans and nature, and the coordination between domestic development and opening to the outside world. Taking the basic requirements of the scientific view of development into account, it ran through Marxist standpoints, viewpoints, and methods. It was the application and expansion of the Marxist outlook, values, and methodology to the issue of development. In its implementation in the practice of development, it adhered to the "Five Coordinations," the Party's basic action-oriented policy leading the social and economic development. An accurate application of the "Five Coordinations" would naturally result in comprehensive, coordinated, and sustainable development. It was overall economic development and social progress, and harmony between humans and nature. In essence, the Scientific View of Development was a unique dialectical theory of development that embodied the basic unified principles of dialectical materialism to achieve a unified world view and methodology, reflecting the development of the purpose and means of consistent development.

Finally, the Scientific View of Development was people-oriented, embodying Marxist values. Taking humans as a foundation, it was a consistent social value of Marxism that was oriented toward people. It emphasized respect for the value of human existence and the value of demand and development, and it was an important feature of the Marxist theory of social development. The simultaneous scientific exposition of historical materialism and development values also pointed out that it is people that create the laws of history. The Scientific View of Development clearly emphasized that its "essence and core" were completely for the people, completely relying on the people as the main body and basic power for promoting development, and taking the meeting of the people's growing material and cultural needs as its foundation and the starting point, which fully embodied a Marxist political party's fundamental value orientation and the outstanding performance of socialist values. Therefore, it was an inevitable conclusion resulting from the integration of a people-oriented principle of historical materialism with the Party's nature and the purpose of serving the interests of the people and governing for the people.

III

Major Strategic Decisions for Scientific Development

The building of a moderately prosperous society in an all-round way and the formulation of a Scientific View of Development provided a guarantee that Chinese society would embark on the road to scientific development. On this basis, the Party ensured the health of Chinese society by launching a series of major strategic decisions to accelerate development.

The Scientific View of Development had been a part of the Party's experience for the previous twenty years of Reform and Opening Up. It reflected the Party's new understanding of development issues, reflecting the urgent requirements for building a moderately prosperous society that both conformed to the development trends of the times and remained in line with contemporary China's national situation.

To effectively implement the Scientific View of Development and to promote scientific development, the Central Committee and State Council adopted a series of major initiatives. The first of these initiatives involved strengthening and improving control at the macro level. Given new problems concerning food, investment, coal, electricity, transportation, and other areas of economic life, the Central Government seized the main conflicts, seeking to lay hold of the key link, targeting its control measures in credit, property, agricultural production, and other areas to curb uncertainties and instabilities in economic operations and seeking to avoid drastic rises and falls in the national economy and maintain the momentum for rapid, sustained economic growth.

The second initiative was an improvement of the socialist market economic system. At the Third Plenary Session of the Sixth National Congress of the Central Committee in October 2003, the Decision on Issues Relating to the Improvement of the Socialist Market Economic System (referred to as the Decision) was passed, clearly putting forward the goal of improving the socialist market economic system as the main task. The main objectives proposed by the Decision were based on the requirements of 1) coordinating urban and rural development, 2) coordinating regional development, 3) coordinating social and economic development, 4) coordinating the harmonious development of humans and nature, and 5) coordinating domestic development and opening up to the outside world. This gave greater play to the market's fundamental role in allocation of resources to enhance the vitality and competitiveness of enterprises and improve the national macro-control system and improve the government's social management and public service functions in order to provide a strong institution as a guarantee for building a moderately prosperous society. The main mission was to improve the basic economic systems with public ownership as the core and diversified ownership in common development, to build a system conducive to steadily changing the binary urban-rural economic structure, to establish a mechanism boosting coordinated development of the regional economy, to construct a unified, open, competitive, and orderly modern market economic system, to improve the macro-control systems, administrative systems, and economic and legal systems, to solidify employment, income distribution, and social security, and to establish mechanisms to promote sustainable socio-economic development. The Decisions embodied the requirements of the scientific view of development, clarifying the objectives of economic reform. It was a key document in the programmatic development of the socialist market economy in China.

The third initiative put forward an overall strategy for coordinated regional development. According to the requirements of the scientific view of development, the Party maintained comprehensive, rational planning, giving full play to the advantages of the policy as it was implemented, particularly sending new deployments aimed at the coordination of regional development. In March 2004, the State Council issued A Number of Opinions on the Further Development of the Western Region, in which it proposed to strengthen the economic exchange and cooperation between the western, eastern, and central regions through market-oriented, cross-regional, and cross-enterprise cooperation mechanisms. The eastern and central capital, technology, and talent would be combined with western resources, markets, and labor for the sake of mutual advantages, benefits, and development. In October 2005, the Fifth Plenary Session of the Sixteenth National Congress of the Central Committee summed up the basis of China's experience of socialist modernization construction and further advanced an overall strategy for regional development in China, emphasizing the continued development of the western region, the revitalization of the old industrial base in the north, and the promotion of the central region, encouraging the eastern region to take the lead in establishing a reasonable pattern for regional development. The Fifth Plenary Session started from the actual situations in various regions and, in accordance with comparative advantage, sought to strengthen weak links, promote the coordinated development of the requirements, clarify the development orientation and overall thinking of each region, and emphasizing the need to implement the strategy of coordinated regional development by improving the mechanism for coordinated regional interaction, clarifying the functional orientation of different regions and promoting healthy development of urbanization.

The fourth initiative was the development of the Eleventh Five-Year Plan. In October 2005, the Fifth Plenary Session of the Sixteenth National Congress of the Central Committee adopted the Recommendations for the Formulation of National Economic and Social Development in the Eleventh Five-Year Plan (called the Recommendations). The Recommendations established an all-round consideration of the development trends and conditions in China over the next five years, upon which the Eleventh Five-Year Plan proposed a goal of doubling the per capita GDP by 2010 over the 2000 figure. With the reduction of energy consumption by about 20% by the end of the Tenth Five-Year Plan, deterioration of the ecological environment had been basically curbed and the reduction of arable land was effectively controlled. A number of strong enterprises had been formed with their own intellectual property rights and well-known brands, as well as competitive advantages on the international scale. The socialist market economic system was near perfect, and the open economy had reached a new level, with international income and expenditure basically balanced. Nine years of compulsory education had been consolidated and universalized, and jobs in urban areas continued to increase. The social security system was sound, and poverty continued to decrease. Urban and rural residents enjoyed a higher quality of life, overall prices were stable, and general living conditions, transportation, education, and cultural, health, and environmental conditions had greatly improved. Democracy, the legal system, and spiritual cultivation were making new progress. Public security and safety in production were improving, and building a harmonious society was moving toward further progress. China's socialist modernization continued to advance in accordance with the above objectives.

The fifth initiative was the strengthening of the new socialist countryside, further deepening of rural reform, and effectively strengthening the basic status of agriculture. In December 2002, the Politburo held a meeting in which they emphasized the need to develop agriculture and the rural areas, putting agricultural issues as the top priority in Party work, giving it a more prominent position. From 2004 through 2008, the Central Government issued five consecutive "Top Documents" as a way of emphasizing the "three rural" issues. In 2005, the Fifth Plenary Session of the Sixteenth National Congress of the Central Committee put forward the historical task of building a new socialist countryside, determining that the goal was to "develop production, live well, civilize rural areas, clean and tidy up villages, and manage democracy." At the beginning of 2006, the Central Government issued the Opinions of the State Council of the CPC Central Committee on the Promotion of Construction of a New Socialist Countryside in the form of a "Top Document," in which the construction of the new socialist countryside was fully deployed. In order to speed up construction of the new socialist countryside, the Party Central Committee conformed to the changing stages of socio-economic development, clearly proposing to establish and "promote agriculture through industry, and bring the city to the village," a long-term mechanism adhering to the approach of "doing more, taking less" that focused the "more" on work to promote and modernize agriculture and to offer industrial support to the construction of the new socialist countryside. In deepening rural reform, the Central Committee was accelerating the tax reform process, gradually reducing the agricultural tax by further cancellation of agricultural taxes. On December 29, 2005 the Nineteenth Session of the Tenth National People's Congress Standing Committee formally decided that, from January 1, 2006, onwards, the "agricultural tax regulations" would be officially abolished. The abolition of the agricultural tax brought an end to two thousand years of "imperial grain taxes" in China, marking a historical change in the distribution pattern of the national income. As a result, rural reform had entered a stage of comprehensive reform, focusing on the reform of the township institutions, compulsory education in the rural areas, and fiscal reform in counties and villages.

The sixth initiative was the building of an innovative country. Innovation is the soul of national progress, the inexhaustible driving force for a thriving nation. Since the Sixteenth National Congress, the Central Committee was building a prosperous society in a well-rounded way under the new socialist situation, promoting independent innovation, and building an innovative nation. After nearly five years of improvement and development, in January 2006, at the opening ceremony of the national branch of the science and technology conference, Hu Jintao formally put forward China's construction of an innovative nation as the main goal, saying that by 2020, China's independent innovation capabilities should have significantly enhanced science and technology to promote social and economic development, significantly enhancing the ability to guarantee national security. In addition, it should have gained a number of significant scientific and technological achievements on the world stage, moving into the ranks of innovative nations and providing strong support for the overall construction of a prosperous society.

The seventh initiative was the promotion of socialist democratic political construction in an orderly manner, striving to build a socialist political civilization. The Sixteenth National Congress of the CPC made the development of socialist democratic politics, the building of a socialist political civilization, and the cultivation of a prosperous society important goals, requiring that the promotion of the political system be carried out continuously, actively, and steadily. After the Sixteenth National Congress, the Central Committee maintained and perfected the people's congress system and strengthened multi-party cooperation and political consultation, while continuing to promote the construction of the material and spiritual civilization. They constantly expanded grassroots democracy and steadily promoted socialist rule of law and other aspects of construction so that the political institutional reform might constantly adapt to the goal of building a socialist political civilization.

The eighth initiative was the deepening of the reform of the cultural system, advancing socialism toward a prosperous culture. With the economic transition and social transformation, China's cultural construction and the development of the economic base, institutional environment, and social conditions gave birth to profound changes. The Sixteenth National Congress asked the comrades throughout the Party to understand the strategic significance of cultural construction, promoting the development and prosperity of the socialist culture and putting forward the idea of focusing on the development of the cultural reform system. From June 27–28, 2003, the National Work Conference for Pilot Reform of the Cultural System studied the issue and deployed pilot reform on the cultural system. On December 23, 2005, the Central Committee and State Council issued A Number of Opinions on the Deepening of Reform of the Cultural System, clearly putting forward the objectives and tasks of the reform of the cultural system. These included development as the theme, reform as the driving force, and national innovation as the focus, forming a scientific and effective macro cultural management system, an efficient micro-operation mechanism for cultural production and service, a cultural industry pattern with public ownership as the main body and a variety of ownership in common development, and a unified, open competitive and orderly modern cultural market system. It further included the formation of a sound cultural innovation system and an open cultural pattern with national culture as the main body, allowing it to absorb foreign cultures and to promote Chinese culture around the world. In March 2006, the National Cultural System Reform Work Conference summed up the pilot work on reform of the cultural system, promoting specific deployment of the cultural system reform. In this way, the cultural system reform was brought into a new stage. In accordance with the principles of "separation of government and enterprises," "separation of governance and administration," and "separation of management and government regulation," the pilot areas further changed the function of the government. Public Welfare Culture Reform was deepened, and significant improvements were made in the capacity and level of public service. By operating cultural institutions as enterprises and employing market-oriented management to achieve a breakthrough, many large-scale cultural groups were formed.

In the process of promoting scientific development, the Central Committee developed a clear understanding of the new situation and problems that had developed as a long-term product of the contradictions within the old institutional mechanisms moving toward the goal of deepening economic and social development according to objective laws. Grasping the laws of development and innovation, they changed the development model, solved development problems, and improved the quality and efficiency of development, gradually gaining the consensus of the entire Party. On this basis, the Central Committee put forward the "good and fast" requirement for development.

In December 2006, The Central Economic Work Conference made it clear that "there must be a profound understanding of sound, rapid development for the full implementation of the Scientific View of Development's essential requirements." From the previous "fast and good" approach, it had moved to one that was "good and fast." Though the two words merely change order, the latter phrase better embodies the Scientific View of Development and its inherent requirements, reflecting the development of the Party's guiding ideology and its subtleties, so that the entire Party might grasp the overall law of the new stage of development regulations more firmly and guide the development policy with the actual tools for solving development problems more firmly in hand.

IV

Strengthening the Party's Governing Capabilities and Advanced Nature

Increasing the Party's ability to govern – elevating both the ability to govern and the level of governance – was always an important part of the thinking on which the Party was built. As early as the beginning of the Soviet regime, Lenin said that the consolidation of the ruling party was a "new, challenging cause," and "this is why the Soviet Communist Party must accumulate all human knowledge." It was an important requirement, then, that the Party must "constantly apply the wealth of human knowledge to our own minds" in order to continually approve its ability in and level of governance. After the founding of New China, several generations of the Communist Party had consistently focused on strengthening the Party's ability to govern. At the beginning of the new century, with the new situation under the new Secretary General, Hu Jintao, there were new tasks and new demands specifically aimed at strengthening and building the Party's ability to make decisions. On the eve of the founding of New China, faced with the prospect of the CPC becoming the ruling Party, Mao Zedong had warned the whole Party that "this is the first step in the long march to victory," adding, "but now the longer revolution starts, and the work will be both greater and more difficult." To govern the entire nation was somewhat like going to the "Beijing exam." Mao's ideas were initially put forward to strengthen the Party's ability to govern. After the adoption of the Reform and Opening Up policy, the Party always gave attention to addressing the Party's ability to lead and the level of governance. In the new century, the international and domestic political and economic situation underwent profound changes, and the Party's ability to govern and its leadership level faced severe challenges, with new, higher expectations arising.

Adapting to the requirements for development in the new system, based on the historical time and circumstances and the historical mission, the Sixteenth National Congress focused on the cause of advancing socialism with Chinese characteristics. Working from the Party's long-term strategy, they clearly put forward five basic requirements for continuing to build the ability to govern: 1) continue to improve the ability to judge the situation scientifically, 2) continue to improve the ability to drive the market economy, 3) continue to improve the ability to cope with complex situations, 4) continue to promote the ability to govern according to law, and 5) continue to improve the overall capacity for leadership.

In order to get a handle on the problem of building the Party's ability to govern, on September 7, 2004, the new Central Committee convened a meeting of the Politburo to discuss the work of the Politburo after the Third Plenary Session of the Sixteenth National Congress of the Central Committee, a step toward strengthening the building of the Party's ability to govern and other issues. At the Fourth Plenary Session of the Sixteenth National Congress held in Beijing on September 19, the Central Committee issued the Decisions on Strengthening the Party's Ability to Govern, a comprehensive analysis of the current situation and tasks and a scientific summary of the Party's ability to govern. It clearly put forward the strengthening of the Party's governance as a guiding thought, as well as the overarching goal and main task.

The Party's ability to govern included the Party advancing and employing correct theories, methods, policies, and strategies to lead the development and implementation of the constitution and the law and adopting a scientific leadership system and governing body to mobilize and organize personnel to manage national and social affairs, as well as economic and cultural undertakings, in accordance with the law.

The guiding ideology behind the Party's ability to govern the nation and build a modern socialist country was that it was necessary to adhere to Marxism-Leninism, Mao Zedong Thought, Deng Xiaoping Theory, and the "Three Represents" as guides for the scientific view of development, to fully implement the Party's basic line, basic program, and basic experience with maintaining a tight bond between the Party and the people at its core, building a team of highly competent cadres as the key, reforming and improving the Party leadership system and working mechanism as the central focus, and strengthening the Party's grassroots organizations and Party members as the foundation, so as to demonstrate the spirit of the times, grasp the natural law of development, and work in a creative way.

The overall objective of strengthening the Party's ability to govern was to work together through the efforts of the whole Party and finally become a Party for the people. The ruling Party must rule for the people, becoming a scientific ruling Party governing democratically and according to the rule of law. It must become pragmatic, pioneering, and innovative, diligent and efficient, and a clean, honest ruling Party. In the final analysis, it had to always achieve the "Three Represents," always maintain an advanced nature, and be a Party that withstood all manner of storms through its commitment to Marxism.

The main tasks in strengthening the Party's ability to govern were to promote a socialist material civilization, a political civilization, and a spiritual civilization coordinated with the requirements of development. It was important to consistently improve management of the socialist market economy, to develop socialist democratic policies, to build an advanced socialist culture, and construct a harmonious socialist society able to cope with the international situation and deal with international affairs.

In addition, the Fourth Plenary Session of the Sixteenth National Congress of the Central Committee adopted the Decisions on Strengthening the Party's Ability to Govern. On the basis of the Five Aspects of the Ability to Rule that they had inherited, they built a specific, strategic plan for improving the Party's ability to govern. According to the relevant arrangements by the Central Government, in order to effectively strengthen the Party's ability to govern, to ensure that the Party was always progressing, and to better shoulder its historical mission, on

November 7, 2004, the Central Committee issued Opinions on Carrying Out the Practice of the "Three Represents" as an Important Component of the Party's Advanced Education Activities (referred to as the Opinions). With regard to advanced education activities, the government stated:

> Based on the target requirements, in general, we must improve the competence of Party members, strengthen grassroots organizations, and serve the people as we promote the work in various fields. Regarding the overall process, we will issue directives in three batches, approximately once every six months. The first batch will include some county Party and government organizations, along with some enterprises and institutions. This will begin in January 2005, and will be basically completed by June 2005. The second batch will address city grassroots organizations and township authorities. It will begin in July 2005 and be basically completed by December 2005. The third batch includes rural and partial government organs. This will begin in January 2006 and be basically completed in June 2006. In methodical steps, the centralized education will roll out in three stages, the mobilizing, analyzing and evaluation, and rectification stages.

After the Opinions were issued, the Central Committee held a work conference on January 5–6, 2005, for Party members on the advanced nature of educational activities during which they specified the deployment of advanced education. According to the overall arrangement of the Central Committee, the Standing Committee of the Politburo undertook the first batch of advanced educational activities. In a speech on January 14, in a special report on maintaining the advanced nature of education in the new era, Hu Jintao asked all Party members to actively participate in advanced educational activities to strengthen the Party's advanced construction and to carry out the importance of advanced educational activities. He urged leading cadres in particular to play an exemplary role, putting advanced education into practice.

After the work conference, from January 2005 through June 2006, the CPC rolled out the advanced educational activities in three successive batches. During this eighteen month period, a total of more than 3.5 million grassroots Party organizations with nearly 70 million members participated in the educational activities related to advanced construction. From the practical perspective, the whole process was healthy and orderly, producing solid work and progressing smoothly. It produced noticeable results in the Party's advanced construction and governance capacity-building, getting positive feedback from the majority of Party members and cadres as well as from various sectors across the nation.

V

Adherence to Peaceful Development for Building a Harmonious World

The new century ushered in a new stage, bringing new opportunities to apply new strategies to China's drive toward socialist modernization. With Hu Jintao as General Secretary, the Central Committee led the Party and the people, faced with an environment in which were seen a series of changes on the international and domestic front, to accelerate economic development, while focusing on the modernization of the military and the national defense system to actively carry out diplomatic work, and to strive for the peaceful reunification of the motherland and gain the most out of a period of strategic opportunity.

To achieve the simultaneous development of national defense and the national economy, and to adapt to the 21st century in line with the changing international military situation, the Central Committee asked the army to work to meet the world's new military reforms, a serious challenge, to urgently promote military reform with Chinese characteristics, and to complete mechanization and the construction of communication infrastructure, a dual historical task, and to move unswervingly toward the construction of an information-based military that would be able to win the information war. On September 20, 2004, at the Central Military Commission Expanded Meeting, the newly appointed Chairman Hu Jintao proposed to "continue to strengthen the army, to strengthen ideological and political construction, to take hold of the troops to further capabilities in the right direction, and to continually improve the leadership of the military as we struggle to prepare the troops for information combat, constantly improving military reform with Chinese characteristics and promoting the mechanization of troops and the construction of information capabilities. We must constantly improve according to military law, strengthening the regular construction of the troops."[11]

On March 13, 2005, in an important speech on the army's mission at the Third Session of the Tenth National People's Congress of the People's Liberation Army delegation, Hu proposed new requirements on behalf of the Central Military Commission. He said it was necessary "to consolidate the ruling position for the Party to provide an important guarantee for the maintenance of national interests in order to provide strong strategic support for the maintenance of world peace and to play a role in promoting common development." The Central Committee and the Central Military Commission delivered this new mission, with its epoch-making significance.

In order to carry out this mission, the Chinese army's path to developing an elite military with Chinese characteristics was accelerated and reform stepped up. Following the disarmament of one million troop members in the mid-1980s and of another half million in the middle to late 1990s, in September 2003, the Chinese government decided that by 2005, the number of troops would be reduced by 200,000.[12] At the same time that troops were being streamlined, the government increased its input in national defense construction. Officers and men throughout the ranks of the military had been greatly improved, and weapons, equipment, and national defense science and technology businesses had also seen rapid development.

Since the Sixteenth National Congress of the CPC, the most striking feature of Chinese diplomacy had been the advocacy and promotion of a "harmonious world." This international strategic line of thought embodied the CPC's basic evaluation of the international situation, global issues, and the human fate, alongside the values the Party pursued. It was a new period characterized by new generalized goals for independence and peaceful foreign policy.

On April 22, 2005, at the Asia-Africa Summit in Jakarta, Hu Jintao went to the countries of the world with a call for "the promotion of friendship and harmony among different civilizations, employing equal dialogue, development, and prosperity to build a harmonious world." This marked the first instance that he put forward the notion of "a harmonious world." On July 1, at the China-Russia Summit meeting, the concept of "a harmonious world" was written into the China-Russia Joint Declaration on International Order in the 21st Century, the first time it was brought into consensus between two nations. On September 15, on the occasion of the 60th anniversary of the founding of the United Nations, Hu Jintao delivered a speech entitled "Efforts to Build Lasting Peace and Common Prosperity in a Harmonious World." In the speech, he said, "In the face of today's complex world, we should pay more attention to harmony, emphasizing and promoting it, and building a harmonious world featuring lasting peace and common prosperity." He went on to expound on all aspects of the rich connotation of this "harmonious world." In August 2006, the CPC held a national foreign affairs work conference, setting the building of a "harmonious world" as the goal of diplomatic work.

To promote the building of a harmonious world, the Chinese government actively carried out a series of fruitful diplomatic activities. The relationship between China and large nations continued to maintain stability and to develop, and friendly relations with neighboring countries continued to be consolidated.

In 2003, the Second China-Africa Cooperation Forum adopted the Action Plan for Addis Ababa (2004–2006), outlining a plan for trade and economic exchange, along with social development and other areas of cooperation over the next three years. After China and ASEAN countries signed the China-ASEAN Comprehensive Economic Cooperation Framework Agreements in 2002, the two sides signed the Agreement on Trade in Goods and the Dispute Settlement Mechanism Agreement in November 2004, agreeing to gradually cancel most bilateral trade tariffs and other trade barriers by 2010. On November 28–30, Wen Jiabao visited Laos and attended the Eighth ASEAN and Chinese Leaders' Meeting in Vientiane (10+1), and published the China-ASEAN Strategic Partnership for Peace and Prosperity Action Plan. In April 2005, Wen Jiabao visited Pakistan, Bangladesh, Sri Lanka, and India and attended the fourth meeting of foreign ministers of the Asian Cooperation Dialogue in Islamabad. During the visit, China jointly announced the establishment of strategic partnerships with Pakistan and India and the establishment of a comprehensive partnership with Bangladesh. China and India signed the Agreement on Guiding Principles for the settlement of Political Boundary Issues, identifying for the first time the idea that the existing boundaries should be adjusted. In the same month, Hu Jintao attended the Asia-Africa Summit in Indonesia and the 50th Anniversary of the Bandung Conference, and issued a comprehensive statement of cooperation with Asian and African countries that articulated a clear position that politically, it was important to have mutual respect and mutual support; economically, it was to be a complementary, mutually beneficial, win-win relationship; culturally, there would be mutual learning; and in security, there would be equality, mutual trust, dialogue, and cooperation. On June 2, at the China-Russia Tokk Exchange in Vladivostok, the Supplementary Agreement Between the People's Republic of China and the Russian Federation on the Eastern Sector of the China-Russia Border was ratified, an agreement that effectively settled the final lingering historical problem of border disputes between the two countries. Regarding the issue of peace on the Korean Peninsula, with China's influence, the two sides finally reached the North Korea Denuclearization Target Document in September 2005. On November 20, when Hu Jintao met with US President George W. Bush, it marked a step forward in the development of constructive cooperation between the US and China, and five suggestions for further promoting constructive relations between the two countries were put forward.

By 2008, China had participated in more than 100 international intergovernmental organizations, more than 300 international public meetings, and 22 United Nations peacekeeping operations. The cumulative number of peacekeeping personnel deployed numbered in the thousands, the most sent out by any of the five permanent member nations. China has been actively involved in international and regional affairs and earnestly fulfilled its corresponding international duties, helping it to become an important member of the international community.[13]

After active efforts, China's bilateral and multilateral diplomatic relations had advanced, its traditional and non-traditional security had gained new weight, and its political, economic, diplomatic, military, cultural, and other aspects complemented and promoted each other, forming new models for development.

Since the Sixteenth National Congress, the new central leadership had strictly observed the "one country, two systems" principle to address the issues relating to the Hong Kong and Macau Special Administrative Regions and implemented some important measures given the new situations concerning their developments. In cross-straits relations, the Central Government had taken some significant, positive steps to oppose "Taiwanese independence," making new progress toward safeguarding national sovereignty.

Since Hong Kong and Macau had returned to the motherland, the Central Committee and State Council had always maintained that Hong Kong and Macau were stable and prosperous, making developing the fundamental interests of their compatriots in both regions a starting point for finding a basic solution to issues there. With an unwavering implementation of the "one country, two systems" policy, Hong Kong and Macau had a high degree of autonomy, with "Hong Kong's people governing Hong Kong" and "Macau's people governing Macau." Both had the firm support of the Chief Executive and the Government of the Special Administrative Region, which were governed by the rule of law.

The Central Government had given full support to the prosperity and stability of Hong Kong and Macau. Not only had they taken effective measures to help both places succeed in ridding themselves of the negative impacts of the Asian financial crisis, but they had also carried out exchanges and cooperation in many areas, hoping to strengthen the links between the Mainland, Hong Kong, and Macau. These initiatives included the implementation of the Pan-Pearl Delta Domain Cooperation and a series of policy measures to promote Hong Kong and Macau alongside the development of the Mainland, creating a broader space for development, stability, and prosperity. With the support of the Central Government and their compatriots from the Mainland, the economics of Hong Kong and Macau grew more prosperous, and development more democratic and orderly. The people lived and worked in peace, and enjoyed social stability. The majority of people in Hong Kong and Macau had an overarching love of the motherland and a deep concern for their own home cities, evident in the struggle for development typical of the spirit there.

After the reunification of Hong Kong and Macau to the motherland, cross-straits relations received closer attention from the CPC and the Chinese people. The Central Committee proposed new ideas in connection with cross-straits relation there, based on the existing policy and the changes in relations with Taiwan, and adopted a number of new measures to promote the continued development of cross-straits relations.

On March 4, 2005, Hu Jintao put forward four points concerning cross-straits relations under the new circumstances, emphasizing the need to never waver from the One China principle, to never give up in the effort to strive for peaceful reunification, to never lose the hope that the Taiwanese people's policy would change, and to never fail to oppose any suggestion of compromise with the "Taiwanese Independence" separatist activities. These "Four Nevers" received a huge response from the international community, which had generally been welcoming of the principles it advocated. On March 14, the Third Plenary Session of the Tenth National Congress of the Central Committee passed the Anti-Secession Law, marking the Central Government's settlement of the Taiwan question. The Law made the split of the motherland a violation of fixed law. The formulation and adoption of this law fully embodied the greatest sincerity of the CPC. The Party had taken the great position of striving for peaceful reunification, the unity of the Chinese people, and territorial integrity, and it was firm in its determination.

Under the impetus of the correct policy of the CPC, with great effort on the part of both parties, the political parties of the two sides exchanged views, opening the way for discussion. In 2005, Taiwan's Chinese Kuomintang Chairman Lien Chan, the People First Party Chairman James Soong, and the new Party Chairman Yu Muming led a delegation to visit the Mainland, where Hu Jintao met and held talks with them. A communiqué was published, the 1992 Consensus, which opposed "Taiwanese Independence" and advocated smooth development of cross-straits relations, among other agreements. The Communist Party of China and the Chinese Kuomintang Party held three cross-strait economic and trade forums, and the Mainland launched a total of 48 initiatives to promote cross-strait exchange and cooperation, including policy measures to benefit their Taiwanese compatriots, such as allowing the sale of Taiwanese agricultural products in the Mainland, recognition of Taiwanese institutions of higher education approved by Taiwan's education ministry, and permission to meet the requests of the Taiwan compatriots who applied to practice in the Mainland long-term or short-term. The CPC and KMT held a Cross-Strait Elite Forum. Through extensive exchanges and cooperation between the political parties on both sides of the strait, the situation was further opened, especially with the new situation of curbed "Taiwanese Independence" separatist activities and the promotion of developing cross-strait relations. Taiwan's Legal Independence, New Constitutional Referendum, and other initiatives such as its application to the United Nations or the "Taiwanese Independence" movement had surfaced again and again. Opposition to "Taiwanese Independence" was widely influenced by the international community, and carried out with international understanding and support. Many countries with significant influence consistently reaffirmed their commitment to the One China policy. In September 2007, the 62nd Session of the United Nations General Assembly overwhelmed the Chen Shui-bien authorities when a very small minority made the proposal that Taiwan be allowed to join the UN. In March 2008, Taiwan held a general election, and the Chen Shui-bien authorities, who were going farther and farther along the "Taiwanese Independence" road, were finally abandoned by the people of Taiwan. The KMT regained its ruling status, and cross-strait relations witnessed new changes favoring peaceful development.

CHAPTER 12

The Implementation of a Scientific Outlook on Development and the Building of a Harmonious Socialist Society

After the Sixteenth National Congress of the Communist Party of China, under the leadership of Hu Jintao, the Central Committee clearly put forward the Scientific View of Development in the practice of building a moderately well-off society in an all-round way, in order to promote sound, rapid development of China's socialist modernization, further generalized the theoretical system of socialism with Chinese characteristics, and, under the guidance of the Scientific View of Development, put forward a new outline for the goal of building a moderately well-off society in an all-round way to promote the construction of a harmonious society and deepen the transformation of administrative systems and rural reform, along with a series of strategic decisions to drive the scientific social development of China in an attempt to ensure the healthy development of Chinese society.

I

A New Summary of the Theoretical System of Socialism with Chinese Characteristics

From October 15–21, 2007, the Seventeenth National Congress of the Communist Party of China was held in Beijing. The theme of the conference was to uphold the great banner of socialism with Chinese characteristics, take Deng Xiaoping Theory and the "Three Represents" as guidance, further carry out the scientific development concept, continue to emancipate the mind, adhere to Reform and Opening Up, promote scientific development and social harmony, and strive for a new victory in building a moderately well-off society in an all-round way. On behalf of the Sixteenth Central Committee, Hu Jintao delivered a report to the General Assembly entitled "Upholding the Great Banner of Socialism with Chinese Characteristics and Striving for a New Victory in Building a Moderately Well-off Society in an All-round Way." The General Assembly elected a new Central Committee and Central Discipline Inspection Commission. It adopted resolutions on the report of the Sixteenth Central Committee, on the work of the Central Discipline Inspection Commission, and on the Constitution (Amendment) of the Communist Party of China.

The report of the Seventeenth National Congress scientifically answered such important questions as what banner the Party should uphold, what path it should take, what attitude it should present, and what development goals it should continue to move forward in the critical stage of reform and development. It devised a comprehensive plan for continuing to promote Reform and Opening Up, socialist modernization, and achieving the grand goal of building a moderately well-off society in an all-round way. It also put forward clear requirements to promote the new great projects of the Party's construction in a well-rounded way with the spirit of reform and innovation.

The report of the Seventeenth National Congress comprehensively reviewed the historical changes that had taken place with the outlook of the Chinese people, socialist China, and the Communist Party of China over the previous thirty years of Reform and Opening Up. It scientifically summarized the valuable experience of shaking off poverty, speeding up modernization, and consolidating and developing socialism in a developing country with a population of more than

1 billion. The report pointed out that the fundamental reason the Party had made so many achievements and so much progress since Reform and Opening Up was that it had blazed a path of socialism with Chinese characteristics and formed the theoretical system of socialism with Chinese characteristics.

Under the leadership of the Communist Party of China, the path of socialism with Chinese characteristics was to build a socialist market economy, socialist democratic politics, advanced socialist culture, and a harmonious socialist society, based on the fundamental national conditions, centering on economic construction, adhering to the four basic principles and Reform and Opening Up, liberating and developing social productive forces, consolidating and improving the socialist system, and building a prosperous, strong, democratic, civilized, and harmonious socialist modern country.

The theoretical system of socialism with Chinese characteristics was a scientific theoretical system including Deng Xiaoping Theory, the "Three Represents," and the strategic scientific development concept.

The new proposition of "the theoretical system of socialism with Chinese characteristics" was a scientific integration of the Party's innovative theory in the new historical period of Reform and Opening Up, a scientific expression of the open characteristics of the Party's theoretical achievements since Reform and Opening Up, a major theoretical contribution to the Seventeenth National Congress, and the latest achievement in the localization of Marxism. In the previous thirty years, through the great historical process of Reform and Opening Up and socialist modernization, the Party had persisted in emancipating the mind, seeking truth from facts, and keeping pace with the times, constantly pushing forward the process of the localization of Marxism, and had made significant theoretical innovations, thus forming a theoretical system of socialism with Chinese characteristics.

From the Third Plenary Session of the Eleventh Central Committee, following the dangerous situation created by the Cultural Revolution, in the previous decade, the Communist Party of China, represented mainly by Deng Xiaoping, scientifically evaluated Mao Zedong and Mao Zedong Thought with great theoretical and political courage, totally denied the wrong theory and practice of "taking class struggle as the guiding principle," and formulated the policy of "taking economic construction as the center" and carrying out Reform and Opening Up. The historic decision opened up a new period for the development of the socialist cause. Through continuous summary of experience and practical theoretical exploration, the Party gradually acquired a clearer understanding of what socialism was and how it should be built, gradually forming Deng Xiaoping Theory.

After the Fourth Plenary Session of the Thirteenth Central Committee, the Communist Party of China, with Jiang Zemin as its main representative, upheld the great banner of Deng Xiaoping Theory, adhered to the Reform and Opening Up policy, and kept pace with the times, successfully pushing the cause of socialist modernization with Chinese characteristics into the 21st century and deepening their understanding of "what is socialism and how to build it" and "what kind of Party should we build and how do we build it" in the practice of building socialism with Chinese characteristics. The Party also formed the "Three Represents," thus enriching and developing the theory of socialism with Chinese characteristics.

After the Sixteenth National Congress, with Hu Jintao as its General Secretary and based on the new requirements for development and the basic national conditions of the primary stage of socialism, through constant summing up of the development experience of China and drawing lessons from the development experience of foreign countries, the Central Committee offered preliminary answers to such important theoretical and practical questions as "aiming at what kind of development and how to achieve it," and put forward a series of strategic thoughts such as the concept of scientific development. The scientific outlook on development was the inheritance and development of the key theories of the three generations of the Party's central leading collectives on development, the concentrated embodiment of the Marxist world view and methodology on development, and the scientific theory that was in line with Marxism-Leninism, Mao Zedong Thought, Deng Xiaoping Theory, and the "Three Represents," and also a scientific theory that kept pace with the times. It was the development of China's economy and society. Guiding principles were important strategic ideas that must be adhered to and implemented in the development of socialism with Chinese characteristics.

Deng Xiaoping Theory and the "Three Represents" were written into the Party Constitution at the Fifteenth and Sixteenth National Congresses of the Party and were established as the guiding ideology of the Party. The Seventeenth National Congress of the CPC unanimously agreed to incorporate the concept of scientific development into the Constitution of the Party.

The theoretical system of socialism with Chinese characteristics adhered to and developed Marxism-Leninism and Mao Zedong Thought. It condensed the wisdom and painstaking effort of several generations of Chinese Communists to lead the people in their unremitting exploration. It was the latest achievement in the localization of Marxism in China, the most valuable political and spiritual wealth of the Party, and the common ideological basis for the unity and struggle of the people of all ethnic groups in the country. The theoretical system of socialism with Chinese characteristics was an open and developing theoretical system. Practice over the previous 160 years since the publication of the *Communist Manifesto* had proven that only by combining Marxism with its own national conditions, developing with the times, and advancing with the people could it radiate strong vitality, creativity, and inspiration. In contemporary China, to adhere to the theoretical system of socialism with Chinese characteristics was to truly adhere to Marxism.

II

New Requirements for Building a Moderately Well-off Society in a Comprehensive Way and the Overall Layout of the "Four-in-One" Construction

To adhere to the theoretical system of socialism with Chinese characteristics was to adapt in practice to the new changes in the situation in China and abroad, to meet the new expectations of the people of all ethnicities for a better life, and to carry out and strive to achieve the new requirements for the goal of building a moderately well-off society in an all-round way, as put forward by the Seventeenth National Congress of the Communist Party of China.

1. New Requirements for the Goal of Building a Moderately Well-off Society in an All-round Way

By this time, China had taken solid steps toward the goal of comprehensively building a moderately well-off society, as had been established by the Sixteenth National Congress. It would continue to strive to ensure that the goal of building a moderately well-off society would be achieved by 2020. To this end, the Seventeenth National Congress of the CPC further advanced the several new requirements.

1) To strengthen the coordination of development and strive to achieve sound and rapid economic development. Significant progress had been made in transforming the mode of development. On the basis of optimizing the structure, improving efficiency, reducing consumption, and protecting the environment, GDP per capita would quadruple by 2020 compared with that of 2000. The socialist market economic system had been improved, independent innovation capability had been significantly improved, and the contribution rate of scientific and technological progress to economic growth had increased significantly, and China had entered the ranks of innovative countries. The consumption rate of residents had steadily increased, and a growth pattern driven by consumption, investment, and export had been formed. The mechanism of coordinated and interactive development between urban and rural areas and regional areas and the layout of main functional areas had basically taken shape. Significant progress had been made in building a new socialist countryside. The proportion of urban population had increased significantly.

2) To expand socialist democracy and better safeguard the rights and interests of the people and social equity and justice. Civil political participation had expanded in an orderly manner. The basic strategy of governing the country by law had been thoroughly implemented, the concept of the legal system had been further strengthened in the whole society, and new achievements had been made in the construction of a government ruled by law. The democratic system at the grassroots level would continue to improve, while the ability of the government to provide basic public services had been significantly enhanced.

3) To strengthen cultural construction and obviously improve the quality of national civilization. The socialist core value system was deeply rooted in the hearts of the people, and the positive ideological and moral customs had been further promoted. The public cultural service system covering all of society had been basically established, the proportion of cultural industry in the national economy had been significantly increased, the international competitiveness had been significantly enhanced, and cultural products adapted to the needs of the people had become more abundant.

4) *To accelerate the development of social undertakings and improve people's lives overall.* The modern national education system was greatly improved, the lifelong education system basically formed, and the education level of all the people and the training level of innovative human resources obviously improved. Social employment was more adequate. The social security system covering urban and rural residents had been basically established, and everyone enjoyed basic living security. A rational and orderly pattern of income distribution had basically taken shape, with the majority of people falling in the middle-income range and absolute poverty eliminated. Everyone had access to basic medical and health services, and the social management system was more sound.

5) *Initial formation of an ecological civilization, the industrial structure, the mode of growth, the mode of consumption of saving energy resources, and protection of the ecological environment.* The circular economy had been formed on a large scale, and the proportion of renewable energy had increased significantly. The discharge of major pollutants had been effectively controlled, and the quality of the ecological environment had been significantly improved. The concept of an ecological civilization was firmly established throughout society.

By 2020, when the goal of building a moderately well-off society in an all-round way would be realized, China's ancient civilized country with a long history and a large developing socialist nation would become a country with the basic realization of industrialization, remarkable enhancement of comprehensive national strength, the overall scale of the domestic market sitting at the forefront of the world, a country with a generally improved individual wealth, a markedly improved quality of life, and a good ecological environment, and it would be a country with a good livelihood for its people. Countries enjoying fuller democratic rights and having a higher quality of civilization and spiritual pursuits would be much better in all aspects of the system, more vibrant, stable, and united in society, more open to the outside world, and with more affinity for and greater contributions to human civilization.[1]

To implement these new requirements aimed at building a moderately well-off society in an all-round way, all Party members needed to "grasp the scientific connotation and spiritual essence of the scientific concept of development in an all-round way, enhance the consciousness and firmness of implementing the scientific concept of development, strive to change the ideological concepts that did not conform to the scientific concept of development, strive to solve the outstanding problems affecting and restricting scientific development, and develop the whole society." It was important to show enthusiasm to guide scientific development and implement the scientific concept of development in all aspects of economic and social development.[2]

One of the most important tasks of thoroughly implementing the new requirements for the goal of building a moderately well-off society in an all-round way was to actively build a harmonious socialist society. This was because scientific development and social harmony were inherently unified. Without scientific development, there would be no social harmony, and without social harmony, it would be difficult to achieve scientific development. Therefore, in order to implement the new requirement of building a moderately well-off society in an all-round way, it was necessary to always do a good job of building a harmonious socialist society.

2. Efforts to Build a Harmonious Socialist Society

Constructing a harmonious socialist society was an important strategic decision made by the Party in accordance with the basic principles of Marxism and the practical experience of socialist construction in China, in accordance with the new requirements of economic and social development in the new century and new stage, as well as the new trends and characteristics of Chinese society. It was also an important achievement made by the Party in guiding the new social practice with the development of Marxism.

1) *Proposal of the thought of building a harmonious socialist society.* A harmonious socialist society was the goal of the Party's unremitting struggle and the common social ideal of all ethnic groups in China. Since the founding of New China, the Party had established a socialist system in which the people were the masters of the country, eliminated the root causes of social antagonism and disharmony, and opened up a broad path for building a harmonious society. However, due to the long period required for understanding the laws of socialist construction, it had also made mistakes in its understanding of what socialism was and how to build it, including serious mistakes such as the Cultural Revolution, which was expansive and long-lived. After the Third Plenary Session of the Eleventh

Central Committee, the Party resolutely abandoned the policy of "taking class struggle as the guiding principle," shifted the focus of the Party's and the state's work to socialist modernization construction, adhered to economic construction as the center, unswervingly promoted Reform and Opening Up, actively driven economic development and social progress in an all-round way, and vigorously pushed forward the construction of a harmonious society.

Over a long period of time, through the joint effort of the Party and the people, Chinese society had generally reached a harmonious state. However, there were contradictions and problems affecting social harmony, such as unbalanced regional, economic, and social development in urban and rural areas, increased pressure on the population, resources, and environment, employment, social security, income distribution, education, medical treatment, housing, safety in production, and other issues related to the vital interests of the masses, imperfect institutional mechanisms, and the democratic legal system. It was not perfect, some members of society lacked honesty and morality, some leading cadres' qualities, abilities, and styles were not adapted to the requirements of the new situation and tasks, corruption in some areas was still serious, and infiltration and destruction of hostile forces endangered national security and social stability. The existence of these contradictions and problems indicated that the task of building a harmonious socialist society in China was still arduous. Faced with this difficult historical task, the Sixteenth National Congress of the Communist Party of China put forward "a more harmonious society" as one of the goals of building a moderately well-off society overall.

2) *Further systematization and theorization of the thought of building a harmonious society.* After the Sixteenth National Congress, the Party deepened its understanding of social harmony, and the position of building a harmonious socialist society in the overall layout of the cause of socialism with Chinese characteristics became increasingly clear.

In November 2002, the Sixteenth National Congress of the Communist Party of China put forward the goal of "six more" in building a moderately well-off society in an all-round way, one of which was "a more harmonious society." In September 2004, the Fourth Plenary Session of the Sixteenth Central Committee of the Communist Party of China deliberated and adopted the Decision on Strengthening the Construction of the Party's Ruling Ability, which put forward the proposition of building a harmonious society and regarded improving the ability to build a harmonious society as one of the main tasks of construction of the Party's ruling ability.

On February 19, 2005, Hu Jintao preliminarily summarized the basic characteristics of a harmonious socialist society at a seminar on Improving the Ability to Build a Harmonious Socialist Society for leading cadres at provincial and ministerial levels. He clearly pointed out that the harmonious socialist society the Party aimed to build should be a society of democracy and rule of law, fairness and justice, honesty and fraternity, full of vitality, stability, order, and harmonious coexistence between man and nature. Democracy and rule of law meant that socialist democracy was fully developed, the basic strategy of ruling the country by law was effectively implemented, and all positive factors were widely mobilized. Fairness and justice meant that the interests of all sectors of society were properly coordinated, contradictions among the people and other social contradictions were correctly handled, and social fairness and justice were effectively maintained and realized, while honesty and fraternity would help the Party achieve these goals. Everyone in society would help each other, be honest and trustworthy, and live in equality, friendship, and harmony with others. Being full of vitality meant that all creative desires conducive to social progress would be respected, creative activities supported, creativity brought into play, and achievements affirmed. Stability and order meant a sound social organization mechanism, sound social management, good social order, and strong people. People would live and work in peace and contentment, and society would remain stable and united. Harmonious coexistence between man and nature meant the development of production, a prosperous life, and a good ecology. Hu also stressed that building a harmonious socialist society was organically integrated with building a socialist material, political, and spiritual civilization. They were not only closely linked, but had their own special fields and laws. Building socialist material, political, and spiritual civilizations could provide a solid foundation for building a harmonious socialist society, which could provide important conditions for building the socialist material, political, and spiritual civilizations.

In October 2006, the Sixth Plenary Session of the Sixteenth Central Committee of the Communist Party of China issued the Decision on Several Major Issues Concerning the Construction of a Harmonious Socialist Society (hereinafter referred to as the Decision), forming a programmatic document for the construction of a harmonious socialist society. Beginning with the importance and urgency of building a harmonious socialist society, the Decision first clarified the nature and orientation of a harmonious socialist society. The harmonious socialist society the Party aimed to build was not only different from the Great Harmony World that some thinkers in history longed for, it was also different from the Utopia described by utopian socialists. It was the product of the combination of Marxist ideas on social harmony and contemporary Chinese reality. The Decision pointed out that it was necessary to build a harmonious socialist society on the path of socialism with Chinese characteristics. The Communist Party of China led all the people in the nation to build and enjoy a harmonious society together. This clarified the core of leadership, the path of development, the subject of practice, and the fundamental purpose of building a harmonious socialist society.

To build a harmonious socialist society, it was necessary to have a correct guiding ideology. The Decision emphasized that the Party must adhere to the guiding principles of Marxism-Leninism, Mao Zedong Thought, Deng Xiaoping Theory, and the "Three Represents," to the Party's basic line, basic program, and basic experience, to the Scientific View of Development as the guide for overall economic and social development, and to the democratic rule of law, fairness, justice, honesty, and fraternity, full of vitality, stability, order, and harmony between man and nature. The general requirement of harmonious coexistence was to focus on addressing issues of the greatest concern and realistic interests of the people. It focused on developing social undertakings, promoting social fairness and justice, building a harmonious culture, improving social management, enhancing social creativity, taking the path of common prosperity, and promoting the coordinated development of social and economic, political, and cultural constructions.

3) *According to the goal of building a moderately well-off society in an all-round way established by the Sixteenth National Congress of the Communist Party of China and the general requirement of building a harmonious socialist society, the Decision put forward the goal and main task of building a harmonious socialist society by 2020, which was to improve the socialist democratic and legal system and to ensure the policy of governing the country according to fully implemented law, and people's rights and interests effectively respected and guaranteed.* Further, the trend of a widening gap between urban and rural and regional development was to be gradually reversed, and a rational and orderly income distribution pattern to be basically formed. In

addition, family property was to be generally increased, and people were to live a more prosperous life, while social employment would be adequate and the social security system covering urban and rural residents would be basically established. In addition, the basic public service system would be better established, the level of government management and service greatly improved, and the ideological and moral quality, scientific and cultural quality, and health quality of the whole nation would be significantly improved, and good moral customs and harmonious interpersonal relationships be further formed. Beyond this, the creativity of the whole society would be significantly enhanced, and an innovative country be basically built, while the social management system would be improved and social order well established. The efficiency of resource utilization would likewise be significantly improved, and the ecological environment greatly advanced. In this way, the goal of building a moderately well-off society at a higher level that would benefit more than a billion people in a holistic way would be achieved and efforts would be made to form a situation in which all the people lived in harmony as much as possible.

To build a harmonious socialist society, it was necessary to follow the correct principles. The Decision of the plenary session put forward the principles of "six firm adherences." The first item to be adhered to was people-orientation, the second scientific development, the third Reform and Opening Up, the fourth democracy and rule of law, the fifth proper handling of the relationship between reform, development, and stability, and the sixth jointly building society under the leadership of the Party.

3. Preliminary Clarification of the Overall Layout of the Four-in-One Socialist Construction

The strategic task of building a harmonious socialist society was put forward to move the overall layout of the cause of socialism with Chinese characteristics more clearly from the trinity of socialist economic, political, and cultural construction to the four-in-one approach of socialist economic, political, cultural, and social construction. Generally speaking, it was evident that the socialist political construction aimed mainly to solve the basic political structure of socialism with Chinese characteristics and constantly improve the socialist political system, so that political governance grew more scientific, rational, and effective. Socialist economic construction aimed mainly to gradually build up the basic socialist economic system to resolve social problems. The driving force and efficiency of the development of socialist society provided a solid material foundation for the consolidation of socialism. In the course of building socialist culture, it was important to mainly form the core value theory of socialism and the healthy and uplifting humanistic idea, construct an advanced, scientific socialist ideological theory and social and cultural atmosphere, and create strong humanities for the better development of socialism. In order to better solve the overall layout of socialist modernization, it was important to focus on solving the historical issue of social development and progress while promoting political, economic, and cultural development. The proposition of the four-in-one development layout enriched and developed the theory of socialism with Chinese characteristics from the aspects of social driving force, development, and progress, and became an inherent part of the cause of socialism with Chinese characteristics. It further clarified the issues of social value orientation and the development objectives of socialism, and not only innovated the balanced mechanism of socialist society, but developed the dynamic mechanism of socialist society. Therefore, the proposition of this idea made the task of social construction more prominent, the overall layout of socialist modernization more reasonable, and the development model of socialism with Chinese characteristics clearer.

The strategic idea of building a harmonious socialist society conformed to the basic principles of Marxism and the scientific assumptions of Marxist socialist society. It was the new progress of the Party in the theory and practice of socialist social construction. This was not only a summary of the Party's governing experience, but also a reference to some foreign governing parties' governing experience and lessons. It was a deepening of the understanding of the laws of socialist construction in China, as well as the rules of the Communist Party's governing, socialist construction, and human social development. It was not only an enrichment and development of the theory of socialism with Chinese characteristics, but also a deepening of the understanding of the laws of Marxism regarding the enrichment and development of socialist construction theory.

III

Deepening Reform in Administrative Systems and the New Deployment of Rural Reform

From February 25–27, 2008, the Second Plenary Session of the Seventeenth Central Committee of the Communist Party of China was held in Beijing. The plenary considered and adopted the Opinions on Deepening the Reform of Administrative Management System and the Plan for the Reform of State Council Institutions, which were put forward on the basis of extensive consultation, and it was agreed that they be submitted for consideration for inclusion in the Plan for the Reform of State Council Institutions to the First Session of the Eleventh National People's Congress.

1. Suggestions on Deepening the Reform of the Administrative System

The Party Central Committee and the State Council had always attached great importance to the reform of the administrative system. Since Reform and Opening Up, and especially since the Sixteenth National Congress, the Party had continuously pushed forward the reform of the administrative system and strengthened the construction of the government itself, achieving remarkable results. Generally speaking, the administrative system basically met the requirements of economic and social development, effectively guaranteeing the development of Reform and Opening Up and socialist modernization. Clearly, in the face of the new situation and new tasks, there were still some incompatible aspects in the current administrative system, such as that the transformation of government functions was not in place, excessive interference in the operation of the micro-economy, the relative weakness of social management and public services, the problems of intersection of departments' responsibilities, separation of powers, and responsibilities and inefficiency, inappropriate setup of government institutions, imperfect administrative operation and management systems and supervision and restriction mechanisms of administrative power, abuse of power, and seeking personal gains by power, corruption, and other such phenomena. These problems directly influenced the government to perform its functions properly and comprehensively, and to a certain extent restricted economic and social development. Deepening the reform of the administrative system was crucial.

1) *The objectives and requirements of deepening the reform of the administrative system.* With regard to the overall goal of deepening the reform of the administrative system, the Opinions on Deepening the Reform of the Administrative System clearly put forward that a relatively perfect socialist administrative system with Chinese characteristics should be established by 2020. Through reform, China would realize the fundamental transformation of government functions to create a good environment for development, provide high-quality public services, safeguard social equity and justice, realize the fundamental transformation of government organizations and staffing to a scientific, standardized, and legalized one, realize the fundamental transformation of administrative operation mechanism and government management mode to a standard, orderly, open, transparent, convenient, and efficient one, and build a government to the people's satisfaction.

2) *Accelerating the transformation of government functions as the core of deepening the reform of the administrative system.* It was imperative to rationally define the functions of government departments, clarify the responsibilities of departments, and ensure the consistency of powers and responsibilities. The Party needed to rationalize the division of responsibilities among departments and adhere to the principle that one department should be responsible for one thing, while some needed to be managed by multiple departments. It needed to clarify the leading departments and distinguish primary and secondary responsibilities. It would improve inter-departmental coordination and coordination mechanisms and effectively speed up the separation of government and enterprises, government and capital, government affairs and market intermediary organizations, and transfer matters that should not be managed by the government. It would also effectively manage matters that should be managed by the government, better play the basic role of the market in resource allocation in the system, and give better play to citizens' and social organizations' roles in the management of social and public affairs, while more effectively offering public goods.

3) *Exploring the system of large departments and improving the administrative operation mechanism.* Promoting the reform of government institutions was mainly based on the principle of streamlining the unified efficiency, the requirements of mutual restriction, and the coordination of decision-making power, executive

power, and supervisory power, while closely focusing on the transformation of functions and rationalizing the relationship of responsibilities, further optimizing the organizational structure of the government, standardizing the establishment of institutions, exploring the implementation of a large department system with organically unified functions, and improving the administrative operation mechanism.

4) *Strengthening administration and system construction according to law.* It was important to strictly administer according to law, insist on using the system to manage power, affairs, and people, improve the supervision mechanism, strengthen investigation accountability, and earnestly ensure that rights must be responsible, rights to use should be supervised, and violations of the law should be investigated. The Party should further accelerate the construction of a government ruled by law, implement the system of government performance management and administrative accountability, improve the supervision system of administrative power, and strengthen the construction of civil servants.

2. Institutional Reform Program of the State Council

According to the spirit of the Seventeenth National Congress and the Second Plenary Session of the Seventeenth Central Committee, the main task of the institutional reform of the State Council was to change the functions of the government and rationalize the responsibilities of the departments, explore and implement a large department system with organically unified functions, rationally allocate the functions of the macro-control departments, strengthen the energy and environment management institutions, and integrate and improve the management systems of the industries of industry, information technology, and transportation. The Party should focus on improving people's livelihoods and strengthen and integrate the social management and public service sectors.

1) *Rationally allocate the functions of macro-control departments.* The National Development and Reform Commission needed to further transform its functions, reduce micro-management matters and specific approval matters, and concentrate on macro-control. The Ministry of Finance needed to reform and improve budgetary and tax administration, improve the system of matching central and local financial resources and powers, and improve the public financial system. The People's Bank of China needed to further improve the monetary policy system,

strengthen the overall coordination with the financial supervision departments, and safeguard the national financial security. The National Development and Reform Commission, the Ministry of Finance, the People's Bank of China, and other departments needed to establish and improve the coordination mechanism and form a more perfect macro-control system.

2) *Strengthen energy management institutions.* As a high-level deliberative and coordinating body, the National Energy Committee needed to be established. The National Energy Committee would be established and administered by the National Development and Reform Commission. The functions and agencies of the National Development and Reform Commission in energy industry management would be integrated with those of the Office of the National Energy Leading Group and the Nuclear Power Management of the National Defense Science, Technology, and Industry Commission. The work of the Office of the National Energy Commission would be undertaken by the State Energy Administration. The National Energy Leading Group and its offices would no longer be retained.

3) *Establishing the Ministry of Industry and Information Technology.* The responsibilities of the National Development and Reform Commission in industrial management, the National Defense Science and Technology Industry Commission in nuclear power management, the Ministry of Information Industry, and the Information Office of the State Council would be integrated into the Ministry of Industry and Information Technology. The State Bureau of Defense Science, Technology, and Industry would be established and administered by the Ministry of Industry and Information Technology. The State Tobacco Monopoly Bureau would be managed by the Ministry of Industry and Information Technology. The National Defense Science, Technology, and Industry Commission, the Ministry of Information Industry, and the Information Work Office of the State Council would no longer be retained.

4) *Establishing the Ministry of Transportation.* The responsibilities of the Ministry of Communications, the General Administration of Civil Aviation of China, and the Ministry of Construction in guiding urban passenger transport would be integrated into the Ministry of Transportation. The State Civil Aviation Administration would be established and administered by the Ministry of Transportation, and the State Post Office would be managed by the Ministry of Transportation. The Ministry of Railways would be retained and reform would

continue. The Ministry of Communications and the General Administration of Civil Aviation of China would no longer be retained.

5) *Establishing the Ministry of Human Resources and Social Security.* The responsibilities of the Ministry of Personnel and the Ministry of Labor and Social Security would be integrated into the Ministry of Human Resources and Social Security. The establishment of the National Civil Service Bureau would be managed by the Ministry of Human Resources and Social Security. The Ministry of Personnel, the Ministry of Labor, and Social Security would no longer be retained.

6) *Establishing the Ministry of Environmental Protection.* The State Environmental Protection Administration would no longer be retained.

7) *Establishing the Ministry of Housing and Urban-Rural Construction.* The Ministry of Construction would no longer be retained.

8) *Re-administration of the State Food and Drug Administration by the Ministry of Health.* The Ministry of Health was responsible for coordinating food safety across the board and organizing the investigation and handling of major food safety incidents.

3. Five Major Changes in the Administrative System

As an important part of the national reform, China's administrative system reform would undergo five changes.

First, the management concept of the government had changed, and the administrative base point had become scientific. Further change would arise from the management concept of the planned economy to the management concept of the socialist market economy. The change of concept was embodied in changing the idea that the state-owned economy was the only form of socialism and the essential attribute of socialism, changing the idea that development was economic development through serving the state-owned economy to serving all the economic elements conducive to the development of productive forces, changing the idea that development was merely economic development, changing the government's commitment to GDP growth to improving economic quality and economic efficiency and coordinated development of an economic society in an all-round way. This change promoted a series of institutional and policy adjustments and reforms.

Second, the scope of management had changed and the functions of the government had grown increasingly reasonable. Through the separation of government and enterprise, the reform of state-owned asset management systems, and the adjustment of state-owned economic distribution, the government had changed from overall management to economic regulation, market supervision, social management, and public services, from direct engagement and intervention in economic activities to effective implementation of macro-control and creation of a market environment, and from purely pursuing high-speed economic growth to promoting economic growth. The combination of degree, quality, structure, and benefit would promote the coordinated development of the economy and society and the harmonious coexistence between man and nature.

Third, the administrative mode had changed and the management means had been constantly improved. To promote the reform of the administrative examination and approval system, the central and provincial governments had drastically reduced the items of examination and approval, adopted new modes of examination and approval, such as approval and registration and filing, standardized and simplified the examination and approval procedures, and provided "one-stop" examination and approval services, online examination and approval, and so forth.

Fourth, the administrative basis had changed and the government's behavior had become increasingly standardized. Since Reform and Opening Up, six different reforms had been carried out to strengthen the institutions engaged in economic regulation, supervision, and social management services, reduce the overlapping responsibilities among departments, streamline the number of government staff, and promote the transformation of government functions and efficiency.

Fifth, the quality of cadres had changed and administrative ability had been effectively improved. To establish a strict mechanism for the selection of administrative personnel or civil servants, all staff members who entered the state administrative organs were required to pass the examination. The Party needed to establish a scientific mechanism for selecting and appointing leading cadres and carry out open selection and competitive induction systems. The Civil Servants Law of the People's Republic of China, promulgated in 2005, had become an important symbol of the legalization of the construction and management of civil servants.

4. Deployment of Deepening Rural Reform

From October 9–12, 2008, the Third Plenary Session of the Seventeenth Central Committee of the Communist Party of China was held in Beijing. The plenary session proceeded from the new requirements of the Seventeenth National Congress to achieve the goal of building a moderately well-off society in an all-round way, formulating a comprehensive plan for further deepening rural reform.

1) *The objective and task of deepening rural reform.* According to the new requirements of realizing the goal of building a moderately well-off society in an all-round way put forward by the Seventeenth National Congress and the requirements of building a new socialist countryside featuring production and development, a well-off life, a civilized rural style, clean and tidy villages, and democratic management, the basic objectives and tasks of rural reform and development by 2020 were to improve the rural economic system and basically establish an integrated system of urban and rural economic and social development, make significant progress in the construction of modern agriculture, improve the comprehensive production capacity of agriculture, guarantee national food security and the supply of major agricultural products, and effectively double the per capita net income of farmers compared with 2008, while raising the level of consumption and eliminating absolute poverty. Further, the construction of grassroots organizations in rural areas should be further strengthened, the villagers' autonomy system improved, and the democratic rights of farmers guaranteed. Equalization of basic public services in urban and rural areas should be promoted, rural culture further prospered, and farmers' basic cultural rights and interests better implemented, and everyone in rural areas should be given the opportunity to receive a good education. Rural basic living security and basic medical and health systems, the rural social management system, and the basic form of resource-saving and environmentally friendly agricultural production systems should be improved. As a result, rural human settlements and the ecological environment would improve significantly, and the ability of sustainable development be continuously enhanced.

2) *Important principles that must be followed in deepening rural reform.* To achieve the basic goals and tasks of rural reform and development by 2020, it was important to follow several major principles.

First, it was necessary to consolidate and strengthen the basic position of agriculture and always make it a top priority to solve the problem of feeding more than a billion people. It was important to adhere to the principle of realizing basic self-sufficiency of grain at home, strengthen the support and protection of agriculture by the state, carry out the strategy of revitalizing agriculture through science and education, speed up the construction of modern agriculture, realize the comprehensive and stable development of agriculture, and lay a solid foundation for promoting economic development, promoting social harmony, and safeguarding national security.

Second, it was necessary to effectively protect the rights and interests of farmers, always taking the realization, maintenance and development of the fundamental interests of farmers as the starting point and the foothold of all rural work. It was important to adhere to a people-oriented approach, respect the wishes of farmers, focus on solving the greatest concerns and realistic interests of farmers, safeguard their political, economic, cultural, and social rights and interests, improve their comprehensive quality, promote their all-round development, give full play to their main role and initiative, and firmly rely on hundreds of millions of farmers to build a new socialist countryside.

Third, it was necessary to constantly emancipate and develop rural social productive forces and always regard reform and innovation as the fundamental driving force of rural development. The Party should unremittingly promote rural reform and institutional innovation, improve the scientific nature of reform decision-making, enhance the coordination of reform measures, give full play to the fundamental role of the market in the allocation of resources, strengthen and improve the state's control and guidance of agricultural and rural development, improve the rural economic system that met the requirements of the socialist market economy, and adjust the production relations and superstructure that failed to meet the requirements of the rural social productivity development, so as to inject vitality into rural economic and social development.

Fourth, the Party was to coordinate the economic and social development of urban and rural areas, always focusing on building a new type of industrial-agricultural, urban-rural relations as a major strategy to accelerate modernization. The key tasks included coordinating the construction of industrialization, urbanization, and agricultural modernization, speeding up the establishment and improvement of a long-term mechanism of promoting agriculture by industry and leading the countryside by cities and towns, adjusting the distribution pattern of the national income, consolidating and perfecting the policy of strengthening agriculture and benefiting the peasants, focusing on the construction of the national infrastructure and the development of social undertakings in rural areas, promoting the equalization of basic public services in urban and rural areas, realizing the coordinated development of urban and rural areas and regions, and urging peasants to participate in the modernization process and share the achievements of reform and development.

Fifth, it was necessary to adhere to the Party's management of rural work and always take strengthening and improving the Party's leadership of rural work as a political guarantee to promote rural reform and development. The Party should adhere to all its basic policies in the countryside, strengthen the construction of grassroots organizations and political power in the countryside, improve the system, mechanism, and methods of its management of rural work, maintain its flesh-and-blood relationship with the peasants, consolidate its ruling foundation in the countryside, and form a strong synergy to promote rural reform and development.

3) *Instituting a comprehensive plan for the construction and innovation of the rural system.* Institutional construction was fundamental, overall, and long-term. The plenary accurately grasped the basic national conditions and the characteristics of the current stage of development in China's primary stage of socialism, closely focused on the major issues in the current rural reform and development, grasped the important areas and key links of rural system reform, and emphatically deployed six major institutional constructions, including stabilizing and improving the basic management system in rural areas and perfecting the strict, standardized rural land management system. It was important to improve the system of supporting and protecting agriculture, establish a modern rural financial system, establish an integrated system to promote the economic and social development of urban and rural areas, and improve the democratic management system in rural areas.

At the Third Plenary Session of the Seventeenth Central Committee of the Communist Party of China, a series of new deployments, such as deepening the objectives, tasks, major principles, and system construction of rural reform and development, as well as actively developing modern agriculture and improving the comprehensive production capacity of agriculture, accelerating the development of rural public utilities and promoting the overall progress of rural society, strengthening and improving the leadership of the Communist Party, and providing a strong political guarantee for the promotion of rural reform and development were made. Further deepening rural reform provided a general idea, which was an important step toward realizing the strategic goal of rural development and promoting modern agriculture with Chinese characteristics. It was of great, far-reaching significance to the acceleration of the construction of a new socialist countryside and the vigorous promotion of the overall development of urban and rural areas.

IV

A Summary of Thirty Years of Reform and Opening Up and the Implementation of the Scientific Outlook on Development

As the Central Committee, with Hu Jintao as its general secretary, was leading the whole Party and all the people in their efforts to build a moderately well-off society in an all-round way, China ushered in the 30th anniversary of Reform and Opening Up. Over the previous thirty years, the Party had consistently taken Reform and Opening Up as a powerful driving force. On the basis of the twenty-nine years since the founding of New China, it had opened up a road of socialism with Chinese characteristics and made remarkable achievements in various undertakings.

On December 18, 2008, on behalf of the Central Committee, Hu Jintao made a scientific summary of the achievements and basic experience gained over the previous thirty years of Reform and Opening Up. The achievements made over the previous thirty years included resolutely pushing forward the reform of all aspects of the system, successfully realizing the historical turning point from a highly centralized planned economy system to a vibrant socialist market economy system, constantly expanding China's opening to the outside world, successfully realizing the historical turning point from closed and semi-closed to an all-round opening, persisting in taking economic construction as the center and taking comprehensive national strength to a new stage, making great efforts to safeguard and improve people's livelihood so that the people's living standards generally reached a well-off level, vigorously developing socialist democracy to ensure that the people's right to be masters of the country was better guaranteed, vigorously developing advanced socialist culture to make sure that the people's growing spiritual and cultural needs would be better met, vigorously developing social undertakings to consolidate and develop social harmony and stability, and adhering to the absolute leadership of the Party over the army to make significant achievements in national defense and army building. The Party had also successfully implemented the basic principle of "one country, two systems" to lead to significant strides in the great cause of peaceful reunification of the motherland, adhered to an independent foreign policy of peace for the achievement of all-round diplomacy, adhered to the Party's governance over itself, and exerted strict self-discipline to ensure that the Party's leadership and ruling level and its ability to resist corruption, change, and risk had been remarkably improved.

Thirty years of practice fully indicated that, through the baptism of the great revolution of Reform and Opening Up, the Chinese nation had caught up with the trend of the times. Socialist China stood firmly in the east, and the Communist Party of China stood at the forefront of the times.

Over the previous thirty years, the fundamental reason China had seen such brilliant achievements and historic progress could be summed up in one point. It had combined the basic principles of Marxism with China's specific reality, followed its own path, and built socialism with Chinese characteristics. In the creative practice of the previous three decades of Reform and Opening Up, the Party had acquired valuable experience through arduous exploration. This was the Ten Combinations clarified by the Seventeenth National Congress of the Communist Party of China. These clarifications included:

1) The Party should combine the adherence to the basic principles of Marxism with the promotion of the localization of Marxism and should not only adhere to the basic principles of Marxism, but also continuously promote the localization of it according to the practice and development of contemporary China, so that Marxism could better play its guiding role in developing the practice of socialism with Chinese characteristics and give contemporary Chinese Marxism a vigorous life.

2) The Party should combine adherence to the Four Basic Principles with adherence to Reform and Opening Up, not only guaranteeing the correct direction of Reform and Opening Up with the Four Basic Principles, but also endowing the Four Basic Principles with the new era's connotation

through Reform and Opening Up. It should educate and guide the whole Party and the people of all ethnicities to deeply understand the dialectical relationship and great significance of adherence to the Four Basic Principles and adherence to Reform and Opening Up, while focusing on the center and adhering to the Four Basic Principles, unifying Reform and Opening Up in the practice of developing socialism with Chinese characteristics.

3) The Party should combine respecting the initiative of the masses with strengthening and improving the leadership of the Party, adhere to the Marxist scientific principle that the people create history, sincerely represent the fundamental interests of the overwhelming majority of the Chinese people, rely closely on the people, mobilize the enthusiasm, initiative, and creativity of the masses of the people in the widest possible way, gather strength, absorb wisdom from the people, and constantly strengthen and improve the Party's leadership, so that the Party could be fully trusted and supported by the people and always play a central leading role.

4) The Party should combine the adherence to the basic socialist system with the development of the market economy, adhere to the basic socialist system throughout profound and extensive changes, and develop the market economy under socialist conditions, so that economic activities would follow the requirements of the law of value, constantly liberate and develop social productive forces, enhance comprehensive national strength, improve people's living standards, and better realize the economy. Economic construction was thus the central task.

5) The Party should combine the promotion of economic base reform with the promotion of superstructure reform. It should actively promote both economic and political system reform, develop socialist democratic politics, build a socialist country ruled by law, ensure that the people remained the masters of the country, constantly promote the adaptation of the socialist superstructure to the economic base, and provide institutional and legal guarantees for the reform, opening up, and construction of socialist modernization.

6) The Party should combine the development of social productive forces with the improvement of the quality of national civilization. It should attach importance to both material development and the improvement of the quality of national civilization. It should also adhere to both material and

spiritual civilization, vigorously develop socialist culture, build the socialist spiritual civilization, and strive to cultivate citizens with ideals, morality, culture, and discipline to provide a strong spiritual impetus and intellectual support for economic and social development.

7) The Party should combine improving efficiency with promoting social equity. It should attach great importance to promoting development through improving efficiency and promoting social harmony through realizing social equity on the basis of economic development. It was important to adhere to a people-oriented approach, focusing on solving the greatest concerns and the realistic interests of the people, focusing on developing social undertakings and improving the income distribution system. The Party should ensure and improve people's livelihood, take the path of common prosperity, and strive to form a situation in which all the people lived in harmony while doing their best.

8) The Party should combine adherence to independence with participation in economic globalization, not only highly cherishing and unswervingly safeguarding the independent rights of the Chinese people after a long struggle, but also adhering to the basic national policy of opening to the outside world. It should always look at the development of China and the world from the perspective of interconnection between the international and domestic situations, consider and formulate China's development strategy, and adhere to independent foreign policy of peace, to the path of peaceful development, to the mutually beneficial and win-win strategy of opening up, and promoting the building of a harmonious world of lasting peace and common prosperity.

9) The Party should combine the promotion of reform and development with the maintenance of social stability. It should not only vigorously promote reform and development, but also correctly handle the relationship between reform, development, and stability. It should adhere to the principle of reform as the driving force, development the goal, and stability the prerequisite. It should integrate the strength of reform, the speed of development, and the degree of social affordability, taking the continuous improvement of people's lives as the conjuncture of reform, development, and stability, so as to promote reform and development in social stability and consolidate social stability through reform and development.

10) The Party should combine the great cause of advancing socialism with Chinese characteristics with the great project of advancing the Party's construction. It should not only promote the Party's construction closely around advancing the cause of socialism with Chinese characteristics, but also promote the cause of socialism with Chinese characteristics by strengthening and improving the Party's construction, constantly improve the Party's governing ability, maintain and develop the Party's advanced nature, and constantly strengthen the Party's class foundation and expand the Party's mass basis, while continuously improving the ability to resist corruption and risk so that the Party would always remain the strong leading core of the cause of socialism with Chinese characteristics.

The Ten Combinations was a new generalization full of the flavor of the times. To sum up, the Party had creatively explored and answered such important theoretical and practical questions as what Marxism was and how to treat it, what socialism was and how to build it, what kind of party to build and how to build it, what kind of development to achieve, and how to achieve it. One of the important features was that it embodied the concept of the "combination" of the second historic leap. It was the concrete development of the general requirement of the combination of the basic principles of Marxism with the practice of contemporary China and the characteristics of the times. Formulating the Ten Combinations was a valuable experience for China, a large developing country with a population of more than 1 billion, allowing it to rid itself of poverty, accelerate modernization, and consolidate and develop socialism. It was also an extremely valuable spiritual wealth gained by the Party and the people through long-term practice and arduous exploration. Hu Jintao's historic summary of thirty years of Reform and Opening Up, which was a height, profound in thought, and rich in connotation, and had a strong theoretical, strategic, and guiding significance. The entire article radiated with the brilliance of Marxist truth, further enriched the theoretical system of socialism with Chinese characteristics, and was a programmatic document guiding China to continue to promote the great cause of Reform and Opening Up.

Drawing on and insisting on using these valuable experiences, the Party would constantly enrich and develop the practice of building socialism with Chinese characteristics. It would persist in emancipating the mind, seeking truth from facts, advancing with the times, daring to change and innovate, never growing rigid or stagnant, never fearing any risks, and never confused by any interference. The development and innovation of the guiding ideology of the Communist Party of China would lead to even greater achievements.

Summarizing the historical experience of the CPC since its ruling and Reform and Opening Up, the Party made a great step forward on the road to integrating Marxism into China. On the other hand, new developments in the localization of Marxism were promoted by the CPC to form a new understanding of the laws of China's reform, opening up, and socialist modernization.

New knowledge arose from new practice. During the Eleventh Five-Year Plan period, facing the complex situation in China and abroad and a series of major risks and challenges, the Communist Party of China united and led the people of all ethnicities throughout the country and comprehensively promoted Reform and Opening Up and socialist modernization, while the national landscape underwent historic changes. China's social productivity and comprehensive national strength improved markedly, various social undertakings accelerated their development, people's lives improved greatly, Reform and Opening Up made significant progress, and its international status and influence improved significantly. Major breakthroughs were made in the frontier sciences and technology of manned space flight, lunar exploration, and supercomputers, and significant achievements were made in the modernization of national defense and the military. In particular, these achievements were made under the difficult conditions of the impact of the international financial crisis, the major earthquakes in Wenchuan and Yushu, and frequent natural disasters, such as the great mountain torrents and debris flows in Zhouqu. On the basis of summarizing the above achievements and experiences, in October 2010, the Fifth Plenary Session of the Seventeenth Central Committee of the Communist Party of China adopted the Suggestions on Making the Twelfth Five-Year Plan for National Economic and Social Development, clearly putting forward the guiding ideology for formulating the Twelfth Five-Year Plan, which was to uphold the great banner of socialism with Chinese characteristics, and to refer to Deng Xiaoping Theory and the important idea of Guiding and Implementing the Scientific View of Development, adapting to the new changes in the situation in China and abroad, meeting the new expectations of the people of all ethnic groups, taking scientific development as the theme, taking accelerating the transformation of the mode of economic development as the main line, deepening Reform and Opening Up, safeguarding and improving people's livelihoods, consolidating and expanding achievements while dealing with the impact of the international financial crisis, and promoting long-term stable, rapid economic development, social harmony, and stability. This would lay a decisive foundation for building a moderately well-off society in an all-round way. In March 2011, the Fourth Session of the Eleventh National People's Congress considered and adopted the Outline of the Twelfth Five-Year Plan for National Economic and Social Development of the People's Republic of China. The outline of the Twelfth Five-Year Plan approved by the General Assembly held high the great banner of socialism with Chinese characteristics, guided by Deng Xiaoping Theory and the "Three Represents," carried out the Scientific View of Development, adhered to the strategic adjustment of the economic structure as the main direction of accelerating the transformation of the mode of economic development, and adhered to ensuring and improving people's livelihood as the Party accelerated the transformation of economic development. The fundamental starting point and end-point of the model were to build a sustainable, environmentally friendly society as an important focus for speeding up the transformation of the economic development mode, to persist in taking Reform and Opening Up as a powerful driving force for accelerating the transformation of the economic development mode, to clarify the main objectives of China's economic and social development during the Twelfth Five-Year Plan period, and to draw a blueprint for the next five years. The outline also specified the main objectives of China's economic and social development in the next five years. These goals not only achieved the organic combination of five years and ten years, current and long-term, but also closely linked up with the goal of building a moderately well-off society in an all-round way, taking into account future development trends and conditions.

In an overview of the Twelfth Five-Year Plan, the magnificent blueprint and grand goal inspired people to forge ahead. The action plan formulated by the Central Committee clearly outlined the road map for the third five years of the new century with realistic, pragmatic, and inspiring strokes, pointing out the direction for China's future development and filling the people of all ethnicities with hope for the future of socialist China.

POSTSCRIPT

To commemorate the 90th anniversary of the founding of the Communist Party of China, Party members Wu Guoyou and Ding Xuemei co-authored the third volume of *An Ideological History of Communist Party of China*. Wu Guoyou wrote the outline of the book and chapters one to four, while Ding Xuemei wrote chapters five to twelve. In the process of writing, we also absorbed the valuable opinions of Party members Zheng Qian, former director of the Second Research Department of the Central Party History Research Office, and Party member Huang Yibing, deputy director of the Second Research Department. In addition, CPC members He Shifen, Zhou Yiqun, Gu Benda, Bai Weiping, Jiang Haoli, Zheng Youxin, Qin Kejia, Ge Youchang, Bai Siyi, Zhang Guangren, Zhang Huiqin, Zhang Wenju, Liu Huiyan, Hu Tongjie, Li Qiushi, He Xingjiang, and Yuan Qizhang also provided us with information and participated in the verification of the information. Meanwhile, the leaders and editors of Guangdong Education Publishing House have provided great help to the publication of this book. We would like to express our heartfelt gratitude to all.

Due to the pressing time for writing and our limited competence, there are inevitable problems and faults with the book. At the time of publication, we sincerely hope that readers and our counterparts will grant us your invaluable criticism and suggestions.

The Authors
May, 2011

NOTES

Introduction

1. *Anthology of Deng Xiaoping's Works.* Beijing: People's Publishing House, 1993. p. 269.

Chapter 1

1. Translator's note: meaning "mourning Zhou together".
2. Dai Huang. *Hu Yaobang and the Redressing of Unjust and False Cases.* China Federation of Arts and Culture Publishing Company, Xinhua Publisher, 1998. p. 65.
3. *A Hundred-Year Wave.* Issue 12, 2006.
4. Chen Danqing: "Upbringing and Humanity." *Wenzhai Newspaper,* September 16, 2008.
5. *The Chronicles of Deng Xiaoping* (1975–1997), Volume 1, ed. The Documentation Research Department of the Central Committee of the Communist Party of China, Central Documents Publishing House, 2004. p. 345.
6. *The Chronicles of Deng Xiaoping* (1975–1997), Volume 1, ed. The Documentation Research Department of the Central Committee of the Communist Party of China, Central Documents Publishing House, 2004. p. 319–320.

Chapter 2

1. *Selected Works of Deng Xiaoping, Volume 2.* People's Publishing House, 1994. p. 243.
2. *Selected Works of Deng Xiaoping, Volume 2.* People's Publishing House, 1994. p. 243–244.
3. Translator's Note: the intersection of Shandong, Henan, Anhui, and Jiangsu Provinces, named after its position to the west of the four lakes, Weishan, Nanyang, Dushan and Shaoyang Lakes.
4. *Selected Works of Deng Xiaoping, Volume 2.* People's Publishing House, 1994. p. 187.

5. *General Situation and Documents of All Previous National United Front Work Conferences.* China Archives Publishing House, 1988. p. 443.
6. Ibid.
7. *Selected Documents of the United Front in the New Period,* 1985 edition of the Party School Press of the Central Committee of the Communist Party of China. p. 164.
8. *Selected Documents of the United Front in the New Period,* 1985 edition of the Party School Press of the Central Committee of the Communist Party of China. p. 163.
9. *Selected Works of Li Weihan.* People's Publishing House, 1987. p. 635–636.
10. *Selected Works of Deng Xiaoping, Volume 2.* People's Publishing House, 1994. p. 205.
11. *Selected Documents of the United Front in the New Period,* 1985 edition of the Party School Press of the Central Committee of the Communist Party of China. p. 165.
12. *Selection and Compilation of Important Documents since the Twelfth National Congress, Volume 1.* People's Publishing House, 1986. p. 36.

Chapter 3

1. Edited by the Documentation Research Department of the Central Committee of the Communist Party of China. *The Chronicle of Deng Xiaoping (1975–1997) Volume 1.* Central Documentation Publishing House, 2004. p. 461–462.
2. "Promoting Democracy and Realizing the Four Modernizations." *People's Daily.* January 3, 1979.
3. Hu Yaobang. *Introduction to the Meeting of Theoretical Work.* January 18, 1979.
4. Edited by the Documentation Research Department of the Central Committee of the Communist Party of China. *The Chronicle of Deng Xiaoping (1975–1997), Volume 1.* Central Documentation Publishing House, 2004. p. 401.
5. Deng Xiaoping. *Speech at the Report Meeting on the Situation of Vietnam's Self-Defense Counter-Strike,* held by the Central Committee of the Communist Party of China, March 16, 1979.
6. Edited by the Documentation Research Department of the Central Committee of the Communist Party of China. *The Chronicle of Deng Xiaoping (1975–1997), Volume 1.* Central Documentation Publishing House, 2004. p. 499–500.
7. *People's Daily.* June 7, 1979.
8. *Selection of Important Documents after the Third Plenary Session of the Central Committee, Volume 1.* People's Publishing House, 1991. p. 239.

Chapter 4

1. *Selected Works of Deng Xiaoping, Volume 3.* People's Publishing House, 1993. p. 83.
2. Speech by Hua Guofeng at the Plenary Session of the Central Military Commission,

December 12, 1977.
3. "Grasping the Outline and Ruling the Army for War." Ye Jianying's Report at the Plenary Session of the Central Military Commission, December 12, 1977.
4. Speech by Hua Guofeng at the Plenary Session of the Central Military Commission, December 12, 1977.
5. *Selected Works of Deng Xiaoping, Volume 2*. People's Publishing House, 1994. p. 77.
6. Deng Xiaoping's Speech at the Plenary Session of the Central Military Commission, December 28, 1977.
7. *Selected Works of Deng Xiaoping, Volume 2*. People's Publishing House, 1994. p. 241.
8. *The Chronicle of Deng Xiaoping Thought*. Compiled by the Literature Research Department of the Central Committee of the Communist Party of China, 1998 edition, Central Literature Publishing House. p. 152–153.
9. *Selected Works of Deng Xiaoping, Volume 2*. People's Publishing House, 1994. p. 77.
10. Ibid, p. 417.
11. Xie Yixian, ed. *Contemporary Chinese Diplomatic History (1949–2001)*. China Youth Press, 2002. p. 419.
12. Edited by the Documentation Research Department of the Central Committee of the Communist Party of China: *The Chronicle of Deng Xiaoping (1975–1997), Volume 1*. Central Documentation Publishing House, 2004. p. 507–508.
13. Han Nianlong, Contemporary Chinese Diplomacy, China Social Sciences Press, 1988. p. 233–234.
14. Han Nianlong. *Contemporary Chinese Diplomacy*. China Social Sciences Press, 1988. p. 347.
15. Ibid, p. 346–347.
16. Ibid, p. 347–348.
17. Qian Qichen: Ten Records of Diplomacy, World Knowledge Publishing House, 2003. p. 6.
18. Ibid, p. 9–10.
19. Qian Qichen. *Ten Records of Diplomacy*. World Knowledge Publishing House, 2003. p. 23–25.
20. *The Chronicle of Deng Xiaoping Thought*. Compiled by the Literature Research Department of the Central Committee of the Communist Party of China, 1998 edition of the Central Literature Publishing House. p. 359–360.
21. *People's Daily*. September 17, 1988.
22. Zheng Qirong. *Diplomacy in China since Reform and Opening up*. World Knowledge Press, 2008. p. 297.
23. Documentation Research Department of the Central Committee of the Communist Party of China, ed. *The Chronicle of Deng Xiaoping (1975–1997) (Part 2)*. Central Documentation Publishing House, 2004. p. 1134.
24. Qian Qichen. *Ten Records of Diplomacy*. World Knowledge Publishing House, 2003. p. 36.
25. Shen Xueming. *The Beginning and Ending of the Normalization of Sino-Soviet Relations*. No. 3 of the 1996 Documents of the Party.

26. Han Nianlong. *Contemporary Chinese Diplomacy.* China Social Sciences Press, 1988. p. 375.
27. Selection and Compilation of Important Documents since the Twelfth National Congress. People's Publishing House, 1986. p. 964.
28. Han Nianlong. *Contemporary Chinese Diplomacy.* China Social Sciences Press, 1988. p. 385.
29. Ibid, p. 388.

CHAPTER 5

1. *People's Daily.* September 30, 1987.
2. *Selected Works of Deng Xiaoping, Volume 3.* People's Publishing House, 1993. p. 212.
3. *People's Daily.* April 27, 1982.

CHAPTER 6

1. *Selected Works of Deng Xiaoping, Volume 2.* People's Publishing House, 1994. p. 208.
2. Ibid, p. 367.
3. Ibid, p. 382.
4. Ibid, p. 404.
5. *Selected Works of Deng Xiaoping, Volume 2.* People's Publishing House, 1994. p. 409.
6. *Selected Works of Deng Xiaoping, Volume 3.* People's Publishing House, 1993. p. 143–144.
7. *Selection and Compilation of Important Documents since the Third Plenary Session of the Central Committee, Volume 1.* People's Publishing House, 1982. p. 234.
8. *Selected Works of Deng Xiaoping, Volume 2.* People's Publishing House, 1994. p. 367.
9. *Selection and Compilation of Important Documents since the Third Plenary Session of the Central Committee Part 2.* People's Publishing House, 1982. p. 784, 788.
10. Records of Major Events in the Construction of Socialist Spiritual Civilization since the Reform and Opening Up, organized compilation by the Central Civilization Office. Liaoning People's Publishing House, 2001. p. 121–122.
11. Resolution of the Central Committee of the Communist Party of China on Guidelines for the Construction of Socialist Spiritual Civilization. *People's Daily.* September 29, 1986.
12. *Selected Works of Deng Xiaoping, Volume 3.* People's Publishing House, 1993. p. 43.
13. Ibid, p. 39, 40, 45.
14. Ibid, p. 181, 182.
15. Wang Binglin. "Against Bourgeois Liberalization." Guo Dehong, et. al., ed. *Special History of the People's Republic of China (Reform).* Sichuan People's Publishing House, 2004.
16. *Selected Works of Deng Xiaoping, Volume 2.* People's Publishing House, 1994. p. 403, 404.
17. *People's Daily.* July 27, 1983.

18. *People's Daily.* August 1, 1985.
19. *Selected Works of Deng Xiaoping, Volume 3.* People's Publishing House, 1993. p. 305, 307.
20. *Selection and Compilation of Important Documents since the Thirteenth National Congress.* People's Publishing House, 1991. p. 678.
21. *Selected Works of Deng Xiaoping, Volume 3.* People's Publishing House, 1993. p. 354.
22. Ibid, p. 356.
23. *Selected Works of Deng Xiaoping, Volume 3.* People's Publishing House, 1993. p. 370–371.
24. Ibid, p. 372.
25. *Selected Works of Deng Xiaoping, Volume 3.* People's Publishing House, 1993. p. 364.
26. Ibid, p. 203.
27. Ibid, p. 373.
28. Ibid, p. 225.
29. *Selected Works of Deng Xiaoping, Volume 3.* People's Publishing House, 1993. p. 373.
30. Ibid, p. 377.
31. Ibid, p. 375.
32. *Selected Works of Deng Xiaoping, Volume 3.* People's Publishing House, 1993. p. 378.
33. Ibid.
34. Ibid, p. 365.
35. Ibid, p. 380.
36. *Selected Works of Deng Xiaoping, Volume 3.* People's Publishing House, 1993. p. 379–380.
37. Ibid, p. 382.
38. Ibid, p. 383.
39. *Selected Works of Jiang Zemin, Volume 2.* People's Publishing House, 2006. p. 10.
40. *Selection and Compilation of Important Documents since the Thirteenth National Congress, Volume 1.* People's Publishing House, 1991. p. 57.
41. *Selection and Compilation of Important Documents since Fourteenth National Congress of the Communist Party of China, Part 1.* People's Publishing House, 1996. p. 10, 13, 39.

Chapter 7

1. Edited by the Documentation Research Department of the Central Committee of the Communist Party of China. *The Chronicle of Deng Xiaoping (1975–1997), Volume 1.* Central Documentation Publishing House, 2004. p. 445–446.
2. *Selected Works of Chen Yun, Volume 3.* People's Publishing House, 1995. p. 245.
3. Ibid, p. 247.
4. *Selected Works of Deng Xiaoping, Volume 2.* People's Publishing House, 1994. p. 236.
5. *Selected Works of Deng Xiaoping, Volume 3.* People's Publishing House, 1993. p. 148.
6. Ibid, p. 148–149.
7. *Selected Works of Deng Xiaoping, Volume 3.* People's Publishing House, 1993. p. 203.
8. Ibid, p. 306.

9. Ibid, p. 364.
10. Ibid, p. 367.
11. *Selected Works of Jiang Zemin, Volume 1.* People's Publishing House, 2006. p. 202.
12. *Chronicle of Deng Xiaoping (1975–1997), Volume 2.* Central Literature Published in 2004. p. 1347.
13. *Selected Works of Deng Xiaoping, Volume 3.* People's Publishing House, 1993. p. 193.
14. Ibid, p. 366.
15. *Selection and Compilation of Important Documents since the Fifteenth National Congress.* People's Publishing House, 2000. p. 10.
16. *Selection and Compilation of Important Documents since the Fifteenth National Congress, Volume 1.* People's Publishing House, 2000. p. 13–14.
17. *Selection of Important Documents since the Fifteenth National Congress, Volume 1.* People's Publishing House, 2000. p. 15–16.
18. Ibid, p. 17.
19. *Selected Works of Deng Xiaoping, Volume 2.* People's Publishing House, 1994. p. 208.
20. *Selected Works of Jiang Zemin, Volume 1.* People's Publishing House, 2006. p. 153.
21. Ibid, p. 155.
22. Ibid, p. 158.
23. Ibid, p. 161.
24. *Selected Works of Jiang Zemin, Volume 2.* People's Publishing House, 2006. p. 18.

CHAPTER 8

1. *People's Daily.* July 14, 1995.
2. *Selection and Compilation of Important Documents after the Fifteenth National Congress, Volume 1.* People's Publishing House, 2000. p. 687–688.
3. Jiang Zemin. *On the "Three Representatives."* Central Documents Publishing House, 2001. p. 47.
4. *Selected Works of Deng Xiaoping, Volume 3.* People's Publishing House, 1993. p. 179.
5. Ibid, p. 176–177.
6. *Selection and Compilation of Important Documents after the Fifteenth National Congress, Volume 1.* People's Publishing House, 2000. p. 34–35.
7. *Selection and Compilation of Important Documents since the Fifteenth National Congress.* People's Publishing House, 2000. p. 31.
8. *Jiang Zemin's Theory on Socialism with Chinese Characteristics (Selected Works).* Central Literature Publishing House, 2002. p. 302–303.
9. Documentation Research Department of the Central Committee of the Communist Party of China. *Chronicle of Deng Xiaoping (1975–1997), Part 2.* Central Documentation Publishing House, 2004. p. 1262.

10. *Jiang Zemin's Theory on Socialism with Chinese Characteristics (Selected Works)*. Central Literature Publishing House, 2002. p. 211.
11. *Jiang Zemin's Theory on Socialism with Chinese Characteristics (Selected Works)*. Central Literature Publishing House, 2002. p. 314.
12. *Selection and Compilation of Important Documents since the Fourteenth National Congress, Volume 1*. People's Publishing House, 1996. p. 29.
13. *Selection and Compilation of Important Documents after the Thirteenth National Congress.* People's Publishing House, 1993. p. 626, 627.
14. *Selection and Compilation of Important Documents after the Thirteenth National Congress, Volume 2*. People's Publishing House, 1993. p. 1644, 1645.
15. *Selection and Compilation of Important Documents after the Fifteenth National Congress, Volume 1*. People's Publishing House, 2000. p. 35.
16. Jiang Zemin. *On the "Three Represents."* Central Documents Publishing House, 2001. p. 3.
17. Jiang Zemin. *On the "Three Represents."* 2001 edition of Central Documents Publishing House. p. 157.
18. Ibid, p. 158.
19. Ibid, p. 158.
20. Ibid, p. 158–159.
21. *Selection and Compilation of Important Documents after the Thirteenth National Congress, Volume 2*. People's Publishing House, 1993. p. 1645.
22. Jiang Zemin. *On the "Three Represents."* 2001 edition of Central Documents Publishing House. p. 159.
23. *Jiang Zemin's Theory of Socialism with Chinese Characteristics (Selected Works)*. Central Literature Publishing House, 2002. p. 400.
24. *Selected Works of Deng Xiaoping, Volume 3*. People's Publishing House, 1993. p. 275.
25. *Jiang Zemin's Theory on Socialism with Chinese Characteristics (Selected Works)*. Central Literature Publishing House, 2002. p. 275.

Chapter 9

1. *Selected Works of Deng Xiaoping, Volume 3*. People's Publishing House, 1993. p. 277–278.
2. Han Zhiguo. "Development and Innovation of China's Joint-stock Economy." *People's Daily,* May 26, 2001.
3. Group of the Research Office of the State Council. *Learning Guidance for the Report on the Outline of the Tenth Five-Year Plan of the Fourth Session of the Ninth National People's Congress.* China Yanshi Publishing House, 2001. p. 137–138.
4. Compiled by the Taiwan Work Office of the Central Committee of the Communist Party of China and the Taiwan Affairs Office of the State Council. *Question and Answer on Jiang Zemin's Eight Proposals.* Jiuzhou Publishing House, 2003. p. 63.

562 NOTES

5. "White Paper on China's National Defense in 2002. *PLA Newspaper*, December 10, 2002.
6. Ibid.
7. *PLA Newspaper*. January 1, 2002.
8. *People's Daily*. September 21, 2004.
9. *People's Daily*. December 28, 2004.
10. Zheng Weiping and Liu Mingfu, ed. *On the New Historical Mission of the Army*. People's Armed Police Press, 2005. p. 1.

Chapter 10

1. *Selection and Compilation of Important Documents after the Fourteenth Congress*. People's Publishing House, 1997. p. 961.
2. Jiang Zemin. *On Party Building*. Central Documents Publishing House, 2001. p. 221.
3. Jiang Zemin. *On Party Building*. Central Documents Publishing House, 2001. p. 103–104.
4. Jiang Zemin. *On Party Building*. Central Documents Publishing House, 2001. p. 381.
5. *Selected and Edited Important Documents after the Fifteenth National Congress (C)*. People's Publishing House, 2001. p. 1139, 1140.
6. *Selection and Compilation of Important Documents after the Fifteenth National Congress*. People's Publishing House, 2001. p. 1407.
7. Jiang Zemin. *On the "Three Represents."* Central Documents Publishing House, 2001. p. 129.

Chapter 11

1. *Selection and Compilation of Important Documents since the Thirteenth National Congress, Volume 2*. People's Publishing House, 1991. p. 1374.
2. *Selection and Compilation of Important Documents since the Fourteenth National Congress, Volume 2*. People's Publishing House, 1997. p. 1480.
3. *Selection and Compilation of Important Documents since the Fifteenth National Congress, Volume 2*. People's Publishing House, 2001. p. 1369.
4. Ibid.
5. *Selection and Compilation of Important Documents since the Sixteenth National Congress, Volume 1*. Central Literature Publishing House, 2005. P. 14–15.
6. *People's Daily*. April 16, 2003.
7. *Selection and Compilation of Important Documents since the Sixteenth National Congress, Volume 1*. Central Literature Publishing House, 2005. p. 395.
8. Ibid, p. 396–397.
9. Ibid, p. 483.

10. *Selection and Compilation of Important Documents since the Sixteenth National Congress, Volume 1.* Central Literature Publishing House, 2005. p. 849–850.
11. *People's Daily.* September 21, 2004.
12. Institute of Military History Academy of Military Sciences. *80 years of the People's Liberation Army.* Military Science Press, 2007. p. 507.
13. Hu Jintao's Speech at the Boao Forum. Xinhua News Agency. April 11, 2008.

Chapter 12

1. *Compilation of Documents from the Seventeenth National Congress of the Communist Party of China.* People's Publishing House, 2007. p. 18–21.
2. Ibid, p. 18.

INDEX

A

A Mao Zedong Anthology **Vol. 1**: 493
"A Single Spark Can Start a Prairie Fire" **Vol. 1**: 179, 181, 331, 411
AB League **Vol. 3**: 102
Abe Awang Jinmei **Vol. 3**: 119
Abolition Party **Vol. 3**: 102
"Absorbing a Large Number of Intellectuals" **Vol. 1**: 210
Accelerating the Training and Education of Young Cadres **Vol. 3**: 457, 459
Accelerating the Progress of Science and Technology **Vol. 3**: 398
Active Military Officers Law **Vol. 3**: 436
advanced socialist culture with Chinese characteristics **Vol. 3**: 386, 387, 388, 389, 391, 394, 466, 474, 476, 487, 514, 525, 546
African Union **Vol. 3**: 216
agrarian revolution (Agrarian Revolutionary War) **Vol. 1**: 43, 65, 80, 95, 105, 110, 130, 136, 137, 143, 144, 151, 163, 165, 167, 168, 172, 174, 175, 176, 179, 182, 183, 188, 254, 277, 279, 284, 288, 296, 298, 311, 326, 329, 331, 334, 336, 341, 344, 350, 361, 371, 379, 382, 385, 389, 393, 405, 420, 434, 459, 467, 481, 486, 525, 531, 533; **Vol. 2**: 49
Agreement on Trade in Goods Vol 3: 518
Agriculture, Sixty Articles of **Vol. 2**: 235, 236, 238, 254, 255
agricultural cooperatives **Vol. 2**: 71, 73, 75, 76, 108, 113, 118, 122, 123, 124, 125, 126, 182, 188, 192, 193, 194, 236

Air Force Engineering University Vol 3: 434
Ali Hassan Mwinyi **Vol. 3**: 264, 265
All-China Federation of Industry and Commerce Vol 3: 242
All-China Federation of Trade Unions **Vol. 1**: 126; **Vol. 2**: 40
All-China Women's Federation Vol 3: 312
Allied Army of the World Socialist Revolutionary Front **Vol. 1**: 110, 112, 118
Allied League **Vol. 1**: 62
American Association in Taiwan Vol 3: 213
An Overview of Social Issues **Vol. 1**: 9
An Ziwen **Vol. 2**: 67; **Vol. 3**: 72
Anguo County **Vol. 2**: 204
Anhui Province **Vol. 1**: 79, 171, 352; **Vol. 2**: 328; **Vol. 3**: 102, 103, 106, 155, 318, 384
Anti-Encirclement **Vol. 1**: 82, 157, 158, 159, 183, 194, 319, 334, 341
anti-Japan base (anti-Japanese base area) **Vol. 1**: 66, 73, 108, 198, 199, 200, 201, 202, 203, 210, 231, 241, 262, 318, 334, 336, 493, 530; **Vol. 2**: 32, 46, 269, 308
Anti-Japanese Guerrilla War **Vol. 1**: 184, 198, 298, 311, 329
Anti-Japanese National United Front **Vol. 1**: 66, 68, 69, 79, 80, 81, 108, 200, 201, 204, 228, 229, 230, 232, 233, 234, 235, 236, 237, 238, 239, 240, 241, 243, 249, 280, 289, 300, 400, 514, 515, 542; **Vol. 3**: 106
Anti-Japanese Salvation **Vol. 1**: 199
anti-landlord class **Vol. 1**: 50

anti-Leftism movement **Vol. 2**: 203, 220
anti-Marxist **Vol. 1**: 164; **Vol. 2**: 177, 290, 294, 327
anti-Party **Vol. 2**: 280, 294, 315; **Vol. 3**: 23, 76, 91, 100, 101, 102, 323
anti-rash advance (anti-rash progress) **Vol. 2**: 188, 189, 190, 207, 246, 255
Anti-Revolt Campaign **Vol. 3**: 102, 103
anti-revolutionary group **Vol. 1**: 49, 52, 283; **Vol. 2**: 320; **Vol. 3**: 100, 103, 105, 170
Anti-Rightist Movement **Vol. 1**: 58; **Vol. 2**: 152, 173, 174, 178, 180, 182, 183, 184, 186, 188, 190, 191, 192, 207, 220, 222, 230, 231, 239, 241, 242, 245, 246, 251, 253, 254, 255, 257, 258, 274; **Vol. 3**: 83, 84, 85, 88, 90, 93
anti-Socialist Vol 2: 294; **Vol. 3**: 91, 323
anti-war movement **Vol. 1**: 260, 274; **Vol. 2**: 263
April 5th Movement (*see* Tiananmen Incident) **Vol. 2**: 309, 316; **Vol. 3**: 9, 10, 11, 12, 15, 53, 54
Arkhipov, Ivan **Vol. 3**: 219
Armed Division of Workers and Peasants **Vol. 1**: 164, 166, 169, 170, 172, 173, 174, 175, 176, 178, 180, 188
armed revolution **Vol. 1**: 143, 283, 284, 361
armed struggle (theory or doctrine) **Vol. 1**: 36, 37, 43, 45, 55, 78, 83, 91, 102, 149, 171, 173, 174, 175, 176, 184, 187, 273, 274, 275, 276, 277, 278, 279, 282, 283, 284, 285, 286, 287, 331, 333, 336, 337, 361, 364, 366, 368, 372, 491; **Vol. 2**: 135, 292; **Vol. 3**: 72, 106
arming the masses **Vol. 1**: 210, 305
ASEAN and Chinese Leaders' Meeting **Vol. 3**: 518
Asia-Africa Summit **Vol. 3**: 517–518
Asian Cooperation Dialogue **Vol. 3**: 518
Association for Cross-Strait Relations **Vol. 3**: 414
Association for Relations Across the Taiwan Straits (ARATS) **Vol. 3**: 414
Audio-Visual Products Management Regulations **Vol. 3**: 394
Audit Office **Vol. 3**: 278
August defeat **Vol. 1**: 170, 173
August 7th Meeting **Vol. 1**: 43, 44, 46, 47, 48, 51, 53, 55, 57, 151, 154, 166, 167, 169, 277, 364, 420, 421
Autumn Harvest Riots **Vol. 1**: 151, 154, 167, 168, 174, 189, 306, 315, 323, 324, 361

B
Basic Law of the Hong Kong Special Administration Region **Vol. 3**: 236, 266
bad elements **Vol. 1**: 423; **Vol. 2**: 167; **Vol. 3**: 113, 126, 145, 146, 147, 309
Bai Chongxi **Vol. 1**: 234
Baiwan Village **Vol. 3**: 199
Bakunin, Mikhail **Vol. 1**: 6, 396
Bakuninists **Vol. 1**: 396, 430
balanced development **Vol. 1**: 62; **Vol. 3**: 285, 301, 302, 303, 305, 306, 307, 309, 310, 362, 486
Bao'an County **Vol. 3**: 277
Bao Huiceng **Vol. 1**: 19
Baoding **Vol. 2**: 204; **Vol. 3**: 313
Basel Conference **Vol. 1**: 396
Basic Program for the Rectification of the Party **Vol. 1**: 512
Basic Views and Policies on Religious Issues in the Socialist Period of China **Vol. 3**: 116, 127
Battle of Guangzhou **Vol. 1**: 36
Battle of Pingjin **Vol. 1**: 354
Bebel, August **Vol. 1**: 430
Becker, Johann Philipp **Vol. 1**: 430
Beidaihe **Vol. 2**: 191
Beidaihe Working Conference (Beidaihe Work Conference) **Vol. 2**: 195, 196, 212, 256, 257
Beijing **Vol. 1**: 3, 14–19, 61, 92, 162, 214, 256, 267, 275, 376, 510; **Vol. 2**: 61, 78, 205, 233, 243, 318, 319, 324, 326, 336; **Vol. 3**: 11, 12, 23, 24, 30, 31, 35, 43, 52, 53, 59, 72, 75–79, 99, 112, 123, 138, 139, 142, 143, 147, 173, 178–180, 199, 200, 210, 218, 219, 221, 227, 234, 236, 237, 263, 280, 305, 317, 318, 322, 323, 325, 372, 408, 414, 416, 417, 450, 455, 458, 462, 470, 472, 482, 513, 524, 536, 542
Beijing Coup **Vol. 1**: 92, 214
Beijing Communist Party Organization **Vol. 1**: 18

Beijing Daily **Vol. 3**: 11
Beijing Military Region **Vol. 3**: 76, 77
Beijing Normal University **Vol. 1**: 18; **Vol. 3**: 317
Beijing-Qinhuangdao Railway **Vol. 3**: 210
Beijing Treaty **Vol. 3**: 234, 416
Beijing University (*see* Peking University)
Beiping Way **Vol. 1**: 356
Beiyang government **Vol. 1**: 267
Beiyang Warlords (*see also* Northern Warlords) **Vol. 1**: 136
Bengbu **Vol. 1**: 354
Bertram, James **Vol. 1**: 231, 316
Big Bang Theory **Vol. 2**: 285
Big Character Poster **Vol. 2**: 182, 300; **Vol. 3**: 78, 79
Blowe, Mitchell **Vol. 2**: 18
Bo Yibo **Vol. 1**: 500; **Vol. 2**: 42, 238; **Vol. 3**: 53, 74, 81, 189, 283
Bo Yibo Group **Vol. 3**: 54
Bohai Sea **Vol. 3**: 210
Bolshevik **Vol. 1**: 59, 358
Bolshevik Party **Vol. 1**: 38, 358, 366, 367, 370, 375, 377, 382, 398, 400, 430, 458, 459; **Vol. 2**: 54, 118, 122, 137, 209, 210, 213, 217
Borodin, Mikhail **Vol. 1**: 40
bourgeois law **Vol. 2**: 268
bourgeoisie (bourgeois) **Vol. 1**: 5, 7, 9, 13, 25–32, 34, 35, 37, 41, 44, 46–47, 51–57, 60, 62, 63, 70–76, 80–81, 87, 92–94, 96–98, 100–118, 120–129, 131, 134, 138–146, 150, 172, 181, 185–186, 195, 199–200, 210, 213–219, 221–226, 230, 233–234, 237–244, 246, 253, 258, 261–263, 269–272, 277–278, 283, 292–293, 295, 298–299, 301, 308–310, 322, 329, 358, 360, 362–365, 370–375, 377–378, 381–384, 421, 427–428, 447, 466–468, 487, 495, 502–503, 507, 509, 513, 514, 516–519, 521–524, 526, 528, 530, 533–535, 540–544, 546; **Vol. 2**: 4, 10, 17, 26–29, 31–34, 36–37, 39, 41–43, 45–47, 49–50, 59–64, 69–70, 79–80, 83, 91–95, 103–105, 109, 116, 125–129, 136, 170, 181, 183–186, 191, 197, 201–202, 212, 241, 251, 257, 259, 265, 268–271, 273, 275, 279–291, 293–297, 307, 315, 328; **Vol. 3**: 22–24, 27, 54, 81, 88, 113, 160, 247, 255, 304, 315–316, 318, 323
bourgeois civil rights revolution **Vol. 1**: 51, 52, 53, 54, 103, 105
bourgeois republic **Vol. 1**: 71, 106, 467, 517
bourgeois revolution **Vol. 1**: 5, 28, 52, 107, 118, 121, 122, 123, 134, 301, 466
Branch Office **Vol. 1**: 503; **Vol. 3**: 143
Brezhnev, Leonid **Vol. 2**: 264, 287, 289; **Vol. 3**: 217
bribery **Vol. 2**: 104; **Vol. 3**: 294, 298, 299, 304, 309, 321
British colonial rule (Hong Kong) **Vol. 3**: 234, 416
Buddhist temples (in Han areas) **Vol. 3**: 127
Bukharin, Nikola Ivanovic **Vol. 1**: 153; **Vol. 2**: 164
Bureau of Religious Affairs (Religious Affairs Bureau) **Vol. 3**: 127
bureaucracy **Vol. 1**: 136, 203, 380, 383, 414, 430, 431, 432, 440, 458, 473; **Vol. 2**: 104, 138, 153, 160–161, 163, 167, 175–182, 297; **Vol. 3**: 47, 57, 146, 271, 281, 284, 372
bureaucratic capitalism **Vol. 1**: 88, 130–131, 133, 138, 245–247, 253, 262–263, 265, 268, 283, 287, 350, 467, 520, 525–534; **Vol. 2**: 26, 37, 87; **Vol. 3**: 148, 252
Bush, George H. W. **Vol. 3**: 215
Bush, George W. **Vol. 3**: 519
Business Group of the United Front Work Conference **Vol. 2**: 92
Business Performance Management Regulations **Vol. 3**: 394

C

Cadre Censorship Bureau **Vol. 3**: 17
Cadre Education **Vol. 3**: 449
cadre retirement system **Vol. 3**: 288
Cadre Route **Vol. 3**: 13
cadre system **Vol. 3**: 185, 286–287, 291, 458, 460
Cai Chang **Vol. 3**: 288
Cai Hesen **Vol. 1**: 16, 17, 29, 30, 49, 52, 53, 92, 102, 167, 219, 399, 400, 507
Cai Tingkai **Vol. 1**: 233, 264
Cai Xitao **Vol. 3**: 30

Cai Yuanpei **Vol. 1**: 14, 233
Cao Diqiu **Vol. 3**: 75
Cao Juren **Vol. 3**: 227
Caolanzi Prison **Vol. 3**: 74
capitalism **Vol. 1**: 3, 5, 6, 7, 8, 10, 12, 13, 20, 26, 30, 31, 39, 53, 54, 76, 88, 94–98, 102–105, 107, 108, 109, 111, 112, 113, 116, 117, 118, 130, 131, 133, 138, 139, 140, 145, 146, 161, 186, 216, 245, 246, 247, 253, 262, 263, 265, 268, 277, 283, 285, 287, 350, 358, 377, 397, 466, 467, 487, 488, 496, 510, 518, 520, 522, 524, 526, 528, 529, 530, 533–538, 543; **Vol. 2**: 4–6, 14, 17–19, 26, 28–35, 37, 39, 41, 43–47, 51–52, 58–59, 61–62, 67, 70, 74, 83, 91, 94–95, 103, 107–108, 111, 113–116, 118, 120, 124–128, 131, 135–137, 151–152, 185, 201, 203, 214, 218–219, 234, 257–259, 267, 272–275, 277–281, 283, 286–288, 290–292, 294, 304–305, 331; **Vol. 3**: 21–22, 27, 46, 56, 93, 146, 148, 233, 235, 241, 246–247, 249, 252, 268, 304, 309, 316, 328, 333, 345–348, 382, 487
capitulationism **Vol. 1**: 232, 240, 280
Carter, Jimmy **Vol. 3**: 145, 213–214
cat theory (Deng Xiaoping) **Vol. 2**: 249, 255
Caudine Forks of capitalism **Vol. 2**: 135
Central Action Committee **Vol. 1**: 61
Central Advisory Committee **Vol. 3**: 67, 180, 186, 188–189, 242, 244–245, 269, 290, 311, 410, 450, 453, 464
Central Bureau **Vol. 1**: 20; Vol 2: 64, 73, 77, 233, 234; **Vol. 3**: 67
Central Bureau of the Shaanxi-Gansu-Ningxia Border Region **Vol. 1**: 199
Central Committee Vol 1: 20, 25, 36, 38, 39, 40, 43–46, 48, 50, 51, 55–59, 63, 66, 67, 71, 75, 79, 83, 86, 87, 88, 92, 94, 103, 104, 105, 150–161, 163–169, 176, 178, 181, 183, 189, 199, 203, 204, 205, 207, 210, 211, 222, 226–238, 240, 244, 245, 248, 249, 250, 251–254, 257, 259, 260, 261, 263, 264, 265, 271, 275, 276, 279, 283, 299, 304, 305, 306, 309, 311, 313, 318, 324, 337, 351, 354, 355, 362, 366, 367, 369, 370, 382, 386, 387, 395, 398, 400, 401, 403, 405, 411, 415, 419, 421, 424, 425, 426, 427, 434, 437, 459, 482, 485, 486, 492–496, 499, 500, 501, 503, 504, 505, 510, 511, 532, 537, 538; **Vol. 2**: 3, 5, 9, 11, 16, 22, 29, 32–33, 35–40, 42, 44–45, 49–52, 56–65, 71–79, 81–87, 89, 91–93, 95, 97–99, 101, 103–105, 107, 109–110, 113–114, 116–119, 122–123, 132, 142, 144–145, 148–152, 154–158, 161, 168, 174–181, 183–185, 188–189, 192–193, 195, 199–200, 202–203, 205–207, 209–210, 214–215, 222, 226, 231–238, 240–241, 243–245, 247–252, 254, 256–258, 260, 272, 277, 290, 299–302, 313, 315, 318, 323, 329–332, 334–338; **Vol. 3**: 3, 6, 9–13, 16–17, 34, 37–38, 40, 46, 48, 51–55, 57, 59–83, 85, 87–99, 101–117, 119–129, 131, 135–139, 141–142, 144–145, 147–163, 165–168, 170–171, 173–180, 182–183, 186, 188–189, 192–193, 196, 198–203, 205, 207, 217, 219, 221, 225–227, 232, 234–235, 240–242, 244–249, 252–255, 257–260, 263, 265–266, 268–270, 273–274, 279–281, 283, 286–295, 297–299, 302, 305–327, 334–335, 337–338, 343, 345–348, 350, 352–355, 357–358, 363–364, 368–370, 373–374, 376–377, 379–384, 386, 390–391, 393–394, 397–405, 407–413, 416, 419, 421, 427, 429, 432, 440, 443, 446–450, 452–470, 479, 481–483, 488, 491, 493–497, 499–502, 506–517, 519–521, 523–526, 531–532, 536, 538, 542, 544–545, 550–551
Central Committee for Ethnic Affairs Vol 2: 250
Central Disciplinary Inspection Commission (Central Commission for Discipline Inspection) **Vol. 3**: 60, 62, 77, 80, 93, 180, 186, 188–189, 242, 244–245, 294, 296, 311, 320–321, 410, 450, 453, 462–465, 467, 483, 524
Central Economic Work Conference **Vol. 3**: 512
Central Leading Group **Vol. 2**: 199; **Vol. 3**: 352, 387, 398, 446
Central Military Commission **Vol. 1**: 59, 61, 238, 239, 313, 314, 346, 351, 355; Vol 2: 326, 331; **Vol. 3**: 10, 42, 73, 75, 189, 203, 282, 307, 429–432, 434, 437–439, 516–517
Central Organizational Department **Vol. 2**: 67; **Vol. 3**: 14–17, 54, 66–68, 70–72, 77, 79, 81, 84–86, 89–90, 93–99, 101, 103–104, 106–108, 111, 114–117, 245, 278–279, 296, 311, 373, 410, 450–454, 460, 464, 471
Central Party School **Vol. 1**: 391; **Vol. 2**: 30,

322; **Vol. 3**: 14, 35–36, 90, 154, 269, 348, 358, 449–450, 472, 502
Central People's Government **Vol. 1**: 268; **Vol. 2**: 77–78, 80; **Vol. 3**: 103, 273
Central Plains **Vol. 1**: 59, 351, 352, 505; **Vol. 3**: 107–108
Central Political Report **Vol. 1**: 39
Central Political System Reform Seminar Group **Vol. 3**: 269–270
Central Project Group **Vol. 3**: 71
Central Provisional Politburo Vol 1: 48, 167
Central Secretariat **Vol. 1**: 238, 482; **Vol. 2**: 154, 251; **Vol. 3**: 99, 115, 117, 218, 235, 269, 273, 311–312
Central Soviet Area **Vol. 1**: 157, 341; **Vol. 3**: 15, 102
Central Soviet Government **Vol. 1**: 61
Central Special Task Force **Vol. 3**: 54, 70, 100
Central Steering Committee for Party Consolidation **Vol. 3**: 281–283
Central Task Force **Vol. 3**: 72, 81
Central United Front Department (Ministry) **Vol. 2**: 80; **Vol. 3**: 89–90, 111, 113, 126
Central Working Conference **Vol. 2**: 103, 237–238, 240, 243, 257, 259, 336; **Vol. 3**: 11–12, 48, 52, 54, 59–61, 73, 93, 100, 123, 135, 138, 259, 286, 305
centralism **Vol. 1**: 190, 359, 365, 368, 369, 379, 387, 394, 395, 397–403, 408–419, 427, 450, 452, 474, 475, 488, 499, 509, 515, 518, 523; **Vol. 2**: 26, 48–49, 159–160, 169, 190, 221–222, 243–244, 246; **Vol. 3**: 57–58, 62, 136, 150, 161, 163, 172, 176–177, 184–185, 190, 281, 370
Chairman of the General Committee **Vol. 1**: 395
Chaling County **Vol. 1**: 189
Changchun **Vol. 1**: 353; **Vol. 3**: 115
Changsha **Vol. 1**: 16, 19, 25, 58, 61, 151, 152, 168, 174, 376; **Vol. 2**: 233
Changxindian Railway Vol 1: 14
Chen Boda Vol 1: 483; **Vol. 2**: 194, 204, 278; **Vol. 3**: 73–75, 77, 79
Chen Chi **Vol. 3**: 30, 74
Chen Duxiu **Vol. 1**: 4, 7, 8, 12, 14, 15, 17–20, 29, 33–34, 38–41, 44, 46–47, 92–93, 101–102, 121–122, 125, 218–219, 227–228, 230, 277, 371, 378, 399, 411, 420, 545
Chen Geng **Vol. 1**: 352
Chen Gongbo **Vol. 1**: 19
Chen Gongpei Vol 1: 19
Chen Jingrun **Vol. 3**: 30
Chen Jiongming **Vol. 1**: 24, 274
Chen Jitang **Vol. 1**: 234
Chen Lifu **Vol. 1**: 246, 531
Chen Mingshu **Vol. 1**: 233
Chen Muhua **Vol. 3**: 189
Chen Pixian **Vol. 3**: 189
Chen Qiyou **Vol. 1**: 264
Chen Shaomin **Vol. 3**: 107–108
Chen Shui-bian **Vol. 3**: 419
Chen Tanqiu **Vol. 1**: 19
Chen Wangdao **Vol. 1**: 18
Chen Yeping **Vol. 3**: 71
Chen Yi **Vol. 1**: 172, 327, 351, 352, 484; **Vol. 2**: 156, 251, 300; **Vol. 3**: 73
Chen Yun Vol 1: 195, 424, 426, 427, 464, 476, 477; **Vol. 2**: 62, 150, 188, 246–249, 304, 324; **Vol. 3**: 11, 14–15, 33–34, 49, 53, 56, 62, 167, 179, 186–189, 193, 200, 245–246, 285, 289, 344
Chen Zaidao **Vol. 3**: 62, 72
Chendai Town **Vol. 3**: 320
Chiang Ching-kuo **Vol. 1**: 271; **Vol. 3**: 413
Chiang Kai-shek **Vol. 1**: 38, 42, 66, 69–70, 85–88, 93–94, 131, 163, 217–218, 221–222, 226, 234, 236, 245–248, 250, 253, 256, 258, 263, 269, 271, 276, 281, 284, 290, 292, 328, 346, 350, 353, 494, 531, 533; **Vol. 3**: 145, 225–228, 252
China Agenda for the 21st Century **Vol. 3**: 250, 424
China Buddhist College **Vol. 3**: 127
China Catholic Theological and Philosophical College **Vol. 3**: 127
China Christian Nanjing Jinling Union Theological College **Vol. 3**: 127
China Democratic League **Vol. 1**: 264
China Human Rights Alliance (China Human Rights League) **Vol. 3**: 142
China Human Rights League (*see* China Human Rights Alliance) **Vol. 3**: 143
China Islamic Economics College **Vol. 3**: 127

China News **Vol. 1**: 10
China Petrochemical Group Corporation **Vol. 3**: 405
China Petroleum and Natural Gas Corporation **Vol. 3**: 405
China Taoist College **Vol. 3**: 127
China Tibetan Language Department Senior Buddhist College **Vol. 3**: 127
China-Africa Cooperation Forum **Vol. 3**: 518
China-ASEAN Comprehensive Economic Cooperation Framework Agreement **Vol. 3**: 518
China-ASEAN Strategic Partnership for Peace and Prosperity Action Plan **Vol. 3**: 518
China-ASEAN Summit **Vol. 3**: 425
China-Russia border **Vol. 3**: 519
China-Russia Joint Declaration on International Order in the 21st Century **Vol. 3**: 517
China-Russia Summit **Vol. 3**: 517
China-Russia Tokk Exchange **Vol. 3**: 519
Chinese Academy of Sciences **Vol. 2**: 156, 215; **Vol. 3**: 23
Chinese Academy of Social Sciences **Vol. 3**: 26, 41, 43, 193, 195, 311, 438
Chinese Association of Science and Technology **Vol. 3**: 43
Chinese Buddhist Association **Vol. 3**: 127
Chinese Catholic Patriotic Congress **Vol. 3**: 127
Chinese Christian Three-Self Patriotic Movement Committee **Vol. 3**: 127
Chinese Culture **Vol. 1**: 21, 76, 209, 540, 544–547, 550; **Vol. 2**: 254; **Vol. 3**: 415, 471, 511
Chinese Customs Commission **Vol. 3**: 200, 288, 290
Chinese Federation of Trade Unions **Vol. 1**: 15
Chinese Foreign Ministry **Vol. 3**: 215, 218
Chinese Industry Association **Vol. 1**: 15
Chinese KMT Democratic Promotion Meeting **Vol. 1**: 264
Chinese Land Law **Vol. 1**: 250–251, 255, 532
Chinese Marxism **Vol. 1**: 485–486, 488–491; **Vol. 2**: 261, 267, 273, 299, 304–305, 309–310, 338; **Vol. 3**: 7, 359, 546

Chinese Marxist Workers' Movement **Vol. 1**: 15
Chinese Muslim pilgrimage group **Vol. 3**: 128
Chinese National Liberation Action Committee **Vol. 1**: 233
Chinese National Salvation Congress **Vol. 1**: 264
Chinese Peasants **Vol. 1**: 33, 102, 287, 525
Chinese People's Political Consultative Conference **Vol. 1**: 87, 244, 511, 523; **Vol. 2**: 4, 25, 48, 50
Chinese Red Army **Vol. 1**: 153; **Vol. 3**: 15
Chinese Revolution **Vol. 1**: 23, 25, 27, 29–32, 36–37, 43–45, 47, 49–56, 58–60, 62–63, 65–66, 69, 72–79, 81–84, 86, 91, 93–97, 99–107, 109–110, 112–118, 128–131, 133–134, 136–137, 139–147, 150–153, 157, 159, 161, 163–164, 166, 172–173, 176, 178–182, 184–186, 188, 213, 222, 230, 237, 244, 246, 257, 263, 273, 275–276, 278–287, 292, 299, 308–310, 329–331, 339, 341, 360, 363, 367–368, 371, 379, 385, 388, 390–393, 407, 420, 422, 431, 439–441, 443–445, 448, 452, 466, 468–471, 474, 486–487, 489–494, 504, 507–509, 517, 521–523, 528, 531, 533, 540, 542, 544, 546; **Vol. 2**: 24, 27–29, 32, 35, 38–40, 52, 90, 98, 114, 143–144, 210, 326; **Vol. 3**: 40, 132, 150, 162, 164, 169, 248, 317
Chinese Soviet **Vol. 1**: 160, 191, 194; **Vol. 3**: 105
Chinese Taoist Association **Vol. 3**: 127
Chinese Workers' and Peasants' Red Army **Vol. 1**: 178, 470
Chinese Workers' Movement **Vol. 1**: 16–17, 360, 370, 376, 470; **Vol. 2**: 330
Chinese Youth **Vol. 3**: 11
Chinese Zhi Gong Party **Vol. 1**: 264
Chongqing **Vol. 1**: 152, 167, 281
City-centered Theory **Vol. 1**: 149–151, 153–154, 157, 159–161, 163–164, 166
Civil Morality Construction **Vol. 3**: 391
Civil Servants Law **Vol. 3**: 460, 541
class analysis **Vol. 1**: 33, 80, 103, 121–123, 125
class struggle **Vol. 1**: 8, 10–11, 20, 24, 27–28, 32, 100, 129, 198, 218–219, 236–237, 277, 288–290, 293, 308, 385, 425; **Vol. 2**: 8, 10, 13–14, 47, 65, 103, 136, 138, 167–168, 170, 173–174, 178, 180, 182–187, 189, 207, 219, 221, 224, 226, 245,

256–259, 265, 270–278, 281, 285–286, 292–298, 312, 316, 325, 335; **Vol. 3**: 4, 51, 55, 60, 66, 93, 130, 135, 140–141, 161, 170, 173, 191, 254, 283, 332, 525, 531
class war **Vol. 1**: 59, 159
Classical Marxist Writers **Vol. 2**: 19, 69, 113, 121, 134, 165, 200, 254, 273, 317; **Vol. 3**: 34
Clausewitz, Carl **Vol. 1**: 289
clearing up historical problems **Vol. 3**: 66
clique **Vol. 1**: 235, 242, 248, 271–272, 281; **Vol. 2**: 289–290; **Vol. 3**: 73, 124
Cold War **Vol. 2**: 101, 120, 131, 225; **Vol. 3**: 426–427, 429, 437
collectivization **Vol. 1**: 498, 512, 531, 537–538; **Vol. 2**: 31, 71, 73, 75–76, 85, 99, 115, 120–125, 138, 193, 195, 209
college entrance examination **Vol. 3**: 9, 17–20
Combating Serious Criminal Activities in the Economic Field **Vol. 3**: 306, 319–320
Comintern (*see also* Communist International) **Vol. 1**: 18–20, 25, 38, 40, 42–44, 47, 49, 51–56, 58, 62–63, 65–66, 68, 92, 94, 103–104, 106, 150, 152–154, 157, 164, 169, 178, 214–215, 217–219, 221–228, 232, 362–363, 371, 482, 486, 507–508
Commerce, Forty Articles of **Vol. 2**: 237
Commission for Economic Reform (*see also* State Economic Reform Office) **Vol. 3**: 194
commodity economy **Vol. 1**: 96, 162, 537–538; **Vol. 2**: 6, 8–10, 15, 20, 35–36, 44, 120–121, 137–138, 218, 224, 226, 267–268, 271, 291, 294, 307; **Vol. 3**: 21–22, 192–196, 198–201, 241, 243–244, 249–251, 283, 294, 302, 323, 335–337, 345, 365, 447
Common Program **Vol. 1**: 87, 268, 511, 523, 538–539; **Vol. 2**: 4–5, 25–26, 48, 50–58, 60, 62, 72, 78, 80–82, 89, 99, 103–104, 114, 116, 141
Communications Secretary **Vol. 1**: 395
Communist Alliance **Vol. 1**: 357, 394–396
Communist International (*see also* Comintern) **Vol. 1**: 17, 25, 121
Communist International East Asia Secretariat **Vol. 1**: 17
Communist League **Vol. 1**: 397
Communist Manifesto **Vol. 1**: 79, 97, 374, 458

Communist morality **Vol. 2**: 160
Communist Organization **Vol. 1**: 18
Communist Party of Beijing **Vol. 1**: 18, 406
Communist Party of China (*see also* CPC) **Vol. 1**: 13–14, 18–20, 23–30, 33, 35, 49, 57, 64–65, 73, 75, 78, 89, 93, 97, 103, 107, 114, 123, 129–130, 132, 139, 141–142, 146, 149, 153–154, 215, 224, 229–230, 232, 235, 237, 256, 284, 309, 339, 359, 363, 367, 369, 376, 382, 400–401, 410–411, 419, 466, 468–469, 491, 499, 512, 528; **Vol. 2**: 3, 5, 7, 13, 16, 21, 25, 27, 32, 41, 45, 52–53, 56, 61, 66, 73–74, 84, 86, 89, 97–99, 109, 118, 123, 140, 142, 148, 158, 166, 168, 170, 183, 186, 194–195, 210, 217, 229, 231, 233, 237, 249, 266, 274, 292, 311, 316, 319, 330, 336; **Vol. 3**: 3, 6, 12, 33, 37, 44, 45, 53, 59–61, 63, 65–66, 73, 75, 77–79, 89, 91, 94–95, 99, 102–106, 109–110, 112, 115–117, 119–125, 127–133, 138, 146, 148, 151, 154, 158–159, 161–163, 169, 172–174, 176, 179–182, 186, 194–196, 198, 200, 203, 207, 216, 221, 225–228, 230–231, 239–240, 242, 247–249, 251–255, 258, 260, 262, 265–266, 273, 279–281, 287–289, 291–295, 297–299, 303, 306, 311–316, 318, 320–322, 324–327, 334–338, 340, 343, 345–346, 350, 353, 355, 357, 359–361, 363–364, 366–368, 370–373, 375, 377, 379, 382–384, 388–389, 391, 393–394, 398, 400–401, 411, 413, 415–416, 419, 422, 427–429, 434, 440, 444, 446–447, 450, 457, 459, 461, 466–467, 470, 474–476, 480, 482–483, 490, 521, 523–527, 531–533, 536, 542, 544, 546, 550
Communist Party Political Consultative Conference (*see also* CPPCC) **Vol. 1**: 266, 406
Communist Surge **Vol. 2**: 236
Communist Youth League **Vol. 1**: 40, 61, 314
Comrades Union of the Three People's Principles (Nationalism, Democracy, the People's Livelihood) **Vol. 1**: 264
"Conflict Theory" **Vol. 1**: 389–391
Conference on Educational Work **Vol. 3**: 82, 102
Confucianism **Vol. 1**: 4, 16
Congress of Chinese Literature and Arts Workers **Vol. 3**: 198

Constitution of the People's Republic of China **Vol. 2**: 117; **Vol. 3**: 122, 231, 287, 377, 475

Construction of Socialist Spiritual Civilization **Vol. 2**: 116; **Vol. 3**: 249, 308, 313–314, 368, 383–384

construction of the People's Army **Vol. 1**: 82, 299; **Vol. 2**: 116; **Vol. 3**: 308

contracted production **Vol. 2**: 202, 248, 328

contradiction **Vol. 1**: 118, 367, 412, 437, 516; **Vol. 2**: 14–15, 33, 36, 39–40, 45, 84, 91–92, 94, 102–103, 105–106, 111, 124, 128–129, 139, 146–147, 157, 164–170, 174, 178, 185–186, 218–219, 226, 236, 245, 256, 258–259, 319; **Vol. 3**; 27, 85, 130, 171, 191, 199, 251, 259, 292, 328–329, 344, 346, 362, 430, 433, 491, 494

Contradictions **Vol. 1**: 66, 68, 118, 228; **Vol. 2**: 165

corruption **Vol. 1**: 197, 358; **Vol. 2**: 104, 309; **Vol. 3**: 293–295, 297, 299, 307–309, 319, 323, 325, 331, 447–448, 454, 460–462, 464–467, 474, 531, 536, 546, 549

counter-revolutionaries **Vol. 1**: 124, 143, 193, 284, 514; **Vol. 2**: 57, 167, 252; **Vol. 3**: 104–105, 113, 115

counter-revolutionary **Vol. 1**: 31, 43, 74, 85–87, 112, 122, 127, 160, 181, 192, 214, 250, 268, 272, 275–276, 279, 284, 291, 298, 320, 340, 355, 378, 474, 494, 514; **Vol. 2**: 111, 136, 284–285, 294, 298, 314, 316; **Vol. 3**: 72, 77, 86, 161, 163, 285

countryside Vol 1: 56, 83, 115, 128, 136, 140, 144, 150–151, 154–155, 157, 160–162, 164, 166, 169, 171, 174–175, 178–180, 182, 184–185, 187, 189, 330–331, 334–335, 360–361, 373, 377–378, 420, 495–497, 499, 502, 508, 527, 533; **Vol. 2**: 30, 32, 38, 41, 65–66, 69, 72, 87, 102, 111, 124, 175, 189, 193–194, 196, 206, 248, 259, 301; **Vol. 3**: 4–6, 148, 250, 282–283, 378, 450, 509, 528, 542–545

County People's Congress **Vol. 1**: 515

CPC **Vol. 1**: 20–21, 24–28, 32–45, 47, 49–58, 61, 63, 66–72, 75, 77–79, 82–87, 89, 91–95, 99–101, 103–106, 108–110, 115–116, 118–121, 123, 125–126, 129–134, 139, 141–143, 145–146, 149–158, 160–161, 163–167, 169, 172, 174, 177–178, 183–184, 186–189, 191–192, 198–203, 208–211, 213–245, 247–273, 275, 277–279, 281–282, 284–285, 287–288, 291–294, 299, 301, 304–311, 313–314, 316, 318, 324, 327, 331–333, 337, 351, 354–355, 360–373, 376–379, 381–382, 384, 386–389, 391–393, 399, 401, 403, 405–408, 410, 414–415, 419–425, 428–429, 431–442, 444–456, 458–463, 465–479, 481–482, 484–486, 489, 491–493, 495–497, 499–501, 503–505, 507–510, 512, 515–517, 519–524, 526, 528, 531–532, 534–539, 541–543, 545; **Vol. 2**: 11, 16, 20–22, 26, 28, 30, 32, 40, 48–49, 52–54, 57, 62, 64, 78–81, 90, 99, 105, 109, 117, 130, 133, 135, 140–143, 145, 152–153, 155, 157–162, 170, 173, 176, 202, 210, 220, 222, 249, 264, 267, 274–277, 279, 291–292, 295, 299, 302, 320, 329, 338; **Vol. 3**: 3–7, 10–13, 15, 46, 52, 59, 63, 70, 74, 76–78, 80–84, 86, 91–93, 98, 100, 103, 105–106, 109, 113–114, 126, 128, 132–133, 136, 139, 141, 146–147, 150, 157, 161–163, 168, 174, 177–178, 180, 189, 191, 199, 225–226, 232, 234, 239–240, 242, 247–248, 253, 255, 257, 275, 280, 290, 298–299, 301, 305, 307, 324, 329, 334, 341, 348, 350, 352, 360, 363, 365, 370, 372–373, 375, 381, 390, 394, 397, 415, 417, 419–421, 432, 438, 443–444, 446–447, 449–450, 454, 457, 459, 461, 465–466, 474, 479–484, 486, 488, 494, 509–510, 513, 515, 517–518, 520–521, 526, 528, 550

CPPCC (*see also* Communist Party Political Consultative Conference) **Vol. 1**: 266–268, 272, 511; **Vol. 2**: 48, 55–56, 62, 64, 111, 117, 154, 249, 319; **Vol. 3**: 129, 133, 136, 269, 374, 450, 454

criterion of truth **Vol. 2**: 11, 23, 321, 324, 327–329, 332, 334, 336, 338–339; **Vol. 3**: 32, 35, 37, 40–41, 43–45, 58, 135, 140, 152–154, 157–158, 162

criticism **Vol. 1**: 5, 13, 41, 61, 79, 102, 154, 160, 265, 322, 364, 374, 380, 385–387, 391, 398, 408, 425, 427–428, 430, 432, 437, 439, 446–456, 463, 471, 479–480, 502, 504, 534, 546; **Vol. 2**: 10–11, 23, 62, 73, 76, 139, 141, 143, 156–157, 162–163, 167, 176–177, 179, 182, 184, 202, 207, 219, 225, 242, 244, 246, 255–256, 259, 268–269, 272, 275, 283–287, 291, 295, 299, 301–304, 307, 314–316, 326, 334, 338; **Vol. 3**: 27, 33, 101, 144, 194–196, 280–281, 284, 455–456

Critique of the Gotha Program **Vol. 2**: 90

Crook, Isabel **Vol. 3**: 117
cross-century development **Vol. 3**: 5, 384, 397, 403, 412
cultural construction **Vol. 1**: 82–83, 135, 189, 197, 208–211, 373, 548; **Vol. 2**: 158, 295; **Vol. 3**: 120, 123, 191, 364, 366, 387–388, 393, 395, 503–504, 511, 528, 534
Cultural Revolution **Vol. 1**: 76, 528, 541–544, 548, 550; **Vol. 2**: 10–11, 14, 23, 155, 174, 187, 191, 221, 230, 236, 252, 260–262, 267, 269–270, 272, 274–280, 282–285, 287, 291–293, 295–303, 305–317, 319–322, 325, 329–330, 335, 337–338; **Vol. 3**: 9–10, 12, 14–16, 18–20, 29–33, 35, 37, 42, 44–45, 53–54, 56, 61–63, 69–70, 73–74, 76–88, 92–93, 96, 98, 100–101, 105, 108–110, 114, 117–118, 122–123, 126, 128, 132, 136, 140–142, 159–160, 162–163, 166–168, 170–171, 187, 203, 228, 253, 283–285, 525, 530
Cultural System **Vol. 2**: 156; **Vol. 3**: 251, 389, 393, 511

D

Dabie Mountains **Vol. 1**: 352
Dachen Island **Vol. 3**: 226
Dadan Island **Vol. 3**: 228
Dalai Lama **Vol. 3**: 123–124
Dalian **Vol. 1**: 493; **Vol. 3**: 112, 410
Daqing **Vol. 2**: 269; **Vol. 3**: 21–22
Daqing Oilfield **Vol. 2**: 269
Das Kapital **Vol. 1**: 10; **Vol. 3**: 353
Dazhai **Vol. 3**: 21–22
decentralization **Vol. 2**: 102, 125, 149–150; **Vol. 3**: 271, 352, 356, 445
Decision on the China Issue **Vol. 1**: 152
Declaration of the Second National Congress of the CPC **Vol. 1**: 120, 215
democracy **Vol. 1**: 4–5, 8, 29, 65, 67, 69, 71, 73, 75–79, 81, 83, 85, 87, 89, 99, 101, 106–112, 114, 117, 131, 146, 190, 192, 199–200, 209, 216, 224, 232, 237, 241–242, 244–245, 258, 264, 266, 268, 272, 281, 298, 312, 317, 321–322, 365, 395–396, 398, 401–403, 409–413, 425, 449–450, 467–468, 482, 487, 491, 500–502, 509, 513, 515–516, 518–520, 522–523, 525, 528, 531, 534–537, 539, 542–544, 546, 548; **Vol. 2**: 4, 8, 10, 13, 25–34, 37, 40–42, 45, 47–49, 51–53, 56–59, 62–63, 65, 69–70, 72, 76–79, 81–83, 86–91, 95, 98–99, 104–105, 111–112, 114, 116–117, 119, 121, 130, 136, 141, 152–154, 159, 163, 169, 176, 179, 183, 185–186, 207–209, 221–222, 226, 232, 241, 245–246, 250, 274, 291, 298, 312, 320, 325, 339; **Vol. 3**: 31, 48, 56–58, 62, 129, 136–138, 140–147, 150, 152, 155, 161, 177, 182, 184, 191, 241, 252, 257–258, 269, 272, 305, 314, 316, 318, 364, 367, 369–372, 376–381, 385, 449, 452–453, 458, 460, 484–485, 509–510, 528, 532, 534, 545
Democratic Alliance **Vol. 1**: 224, 527, 535; **Vol. 2**: 30, 49
democratic centralism **Vol. 1**: 190, 359, 365, 368–369, 379, 387, 394–395, 398–403, 408–419, 427, 450, 452, 474–475, 488, 499, 509, 515, 518, 523, 527, 535; **Vol. 2**: 26, 48–49, 159–160, 190, 221–222, 243–244, 246; **Vol. 3**: 57–58, 62, 150, 161, 163, 172, 176–177, 184–185, 190, 281, 370
Democratic Management in Rural Areas **Vol. 1**: 527, 535; **Vol. 3**: 377
democratic parties (other) **Vol. 1**: 87, 120, 224, 256, 262–269, 271–272, 516, 527, 535; **Vol. 2**: 49, 53, 61, 79–81, 127, 129, 152–153, 170, 179, 249–250, 319–320; **Vol. 3**: 128–133, 168, 180, 242, 245, 372–375, 454
Democratic Republic Vol 1: 27, 72, 76, 100, 109–110, 117, 236, 491, 509, 513, 515, 517, 521, 527, 529, 535–536; **Vol. 2**: 28–29, 49
democratic system within the Party **Vol. 1**: 527, 535; **Vol. 3**: 452
Democratic United Front **Vol. 1**: 29, 87–88, 213, 244–245, 254, 256, 259, 261–262, 264, 268–269, 271, 527, 535; **Vol. 2**: 53, 79–80, 87, 153, 170, 320
Deng Enming **Vol. 1**: 19
Deng Liqun **Vol. 3**: 25, 125, 189, 193, 195, 199–200
Deng Xiaoping **Vol. 1**: 158, 200, 351, 352, 410, 485, 500; **Vol. 2**: 9, 11, 18, 21, 23, 142, 153, 160–163, 166, 197, 233, 237–238, 240, 245, 248–249, 251, 254–255, 299, 302–305, 307, 309–310, 312, 316–321, 324–328, 330–332, 334–339; **Vol. 3**: 4–5, 7, 9–11, 14–15, 18, 20, 24–26, 28, 34, 39–40, 45–47, 49–51, 57–60,

62–63, 74, 88, 90, 94, 110, 123, 125, 129, 132–133, 136–138, 140, 144–152, 157, 159, 162–163, 165–168, 178–181, 186, 188–189, 193, 195, 199–200, 202, 205–208, 210–211, 213, 215, 217–219, 221, 225, 229, 231–233, 235–237, 240–242, 245–246, 255, 258–266, 268–269, 286–291, 301, 304–311, 315–319, 323–338, 340, 344–349, 351, 354, 357–364, 366, 368–372, 380, 382, 385, 390, 392–393, 398–401, 406, 415, 427, 430, 440, 446–449, 468, 472–476, 479, 481, 483–484, 492, 500, 502, 504, 514, 524–526, 533, 550–551

Deng Xiaoping Chronology **Vol. 3**: 137

Deng Xiaoping Theory **Vol. 3**: 5, 7, 63, 301, 326, 357–360, 368, 448, 468, 472–476, 483–484, 500, 504, 514, 524–526, 533, 550–551

Deng Xiaoping's Selected Works **Vol. 3**: 372, 448–449

Deng Yingchao **Vol. 3**: 62, 179, 188–189, 288

Deng Zhongxia **Vol. 1**: 14–15, 17, 29, 35, 102, 123–127, 139, 274

Deng Zihui **Vol. 1**: 497; **Vol. 2**: 166, 248

Deng's Six Articles **Vol. 3**: 232

Department of Theory of the Ministry of Publicity and Propaganda **Vol. 2**: 104

Developing Civilized and Courteous Activities **Vol. 3**: 367

Diaoyu Islands **Vol. 3**: 212

dialectical materialism **Vol. 1**: 64, 83, 294–295, 302, 326, 367, 388, 438; **Vol. 2**: 164, 232; **Vol. 3**: 41, 154, 156, 158, 168, 505

dictatorship of the proletariat **Vol. 1**: 13, 27–28, 34, 53–54, 60, 78, 89, 100, 103, 108, 190–191, 194, 227, 458, 507, 513, 519–520; **Vol. 2**: 49–50, 92, 135, 219, 262, 277–282, 290, 294, 296, 299–300, 306, 315, 318–319; **Vol. 3**: 21, 23, 49, 51, 140–142, 145, 147, 149–150, 283, 329

Ding Guangen **Vol. 3**: 245

Ding Guangxun **Vol. 3**: 127

Dingxi County **Vol. 3**: 277

diplomatic guidelines **Vol. 3**: 203

Discipline Commission (provincial or municipal) **Vol. 3**: 164, 200, 288, 294, 298–299, 318, 321–322, 460, 464–465, 467

Dispute Settlement Mechanism Agreement **Vol. 3**: 518

distribution **Vol. 1**: 13, 174, 199, 251, 420, 525, 532; **Vol. 2**: 4, 8, 107, 126, 128, 135, 141, 201, 205, 219, 236, 238, 268, 270, 280, 287, 294, 297, 301, 328, 334; **Vol. 3**: 14, 21–28, 37, 150, 194–195, 201, 249, 292, 329, 337, 349, 351, 355, 365–367, 394, 401, 473–474, 480, 489, 492, 496, 507, 510, 529, 531, 533, 541, 543, 548

District People's Congress **Vol. 1**: 515

doctrinairism **Vol. 1**: 366, 389

dogmatism (dogmatist) **Vol. 1**: 61, 65, 68, 157, 183, 188, 366–367, 391, 437, 441, 463, 485, 491, 546; **Vol. 2**: 8, 11, 13, 15, 17–18, 20, 23, 50, 120, 134, 139–143, 145, 156, 176–177, 184, 197, 204, 209–213, 220, 225, 273–274, 309–310, 312–313, 315–317, 319, 321, 323, 325, 328, 332, 338–339; **Vol. 3**: 332

Dong Biwu **Vol. 1**: 19, 38, 257; **Vol. 2**: 153

Dong Fureng **Vol. 3**: 199

Dong Yingbin **Vol. 1**: 234

Dong Zhentang **Vol. 3**: 104

Dong Zhiyong **Vol. 3**: 299

Double Hundred policy **Vol. 3**: 390

Draft Law of the People's Republic of China **Vol. 3**: 275

Duanjin **Vol. 1**: 191

E

East China Bureau **Vol. 2**: 249

Eastern Europe **Vol. 1**: 522; **Vol. 2**: 15, 40, 46, 50, 133; **Vol. 3**: 247, 323, 326

Economic and Technical Cooperation Agreement for the Construction and Reconstruction of Industrial Projects in China **Vol. 3**: 219

Economic Center of the State Council **Vol. 3**: 194

economic construction **Vol. 1**: 105, 193–197, 204–205, 292–294, 404, 505, 519, 526–528, 538–539; **Vol. 2**: 5–8, 26, 35, 38, 44, 46, 51, 78, 82, 84, 91, 94, 98–99, 101, 118, 120, 122, 131–132, 136, 138, 147–148, 174, 181, 186–188, 190, 192, 197, 202, 205, 211, 245, 268, 270, 306, 335; **Vol. 3**: 4, 21,

45, 47, 61, 148, 150, 161, 170–172, 174, 181–182, 191, 202–203, 207, 225, 243, 251–252, 254–256, 261, 266, 280, 293, 301, 309–310, 314, 318, 328, 334, 336, 339, 364, 386, 399, 408, 412, 433, 435, 484, 501, 503, 525, 531, 535, 545, 547
Economic Research **Vol. 3**: 24, 26, 192
economic system reform **Vol. 3**: 193, 198, 201–202, 241, 268, 313, 334–335, 344–346, 348–352, 354, 367, 378, 428, 488–489
Economic, Trade, and Science and Technology Commission **Vol. 3**: 219
Editorial Department of Philosophical Research **Vol. 3**: 43
egoism **Vol. 2**: 282–284
Eight-Character Principle **Vol. 3**: 132
Eight Conditions for the Standard of Communist Party Members **Vol. 2**: 86
Eight Major Routes **Vol. 2**: 74, 181, 185
Eight-Grade Wage System **Vol. 2**: 294
Eight-Nation Alliance **Vol. 1**: 3
Eighth Five-Year Plan **Vol. 3**: 212, 337, 364, 481
Eighth National Congress of the Communist Party of China **Vol. 2**: 7, 13, 183, 194; **Vol. 3**: 253
Eighth Political Report **Vol. 2**: 183
Eighth Route Army **Vol. 1**: 69, 202, 231, 241, 285–286, 305, 308–309, 311, 336–337, 342, 344
Eleventh Five-Year Plan **Vol. 3**: 177, 503, 508, 530, 550
Eleventh National Congress of the Communist Party of China **Vol. 3**: 3, 177, 530
emancipating the mind **Vol. 1**: 470; **Vol. 2**: 8, 21, 140, 209, 211, 226, 325, 328–329, 332, 334, 339; **Vol. 3**: 35, 57, 60, 68–69, 90, 153–155, 158, 173, 243, 333, 336, 343, 359, 472, 525, 549
Engels, Friedrich **Vol. 1**: 7, 97, 163, 188, 224, 357, 364, 374–375, 381, 384, 393–397, 429–432, 434, 443, 445, 447, 451, 458, 492–493; **Vol. 2**: 12, 53, 113, 125, 135–137, 164, 209, 211–212, 215, 280, 299; **Vol. 3**: 41, 481
Enlightenment Society **Vol. 3**: 143
Enlightenment (Western Enlightenment) **Vol. 1**: 5, 545, 547; **Vol. 3**: 143

equalitarianism **Vol. 2**: 77, 201, 235, 238; **Vol. 3**: 365
Erdan Island **Vol. 3**: 228
ethnic groups (ethnic minorities) **Vol. 1**: 201–202, 228, 258, 266, 268, 289, 298, 449, 466, 516, 545; **Vol. 2**: 22, 53–55, 81–82, 135, 152, 157–158, 250, 298, 332; **Vol. 3**: 119–123, 126, 130, 131, 133, 137, 177, 179, 229, 231, 240, 242, 358, 367, 372, 482, 527, 530, 550
ethnic policy **Vol. 2**: 55; **Vol. 3**: 116, 118–122, 125
ethnic relations **Vol. 2**: 55, 157; **Vol. 3**: 120–122, 125, 130
etiquette system **Vol. 1**: 317
European Capitalist Society **Vol. 1**: 161
European proletarian revolution **Vol. 1**: 161
Exchange and Payment Agreement **Vol. 3**: 219
Executive Committee **Vol. 1**: 33, 35, 38–39, 51, 54, 103–104, 152–153, 190–191, 215–217, 221, 226–227, 232, 275, 363; **Vol. 3**: 105, 537
extremism **Vol. 2**: 305

F
fake party **Vol. 3**: 79
fall of Shanghai **Vol. 1**: 308
Fallaci, Oriana **Vol. 3**: 163, 289
Fan Hongjie **Vol. 1**: 17
Fang Fang **Vol. 1**: 257
Fang Jisheng **Vol. 3**: 32
Fang Lingxuan **Vol. 3**: 32
Fang Lizhi **Vol. 3**: 316, 318
Fang Yi **Vol. 3**: 42, 189
Fang Zhenwu **Vol. 1**: 233
Fang Zhimin **Vol. 1**: 175, 178
February Countercurrent **Vol. 3**: 54, 76
February 7th Movement **Vol. 1**: 36
February Revolution **Vol. 1**: 28, 89
Federal Republic of China **Vol. 2**: 54
Federation of China **Vol. 2**: 54
Federation of Industry and Commerce **Vol. 2**: 127, 319; **Vol. 3**: 242
Feng faction: **Vol. 1**: 215
Feng Wenbin **Vol. 3**: 154
Feng Yuxiang **Vol. 1**: 214, 234, 248
Fenghua **Vol. 3**: 227

Fengtian warlords **Vol. 1**: 214
feudalism **Vol. 1**: 28, 37, 45, 52, 60, 62, 72–74, 88, 92, 94, 96, 98–100, 107, 114, 119–120, 130–131, 133–137, 140, 145, 246–247, 263, 268, 278, 280, 283, 285, 287, 316, 329, 331, 350, 466–468, 487, 509, 520, 525, 530, 535, 540–541, 543; **Vol. 2**: 26, 31, 37, 53, 83, 91, 93, 111, 116, 286; **Vol. 3**: 57, 148, 252, 309
Fifth Anti-Encirclement Campaign **Vol. 1**: 82, 158–159, 194
Fifteenth National Congress of the Communist Party of China **Vol. 3**: 359, 361, 363, 368, 371, 388, 400, 408, 419, 434
Fighting, Criticizing, and Reforming **Vol. 1**: 296
Fighting Egoism and Repudiating Revisionism **Vol. 2**: 283
Figueiredo, João **Vol. 3**: 264
Finance and Economic Commission **Vol. 2**: 37
Financial and Trade Economy **Vol. 3**: 193
First Congress of the Chinese Socialist Youth League **Vol. 1**: 25
First Five-Year Plan **Vol. 2**: 98, 101–102, 106, 131–132, 148–149, 188, 190; **Vol. 3**: 160, 482
First International **Vol. 1**: 357, 395
First National Congress of the Communist Party of China **Vol. 1**: 19, 29, 419
First National Labor Conference **Vol. 1**: 25
First Resolution of the Communist Party of China **Vol. 1**: 20
First World War (*see also* World War I) **Vol. 1**: 4; **Vol. 2**: 54
Five Always **Vol. 3**: 468
Five Coordinations **Vol. 3**: 495, 505
Five Determinations **Vol. 2**: 238
Five Emphases and Four Beauties **Vol. 3**: 312
Five Emphases, Four Beauties, and Three Loves **Vol. 3**: 313
Five Guarantees **Vol. 2**: 238
Five Oppositions Campaign **Vol. 2**: 94, 103–105, 109, 259, 292; **Vol. 3**: 93
Five Principles of Peaceful Co-existence **Vol. 3**: 206–208, 221, 426–427
Five Surges **Vol. 2**: 230, 232

Five-Year Plan **Vol. 1**: 498, 511; **Vol. 2**: 98, 101–102, 106, 114, 117–119, 124, 131–132, 147–149, 183, 188–190, 209, 260–261; **Vol. 3**: 160, 183, 212, 254, 261–262, 265, 286, 313, 337, 364, 381, 384, 399, 401–402, 481–482, 503, 508, 550–551
focus of work **Vol. 1**: 155; **Vol. 2**: 136, 145, 185, 330, 332; **Vol. 3**: 49, 51–55, 60–61, 254
Foreign Experts **Vol. 3**: 116–118
Foreign Language Bureau **Vol. 3**: 117
Foreign Language Institute **Vol. 3**: 117
Foreign Liaison Department **Vol. 3**: 82
Former Businessmen **Vol. 3**: 113–114
Four Adherences **Vol. 3**: 155
Four Basic Principles **Vol. 3**: 4, 136, 144, 148–152, 154–155, 162, 241, 243, 252, 254–256, 259, 281, 305, 310, 314, 318, 323–324, 336, 339, 525, 546–547
Four Cardinal Principles **Vol. 3**: 135, 484
Four Clean-ups **Vol. 2**: 259, 269; **Vol. 3**: 93–96
Four Clean-ups Movement **Vol. 2**: 269; **Vol. 3**: 93–96
Four Clearance Movement **Vol. 2**: 221
Four Little Dragons **Vol. 3**: 331
Four Modernizations **Vol. 2**: 03, 309, 327, 333–335, 339; **Vol. 3**: 28, 47, 49, 51, 53, 58, 64, 70, 115, 129–130, 136–137, 140, 145, 147–149, 154, 158, 175, 229, 258–261, 263, 267, 286–287, 290–292, 307, 309, 311, 319, 398, 458
Four Nevers **Vol. 3**: 520
Four Obediences **Vol. 3**: 453
Four Purifications Movement **Vol. 3**: 83, 85, 92
Four Subordinations **Vol. 1**: 410–411, 417
Fourth Army **Vol. 1**: 69, 202, 241, 285–286, 299, 307, 311, 323, 336–337; **Vol. 3**: 106–107
Fourth National Congress of the Communist Party of China **Vol. 1**: 30–34, 101–102, 125–126, 128, 139, 218, 220, 225–226, 400, 507; **Vol. 2**: 277, 302
Fourteen Articles for Scientific Research **Vol. 2**: 285
Fourteen Articles of Science **Vol. 2**: 240, 254
free market **Vol. 2**: 151, 287
French Revolution **Vol. 1**: 105, 165
Front Line Committee **Vol. 1**: 307

Fu Chongbi **Vol. 3**: 75–76
Fu Zuoyi **Vol. 1**: 234
Fujian Front Force **Vol. 3**: 228
Fujian Province **Vol. 1**: 299; **Vol. 3**: 96, 298, 313, 320–321
Further Development of the Western Region **Vol. 1**: 263; **Vol. 3**: 337, 508

G

Gang of Four **Vol. 2**: 303, 309–310, 313–317, 319, 321, 323–324, 326, 334–335, 337; **Vol. 3**: 9–14, 17, 20–23, 28–29, 32–34, 36, 40, 47, 49–52, 54, 60, 65, 72–73, 75–77, 79, 81, 83, 85, 88, 92–93, 100–101, 110, 118, 121, 126, 128, 130, 147–151, 154, 156, 159, 161, 163–164, 170, 175, 187
Gansu Province **Vol. 3**: 277
Gao Gang **Vol. 3**: 101
Gao Shanquan **Vol. 3**: 199
Gao Shuxun **Vol. 1**: 248
Gaozhou City **Vol. 3**: 456
General Administration of Civil Aviation of China **Vol. 3**: 539–540
General Administration of Customs **Vol. 3**: 278
General Administration of Radio and Television **Vol. 3**: 455
General Assembly **Vol. 1**: 19–20, 153, 202, 221, 232, 369–370, 387, 395, 403, 421, 504; **Vol. 2**: 148, 160, 212, 243, 245, 304, 319; **Vol. 3**: 139–141, 179–180, 182, 185–188, 190, 220, 224, 240, 244, 360, 473, 521, 524, 551
General German Workers' Association **Vol. 1**: 430
general line of the new democratic revolution **Vol. 1**: 143
General Political Department (PLA) **Vol. 3**: 82, 106, 156, 306, 432
General Secretary **Vol. 1**: 395; **Vol. 3**: 6, 78, 123, 189, 207, 211, 219, 221, 245, 324, 497, 516, 526, 545
Geng Biao **Vol. 2**: 317
German Democrats **Vol. 1**: 224
German Social Democratic Labor Party **Vol. 1**: 357
"going global" **Vol. 3**: 402

Gong Yuzhi **Vol. 2**: 3; **Vol. 3**: 199
Gorbachev, Mikhail **Vol. 3**: 219–221
Gotha Program **Vol. 1**: 430; **Vol. 2**: 90
governance **Vol. 1**: 119, 208, 439; **Vol. 2**: 292; **Vol. 3**: 4–5, 234, 241, 301–302, 325, 366, 440, 449, 465, 503, 511–513, 516, 534, 546
Government of the Ningkang County Workers, Peasants, and Soldiers **Vol. 1**: 136, 189, 202, 255
Government of the Workers and Peasants of Chaling County **Vol. 1**: 136, 189, 202
Government of the Workers, Peasants, and Soldiers of Suichuan County **Vol. 1**: 136, 189, 202, 255
Government of the Yongxin and Lianhua County Workers, Peasants, and Soldiers **Vol. 1**: 136, 189, 202, 255
Government Work Report **Vol. 1**: 136, 202; **Vol. 3**: 254, 262
Gramsci, Antonio **Vol. 2**: 18
Grasping Revolution and Promoting Production
grasping with both hands ("two handed grasp") **Vol. 3**: 302, 304, 309, 331, 364, 382
grassroots autonomy **Vol. 1**: 36 **Vol. 3**: 376
Great Hall of the People **Vol. 3**: 148, 239, 242
Great Harmony World **Vol. 3**: 533
Great Ideological Liberation Movement **Vol. 2**: 311
Great Leap Forward **Vol. 2**: 8–9, 130, 185, 187–193, 197, 199–200, 203–204, 206, 208–209, 211–216, 218–222, 226, 230–232, 234, 237–244, 246, 250, 253–254, 267–268, 270, 273, 276, 293, 325; **Vol. 3**: 332
Great Proletarian Cultural Revolution (*see* Cultural Revolution)
Great Revolution **Vol. 1**: 29, 42–47, 52, 58, 65, 79, 82, 112, 137, 145, 149–150, 152, 154, 163, 167, 172, 176, 180–181, 185, 189, 217, 222, 228, 234, 249, 278, 284, 361, 377–378, 419–420, 488, 494, 504, 508; **Vol. 2**: 170, 332–333; **Vol. 3**: 49, 51, 359, 546
Gu Bai **Vol. 1**: 158
Gu Mu **Vol. 2**: 331; **Vol. 3**: 46, 189

Gu Zhenfu **Vol. 3**: 414, 419
Gu Zhun **Vol. 2**: 307–309
Guangdong Province **Vol. 1**: 33; **Vol. 3**: 277, 322, 331, 456, 468, 500
Guangdong Province Second Peasant Congress **Vol. 1**: 33
Guangdong Provincial Committee **Vol. 3**: 322
Guangming Daily **Vol. 2**: 322; **Vol. 3**: 12, 24, 35–36, 53
Guangxi Province **Vol. 1**: 234; **Vol. 3**: 80, 96, 106, 125, 284, 455
Guangxi Student Army **Vol. 3**: 106
Guangzhou **Vol. 1**: 16, 18–19, 24, 36, 51, 61, 151, 165, 214, 353; **Vol. 2**: 235, 251, 254; **Vol. 3**: 143, 468–469
Guangzhou Conference **Vol. 2**: 254
Guangzhou National Government **Vol. 1**: 214
Guangzhou Uprising **Vol. 1**: 151, 165
guerrilla forces **Vol. 1**: 331, 333
guerrilla war **Vol. 1**: 83, 152, 169, 184, 198, 231, 298, 311, 329, 333, 373, 383
Gui Shifu **Vol. 3**: 199
guiding ideology **Vol. 1**: 3, 5, 7, 9, 11, 13, 15, 17, 19, 21, 23, 25, 27, 29, 31, 33, 35, 37, 39, 41, 43, 45–47, 49, 51, 53, 55, 57–59, 61, 63, 84, 157, 199, 205, 313, 370, 376, 384, 469, 485, 491; **Vol. 2**: 82, 125, 144, 157, 161, 171, 179–180, 203, 209, 229, 246, 255, 260, 277, 293, 314, 317–318; **Vol. 3**: 3, 6–7, 20, 51–53, 55, 59, 61, 63, 67, 95, 118, 141, 152, 158, 163, 169, 171–172, 174, 181, 283, 313, 334, 360, 365, 384–385, 387, 389, 443, 465, 468, 473–476, 492, 501, 512, 514, 526, 533, 550
Guidong County **Vol. 1**: 323
Guiyang City **Vol. 3**: 94
Guizhou Province **Vol. 1**: 323; **Vol. 3**: 78–79, 94–96
Guo Fan **Vol. 1**: 405
Guo Hongtao **Vol. 3**: 105
Guo Junyu **Vol. 1**: 17
Guo Moruo **Vol. 1**: 264
Gutian Congress **Vol. 1**: 178
Gutian Meeting **Vol. 1**: 289, 304, 307, 316, 321, 364, 366, 382, 400, 410

H

Ha'erbin (Harbin) **Vol. 1**: 16: **Vol. 3**: 277–278
Hai Rui **Vol. 2**: 222
Hainan Island **Vol. 3**: 226, 320–321
Han **Vol. 1**: 201; **Vol. 2**: 55, 81, 157; **Vol. 3**: 11, 62, 120–121, 124–125, 127, 189
Han Tianshi **Vol. 3**: 189
Han Zhixiong **Vol. 3**: 11
Handan **Vol. 2**: 204
Handicrafts, Thirty-five Articles of **Vol. 2**: 236
handicraft workers **Vol. 1**: 128, 292, 525, 539; **Vol. 2**: 62, 125
Handling Cases before the Cultural Revolution **Vol. 2**: 152; **Vol. 3**: 87
Hangzhou **Vol. 1**: 260, 355
Hankou **Vol. 1**: 18, 34, 40, 42–43, 166–167, 222
Hankou Special Meeting **Vol. 1**: 222
Hao Jianxiu **Vol. 3**: 189
Harmonious Socialist Society **Vol. 3**: 466, 514, 523, 525, 530–535
harmonious world **Vol. 3**: 516–518, 548
Hartling, Paul **Vol. 2**: 280; **Vol. 3**: 22
He Changgong **Vol. 3**: 288
He Kaifeng **Vol. 1**: 492
He Long **Vol. 1**: 178; **Vol. 3**: 81
He Mengxiong **Vol. 1**: 17
He Shuheng **Vol. 1**: 19
He Xiangning **Vol. 1**: 264
He Zhigui **Vol. 3**: 299
Heath, Edward **Vol. 3**: 139, 235
Hebei Province **Vol. 3**: 277
Hegel, Georg Wilhelm Friedrich **Vol. 1**: 374
hegemony **Vol. 2**: 263, 305; **Vol. 3**: 160, 181–182, 184, 203–207, 327, 421, 426, 437
Heilongjiang Province **Vol. 3**: 122, 299
Henan Province **Vol. 2**: 204; **Vol. 3**: 90, 277
Higher Education, Sixty Articles of **Vol. 2**: 240, 254
historical idealism **Vol. 1**: 92, 456
historical materialism **Vol. 1**: 7–11, 92, 302, 326, 374, 435–436, 444, 456–457, 461, 546; **Vol. 2**: 135, 164, 327; **Vol. 3**: 50, 84, 168, 329, 332–333, 506
History and Class Consciousness **Vol. 2**: 17

History of the Communist Party of China **Vol. 2**: 118
Hong Kong **Vol. 1**: 25, 34, 36, 228; **Vol. 2**: 42; **Vol. 3**: 56, 132, 134, 182, 216, 227, 231–237, 260, 266, 416–417, 420, 519–520
Hong Kong Business Group **Vol. 3**: 233
Hope Project **Vol. 3**: 383–384
"How Can the Party Last?" (article) **Vol. 1**: 193, 365
Howe, Jeffrey **Vol. 3**: 263
Hu Fuming **Vol. 3**: 35
Hu Jintao **Vol. 3**: 6, 439, 455, 458–459, 465, 499–503, 510, 512, 515–521, 523–524, 526, 532, 545
Hu Jiwei **Vol. 3**: 12, 42, 139
Hu Qiaomu **Vol. 1**: 483; **Vol. 3**: 22, 25, 28, 48, 62–63, 72, 139, 145, 165, 178, 185, 189
Hu Qili **Vol. 3**: 189, 245
Hu Sheng **Vol. 2**: 40, 229; **Vol. 3**: 139
Hu Shih **Vol. 1**: 10–11, 14, 24
Hu Yaobang **Vol. 2**: 322, 326; **Vol. 3**: 12–17, 33, 35, 38, 62–63, 67, 71, 96, 107, 111, 123–125, 133, 136–140, 145, 165, 177–179, 182, 186, 189, 199–200, 206–207, 211, 218, 245, 317, 323
Hu Zhaopei **Vol. 3**: 193
Hu Zongnan **Vol. 1**: 352
Hua County **Vol. 3**: 277
Hua Gang **Vol. 1**: 483
Hua Guofeng **Vol. 2**: 317, 324, 331, 333; **Vol. 3**: 10–12, 22, 40, 52, 54, 57, 59, 63, 136, 138, 171, 179, 203, 289
Hua Luogeng **Vol. 3**: 30
Huadong Field Army Corps **Vol. 1**: 351
Huaibei Base **Vol. 3**: 106
Huaihai **Vol. 1**: 327–328, 342, 352–355
Huainan Base **Vol. 3**: 106
Huairen Hall **Vol. 3**: 380
Huang Baitao Corps **Vol. 1**: 354
Huang Chao **Vol. 1**: 332
Huang Hua **Vol. 3**: 217
Huang Huoqing **Vol. 3**: 62
Huang Kecheng **Vol. 3**: 62, 81, 91, 164, 189, 288
Huang Lingshuang **Vol. 1**: 12
Huang Rikui **Vol. 1**: 17

Huang Zhen **Vol. 3**: 104, 139
Huang Zhongyue **Vol. 3**: 104–105
Huangpu Student Army **Vol. 1**: 274
Hubei Province **Vol. 1**: 43; **Vol. 2**: 109; **Vol. 3**: 85
Hubei Provincial Party Committee **Vol. 3**: 72–73, 108
Hume, David **Vol. 3**: 41
Hunan Peasant Movement **Vol. 1**: 331, 389
Hunan Province **Vol. 1**: 38, 169, 323; **Vol. 2**: 233
Hunan Provincial Party Committee **Vol. 1**: 151, 169, 174
Hunan-Guangdong-Guangxi Border War **Vol. 1**: 59
Hundred Days Reform Movement **Vol. 1**: 540
Hungarian Incident **Vol. 2**: 181
Huxi **Vol. 3**: 84, 105–106

I

ideological and cultural education **Vol. 2**: 82
ideological construction **Vol. 1**: 364, 373–376, 378–382, 384, 388, 400, 422, 427; **Vol. 3**: 432, 448
ideological emancipation **Vol. 2**: 11–12, 142, 186, 222, 312–313, 320–321, 325, 327, 329–330, 332, 334, 338–339; **Vol. 3**: 24, 32, 44–45, 69, 118, 136, 154–155
Ideological Liberation Movement **Vol. 2**: 311, 339
ideological line **Vol. 1**: 63–64, 66, 366–367, 378–379, 388–391, 393, 427, 438, 548; **Vol. 2**: 5, 11, 203, 232–235, 313, 316, 324, 327, 329, 338; **Vol. 3**: 34, 55, 58, 60, 69, 135, 153–158, 254, 472
imperialism **Vol. 1**: 3–4, 13, 24–27, 30–31, 34, 37, 44, 51–54, 56, 60–62, 66, 72–74, 87–88, 92–95, 98–100, 105, 107–108, 111–115, 119–123, 125–127, 130–131, 133–137, 140, 145, 160, 173, 187, 238, 243, 245–247, 253, 263, 268, 272, 275, 280, 283, 285, 287, 289, 292, 326, 329, 331, 350–351, 358, 375, 377, 397, 400, 434, 466–468, 487, 509, 514, 517, 519–520, 525–526, 530, 535, 540–541, 543–545; **Vol. 2**: 16, 18, 26, 31, 33, 37, 40–41, 53, 55, 60–61, 83, 91, 116, 136, 262–266, 274, 285, 288; **Vol. 3**: 145, 148, 172, 182, 226, 234, 252, 332, 416

Indies Social Democratic Alliance **Vol. 1**: 224
industrialization **Vol. 1**: 251, 497–498, 519, 533; **Vol. 2**: 5–6, 31, 64–65, 73, 76–78, 85–86, 88, 100–102, 104–105, 107–110, 112–115, 117–120, 122, 130–131, 137–138, 141, 146–150, 183, 187, 209–210, 218, 223, 225; **Vol. 3**: 253, 485, 490, 499, 529, 543
Industry, Seventy Articles of **Vol. 2**: 238–239, 254
Information Engineering College **Vol. 3**: 434
Information Work Office **Vol. 3**: 539
informationization **Vol. 3**: 437, 439
initial stage of capitalism **Vol. 1**: 475
Inner Mongolia **Vol. 1**: 202; **Vol. 3**: 15, 116, 122, 125, 277, 455
Institute of Philosophy **Vol. 3**: 43
institution building **Vol. 3**: 279
institutional reform program **Vol. 3**: 276, 538
Instructions on Land Issues (May 4th Instructions) **Vol. 1**: 249, 532
integrating Marxism into China **Vol. 1**: 77, 489, 491, 550; **Vol. 2**: 27, 273, 299, 303, 306, 310; **Vol. 3**: 550
intellectuals **Vol. 1**: 5, 7, 11–12, 14–16, 20, 46, 57, 72, 76, 113–114, 117, 128, 144, 198, 210, 215, 241, 253–254, 262–263, 288, 293, 367, 383, 399, 471, 488, 495, 499, 501, 513; **Vol. 2**: 61–62, 80–81, 130, 154–155, 157, 177, 179, 239, 241–243, 250–251, 254, 259, 263–264, 270, 288, 291, 301, 309–310, 320; **Vol. 3**: 18, 20, 30, 88, 110–112, 129–131, 145, 185, 242, 308, 317, 339, 372
International Law Commission **Vol. 3**: 224
International Monetary Fund **Vol. 3**: 224
International General Committee **Vol. 1**: 396
International Labor Day Commemorative Event **Vol. 1**: 15
International Workers' Association **Vol. 1**: 395–396
intra-Party struggle **Vol. 1**: 490; **Vol. 3**: 141
Iskra **Vol. 1**: 399
Islamic Union **Vol. 1**: 224

J

James Soong **Vol. 3**: 521
Jameson, Friedrich **Vol. 2**: 18–19
January Revolution **Vol. 3**: 66, 75
Japan **Vol. 1**: 9, 18–19, 30, 73, 75, 81, 229–230, 233–240, 242–243, 290, 297, 376, 400, 514, 532; **Vol. 2**: 263–264, 330; **Vol. 3**: 46, 106, 210–212, 228–229, 241, 347, 419, 423–425
Japanese imperialism **Vol. 1**: 61, 66, 73, 80, 98–99, 160, 238, 243, 289, 326, 400, 526, 530
Ji Dengkui **Vol. 3**: 70, 104
Ji Pengfei **Vol. 3**: 104
Jia Shuang **Vol. 3**: 299
Jiang Qing **Vol. 2**: 292, 294, 300, 304, 310, 313, 320; **Vol. 3**: 75–77, 79, 86, 170, 187, 285
Jiang Qing Anti-Revolutionary Group **Vol. 3**: 170
Jiang Zemin **Vol. 2**: 21; **Vol. 3**: 6, 245, 324–326, 338, 348–349, 351–352, 358–360, 364–365, 368–371, 375, 378–380, 383, 387–388, 390–392, 397, 401–402, 408, 410, 415, 417, 419, 421, 423–424, 426–427, 429–431, 433–435, 438, 444, 446–447, 454, 456, 458–459, 462, 468–472, 484, 526
Jiangshan Island **Vol. 3**: 226
Jiangsu Province **Vol. 1**: 352; **Vol. 3**: 53, 87, 105, 141, 263
Jiangxi Province **Vol. 1**: 38, 41, 178, 299; **Vol. 3**: 91
Jiangxi Provincial Political Committee **Vol. 1**: 38
Jiao Ren **Vol. 3**: 414
Jicheng County **Vol. 3**: 277
Jilin Province **Vol. 3**: 39, 122
Jin-Cha-Ji Territorial Doctrine **Vol. 3**: 76–77
Jinan **Vol. 1**: 19; **Vol. 3**: 38
Jinchaji **Vol. 1**: 202, 211, 493
Jinchaji Daily **Vol. 1**: 493
Jinggangshan (Jinggangshan Revolutionary Base) **Vol. 1**: 105, 168–170, 173–174, 189, 191, 306, 315, 317, 319, 323, 331, 336, 345, 361, 365, 382, 404
Jingxi Hotel **Vol. 2**: 300
Jinjiang Region **Vol. 3**: 298, 320–321
Jinjiluyu Central Bureau **Vol. 1**: 493
Jinmen Islands **Vol. 3**: 228

Jinsui Cadres Meeting **Vol. 1**: 533
Jinzhai County **Vol. 3**: 384
Jinzhou **Vol. 1**: 353–354
Joint Commission **Vol. 1**: 395
Joint Statement of the People's Republic of China and the Government of Portugal on Macao **Vol. 3**: 237
joint-stock enterprises **Vol. 3**: 406
July 1st Speech (Jiang Zemin) **Vol. 3**: 115, 471

K

Kang Sheng **Vol. 2**: 279; **Vol. 3**: 54, 73, 77, 79, 100–101
Kant, Immanuel **Vol. 3**: 41
Khrushchev **Vol. 2**: 143, 256, 264, 289; **Vol. 3**: 163, 247
KMT Legislative Body **Vol. 1**: 258, 260
KMT Revolutionary Committee **Vol. 1**: 258, 264
KMT ruling clique **Vol. 1**: 258, 271, 281
Kong Xiangxi (H H Kung) **Vol. 1**: 246
Korean War **Vol. 2**: 84–85, 99; **Vol. 3**: 226
Kosygin **Vol. 2**: 287, 289
Kowloon **Vol. 3**: 234, 416
Kropotkin, Peter **Vol. 1**: 6
Kung, H H (*see* Kong Xiangxi)
Kuomintang (*see also* Nationalist Party) **Vol. 1**: 24, 26, 29, 32–33, 35, 41, 48–49, 66, 69, 85, 102, 115, 123, 126, 136, 153, 192, 197, 215, 223, 235, 239, 248, 254, 257, 261, 467; **Vol. 2**: 37, 43, 49–50, 57, 60–61, 91–93, 116; **Vol. 3**: 79, 104, 107, 130–131, 226–228, 230, 232, 413, 419, 521
Kuomintang New Army **Vol. 1**: 33, 136
Kuybyshev, Valerian **Vol. 2**: 118

L

labor market **Vol. 3**: 354
labor-based distribution **Vol. 3**: 21, 23–27, 37
Lakeside Prefectural Committee **Vol. 3**: 105
Lan Gongwu **Vol. 1**: 11
land ownership **Vol. 1**: 51–52, 136–137, 143, 162, 523, 527, 532–533; **Vol. 2**: 26, 63–65, 123
Land Reform **Vol. 1**: 87, 250–256, 263, 271, 370, 439, 531–533; **Vol. 2**: 39, 57, 61, 63–67, 69, 71, 73–77, 87, 92, 94, 98, 102, 107, 111, 116; **Vol. 3**: 166
landlord class **Vol. 1**: 37, 52–54, 56, 75, 87, 93, 98, 129, 131, 135–138, 171, 185, 200, 246, 249–252, 271, 280, 288, 293, 371, 468, 528, 531–533; **Vol. 2**: 61, 64, 105, 286
landlords **Vol. 1**: 33, 46, 74–75, 80–81, 122, 129, 136–138, 143–145, 201, 237–238, 240, 249–255, 271, 278, 336, 377, 427, 467, 530, 532–533; **Vol. 2**: 64, 136, 257; **Vol. 3**: 112–113
Law of the Unity of Opposites **Vol. 2**: 168, 281; **Vol. 3**: 236
leadership of the CPC **Vol. 1**: 42, 87, 108, 115, 142, 172, 174, 178, 186, 198, 200, 229, 262, 264–265, 267, 272, 307, 310, 313, 368, 414, 466–467, 469, 521; **Vol. 2**: 152–153; **Vol. 3**: 257, 270, 483, 486
leadership system **Vol. 1**: 368–369, 415, 418; **Vol. 2**: 161, 186, 223, 230; **Vol. 3**: 3, 188, 241, 244, 268, 270, 337, 371, 449, 454, 513–514
League membership **Vol. 3**: 92
Lee Teng-hui **Vol. 3**: 418–419
Left-Wing Corps **Vol. 1**: 310
leftism **Vol. 2**: 138, 175, 200, 202–204, 206–208, 213, 216, 230–231, 234, 247, 252–253, 262, 302–303, 312; **Vol. 3**: 155
Leftist bias **Vol. 1**: 252, 254, 372; **Vol. 2**: 64
Leftist errors (*see also* Leftist mistakes) **Vol. 1**: 47, 58, 63, 251, 285, 378; **Vol. 2**: 10, 42, 95, 250, 258, 260, 277, 298, 319, 321; **Vol. 3**: 28, 31, 62–63, 66, 98, 126, 131, 135, 159, 162, 164, 171
Leftist mistakes (*see also* Leftist errors) **Vol. 1**: 55, 534; **Vol. 2**: 8, 10, 59, 175, 239, 246, 336; **Vol. 3**: 92, 174, 185, 250, 252, 334
Leftist tendencies **Vol. 1**: 105, 370; **Vol. 2**: 62, 74; **Vol. 3**: 283
Legislative Adjustment Bill **Vol. 3**: 213
Legislative Law Lecture **Vol. 3**: 380
Lenin, Vladimir **Vol. 1**: 6, 25, 149–150, 163, 188, 289, 291, 358–359, 364, 375–376, 379, 381, 384, 393–394, 397–399, 411, 430–432, 434, 443, 445, 447, 458–459, 492–493, 520; **Vol. 2**: 16, 18–19, 45, 54, 66, 118–119, 121, 126–127, 136–137, 140, 164, 181, 209, 211–212, 215, 266, 274, 280, 299;

Vol. 3: 28, 39, 147, 246, 332, 512
let a hundred flowers bloom and a hundred schools of thought contend **Vol. 2**: 156–157, 178, 183, 241; **Vol. 3**: 365, 390
Letter to Taiwan **Vol. 3**: 228
"letting in" and "reaching out" **Vol. 3**: 402–403
Li Chang **Vol. 3**: 189, 311
Li Da **Vol 1**: 9, 12, 18–20; **Vol. 3**: 104
Li Dazhao **Vol. 1**: 7–8, 10–12, 14, 16–19, 21, 29, 33, 102, 127, 399, 545, 547
Li Dingming **Vol. 1**: 202
Li Fuchun **Vol. 1**: 38; **Vol. 2**: 101, 156, 238; **Vol. 3**: 73
Li Hanjun **Vol. 1**: 9–10, 18–20
Li Honglin **Vol. 3**: 139
Li Jiantong **Vol. 3**: 100
Li Jingquan **Vol. 3**: 94, 288
Li Jishen **Vol. 1**: 248, 264
Li Jun **Vol. 1**: 17
Li Kenong **Vol. 1**: 234
Li Lisan **Vol. 1**: 52, 58–62, 105, 157, 285; **Vol. 2**: 40, 166; **Vol. 3**: 72
Li Peng **Vol. 3**: 221, 245, 275
Li Ruihuan **Vol. 3**: 245
Li Shangyin (Tang Dynasty poet) **Vol. 3**: 187
Li Siguang **Vol. 3**: 30
Li Tieying **Vol. 3**: 245
Li Weihan **Vol. 1**: 95; **Vol. 3**: 189
Li Xiannian **Vol. 2**: 300, 324, 326, 328, 333; **Vol. 3**: 11, 40, 48–49, 73, 179, 188–189, 200, 215, 246, 289
Li Ximing **Vol. 3**: 245
Li Zhangda **Vol. 1**: 264
Li Zicheng **Vol. 1**: 332
Li Zongren **Vol. 1**: 234
Liang Qichao **Vol. 1**: 5, 7
Liaoning Province **Vol. 3**: 122, 141
Liao Chengzhi **Vol. 3**: 189
Liao Jili **Vol. 3**: 198
Liao Zhongkai **Vol. 1**: 7
Liaoshen **Vol. 1**: 327–328, 342, 352–355
Liberation **Vol. 1**: 27–28, 37, 53, 76, 85–88, 105, 111, 113, 130, 132, 135–137, 142, 188, 203, 210, 224, 233, 244–245, 247–248, 255, 258, 261–263, 265, 267, 269–271, 278, 281, 284–286, 300, 305–306, 309, 311–313, 317, 320–321, 324, 327–329, 334, 337–338, 342, 344, 346–347, 350–351, 353, 355, 372, 383, 388, 403, 410, 421, 433, 466–467, 470, 475, 477, 484, 486, 491, 494, 500, 516, 522, 531, 534–535; **Vol. 2**: 32, 41–42, 49, 53–54, 99, 141, 252, 263, 272, 278–280, 295, 311, 327, 339; **Vol. 3**: 23, 29, 41, 65, 82, 97, 106, 109, 114, 137, 148, 153, 162, 169, 178, 225–229, 240, 244, 309, 327, 358, 433, 435, 487, 496, 517
Liberation Army Daily **Vol. 2**: 278–279; **Vol. 3**: 41, 137
Lien Chan **Vol. 3**: 521
Lihuang Municipal Committee **Vol. 3**: 106
Lin Biao **Vol. 1**: 179; **Vol. 2**: 269, 280, 300–301, 303, 310, 316, 320–321, 324, 326; **Vol. 3**: 40, 60, 72–77, 79, 83, 85–86, 93, 100–101, 121, 126, 130, 147–148, 150, 154, 156, 159, 161, 163–164, 170, 175, 187, 285
Lin Feng **Vol. 3**: 72
Lin Jianqing **Vol. 3**: 139, 199
Lin Zuhan **Vol. 1**: 38
lingering historical issues (post Cultural Revolution) **Vol. 3**: 53, 55, 82–88, 103
linking theory and practice **Vol. 1**: 423, 436, 440, 445, 471
Lisan Road **Vol. 1**: 157
literature and art **Vol. 1**: 198, 210, 300, 549; **Vol. 2**: 240, 242, 254, 259; **Vol. 3**: 32, 304–305, 315, 393
Literature and Art, Ten Articles of **Vol. 2**: 240
Literature and Art, Eight Articles of **Vol. 2**: 240, 254
Liu Binyan **Vol. 3**: 316, 318
Liu Bocheng **Vol. 1**: 347, 351; **Vol. 2**: 249; **Vol. 3**: 288
Liu Changsheng **Vol. 1**: 257
Liu Demin **Vol. 3**: 299
Liu Guoguang **Vol. 3**: 195
Liu Jingfan **Vol. 3**: 100
Liu Lantao **Vol. 3**: 72
Liu Renjing **Vol. 1**: 17, 19, 21
Liu Shaoqi **Vol. 1**: 34, 102, 249, 360, 367, 369, 381, 402, 410, 412, 425, 438, 460, 471, 475,

484, 489–490, 493, 496, 510–512, 522; **Vol. 2**: 33–34, 36, 42–44, 46–48, 50, 59, 64, 67–69, 72–74, 76, 78, 82–83, 85–86, 89, 91, 99–100, 109, 116–117, 129, 142, 147, 151, 153, 158–159, 165, 178, 188, 193–194, 212, 216, 219, 222, 233, 243, 247–248, 254, 257, 295, 299–300; **Vol. 3**: 15, 66, 77–78, 81
Liu Shaoqi Memorial Conference **Vol. 3**: 78
Liu Wenhui **Vol. 1**: 234
Liu Xiang **Vol. 1**: 234
Liu Xiao **Vol. 1**: 257, 259
Liu Xinwu **Vol. 3**: 30
Liu Zhidan **Vol. 3**: 66, 100–101
local nationalism **Vol. 2**: 149, 157; **Vol. 3**: 121
local religious organizations **Vol. 2**: 149; **Vol. 3**: 126
localization of Marxism **Vol. 1**: 481, 484; **Vol. 2**: 3–5, 8, 10–11, 13, 16–17, 20–25, 27–28, 41, 54, 57, 89–90, 95, 120, 125–126, 132–134, 145–146, 158, 163–164, 168, 170–171, 173–174, 182, 186, 191–192, 197, 200, 203, 206–208, 220–223, 225–227, 230–232, 234, 238, 245, 252–254, 258, 260–261, 299, 310–313, 315, 319, 321, 328–330, 332, 335–339; **Vol. 3**: 3, 6–7, 169, 335, 341, 376, 395, 417, 443, 461, 525, 527, 546, 550
localized Marxism **Vol. 1**: 444; **Vol. 2**: 170
Lominadze, Vissarion **Vol. 1**: 43, 56–58
Long March **Vol. 1**: 159–160, 286, 311, 341, 504; **Vol. 3**: 37, 104, 140, 154, 513
Long Yun **Vol. 1**: 234
Longhai Line **Vol. 1**: 352
Lu Dingyi **Vol. 1**: 483; **Vol. 2**: 193; **Vol. 3**: 72, 81
Lu Ping **Vol. 3**: 78–79
Luanchuan **Vol. 1**: 323
Lukács, György **Vol. 2**: 18
Luo Ronghuan **Vol. 3**: 105
Luo Ruiqing **Vol. 2**: 326; **Vol. 3**: 42, 76, 81
Luo Yinong **Vol. 1**: 276
Luo Yunguang **Vol. 3**: 299
Luo Zhanglong **Vol. 1**: 17
Luojing Mountains (Luojing Mountain Rage) **Vol. 1**: 169, 171
Lushan Conference **Vol. 2**: 175, 186, 191, 208, 216–217, 219–222, 226–227, 229–231, 255; **Vol. 3**: 91, 164
Lushan Preparatory Conference **Vol. 2**: 200
Lutai **Vol. 1**: 354
Luxemburg, Rosa **Vol. 2**: 18
Luyu District **Vol. 1**: 351

M

Ma Bufang **Vol. 1**: 356
Ma Guorui **Vol. 3**: 189
Ma Hong **Vol. 3**: 28
Ma Hongkui **Vol. 1**: 356
Ma Mingfang **Vol. 3**: 15
Ma Mingshan **Vol. 3**: 299
Ma Wanqi **Vol. 3**: 237
Ma Xulun **Vol. 1**: 264
Macao **Vol. 3**: 132, 134, 182, 231–234, 237, 416–417, 420
MacLehose, Barry **Vol. 3**: 234
macro-control (of the economy) **Vol. 3**: 302, 347, 349–351, 354–356, 365–366, 480, 491–492, 495–496, 505, 507, 538–539, 541
mandatory planning **Vol. 3**: 191
Malenkov, Georgy **Vol. 2**: 118
Malthusian theory **Vol. 1**: 8
Malyn, **Vol. 1**: 19
Manabendra Nath Roy **Vol. 1**: 222
Manchu **Vol. 1**: 201
Mao Zedong **Vol. 1**: 16, 19, 29–31, 33, 46, 51–53, 57, 66–79, 81–86, 89, 91–92, 95, 99, 102, 105–117, 127, 129–133, 139–141, 143, 146–147, 150, 158–161, 164, 166–176, 178–199, 203–210, 216, 228–249, 252–258, 262, 264, 266, 269–271, 273, 276–286, 288–292, 294–302, 304–308, 310–313, 315–324, 326–350, 353–356, 361–363, 365–369, 377, 379–382, 384–389, 391–401, 403–411, 416, 423–424, 426–428, 431–438, 440, 443–445, 448, 452–454, 459, 461–464, 469–470, 472, 474, 476, 478–479, 481–497, 499–501, 503–549; **Vol. 2**: 5–8, 11, 13–14, 16, 18, 20, 22–24, 27–32, 34, 37–41, 43, 47, 49, 51–53, 55, 59–65, 74–77, 79–82, 84–85, 88, 91–93, 97, 99–101, 103–105, 109–111, 114–117, 119–120, 122–123, 126–127, 130, 132, 134, 141, 143–144, 146–157, 161, 163, 166–170, 174–181,

184–191, 193–194, 196–197, 199–217, 220–222, 227, 231–235, 238, 244–245, 254, 256–259, 262, 265–267, 269–280, 282–283, 286, 291–292, 294–296, 299, 301–305, 307–308, 311, 313–319, 321–327, 329, 334, 336–339; **Vol. 3**: 10, 22–23, 33–40, 42, 58, 60, 62–63, 66, 73, 79, 93, 104, 126, 128, 132, 135–136, 140, 142–151, 154, 157, 161–170, 173, 180, 184, 204, 226–227, 234, 247–248, 252, 259, 280, 285, 315, 325, 327, 332, 337, 340, 358–360, 364–365, 385, 393, 416, 444, 472–476, 483, 500, 504, 513–514, 525–527, 533

Mao Zedong Thought **Vol. 1**: 81, 83–85, 183, 188, 279, 312–313, 363, 382, 394, 424, 459, 469–470, 479, 481–495, 497, 499, 501, 503, 505, 507, 509, 511, 513, 515, 517, 519, 521, 523, 525, 527, 529, 531, 533, 535, 537, 539, 541, 543, 545, 547, 549; **Vol. 2**: 13, 22, 82, 88, 143, 161, 170, 262, 272–273, 278, 282–283, 286, 303, 307, 313, 315–319, 321–324, 326–327, 329, 336–338; **Vol. 3**: 33–37, 39–40, 42, 58, 60, 62–63, 126, 128, 140, 142–145, 147, 149–151, 154, 157, 161–169, 173, 180, 184, 280, 325, 337, 340, 359–360, 365, 385, 393, 472–476, 483, 500, 504, 514, 525–527, 533

Maoism/Maoist **Vol. 1**: 483, 492; **Vol. 2**: 264, 303

Maoming City **Vol. 3**: 468

Mari Incident **Vol. 1**: 166

Marin (Jakob Rudnick, Comintern leader) **Vol. 1**: 215, 224

market economy **Vol. 1**: 54, 507; **Vol. 2**: 4, 13, 15, 23, 152, 196, 222, 225–226, 291; **Vol. 3**: 6, 195, 200, 328–329, 344–354, 357, 362, 366, 371, 379–382, 385–386, 391, 393, 404–405, 410, 432, 436, 444–447, 454, 461, 467, 480, 488–489, 492–497, 507, 513–514, 525, 540, 543, 545, 547

market regulation **Vol. 2**: 14, 288; **Vol. 3**: 191–197, 199, 344–348, 350, 365, 488

Marx, Karl **Vol. 1**: 7–8, 97, 163, 188, 224, 357, 364, 374–376, 381, 384, 392, 394–397, 429–431, 434, 443, 445, 447, 456, 458, 493; **Vol. 2**: 12, 19, 53, 90, 113, 119, 125, 127, 135–137, 144, 164, 209–212, 215, 266, 280, 299; **Vol. 3**: 39, 332

Marxism **Vol. 1**: 3, 5–19, 21, 23, 27, 29, 37, 63, 65, 67–71, 77, 79, 81, 92, 102, 134, 141, 149–151, 163–164, 302, 308, 311, 358–359, 367, 374–375, 381, 385, 389–393, 405–407, 420, 431, 433–435, 437, 440–442, 444, 446, 448, 451, 456–457, 464, 473, 481–486, 488–491, 496, 502, 509, 535, 541, 546, 550; **Vol. 2**: 3–28, 30, 39, 41, 47, 50, 54, 56–57, 66, 73, 77, 82, 87–90, 94–95, 104, 113, 120, 125–126, 130–134, 136, 139–140, 142–146, 148, 156–158, 163–164, 168, 170–171, 173–174, 177, 182, 186–188, 191–192, 195, 197, 200, 202–204, 206–210, 215–216, 219–227, 230–232, 234, 238, 245, 252–254, 258, 260–262, 264–268, 271–274, 276–278, 282, 284, 290–291, 294, 298–306, 309–316, 319, 321–325, 327–330, 332, 335–339 **Vol. 3**: 3, 6–7, 28, 36–37, 39, 41, 63, 110, 169, 181, 185, 191–192, 202, 233, 243, 250–251, 315–317, 329, 332–335, 338, 340–341, 346, 357, 359–360, 368, 376, 388–389, 395, 397, 403, 417, 443, 461, 468, 475–477, 487, 495, 497, 504–505, 514, 525, 527, 530, 535, 546, 549–550

Marxism with Chinese characteristics **Vol. 1**: 6, 481; **Vol. 3**: 334

Marxism-Leninism (*see also* Marxist-Leninist Thought) **Vol. 1**: 26, 63, 65, 67–68, 79, 82–84, 89, 99, 106, 116, 128, 130, 144, 150, 164, 188, 218, 276, 311–313, 357, 359–360, 363, 371, 373, 376, 379–384, 387, 392, 405–406, 424–425, 439, 441, 459, 468–470, 479, 482–486, 490–492, 502, 517; **Vol. 2**: 8, 14, 21, 28, 54, 82–83, 128, 143–144, 162, 210, 233, 244, 283, 286, 322–324, 326–327, 329–330, 336–337; **Vol. 3**: 33–35, 37, 39–40, 58, 60, 62, 126, 128, 140, 143, 145–147, 149–151, 154, 157, 169, 184, 280, 325, 340, 359–360, 365, 385, 393, 472–474, 476, 500, 504, 514, 526–527, 533

Marxist Economic Theory **Vol. 1**: 7, 9; **Vol. 3**: 20, 488, 493

Marxist epistemology **Vol. 1**: 409, 444, 463; **Vol. 3**: 41, 137, 452

Marxist line **Vol. 2**: 321; **Vol. 3**: 241

Marxist line of thought **Vol. 2**: 321

Marxist-Leninist Thought (*see also* Marxism-Leninism) **Vol. 1**: 24, 65; **Vol. 2**: 262, 265, 272, 277–279, 281, 298; **Vol. 3**: 483, 504

Marxist Research Society of Peking University **Vol. 1**: 17

Marxist Studies **Vol. 1**: 7, 20

INDEX 585

Masayoshi Ōhira **Vol. 3**: 210, 260
mass historical view **Vol. 1**: 41, 456–458
mass line **Vol. 1**: 41, 326, 366, 380, 409, 459–461, 463, 470–471, 474–475, 488; **Vol. 2**: 161, 219, 243, 246, 319; **Vol. 3**: 16, 72, 155, 163, 169, 177, 296, 452, 457–458
mass movement **Vol. 1**: 39, 41–42, 220, 228, 231, 259, 285; **Vol. 2**: 190, 193, 299; **Vol. 3**: 12, 50, 52, 60, 93
masses (peasant masses) **Vol. 1**: 9, 13–15, 24, 33, 35, 37–38, 42–44, 48, 52–53, 58–59, 73, 75, 85–86, 95, 108–109, 124, 130–131, 133, 143, 150, 156, 168, 171, 173–177, 179–181, 183–185, 187, 190–194, 198, 200–201, 207, 209–212, 218, 226, 237, 241–242, 247, 249, 251–252, 254–256, 258–261, 267, 270, 277–278, 284–287, 293, 300–307, 310–312, 315, 317, 320–321, 326, 328–329, 332–335, 337–338, 358, 363, 366–367, 372, 374, 376–377, 380, 384, 387, 389, 393, 396, 402, 404–409, 412–413, 415, 417, 419–420, 424, 426–428, 430, 432, 435–436, 439, 444, 449–450, 456–465, 469–475, 477–480, 484, 487, 502, 506, 518, 548–549; **Vol. 2**: 9, 65, 67, 78, 80, 84, 104, 124, 129, 159–163, 175–176, 179, 181, 188, 190–192, 206, 218–219, 224, 234–236, 241, 244–245, 249, 252, 261, 269, 276, 286, 292, 295, 297–298, 301, 303, 305–306, 309, 311–312, 314, 316–318, 323, 327, 339; **Vol. 3**: 10, 12–13, 15, 19, 38, 53–54, 58, 69, 72–75, 77, 81, 83, 85, 102, 106, 109, 113–114, 121–122, 126, 142–143, 146–147, 150, 157–158, 161, 177, 184–185, 202, 252–253, 257, 271–272, 281–282, 284–285, 291, 308–309, 323, 338–339, 362, 367, 377–378, 380, 382, 386, 388, 393, 418, 445, 447, 451, 453, 456–459, 471, 476, 531, 547
material stimulus **Vol. 2**: 31 **Vol. 3**: 183
May Day **Vol. 1**: 16
May 7 Instructions **Vol. 2**: 269–272
May 16 Notice **Vol. 2**: 270
May Instructions **Vol. 1**: 223
May 4th Movement (May Fourth Movement) **Vol. 1**: 5, 7, 12, 14, 19, 36, 72, 81, 110, 114–116, 139, 259, 267, 363, 376, 508, 541–542, 546–547; **Vol. 3**: 31
May 19th Movement **Vol. 1**: 108

May 30th Movement **Vol. 1**: 29–34, 36, 274
May 4th Instructions **Vol. 1**: 250–251, 254
Mazu **Vol. 3**: 228
McNamara, Robert **Vol. 3**: 205
means of production **Vol. 1**: 6, 12, 162; **Vol. 2**: 6, 65, 112, 115, 118–119, 122, 124–128, 133, 135–136, 138, 141, 147, 165, 181, 185, 196, 216, 218, 223, 281; **Vol. 3**: 149, 193–195, 250, 355, 365
Meeting of Theoretical Work **Vol. 1**: 215, 265; **Vol. 3**: 137–139, 141
Meng Zi **Vol. 1**: 305
Mengcheng **Vol. 1**: 354
Mensheviks **Vol. 1**: 398; **Vol. 2**: 54
militant communism **Vol. 2**: 268, 271
Military and Civilian Congress of the Jinchaji Border Region **Vol. 1**: 211
Military Commission Symposium **Vol. 2**: 335
Military Committee **Vol. 1**: 172
Military Dialectics **Vol. 1**: 288
military drills (Taiwan) **Vol. 3**: 418
Military Facilities Protection Law **Vol. 3**: 436
Military Movement Resolution **Vol. 1**: 275
military reform **Vol. 3**: 429, 431, 438–439, 516
Military Region **Vol. 1**: 503 **Vol. 3**: 43, 50, 73, 76–77
military revolution with Chinese characteristics **Vol. 3**: 429
Military Service Law **Vol. 3**: 436
Min Xing **Vol. 1**: 6
Ming Pao Daily **Vol. 3**: 233
Ministry of Central Organizations **Vol. 3**: 97, 99
Ministry of Civil Affairs **Vol. 3**: 89–90, 103, 378
Ministry of Communications Vol 3: 539–540
Ministry of Construction Vol 3: 539–540
Ministry of Culture **Vol. 3**: 39, 82, 312
Ministry of Culture (Japan) **Vol. 3**: 212
Ministry of Economy and Trade **Vol. 3**: 322
Ministry of Education **Vol. 2**: 240; **Vol. 3**: 18–19, 67, 312, 455
Ministry of Environmental Protection **Vol. 3**: 540
Ministry of Finance **Vol. 3**: 455, 538–539
Ministry of Foreign Affairs **Vol. 3**: 217
Ministry of Health **Vol. 3**: 312, 540

Ministry of Housing and Urban-Rural Construction **Vol. 3**: 540
Ministry of Human Resources and Social Security **Vol. 3**: 540
Ministry of Information Industry **Vol. 3**: 539
Ministry of Land and Resources **Vol. 3**: 455
Ministry of National Defense **Vol. 3**: 91
Ministry of Organizations and Personnel of the Central Committee **Vol. 3**: 279
Ministry of Personnel **Vol. 3**: 277, 279, 540
Ministry of Propaganda **Vol. 2**: 104, 156, 240; **Vol. 3**: 37–38, 312, 384, 471
Ministry of Public Security **Vol. 2**: 104, 215; **Vol. 3**: 67, 89–90, 117, 312
Ministry of Publicity **Vol. 3**: 138, 312
Ministry of Railways **Vol. 3**: 87, 298–299, 539
Ministry of the Machinery Industry **Vol. 3**: 47
Ministry of Transportation **Vol. 3**: 539
minority ethnic groups **Vol. 2**: 157; **Vol. 3**: 121
moderately well-off society (moderately prosperous society) **Vol. 3**: 4, 260, 263, 266, 347, 479–488, 491, 495, 497, 501, 506–507, 523–524, 527–531, 533–534, 542, 545, 551
modern enterprise system **Vol. 1**: 24; **Vol. 3**: 351–353, 404–406, 410–412, 451, 494
modernization **Vol. 1**: 35–137, 463, 538; **Vol. 2**: 12, 15–17, 19–20, 23, 71, 76, 113, 130, 139–140, 181–182, 197, 210, 213, 216–217, 220–221, 225, 227, 253, 260–263, 267–268, 271–272, 284, 298, 302, 316, 325, 329–330, 332, 336–338; **Vol. 3**: 3–5, 7, 46–47, 49–52, 55, 57–63, 118, 130, 133, 136–137, 148–149, 151, 171–175, 177, 179–182, 185–186, 190, 192, 202, 205, 207, 210, 223, 225, 239–240, 243–245, 251, 254–260, 262–263, 266–268, 270, 279–280, 286–287, 290, 299, 303, 305, 307, 309–312, 314–315, 318–319, 322, 324, 326, 333–334, 336–337, 339–341, 343, 345, 348, 350, 357–360, 362–364, 366, 369, 373, 383–384, 387, 390, 392, 397–401, 403, 423, 434, 436–437, 441, 443, 446, 473, 475–476, 479, 482–488, 494, 498–500, 502, 505, 508–509, 516, 523–526, 531, 535–536, 543–544, 547, 549–550
modernization of Marxism **Vol. 2**: 12, 15–17, 19–20, 23, 113, 139–140, 182, 210, 216, 220–221, 227, 253, 267–268, 316, 325, 332, 338

Molotov, Vyacheslav **Vol. 2**: 118
Mongolia **Vol. 1**: 61, 202; **Vol. 3**: 15, 116, 122, 125, 201, 218–220, 222, 277, 455
Montargis Conference **Vol. 1**: 17
Mopping-Up Operation **Vol. 1**: 69
Moral Education **Vol. 3**: 383, 466
Moscow Conference **Vol. 2**: 189
multi-ethnic **Vol. 2**: 54–55; **Vol. 3**: 97, 172
multi-party **Vol. 1**: 209, 262, 264–265, 268; **Vol. 2**: 7, 52–54, 79, 152–153; **Vol. 3**: 272, 316, 365, 367, 372–373, 375–376, 510
Mutual Aid Organizations **Vol. 1**: 206; **Vol. 2**: 73, 76
Mutual Assistance Groups **Vol. 2**: 123
My View of Marxism (Li Dazhao article) **Vol. 1**: 7

N

Nakasone Yasuhiro **Vol. 3**: 211, 263
Nanchang **Vol. 1**: 57, 61, 168, 176
Nanchang Uprising **Vol. 1**: 57, 168
Nanjing **Vol. 1**: 18, 34, 61, 93, 156, 231, 235, 249, 256, 260, 354–355; **Vol. 3**: 35, 127, 234, 414, 416
Nanjing Peace Talks **Vol. 1**: 256
Nanjing Treaty **Vol. 3**: 234, 416
Nanning Conference **Vol. 2**: 185
National Army **Vol. 1**: 40, 214–215
national bourgeoisie **Vol. 1**: 27, 31–32, 37, 51–52, 56, 70, 74, 80, 87, 106, 114–115, 127, 138, 143, 145, 213, 216–218, 233–234, 237–238, 240, 242, 244, 253, 258, 261–263, 270–271, 283, 310, 468, 495, 517–519, 523, 540; **Vol. 2**: 4, 26–27, 41–44, 46, 49–50, 59–61, 63–64, 69, 80, 92–93, 103–105, 116, 126–129, 170, 202
national capitalism **Vol. 1**: 98, 138–139, 377, 534
National Civil Service Bureau **Vol. 3**: 540
National Civilization and Politeness Month **Vol. 3**: 312
national conditions **Vol. 1**: 25, 27–28, 66, 81, 91, 94, 130, 133, 140, 150, 161, 163–164, 175, 179–180, 186, 224, 298, 361, 376, 379, 392–393, 432, 508, 519–520; **Vol. 2**: 6–7, 11, 13, 19, 27, 39–40, 46–47, 54, 59, 66, 69, 87, 89, 93, 116, 129–130, 139–140, 144–146, 154, 166, 173, 187, 204, 206–207, 213, 234, 238, 246, 260, 264,

266–267, 296; **Vol. 3**: 170–171, 174, 241, 243, 246–248, 252, 257, 259, 266, 336, 351, 361, 369, 371, 397–399, 421, 488, 525–527, 544
National Conference on Education **Vol. 3**: 37
National Conference on Scientific and Technological Work **Vol. 3**: 264
National Congress of Workers, Peasants, and Soldiers **Vol. 1**: 191, 255; **Vol. 3**: 112
National Cultural System Reform Work Conference **Vol. 3**: 511
National Defense Law **Vol. 3**: 436
National Development and Reform Commission **Vol. 3**: 538–539
National Economic Plan **Vol. 3**: 61
National Energy Leading Group **Vol. 3**: 539
National Ethnic Work Conference **Vol. 2**: 250
National Ethnic Work Plan **Vol. 2**: 158
National Federation of Literature and Arts **Vol. 2**: 240
National Federation of Trade Unions **Vol. 3**: 311, 450
National General Assembly **Vol. 1**: 19
national independence **Vol. 1**: 173, 466, 470
National People's Congress **Vol. 1**: 268, 515; **Vol. 2**: 26, 48, 53, 153, 249, 251, 260, 277, 302; **Vol. 3**: 24, 56–57, 118–119, 123, 198, 217, 224, 226, 228, 230–232, 236, 254, 261–262, 269, 271, 274–275, 287, 299, 319–320, 349–350, 373, 376–377, 380–381, 384, 399, 402, 413, 436, 439, 475, 482, 500, 503, 509, 517, 536, 551
National Planning Conference **Vol. 2**: 333–334; **Vol. 3**: 48
national religious groups **Vol. 3**: 126
national reunification **Vol. 3**: 413, 438
National Revolutionary Groups of the Far East **Vol. 1**: 92
National Riot Plan **Vol. 1**: 61
national salvation **Vol. 1**: 13, 233, 264, 282
National Salvation Times **Vol. 1**: 233
National Science and Technology Commission **Vol. 2**: 240; **Vol. 3**: 42
National Science Congress **Vol. 2**: 332; **Vol. 3**: 20, 45, 110
National Security Bureau **Vol. 3**: 104
National Socialist Party **Vol. 1**: 69

National Statistical Bureau **Vol. 3**: 278
National Symposium on Ethnic Work **Vol. 2**: 250
National United Front Conference **Vol. 2**: 59, 250
National United Front Work Conference **Vol. 2**: 79, 250; **Vol. 3**: 129–131, 133, 375
national unity **Vol. 2**: 157, 250; **Vol. 3**: 119–122, 124, 126, 336, 401
National University of Defense Science and Technology **Vol. 3**: 434
National Workers, Peasants, and Soldiers Congress **Vol. 1**: 105, 191, 255; **Vol. 3**: 112
Nationalism, Democracy, the People's Livelihood **Vol. 1**: 264, 518
Nationalist Party (*see also* Kuomintang) **Vol. 1**: 41, 93, 109, 266
nationalities (*see also* ethnic groups) **Vol. 1**: 523; **Vol. 2**: 26, 157, 249; **Vol. 3**: 314
nationalization of industry **Vol. 2**: 72, 85
nationalization of Marxism **Vol. 2**: 225
Naval Engineering University **Vol. 3**: 434
Navy **Vol. 3**: 156–157, 226
new capitalism **Vol. 2**: 45, 335; **Vol. 3**: 394, 508
New China **Vol. 1**: 72–73, 76, 79, 81, 85–86, 132, 210, 263, 265, 306, 369, 424, 439, 466–467, 494, 498, 510–511, 517; **Vol. 2**: 4, 11–12, 16, 20, 22, 24, 26, 32, 39, 41, 44–45, 48, 52–53, 55–56, 58–59, 61–63, 65–66, 70, 80, 82–83, 87–95, 97–101, 103, 108–111, 114–116, 119, 122, 126, 129, 132, 140, 146, 148, 155–156, 165, 180, 187, 203, 226, 231, 238, 253, 261, 284–285, 293, 296, 298, 308, 312, 315, 320, 325, 333, 335, 337; **Vol. 3**: 6, 15–16, 18, 47, 60, 80, 84, 92, 96, 98, 102–103, 109, 114–115, 119, 126, 128, 130, 141, 145–146, 148, 155, 158–162, 164–168, 170–171, 174, 203, 208, 225, 234, 240, 248, 252, 256, 270, 274, 316, 358, 363, 373, 387, 394, 404, 416, 427, 484, 498, 508, 512–513, 530, 545
New Citizen Study Society **Vol. 1**: 17; **Vol. 2**: 45, 335; **Vol. 3**: 394, 508
New Constitutional Referendum **Vol. 2**: 45, 335; **Vol. 3**: 394, 508, 521
New Cultural Movement **Vol. 1**: 4–5, 8, 10, 541, 546, 548

New Democracy **Vol. 1**: 65, 67, 69, 71, 73, 75–79, 81, 83, 85, 87, 89, 99, 106–108, 110, 112, 117, 131, 146, 199, 209, 268, 467–468, 482, 487, 491, 509, 513, 515, 520, 522–523, 525, 528, 531, 534, 536–537, 539, 542–544, 546, 548; **Vol. 2**: 4, 13, 25, 27–34, 37, 40–42, 47, 49, 51–52, 56–59, 62–63, 65, 69–70, 72, 76–78, 81–83, 86–91, 95, 98–99, 104–105, 111–112, 114, 116–117, 119, 121, 141, 208–209, 274; **Vol. 3**: 252, 364

New Democracy National Founding Program **Vol. 2**: 95

New Democracy Program **Vol. 2**: 4, 57, 63, 69, 81, 87, 117

New Democratic Outline for the Founding of the People's Republic **Vol. 1**: 527, 535; **Vol. 2**: 4

New Democratic Revolution **Vol. 1**: 23, 25, 27, 29, 31, 33, 35, 37, 39, 41, 43, 45, 47, 49, 51, 53, 55, 57, 59, 61, 63, 71–73, 75, 78, 84–85, 89, 91, 93, 95, 97, 99, 101, 103, 105, 107–111, 113, 115–119, 121, 123, 125–127, 129–133, 135, 137–141, 143–147, 188, 199, 245–247, 263, 266, 268, 301, 370, 372, 421–422, 448, 460, 467–470, 487, 494, 508, 511–512, 521, 523, 527–529, 531, 534–536, 543, 548; **Vol. 2**: 3–4, 11, 27–29, 38–39, 41, 48, 53, 56, 63, 69, 72, 87, 89, 94, 98–99, 110, 114, 117, 126, 129, 143–144; **Vol. 3**: 180, 247, 252, 358

New Democratic Revolutionary Theory **Vol. 1**: 130, 507, 512, 527, 535; **Vol. 2**: 25, 32

New Democratic Socialization Theory **Vol. 1**: 527, 535; **Vol. 2**: 25

New Democratic Sociology **Vol. 1**: 527, 535; **Vol. 2**: 27, 41

New Democratic Theory **Vol. 1**: 73, 81–82, 85, 89, 107, 109, 130, 198, 495, 507, 523, 527–528, 535; **Vol. 2**: 4, 70, 93, 105, 117

new deployment of rural reform **Vol. 3**: 536

New Fourth Army **Vol. 1**: 69, 202, 241, 285–286, 311, 336–337; **Vol. 3**: 106–107

New Great Project **Vol. 3**: 443–444, 447–448, 474, 476, 484

New Historical Period **Vol. 3**: 18, 120, 130–131, 170, 182, 191, 254, 311, 457, 525

New Long March **Vol. 3**: 37, 140, 154

New Right (KMT) **Vol. 1**: 41, 93, 216, 221, 226

New Territories (Hong Kong) **Vol. 3**: 234, 416

New Youth (Youth Magazine) **Vol. 1**: 4, 7–8, 12, 16

Ni Zhengyu **Vol. 3**: 224

Ni Zhifu **Vol. 3**: 109

Nie Rongzhen **Vol. 2**: 156, 240, 300; **Vol. 3**: 33, 73, 76, 179, 188–189, 288

Nie Yuanzi **Vol. 2**: 300; **Vol. 3**: 78

Nikolsky, Vladimir **Vol. 1**: 19

Ningdu Uprising **Vol. 3**: 104

Ningxia Province **Vol. 1**: 76, 160, 199, 201, 203–204, 206–209, 211, 530; **Vol. 2**: 30, 323; **Vol. 3**: 122, 125, 455

Ningxiang County **Vol. 2**: 233

Ninth Five-Year Plan **Vol. 3**: 380, 384, 399, 401, 481

Ninth National Congress of the Communist Party of China **Vol. 3**: 179, 380

non-Party democrats **Vol. 2**: 81, 179, 249 **Vol. 3**: 133

non-public enterprises **Vol. 3**: 452

Nong'an County Committee **Vol. 3**: 115

North China Bureau **Vol. 2**: 71–72, 74, 76

North China Finance and Economic Commission **Vol. 2**: 37

North China University **Vol. 1**: 492

North China Territorial Doctrine **Vol. 3**: 76–77

North Korean Denuclearization Target Document **Vol. 3**: 519

Northeast Army **Vol. 1**: 234

Northeast Group **Vol. 3**: 53

Northeast Military Work Committee **Vol. 1**: 234

Northern Expedition **Vol. 1**: 24, 37–38, 40, 110, 150, 171, 221, 226–227, 267, 273, 275, 277, 279, 283–284, 371, 467; **Vol. 3**: 227

Northern War **Vol. 3**: 71

Northern Warlords (*see also* Beiyang Warlords) **Vol. 1**: 137, 150, 226, 467

Northwest Bureau **Vol. 1**: 310; **Vol. 3**: 101–102

Northwest Field Army **Vol. 1**: 356, 532

Northwest United University **Vol. 3**: 97

Northwestern High-level Conference **Vol. 1**:

205
Nuclear Power Management of the National Defense Science, Technology, and Industry Commission **Vol. 2**: 304; **Vol. 3**: 176, 211, 539
Nyers, Rezső **Vol. 3**: 197

O

October Revolution **Vol. 1**: 6–7, 28, 30, 60, 89, 92, 108, 110–113, 150, 154, 162, 164–165, 182, 188, 227, 274, 276, 363, 370, 430, 432, 458, 542; **Vol. 2**: 14, 121, 126, 136, 142, 278; **Vol. 3**: 146
Office of Institutional Reform **Vol. 3**: 277
old cadres **Vol. 3**: 187, 286, 290
Ombudsman **Vol. 3**: 407
On Contradiction **Vol. 1**: 367, 437; **Vol. 2**: 80, 188; **Vol. 3**: 5, 206, 226, 282, 514
"On Investigation" (*see also* "Opposing Doctrines") **Vol. 2**: 233
On New Democracy **Vol. 1**: 491; **Vol. 2**: 27–30, 37, 45, 49, 86, 141
On Practice **Vol. 1**: 367, 437, 443; **Vol. 2**: 136, 174, 211, 233, 313; **Vol. 3**: 332
On Ten Relations **Vol. 2**: 7, 148, 150, 210
On the Correct Handling of Contradictions Among the People **Vol. 1**: 178; **Vol. 2**: 7, 168
On the Party **Vol. 1**: 117, 178, 249, 391, 402; **Vol. 2**: 144, 161, 180, 221, 295; **Vol. 3**: 34, 52, 88
On the People's Democratic Dictatorship **Vol. 1**: 89, 178, 249; **Vol. 2**: 116, 144
"On the People's Democratic Dictatorship" (article) **Vol. 2**: 49
On the Ten Relations **Vol. 1**: 178, 249
"On the United Government" **Vol. 2**: 30, 37, 45
one center, two basic points **Vol. 1**: 349; **Vol. 3**: 227
one country, two systems **Vol. 1**: 349; **Vol. 3**: 227
Open Rural Affairs **Vol. 3**: 377
Opium War **Vol. 1**: 3, 50, 96, 110, 114, 133, 517, 540; **Vol. 3**: 234, 416
opportunism **Vol. 1**: 44, 57, 120, 122, 145, 277, 296, 311, 358, 378, 389, 391, 474; **Vol. 2**: 38, 177, 235, 256; **Vol. 3**: 92, 160
"Opposing Doctrines" ("On Investigation") **Vol. 2**: 233

"Opposing Doctrinairism" (article) **Vol. 1**: 478
Organic Law of the CPPCC **Vol. 1**: 267–268
organization **Vol. 1**: 8, 12–13, 17–20, 45, 56, 68, 78, 80, 88, 140, 142, 144, 184, 187, 190, 208, 210–211, 219–220, 222, 225–226, 228, 233, 241, 255, 258–259, 261, 265–268, 271, 282–283, 285, 290, 304, 307–308, 310, 314, 321, 324, 333, 336, 343, 359, 361, 363–370, 372, 374, 376–377, 379–383, 385, 388, 394–396, 399–400, 402–404, 409–410, 413–415, 417–419, 421–422, 424–425, 427–428, 432, 434, 438–440, 460–461, 471, 488, 495, 513, 523, 531; **Vol. 2**: 49, 78, 116, 159–160, 192–193, 195–196, 223, 288, 292, 295, 298, 302, 322, 338; **Vol. 3**: 15, 17, 71, 79, 91, 93–94, 104, 106, 109, 112, 114, 181–182, 186, 271, 280–282, 296–297, 307, 354, 357, 377, 406, 414, 424, 427–429, 433, 448, 450–452, 465, 532
Organization Newsletter **Vol. 3**: 17, 94
Organizational Communications **Vol. 3**: 90, 447
organizational construction **Vol. 1**: 364–365, 368–369, 379, 394, 403, 408, 419, 428; **Vol. 3**: 280, 447–448, 450, 452
Organizational Work Conference **Vol. 1**: 512; **Vol. 2**: 86; **Vol. 3**: 447
orthodoxy **Vol. 1**: 164; **Vol. 2**: 23, 138
Outline of Vision for 2010 **Vol. 3**: 384
overseas Chinese **Vol. 1**: 228, 258, 261, 266, 268, 516; **Vol. 2**: 53, 250; **Vol. 3**: 67, 132, 134, 182
Overseas Chinese Daily **Vol. 3**: 233
Overseas Chinese Office **Vol. 3**: 67
Overseas Economic Cooperation Fund **Vol. 3**: 210

P

Palace of Hell **Vol. 3**: 82
Pan Hannian **Vol. 3**: 80–81, 98
Pan Keming **Vol. 3**: 299
Paris Commune Uprising **Vol. 1**: 358
Paris Coordination Commission **Vol. 3**: 217
Party Charter **Vol. 1**: 8, 362, 406; **Vol. 2**: 292; **Vol. 3**: 281
Party Committee System **Vol. 1**: 403, 410–411, 503
Party constitution **Vol. 1**: 84, 382, 402, 410–411,

424, 452, 455, 460, 486, 488, 500; **Vol. 2**: 159–162, 244, 314; **Vol. 3**: 151, 177–178, 181, 184–186, 188, 190, 287, 340, 360, 453, 467, 474–475, 526

Party construction **Vol. 1**: 75, 285, 367–368, 372, 376, 432; **Vol. 3**: 451–452

Party discipline **Vol. 1**: 405–406, 411, 424; **Vol. 2**: 160; **Vol. 3**: 62, 280, 298, 320–322, 464–465

Party Group **Vol. 1**: 307; **Vol. 2**: 240; **Vol. 3**: 43, 66, 87, 99, 108, 117, 121, 299, 321

Party leadership **Vol. 1**: 43, 88, 165, 230, 243, 275, 308, 313, 368–369, 404, 408, 422, 429, 439, 466, 469, 471, 478; **Vol. 2**: 180, 276, 288, 300–301, 309; **Vol. 3**: 47, 360, 514

Party Life **Vol. 1**: 200, 365, 413, 418, 420, 427, 440, 450–451, 455, 479

Party membership **Vol. 1**: 57, 364, 419–420, 422–424, 512; **Vol. 2**: 69; **Vol. 3**: 85, 97, 105–108, 188, 287

party organization **Vol. 1**: 18–20, 68, 78, 220, 228, 258, 361–365, 368, 370, 377, 381, 385, 394–395, 400, 403, 409, 413, 421–422, 432, 438, 471; **Vol. 2**: 223, 288, 292, 298; **Vol. 3**: 79

Party spirit **Vol. 1**: 70, 380, 411, 416–417, 423, 432, 436–438, 443–444, 449, 451

party-building **Vol. 1**: 46, 284–285, 357, 359–379, 381, 383, 385, 387, 389, 391, 393–395, 397, 399–401, 403, 405, 407, 409–411, 413, 415, 417, 419, 421–423, 425, 427–429, 431, 433–435, 437, 439, 441, 443, 445, 447–451, 453, 455, 457–461, 463, 465, 467, 469, 471, 473, 475, 477, 479, 488, 491, 497, 500, 504–505; **Vol. 2**: 162–163

Party's absolute leadership of the military **Vol. 1**: 306, 311–313

Party's basic line **Vol. 1**: 404; **Vol. 3**: 4, 152, 174, 239, 243–244, 253–257, 303, 325, 328, 332, 358, 361, 363, 366, 368, 385, 398, 432, 447, 453, 458, 514, 533

Pastoral Work, Forty Articles of **Vol. 2**: 250

Patriotic Education **Vol. 3**: 383

peaceful evolution **Vol. 3**: 323, 332, 447

peaceful reunification **Vol. 3**: 225, 228–230, 232, 340, 414–415, 420, 438, 516, 520–521, 546

peasant class (*see also* peasantry) **Vol. 1**: 33, 72, 109, 113, 127, 129, 141, 143, 185, 253, 283, 288, 310, 330; **Vol. 2**: 41, 49, 80, 83

peasant movements **Vol. 1**: 50, 171

peasant party **Vol. 1**: 153, 361–362; **Vol. 2**: 67, 69–70

peasant revolution **Vol. 1**: 33, 44–45, 47, 49–50, 52, 54, 58, 62, 143, 152, 287, 331

peasant self-defense force **Vol. 1**: 153

peasantry (*see also* peasant class) **Vol. 1**: 33–34, 50, 53–54, 63, 120–123, 125, 127–129, 140–141, 143–144, 163, 168, 191, 194, 196–197, 219, 227, 241, 246, 252–253, 279–280, 282, 309, 330, 362, 371, 378, 420–421, 471, 487, 491, 501, 507–508, 512, 517, 519, 523, 526–528, 532

peasants' allied force **Vol. 1**: 164

Peking Girl's High School **Vol. 1**: 8

Peking People's Art Theatre **Vol. 3**: 32

Peking University (Beijing University) **Vol. 1**: 8, 10, 14–15, 17, 258; **Vol. 3**: 23, 78–79, 434

Peking University Civilians Lecture Group **Vol. 1**: 14

Peng Dehuai **Vol. 2**: 217, 275; **Vol. 3**: 15, 53–54, 81, 91, 93, 101–102

Peng Gongda **Vol. 1**: 57

Peng Peiyun **Vol. 3**: 78–79

Peng Shuzhi **Vol. 1**: 124–125

Peng Zemin **Vol. 1**: 264

Peng Zhen **Vol. 3**: 72, 81, 179, 188–189, 211

Peng, Gao, and Xi Anti-Party Group **Vol. 3**: 101–102

Penghu **Vol. 3**: 228

People's Bank of China **Vol. 3**: 354, 538–539

People's Commune Movement **Vol. 2**: 9, 130, 192, 195–197, 199–200, 204, 206, 211–213, 218, 221–222, 231, 239, 246, 267, 270, 273, 325

People's Congress **Vol. 1**: 190, 192, 268, 509, 515; **Vol. 2**: 7, 26, 48, 50, 53, 77–78, 141, 153, 221, 243, 246–247, 249–254, 256–257, 260, 277, 302; **Vol. 3**: 24, 56–57, 118–119, 123, 198, 217, 224, 226, 228, 230–232, 236, 254, 261–262, 269, 271–272, 274–275, 287, 299, 319–320, 349–350, 365, 367, 373, 376–377, 380–381, 384, 402, 413, 436, 439, 454, 475, 482, 500, 503, 509–510, 517, 536, 551

People's Court (provincial or municipal) **Vol. 3**: 321
People's Daily **Vol. 1**: 7; **Vol. 2**: 117, 143, 166, 179, 188–189, 272, 278–280, 296, 314, 322–323, 328; **Vol. 3**: 12–13, 17, 19, 21, 24, 26, 28, 30, 32, 35–38, 40–42, 53, 79, 137, 153, 165, 195, 217, 318, 373, 394
people's democratic dictatorship **Vol. 1**: 85, 89, 146, 261, 268, 282, 468, 510, 513, 516–521, 523; **Vol. 2**: 7, 25, 32, 41, 48–51, 79–80, 87, 92, 116, 153; **Vol. 3**: 250, 316, 318, 337, 365, 367, 440
People's Democratic United Front **Vol. 1**: 87–88, 244–245, 254, 256, 261–262, 264, 268–269, 271; **Vol. 2**: 53, 79–80, 87, 153, 170, 320
People's Liberation Army (PLA) **Vol. 1**: 86, 188, 247, 258, 261, 281, 286, 305, 309, 311, 313, 342, 494, 500, 516; **Vol. 2**: 53–54, 272, 295; **Vol. 3**: 41, 82, 137, 153, 169, 178, 225–226, 228–229, 433, 435, 517
People's Liberation War **Vol. 1**: 86, 188
People's Literature **Vol. 3**: 30
People's Republic **Vol. 1**: 88, 268, 284–285, 421, 467, 508, 517, 520, 523, 534, 539; **Vol. 2**: 4–5, 25–26, 39, 48, 51–55, 57, 63, 69, 76–77, 79, 82, 86–87, 89–90, 110–111, 117–118, 165, 183, 209, 233, 240, 304; **Vol. 3**: 4, 44, 77, 87, 97, 108, 111, 119, 122, 131, 140, 144, 158–159, 161–163, 165, 167–169, 172, 213–215, 224, 228–229, 233–237, 248, 252–253, 263, 275, 287, 310–311, 333, 335, 345, 376–378, 402, 413, 416–417, 460, 475, 498, 519, 541, 551
People's Republic of China **Vol. 1**: 88, 268, 284–285, 421, 517, 520, 523, 539; **Vol. 2**: 25–26, 39, 48, 51–53, 55, 57, 63, 77, 79, 86, 89–90, 110–111, 118, 165, 183, 233, 240, 304; **Vol. 3**: 4, 44, 77, 87, 97, 108, 111, 119, 122, 140, 144, 158–159, 162–163, 165, 169, 172, 213–215, 224, 228–229, 233–237, 248, 252–253, 263, 275, 287, 310, 345, 376–378, 402, 413, 416–417, 460, 475, 498, 519, 541, 551
People's Self-Defense Force **Vol. 1**: 333–334
personnel system **Vol. 3**: 269, 271, 277, 279, 295, 460
Petőfi Club **Vol. 2**: 259

Pingjiang **Vol. 1**: 61
Pingjin **Vol. 1**: 328, 342, 352–355
Pioneer **Vol. 1**: 13, 16; **Vol. 2**: 338
PLA (*see also* People's Liberation Army) **Vol. 1**: 86–89, 188, 248, 254, 256, 265–266, 268, 280, 285, 290, 298, 306, 315, 317–319, 324–325, 328, 350, 353, 505; **Vol. 2**: 314, 326; **Vol. 3**: 36, 42, 73, 156, 158, 176, 228, 281, 306, 429, 433–434, 436, 438–440
planned economy **Vol. 1**: 202; **Vol. 2**: 13–15, 17, 20, 36, 105–106, 108, 119, 130, 132, 151–152, 174, 186, 223–226, 287–288; **Vol. 3**: 21, 191–192, 194–196, 199–201, 328–329, 335, 344–348, 352, 357, 365, 461, 480, 540, 545
police **Vol. 1**: 260–261, 519; **Vol. 3**: 435, 464
Policies for Foreign Experts and Allies **Vol. 2**: 113; **Vol. 3**: 117
Policy of Intelligence Workers **Vol. 1**: 195
Politburo **Vol. 1**: 42, 45, 48, 51, 55–59, 79, 103–104, 154, 167, 199, 222, 229, 231–232, 240, 400, 482, 495, 501, 503, 511, 516; **Vol. 2**: 32, 51, 60, 63, 85, 105, 110, 143, 156, 166, 188, 191, 214, 240, 247, 257, 300; **Vol. 3**: 10, 12, 16, 38, 52, 54, 59, 62, 71, 73, 91, 138, 165, 168, 175–179, 189, 200, 218, 232, 245–246, 259, 268–270, 273, 286, 306, 309, 319, 323–325, 331, 380, 409, 455–456, 465, 509, 513, 515
political boundary issues **Vol. 3**: 518
political consultation **Vol. 1**: 87, 264; **Vol. 2**: 7, 52–54, 79, 152; **Vol. 3**: 272, 365, 367, 372–373, 375, 510
political line **Vol. 1**: 63–64, 285, 365, 367, 378, 403–404, 433, 470, 482; **Vol. 2**: 306; **Vol. 3**: 4, 13, 28, 53, 157–158, 285, 331, 457
political strike **Vol. 1**: 153
political struggle (*see also* struggle) **Vol. 1**: 35, 115, 122, 259–260, 263, 290; **Vol. 2**: 138, 190, 242, 281
political system reform **Vol. 3**: 244, 255, 268–270, 273, 275, 316–317, 369–372, 376, 380, 547
Political Weekly **Vol. 1**: 103
Polytechnic University **Vol. 3**: 434
populism **Vol. 1**: 55–56, 535; **Vol. 2**: 30, 39
popularization of Marxism **Vol. 3**: 7

Practical Theory **Vol. 1**: 66, 68, 183, 389–391
practice is the sole criterion for testing truth **Vol. 3**: 157
pre-Qin scholars **Vol. 3**: 31
primary stage of socialism **Vol. 2**: 133; **Vol. 3**: 152, 239, 241, 243, 245, 249–252, 254–258, 266, 268, 270, 303, 325, 335, 338, 354, 358, 360–363, 366–368, 493–494, 526, 544
Printing Industry Management Regulations **Vol. 3**: 394
private sector **Vol. 3**: 451
production **Vol. 1**: 4–6, 8, 12, 29, 44, 53, 123, 127, 131–132, 162, 174, 184, 192–193, 196–197, 203–208, 246–247, 255, 270–271, 282, 293–294, 302, 304–306, 312, 328, 335, 361, 383, 393, 457, 468, 473, 496–500, 502, 505–506, 519, 524, 526–527, 529–530, 533, 535–536; **Vol. 2**: 4, 6, 9, 15, 26, 28, 30–31, 33–35, 39–40, 42–44, 51, 57–58, 60, 62, 64–69, 72, 74–76, 84, 87–88, 91, 94, 100, 102–103, 105–108, 112–115, 118–119, 121–128, 131–133, 135–139, 141, 146–148, 150–151, 154–155, 164–165, 168–169, 181, 183, 185, 187, 189–190, 192–193, 195–197, 200–203, 205, 207, 214, 216–219, 222–223, 235–239, 243, 247–250, 253–257, 260–261, 267, 269–271, 281, 284, 286–288, 293–294, 297, 299–300, 302–304, 310, 320, 327–328, 333–334; **Vol. 3**: 3, 10, 21–22, 25–27, 48–51, 55, 61, 64, 72, 75, 142, 149, 171, 183, 192–195, 197–198, 200–201, 209, 250–251, 253, 256, 260, 262, 275, 304, 309, 325, 329, 344, 349, 352–353, 355–356, 365, 394, 406–407, 433, 435, 480, 489, 493, 498, 503, 507, 509, 511, 531–532, 542–544
program of action **Vol. 1**: 246, 543; **Vol. 2**: 48; **Vol. 3**: 244, 343
proletarian (*see also* proletariat) **Vol. 1**: 12, 17, 21, 28, 30, 35, 37, 39, 53, 63, 75, 100, 102, 104, 107–108, 110–114, 116–118, 123, 126–128, 140–142, 149, 153–154, 161, 163–164, 178, 185–186, 188, 194, 213, 217–220, 225, 229, 271, 275–277, 284–285, 288, 299, 301, 306–310, 321, 326, 331, 357–364, 370, 372, 374–378, 380–382, 384–385, 388, 392, 394, 396–399, 406, 421–423, 426, 429, 434, 437, 440, 442–445, 447, 457–458, 461, 472, 474, 479, 487, 507–508, 514, 516, 520, 526, 541–542, 544–545; **Vol. 2**: 18, 20, 27, 33–34, 36, 50–51, 118, 135–136, 139, 143, 152, 166, 208, 262, 274–276, 278–279, 282, 295, 301–302, 315; **Vol. 3**: 77–78, 101, 119, 137, 146, 160–161, 169, 240, 242, 245–246, 316
proletarian dictatorship **Vol. 1**: 12, 363, 514; **Vol. 2**: 34, 50–51, 118, 136, 143, 152, 166; **Vol. 3**: 137, 146
proletarian organization **Vol. 1**: 308, 399
proletariat (*see also* proletarian) **Vol. 1**: 4, 13, 19–20, 26–30, 32, 34–35, 50, 53–54, 57, 60, 63, 72–78, 89, 92, 94, 100–106, 108–118, 122–125, 127–131, 138–146, 149–150, 152, 154, 162–163, 171, 173, 175–176, 180, 190–191, 194, 196–197, 199, 213–215, 217–218, 220–222, 224–225, 227, 230–231, 241, 243, 252, 255, 263, 267, 269, 276–279, 282–284, 286–287, 298, 301, 308–310, 330–331, 357–359, 362, 364–365, 371–372, 374–378, 381, 383, 394, 397, 405, 417, 419–422, 425, 429–431, 433–435, 438, 443–444, 447, 449, 457–458, 466–468, 470–471, 478–479, 487, 490, 497, 504, 507, 509, 513, 515–517, 519–524, 530–531, 534–536, 538, 541–544, 547; **Vol. 2**: 25, 27–28, 31–37, 43–47, 49–51, 53–54, 91–92, 103, 125–126, 135–136, 184–185, 219, 257, 262, 272–273, 275, 277–283, 288, 290, 294–296, 299–300, 306–307, 315, 318–319, 335; **Vol. 3**: 21, 23, 49, 51, 58, 140–142, 145, 147, 149–150, 161, 252, 283, 329
propaganda **Vol. 1**: 7–8, 25, 36, 40, 48, 69, 75, 128, 144, 163, 191, 210–211, 220, 222, 248, 286, 319, 376, 404, 464, 492, 537, 543–544; **Vol. 2**: 6, 56, 72, 82, 85, 104, 110, 115, 117, 135, 156–157, 176–177, 179, 184, 240, 289, 315, 317, 323; **Vol. 3**: 37–39, 55, 63, 68, 82, 89–90, 121–122, 138, 140–142, 144, 154, 158, 312, 316, 325, 373, 383–384, 393, 470–471
Propaganda Outline **Vol. 2**: 6, 110, 115
Protection of Taiwanese Compatriots' Investment **Vol. 3**: 413
Protection of the Rights of Party Members **Vol. 3**: 453, 466
Proudhon, Pierre-Joseph **Vol. 1**: 6

Provincial Civil Affairs Department **Vol. 3**: 108
Provincial Military Control Council **Vol. 3**: 96
Provincial People's Congress **Vol. 1**: 515
Provincial Reform Commission **Vol. 3**: 96
Provincial Reform Committee **Vol. 3**: 72–73
public ownership **Vol. 2**: 6, 8, 14, 103, 106, 108, 114, 118, 120, 124, 130, 141, 165, 193, 195–196, 200–202, 205, 213–214, 219, 223, 237, 297–298; **Vol. 3**: 21, 146, 150, 193–195, 200–202, 249–251, 279, 329, 335, 337, 345, 349–350, 352, 365–366, 410, 473, 489, 491, 493–494, 496, 507, 511
Public Welfare Culture Reform **Vol. 3**: 511
Publicity (Propaganda) Committee **Vol. 1**: 20, 131
Publishing Management Regulations **Vol. 3**: 394
Pudong **Vol. 3**: 4, 354
Pudong District **Vol. 3**: 4

Q
Qi Qi **Vol. 3**: 192
Qian Qichen **Vol. 3**: 220
Qian Ying **Vol. 1**: 257; **Vol. 3**: 72
Qiao Shi **Vol. 3**: 189, 245
Qiliying **Vol. 2**: 204
Qin Jiwei **Vol. 3**: 189, 245
Qing Dynasty (Qing court) **Vol. 1**: 133, 135, 267, 514
Qingdao **Vol. 1**: 34; **Vol. 3**: 277, 410
Qinghai Province **Vol. 3**: 125, 502
Qingming Festival (see Tomb-Sweeping Day)
Qinhuangdao Port **Vol. 3**: 210
Qionglai County **Vol. 3**: 277
Qu Qiubai **Vol. 1**: 29–30, 34, 36, 43, 52–53, 55–56, 58, 102, 105, 126–127, 139, 167, 274; **Vol. 3**: 81
Quanzhou City **Vol. 3**: 320

R
radicalism **Vol. 2**: 262, 264
Radio and Television Management Regulations **Vol. 3**: 394
re-education **Vol. 3**: 121–122
re-employment of laid-off workers **Vol. 3**: 408

reactionary **Vol. 1**: 24, 26, 37, 41, 44, 56, 60, 62, 77, 85–89, 127, 135–136, 138, 149, 163, 172, 181, 197, 216, 242, 245–250, 258, 260, 265, 268–270, 272, 274, 276, 280–282, 288, 291–293, 301, 312, 320–321, 329, 339, 350, 355, 401, 420, 467, 495, 500, 505, 519–520, 528, 533, 535, 540–541; **Vol. 2**: 49, 104, 257, 264, 275, 283, 286, 289–291, 295–297; Vol 3: 22, 151, 226, 228, 304
Reagan, Ronald **Vol. 3**: 215–216
rectification **Vol. 1**: 54, 83–84, 210, 282, 366–370, 380, 385–389, 391, 394, 402, 410, 421, 423, 425, 427–428, 433–434, 437–440, 448, 484–486, 492, 512; **Vol. 2**: 167, 175–182, 184–185, 188–189, 192, 199, 203, 207–209, 211, 213, 215, 220–221, 226–227, 230, 235, 237, 246, 297, 299, 302–303, 309, 312–313, 320, 324, 329, 335–336, 339; **Vol. 3**: 4–5, 10, 19, 65–66, 78, 81, 84, 88, 90, 93–94, 100, 118, 139, 152, 155, 158–159, 175, 183, 186, 280, 282–284, 301–302, 325, 334, 454–457, 515
Rectification Movement **Vol. 1**: 83–84, 210, 282, 367–368, 380, 385–389, 391, 394, 402, 410, 421, 425, 433–434, 437, 439, 448, 484–486; **Vol. 2**: 175–182, 184–185, 189; **Vol. 3**: 155, 457
Red Army **Vol. 1**: 59–62, 66, 153, 156–161, 164, 168–172, 174–176, 178–181, 183, 185, 193, 229–231, 233–236, 279, 285–286, 288, 296, 299–300, 304–305, 307, 311, 316–317, 319, 321, 323, 331–332, 334, 336, 341, 350, 361, 364–367, 382, 420, 459; **Vol. 3**: 15, 104–105, 432
Red Army University **Vol. 1**: 288
Red Flag **Vol. 1**: 59, 170, 176, 279; **Vol. 2**: 190, 194, 278–279, 314, 323; **Vol. 3**: 33, 38, 40, 55, 79–80, 137
Red Flag Party **Vol. 3**: 79–80
Red Guards **Vol. 1**: 175, 332, 334, 336
Red regime **Vol. 1**: 53, 170–173, 179–180, 182, 292, 331, 365
redeployment **Vol. 3**: 124
Reform and Opening Up **Vol. 2**: 22–23, 249, 304, 310, 313, 329–330, 332, 334–338; **Vol. 3**: 3–5, 7, 9, 18, 32, 44–45, 48–49, 51–52, 56, 61, 123, 129, 132–133, 181, 192, 225, 241–243, 251–252, 254–256, 279, 292, 297, 301–306, 310,

313, 318, 323–324, 326–328, 330–337, 341, 343, 348, 350, 352–353, 355, 357–359, 364, 369, 379, 381, 384, 387, 391, 397, 402, 408, 416, 422, 427, 435, 437, 444, 446–447, 454, 461, 475, 480, 482, 484, 488, 497–498, 501–502, 506, 513, 524–526, 531, 534, 536, 541, 545–547, 549–551

Reform Group of the Financial and Economic Committee **Vol. 3**: 193
Reform Movement of 1888 **Vol. 1**: 140
Reform Movement of 1898 **Vol. 1**: 110
reform of the cultural system **Vol. 2**: 20; **Vol. 3**: 389, 393, 511
rejuvenating the nation **Vol. 3**: 398
Religious Affairs Bureau (*see also* Bureau of Religious Affairs) **Vol. 3**: 126, 128
Religious Policy **Vol. 3**: 116, 122, 126, 128
Removing Chaos **Vol. 2**: 327
Ren Bishi **Vol. 1**: 254, 484, 497–498, 501–502, 504–505; **Vol. 2**: 40
Ren Wanding **Vol. 3**: 142
Ren Zhuoxuan (*see* Ye Qing) **Vol. 1**: 70
Republic of China **Vol. 1**: 4, 24, 88, 114, 268, 284–285, 421, 517, 520, 523, 539; **Vol. 2**: 25–26, 39, 48, 51–53, 55, 57, 63, 77, 79, 86, 89–90, 110–111, 118, 165, 183, 233, 240, 304; **Vol. 3**: 4, 44, 77, 87, 97, 108, 111, 119, 122, 140, 144, 158–159, 162–163, 165, 169, 172, 213–215, 224, 228–229, 231, 233–237, 248, 252–253, 263, 275, 287, 310, 345, 376–378, 402, 413, 416–417, 460, 475, 498, 519, 541, 551
Republic of China in Taiwan **Vol. 3**: 233
Republic of Workers and Farmers **Vol. 1**: 508
Resolution of the Central Committee of the Communist Party of China on Some Historical Issues of the Party Since the Founding of the People's Republic of China **Vol. 3**: 3
Resolution on Land Issues **Vol. 1**: 49
Resolution on Relations between the KMT and the CPC **Vol. 1**: 215
Resolution on Several Historical Issues **Vol. 1**: 387, 485; **Vol. 3**: 102, 131, 163, 165, 168, 311, 335
Resolution on the Party's Organizational Issues **Vol. 1**: 45

Resolution on the Relationship between the Communist Party of China and the Kuomintang **Vol. 1**: 35
Resolution on the United Workers and Peasants **Vol. 1**: 32
Restructuring Party **Vol. 3**: 102
revisionism **Vol. 1**: 358; **Vol. 2**: 14, 184, 219, 253, 256, 259, 265–266, 268, 273, 279–280, 282–283, 287–291, 294–295; **Vol. 3**: 27, 161
Revolutionary Army of Workers and Peasants **Vol. 1**: 140, 315
Revolutionary Base Area **Vol. 1**: 36, 82, 140, 174, 176, 189, 329
revolutionary bourgeoisie **Vol. 1**: 101, 121, 140
revolutionary path (se also revolutionary road) **Vol. 1**: 37, 49, 140, 149, 151, 153, 155, 157, 159–161, 163, 165–167, 169, 171, 173, 175, 177–179, 181–183, 185, 187, 189, 191, 193, 195, 197, 199, 201, 203, 205, 207, 209, 211, 361, 379, 389, 466, 470
revolutionary practice **Vol. 1**: 23, 25, 29, 37, 81–82, 140–141, 151, 163, 169, 188, 273, 406, 428, 443–446, 463, 484, 508; **Vol. 2**: 262; **Vol. 3**: 37, 41–42
revolutionary road (*see also* revolutionary path) **Vol. 1**: 140, 149, 163, 176, 178; **Vol. 2**: 5
revolutionary struggle **Vol. 1**: 23, 25, 29, 37, 45, 47, 50–51, 54, 56, 62, 78, 92, 130, 140, 142, 149, 151, 155, 157, 161, 176, 182, 186, 190, 192, 198, 271, 277, 283, 285–286, 300, 308, 312–313, 330, 357, 362–363, 372, 376, 397, 399, 403, 419, 423, 425, 431, 440, 442, 444, 456–457, 464, 466–467, 469, 472–473, 490, 521, 531; **Vol. 2**: 53, 136, 268; **Vol. 3**: 62, 101, 115
Revolutionary United Front **Vol. 1**: 29, 93, 140–141, 218, 227, 235, 244, 268, 372
rich peasant (*see also* wealthy peasant) **Vol. 1**: 536; **Vol. 2**: 63, 65–66, 68–69, 125; **Vol. 3**: 113
right opportunists **Vol. 3**: 66, 87
Right-Wing Correction Office **Vol. 3**: 90
rightism **Vol. 2**: 183, 230, 312
Rightist deviation **Vol. 3**: 91, 93
Rightist errors **Vol. 1**: 46, 58, 232, 391, 401, 550; **Vol. 3**: 252

rightist labels **Vol. 3**: 87
Rightist tendencies **Vol. 3**: 241
riot **Vol. 1**: 48, 61, 151, 156, 165, 167–169, 179, 237, 276, 334
Rogachev, Igor **Vol. 3**: 219
Ruan Ming **Vol. 3**: 139
rule of law **Vol. 2**: 163, 269, 298; **Vol. 3**: 58, 137, 146, 379–381, 436, 499, 510, 514, 520, 532–534
ruling party **Vol. 1**: 285, 308, 370, 430, 458, 465, 504–505; **Vol. 2**: 158–159, 161–163, 183, 185, 190, 296–297; **Vol. 3**: 241, 243, 280, 336, 446, 472, 512–514
Rural People's Commune Work Regulations **Vol. 2**: 9, 235; **Vol. 3**: 52, 60, 112
Rural People's Commune Work Regulations (60 Agricultural Articles) **Vol. 2**: 9
rural policy **Vol. 2**: 63, 235, 328
rural reform **Vol. 3**: 61, 262, 335, 509–510, 523, 536, 542–545
rural revolutionary base **Vol. 1**: 82–83, 157–158, 164, 174–176, 195, 329, 364, 471
Rural Socialist Education Movement **Vol. 3**: 93
rural system **Vol. 3**: 544
rural to urban (transfer) **Vol. 1**: 370, 494–495, 497, 499
rural work **Vol. 1**: 83, 155, 255, 495; **Vol. 2**: 189, 328; **Vol. 3**: 543–544
Russell, Bertrand **Vol. 1**: 18
Russian Bolshevik Party **Vol. 1**: 358
Russian Revolution **Vol. 1**: 56, 113, 149, 152, 379; **Vol. 2**: 54, 137
Russian Social Democratic Labor Party **Vol. 1**: 397–398

S

SACO **Vol. 3**: 109
Saneatsu Mushakoji **Vol. 1**: 6
Sanming City **Vol. 3**: 313
Sanwan Reorganization **Vol. 1**: 315
SARS **Vol. 3**: 500–502
scar literature **Vol. 3**: 31
School of Marxism **Vol. 2**: 73
science education **Vol. 3**: 29
Science, Fourteen Articles of **Vol. 2**: 240, 254

scientific evaluation **Vol. 3**: 135, 159
Scientific View of Development **Vol. 3**: 479, 494, 497, 500–507, 512, 514, 523, 533, 550–551
Second Civil Revolutionary War **Vol. 2**: 46
second combination **Vol. 2**: 7, 14, 143, 145
Second Expanded Plenary Session of the Central Executive Committee **Vol. 1**: 39
Second Leap **Vol. 2**: 3, 9, 11–13, 16–17, 20–23, 133–134, 182, 222, 225–226, 310–313, 329, 332, 335–336, 338; **Vol. 3**: 359, 490
Second National Conference of Workers and Peasants **Vol. 1**: 195
Second National Congress of the Chinese Soviet Workers, Peasants, and Soldiers **Vol. 1**: 191, 255; **Vol. 3**: 112
Second National Congress of the Communist Party of China **Vol. 1**: 26–28
Second National Labor Conference **Vol. 1**: 32, 126
Second National Workers, Peasants, and Soldiers Congress **Vol. 1**: 105, 255; **Vol. 3**: 112
Second Revolutionary Civil War **Vol. 1**: 296; **Vol. 3**: 103
Second World War (*see also* World War II) **Vol. 1**: 113; **Vol. 2**: 19, 46, 138, 187, 263–264, 269; **Vol. 3**: 46
Secondary Education, Fifty Articles of **Vol. 2**: 240
Secretariat in Irkutsk **Vol. 1**: 19
seeking truth from facts **Vol. 1**: 294, 379, 388–391, 424, 453–454, 463, 474, 546; **Vol. 2**: 5, 11, 21, 203, 233–234, 243, 245–246, 313, 316, 319, 321, 324–325, 328–329, 336–337; **Vol. 3**: 20, 33–35, 39, 51, 55, 57–58, 60–61, 63, 67, 69, 74, 83–84, 86, 89, 97, 108, 135, 150, 155, 165, 169, 173, 243, 332–333, 336, 338, 344, 359, 393, 472, 525, 549
Selected Works of Mao Zedong **Vol. 1**: 73, 79, 493–494; **Vol. 2**: 29, 315
self-criticism **Vol. 1**: 322, 364, 385–387, 426–428, 430, 432, 436–437, 446–456, 463, 469, 471, 477, 502, 504; **Vol. 2**: 162, 167, 176, 179, 244–246, 249, 283; **Vol. 3**: 55, 57, 280–281, 284, 455–456
semi-colonial, semi-feudal society **Vol. 1**: 3, 50,

72, 91, 96, 99, 110, 115, 133, 173, 376, 392, 431, 509–510, 521, 525, 540
semi-socialist economy **Vol. 2:** 26, 33, 51
separation of Party and government **Vol. 1:** 191; **Vol. 3:** 269–270, 273, 275
September 13 Incident **Vol. 2:** 122, 306
September Letter **Vol. 1:** 178; **Vol. 2:** 122
serving the people wholeheartedly **Vol. 1:** 299–300, 302, 325, 465, 470; **Vol. 3:** 281, 308, 447–448, 459
Seven Thousand People's Congress (*see also* 7,000 People's Congress) **Vol. 2:** 221
Seventh National Congress of the Communist Party of China **Vol. 1:** 410
Seventh Plenum of the Executive Committee of the Comintern **Vol. 1:** 38
Seventh Regiment **Vol. 1:** 354
Seventeenth National Congress of the Communist Party of China **Vol. 3:** 524, 527, 546
Seventh Five-Year Plan **Vol. 3:** 183, 261, 265, 313
Shaanxi Province **Vol. 1:** 324; **Vol. 3:** 101–102
Shaanxi-Gansu-Ningxia Border Region **Vol. 1:** 76, 199, 201, 203–204, 206–209, 211; **Vol. 2:** 30
Shandong Province **Vol. 3:** 38, 84, 88, 450
Shanghai **Vol. 1:** 4, 6, 11, 15–19, 24–26, 34, 56, 58, 61, 155–157, 162, 167, 223, 256, 259–261, 276, 308, 355, 376, 525; **Vol. 2:** 43, 77, 151, 178, 200, 202, 204, 206, 300; **Vol. 3:** 4, 11, 31–32, 49, 66, 74–75, 141, 143, 147, 263, 318, 324, 327, 347, 354, 405–406, 414, 428
Shanghai Association **Vol. 3:** 414
Shanghai Baoshan Iron and Steel Works **Vol. 3:** 49
Shanghai Bureau **Vol. 1:** 259–261
Shanghai Commune **Vol. 2:** 300
Shanghai Communist Party **Vol. 1:** 18
Shanghai Conference **Vol. 2:** 200, 202, 206
Shanghai General League Strike **Vol. 1:** 61
Shanghai Municipal Committee **Vol. 3:** 75
Shanghai Party Organization **Vol. 1:** 18
Shanghai People's Commune **Vol. 3:** 74–75
Shanghai Stock Exchange **Vol. 3:** 406

Shanghai Xinbao Steel Group Company **Vol. 3:** 405
Shangyu County **Vol. 3:** 277
Shanxi Province **Vol. 1:** 160, 202, 234, 249, 251; **Vol. 2:** 71–76, 85, 108, 122; **Vol. 3:** 277
Shanxi Provincial Party Committee **Vol. 2:** 72–73, 76
Shao Lizi **Vol. 1:** 18
Shao Piaoping **Vol. 1:** 10
Shapiro, Sidney **Vol. 3:** 117
Shatian Village **Vol. 1:** 323
Shen Chong **Vol. 1:** 258
Shen Chong Incident **Vol. 1:** 258
Shen Junru **Vol. 1:** 233, 264
Shen Xuanlu **Vol. 1:** 18
Shen Yanbing Vol.1: 18
Shenyang **Vol. 1:** 353; **Vol. 3:** 50
Shenzhen **Vol. 3:** 277–278, 327–328, 349, 354, 406, 468
Shenzhen Stock Exchange **Vol. 3:** 406
Shi Cuntong **Vol. 1:** 18–19
Shi Yousan **Vol. 1:** 239
Shijiazhuang **Vol. 2:** 204
Shijiusuo Port **Vol. 3:** 210
Shu Tong **Vol. 3:** 14
Shuai Mengqi **Vol. 3:** 72
Sichuan Province **Vol. 1:** 234; **Vol. 2:** 233, 249, 328; **Vol. 3:** 66, 79, 103, 109, 154, 277
Sinicization of Marxism (*see also* integrating Marxism into China) **Vol. 2:** 17
Sino-American Civil Aviation Agreement **Vol. 3:** 213
Sino-American Cooperative Organization (SACO) Prison **Vol. 3:** 109
Sino-American Maritime Transport Agreement **Vol. 3:** 213
Sino-American Textile Agreement **Vol. 3:** 213
Sino-British Joint Statement **Vol. 3:** 236
Sino-foreign joint ventures **Vol. 3:** 293
Sino-French War **Vol. 1:** 110
Sino-Japan relations **Vol. 2:** 304
Sino-Japanese Joint Declaration **Vol. 3:** 424
Sino-Japanese Joint Statement **Vol. 3:** 211
Sino-Japanese relations **Vol. 3:** 210–212, 424–425

Sino-Japanese Treaty of Peace and Friendship **Vol. 3**: 211
Sino-Japanese War **Vol. 1**: 4, 110
Sino-Soviet relations **Vol. 2**: 265; **Vol. 3**: 203, 206, 217–218, 221
Sino-Soviet Treaty of Friendship, Alliance, and Mutual Assistance **Vol. 3**: 217
Sino-US Joint Communiqué **Vol. 2**: 304
Sino-US relations **Vol. 2**: 304–305; **Vol. 3**: 206–207, 213, 215, 217, 423
Sixth Anti-Encirclement Campaign **Vol. 1**: 157
Sixteen-Character Principle **Vol. 3**: 133, 465
Sixteenth National Congress of Communist Party of China **Vol. 3**: 498
Sixth Five-Year Plan **Vol. 3**: 183, 261–262
social class **Vol. 1**: 119, 397, 513, 515; **Vol. 3**: 130, 141, 308, 504
Social Democratic Party **Vol. 1**: 111, 371, 397; **Vol. 3**: 102, 308, 504
Socialism **Vol. 1**: 6–10, 12–13, 16, 18, 24–25, 27, 30–31, 50, 54–56, 70, 75–76, 85, 89, 103–108, 111–114, 116–118, 144, 146, 196, 221, 301, 359, 394, 417, 458, 467–468, 498, 507–512, 517, 519–522, 526, 528, 534–538, 543–544; **Vol. 2**: 4–6, 9, 13–15, 17–20, 22, 27–30, 33, 37, 39–41, 43, 45–47, 50, 52, 56, 58–59, 61–62, 70, 72–73, 76, 80, 83, 85–86, 88–91, 94–95, 97–99, 101–103, 105–121, 123–126, 128–139, 142–145, 151–152, 154–155, 158, 164, 169–170, 173–174, 176, 180–182, 184–185, 187–188, 190, 192–193, 195–197, 199–200, 202, 205, 211–214, 216–219, 223, 226, 229–231, 234–236, 242, 245, 253–255, 257–259, 261–262, 264, 266–272, 274–275, 280–281, 284–285, 291, 294, 296–298, 304–306, 308, 311, 320, 325, 327, 329, 332, 334, 336–338; **Vol. 3**: 4–7, 27–28, 36, 58, 91, 93, 110, 115, 129–135, 141–143, 146–147, 150–152, 159, 170–171, 173–174, 181, 184–185, 189, 191–192, 195, 202, 233, 235, 239, 241, 243–258, 266–268, 270, 283, 286, 301, 303, 309, 312, 314–315, 318, 325–340, 343–348, 350–351, 354, 357–369, 371, 380, 382–383, 385–391, 393, 397, 400, 440, 447–448, 458–459, 468, 472–473, 475–476, 482–484, 486–487, 493–494, 504, 511, 513, 523–527, 530–531, 533–535, 540, 544–547, 549–551
socialism with Chinese characteristics **Vol. 1**: 509; **Vol. 2**: 13, 130, 329, 336–338; **Vol. 3**: 4–7, 134, 142, 152, 173–174, 181, 185, 189, 243–244, 246, 255, 257, 268, 286, 301, 303, 314, 318, 325–327, 331, 333–338, 340, 350–351, 357–360, 362, 364–366, 368–369, 371, 380, 382–383, 385–391, 393, 397, 400, 447–448, 459, 468, 472, 475–476, 483–484, 486, 504, 513, 523–527, 531, 533–535, 545–547, 549–551
socialist commodity economy **Vol. 2**: 9; **Vol. 3**: 22, 77, 192, 201, 241, 249, 302, 335
socialist commodity production **Vol. 2**: 15; **Vol. 3**: 21–22
socialist construction **Vol. 1**: 145, 458–459; **Vol. 2**: 5, 7–8, 13, 15, 22–23, 110, 116, 118–120, 128, 134, 136–138, 141, 145–148, 154–155, 158–159, 165–166, 170, 173, 185, 187–188, 190, 192, 195, 197, 201, 209–210, 212, 214, 217, 221, 225, 244, 268, 270–271, 273, 291–292, 308, 325, 328–330, 337; **Vol. 3**: 20, 27, 61, 63, 77, 123, 126, 142, 159, 171–172, 180–181, 184, 188–189, 191, 218, 253, 335–336, 339, 360, 443, 476, 505, 530, 534–535
Socialist Education Movement (*see also* Four Clean-ups) **Vol. 2**: 258, 269, 275, 292; **Vol. 3**: 93
socialist market economic system **Vol. 3**: 5–6, 63, 77, 202, 334, 343, 348–353, 355–357, 366, 370, 379, 384, 409–411, 447, 465–466, 474, 480–481, 484–486, 488–489, 491–496, 499, 501, 507–508, 528, 534
socialist model **Vol. 2**: 12–13, 21, 23, 87, 121, 139–141, 170, 195, 215, 253, 255–256, 271
Socialist Reform **Vol. 2**: 10–11, 13–15, 23, 138–140, 145, 174, 181, 186, 221, 255, 268; **Vol. 3**: 5, 334, 358
Socialist Youth League **Vol. 1**: 25, 214
Some Historical Issues **Vol. 2**: 6; **Vol. 3**: 4, 158–159, 165, 172, 248, 345
Song Baoqi **Vol. 3**: 30
Song Jiaoren **Vol. 1**: 7
Song of the Heart **Vol. 3**: 32
Song Ping **Vol. 3**: 245

Song Qingling **Vol. 1**: 233
Song Renqiong **Vol. 3**: 62, 68, 81, 189
Song Shuo **Vol. 3**: 78–79
Song Zheyuan **Vol. 1**: 234
Song Ziwen (TV Soong) **Vol. 1**: 246
Songjiang County **Vol. 2**: 77
Soong, TV (*see* Song Ziwen)
South Beijing Riot **Vol. 1**: 61
South China Sea **Vol. 3**: 425
Southern Anhui Incident **Vol. 1**: 79
Southern Expedition **Vol. 3**: 71
Southern Talks (Deng Xiaoping) **Vol. 3**: 327–328, 333, 338, 347, 362, 366
sovereignty (Hong Kong) **Vol. 1**: 524; **Vol. 3**: 203, 212, 231, 235–237, 416–417, 421, 426, 519
soviet **Vol. 1**: 7, 43, 48, 51, 53–54, 59, 61, 63, 66, 79, 84, 109, 113, 149–150, 153, 155, 157–160, 164–165, 180, 189, 191–192, 194–197, 224, 227, 230, 232, 304, 341, 351, 432, 458–459, 482, 484, 486, 507–508, 511, 513–514, 528; **Vol. 2**: 5–8, 12–15, 18–21, 23, 27, 40, 44–46, 50, 54–55, 59, 66, 76, 87, 89, 91, 94–95, 97, 102, 105–106, 108–109, 113, 116–122, 124–125, 129–134, 136–145, 147–153, 156, 159–160, 163, 165–166, 173, 184, 187–189, 191–192, 200, 209–211, 213–220, 231, 238, 252–253, 255, 258, 262, 264–268, 271, 274, 287–291, 298, 305, 308, 325; **Vol. 3**: 15, 38, 47, 84, 102–105, 163, 193, 203–206, 208–209, 213, 217–221, 246–247, 326, 347, 423, 437, 512
Soviet Communist Party **Vol. 1**: 51; **Vol. 2**: 12, 44, 50, 109, 124, 139, 141, 143, 163, 166, 184, 209–210, 213, 288–290; **Vol. 3**: 221, 247, 512
Soviet Government of the Workers, Peasants, and Soldiers **Vol. 1**: 189, 255; **Vol. 3**: 112
Soviet Revisionist Group **Vol. 2**: 288–291
Soviet Union **Vol. 1**: 7, 53–54, 66, 84, 109, 113, 149, 180, 232, 511, 513–514; **Vol. 2**: 5–8, 12–15, 20, 23, 40, 45–46, 50, 54, 59, 66, 89, 91, 102, 106, 108, 113, 116–120, 122, 124, 130–134, 137–144, 148–153, 156, 159–160, 165–166, 173, 191–192, 200, 209–211, 213–214, 216–218, 220, 252–253, 255, 265, 287–290, 305, 308, 325; **Vol. 3**: 47, 104, 193, 203–204, 206, 208–209, 213, 217–221, 246–247, 326, 347, 423, 437

Special Article on the Development of Hong Kong Border Sites **Vol. 3**: 234, 416
Special Case Office **Vol. 3**: 71
Special Committee **Vol. 1**: 172, 174; **Vol. 3**: 373
Speech at Chun Qu Zhai (Liu Shaoqi) **Vol. 3**: 10
Speech at the Yan'an Forum on Literature and Art **Vol. 1**: 300; **Vol. 3**: 10
Stalin, Joseph **Vol. 1**: 51, 94, 113, 227, 283, 364, 371, 381, 384, 393, 430–431, 434, 443, 492–493, 507; **Vol. 2**: 6, 18, 91, 109, 118–119, 121–122, 137, 139, 141, 143, 164–165, 209–212, 214–215, 218, 265, 290; **Vol. 3**: 21, 247
Standing Committee **Vol. 1**: 43, 167, 276, 395; **Vol. 2**: 111, 115, 153, 247, 257; **Vol. 3**: 11–12, 38–39, 50, 53–54, 56–57, 62, 75, 119, 137–138, 156–157, 160, 178–180, 189, 217, 226, 228, 230, 245, 269, 273–274, 298–299, 309, 319–321, 324, 331, 373, 376–377, 381, 413, 431, 455–456, 509, 515
State Bureau of Defense Science, Technology, and Industry **Vol. 2**: 304; **Vol. 3**: 176, 211, 539
State Bureau of Foreign Experts **Vol. 3**: 117
State Civil Aviation Administration **Vol. 3**: 539
State Commission for Reform of Sports and Physical Education **Vol. 3**: 450
State Construction Commission **Vol. 3**: 127
State Council **Vol. 2**: 80, 82–83, 152, 156, 188, 245, 249, 301–302, 314, 331, 333; **Vol. 3**: 10, 21–22, 24–25, 28, 40, 46–48, 51–52, 56, 67, 71, 74, 103, 121–122, 125, 127–128, 160, 193–194, 196, 198, 215, 221, 259, 269, 271, 273–274, 276–278, 289–290, 293–294, 297–299, 306, 313, 318–319, 322, 344, 350, 353–355, 373–374, 377, 380–381, 398–399, 406–410, 413, 419, 436, 461–463, 465, 467, 482, 506, 508–509, 511, 519, 536, 538–539
State Economic Commission **Vol. 3**: 322
State Economic Reform Office (Commission for Economic Reform) **Vol. 3**: 194
State Environmental Protection Administration **Vol. 3**: 540
State Environmental Protection Bureau **Vol. 3**: 278

State Food and Drug Administration **Vol. 3**: 540
State General Administration of Labor **Vol. 3**: 23–24
State Personnel Department **Vol. 3**: 278
State Planning Commission **Vol. 2**: 237; **Vol. 3**: 23–24, 196–197, 262, 346
state power **Vol. 1**: 13, 131, 138, 188, 246, 458, 513, 517–518, 520, 522–523, 538; **Vol. 2**: 26, 34, 41, 48–50, 121–122, 196, 223, 292–293, 298
State Tax Administration **Vol. 3**: 278
state-owned enterprises **Vol. 1**: 195, 496; **Vol. 2**: 238–239; **Vol. 3**: 196–197, 349, 351–353, 378, 402–412, 450–451, 460, 464, 489–490, 494, 496
Stirner, Max **Vol. 1**: 6
Straits Exchange Foundation (SEF) **Vol. 3**: 414–415, 419
Strategic military policy in a high-tech environment **Vol. 1**: 182, 341–342; **Vol. 3**: 429
"Strategy for Opposing Japanese Imperialism" **Vol. 1**: 229
strike **Vol. 1**: 25, 36, 47, 58, 61–62, 124, 153, 156, 185, 187, 192, 243, 258, 261, 278, 280; **Vol. 2**: 175; **Vol. 3**: 127, 142, 304
struggle **Vol. 1**: 8, 10–11, 13–15, 20–21, 23–25, 27–37, 41–43, 45–48, 50–52, 54–56, 58–60, 62, 66–68, 70, 78, 80, 82–83, 86, 88–89, 91–92, 100–103, 105–106, 109, 112–113, 115, 119, 122, 125, 129–130, 133–135, 139, 141–142, 144, 146, 149–151, 155, 157–159, 161, 164–166, 169–171, 173–177, 180, 182, 184–187, 189–190, 192, 198, 210, 212, 218–219, 221, 223–224, 230, 232, 234, 236–245, 247–249, 252–254, 257–261, 263, 265, 269, 271, 273–279, 281–291, 293–295, 297, 299–305, 307–309, 311–313, 315, 317, 319–321, 323, 325, 327, 329–333, 335–339, 341, 343, 345, 347, 349, 351–353, 355–359, 361–369, 371–372, 376, 382, 384–386, 388, 391, 394, 396–399, 401, 403, 406, 408, 412, 419, 421, 423, 425–426, 431, 440, 442, 444, 451, 454–458, 461, 464, 466–467, 469–473, 476, 479, 483, 486, 489–491, 501, 504, 509, 512, 521, 525–528, 531, 538, 540–541, 545; **Vol. 2**: 6, 8, 10, 13–14, 20, 28, 33–34, 36–37, 42–43, 45, 47, 49, 53, 59–61, 65, 91–93, 99, 103, 105, 116, 128–129, 135–136, 138, 153, 161–163, 167–168, 170, 173–174, 178–180, 182–187, 189–191, 207, 219, 221, 224, 226, 230–231, 234, 241–242, 244–247, 251–252, 254–259, 265, 268–279, 281, 285–286, 292–299, 301, 303, 307, 309, 312, 314, 316, 321, 325, 333, 335, 338; **Vol. 3**: 4, 11, 17, 32–33, 40, 48, 51, 55, 60, 62–63, 66, 72–73, 80, 85, 88, 93, 96, 99, 101, 106, 115, 120–121, 130, 135, 140–141, 143, 152, 160–161, 170, 173, 191, 205, 207, 228, 253–254, 257–258, 261, 264, 283, 299, 307, 311, 319, 323, 332, 362, 368, 390, 415, 418, 429, 431–432, 437–440, 454, 460–461, 464–465, 483, 516, 520, 525, 527, 530–531, 548
Struggle, Criticism, and Reform Campaign **Vol. 1**: 425, 450; **Vol. 2**: 272
Stuart, John Leighton **Vol. 1**: 281
Su Hua **Vol. 1**: 50
Su Jin **Vol. 3**: 104
Su Shuyang **Vol. 3**: 32
Su Yu **Vol. 1**: 327, 351
Su Zhaozheng **Vol. 1**: 39
Sun Yat-sen **Vol. 1**: 3, 7, 24, 93, 111, 126, 224–225; **Vol. 3**: 358
Sun Yifang **Vol. 2**: 9, 307, 309
Sunzi **Vol. 1**: 296
superstructure **Vol. 1**: 131, 137, 468; **Vol. 2**: 4, 70, 81, 113–114, 164, 167–169, 189, 239, 245, 253, 281–283, 293–294, 302, 327, 333, 335; **Vol. 3**: 27, 49–50, 57, 64, 191, 250, 256, 329–330, 498, 503, 543, 547
Supreme State Conference **Vol. 2**: 179, 249
sustainable development **Vol. 3**: 372, 398–400, 485, 490, 496, 501, 503, 505, 542
Suzhou **Vol. 1**: 260
Symposium of the Secretary of Culture and Education **Vol. 3**: 37
Symposium on Implementing the Cadre Policy **Vol. 3**: 84

T

Taiping Heavenly Kingdom **Vol. 1**: 133
Taiping Rebellion **Vol. 1**: 110

Taiwan **Vol. 1**: 228, 534; **Vol. 2**: 55, 61; **Vol. 3**: 56, 132, 181, 206–207, 213–217, 225–234, 413–416, 418–420, 520–522
Taiwan Relations Act **Vol. 3**: 206, 214–215
Taiwan Strait **Vol. 3**: 225–226, 229–230, 413–415, 420
Taiwan Strait Exchange foundation **Vol. 3**: 414
Taiwan's Legal Independence **Vol. 3**: 521
Taiwanese independence **Vol. 3**: 438
Taiyue Corps **Vol. 1**: 352
Taking and managing the cities **Vol. 1**: 453
Tan Pingshan **Vol. 1**: 19, 38–39, 57, 226, 264
Tan Zhenlin **Vol. 1**: 189; **Vol. 2**: 300, 326; **Vol. 3**: 40, 72–73, 81, 189
Tang Aoqing **Vol. 3**: 30
Tang Sheng-chih **Vol. 1**: 38
Tang Shubei **Vol. 3**: 414
Tanggu **Vol. 1**: 354
Tangshan **Vol. 1**: 16, 354; **Vol. 3**: 50
Tangxian County **Vol. 2**: 204
Tao Xingzhi **Vol. 1**: 233
Tao Xisheng **Vol. 1**: 94–95
Tao Zhu **Vol. 1**: 483; **Vol. 3**: 15, 53–54, 72, 81
Taoist temples (in Han areas) **Vol. 3**: 127
Ten Combinations **Vol. 3**: 546, 549
Ten Military Principles **Vol. 1**: 86
Ten-Year Summary (Mao Zedong) **Vol. 2**: 130
Tenth Five-Year Plan **Vol. 3**: 401–402, 482, 508
testing truth **Vol. 2**: 21, 233, 322–323, 326; **Vol. 3**: 20, 35–36, 38–42, 44, 58, 60, 137–138, 153–157, 243, 336, 338
Thatcher, Margaret **Vol. 3**: 231, 235
Thaw Society **Vol. 3**: 143
The Chinese Peasant **Vol. 1**: 33
The Chinese Revolution and the Communist Party of China **Vol. 1**: 7, 20, 34, 37, 50–51, 63, 71, 73–75, 79, 97, 100–101, 103, 107, 114, 122–123, 125, 133, 142, 146, 155, 159, 176, 178, 185, 204, 237, 247, 251, 264, 269, 307, 313, 321, 334, 352, 369, 372, 375–376, 384–385, 387, 400, 410, 412, 427, 436, 442, 444, 454, 474, 483, 499, 508, 514–515, 532, 534, 545; **Vol. 2**: 10, 14, 17, 20, 27, 32, 49, 53, 55, 65, 74, 89–90, 142, 144, 147, 155, 160, 165, 169, 201, 214, 224, 237, 246, 268, 294, 314–315, 327; **Vol. 3**: 4, 11–12, 18, 21, 32, 62–63, 73, 75, 88, 99, 127–128, 139, 149, 168, 170, 195, 200, 208, 213–214, 224, 236, 247, 252–253, 259, 265–266, 270, 278, 283, 317, 327, 330, 355, 371, 375, 411, 427, 431, 433, 448, 466, 499–500, 502, 515, 517
The Communist Manifesto **Vol. 1**: 79, 97, 374, 458; **Vol. 3**: 527
The First Program of the Communist Party of China **Vol. 1**: 20
The History of the Communist Party of the Soviet Union (Bolshevik) **Vol. 2**: 118, 122
the masses **Vol. 1**: 7, 9, 14–15, 20, 24, 34–35, 37, 42, 44, 48, 50–53, 58–59, 63, 71, 73–75, 79, 85–86, 95, 100–101, 108–109, 114, 122, 125, 130–131, 133, 142, 150, 155–156, 159, 168, 171, 173–179, 181, 183, 185, 187, 190–194, 198, 200–201, 204, 207, 210–212, 218, 226, 237, 241–242, 247, 251, 254–255, 258–261, 264, 269–270, 277, 286, 293, 301–307, 310–311, 313, 315, 317, 320–321, 326, 328, 332–335, 337–338, 352, 358, 363, 366, 369, 372, 375–377, 380, 384–385, 387, 389, 393, 396, 400, 402, 404–406, 409–410, 412–413, 415, 417, 419, 424, 426–428, 430, 432, 435–436, 439, 442, 444, 449–450, 454, 456–465, 469–475, 477–480, 483–484, 487, 499, 502, 506, 508, 514–515, 532, 534, 545, 548–549; **Vol. 2**: 9–10, 14, 17, 20, 32, 49, 53, 55, 65, 67, 74, 78, 84, 89–90, 104, 142, 144, 147, 155, 159–163, 165, 169, 175–176, 179, 181, 191, 201, 206, 214, 218–219, 224, 234–237, 241, 244–246, 249, 252, 261, 268–269, 276, 286, 292, 294–295, 297, 301, 303, 305–306, 309, 311–312, 314–318, 327; **Vol. 3**: 4, 10–13, 15, 18–19, 21, 32, 53–54, 58, 62–63, 69, 72–73, 75, 77, 81, 83, 85, 88, 99, 106, 109, 113–114, 121–122, 127–128, 139, 142–143, 146–147, 149–150, 158, 161, 168, 170, 177, 184–185, 195, 200, 202, 208, 213–214, 224, 236, 247, 252–253, 259, 265–266, 270, 272, 278, 281, 283–285, 291, 308–309, 317, 323, 327, 330, 338, 355, 367, 371, 375, 377–378, 393, 411, 427, 431, 433, 447–448, 451, 453, 456–459, 466, 476, 499–500, 502, 515, 517, 531, 547
"The Scars" **Vol. 3**: 31

The Socialist Economic Problems of the Soviet Union **Vol. 2**: 139, 165, 209–211, 213–214, 216, 218
"The United Government" (article) **Vol. 1**: 487
The Weekly Review **Vol. 1**: 18
Theoretical Dynamics **Vol. 2**: 322; **Vol. 3**: 36, 340
Theoretical Education of Cadres **Vol. 2**: 118; **Vol. 3**: 340
theoretical work **Vol. 1**: 37, 72, 78; **Vol. 3**: 137–145, 149, 152, 159, 310, 340
Theory of Continuing Revolution (permanent revolution) **Vol. 1**: 359, 362; **Vol. 2**: 277–279, 281–283, 291, 293–294, 296, 298, 310, 319, 322; **Vol. 3**: 170, 493
theory of descent **Vol. 1**: 359, 362; **Vol. 3**: 493
Third Beijing People's Congress **Vol. 2**: 78
Third Five-Year Plan **Vol. 3**: 254
Third Party **Vol. 1**: 233; **Vol. 3**: 102
Third World **Vol. 2**: 263–264, 305; **Vol. 3**: 128, 206, 260, 268, 426
Thirteenth National Congress of the Communist Party of China **Vol. 2**: 3; **Vol. 3**: 112, 151, 239, 241–242, 249, 266, 273, 289, 303, 327, 335–336, 361, 372, 455
Three Advocates **Vol. 3**: 454–457, 468
Three Great Transformations **Vol. 2**: 266
Three Guarantees **Vol. 3**: 490
Three Major Disciplines and Eight Codes of Behavior **Vol. 1**: 322
Three Major Tasks **Vol. 1**: 245, 298, 304–306, 312, 318; **Vol. 2**: 125; **Vol. 3**: 181, 207
Three Orientations **Vol. 3**: 390
Three People's Principles **Vol. 1**: 69–71, 77, 106, 109, 264, 529; **Vol. 3**: 227
Three Principles **Vol. 1**: 8, 223, 243, 280, 315–316, 320, 425, 427, 515; **Vol. 3**: 211, 427
Three Represents **Vol. 3**: 6–7, 388, 432, 443, 468–477, 479, 483–484, 487, 462, 500, 502, 504, 514–515, 524–526, 533, 551
Three Rules for Discipline and Eight Points for Attention (*see* Three Major Disciplines and Eight Codes of Behavior) **Vol. 1**: 312
Tian Jiaying **Vol. 2**: 204, 231
Tian Jiyun **Vol. 3**: 245

Tian Zengpei **Vol. 3**: 219
Tiananmen Incident (April 5th Movement) **Vol. 2**: 316; **Vol. 3**: 9–12, 15, 53–54
Tiananmen Poetry **Vol. 3**: 11
Tiananmen Square **Vol. 3**: 11–12, 142, 323
Tianjin **Vol. 1**: 18, 34, 256, 353–354, 356; **Vol. 2**: 42–44, 59, 70, 204–205; **Vol. 3**: 50, 143, 157, 451
Tianjin speech (Liu Shaoqi) **Vol. 2**: 43–44, 59, 70
Tianjin Way **Vol. 1**: 356
Tibet **Vol. 2**: 55, 61, 201; **Vol. 3**: 116, 123–125, 127, 226
Tomb-Sweeping Day **Vol. 2**: 316; **Vol. 3**: 11, 54
Tong Dalin **Vol. 3**: 139, 199
Tong Dizhou **Vol. 3**: 30
Top Documents **Vol. 3**: 338
Torui Huko **Vol. 3**: 241
Touring Europe (Liang Qichao article) **Vol. 1**: 5
Township People's Congress **Vol. 1**: 515
Trade Union **Vol. 1**: 219; **Vol. 3**: 49
Training and Selection of Excellent Young Cadres **Vol. 3**: 459
transition to socialism **Vol. 1**: 105, 512; **Vol. 2**: 5, 30, 37, 56, 59, 70, 76, 85–86, 89–90, 95, 97–99, 102–103, 105–113, 115–117, 120–121, 124–125, 136
tribalism **Vol. 2**: 157
Trotsky Doctrine Incident **Vol. 3**: 105–106
Trotskyists **Vol. 1**: 95, 116; **Vol. 3**: 84, 105–106
Tsinghua University **Vol. 3**: 317, 434
Turati, Filippo **Vol. 1**: 430
Twelfth Five-Year Plan **Vol. 3**: 550–551
Twelfth National Congress of the Communist Party of China **Vol. 3**: 133, 174, 180, 182, 194–195, 248, 254, 262, 280, 287, 312, 345
Two Directions **Vol. 1**: 61
"Two Step" System **Vol. 1**: 103
Two Theories **Vol. 1**: 389, 391; **Vol. 2**: 25
Two Whatevers **Vol. 2**: 317, 319, 336–337; **Vol. 3**: 55, 173

U
Ulanhu **Vol. 3**: 189

ultra-Leftist **Vol. 2**: 10, 314–315; **Vol. 3**: 30, 79, 92, 150, 156, 175
UN Human Rights Commission **Vol. 3**: 426
Underground Party Organizations **Vol. 3**: 80, 97
UNFPA **Vol. 3**: 225
UNICEF **Vol. 3**: 225
United Front **Vol. 1**: 27, 29, 33, 40–41, 43, 49–51, 66, 71, 74–75, 78–83, 87–88, 93, 108–109, 123, 137, 141–142, 198–201, 204, 210, 213–221, 223, 225, 227–241, 243–247, 249, 251–269, 271, 280, 283, 289, 300, 309, 368, 371–372, 400, 425, 469, 483, 487–488, 491, 511, 514–516, 526–527, 539, 542, 547; **Vol. 2**: 30, 49, 53–54, 59, 62, 64, 79–81, 87, 92, 129–130, 153–154, 157–158, 170, 239, 249–250, 302, 305, 320; **Vol. 3**: 67, 80, 82, 89–90, 106, 111, 113, 118–122, 126, 128–134, 204, 339, 360, 373, 375, 469
United Front Ministry **Vol. 2**: 80, 249; **Vol. 3**: 126
United Front Work Conference **Vol. 1**: 511; **Vol. 2**: 79, 92, 250; **Vol. 3**: 129–131, 133, 217, 375, 469
United Nations **Vol. 2**: 304; **Vol. 3**: 220–221, 224–225, 426–427, 518–519, 521
United States Navy **Vol. 3**: 226
university enrollment **Vol. 3**: 17
Unjust and False Cases **Vol. 3**: 12–17, 61, 66, 68–70, 82–85, 92, 95, 100, 110, 114, 118, 175
Unjust, False, and Wrong Charges **Vol. 3**: 66, 85
urban center **Vol. 1**: 60, 158, 161
Urban Residents' Committee **Vol. 1**: 60
urban work **Vol. 1**: 60, 83, 154, 156, 158, 165–166, 186–187, 494–498; **Vol. 2**: 42, 58–59; **Vol. 3**: 451
US-Taiwan Joint Defense Treaty **Vol. 3**: 214
utopian **Vol. 2**: 69, 73, 76, 193, 196, 212, 284, 298; **Vol. 3**: 329, 533

V

vanguard of the proletariat **Vol. 1**: 308, 419, 421, 429, 431, 433–435, 438, 458, 466, 470–471; **Vol. 2**: 295

Vietnam War **Vol. 2**: 263; **Vol. 3**: 203
Villagers' Committee **Vol. 3**: 377
Voitinsky, Grigori **Vol. 1**: 17–18, 40

W

Wall of Democracy **Vol. 1**: 310; **Vol. 3**: 142–143, 145, 147
Wallace, Mike **Vol. 3**: 288
Wan Li **Vol. 3**: 124–125, 189, 245, 320
Wang Bingnan **Vol. 1**: 234
Wang Congwu **Vol. 3**: 189, 288
Wang Daohan **Vol. 3**: 414, 419
Wang Dongxing **Vol. 3**: 10–11, 23, 26, 37–38, 63, 70
Wang Feng **Vol. 1**: 234
Wang Guangmei **Vol. 3**: 72
Wang Heshou **Vol. 3**: 62, 189
Wang Hongwen **Vol. 2**: 313
Wang Jiaxiang **Vol. 1**: 238, 482, 484; **Vol. 2**: 252
Wang Jingwei **Vol. 1**: 38, 115, 217–218, 222, 239
Wang Jinmei **Vol. 1**: 19
Wang Ming **Vol. 1**: 65–67, 105, 157, 159, 195, 232, 280, 285, 401, 408, 420, 482
Wang Minglu **Vol. 1**: 62
Wang Ninzhi **Vol. 3**: 199
Wang Renzhong **Vol. 3**: 15, 62, 72, 81, 289
Wang Ruowang **Vol. 3**: 316, 318
Wang Shao'ao **Vol. 1**: 264
Wang Xuewen **Vol. 3**: 192
Wang Xuren **Vol. 3**: 105
Wang Yitang **Vol. 1**: 239
Wang Youping **Vol. 3**: 104
Wang Zhen **Vol. 3**: 11, 49, 62, 189, 289
Wang Zhuo **Vol. 3**: 197–198
Wang-Gu Talks **Vol. 3**: 414, 418
War Against Japanese Aggression **Vol. 1**: 130, 297–298, 549
war of aggression **Vol. 1**: 135, 290, 297–298, 400, 549; **Vol. 3**: 204
War of Liberation **Vol. 1**: 85, 87–88, 130, 136–137, 188, 244–245, 248, 255, 262–263, 265, 267, 269, 271, 284–285, 297–298, 305, 311, 317, 320–321, 324, 328–329, 334, 337–338, 342, 344, 346–347, 350–351, 355, 372, 388, 403, 410, 421, 433, 467,

477, 494, 531, 534, 549; **Vol. 2**: 32, 41, 49; **Vol. 3**: 240
War of Resistance Against Japanese Aggression **Vol. 1**: 66–67, 69–70, 72, 79–85, 106, 108, 110, 115, 130–131, 135, 137, 183–184, 186, 198, 200, 202, 204–206, 209–211, 228–229, 231, 240–242, 244, 246–247, 249, 253, 261–262, 267, 279–282, 284–285, 289–290, 297–298, 300, 305, 308, 311, 319, 321, 326, 334, 337, 341, 344, 368, 371, 385, 401–402, 421, 433, 439, 459, 466–467, 486, 493, 500, 526, 528, 532–533, 535, 539, 549; **Vol. 2**: 29, 38, 49, 97, 99, 271; **Vol. 3**: 227, 247, 286
War of Resistance Against US Aggression and Aid to North Korea (*see* Korean War) **Vol. 2**: 99
warlord bureaucrats **Vol. 1**: 26, 98, 135
warlords **Vol. 1**: 4–5, 23–27, 30–32, 34, 36, 40, 56, 92, 100, 105, 120–122, 124–125, 127, 134–137, 150, 171, 173, 185, 214, 216, 226, 274–275, 278, 292–293, 467, 533
Wayaobao Meeting **Vol. 1**: 160, 508
wealthy peasant (*see also* rich peasant) **Vol. 1**: 54, 62, 129, 138, 144, 201, 250–255, 270, 529–532; **Vol. 3**: 112
Wei Guofan **Vol. 3**: 299
Wei Guoqing **Vol. 3**: 137, 189
Wei Jingsheng **Vol. 3**: 143
Wen Jiabao **Vol. 3**: 245, 502, 518
Wenhui Newspaper **Vol. 3**: 31
West Lake Conference **Vol. 1**: 224
Western Enlightenment **Vol. 1**: 5
Western Marxism **Vol. 2**: 18
Westernization **Vol. 3**: 241, 249, 365
Whampoa Military Academy **Vol. 1**: 40
White Area **Vol. 1**: 82–83, 89, 257
White regime **Vol. 1**: 170–171, 173, 332
White Terror **Vol. 1**: 47, 411; **Vol. 3**: 97
wholeheartedly serve the people **Vol. 1**: 447, 460–461
Work and Mutual Aid Group **Vol. 1**: 14
Work of Mixed and Diaspora Ethnic Minorities **Vol. 3**: 121
work style (Party style) **Vol. 1**: 367–368, 380, 388, 428–434, 436–440, 446, 455–456, 462, 471, 478, 488, 505; **Vol. 2**: 180; **Vol. 3**: 111, 444, 461
Workers and Peasants League (Workers' and Peasants' Alliance) **Vol. 1**: 33, 195, 249, 470, 548
Workers and Peasants' Revolutionary Army **Vol. 1**: 548
Workers' Picket Corps **Vol. 1**: 36, 470
working class (*see also* proletariat) Vol 1: 9, 15, 17, 20, 32–34, 36, 45, 53, 72, 74, 87–89, 100, 115, 117, 120–125, 127, 131, 139, 141, 149, 154, 162, 185, 195, 219, 263, 268–269, 271, 276, 300, 321, 357, 360, 371, 373–378, 394, 420–421, 431, 433, 458, 461, 471, 495–497, 499, 501, 504, 517, 519, 538, 543; **Vol. 2**: 17, 30, 39, 41–43, 48–50, 53, 58, 83–84, 87, 91–92, 94, 105, 113, 119, 121, 126–127, 129, 136, 155, 159, 165, 170, 177, 183; **Vol. 3**: 20, 110, 129–130, 185, 337, 365, 367, 412, 440, 451, 468, 474
World Bank **Vol. 3**: 205, 224
World Federation of Taiwan Fellow Citizens **Vol. 3**: 419
World Multi-polarization and the Establishment of a New International Order **Vol. 3**: 424
World Trade Organization (WTO) **Vol. 3**: 357, 427
World War I (*see also* First World War) **Vol. 1**: 4–6, 108, 542
World War II (*see also* Second World War) **Vol. 1**: 117; **Vol. 2**: 113, 274; **Vol. 3**: 438
Worldwide Proletarian Socialist Revolution **Vol. 1**: 113, 544
Wu Bangguo **Vol. 3**: 409
Wu Guozhen **Vol. 1**: 260
Wu Jiang **Vol. 3**: 139
Wu Jichang **Vol. 3**: 30
Wu Lengxi **Vol. 2**: 204; **Vol. 3**: 139
Wu Peifu **Vol. 1**: 214
Wu Yuzhang **Vol. 1**: 257, 492
Wu Zhonghua **Vol. 3**: 30
Wuchang **Vol. 2**: 199, 205–206, 215; **Vol. 3**: 327
Wuchang Conference **Vol. 2**: 199, 206, 215
Wuhan **Vol. 1**: 19, 58, 60–61, 69, 155–156, 223,

355, 376; **Vol. 2**: 214; **Vol. 3**: 72–73, 112, 143, 277, 410
Wuhan Kuomintang government **Vol. 1**: 223
Wuhan-Changsha Railway **Vol. 1**: 61
Wuhan Military Region Party Committee **Vol. 3**: 73

X

Xi Maozhao **Vol. 3**: 109
Xi Zhongxun **Vol. 3**: 62, 72, 81, 100–102, 189
Xi'an **Vol. 1**: 235–236, 282; **Vol. 3**: 101–102, 401, 410
Xi'an Incident **Vol. 1**: 235–236, 282
Xiamen University **Vol. 3**: 193
Xiao Chunu **Vol. 1**: 102
Xiao Jinguang **Vol. 3**: 288
Xibaipo **Vol. 2**: 32
Xidan Wall of Democracy **Vol. 3**: 142–143
Xie Fuzhi **Vol. 3**: 54
Xie Huimin **Vol. 3**: 30
Xie Minggan **Vol. 3**: 199
Xie Weijun **Vol. 1**: 158
Xie Xide **Vol. 3**: 30
Xikou **Vol. 3**: 227
Xin Douyin **Vol. 1**: 276
Xinhai Revolution **Vol. 1**: 3–4
Xinhua Gate **Vol. 3**: 143
Xinhua News Agency **Vol. 2**: 323; **Vol. 3**: 12, 36, 38, 53, 109, 113, 117, 276
Xinjiang **Vol. 1**: 356; **Vol. 2**: 55; **Vol. 3**: 15, 116, 122, 125
Xinmin Congbao **Vol. 1**: 7
Xinxiang **Vol. 2**: 204
Xishan Conference **Vol. 1**: 225
Xiuwu **Vol. 2**: 204
Xu Chi **Vol. 3**: 29
Xu Jun **Vol. 3**: 299
Xu Kexiang **Vol. 1**: 276
Xu Qian **Vol. 3**: 179, 288
Xu Qianfu **Vol. 3**: 189
Xu Qianqian **Vol. 3**: 33, 73, 76, 188–189
Xu Shiyou **Vol. 3**: 189
Xu Xiangqian **Vol. 2**: 300
Xue Muqiao **Vol. 3**: 193, 195

Xushui County **Vol. 2**: 204
Xuzhou **Vol. 1**: 354

Y

Yagodin, Gennadiy **Vol. 2**: 290
Yan Xishan **Vol. 1**: 234
Yan'an **Vol. 1**: 71–73, 76, 106, 116, 199, 210, 230, 232, 240, 281, 300, 366–369, 380, 386–387, 389, 391, 393, 400, 402, 410, 412, 421, 426, 433–434, 437, 439, 448, 482, 484–485, 539, 548; **Vol. 2**: 176–177; **Vol. 3**: 79–80, 104, 155, 457
Yan'an Cadre Conference **Vol. 1**: 281
Yan'an Cadre Trial Campaign **Vol. 3**: 79
Yan'an Rectification Movement **Vol. 1**: 367–368, 380, 386–387, 389, 391, 402, 410, 421, 433–434, 437, 439, 448, 484–485; **Vol. 2**: 176; **Vol. 3**: 155, 457
Yan'an Senior Cadre Conference **Vol. 1**: 199
Yang Anan **Vol. 1**: 9
Yang Dezhi **Vol. 3**: 189
Yang Hucheng **Vol. 1**: 234; **Vol. 3**: 79
Yang Jingren **Vol. 3**: 119
Yang Liyu **Vol. 3**: 232
Yang Mingzhai **Vol. 1**: 18
Yang Qixian **Vol. 3**: 193, 199, 201
Yang Rudai **Vol. 3**: 245
Yang Shangkun **Vol. 3**: 54, 81, 189, 221, 245
Yang Xiguang **Vol. 3**: 12, 35
Yang Yong **Vol. 3**: 189
Yang Zhong **Vol. 3**: 299
Yang, Yu, and Fu **Vol. 3**: 66
Yangtze River **Vol. 1**: 51, 221, 249, 355, 534; **Vol. 2**: 63; **Vol. 3**: 263
Yanshi Railway **Vol. 3**: 210
Yantai **Vol. 3**: 88
Yao Wenyuan **Vol. 2**: 278, 280; **Vol. 3**: 23, 74–75, 100
Yao Yilin **Vol. 3**: 49, 63, 189, 245
Yasukuni Shrine **Vol. 3**: 212
Ye Jianying **Vol. 1**: 231; **Vol. 2**: 300, 317, 324; **Vol. 3**: 11, 14, 57, 73, 104, 137–138, 158, 160–161, 165, 179, 186, 188–189, 230–231, 248, 288, 310, 363, 415
Ye Qing **Vol. 1**: 70, 77

Yellow River **Vol. 1**: 351–352
Yeltsin, Boris **Vol. 3**: 424
Yichang **Vol. 3**: 85
Yokohama Ohira **Vol. 3**: 212
Yongcheng County **Vol. 3**: 90
young and middle-aged cadres **Vol. 3**: 187, 286–287, 290–291
Young Pioneers **Vol. 1**: 334
Youth Magazine (New Youth) **Vol. 1**: 4
Yu Guangyuan **Vol. 3**: 24–25, 28, 139, 199
Yu Lijin **Vol. 3**: 75–76
Yu Muming **Vol. 3**: 521
Yu Qiuli **Vol. 3**: 189
Yu Xiusong **Vol. 1**: 18
Yuan Mu **Vol. 3**: 199
Yuan Shikai **Vol. 1**: 4, 134
Yuan Xuezu **Vol. 3**: 104
Yuanping County **Vol. 3**: 277
Yugoslavian nationalists **Vol. 1**: 113
Yulin **Vol. 1**: 352
Yun Daiying **Vol. 1**: 21, 29, 102, 274, 464
Yunnan Province **Vol. 1**: 160, 176–177, 234; **Vol. 3**: 79, 96–97, 116, 125
Yuquan Mountain **Vol. 3**: 199
Yusui Soviet Area **Vol. 1**: 351

Z
Zedong School for Young Cadres **Vol. 1**: 279; **Vol. 2**: 336
Zeng Qinghong **Vol. 3**: 502
Zeng Tao **Vol. 3**: 12
Zeng Zhi **Vol. 1**: 79
Zenko Suzuki **Vol. 3**: 210
Zhang Bojun **Vol. 1**: 233, 264
Zhang Chunqiao **Vol. 2**: 280, 294, 313; **Vol. 3**: 23, 74–75
Zhang Dongsun **Vol. 1**: 11–12
Zhang Guangdou **Vol. 3**: 30
Zhang Guotao **Vol. 1**: 14, 17–20, 502; **Vol. 3**: 33
Zhang Jieqing **Vol. 3**: 72
Zhang Luping **Vol. 3**: 109
Zhang Naiqi **Vol. 1**: 233
Zhang Pinghua **Vol. 3**: 39
Zhang Ruxin **Vol. 1**: 483

Zhang Shenfu **Vol. 1**: 18–19
Zhang Shizhao **Vol. 3**: 227
Zhang Tingfa **Vol. 3**: 189
Zhang Wentian **Vol. 1**: 50, 68, 71, 95, 195, 230–231, 367, 537–538; **Vol. 2**: 9, 35–36, 306–307, 309; **Vol. 3**: 81, 91
Zhang Xueliang **Vol. 1**: 234
Zhang Zhen **Vol. 3**: 431
Zhang Zhiyi **Vol. 3**: 107
Zhang Zhizhong **Vol. 1**: 249
Zhang Zuolin **Vol. 1**: 214
Zhangqiu **Vol. 3**: 450
Zhao Bosheng **Vol. 3**: 104
Zhao Cangbi **Vol. 3**: 71
Zhao Puchu **Vol. 3**: 127
Zhao Shiyan **Vol. 1**: 19, 276
Zhao Yimin **Vol. 3**: 72
Zhao Ziyang **Vol. 3**: 179, 189, 199–200, 210–211, 215, 221, 224, 240, 242, 245, 324
Zhejiang Province **Vol. 1**: 177–178, 420; **Vol. 2**: 204, 233; **Vol. 3**: 53, 79, 263, 277, 455
Zheng Bijian **Vol. 3**: 199
Zheng Boke **Vol. 3**: 96
Zheng Shaowen **Vol. 3**: 107
Zheng Weisan **Vol. 3**: 107–108
Zheng Zhenduo **Vol. 1**: 5
Zhengding County **Vol. 2**: 204
Zhengzhou Conference **Vol. 2**: 199–202, 204–206, 213–214, 226, 230–231, 236
Zhengzhou Railway Administration **Vol. 3**: 298
Zhongnanhai **Vol. 3**: 143, 196, 199, 380
Zhongshan Warship Incident **Vol. 1**: 221, 226–227
Zhou Enlai **Vol. 1**: 19, 29, 35–36, 57, 71, 102, 178, 181, 231, 234, 257, 259–260, 262, 274, 276, 307, 382, 399, 410, 434, 464, 485, 493, 511; **Vol. 2**: 11, 53, 55–56, 59, 79–80, 82, 86, 92, 111, 115, 142, 147–151, 153–154, 156, 188, 193, 207, 212, 216, 233–234, 237, 245, 249, 251, 254, 260, 299–302, 304–305, 309–310; **Vol. 3**: 11, 32, 74, 226–227, 254
Zhou Fuhai **Vol. 1**: 19
Zhou Hui **Vol. 3**: 62
Zhou Yang **Vol. 3**: 139

Zhu De **Vol. 1**: 175, 231, 234, 238, 288, 299, 304, 328, 334, 338, 461–462, 484, 493, 499; **Vol. 2**: 233, 246; **Vol. 3**: 74
Zhu Muzhi **Vol. 3**: 139
Zhu Wushan **Vol. 1**: 17
Zhu Xuefan **Vol. 1**: 245
Zhu Zhixin **Vol. 1**: 7
Zhuang Autonomous Region **Vol. 3**: 284
Zhuhai **Vol. 3**: 327
Zhuo Jiong **Vol. 3**: 193
Zhuozi Mountain **Vol. 3**: 277
Zong Fu **Vol. 3**: 11
Zong Fuxian **Vol. 3**: 32
Zou Taofen **Vol. 1**: 233
Zunyi Conference (Zunyi Meeting) **Vol. 1**: 63, 84, 159, 182, 285, 311, 364, 366, 379, 421, 482, 485; **Vol. 3**: 285

Numbers

17th Route Army **Vol. 1**: 234
1911 Revolution **Vol. 1**: 25, 33, 92, 134; **Vol. 3**: 234, 358, 416
26th Route Army **Vol. 3**: 104
3-3 System **Vol. 1**: 199–200, 262
57th Army **Vol. 1**: 234
61 traitors (61 People's Case) **Vol. 3**: 74
7/20 Incident **Vol. 3**: 72–73
7,000 People's Congress (*see* Seven Thousand People's Congress) **Vol. 2**: 243, 246–247, 249–254, 256–257

ABOUT THE AUTHOR

Wu Guoyou was born in 1957 in Kailu, Inner Mongolia. A doctoral researcher, he has studied in the Department of Political History of Inner Mongolia Normal University for Nationalities and Marxist-Leninist Thought of Jilin University and the School of Political Science and Law of the Northeast Normal University, and he holds a postgraduate degree and a doctorate in Law. After graduating with a Master's degree in 1990, he worked at the Jilin Academy of Social Sciences and has successively served as deputy director of the Institute of Sociology and director of the Deng Xiaoping Theory Research Center. In 1998, he was transferred to the Party History Research Office of the CPC Central Committee and engaged in the study of the CPC's history in the new era. In August 2002, he was appointed Assistant Director of the Third Research Department of the Party History Research Office of the CPC Central Committee. In July 2005, he was appointed Deputy Director of the No. 3 Research Department of the Party History Research Department of the CPC Central Committee. In October 2010, he was appointed Director of the No. 3 Research Department of the Party History Research Office of the CPC Central Committee. He also served as a member of the National Association of Party Construction Studies and the Chinese Communist Party History Society. In July 2012, he was appointed Director of the No. 2 Research Department of the Party History Research Office of the CPC Central Committee. His publications include *Science and Technology and China's Cross-Century Social Development*, *An Overview of Deng Xiaoping's Strategy to Build a Moderately Well-off Society*, and *The "Three Represents" The Great Achievements of the Party's Guiding Thoughts in Keeping Pace with the Times*, along with more than 50 papers. He has also written, edited, and co-authored more than ten books, including *A History of China's Reform and Opening up Policy*, *The New Theory of Mao Zedong Thought*, and *The Whole History of the Long March of the Red Army (Volume III)*.

ABOUT THE TRANSLATORS

Sun Li is a professor of English Literature, Language, and Translation at Shanghai International Studies University, where she has taught since 1992. Her work includes translation, editing, and teaching. She has been involved in numerous translations of academic and literary writing, and has been a part of the editorial team for the The Cambridge History of American Literature and The New Century Multi-functional English-Chinese Dictionary. Her most recent translation projects include translation of A New Way Forward for Tibet (National University of Singapore Press) and editing the Chinese translation of Journey to the Beginning of the World (Rapscallion Press).

Shelly Bryant divides her year between Shanghai and Singapore, working as a poet, writer, and translator. She is the author of nine volumes of poetry (Alban Lake and Math Paper Press), a pair of travel guides for the cities of Suzhou and Shanghai (Urbanatomy), a book on classical Chinese gardens (Hong Kong University Press), and a short story collection (Epigram Books). She has translated work from the Chinese for Penguin Books, Epigram Publishing, the National Library Board in Singapore, Giramondo Publishing, HSRC, and Rinchen Books, and edited poetry anthologies for Alban Lake and Celestial Books. Shelly's poetry has appeared in journals, magazines, and websites around the world, as well as in several art exhibitions. Her translation of Sheng Keyi's *Northern Girls* was long-listed for the Man Asian Literary Prize in 2012, and her translation of You Jin's *In Time, Out of Place* was shortlisted for the Singapore Literature Prize in 2016. Shelly received a Distinguished Alumna Award from Oklahoma Christian University of Science and Arts in 2017.